THE FEMALE POPULATION
OF FRANCE
IN THE NINETEENTH CENTURY

This book is published in conjunction with a series
on the decline of European fertility.
A publication of the Office of Population Research
Princeton University.

The Female Population
of France in the
Nineteenth Century

A Reconstruction of 82 Départements

ETIENNE VAN DE WALLE

PRINCETON UNIVERSITY PRESS

PRINCETON, NEW JERSEY

Library of Congress Cataloging in Publication data
will be found on the last printed page of this book.

This book has been composed in Linotype Times Roman

Printed in the United States of America
by Princeton University Press

Foreword

This book presents the statistical base for an analysis of the decline of fertility in France. In a sense, it is a by-product—albeit an important one—of the overall European Fertility Project that is being conducted under the auspices of the Office of Population Research at Princeton University. Originated in 1964 and funded by the Rockefeller Foundation, the National Science Foundation, and the National Institutes of Health, the Project seeks to uncover greater understanding of the circumstances under which a major fertility decline occurs through a detailed examination of fertility trends in 700 European provinces over the last century.

France paved the way for the decline of fertility in Europe. Thus, it was necessary to go back much further in time to obtain demographic data than was the case for the other countries included in the Project. In examining the early French data, Dr. Etienne van de Walle concluded that they were inadequate for the kind of analysis required by the overall Project. This led to his decision to construct estimates of the female population of France, by département, throughout the 19th century. It is believed that the results will be of interest to historians, social scientists, and demographers outside the context of the European Fertility Project; for this reason, they are being presented as a separate entity in this volume.

With publication of this book, demographers now have available the estimated female population of 19th-century France by age and marital status, adjusted estimates of births, and estimates of various demographic indices such as marital and illegitimate fertility, age at marriage, and expectation of life at birth. The material is presented in two parts. In Part One, Dr. van de Walle describes the methods used in his reconstruction, and illustrates the results through comparisons between reported and estimated figures. Part Two presents demographic data by département as well as a brief exposition for the French reader.

Dr. van de Walle describes trends revealed by the data in the last two chapters of Part One. A more detailed examination of the actual fertility decline as well as the effects, if any, of various social, cultural, and economic factors on the birth rate in France will be presented in the book he is currently writing as his contribution to the European Fertility Project.

Ansley J. Coale
Director
Office of Population Research
Princeton University

Preface

This study originated in the need for usable estimates of fertility—in particular marital fertility—for the départements of France, as part of a larger project tracing the decline in fertility by region in Europe. In its first stage, the overall project aims at computing standardized indices of fertility and nuptiality for each province-sized administrative area in Europe, at census dates when the population was enumerated by age and marital status and the vital registration recorded the number of births. The second stage will consist of the analysis of this information and a search for explanations—or at least correlates—of the fertility decline in Europe during the 19th century.[1] In France, the units of observation are départements, administrative creations of the French Revolution which remain almost constant throughout the 19th century, and for which demographic information is tabulated in detail. The present book is devoted to the first stage of the study, i.e. to the computation by département of the basic indices that will later be used to analyze the determinants of the long-term drop in fertility. The fact that our unit of observation is the département imposes special constraints. The available data are official censuses and vital statistics. This imposes a *terminus a quo* to the study: the creation of the French vital statistics and the publication of yearly data by départements starting in 1800, and the first published French census, i.e. the 1801 enumeration. At the other end of the range, the 1901 and 1906 censuses give a more artificial *terminus ad quem*. It could be argued that 1914 constituted the end of an historical period, and that the last census to be taken before the war, in 1911, should have delimited our study. But in French population statistics, 1901 marked a new era in census-taking as well as a new century. In 1901, for the first time, all census returns had to be sent to Paris, where the processing of the data was centralized and standardized (Dupâquier, 1965, p. 37). Improved techniques of tallying, including the use of adding machines in 1901 and of

---

[1] The project is described in Coale, 1969. (Full bibliographical references are given at the end of the book.)

[vii]

Hollerith machines in 1906, were probably responsible for the marked improvement of quality of the published results. Similarly, a reform of vital registration in 1907 introduced the use of individual bulletins for each event, and centralized the processing in Paris, so that the local registrars were freed from the statistical functions they had assumed since the Revolution (Huber, 1938, Vol. II, p. 69).

This study will be limited to a reconstruction of the female population of France. The genesis of this project—the interest in fertility, best considered from the female angle—as well as the fact that the female population is less disturbed by migration and less exposed to exceptional mortality in times of war, and therefore can be reconstructed more easily, suggested this choice. The methods developed here, however, could be adapted to the men with a few changes. The types of biases encountered in the study of women are also present in the other sex's statistics. For technical reasons— the disruptive impact of massive migration in four urban départements—we have also limited the study to 82 départements.

The aim of the present book is to fill the gaps in our knowledge about the female age and marital status distribution of France in the 19th century in order to allow the computation of indices of total, marital, and illegitimate fertility as well as indices of nuptiality. A secondary aim is to evaluate the quality and completeness of those parts of the record for which detailed published statistics exist. As will be shown, there are persistent and grave errors in the censuses, even during the second half of the century. New age and marital status distributions are presented here to replace those given in the official documents, and to supplement the official statistics before 1851. There are also biases of various sorts in the vital registration, and new estimates of the number of births are offered, starting at the beginning of the century.

The first chapter of this book will provide some background for the study of the decline of fertility in France. We shall devote the second chapter to a description of the existing data. Chapter 3 discusses our methods of reconstructing the female population by age; Chapter 4 will deal with the methods of reconstructing marital status. Chapter 5 presents the results for the whole of France, and Chapter 6 examines some of the patterns of bias found in the French statistics by département. The main results are summarized in the two last chapters. In Chapter 7, we examine the general trends in fertility and nuptiality. Chapter 8 presents some by-products of this study, namely estimates of mortality (expectation of life at birth) and of migration for the départements. Finally, in a separate section we present the detailed results of the study for each département, preceded by a note that explains the methods used in the reconstruction and draws attention to some of the more common defects of the data.

As we hope that French regional historians will be among the users of this book, since it presents data by départements and the means to evaluate the quality of the local statistics during the 19th century, we have included a French summary at the end.

Discussion and interpretation of the findings will not be very detailed in this book, which represents only the first part of a larger study of the French fertility decline. A second book will deal with the correlates of fertility and will discuss the causes of the decline. It will use the data that have been reconstructed here, in combination with other sets of statistical material. The limitations of time, space, and subject matter which restrict the scope of the present book will then be abandoned.

I wish to acknowledge here my intellectual indebtedness to Professor Ansley J. Coale, who has devised many of the methods of population reconstruction used in this book and has advised me on their application to the case of France. He has been constantly associated with this research, and deserves far more credit than I can give in a small paragraph. I must also recognize the invaluable help of the two persons who have assumed the tedious and repetitive care of individual estimations and corrections for each of the départements—Elise F. Jones for the reconstruction of the population, and Francine van de Walle for the reconstruction by marital status. Patricia Taylor edited the tables and figures and managed the final assembly of the manuscript. I thank all those who have contributed useful advice or information, or read critically the whole or part of the manuscript; among them André Armengaud, Dr. Jean-Noël Biraben, Jacques Dupâquier, Léon H. Dupriez, Etienne Hélin, Louis Henry, and Guillaume Wunsch. And last but not least, I must acknowledge the good humor and patience of Hazel Chafey, who typed an arid text in successive versions. I thank the National Institutes of Health, whose generous support has made this project possible.

A NOTE ON TERMINOLOGY

In this book I have used systematically the term "reconstruction" to describe the process of simulating populations from aggregate vital registration data, as opposed to "reconstitution," which attempts to reassemble families from individual, usually nominal, information drawn from a variety of sources (census lists, registers of baptism, marriage and burial, etc.), or to retrace the life history of individuals. In this sense, the studies of Crulai (Gautier and Henry, 1958) and of the British peerage (Hollingsworth, 1964) are based on reconstitution; Bourgeois-Pichat reconstructed the population of France (1951). The present work is a reconstruction. The choice of terms is somewhat arbitrary and not widely accepted. Bourgeois-Pichat himself talks about reconstitution (p. 638). I receive some support from Webster's *Third International Dictionary*: to reconstitute is "to build up again by putting back together the original parts or elements"; while reconstruction is described as:

2. something reconstructed: as *a*: a model or replica of something *b*: something reassembled (as from parts) into its original form or appearance.

The noun "département" and the adjective "départemental" are used throughout in their French spelling, without italics.

[x]

Contents

CONTENTS

List of Tables

TABLES

List of Maps and Figures

[xvi]

[xviii]

Part One

METHODS

CHAPTER 1: The Background

I. France and the population transition

Toward the end of the 19th century, the fertility of most countries of Europe was launched upon a course of sustained decline. The near-simultaneity of this change in Europe is somewhat hidden by the substantial regional differences in nuptiality that existed at the time. Marriage was generally later, and a smaller proportion of all persons got married in Western Europe than in Eastern Europe, so that important differences in the crude birth rate continued to be observed into the 20th century. But a discernible decline in marital fertility occurred between 1870 and the First World War in an overwhelming majority of European provinces or province-size units. In an attempt to date the beginning of the decline of marital fertility for entire countries, a series of European States were ranked in function of the time when their marital fertility had undergone a 10-percent continuous decline from its highest value, never to recover to its previous level (van de Walle and Knodel, 1967). The decline was to continue well into the 20th century, until marital fertility stabilized at under 50 percent of its predecline level; but the 10-percent threshold marked the point at which the incipient decline can be distinguished from the temporary fluctuations of high marital fertility in earlier times. In most instances, a sharp downturn could be recognized in the European series, and these downturns were remarkably concentrated in time. From Belgium (1882) to Bulgaria (1912) the 10-percent declines occurred usually within a thirty-year period prior to the First World War. There were a few stragglers, such as Ireland in 1929 and Albania at some time in the 1950s. And there was one remarkable forerunner: France, where the beginning of the decline of marital fertility would have to be dated prior to 1830.

A detailed look at the provinces, rather than the national units, does not modify this picture substantially. There appears to have been an isolated example of very early fertility decline in a small area of Hungary (Andorka, 1971). Otherwise, the only province-size unit outside of France engaged in its long-term fertility decline before 1860 in Europe was the canton of Geneva, an urbanized French-speaking area with numerous contacts with France. By 1860, however, only a few islands of high fertility were left behind in France, and a majority of the départements had undergone a substantial reduction of their marital fertility. France represents a clear exception to the regular pattern. Therefore it deserves a special place in the history of European demography.

The general explanations of the European fertility decline have usually been summarized under one of several forms of the theory of demographic transition. This theory itself is based on the idealized description of the trends of Western vital rates under the impact of modernization. The theory has at least two common characteristics in its different versions: (a) It interprets the change in demographic characteristics as a response to the economic and social changes that occur as a society evolves from an essentially agrarian to a mostly industrialized state, and (b) it postulates a sequence of recognizable stages in the decline of mortality and fertility and in population growth rates. A typical sequence of this kind would have mortality declining first, with fertility lagging behind, and natural increase reaching a peak before fertility in its turn comes down.

As stated by Freedman in his review of "The Sociology of Human Fertility" (1961–1962):

Most sociologists and demographers would probably agree . . . that the basic causes of the general decline are: (a) a major shift in functions from the family to other specialized institutions, so that there was a decrease in the number of children required to achieve socially valued goals, and (b) a sharp reduction in mortality which reduced the number of births necessary to have any desired number of children (p. 53).

Freedman grants later that:

Given the general theory that urban-industrial development led to changing family organization and lower fertility, there are

[4]

still no satisfactory answers to some important comparative historical questions: e.g., why did fertility begin to decline much earlier in France than in England, where urban-industrial development was earlier and more intense (p. 56)?

Here too, France seems not to conform to the standard explanation unless it can be shown that the shift of functions from the family to specialized institution had occurred in an original way in France, or that infant mortality had started to decline earlier than elsewhere on the continent. The usual sequence of stages described by the theory of transition does not seem to apply. But it will not do to relegate France to a footnote in the history of the fertility decline, no more than it would to treat England as an exception to the industrial revolution, merely because it is the harbinger of things to come. France is of a special interest because of its very singularity, and any general theory of the transition to low fertility would have to take it into account. The need for overall economic and social modernization before fertility starts to decline has often been invoked as an obstacle to the success of birth-control programs in the underdeveloped world. If France can be presented as an instance where fertility came down among agrarian populations in the absence of wide-scale urbanization, literacy, and rise in expectation of life, the argument may have policy implications. If, on the contrary, France is shown to conform to the general pattern of demographic transition theory, the predictive value of the latter will be enhanced.

One of the major difficulties of the analysis lies in the early date of French fertility decline. Whereas most European countries had a full and detailed system of vital statistics and enumerations by the time their fertility started to decline at the end of the century, there are no adequate official data to analyze the early beginning of the French drop in marital and total fertility. Not only are the official records scanty and unreliable for the first half of the 19th century— a condition that the present book attempts to remedy by extensive reconstruction of the population—it is clear also that a complete study must extend even further back in time than the period covered by censuses and vital records. As we will show, available measures of fertility for départements at the beginning of the 19th century reveal uncommonly low birth rates in a very large part of the country. The beginning of the 19th century is somewhat late for the purpose of an analysis of the correlates of the fertility decline; but there is little hope of finding a comparable wealth of statistical data available by regions at an earlier date, so we have to be satisfied with the type of data that this book makes available. We must, however, indicate how our study stands in relation to the work of other scholars who have probed the history of French fertility.

II. *Research on the demographic history of France*

The literature on the decline of fertility in France is voluminous. Much of it is polemical, and was written in an intellectual climate best summarized by the title of one of the most valuable books on the subject: *France Faces Depopulation* (Spengler, 1938). A bibliographical list compiled in 1902 included "216 works on population, the majority of which dealt with depopulation" (Spengler, 1938, p. 122). The tide of printer's ink was still rising then, and many more works were to be written in France and abroad on the subject before the recovery of French fertility after the Second World War. Spengler's work provides an invaluable introduction to this literature, most of which is forgotten today. In general, its statistical content is weak and outdated, and it provides little more to today's scholars than a storage of hypotheses to be tested: the role of "social capillarity" (Dumont, 1890), or "civilisation" (Leroy-Beaulieu, 1913) in the decline of fertility; the influence of inheritance laws and kinship systems on the birth rate (Le Play, 1866), and so on. One must also cite Landry's work and his formal statement of transition theory in application to France (Landry, 1934). More recently, Ariès has proposed a cultural theory of the decline of fertility, which tried to encompass some of the regional variation in demographic history (Ariès, 1948). All these works were written before the great renewal of demographic techniques and theories in France that coincided with the creation of the National Institute for Demographic Studies (INED) after the war.

Of course much valuable statistical work had been accomplished in the past. The work of the *Statistique générale de la France* has been the basis of practically every analysis, for the whole of France as well as for the départements; it provides the material for the present book. The most significant recent progress in our knowledge of the past, however, has a different origin, and it deals mostly with an earlier period, that prior to the French Revolution. Although the official records—censuses and vital registrations—become usable only after 1800, another approach has been followed with great success to study the population of France during the Old Regime: the analysis of parish registers and, subsidiarily, of genealogies, either by aggregate methods or by the reconstitution of families. This approach has been pioneered by Louis Henry and his colleagues and has produced numerous monographs of parishes (many unpublished) mostly for the period prior to the Revolution. The religious registers are most complete for the 18th century, or more specifically for a period between the civil ordinance of 1667 and the creation of civil registration in 1793. Only a few studies carry over into the 19th century by nominal exploitation of the civil register after 1793 to supplement the interrupted parish records. The parish monographs deal with all aspects of the population, but the method of family reconstitution permits the investigation of marital fertility and its evolution. A detailed review of their findings cannot be attempted here; it will be sufficient to point out that there are a number of rural parishes where couples who married before the French Revolution show evidence of contraceptive behavior (Ganiage, 1963; Deniel and Henry, 1965; Dupâquier and Lachiver, 1969). Moreover, the study of genealogies allows the pinpointing of the incipient decline of fertility among certain closed social groups at a much earlier date: fertility control has been identified among the higher aristocracy since the beginning of the 18th century at least (Levy and Henry, 1960).

Henry and his colleagues have endeavored to provide a more systematic survey of the period (extended to 1829 by civil registration data) by studying a sample of parishes and communes representative of the entire country (Fleury and Henry, 1958; Biraben, Fleury, and Henry, 1960). A large part of this project uses aggregate data, but the study is complemented by nominal reconstruction on a subsample. The study is not finished, and the most important results presented up to now are the result of a pilot exploitation of the data on Brittany and Anjou (Blayo and Henry, 1967). This project will throw much light on the course of French fertility during the 18th century, on the period of the French Revolution that has been difficult to study in parish monographs because of the transition to a civil registration in 1793, and on the beginning of the 19th century. On the other hand, because the study is restricted to a limited sample, it will not give much information on regional differentials; in particular, no meaningful results will emerge at the level of the départements.

On the whole, the département has been neglected as a level of aggregation, and the most significant work has been done either at the level of the commune or the parish or at that of the nation. The historical demographers are now moving to the 19th century, exploiting either civil registration (Houdaille, 1967 and 1971; Deniel and Henry, 1965) or the rich supply of nominal lists elaborated at the time of the censuses (Blayo, 1970). At the national level too, there are some significant studies.[1]

The 19th-century official records have been used by Bourgeois-Pichat in a reconstruction of the population of France as a whole (1951 or 1965). In Chapter 5 of this book, we shall compare our results for the entire country to those of Bourgeois-Pichat. His reconstruction was based on the distribution of deaths by age and sex, available for the whole country since 1806. Each cohort alive at the end of the century was rejuvenated back to its date of birth by restituting the persons recorded as dead along the way. Before 1806, the estimate was based on the life table computed by Duvillard. Bourgeois-Pichat assumed that migrations were negligible, that the registration of deaths was complete, and that Duvillard's

---

[1] A useful bibliographical indication of recent studies of the 19th century is included in Armengaud, 1971b.

table reflects the mortality of 1770—and all these assumptions are questionable. Therefore, his conclusion about fertility is presented here as a challenge rather than as an established point: the gross reproduction rate in France would have started to decline around 1770 at least, and it had undergone a substantial cut by 1801, from 2.5 in 1771–1775 to 2.0 in 1801–1805 (Bourgeois-Pichat, 1965, p. 489). Although the article's conclusions have not been confirmed by the parish reconstitutions, its findings are often reproduced by historians and retain considerable authority to this day. Our impression is that Bourgeois-Pichat underestimated the speed of the decline in the early 19th century by overlooking the possibility of underregistration and that he exaggerated the earlier trends.

A team engaged in the macro-economic study of French history has devoted a volume to the population of France between 1700 and 1900, which concentrates on numbers, growth, urban-rural and professional distribution, and literacy (Toutain, 1963). No regional information is provided. The valuable summary by Armengaud (1971a) remains very sketchy. The synthesis of the world's population history by Rheinhard, Armengaud, and Dupâquier (1968) gives special attention to France, but a work of that scope could not be very detailed. One should also note the existence of a number of good regional monographs that integrate population data with the economic and social description of one or several départements or of a city (for example: Armengaud, 1961; Chevalier, 1950; Pinchemel, 1957).

In general, there have been few unified attempts to cover the demographic history of France by département during the 19th century. The most detailed study was done at the end of the 19th century, by Levasseur (1889–1891). This work remains a valuable source of statistics if used critically: so does the pioneering compilation of social statistics in the early 19th century by d'Angeville, recently re-edited by Le Roy Ladurie (1969). Pouthas's work (1956) leaves much to be desired because of his blind faith in the face value of the statistics of the time. Pouthas is mostly concerned about the distribution and the pace of population growth, and gives special attention to migration. His conclusions have to be treated with caution. Other authors have concentrated on various demographic aspects of the 19th century, and the next paragraph will briefly review some of the work done on fertility, nuptiality, mortality, and migrations at the national or départemental level.

The early history of the crude birth rate by département has been computed from the raw data and published by A. Bertillon (1852–1880) for 1801 to 1869, in ten-year periods. Later rates can be found in the official French publications. Depoid (1941) published a series of départemental estimates of the Gross Reproduction Rate, starting in 1860. As a rule, no distinction between marital and general fertility has been made; Chasteland and Henry (1956) mapped marital fertility at the end of the 19th century and followed its geographical evolution until after the Second World War. All these studies have shown that uncommonly low birth rates had been reached in several regions of France by midcentury and that islands of high fertility subsisted even at the end of the 19th century, most strikingly in Brittany and the Massif Central (the Lozère département and its immediate neighbors).

The general evolution of nuptiality has been analyzed by cohort for France as a whole since 1851 by Chasteland and Pressat (1962). Age of marriage undergoes a steady decline, while proportions marrying stay almost constant throughout the history of French censuses. The ages of marriage are given by département by Duplessis for the second half of the century (Duplessis-Le Guelinel, 1954; see also Camp, 1961). The relationship in space of late marriage and high fertility has been noted by Duplessis (1954) and by Spengler (1938).

The evolution of mortality is described by Bourgeois-Pichat for the entire country; he concludes that there was a steady rise of the expectation of life at birth between 1770 and our time, but that infant mortality changed only a little during the 19th century, although it was improved before 1800 by inoculation and vaccination against smallpox, and after 1900 by the spread of hygiene (Bourgeois-Pichat, 1951 or 1965, pp. 484-488). Delaporte (1941) used the existing French life tables to follow the evolution of mortality by cohort. We know of no systematic study of the regional evolution of mortality.

The study of migration has usually relied on one of two methods: the use of the balance equation or of the difference between natural increase and intercensal population growth (Pouthas, 1956) on the one hand; and the exploitation of information on place of birth and place of residence, included in several censuses since 1891 (Courgeau, 1970; Tugault, 1970), on the other hand.

Our own work has to be situated in the larger framework of the research just described. It relies almost entirely on the published material assembled by the French administration through censuses and vital registration during the 19th century. The analysis proceeds at the level of the départements. Within these constraints, we present a unified body of estimates of fertility, nuptiality, mortality, and migration—although the emphasis lies on the first two variables. New estimates for each of the variables are derived from a reconstruction of the population by age and marital status, and this must necessarily ensure a degree of internal consistency between the components of population change.

The following three chapters are devoted to a description of the data and of the methods used to adjust the information in order to obtain new estimates. The estimates' value hinges on the acceptability of the methods used, and therefore the latter must be presented in detail. The reader who is primarily interested in a summary of the results may turn to Chapter 7 for a description of some general trends of fertility and nuptiality, or to Chapter 8 for the results on mortality and migration.

Map 1.1 presents the départements of France during two periods: 1815–1860, from the end of the Empire to the acquisition of Nice and Savoie; and 1872–1914, the interwar period after the loss of Alsace and Lorraine.

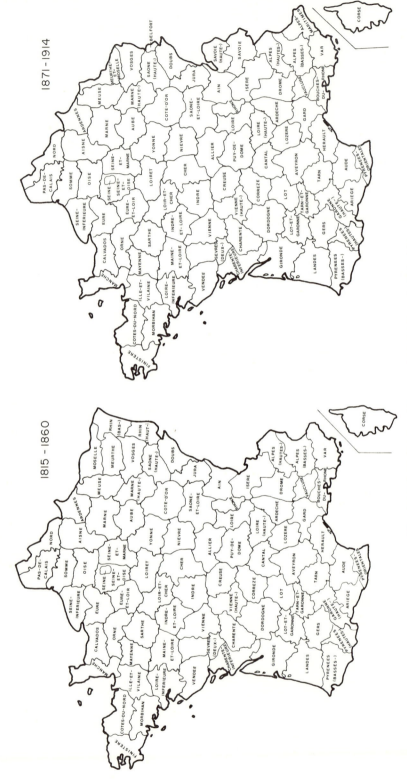

Map 1.1 Départements of France: 1815-1860 and 1871-1914

CHAPTER 2: The Data

I. *Introduction*

In this chapter, we describe the censuses and vital registration from which we draw our information for France in the 19th century. This is the time when most European States set up their statistical systems, in the absence of accepted rules and standard practices. The general recognition of a need for detailed censuses and for their detailed publication was a phenomenon of the 19th century. Of course there are isolated examples of censuses in the 18th century, but they require careful scrutiny before they can be accepted at face value. Typically, they are not detailed, and their publication may occupy only a few pages. The Belgian census of 1846 organized by Quetelet has been heralded as the "first scientific census" (Levasseur, I, 1889, p. 61). The form of the questionnaire and the instructions to the interviewers were given in the census volume, and an attempt was made in the introduction to evaluate the completeness of the enumeration by a comparison of the results at younger ages with the birth and death registration. Quetelet himself was extremely active in international meetings of statisticians, and he contributed to the establishment of uniform standards of census-taking. The modern user can feel at home with the European censuses taken after midcentury. According to Legoyt, the French administration decided to include age, religion, profession, and nationality among census questions in 1851 because its "zeal was stimulated by the example of England, Belgium, the Netherlands, Saxony and Sweden" (Legoyt, 1862, p. 266).

Similar remarks could be made about vital registration. The first half of the century was a period of experimentation and of setting standards. It was also a time when the administration strove to achieve more than a modicum of efficiency and centralization. The vital registers (and the census forms) were not unified throughout France; and statistical practices varied a great deal. The guidelines emanating from the capital were often imperfectly understood or followed.

Thus, in most countries vital registration and census-taking did not immediately reach the stage where the evidence of completeness and accuracy of the records is quite conclusive. There comes a time when various rates computed from the demographic data are at least not patently wrong, and the threshold of meaningful analysis has been crossed. But careful examination will reveal some defects, and, if the defects are important, the conclusion drawn from the unadjusted data may be misleading. It is important to go back in time as far as the data allow; but the data are often less and less detailed, so that their reliability cannot be easily tested. Since in France the more detailed information after midcentury contains obvious inconsistencies and can often be shown to be biased and misleading, it is likely that similar and perhaps worse errors existed prior to 1850.

Although common sense suggests accordingly that one should always be careful when using the official French statistics of the 19th century, there has been surprisingly little critical treatment of the quality of the published data. Only recently have there been signs of interest in the problems of quality and completeness, as the historical demographers shift their attention from their former hunting grounds in the Old Regime to what Armengaud has called "the neglected Nineteenth Century" (1971b). The greatest contribution by historical demography has been the return to the primary document, beyond the published tabulations. The failings and the biases of the data can be exposed when the processes of data collection, tabulation, and centralization are understood. Furthermore, the perusal of the archives of statistical offices reveals the extent to which the very agencies entrusted with the collection and tabulation of population data had misgivings about their quality.

These opinions have left few traces in the literature. Until recently, scholars as well as the public accepted the infallibility of the printed figures. Classic demographic texts, from Levasseur (1889) to Landry (1945), devote little attention to possible defects and biases of the data. When a particular subject is singled out for critical evaluation, the comments are sometimes frankly misleading (as our discussion of the respective values of the 1801

[14]

and 1806 censuses will show). Past users of French 19th-century statistics have often been surprisingly careless and uncritical. What remains the most often-quoted book on the population of France during the first half of the 19th century, published in the most reputable demographic collection in print (Pouthas, 1956), was recently the target of a thorough criticism which demonstrated the presence of abundant errors, careless computations, and faulty interpretations (Spagnoli, 1972).

In this chapter we shall try to survey some of the contemporary writings dealing with the quality of the statistics, as well as some recent research which has revealed the existence of errors and has discussed their nature. We shall treat separately censuses and vital registration, and consider the nature of the available data and their possible biases.

II. *The censuses*

A. THE AVAILABLE DATA

Many censuses were made under the Old Regime, for fiscal, administrative, or religious purposes. But census-taking was a prerogative of local authorities, and the experts were skeptical concerning the possibility of a national census. Moheau himself had had much experience with local censuses (1778, p. 16):

> The means of having accurate enumerations, is to start at one end of the enumerated area, to follow through until the other end, and to write down in order the inhabitants of each house, with their names, professions or qualities . . . ; but if these procedures were extended to an entire kingdom, let alone the fact that they would become very expensive, it would be very difficult, in view of the number of the clerks [*rédacteurs*] to be employed, and the difficulty of checking on their mistakes, to avoid considerable errors.

The Revolution led to a drastic reconsideration, inspired by faith in rational approaches and by the need of data for political and administrative reorganization. There were at least ten attempts to

[15]

take a national census during the revolutionary period. In 1790–1791, four different agencies or ministries were attempting such a census independently; their concerns included the setting up of départements with populations of comparable sizes, electoral representation, poverty relief, and taxation (Biraben, 1970, p. 359). This uncoordinated enthusiasm was eventually consolidated into the so-called Census of the Year II (1793). The difficulty of obtaining returns from local administrations during a time of unrest—if not civil war—and despite the departure of many of the local literate elites, must have dampened the zeal of the statisticians. There are numerous tracks of aborted or partly successful censuses and demographic surveys in the French archives for the period of the Revolution and the Empire (Biraben, 1962).

In principle at least, the obligation of a permanent population list, updated every year, existed after 1791 in each municipality (Biraben, 1970, p. 365). According to a law of *10 vendémiaire an IV* (October 1, 1795), a yearly census of the population was to be taken for police purposes in local areas. The information collected was to be extensive, and included age and marital status.[1] But the legislation does not seem to have been heeded throughout the country, although there are communes where such censuses were taken regularly for some time. In Crulai, the series exists between 1795 and 1812, with an isolated further example in 1820. Standard forms were used, including room for the number of children under 12 (without indication of sex) (Gautier and Henry, 1958, p. 205).

The census of 1801 is usually considered the first general population census of France (Huber, 1938, ii, pp. 2, 10). It is certainly the first census of the entire country to be published by département in a standardized way. Although the results had been known and used, their publication, together with that of several other censuses up to and including that of 1836, was a result of the creation of

---

[1] *"Titre II.* Moyen d'assurer la police intérieure de chaque commune. *Article premier.* Il sera fait et dressé dans chaque commune de la République un tableau contenant les noms, âge, état ou profession de tous les habitans au-dessus de l'âge de douze ans, le lieu de leur habitation et l'époque de leur entrée dans la commune." (Quoted by Gautier and Henry, 1958, p. 205.)

the *Bureau de la Statistique Générale* in 1833 (France, 1837). Moreau de Jonnès, the head of the new bureau, and his colleagues were already far removed from the time of the censuses of 1801 and 1806. The following comments appeared in the official volume (France, 1837, p. xxiii):

> The census of 1801 was executed with care, and met success, which may seem surprising considering the time of its execution. The one in 1806 appears to have been less favored by circumstances. The one in 1811 was nothing but an estimation in globo and by approximation of the population of each département. . . . The census of 1821 was satisfactory; but the one in 1826, executed under the administration of Mr. Corbière, was estimated only by adding to the population of each *arrondissement* in 1821, the increase produced by the excess of births over deaths during the five following years. The censuses of 1831 and 1836 are without doubt the best, most of all the last one, which was taken on individual census forms. The age of each person enumerated was indicated on the forms, so that it would be possible to obtain from this enumeration a series of numerical terms such as no other census could yet give; but it would require an immense labor to extract this knowledge out of such a great mass of documents.

This evaluation of the respective quality of the 1801 and 1806 censuses did not correspond to the opinions of contemporaries and has not been vindicated by modern research. Both censuses were to a large extent the result of estimations without enumeration. Communes were under the obligation of keeping population lists (described above), but the laws of 1791 and of the year IV were not in effect in many areas. On the other hand, the requests of the Ministry of Interior activated these laws concerning the local censuses, and communal archives still contain many more nominal lists for 1800 and 1806 than for any other year before the end of the Empire (Biraben, 1970, p. 367). Many communes appear to have sent in no returns in 1800–1801, and the prefects (of the départements) had to use the results from a previous census instead,

[17]

that of the year VII (1799). Several prefects thought that the figures were underestimated, either because young men sought to avoid conscription, or because the mayors feared that the results would be used to determine the burden of taxation, or otherwise suspected the motives of the Revolutionary administration (Biraben, 1970, pp. 369-370). Detailed population figures for cities are often obviously rounded, summary estimates. (See, for example, in Table 2.1 the results for the *chef-lieux d'arrondissement*, or administrative capitals of the Seine-Inférieure département in 1801 as compared to 1821.)

TABLE 2.1

TOTAL POPULATION, ADMINISTRATIVE CAPITALS, SEINE-INFERIEURE:
1801 AND 1821

Administrative Capital	1801	1821
Rouen	87,000	86,736
Dieppe	20,000	16,664
Le Havre	16,000	21,108
Yvetot	10,000	9,758
Neufchatel	2,838	3,196

SOURCE: France, 1837.

It is said that no less an authority than the mathematician Laplace suspected the total figure for France, and that he initiated a sample survey designed to check on the results. Laplace's criticism led to renewed care at the time of the 1806 census (Legoyt, 1862, pp. 264-265). The letter of instruction ordering the new census cautioned against past errors (Levasseur, I, p. 300-301). Duvillard, who had been involved in the operation and had requested recounts in 16 départements with incomplete or obviously faulty returns, thought that "for the first time, one had, more or less, the population by commune." In general, the 1806 census was considered at the time to have been more successful than the 1801 operation (Biraben, 1970, p. 370).

Studies at the parish level by historical demographers seem to confirm that 1806 is the better census and that "the 1801 census very often gives too low figures" (Henry, 1967, p. 56; see also Deniel and Henry, 1965, p. 567). It is therefore strange that the 1806 census has been more mistrusted by a majority of scholars, from Moreau de Jonnès to our days. Pouthas took the 1801 census as benchmark because "it is recognized that the 1806 one is clearly biased by exaggerations" (1956, p. 17). One author claims that "in 1806, the Emperor had insisted upon inflating artificially the number of Frenchmen, particularly in the old départements" (Vidalenc, 1956, p. 161). It would seem that the basis for this persisting opinion is the computation made by members of the Statistical Bureau in 1835, who added the births to, and subtracted the deaths from, the 1831 census total without accounting for military casualties that were not registered (Biraben, 1970, p. 370). As we shall show, the same kind of computation restricted to the female part of the population confirms the estimate of 1806 rather than the earlier one. Achille Guillard, the inventor of the term "demography," who was fiercely opposed to the second Empire, used the argument to accuse Napoleon I of falsification: "If a conqueror wants to intimidate his outside enemies, and at the same time deceive his subjects on the losses of blood that he is causing them, he will find compliant census takers who will inflate population records" (Guillard, 1855, quoted by Biraben, 1970, p. 370).

The nominal date of the early censuses was assigned later, when a periodicity of five years had been established. The returns of the so-called 1801 census were sent by the prefects over a period of more than three years, with an overwhelming majority during the second half of 1800. The results of 1806 were more concentrated in time, with a fourth of the départements' returns sent in 1807.[2] There was no national census in 1811 or in 1816, and what is usually designated as the 1821 census was taken at widely different dates between 1817 and 1821. The forms and the methods of enumeration varied from département to département. In Paris and

[2] The distribution over time is given in Biraben, 1970, p. 368.

in Seine-et-Oise at least, the 1817 census was taken on nominal lists by household, and included mention of age and profession; in Paris marital status was recorded.[3]

The results of censuses taken over a number of years were authenticated as making up the population of France on January 1, 1821, and as being valid for five years. A new estimate therefore became necessary in 1826, and it was derived from population movements recorded by vital registration. The census of 1831 begins the series of truly quinquennial censuses. Outwardly, from the mode and format of the publication, there is little to distinguish the censuses between 1831 and 1846. The distribution by marital status is comparable in each census: total children plus single women, married women, widows. There was still no distribution by age. But there were some methodological changes in the census procedures and, on the whole, a steady improvement of the operations. The 1836 census is the first one which was organized on a national basis. Prior to 1836, the instructions from the Ministry contained no more than the general prescription to enumerate the population. The innovation was that detailed instructions, standardized for the country, were sent out; they included the mention of age and the use of *bulletins nominatifs* (nominal census forms), or forms with distinction of households and one line per individual. The census was *de jure*, which was not an innovation, as the 1806 instructions specified that the military should be enumerated at their domicile, and the transient population left out, and as later censuses left the matter to the prefects. In 1836, it was specified that soldiers, travelers and prisoners away from their commune must be reported there, while boarders, nurslings, and foundlings must be excluded.

According to Moreau de Jonnès, Director of the French Statistical Bureau from 1834 on, it was a mistake that the census was taken on a *de jure* basis, and "an inextricable confusion resulted" (Moreau de Jonnès, 1856, p. 69). In 1841, however, the Ministry

---

[3] See the invaluable inventory for Seine-et-Oise (Dupâquier, 1965). The results of the census of Paris, designed by the mathematician Fourier, were published in France, 1855.

admitted that "numerous protests, uncountable omissions and difficulties of various kinds have demonstrated that it was indispensable to come back to the actual residence . . ." (quoted by Dupâquier, 1965, pp. 15-16). The decision led to vigorous protest, as increases in population had some fiscal consequences, and it was therefore decided that institutional populations would be counted separately. In Seine-et-Oise, center of the wet-nurse industry, the *de facto* principle may have led to a substantial rise in population because of the inclusion of nurslings (Dupâquier, 1965, pp. 16-17). Elsewhere, there is a possibility that the fiscal issue led to underenumeration. The link between taxation and population is important, and we will consider it here once and for all.

In the 19th century, there were four kinds of direct taxes in France. The land tax was by far the most important and was in no way affected by population. The *contribution personnelle et mobilière* was a tax on the letting value of furnished houses. The tax on doors and windows varied according to the size of the commune, and so did the rate of the tax on commercial, industrial, and professional licenses (*contribution des patentes*). Population had an important bearing on the two latter taxes following the tax reforms of 1832 and throughout the century. The impact of the second tax, the one on letting value, was restricted to the census of 1841. According to Legoyt (1862, p. 266):

> . . . it was executed under the sorry influence of serious events brought about by the census of letting values. Presented by a hostile press as an annex to that delicate operation, it encountered strenuous resistance on the part of the population and of the municipal authorities themselves, with numerous omissions as a result.

The two operations were completely distinct, but they were occurring at about the same time. There were violent riots in Toulouse and Clermont, and, as a result of the crisis, the administration abandoned the principle of periodic readjustment of the basis of the tax on letting values, which had been proclaimed in

1832 but was to be first carried out in 1842.[4] It is possible that the quality of the population census was seriously affected in places by these events.

The recurrent problem, existing in all censuses after 1832, related to the taxes on doors and windows and on licenses, because the amount to be paid per unit increased step-wise as a function of the size of the community. The prefect of Seine-et-Oise recommended for 1841, "scrupulous checking . . . of the census of those communes that populations of 4,000 [it should probably be 5,000], 10,000, 25,000, 50,000 and 100,000 inhabitants would subject to a higher taxation rate. There are some of these communes from which 4, 8, 12 and up to 15,000 inhabitants were subtracted, by eliminating several streets in the tables sent to the Prefects . . ." (Dupâquier, 1965, p. 17).

The same source of bias persisted in census after census. I am indebted to Professor Armengaud for the reference to a study of Toulouse which shows that successive municipal administrations falsified censuses after 1895 in order to keep the population under 150,000 (Coppolani, 1953). Sections of streets, and sometimes entire streets, were simply deleted from the records.

Our discussion of the successive censuses has now led us to that of 1846, which was probably executed under better conditions than the previous one. It had been granted that the floating population would not be included in the tax basis; the new instructions also provided that the floating population be enumerated on a single day (June 14). For the first time, the size of the agglomerated population (i.e. living in uninterrupted clusters of houses or fenced properties) was to be indicated by commune. These results determined the rural and the urban population. The mention of age, attempted nationally in 1836, had since been abandoned. Moreau de Jonnès did not believe that meaningful data could be collected

---

[4] There may even have been a further problem in areas of the South, where the cadastre was being established at this very time. The cadastre is the land register which serves to allocate the land tax, and was in process since the beginning of the century. Levasseur, who alludes to it in connection with the Toulouse riots, may have confused his taxes (Levasseur, 1889, I, p. 303). The story of the 1841 riots is told in Marion, 1928, v, pp. 193-197.

on the subject of age. He wrote that "it is almost impossible to collect the age of persons with any precision, because some people do not know it, and others are concealing it . . . ," and he quoted Rickman in England as saying that he was never successful in that matter even in his own house "where he never could ascertain the age of his wife and of his maid" (Moreau de Jonnès, 1856, p. 70). There was no change in procedures until a new director of the Statistical Bureau (Legoyt) and the census of 1851.

The census of 1851 represented a new orientation, and was the first detailed French census. It contained information on age by marital status. Ages were published by single years for all the départements, and this allows us to observe very considerable age heaping. From 1856 until 1901, age was published by marital status in five-year age groups in all censuses. Further information on various subjects such as profession, religion, place of origin and nationality, and literacy were included at least in certain censuses from 1851 on or later. But our main concern here is with the population figures by sex, age, and marital status. (In 1906, the full distribution of marital status by age was omitted for reasons of economy, although it was given again in 1911 and after the First World War, in abbreviated form. But we are restricting our discussion to the 19th-century censuses plus the census of 1901.)

The central administrations were constantly attempting to improve the censuses of the second half of the century.[5] Several ministries were involved in writing separate instructions. In 1856, 1861, and 1866, the Ministry of Agriculture and Commerce requested the establishment of separate forms per household, whereas the Ministry of Interior required only a nominal list, i.e. a long series of names and characteristics whose order was determined by the sequence of enumeration. The household form thus became the primary document from which the information was copied onto the list, or, rather, on two copies of the list (one being kept in the commune).

In 1872, the Ministry of Agriculture innovated again by impos-

---

[5] I am here following Biraben (1963) and Dupâquier (1965). Huber (1938) is misleading on more than one point.

ing the individual bulletin.[6] Forms for every person in the household were bound together. The use of the individual form was hailed as great progress by statisticians such as Jacques Bertillon and Huber, and it is therefore puzzling that its use coincided with a marked deterioration of the quality of census results. We shall see in particular that age distributions are much less reliable between 1872 and 1896 than before or after these dates. In 1901, the individual census forms were centralized in Paris and tallied with the help of adding and classifying machines (Huber, I, p. 50). Before incriminating the 1872 innovation of the individual forms, one would have to know at what stage the mistakes were made (in filling the primary form, in transferring the information to the nominal list, or in tallying the latter's information?). Dupâquier reproduces a form for 1876 (p. 28). The question of age may appear confusing ("indicate exactly the year of birth and subtract from the date 1876") and does not elicit age at last birthday as did earlier census forms. I have not seen a copy of the forms in the next censuses. By 1891, the question asked is "completed years of age" (France, 1894, p. 22).

The main advantage of the household or the individual form was that it could be left with the persons to be enumerated and collected on census day. This was done from 1881 on, the first census to be held on a fixed date for the whole of France (December 18). The problems of self-enumeration had been underestimated, and there was an insufficient number of enumerators in many communes—a situation that was improved by law in later censuses.

To conclude this section, we must say one word about the date of the censuses. This has varied greatly during the century, from the early censuses, taken over a period of several years, to the fixed census day at the end of 1881 and at the beginning of subsequent census years (May 1886, April 1891, March 1896 and 1901). The dates were determined by the Ministries from 1836 on, and vary usually between April and June, with one or two months to carry out the fieldwork. The census that was to be held in 1871 was

[6] According to Dupâquier (1965, p. 25) this was not compulsory in Seine-et-Oise in 1872, but the practice was recommended by the prefects to the mayors.

postponed to 15 April/15 May 1872 (with the first of May for the floating population) because of the war with Prussia. International recommendations pushed the date back to the end of the year in 1876 and 1881. The full list of dates is given in Biraben (1963, p. 324-327).

B. A PRELIMINARY CHECK OF THE QUALITY OF CENSUSES

We have dealt at some length with the changes of statistical and administrative procedures because they may illuminate some of the defects that we indicate from internal evidence in later parts of this book. Errors must be expected. One must remember that France was taking a census of 30 million people every five years, at a time when census operations were entirely manual. In sheer material amount of work, the problems of organization were tremendous, and it is not implausible that the quality of the results would have been better had censuses been spaced at wider intervals. Of course, there were the added problems of organizing a standardized operation in a large country with widely scattered and diversified populations. A large part of the French population was still illiterate at midcentury, and the cultural homogeneity that we know today did not exist, for instance, in matters of language. It would thus be surprising if the censuses showed no biases and errors. We should expect systematic errors in the reporting of ages, for example, such as are encountered in censuses of underdeveloped countries today. Of the French censuses, Bourgeois-Pichat says that "it is well known . . . that the number of people in the 20–24 age-group is always exaggerated, as adolescents tend to exaggerate their ages and adults to understate them" (Bourgeois-Pichat, 1965, p. 477). This is true, as we shall see, in some censuses at least, but not in all of them. The introductory comments accompanying the 1886 census (France, 1888, p. 91) note the "abnormal" age-group 20–24 in the censuses taken after 1866 and states two hypotheses:

> . . . the first is based on the possible understatement of age in the declarations of the feminine sex; the second, on the known presence of a large number of foreigners temporarily established in France.

[25]

The same report recognizes that the very young children were probably underenumerated in 1881 and 1886, and suggests that the nurslings away from their parents' home, who should have been recorded as visitors, were left out (p. 92). The underenumeration of children under age 5 is a well-recognized feature of many censuses over the world, and France has not avoided it. Tabah estimated that 12 percent of that age-group had been left out in 1851 (1947). But it is sometimes difficult to recognize underenumeration of the children with complete certainty. The misreporting of ages may affect the age distribution in a way which appears to reflect underreporting of an age-group. Deniel and Henry performed an interesting test in a parish where they matched birth certificates since 1845 with the children under 5 on the nominal list of the 1851 census; the conclusion in that instance was that there were very few, if any, omissions, but that children aged four and a half were often recorded as five years old (1965, p. 570).

In addition to the systematic biases, which are apparent when one deals with the entire population of France, there are many unsystematic errors affecting individual départements in a particular census. Sometimes these are clearly errors of tabulation and addition made during processing and publishing. In other instances, it may be very difficult to identify the source of the error. There may be cases of apparent and unexplained overestimation. Or the age and marital status distribution in one year may be completely unrelated to that of any other year.

The natural tendency of most users of censuses for other purposes than demographic analysis—historical studies, regional monographs, etc.—has been to accept the recorded figures at face value, unless some very definite causes of errors and omission could be traced. Usually monographs on départements are of little help in tracing such causes precisely because they often place unwarranted confidence in the accuracy of the data. In the next pages, we turn to a first look at the quality of data from the censuses. The conclusion of this examination will be that considerable bias exists, and that the data cannot be trusted but must be corrected in some way. To this correction—actually a reconstruction of the population—we shall turn in the next chapter. We shall have abundant opportunity later to come back to the various biases of the reported enumeration. At this early stage, we restrict ourselves to a preliminary review of the data, retracing as it were the process which led to the writing of this book. It was dissatisfaction with the quality of the data, in simple tests such as those that will follow, that convinced us that extensive reconstruction was needed.

The main indication of the unreliability of the censuses is the incompatibility of one census total, or of one census cohort, with the surrounding censuses. If there is a perceptible trend in the growth of the population of a département, a census that yields a figure outside of the trend is suspect. This is true not only for the total female population of the département but also for more specific aggregates, such as the total married population, or the women aged 15–49. Violent fluctuations of these aggregates should not occur often in the five years between two censuses. The same reasoning has other applications as well. For instance, the same cohort, followed from census to census, should not fluctuate in an irregular fashion, but should be smaller and smaller as it progresses through life; or the proportion married at a certain age should evolve rather smoothly from census to census, barring catastrophic events that may affect it radically.

As demonstrated by the quotation from the 1886 census report above, the main objection to this general method is based on the possibility of migratory movements. Indeed, migration appears to be the *deus ex machina* which explains all the unaccounted quirks and vagaries of the data. An accepted method of computing migrations is to subtract the balance of births and deaths from a census population, and to compare the result to the next census. The unexplained residual is then attributed to migration.[7] We shall discuss migration in more detail later. Let it be said here that migration can be investigated in this way when reliable censuses are taken sufficiently separated in time, so that small fluctuations in the completeness of enumeration are not important compared to the residual which is accepted as a result of migration; but the

[7] For an application of this method to French data, see Pouthas (1956, p. 121ff.).

comparison of two censuses close in time may yield very misleading results. Furthermore, it is plausible that migration follows definite patterns, changes only progressively in intensity, and only very exceptionally causes deep fluctuations from one census to the next. Also, women migrate less than men. The likelihood that population movements will explain a deviation from a clear trend is indeed small.

The first test of consistency of the data, then, is to look at the progression of the total female population and of the total number of married women from census to census. At a later stage, we shall look at the distribution by age both of total women and of married women. It will become clear that the départements discussed here are only examples, and that the types of biases that will become apparent are very widespread during the 19th century. We shall discuss them in a more systematic fashion in Chapter 5.

CONSISTENCY IN THE SERIES OF CENSUS TOTALS

Some useful hints are gained from the systematic graphing of the series of total population (females), total married women, women aged 15–49 years, and married women aged 15–49 in the censuses. To these four series, we add the five-year total of legitimate births centered on the census. Figure 2.1 presents these series for Charente between 1851 and 1901 as an illustration of the reasoning.

Of course, we do not expect all the series on Figure 2.1 to behave in a parallel way. The total population may decrease over time while the number of females aged 15–49 is still increasing, if the age distribution is changing as a result of changing fertility. The number of married women (both in the total population and aged 15–49) may be increasing at a faster pace than the total number of women if an increased proportion marries. The married women at the fecund ages, in turn, will not increase strictly in the same way as all married women, although they represent a very large proportion of the latter group. But the forces that lead to an independent trend in these various aggregates move slowly. Many of the females in any of these aggregates at one census remain in it at the

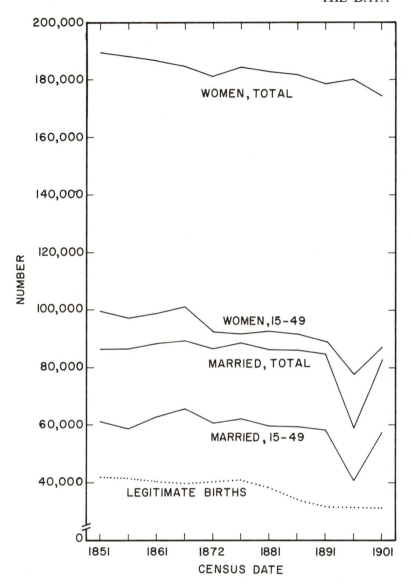

NOTE: Legitimate births refer to five-year totals.

Figure 2.1 Female Population, Total and Age 15-49, Married Women, Total and Age 15-49, and Legitimate Births, Charente: 1851 to 1901

next. The proportion married, for instance, does not tend to change drastically in five years, even if there is a marked change in the number of new marriages; data of the stock type are much less sensitive than data of the flow type. Therefore, it is legitimate to ask whether the various series are consistent, whether some or all of them undergo variations at the same time, and whether their trends are compatible. The married women aged 15–49 represent typically about 3/4 of all married women. Therefore a fluctuation in the former series which finds no echo in the latter may very well be due to a misreporting of ages that has shifted some women inside or outside of the category 15–49. And finally, the series of legitimate births is closely related to the number of married women aged 15–49, and a large fluctuation in the latter's number should cause a fluctuation in the birth series. An increase in the number of married women in one census would normally be caused by new marriages, and these would involve, more often than not, young women capable and willing to have children not long after marriage. In Figure 2.1, on the contrary, the abrupt decline in the number of married women aged 15–49 at the time of the 1896 census does not exert any visible effect on the birth series. The incompatibility of the curves in 1896 points very strongly toward an error in the figures.

The 1896 enumeration in Charente yields results which cannot be explained in a satisfactory fashion by demographic movement. The total female population is in line with the results obtained in previous and later censuses. The series of numbers for women 15–49, for total married women, and for married women aged 15–49, all experience a dip of several thousand units in 1896, compared to both the previous and the following census. A comparison of census figures is given in Table 2.2 for the three censuses. There seems to be an excessive number of single girls, but the error is not simply one of misreporting marital status, since there are also too many young girls under age 20. There is no obvious, logical way to explain how married women over 20 might have been enumerated as single women under 20. The pattern among males is very similar. The cause of the error is unknown; but it is certain that no migratory movement can explain the resulting figures. One might add that the censuses after 1901, not shown in Figure 2.1, are in line with the earlier censuses, and that 1896 is aberrant also when compared with a series extended into the 20th century.

The instance of the Creuse département is very similar (see

TABLE 2.2

MARITAL STATUS OF WOMEN, TOTALS AND SELECTED AGE
GROUPS, CHARENTE: 1891, 1896, AND 1901

	1891	1896	1901
TOTAL WOMEN	178,726	180,344	174,393[a]
Aged 15-49	89,018	77,796	87,000[b]
TOTAL SINGLE	72,932	109,496	67,775
Aged 0-15	43,994	56,383	40,980
Aged 15-49	26,511	35,870	24,375
TOTAL MARRIED	84,506	56,699	82,509
Aged 15-49	58,308	40,730	57,220
TOTAL WIDOWED AND DIVORCED	21,288	11,149	24,109
Aged 15-49	4,199	1,196	4,039

SOURCES: France, 1894, 1899 and 1906, vol. 4.

[a] Includes 1,600 women of undeclared marital status.
[b] Includes 1,366 women of undeclared marital status.

Figure 2.2). In 1886 and in 1881, the number of married women is clearly underestimated. The underestimation of the women 15–49 is restricted to the 1886 census and is less spectacular. The trends in the total female population and in the number of births per quinquennium are uninterrupted. If the disappearance of over a third of the married women in the fecund ages was not an error in the statistics, but was the result of heavy migration, the number of births would certainly have undergone fluctuations. As in the case of Charente, the error in Creuse appears to be well circumscribed.

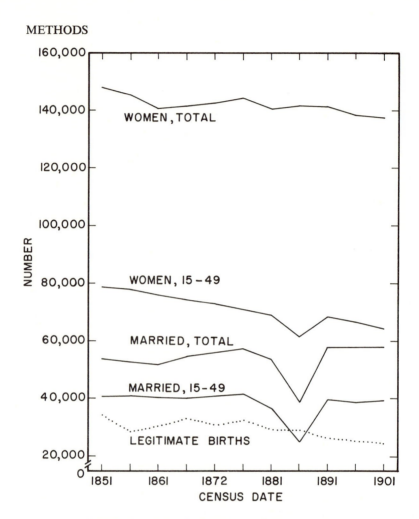

NOTE: Legitimate births refer to five-year totals.

Figure 2.2 Female Population, Total and Age 15-49, Married Women, Total and Age 15-49, and Legitimate Births, Creuse: 1851 to 1901

Unfortunately, there are many départements where the trend is not at all so obvious, and where several censuses in succession appear to be in error or at least incompatible. The criterion of consistency can be applied only when a reasonable body of evidence tells the same story. Of course at the limit, if all the censuses are in error, no trend can be recognized. Two instances of more erratic series are presented in Figure 2.3: Landes, and Figure 2.4: Finistère. In

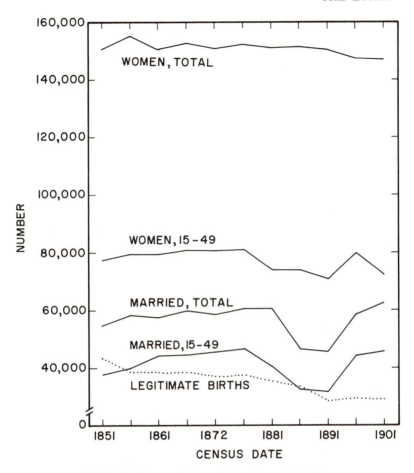

NOTE: Legitimate births refer to five-year totals.

Figure 2.3 Female Population, Total and Age 15-49, Married Women,
Total and Age 15-49, and Legitimate Births, Landes: 1851 to 1901

all the examples shown (but by no means in all départements),
the total number of women follows a regular progression, and clear
deviations (as in Finistère, 1866–1872) do not exceed a few
percent of the total population. The number of married women is
much more erratic. And deviations in the age distribution (reflected
here by fluctuations in the number of women reported as aged
15–49) are very conspicuous. We now turn to a more detailed look
at the age distribution.

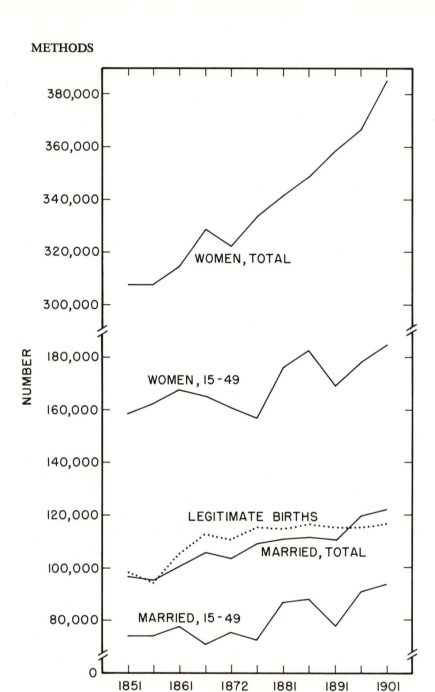

NOTE: Legitimate births refer to five-year totals.

Figure 2.4 Female Population, Total and Age 15-49, Married Women,
Total and Age 15-49, and Legitimate Births, Finistère: 1851 to 1901

THE AGE DISTRIBUTION

A systematic graphing and examination of age distributions for départements yields pictures of unaccountable defects of the most extraordinary kind. These mistakes are swamped in a presentation of the age distribution for the whole country, but they will severely affect the computation of fertility indices on a départemental basis. We illustrate this point first with the age distribution of Hérault in successive censuses, graphed in Figure 2.5 by year of birth so that

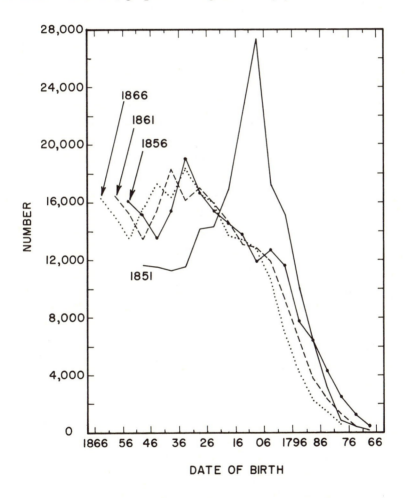

Figure 2.5 Distribution of Female Population by Date of Birth, Hérault: Censuses of 1851, 1856, 1861, and 1866

the birth cohorts can be compared. In 1856, 1861, and 1866, the age distribution has similar traits. The age-group 10–14 is uncommonly small, the age-group 20–24 overly large. There is no hint of cohort effect here, and these features of the age-distribution must almost certainly be attributed to a systematic pattern of age misreporting (including probably underreporting at young ages). However, the shape of the 1851 age distribution cannot be accounted for by the same persistent and conventional biases. It is entirely *sui generis*, and the pattern probably originated, not in the misreporting of ages by respondents, but in some incomprehensible error of tabulation. Hérault is not an isolated case in 1851. Several départements, including Pyrénées-Orientales and Loire-Inférieure, have equally peculiar age distributions, unparalleled in later censuses of the same area. But unfortunately, the 1851 census has no monopoly on extraordinary features. There are many instances of cohorts that undergo extreme fluctuations from census to census.

Figure 2.6 plots the age distributions 15–49 (classified by date of birth, in order to show the cohorts) in all the censuses of Finistère between 1851 and 1901. There appears to be a complete breakdown in age reporting between 1872 and 1886. Before and after those dates, the censuses present a certain consistency, and there is a normal attrition of the cohorts. It seems certain that the recorded figures do not reflect the true state of the population at the time of those four censuses, and that no demographic events could possibly have brought about such a helter-skelter behavior of the data. In 1886, for instance, an extraordinarily large number of women are reported as aged 20–24 years. The census volume for 1886 reproduces the age pyramid for Finistère and attributes the excess of women in that age-group to migration. The explanation is not convincing in the context of the other censuses of the same département. The age-group is back to normal in 1891, and so is the cohort. If one follows the same birth cohort of women as they grow older in successive censuses, it is most unlikely that the number of women aged 20–24 in 1872 would have been reduced by more than half in 1876 (as a result of out-migration this time) but would have gone back to normal by 1881. These discrepancies

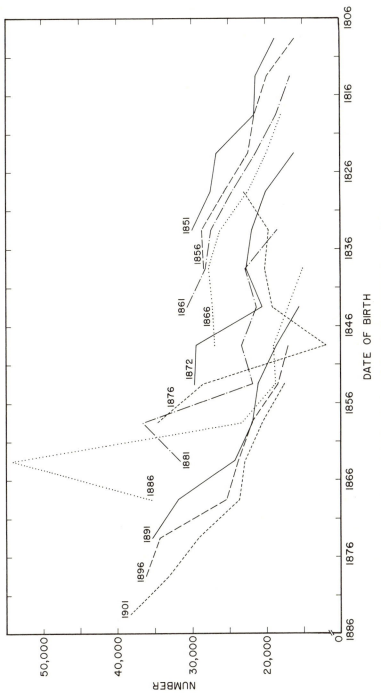

Figure 2.6 Distribution of Female Population Age 15-49 by
Date of Birth, Finistère: Censuses from 1851 to 1901

point to major errors in tabulation or in reporting. The instance of Finistère, unfortunately, is far from isolated. There are few départements where the series of censuses is completely consistent, and it seems advisable to adjust the age distribution before one uses it for analytical purposes.

THE DISTRIBUTION BY MARITAL STATUS

The biases in the age distribution just described affect the proportion married at successive ages. Indeed, it is unlikely that the transfer of women from one age-group to another, as a result of misreporting or mistabulating, would be of such a nature as to leave the proportions married unaffected. This could only happen if the errors on age were independent of the marital status of the women, and if marital status were always correctly recorded. Neither of these conditions is fulfilled, as the instance of Finistère once again demonstrates. Figure 2.7 presents proportions married by age in successive censuses. In 1886, the proportion married aged 20–24 is exceptionally large at the very time when the age-group is inflated; married women seem to have been attracted preferentially to the age-group by the age misreporting. On the other hand, the dip in the proportions married between 30–39 must probably be due to a misclassification of marital status. It is not likely that the proportion married aged 30–34 in 1861 was really higher than the proportion married aged 35–39 in 1866: after all, women who were married five years before are unlikely to massively change their marital status in the midst of the childbearing years, in so short a time. Such abrupt changes, if real, could only result:

1) from a sudden change in marital status, e.g. in the prevalence of widowhood;
2) from the sudden in-migration of widows, and out-migration of married women.

Neither of these events is very likely, as the situation is back to normal by 1872. In Table 2.3, we compare the numbers and proportions in each marital category for the same cohort of women in

two censuses, 1861 and 1866. There is an abnormal increase in the
number of widows, restricted to the age-group 35–39 in 1866,
suggesting misclassification of married women as widows. The
proportion single, but not the number single, increases.

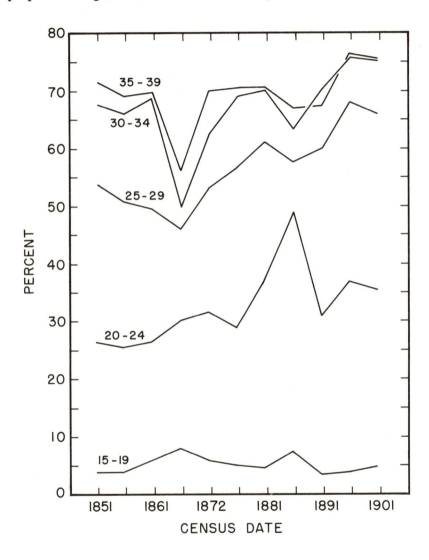

Figure 2.7 Proportion Women Married, by Selected Age-Groups,
Finistère: 1851 to 1901

METHODS

Because of the various possibilities of changes, including changes in marital status, it is convenient to aggregate married women and widows as ever-married. The change from the status of single to that of ever-married is irreversible. If genuine, an increase in the proportion single with age in a cohort logically can only be attributed to a peculiar pattern of migration or mortality. Differential mortality by marital status is unlikely to cause large changes in the proportions ever-married by age, at least until old age. Migration is not likely to affect the proportion single by age in one single census to the exclusion of later ones. We take another département

TABLE 2.3

MARITAL STATUS OF WOMEN, AGED 30-34 IN 1861 AND

AGED 35-39 IN 1866, FINISTÈRE

Age	Date	Single		Married		Widows		Total	
		Number	Percent	Number	Percent	Number	Percent	Number	Percent
30-34	1861	6,742	27.4	16,829	68.4	1,044	4.2	24,615	100
35-39	1866	6,382	29.1	12,205	55.7	3,342	15.2	21,929	100

SOURCE: France, 1864 and 1869.

as an example and plot in Figure 2.8 the trend in proportions ever-married by age in Creuse. A collapse in the proportions ever-married in 1881 and 1886 cannot warrant any logical interpretation other than a massive error in reporting or tabulating. It is almost inconceivable that the proportion single at 25–29 in a cohort would *decrease* by the time these women have reached 35–39, ten years later, as the data indicate between 1876 and 1886.

The choice of the graphic examples in this chapter is arbitrary, and similar points could be illustrated for almost any département in France. The series of censuses, either for the total female, or by age and marital status, show inconsistencies and fluctuations that can only be explained by biases and misreporting. We now turn to a similarly impressionistic look at the vital registration, before we indicate a general method to adjust the data and investigate the extent of misreporting.

[40]

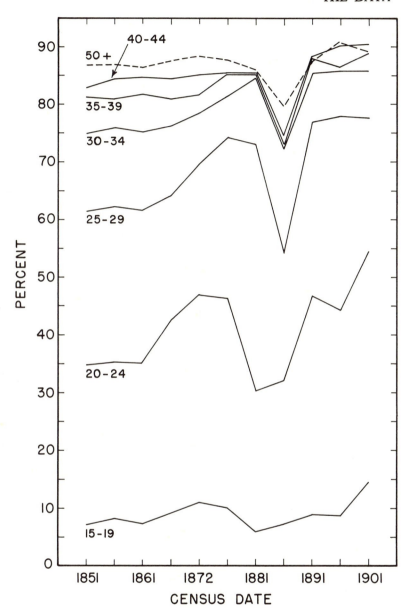

Figure 2.8 Proportion Women Ever-Married, by Selected Age-Groups,
Creuse: 1851 to 1901

III. *Data from vital registration*

Although the recording of marriages, baptisms, and burials was a prerogative of the Catholic clergy, there was a great deal of administrative interest in the registration even before the Revolution. The records had long ceased being purely religious documents, and the state had imposed registration as early as 1539 in an edict of François I. Since 1667, the parish priests had had to send annually a duplicate of their registers to the judiciary authorities. But the credit for attempting to centralize and use these documents for demographic purposes goes to the Abbé Terray, a *Contrôleur Général* (the equivalent of Finance Minister). In 1772, he sent a letter to the *Intendants* (or provincial heads) ordering them to compile an annual statistic of baptisms, marriages, and burials. The information was to be gathered from the duplicates held by the courts or, if the priests had failed to send those in, from the parish registers; provision was made for the vital events of non-Catholics. Terray's successors concurred with his views on the importance of these data, and the *Intendants* sent them regularly until the Revolution. Thus an estimate of the number of vital events by year exists between 1770 and 1789 (Esmonin, 1964). The material is clearly of great interest, although spotty and often unreliable in its present state. It has been used to check the results of the sample inquiry of INED on the past population of France (Blayo and Henry, 1967) and, in conjunction with various prerevolutionary and revolutionary censuses, to estimate the trend in the birth rate (Biraben, 1966; Le Roy Ladurie, 1965).

The renewed interest in birth registration, at the end of the Old Regime, originated to a large extent in the belief that it would be difficult to take a general census of the population of France. Such an endeavor would have been viewed with extreme suspicion by a tax-scarred population, and its administrative complexity was deemed too great by most experts. Various population writers of the time, however, thought that a substitute estimation of the French population could be derived by multiplying the annual number of births by a constant coefficient. Although the idea was essentially wrong in a country where fertility had started to decline, and was rapidly abandoned when censuses began to be taken regularly, it contributed to a tradition in matters of vital registration for demographic purposes. This tradition was much more deeply anchored in France than, say, in England, and the relative homogeneity of the parish records in Catholic France makes them more reliable and easier to handle as demographic sources. Of course, the organization of official vital registration occurred later in England than in France, namely at the time of the registration law of 1836.

The Revolution upset the data-gathering efforts of the central administration as well as the registration in the villages. A law of 20 September 1792 transferred the official function of registrar from the parish priests to the mayors of the communes. There appeared to be a great deal of confusion at the top about what agency would be responsible for the compilation of vital statistics (see Biraben, 1970; Reinhard, 1950). The personal interest in population questions of François de Neufchateau, Minister of the Interior in 1798 and 1799, determined the final allocation of vital registration in that Ministry. But not until the year IX (1800-1801) did the numerous instructions, requests for data, and reminders sent out by the Bureau of Statistics elicit sufficiently complete responses from the prefects to warrant publication at the départemental level (France, I, 2, 1837). Thus, the official vital statistics for France really started at the beginning of the century. By then, each prefect was sending in the data on births, deaths, and marriages for the year that he had himself received from the mayors of his départements. Even so, the returns from the communes might not be complete, and only a thorough search in the départemental archives would turn up the list of communes that had sent their yearly data. Occasional checks of this nature show that some local administrations were delinquent in the beginning of the century. It is important to note that the obvious defects of the birth or death series must not be attributed necessarily to underregistration, but may well be the result of incomplete centralization of the information, or even of faulty tabulation and addition.

Passing an overall judgment on the quality of the registration itself is very difficult. On the whole, it seems to have been excellent, but some criticism was voiced at the time. A priori, one would expect a sharp discontinuity in the records in 1792, when the civil authorities took over registration from the church. There was a shortage of competent, and even of literate, registrars. Furthermore, civil unrest and overt resistance to the new regime precluded complete registration. At least in some regions, one must expect a gap between the statistics of the old and of the new regime (Reinhard, Armengaud, and Dupâquier, 1968, p. 297). And the period of transition may have been long. The unreliability of the records may well have persisted into the 19th century. Among the causes (Biraben, 1970, p. 365):

. . . the underadministration of certain regions perturbed by the wars and where the municipal staffs were not re-established before the Year IX or even the Year X [1800–1802]; the great number of people in hiding because of political events, who did not register the facts concerning them (many births of the period of the Revolution and Empire will be established by an *acte de notoriété* [a court judgment ascertaining a person's identity] under the Restoration). . . .

Biraben also mentions the ambiguity of the administrative instructions received from Paris as a further factor contributing to the unreliability of the records.

The central administration at least was taking seriously registration as a tool of administration. There are stories of conscripts burning the duplicate copy of registers in 1805 to prevent its use for the draft. It is even possible that parents did not register some male births in Ariège, so that their sons could avoid military service (Armengaud, 1961, p. 17). The mayors collaborated intermittently by inscribing false marriages (because married men were spared the draft). Archives contain many horror stories about the registration; yet the central authorities relentlessly pressed for their improvement and initiated controls and checks. Some writers have referred to the revolutionary period, and blame "the frightening disorder of the registers" on ill will as much as on ineptitude on the part of the newly appointed municipal staff (Bougard and Reinhard, 1964, p. 29). But the criticism had not abated by 1820 when the *procureurs du roi* (attorney generals) were requested to inquire into the state of the registers. According to R. Le Mée, who investigated their reports in the archives, they often found poorly kept registers, and sometimes communes without printed forms, or without registers at all. In Pas-de-Calais, an 1818 letter of a *procureur* to the mayors of an *arrondissement* referred to "the poor keeping and the irregularity of most of the registers" and mentioned that "some mayors are careless to the point of inscribing all the acts together at the end of the year . . ." (Bougard and Reinhard, 1964, p. 30).

The most pessimistic contemporary statement about the quality of the annual population movements' statistics in the thirties and forties, and about "the degree of confidence that can be expected from administrative records," was that of Legoyt, and it should not be dismissed lightly in view of his future career in the statistical service (Legoyt, 1843, p. iii). Legoyt had no confidence in the competence of the mayors in rural France, and he noted the absence of central control in the various steps that led to the compilation of the statistics.[8] The very strong phrasing of Legoyt's indictments is perhaps excessive, but some caution is obviously required.

[8] The text is worth quoting: ". . . le relevé que l'on exige de l'autorité municipale est à la fois trop long et trop compliqué surtout pour les maires des communes rurales, qu'effrayent avec raison les nombreuses divisions du cadre modèle, et qui n'en comprennent même pas toujours les titres . . . remplir un pareil cadre ne constitue pas seulement pour les fonctionnaires municipaux une opération fort longue et fort détaillée, mais elle exige encore d'eux un degré d'intelligence qu'on ne saurait leur supposer, au moins dans les communes rurales, les plus nombreuses du royaume . . . ." Legoyt refers in this connection to the "avènement aux dignités municipales d'une foule d'hommes complètement illettrés ou hostiles." He then goes on to indict: ". . . le défaut d'inspection des registres de l'état civil, et de collation des extraits destinés à faire connaître le mouvement de la population; puis l'absence d'une surveillance spéciale . . . qui permette de vérifier, controler, rectifier les expressions numériques de plus de deux millions de mutations en décès, mariages et naissances; c'est encore le grand nombre d'éditions des relevés des maires, inconvénient dont le résultat est de soumettre ces relevés, dans leurs différentes transformations, à des altérations à peu près inévitables; c'est enfin l'irrégularité des registres de l'état-civil, l'absence d'uniformité dans la rédaction et dans la nature même des actes, malgré tous les efforts de l'administration centrale pour faire cesser un pareil état de choses."

This evidence of failings in the system should not lead to an extremely negative overall evaluation. In their efforts to improve the quality of registration, contemporary critics underlined the glaring deficiencies and may have failed to comment on the smooth accomplishment of their task by a majority of communes. Therefore, the testimony of modern scholars who have worked with representative registers of the time is precious. Unfortunately, there are few parish studies that bridge the gap between the prerevolutionary period and the 19th century. In a few instances at least, the transition was smooth enough (Deniel and Henry, 1965, p. 565; Houdaille, 1971, p. 1069-1070). Henry and his colleagues, working on the great INED sample survey of France between 1740 and 1829, grant that the revolutionary period marks at least a partial deterioration of a registration system that had reached a high level of efficiency at the end of the Old Regime. For example, there is obvious underregistration of vital events in the Royalist Vendée and Maine-et-Loire départements during 1790–1799 (Blayo and Henry, 1967, p. 105). There are flurries of false marriages here and there to avoid conscription.

In some backward areas of southern France, where even the church registers were not well kept, there is clear evidence of underregistration of deaths. Louis Henry has found one commune of Dordogne, included in the INED sample, where approximately 10 percent of the births were omitted in the period 1815–1825. But careful perusal of existing registers by historical demographers leads to no general indictment of the registration at the beginning of the 19th century. In a most interesting test, Blayo and Henry compared a sample of registers in Brittany and Anjou with the official statistics. There conclusion is that there were counting errors on the part of the communal officials—or that some did not send in their returns—but that genuine underregistration was very infrequent at the time (Blayo and Henry, 1967, p. 167-169). This judgment, however, may not apply for other parts of France where the quality of the parish registers had also been more uncertain.[9]

[9] Most family reconstitutions outside of the INED sample had been using parish records of the northern half of France. An exception is Valmary (1965) on two

It is probably safe to conclude that, although there were instances of faulty registration, vigorous efforts were made to insure high quality and completeness. The importance of vital registration was realized by the reorganizers of the French administration and the authors of the Napoleonic Code. The French term for the registration of vital events—*état civil*, or literally "civil status" —indicates well the orientation of the system toward an identification of the individual and of his legal rights. The English term *vital registration* indicates the concern of the British with public health. In France, insofar as a child dying before being registered had no legal existence, he was of little interest to the vital registration. In England, however, the death of children would be a foremost concern of the system.

In France the term "stillbirth" covers not only those born dead but also children dying before the registration of their birth. For the entire period covered here, there was a systematic underreporting of live births because of this definition of stillbirth. Its extent, however, must have been variable. Henry has found birth registration entries for children who died within the first hour of their life, and he believes that precise rules on reporting children who had died before registration did not exist at the beginning of the century (Henry, 1967, p. 120). There is confusion in the practice, even in the official circulars emanating from the Paris administrations. Should the stillbirths be included among the births, among the deaths, or classified entirely apart? To avoid double counts, Duvillard (then with the Bureau of Statistics) sent out a circular letter in July 1806, instructing the use of a separate column on the register of deaths (Biraben, 1970, p. 365). No less an authority than Legoyt, however, believed that the children "presented without life" should be inscribed both in the registers of births and of deaths according to the Imperial decree of July 4, 1806,[10] but that most registrars were treating them as deaths without corresponding

---

parishes of the Lot département. According to L. Henry in the introduction of this book, "les registres du Sud-Ouest de la France ont été, dans l'ensemble, assez médiocrement tenus et conservés" (p. 13).

[10] Is Legoyt referring to, and misinterpreting, Duvillard's circular, or was there such a decree?

births (Legoyt, 1843, pp. iii-iv). The Ministry of the Interior attempted to impose this practice in a circular of January 1844 which is in direct contradiction to a June 1839 circular of the Ministry of Commerce reiterating Duvillard's instructions, and recommending exclusion from the stillbirths of those children who had died before registration (Dupâquier, 1965, p. 7).

Thus, it is only rather late that the practice of only considering as live births those children who had been registered alive became well established. Fortunately, the fluctuations in underregistration of live births due to this rule must be rather small. The evidence for this statement comes from Belgium, also a Napoleonic Code country, where stillbirths were defined in a similar way. For statistical purposes between 1848 and 1867 a record of whether the child had lived or was born dead was included in special registers kept in each Belgian commune. The practice was discontinued because the accuracy of the information seemed questionable, but it was resumed in 1879, with somewhat different categories (Belgium, 1885, pp. 562-563). The new results showed a much smaller proportion of false stillbirths. Part of the difference may be due to the category "dead during delivery," which existed only before 1867. Most of these are probably children who should be counted as stillbirths according to modern statistical practices. The criterion used after 1867 was that the child should come out of the womb of his mother alive. The result of these Belgian investigations is given in Table 2.4. There is no reason to believe that the underestimation resulting from this practice was larger in France at the time, and the resulting underestimation may be of the order of 1 percent. A birth rate given as 30 per thousand would thus actually be about 30.3 or so; the adjustment seems too small to matter.

An unknown, variable, proportion of the live births was recorded as stillbirths in conformity with the Napoleonic Code's provisions in matters of inheritance. Furthermore, the stillbirths included a number of what we would call abortions or miscarriages, when the pregnancy had lasted for less than 6 months; those were systematically eliminated from the records of stillbirths only after 1920. Before this elimination, the ratio of so-called stillbirths per thou-

TABLE 2.4

INFANT DEATHS BEFORE REGISTRATION ("FALSE STILLBIRTHS") AS PERCENTAGE OF
STILLBIRTHS AND LIVE BIRTHS, BELGIUM: 1851-1855 TO 1861-1865 AND
1881-1885 TO 1896-1900

	Deaths before registration					
	As percentage of stillbirths			As percentage of live births		
Date	Legitimate	Illegitimate	Total	Legitimate	Illegitimate	Total
1851-1855	42.6	38.0	42.1	1.9	2.3	2.0
1856-1860	--	--	41.1	--	--	1.9
1861-1865	40.1	35.0	39.5	1.9	2.4	1.9
1881-1885	11.6	10.9	11.5	0.5	0.7	0.5
1886-1890	16.7	17.7	16.8	0.8	1.1	0.8
1891-1895	16.2	15.6	16.1	0.7	1.0	0.8
1896-1900	16.8	17.7	16.9	0.8	1.1	0.8

SOURCES: Belgium, 1880. Belgium, 1885 and 1870 to 1900, passim.

sand live births was 49.2, 47.1, 45.5, and 46.7, respectively, in 1891–1900, 1901–1910, 1911–1913, and 1914–1919 (Landry, 1945, p. 290). The proportion of stillbirths and neonatal deaths was changing as a function of the general mortality decline, but much less so than infant mortality itself. We suspect of inaccuracy any ratio of the so-called stillbirths to live births which is below 4 or 5 percent. No information is given on the subject in the vital statistics before 1836. The distribution of stillbirth frequency by départements between 1836 and 1903 is given in Table 2.5. The data suggest a clear trend toward better registration of stillbirths. The results are plotted in Figure 2.9.

We now turn to an examination of the sex ratios at birth (number of male births per hundred female births). The discussion is based on groups of births for five years, beginning in 1804—i.e. 1804–1808, 1809–1813, . . . 1894–1898. The births are regrouped so as to be centered on the normal census years ending in 1 or 6. It is not truly at birth that the relationship between the sexes can be observed, but at registration. Since male mortality is higher than female mortality during the first hours of life, we would expect a

METHODS

TABLE 2.5

RATIO OF STILLBIRTHS TO LIVE BIRTHS, DISTRIBUTION OF DEPARTEMENTS: 1836-1838
TO 1894-1898

Date	Number of départements with a stillbirth ratio of				Total départements
	Less than 2	2-3	4-5	More than 6	
1836-1838	33	42	9	2	86
1839-1843	23	45	17	1	86
1844-1848	14	48	23	1	86
1849-1853	10	40	34	2	86
1854-1858	4	37	39	6	86
1859-1863	3	32	45	6	86
1864-1868	1	31	49	8	89
1869-1873	1	29	49	8	87
1874-1878	0	30	50	7	87
1879-1883	0	33	47	7	87
1884-1888	1	25	54	7	87
1889-1893	1	20	58	8	87
1894-1898	0	18	60	9	87

NOTE: Stillbirth ratio is the number of stillbirths per 100 live births.
SOURCE: France, passim.

sex ratio in France somewhat below that prevailing in European countries where all live births are recorded. These considerations would lead us to expect a sex ratio of 104 or 105 as most probable for France. This ratio might have been somewhat higher at the beginning of the century when children dead before registration were often counted as live births. On the other hand, neonatal mortality was probably also higher at that time, and the toll among males was then proportionately heavier. On the whole, one would not expect any clear trend with time, and therefore it comes as a surprise that the sex ratios for France as a whole decline from 107 in 1809–1813 to 104.1 in 1894–1898 (Table 2.6). It is therefore appropriate to inquire whether this change might reflect an improvement of the vital statistics.

At the départemental level, one would expect not only lasting differences in the level of the sex ratio, but also random fluctuation over

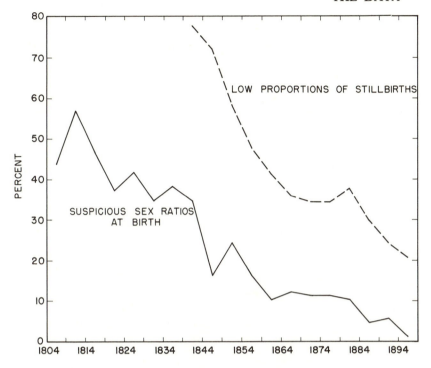

Figure 2.9 Percentage Départements with Suspicious Sex Ratios at Birth
and Low Proportions of Stillbirths: 1804-1808 to 1894-1898

time. One hundred and five is only an average value; levels between 103 and 107 cannot be rejected offhand and have been reliably observed in certain populations over long periods of time. For example, the Seine département maintains a sex ratio close to 103 during the whole century. Random fluctuation around the expected level should be distributed normally, and it is possible to compute the normal confidence interval, within which 95 percent of the cases should be found, by means of the following formula which takes into account the number of births.

$$\sigma(p) = \sqrt{\frac{pq}{n}}$$

where p is the expected proportion of male births, q the expected proportion of female births, and n the observed number of births of both sexes (Visaria, 1963, pp. 75-76). Table 2.6 gives for every

[51]

METHODS

TABLE 2.6

SEX RATIOS, DISTRIBUTION OF DEPARTEMENTS WITH RESPECT TO CONFIDENCE LIMITS:
1804-1808 TO 1894-1898

Date	Sex Ratio	Distribution with respect to confidence limits			Total départements
		Under	Within	Above	
1804-1808	106.4	6	42	37	85
1809-1813	107.0	5	32	49	86
1814-1818	106.6	4	42	40	86
1819-1823	106.4	4	50	32	86
1824-1828	106.4	6	44	36	86
1829-1833	106.2	5	51	30	86
1834-1838	106.2	7	46	33	86
1839-1843	106.0	6	50	30	86
1844-1848	105.4	7	65	14	86
1849-1853	105.4	7	58	21	86
1854-1858	105.3	6	66	14	86
1859-1863	105.1	9	68	9	86
1864-1868	105.0	7	71	11	89
1869-1873	104.9	10	67	10	87
1874-1878	104.8	11	66	10	87
1879-1883	104.7	12	66	9	87
1884-1888	104.6	9	74	4	87
1889-1893	104.6	9	73	5	87
1894-1898	104.1	12	74	1	87

NOTE: The expected sex ratio is 105 male births per 100 female births.

SOURCE: France, passim.

period the number of instances where the sex ratio is above, within, or below the normal confidence interval of 1.96 sigma, assuming 105 as the expected sex ratio. There is a clear trend toward a lower sex ratio as time goes by and the départements conform increasingly to the expected norm. Although this could be the result of some real trend in the masculinity of births, there are also less fluctuations in the ratios from period to period. The evidence seems to point to an improvement of the records, particularly in the registration of female births.

[52]

Some regional patterns emerge from the data presented here. The quality of reporting seems better in the North than in the South of France. We turned to linear correlation coefficients to express this relationship between the geographical distributions. We shall also include in the correlations the infant mortality at the time when the deaths by age are first given in the official publications by département, in order to test whether a low infant mortality, which may be caused at least in part by a faulty reporting of infant deaths, is related to below-normal reporting of stillbirths and to high sex ratios. Furthermore, as a possible factor explaining the differential quality of the reporting, we shall correlate the variables described above with the proportion of illiteracy by département.[11]

The zero-order correlation coefficients are given in Table 2.7.

TABLE 2.7

ZERO ORDER CORRELATION BETWEEN INFANT MORTALITY, STILLBIRTH RATIO,
SEX RATIO, AND ILLITERACY: SELECTED DATES

	Infant mortality 1864-1868	Stillbirth ratio 1839-1863	Sex ratio 1839-1863
Stillbirth ratio 1839-1863	0.224		
Sex ratio 1839-1863	-0.281	-0.363	
Illiteracy 1866	-0.460	-0.561	0.254

NOTES: N = 86.
  Infant mortality refers to the number of deaths of children under 1 year per 1,000 live births.
  Stillbirth ratio is the number of stillbirths per 100 live births.
  Sex ratio is the number of male births per 100 female births.
  Illiteracy is the percentage of females, aged 20-24, illiterate.

[11] Our index of illiteracy is derived from the census of 1901. It is the proportion of illiterate women who would have been between the ages of 20 and 29 at the time of the 1866 census. In 1901, they were between 60 and 69 years of age. This is a legitimate index of illiteracy at an earlier period, since literacy generally is acquired before 20 and changes little after that.

METHODS

There were 86 départements at the time. The correlation coefficients are thus all significant at the 95 percent level. Of course, one would normally expect significant correlations between some of the variables considered. For instance, infant mortality and the proportion of stillbirths should both reflect the state of health in the départements. But it appears that the weak r of 0.224 found between the two variables is the result of their common association with literacy. When a partial correlation is computed, "holding constant" illiteracy, the association between infant mortality and the proportion of stillbirths becomes negative and ceases to be significant (see Table 2.8). Also, a large proportion of true stillbirths and deaths

TABLE 2.8

PARTIAL CORRELATIONS BETWEEN INFANT MORTALITY, STILLBIRTH RATIO, AND
SEX RATIO, CONTROLLING FOR ILLITERACY: SELECTED DATES

	Infant mortality 1864-1868	Stillbirth ratio 1839-1863
Stillbirth ratio 1839-1863	-0.046	
Sex ratio 1839-1863	-0.191	-0.275

NOTES: N = 86.
Infant mortality refers to the number of deaths of children under 1 year per 1,000 live births.
Stillbirth ratio is the number of stillbirths per 100 live births.
Sex ratio is the number of male births per 100 female births.
Illiteracy is the percentage of females, aged 20-24, illiterate.

before registration, with their high masculinity, might decrease the sex ratio at birth. However, one would expect a high ratio of illiteracy to be positively associated with mortality, and not negatively as is found in the French data. Indeed, an educated population should be expected to provide better care to mother and child, and the départements where education is more widespread should also have the lower mortality. On the other hand, it is likely that illiterate persons would report their vital events less completely and less accurately. And the general association of low infant mortality, low proportion of stillbirths, and high sex ratio with a high prevalence of illiteracy suggests that misreporting or under-registration of infant deaths, of "stillbirths" (including infant deaths before registration), and of female births might be a more likely explanation of the relationships encountered. Partial correlations meant to account for the common association with literacy decrease the correlations between the other variables (see Table 2.8).

We may thus conclude that there is prima facie evidence that the reporting of vital events was biased or incomplete, that it is likely that the period under review witnessed an improvement of registration, and that there are regional differences in the quality of the records. These conclusions warrant a further study of the extent of underreporting.

Similarly, the poor quality of the censuses, discussed earlier, will hamper the study of the fertility trends by départements in France. The following chapters explore a method to reconstitute the demographic history of the French population and to evaluate the extent of underregistration of births and of misreporting in censuses.

CHAPTER 3: Reconstruction of the Female Population by Age

I. *General description of the method*

The available data have been described in the previous chapter, and some preliminary indications have suggested that both censuses and vital registration were deficient, at least in some regions and at some times during the 19th century. This chapter attempts to reconstruct estimates of the female age distribution and the female birth series, parallel to the official ones, i.e. using the same geographical classification (the départements) and the same dates as the published censuses and vital registration. Despite all its defects, the French material is exceptionally complete in its coverage. There are frequent censuses: every five years over most of the century. And although the early censuses are not detailed, information exists at least on the size of the population by sex and marital status. Vital registration was uninterrupted from 1800 on.

The area of départements remained extremely stable. The following border changes are recorded:[1]

(1) In 1808, the département of Tarn-et-Garonne was formed out of areas taken from the départements of Lot, Garonne (Haute-), Lot-et-Garonne, Gers, and Aveyron.

(2) The Treaty of Paris (November 21, 1815) determined the new borders of France at the end of the Napoleonic wars. Of course, the statistical data had been collected on the borders of the time; but when the newly founded Bureau of Statistics endeavored to publish the results of past censuses and vital registration in 1837, it reorganized the data to fit the new borders. Unfortunately, all the necessary corrections were not made. In particular, the published data for the population of Ain in 1801 omits the *arrondissement* of Gex, and includes two cantons lost by Ardennes in 1815.[2]

---

[1] Many details about border changes are given in France, 1923, pp. 31-37.

[2] The *Centre de démographie historique* in Paris, under the leadership of Jacques Dupâquier, has traced all the border changes of the early part of the century, but this became known to the author too late to make use of the information here.

(3) A small part of Pyrénées (Basses-) was annexed to Landes in 1857.

(4) In 1860, Savoie and Nice were annexed to France, and three new départements were created: Savoie, Savoie (Haute-), and Alpes-Maritimes (the latter including a part of Var).

(5) In 1871, at the end of the Franco-Prussian war, Alsace and Lorraine, a large chunk of France which did not exactly correspond to previous administrative units, was annexed by Germany. The départements of Moselle, Rhin (Bas-), and Rhin (Haut-) ceased to exist, and Meurthe-et-Moselle was assembled out of the remaining parts of Moselle and Meurthe; what remained of Rhin (Haut-) became the Territory of Belfort. Vosges also lost part of its territory.

As a result of the border changes, we have not attempted the reconstruction of the demographic history of the following départements: Alpes-Maritimes, the Territory of Belfort, Meurthe-et-Moselle, Savoie and Savoie (Haute-).

We have also left out the most urbanized départements, i.e. Seine and Seine-et-Oise (the Paris region), Rhône (including Lyon), and Bouches-du-Rhône (Marseilles). This is an important and in many ways regrettable omission, but the importance of migration streams made these départements intractable to the standard methods of reconstruction presented in this volume. They present an analytical problem that has to be tackled separately.

In all, we reconstructed the female population of 82 départements between 1801 and 1906 by age, and corrected the birth series during the same period. The reconstruction attempts to use, as much as possible, the existing census data and the vital registration. We know that no great confidence should be given to any part of the grid of demographic information that we possess, coming from either censuses or vital registration. However—and this is the idea behind our method—from the coherence of the information considered as a whole, we can assess the reliability of the details. We possess information about the same people at various points in time. A birth cohort, of which the initial size is given by the registration, can be followed as it grows older through several censuses, being successively depleted by mortality and affected by migration. If

[57]

there is an inconsistency between the various sources, it can usually be traced to its origin. For instance, assuming that the given levels of mortality and migration are known or estimated, the under-reporting of a cohort at birth becomes apparent if successive censuses indicate that there are relatively too many survivors, so that the cohort cannot have originated in the recorded number of births. Similarly, an unusually large age-group in a census that is not related to a large cohort (i.e. that is not unusually large in other censuses and originating in a large number of births) becomes suspect and can probably be traced to a defect of that census itself.

These general principles are used in this chapter to estimate age distributions covering the entire 19th century, five years apart, and to correct the birth series. The main sets of data used were:

a) The series of female births and deaths in five-year spans, starting in 1801; i.e. 1801–1805, 1806–1810, . . . 1901–1905.
b) The total female population at the time of the censuses, or interpolated values when there was no census (in 1811, 1816, and 1826). We have assumed, despite the variability of dates at which the censuses were actually taken, that the figure was valid for January 1st of 1801, 1806, . . . 1906.[3]

We always used the above data, as recorded, in a preliminary reconstruction of the population. The ground was thus laid for an eventual correction of the inputs when they led to inconsistent results.

Using these data, we rounded out the model with three basic sets of assumptions:

1) The age distribution in 1801 was assumed to conform to a stable population of either the West or the North Model tables.[4]
2) Schedules of mortality of the West or the North pattern were used to project the population, five years ahead at a time.
3) An identical pattern of migration by age was used every-where.

[3] This involved another approximation: Censuses were at some times taken late in the year, and the date of one of them, in April-May 1872, was quite remote from January 1st of the assumed year, 1871.
[4] The stable populations and mortality schedules at various levels were taken from Coale and Demeny, 1966.

The use of these three basic sets of assumptions will be justified in more detail. At this point, we are attempting to give a general overview of the method. The reconstruction of the female population of any département for which no border change intervened between 1801 and 1906 is essentially a projection of the assumed 1801 population by age, and of the births occurring after 1801 in five-year periods. These births make up the youngest age-group at the end of the period and are projected ahead together with the 1801 survivors in their respective age-groups. The deaths by age in five-year periods after 1801 are distributed according to a model pattern of mortality applied to the estimated population at the beginning of the period and to the births occurring during the period. The level of mortality is determined by the total number of deaths reported in the five-year period. Finally, the difference between the projected population size and the one recorded at the next census is attributed to in- or out-migration or to small random errors in the data and allocated by age according to the schedule of migration. In algebraic notation:

if PT_n is the total female population at census n;

if $(_5P_a)_n$ is the female population aged between a and $a + 5$ at census n;

if B_N and D_N are, respectively, the female births and deaths recorded in the five-year period N between time n and $n + 5$;

if l_0, $_5L_a$ and T_a are conventional life table symbols for, respectively, the radix of the table, the stationary population between age a and $a + 5$, and the stationary population above age a in the appropriate model life table;

then we have the following equations:

$$PT_n = \sum (_5P_a)_n ; \tag{1}$$

$$(_5P_0)'_{n+l} = B_N \frac{_5L_0}{5l_0} ; \tag{2}$$

$$(_5P_a)'_{n+5} = (_5P_{a-5})_n \cdot \frac{_5L_a}{_5L_{a-5}} \tag{3}$$

[59]

where a is a multiple of 5 greater than 5;

$$D_N = B_N \left(1 - \frac{{}_5L_0)}{5l_0)}\right) + ({}_5P_0)_n \left(1 - \frac{{}_5L_5)}{{}_5L_0)}\right) + \ldots$$

$$+ ({}_5P_{70})_n \left(1 - \frac{{}_5L_{75})}{{}_5L_{70})}\right) + (P_{75+})_n (1 - T_{80}/T_{75}) ; \quad (4)$$

and

$$PT'_{n+5} = \sum ({}_5P_a)'_{n+5}. \quad (5)$$

Because of intercensal migrations during the period, PT'_{n+5} is not equal to PT_{n+5}. The difference we call M_{n+5}, so that

$$M_{n+5} = PT_{n+5} - PT'_{n+5}. \quad (6)$$

We allocate M_{n+5} by age according to migration weights by age ${}_5w_a$; so that finally

$$({}_5P_a)_{n+5} = ({}_5P_a)'_{n+5} + {}_5w_a \cdot M_{n+5}. \quad (7)$$

The migration weights will be discussed later. At this point, for the sake of presenting the model, we assume that there was no migration, or that it was distributed evenly among the age-groups, proportionally to their size. In other terms, we assume provisionally for each estimation that

$$\,_5w_a = \frac{({}_5P_a)'_{n+5}}{PT'_{n+5}} . \quad (8)$$

Incidentally, this simplification takes care for the time being of any difference between the sizes of the projected population and the one enumerated at the end of each five-year period that might be due to fluctuations in the completeness of registration or of census enumeration. These differences are allocated proportionately to the age groups in the later population.

We make two further simplifying assumptions. At this stage, for exposition's sake, we shall take for granted (a) that the 1801 population was stable and had the age distribution implied in the crude birth and death rates of 1801–1805; (b) that the West pattern of mortality was valid. We shall devote two sections of this chapter, respectively, to a review of the criteria used to evaluate and correct the data and to a discussion of the above three assumptions about the 1801 stable population, the mortality pattern, and the migration pattern. Each of these preliminary assumptions will have to be revised or qualified at a later point.

To illustrate the procedure, we reconstruct the population of Calvados, in Normandy. The original data for Calvados are presented in Table 3.1: the census-enumerated total female population and the births and deaths between census dates. Population totals for the years when there was no census were obtained by linear interpolation between the two censuses nearest to the estimated value's date, and are given between brackets. (For example, 1826 is the average of the population total for 1821 and 1831.) We assume that all population numbers are valid for the first of January of the year, and that the intercensal period coincides with the five years spanned by the vital registration. The reconstruction presented here constitutes only a preliminary test of the hypotheses. The problems encountered with Calvados suggest solutions that can be applied at a later point to similar data.

At least one of our assumptions does not strain the facts greatly: there was apparently little net migration to or from Calvados during the century, and the balance of reported births and deaths accounts nicely for intercensal increases. The censuses were fairly good and were also consistent with the vital registration in most cases; the exceptions are clearly in error. The total census population size in 1801 is markedly smaller than the estimate obtained by subtracting births and adding deaths to the 1846 base population, whereas the two figures agree reasonably at the other census dates. The presumption of underenumeration in 1801 becomes overwhelming when a similar drop of the R/CB ratio is found in département after département. We note that we shall have to inflate the census figure for that year, in order to make it consistent with the rest of the series.

The initial population in 1801 has the size recorded at the 1801 census—240,049 people—and the crude birth and death rates of the period 1801–1805—i.e. the 28,163 female births and 24,996 female deaths registered in the interval, divided by five (for five years) over the average of the 1801 and 1806 population figures. A crude birth rate of 22.42 and a crude death rate of 19.90 per

METHODS

TABLE 3.1

REPORTED FEMALE POPULATION COMPARED WITH COMPUTATION BASED ON FEMALE
BIRTHS AND DEATHS, CALVADOS: 1801 TO 1906

Date	Reported total (R)	Female births	Female deaths	Computed total (CB)	R/CB ratio
1801	240,049			257,108	.934
		28,163	24,996		
1806	262,349			260,275	1.008
		27,516	24,698		
1811	262,766[a]			263,093	.999[a]
		26,105	24,990		
1816	263,183[a]			264,208	.996[a]
		26,704	25,060		
1821	263,600			265,852	.992
		27,318	26,801		
1826	263,340[a]			266,369	.989[a]
		26,295	26,786		
1831	263,080			265,878	.989
		25,838	26,619		
1836	266,323			265,097	1.005
		25,006	25,247		
1841	262,399			264,856	.991
		23,656	25,480		
1846	263,032			263,032	1.000
		22,879	27,045		
1851	257,629			258,866	.995
		22,869	28,553		
1856	252,918			253,182	.999
		23,675	27,159		
1861	251,581			249,698	1.008
		23,812	28,079		
1866	247,287			245,431	1.008
		22,990	28,540		
1871	237,402			239,881	.990
		22,392	30,222		
1876	234,793			232,051	1.012
		22,243	25,735		
1881	228,574			228,559	1.000
		22,092	24,418		
1886	223,997			226,233	.990
		21,851	25,371		
1891	226,129			222,713	1.015
		21,061	26,570		
1896	218,026			217,204	1.004
		20,670	24,180		
1901	212,559			213,694	.995
		20,646	22,321		
1906	206,678			212,019	.989

NOTE: The computed total is derived from the balance of births and deaths
over the 1846 reported population.

[a]Interpolated values.

thousand determine a unique stable population in the Model West tables. This stable population is projected from 1801 on to 1906 as explained above.

With the published detailed age distributions after 1851, we are able to compare the estimated population by age to the recorded one. This comparison has taken the form of ratios of the reported population over the estimated one (called hereafter R/E ratios), and is shown in Figure 3.1 by solid lines. Perfect agreement would produce R/E ratios of 1.0 overall, and the divergences which we encounter require an explanation.

One striking feature of Figure 3.1 is that the tail of the four first census age distributions consistently appears to contain more people than are projected from 1801 in the estimate. This can be noted by observing the R/E ratios for ages 50–54 and over in 1851, for ages 55–59 and over in 1856, and so on. The most striking discrepancy is for the three cohorts that were, respectively, aged 0–4, 5–9, and 10–14 in 1801. The discrepancy originates in the stable population estimated for 1801. As we showed before, the overall size of the enumerated population in 1801 was underreported (a feature that is adjusted for to some extent by the application of formula [7] in 1806). But in addition, its age distribution is also not steep enough. The size of the three first age-groups estimated in 1801 is inconsistent with the number of their survivors enumerated in the censuses of 1851, 1856, 1861, and 1866. These four censuses as a rule are better than later ones, at least before 1901. We attempt to find a stable age distribution in 1801 such that, for the accepted population size in that year[5] and taking into account the deaths between 1801 and 1866 distributed according to model mortality schedules by age, the sum of the number of survivors to 1851, 1856, 1861, and 1866 in the cohorts born in 1786–1790, 1791–1795, and 1796–1800 is equal to the sum of the population at the relevant ages in the four censuses. Concretely, we instructed the computer to modify the rate of growth of the initial stable population first computed from the

[5] I.e., the new population size of 257,108, corrected for underenumeration in 1801 by substitution of the result computed by the balance of births and deaths (see Table 3.1).

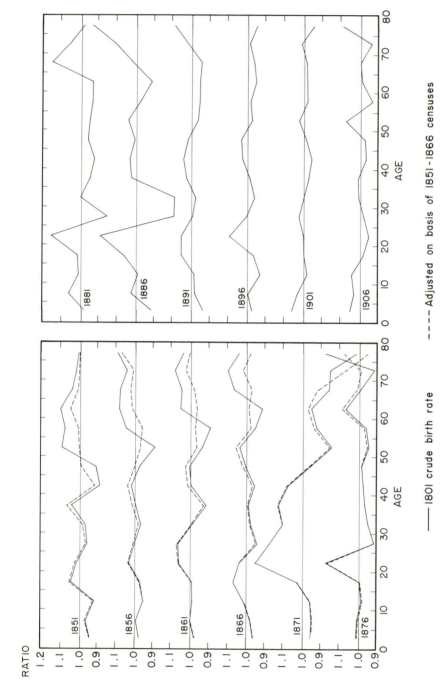

Figure 3.1 Ratios of Reported to Estimated Female Population as Calculated
from Two Different Stable Populations, by Age, Calvados: 1851 to 1906

—— 1801 crude birth rate   - - - - Adjusted on basis of 1851-1866 censuses

crude birth and death rates for 1801, keeping the same mortality level, until the projected three age-groups in the four more reliable censuses of 1851, 1856, 1861, and 1866 added up to the actual reported number.[6] This new stable population was supposed to be the one valid for 1801 at all ages. The degree of imprecision introduced by this procedure will be discussed later. It must be remarked at this stage that the age distribution of 1851 is determined up to age 50 by the births and deaths recorded in the vital registration, and that the influence of the initial 1801 estimate decreases in importance as one advances through the century. The results of the new set of assumptions is plotted in broken lines on Figure 3.1. After 1876, the two lines are almost indistinguishable, and only solid lines are shown.

II. *Evaluation of the data*

We still assume at this point that the model's assumptions about mortality and migration are valid. This section is devoted to setting out some criteria for the evaluation of the data. The data are part of our model; but at the same time their correction is among the goals of the reconstruction. It is convenient to use the ratios of the reported over the estimated population (R/E ratios in short) to analyze and correct both the vital statistics series, which served to construct the estimated population, and the series of censuses which provides the reported population.

If vital registration were perfect, then deviations from unity of the R/E ratios would have to be attributed to age misreporting or to omissions and double counts. We cannot assume, however, that all the data errors originated in the censuses. When the biases are clearly age specific, i.e. when they are either found repeatedly in successive censuses at the same age or characterize one age group at one particular census without being found again cohort-wise at the corresponding ages in previous or later censuses, then it is safe to blame them on the census. (Examples of typical age specific

[6] We shall present much evidence concerning the fact that these four censuses were the best taken during the century. By averaging a cohort over four censuses, we further reduce the uncertainty of the procedure.

biases are underreporting of the first age group 0 to 4 in many départements, and heaping on the age group 20–24.) A deficiency in the birth series, on the contrary, will result in a cohort effect, found repeatedly in successive reconstructed age distributions as the generation originating in the misreported births moves on in age.

Figure 3.1 gives examples both of age specific and of cohort deviations in Calvados. Heaping on the age-group 20–24 is very frequent between 1871 and 1896. In 1876, 1881, and 1886, the next age-group is much smaller, as if women who in fact belonged to the age group 25–29 had reported themselves as aged 20–24. The 1872 census appears to be defective overall;[7] a priori, no known pattern of migration could explain such discrepancies between the estimated population and the reported one. Since the estimated populations are more consistent—that is, more compatible with the combined evidence of neighboring censuses and of the vital registration—we have grounds for believing that the discrepancies are due to serious defects in the 1872 census. Thus, our reconstruction can be used as a standard against which we measure the accuracy of a census.

However, this is only legitimate within limits. The reconstruction may have its own defects, and insofar as the defects are not due to our assumptions but to the data inputs, they may point to the vital statistics used as the source of bias. A deficit in the number of births will appear as a cohort with an inflated R/E ratio in census after census. One such cohort in Figure 3.1 can be traced back to the births between 1811 and 1815. The girls born during these years were aged 35 to 39 years in 1851, 40 to 44 in 1856, and so on. In most censuses since 1851, the R/E ratio for the cohort 1811–1815 is larger than 1.0, suggesting that the estimated number is too small, and that too few births are given for these years. To adjust the cohort, we inflate the number of births by the average of the R/E ratios at census dates that appear to have consistent population

___

[7] The comparison with our estimate for January 1, 1871, is not entirely legitimate, but since the population of Calvados was growing very slowly at the time, since the département was remote from the scenes of battle, and since there is little evidence of migration, the real age distributions of January 1871 and of April-May 1872 must have been very similar.

sizes for the age-group: in the present instance, 1851, 1856, 1861, and 1866. The computation is as follows:

Cohort	1851	R/E Ratio in: 1856	1861	1866	Average 1851-1866	Births 1811-1815 Reported	Adjusted
1811-1815	1.073	1.042	1.028	1.060	1.051	26,105	26,105 x 1.051 = 27,436

There are other birth cohorts that might also require a correction, but their existence is more doubtful. For instance, it is possible that an insufficiency of births between 1831 and 1836 caused a series of high R/E ratios starting at age 15–19 in 1851 (see Figure 3.1). However, the cohort ceases to be noticeable from 1866 on, so we made no adjustment.

It is easier to conceive of a deviant cohort originating in the deficiency of births (R/E above 1.0) than in their excess (R/E under 1.0).[8] Therefore, we hesitate to correct the 1821–1825 births, although there is a cohort which is out of line (starting at age 25–29 in 1851). It may find its origin in an incorrect total population estimate for 1826 (witness the effect of inflating the 1801 census total on the 1801–1805 birth cohort) or in the underestimation of mortality.

The effect of understating the number of deaths is more difficult to assess than that of the number of births, although both may occur. If deaths were omitted randomly, they will not affect the age distribution greatly. If, however, some systematic underregistration was occurring, the deaths most likely to go unreported were those of young children; and the effect on the age distribution would be very similar to that of an overstatement of births. The simultaneous omission of births and of deaths of young children thus would have compensating effects on the age distribution. This is likely to have happened, since one may presume that registration of births and deaths was bad at the same time in the same areas, or that mayors would have abstained from sending returns which included both the

[8] We talk of deficiency, or excess, rather than of under- or overregistration, as the source of the most frequent problem must have been with the tabulating and centralizing of the already-registered events, rather than with their recording in the communes (see Chapter 2).

births and deaths of their communes. As a rule, we have made no adjustments for the faulty totaling of deaths.

In the instance of Calvados, a département that has comparatively good data, the need to correct the series of births may be doubtful. There are, however, a large number of départements where there are obvious deficiencies which leave a clear imprint on the R/E ratios by showing a deficient number of women in successive projected age-groups in the series of estimates. When the results are graphed, they show a characteristic hump moving cohortwise from census to census. The example of Indre-et-Loire in Figure 3.2 is particularly convincing. The solid line represents the results of the reconstruction with unadjusted data. The births in 1811–1815 (and probably in 1806–1810 as well) were clearly underestimated. A less common instance of excessive number of births occurs in 1866–1870. In the latter case, the blame must almost certainly lie with a clerical mistake. In 1867, the published figure is 7,116 female births as compared with 3,872 male births for the same year, and 3,113 female births in 1868. We also show in the figure, in broken lines, the reconstruction after correcting for the deficient birth cohorts and after a few minor adjustments, such as that of the population size in 1801. The corrected series is based on the population given for Indre-et-Loire in the second part of this book. After the birth correction, the erratic fluctuations of the R/E ratios are probably due mostly to faulty reporting in the census. The 1856 census was particularly deficient. Some familiar patterns of errors are often present, such as the shortage of children under age 5 and an excess between 20 and 24.

III. *A review of the assumptions*

We have assumed until now that the French mortality pattern in the 19th century could be approximated by model life tables. This hypothesis must now be discussed. In later parts of this section, we shall deal with two other critical assumptions used in our model, namely the use of a stable population in 1801 and the estimation of migration.

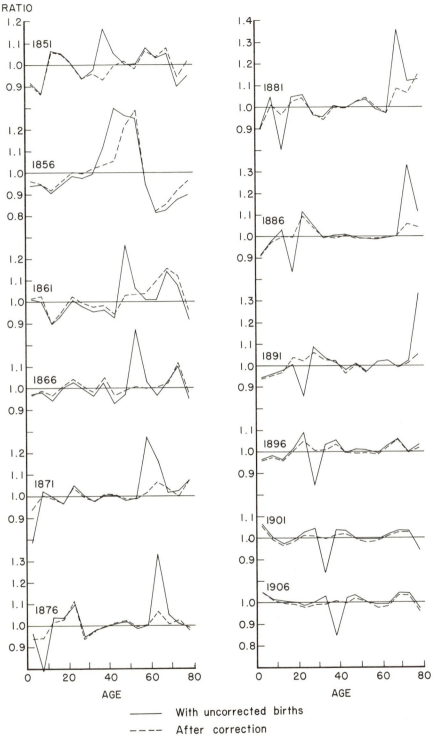

RATIO

Figure 3.2 Ratios of Reported to Estimated Female Population as Calculated
from Adjusted and Unadjusted Births, by Age, Indre-et-Loire: 1851 to 1906

METHODS

A. MORTALITY PATTERN

We must recognize quite candidly that we possess little information concerning mortality patterns during the 19th century, particularly by regions or by départements. Published distributions of deaths by age for the whole of France do exist from the beginning of the century.[9] The official statistics give deaths by age by département from 1861 on, although the data had been assembled previously and can sometimes be found in départemental yearbooks or regional monographs.[10] However, these distributions are not necessarily accurate. They may be somewhat more accurate than the age distributions of living populations, because the registrar could check the birth entry when a death was reported in the commune of birth. However, we know that the French statisticians of the time did not think the reliability of death distributions was such as to deserve publication.[11]

Even if the recorded distributions of deaths by age were inaccurate, there is no certainty that the true distribution conformed to a standard pattern of mortality tabulated in the model life tables. The experience of mortality in 19th-century France may have been different from that in the countries from whose experience the models were derived. It is true that French life tables were actually used in the derivation of the West model, but they were themselves a by-product of the reconstruction of the population done by Bourgeois-Pichat (1951). Some of their characteristics may be due to idiosyncrasies of that reconstruction. There is no doubt that the application of model life tables to the past presents problems. Cer-

[9] The number of deaths by year from 1806 to 1859 is given in the Appendix to France, 1863. The total number of deaths does not always agree with that given in tabulations that do not include age; varying numbers of départements are omitted, mostly during the 1820s.

[10] Unpublished data by département exist in the National Archives in Paris. Their existence was unknown to the author at the time he was preparing the reconstructions presented in this book.

[11] Legoyt, the future head of the French Bureau of Statistics, wrote that "the age of the deceased was a certain cause of error, the mayors being obliged to accept the more or less exact declarations of the witnesses on the death certificate . . ." (Legoyt, 1843, p. IV).

[70]

tain diseases which were typical of the time affected the population by age in characteristic ways. The example of tuberculosis is well known. Historically, tuberculosis has affected certain birth cohorts —particularly in the 19th century and early 20th century—in ways which were not clearly dependent on the general mortality level of the population, and tubercular mortality has "followed" these cohorts from period to period (Frost, 1940). The age pattern of tuberculosis deviates from the standard one most of all from age 5 to 35 or 40 (Coale and Demeny, 1966, p. 13-14). Cholera, a great killer in the 19th century, seems to have killed mainly adults and to have affected very young children rather little (Chevalier, 1958, pp. 81-85, 95, 119).

In Figure 3.3 we compare for Calvados the distribution of deaths by age reported during various intercensal intervals, with the estimated distribution resulting, for the same total number of deaths, from the application of a model West mortality schedule to the age distribution estimated for the time. The West model produces entirely satisfactory results for 1901-1905, and conforms very closely to the recorded distribution. In earlier years, however, the approximation is less satisfactory. In the 1890s, more deaths are estimated than reported at most ages; the difference is made up by the large number of reported deaths of old people (75 and over). There may of course have been a tendency toward reporting dead people as older than they were. In the beginning of the series (e.g. 1861–1865) the number of deaths reported under 30 is much greater than the estimated number. This may have been the impact of diseases such as tuberculosis—but the evidence is slim. The use of the North mortality pattern gives a distribution of deaths which is closer to the recorded one in some years. But the West model approximates the enumerated population more closely; and, by the end of the century, the West distribution of deaths is clearly better. These two criteria appear sufficient to choose the West model in the instance of Calvados. In other départements, we may have to accept empirically another pattern if it produces a better fit.

It is well to remember that the age distribution of deaths is more

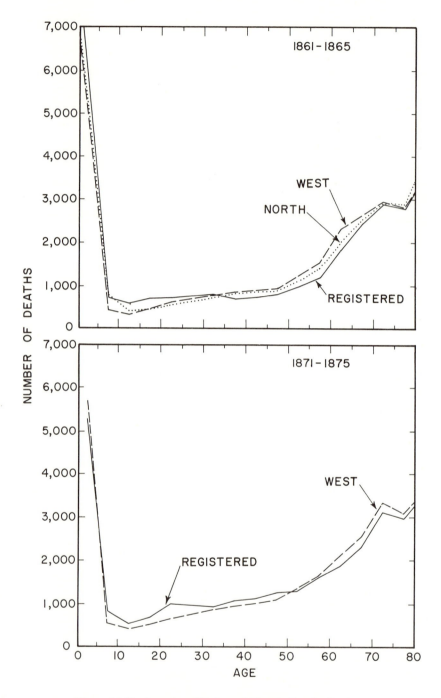

Figure 3.3 Registered and Estimated Female Deaths, by Age,
Calvados: 1861 to 1905

[72]

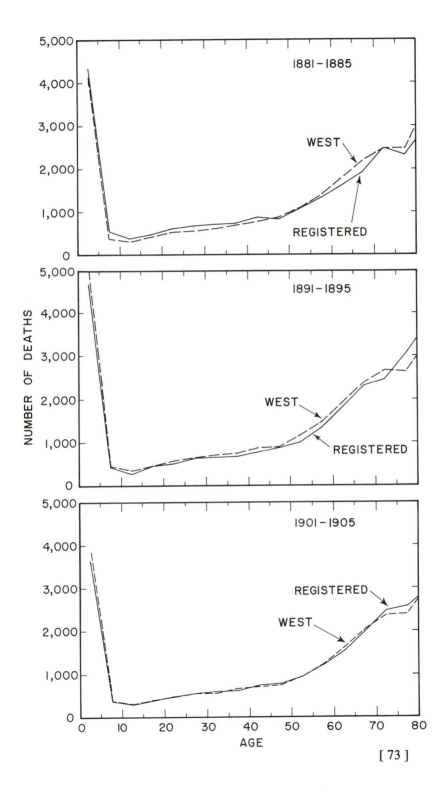

sensitive to variations in mortality pattern and age distribution than the proportions surviving actually used in the projection.[12] One must also keep in mind that cohorts, as they are projected, are successively subjected to the mortality of various age-groups. Thus, the depletion of a birth cohort involves a cumulative effect, where the biases in opposite directions have an opportunity to compensate.

We may conclude in this section on mortality patterns that the question of their adequacy is an empirical one that cannot really be settled a priori. In Calvados, at least, the use of the West model permits us to reconstruct age distributions which are reasonably close to some of the censuses that appear most reliable. This fit at some dates is our best indication that a standard mortality pattern is appropriate. As a rule, we have used the same family of models (either West or North) throughout for a département, although in reality there may of course have been shifts in time. This means also that the stable population chosen in 1801 had the same mortality pattern as the survivorship ratios by which the population was projected.

It is somewhat reassuring that the areas where the West or the North pattern was used, purely on the basis of internal evidence, fell nicely into regional patterns when they were mapped at the end of the départements' reconstruction (see Map 3.1). A large area in the North of France seems to conform to the North pattern; three neighboring départements of Provence were also reconstructed on the basis of the North tables. It might be of interest to note that, although the West model life tables seem to conform to the experience of France as described by the official life tables from the second part of the 19th century on, they do not adequately fit the death series and the generational life tables computed by Blayo and Henry for Brittany in the 18th and early 19th centuries. North in that case seems much closer than the U.N. model tables and, therefore, than the West family which is close to the latter (Blayo and Henry, 1967, p. 155; van de Walle, 1972).

[12] In life table notation: if the registered deaths tend to have the biases present in the age distribution, the variation of mortality will be less expressed in q_x and m_x than in d_x. Furthermore, p_x, used in the projection, varies much less than q_x, since it is equal to $1-q_x$.

North

West

x Not applicable

Map 3.1 Mortality Pattern, Model Used in Reconstruction, by Département

B. A STABLE POPULATION IN 1801

We must now turn to the second assumption used in the recon-struction, namely the use of a stable population to approximate the age distribution in 1801. Information from the census and the vital registration for Calvados about 1801 or 1806 point to a crude birth rate between 20 and 25 per thousand. It seems therefore that the area had already undergone a decline of fertility. In much of France, moreover, the early 1800s were a time of hardship; and external wars compelled the conscription of young men, delaying or hastening their marriages and causing fluctuations in the number of births. We can say a priori that the age distribution of 1801 will not be perfectly simulated by a stable population. The fact remains, however, that stable population theory provides a convenient model to reconstruct age distributions on the basis of crude birth and death rates and recorded population size. In regions of France where fertility had not yet declined, and where the census and vital regis-tration can be trusted, the approximation to the real age distribution in 1801 must be close enough.

We are not worrying here about a possible underestimation of the birth rate or of the population size enumerated in the census, since the reconstruction procedure provides means to correct these de-fects, and the projection can be redone with corrected inputs. (As for an underestimation of mortality, the effect on the estimated age distribution is relatively inconsiderable.) The crucial question is whether the stable population, based on the vital rates of 1801–1806, can be used when fertility had started to decline before the turn of the century—as it had in Calvados. The extent to which the age distribution had been affected will depend both on the speed and on the duration of the decline. As an illustration—a purely hypothetical one—let us consider two different paces of fertility reduction with constant mortality, from an initial situation, charac-terized by an $e_0^0 = 40$, and a GRR(29) $= 2$ in the West model stable populations. We project this base population assuming in the first instance (Decline #1) that the GRR decreases at 1 percent per year during thirty years; in the second instance (Decline #2) that it decreases at 2 percent a year for fifteen years. The age distribution and the crude birth and death rates are given in Table 3.2. If we now look for a stable population defined by the same crude birth and death rates, its age distribution will be different—and notably so (see the third column of Table 3.2).

We are very much in the same predicament when we attempt to approximate the population of Calvados in 1801 by a stable population with some estimated crude birth and death rates, except that we do not know the pace of the fertility decline. As indicated before, we have attempted a simple correction to account for the size of the cohorts born in 1786–1800, aged, respectively, 0 to 15 in 1801, and 50 to 64 in 1851, 55 to 69 in 1856, 60 to 74 in 1861, and 65 to 79 in 1866. The R/E ratios for the censuses of 1851 to 1866 give us some indications about the correct size of the three first age-groups in 1801. For a given level of mortality, the slope of the stable age distribution in 1801 can be easily modified by changing the growth rate, in order to generate a population that can be projected to yield a reasonable number of people in the relevant age-groups in 1851 and later. To go back to our illustration of Table 3.2, it is possible to find stable populations which, for the level of mortality of the initial stable, have the same number under age 15 as either the #1 or the #2 instance of declining fertility. These populations are shown in Table 3.2, as well as the ratio of each age-group to that of the #1 or #2 population. It is clear from the illustration that it would be very difficult to simulate perfectly the age distribution in 1801 from the limited information we possess on the reality and the pace of decline in French départements.

This raises a serious objection to our procedure, at least in those areas where the fertility decline had been early and steep. However, the effects of the assumption become increasingly less important as we move in time. Since the population present at the 1801 census is aged over 50 in 1851, the initial assumption of stability will carry little weight after midcentury. By then, the population is estimated almost entirely on the basis of the birth and death records, at least at the fecund ages that are more important in our reconstruction. The question is somewhat different when one considers the validity

TABLE 3.2

AGE DISTRIBUTION OF INITIALLY STABLE POPULATIONS AFFECTED BY HYPOTHETICAL DECLINES IN FERTILITY

| Age | #1: Decline of gross reproduction rate by 1% for 30 years | | | | #2: Decline of gross reproduction rate by 2% for 15 years | | | |
	Population with fertility decline (1)	Initial stable population (2)	Corrected stable population (3)	Ratio (3)/(1)	Population with fertility decline (1)	Initial stable population (2)	Corrected stable population (3)	Ratio (3)/(1)
0-4	951	957	979	1.03	958	958	1,031	1.08
5-9	896	879	894	1.00	933	879	934	1.00
10-14	891	853	865	.97	968	853	894	.92
15-19	880	827	835	.95	954	826	855	.90
20-24	861	795	801	.93	887	794	812	.92
25-29	834	760	762	.91	818	759	766	.94
30-34	784	723	722	.92	750	721	719	.96
35-39	715	682	679	.95	683	681	671	.98
40-44	646	640	635	.98	619	640	623	1.01
45-49	582	598	591	1.02	556	597	573	1.03
50-54	514	550	541	1.05	492	549	521	1.06
55-59	442	492	483	1.09	423	492	461	1.09
60-64	363	422	413	1.14	347	422	391	1.13
65-69	278	337	329	1.18	266	339	309	1.16
70-74	191	244	237	1.24	182	245	222	1.22
75-79	111	150	146	1.32	106	152	136	1.28
80+	61	91	88	1.44	58	93	82	1.41
Total	10,000	10,000	10,000		10,000	10,000	10,000	
Expectation of life at birth	40	42.8	42.8		40	43.4	43.4	
Crude birth rate	23.81	23.81	24.39		23.68	23.68	25.66	
Crude death rate	23.27	23.27	22.59		22.84	22.84	22.32	

NOTES: Column (1) simulates a population which has undergone fertility decline.
Column (2) gives a stable population with the same crude birth and death rates, as might be used as the initial stable population of a reconstruction.
Column (3) corrects the stable population for the age distribution implied on the basis of the

of the reconstruction before 1851. The initial stable population contributes growing sections of the age distribution as we go back in time, and the reconstruction of the period 1801 to 1851 becomes increasingly doubtful. For the purpose of fertility estimation and marital status evaluation it seems that we can push backward in time for fifteen or twenty years, provided the estimated cohorts 1786 to 1800 conform closely enough to their reported equivalents (as expressed by the R/E ratios) in the censuses between 1851 and 1866. When the fit is not good in those censuses, we can improve it by changing the slope of the age distribution of 1801 (that is by modifying the rate of growth for the level of mortality implicit in the recorded mortality, as was done above in Calvados). In the instance of Calvados, the agreement of reported and estimated at the relevant ages between 1851 and 1866 is close enough; no suspicious cohorts show up. By 1831, a large enough segment of the population has been estimated from the registered births, and the three cohorts (1786–1790, 1791–1795, and 1796–1800) can be checked against the enumerated numbers in 1851–1866 and adjusted accordingly. We have sufficient guarantees to be reasonably confident of a close approximation of the age structure at that date. Prior to 1831, the essential purpose of the estimated population is to allow an approximate distribution by age of the deaths for the projection. (We give, with reservations, the estimated population prior to 1831, but will not attempt to estimate the marital distribution nor fertility indices other than the CBR for that period.)

C. MIGRATION

A reconstruction of the population by département encounters an important problem that is almost negligible in the reconstruction of the population of the entire country: the effect of migration on the age distribution. Bourgeois-Pichat, in his estimation of the population of France, neglected migration altogether. We must cope with the problem of internal migration. Calvados, the département used until now as our example, has little recognizable migration, insofar as this would be apparent if the cumulated balance of births and deaths were different from the real increase from census to census (see Figure 3.4). We select one département, Pyrénées (Hautes-), where the cumulated effect of migration is clearly recognizable, and we assume that all other problems (underregistration of birth cohorts, etc.) have been solved. Table 3.3 gives the enumerated population, the population obtained by adding or subtracting the balance of births and deaths to the 1846 enumerated number of women, and the ratio of these two figures. (We call the latter ratio R/CB, for Reported/computed by balance). The R/CB ratio for Pyrénées (Hautes-) is plotted in Figure 3.4. By 1901, the computed value based on 1846 and the intervening vital events, is 20 percent larger than the recorded figure. The difference must be attributed to migration. A reconstruction of the population which

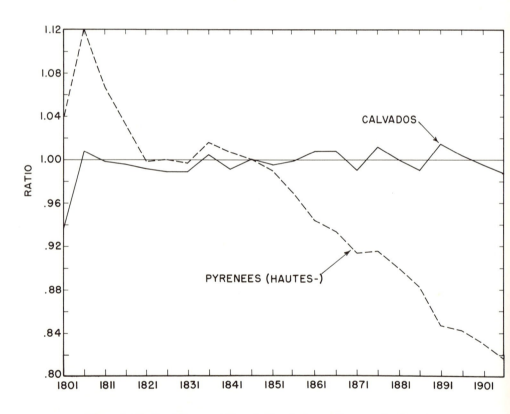

Figure 3.4 Ratio of Reported Female Population to Computation Based on Female Births and Deaths, Calvados and Pyrénées (Hautes-): 1801 to 1906

TABLE 3.3

REPORTED FEMALE POPULATION COMPARED WITH COMPUTATION BASED ON FEMALE BIRTHS
AND DEATHS, PYRENEES (HAUTES-): 1801 TO 1906

Date	Reported total (R)	Computed total (CB)	R/CB ratio
1801	88,779	85,682	1.036
1806	100,877	89,930	1.122
1811	102,902[a]	96,433	1.067[a]
1816	104,927[a]	101,680	1.032[a]
1821	106,952	107,029	0.999
1826	111,877[a]	111,823	1.000[a]
1831	116,801	117,170	0.997
1836	123,022	121,122	1.016
1841	125,116	124,246	1.007
1846	128,121	128,121	1.000
1851	128,608	129,906	0.990
1856	127,598	131,670	0.969
1861	124,257	131,687	0.944
1866	123,515	132,226	0.934
1871	120,829	132,169	0.914
1876	121,172	132,232	0.916
1881	119,829	133,124	0.900
1886	117,840	133,409	0.883
1891	112,322	132,554	0.847
1896	109,645	130,104	0.843
1901	106,551	128,176	0.831
1906	103,996	127,099	0.818

NOTE: The computed total is derived from the balance of births and deaths over the 1846 reported population.

[a]Interpolated values.

does not adjust the population by age produces estimates that are clearly deficient; such a reconstruction is presented in solid lines on Figure 3.5. The ratios of the reported over the estimated age group (or R/E ratios) are consistently under 1.0 at ages where the impact of migration would be strongest. This excess in the estimated population is compensated for at other ages, for the young and old.

[81]

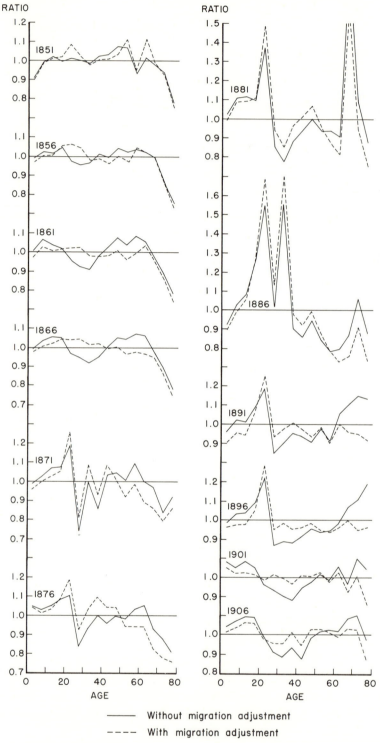

Figure 3.5 Ratio of Reported to Estimated Female Population, with and without Migration Adjustment, Pyrénées (Hautes-) : 1851 to 1906

Instead of reallocating migrants proportionately to the size of the age-group, as was done until now, it becomes necessary to use an age schedule of migration.

At this point, some simplification is inevitable. It is practically impossible to select for each département an age pattern of migration, let alone to change it during the 19th century. On the other hand, the assumption of a uniform pattern is contrary to fact; there were regional differences and fluctuations over time. Fortunately, the effect of even a very arbitrary pattern of migration may not greatly differ from that of another of the same sign, provided streams of migration are regular and fairly constant in size. Suppose for one moment that we ascribed all migrations to age 20 over a long period; in due time, each age-group over 20 would be affected as the affected age-group became older. This example suggests that even the use of an inaccurate pattern may be adequate under certain circumstances.

The actual choice of a schedule was inspired by the fact that the Seine département (where Paris is located) receives a very substantial proportion of the total French internal migration. Therefore, the Parisian pattern of migration by age might be a valid one for the entire country. Unfortunately, we do not possess direct information of internal migration by sex and age during the 19th century, for Paris or elsewhere, on a sufficiently wide scale. With good statistics, however, changes in age distribution between one census and the next that are not accounted for by mortality and fertility must be attributed to migration. We projected the population of the Seine département from 1861 to 1866, with a West mortality pattern at the appropriate level, and compared the resulting hypothetical 1866 population with the recorded one.[13] The differences between the projection and the enumeration were attributed to migration. The results were expressed by age in percent of the total migration so as to provide age-specific migration quotas. The computation was also made for 1896–1901, and the

[13] The level of mortality is that for which m_x's, applied to the average of the reported 1861 and 1866 female populations by age corrected for underreporting of the age-group 0-4, produce the number of female deaths registered between 1861 and 1866.

results were averaged with the ones for 1861–1866. Figure 3.6 presents the age pattern for both periods, and Table 3.4 the migration weights that were finally obtained for each age-group. These weights by age are substituted for $_5w_a$ in equation (7).

One uncertainty in the procedure comes from the abundant migration of very young children—nurslings or orphans—out of Paris to the neighboring départements. This characteristic of the Paris

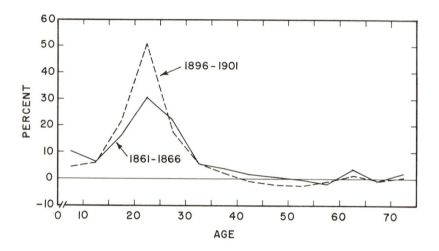

Figure 3.6 Age Distribution of Female Migrants, by Percentage of
Total Female Migration, Seine: 1861-1866 and 1896-1901

migration cannot be generalized to the entire country. In the French départements, where we apply the migration pattern, we assumed that there was typically no migration in the 0-4 age group. The nurslings constitute a large stream of temporary out-migrants, who either died away from Paris or came back within a few years. A special adjustment will be indicated later for the départements with the largest quota of nurslings.

The weights in Table 3.4 exhibit a sharp maximum in the age-group 20–24. The 1861–1866 distribution of migrants was less abrupt than the 1896–1901 one, and it is possible that the intensity of migration patterns changed through time. As a rule, there

TABLE 3.4

WEIGHTS FOR APPORTIONING FEMALE MIGRANTS,

BY AGE OF MIGRANT

Age	Weight (percent)
0-4	0
5-9	6.7
10-14	6.3
15-19	20.1
20-24	42.3
25-29	20.3
30-34	5.7
35-39	2.9
40-44	0.3
45-49	-0.9
50-54	-1.9
55-59	-1.8
60+	0
	100.0

NOTES: These weights are valid for in-migration.
For out-migration, the sign must be
inversed.
Computation based on 1861-1866 and
1896-1901 migration into Seine.

does not seem to be any need for the migration adjustment prior to midcentury—not that there was no migration, but probably because it was better distributed over all ages. The R/E ratios in the first available census age distributions for départements with strong migration streams do not as a rule show a marked age-specific pattern. In many instances, the migration weights of Table 3.4 appear excessive in the young adult ages. Although we first attempted in all instances to introduce the migration adjustment in the period 1846–1851, we modified the procedure wherever its application at full strength from 1846–1851 on appeared to concentrate the migrants too heavily in the twenties of the age distribution. In those départements we switched to the migration weights in a progressive manner, and applied what we call the "gradual" adjustment.[14] By the end of the century, however, the full pattern was everywhere in force. In Pyrénées (Hautes-), our example, we use it from 1846 on. Map 3.2 shows to which départements we applied the adjustment with full strength, and to which départements the gradual one.

Theoretically the number of migrants reallocated with the migration weights should be equal to the difference between the enumerated population and the population calculated from the balance of births and deaths since the previous census. In brief:

$$M = PT_{n+5} - PT_n - B + D \qquad (9)$$

where M is the intercensal migration, PT_n and PT_{n+5} are the census populations at either end of the interval, and B and D are the intercensal births and deaths, respectively. However, the variable completeness of the enumeration at the time of the censuses may easily create the fictitious appearance of migration. When we deal with actual data, the equation above must be rewritten

$$M + E = PT_{n+5} - PT_n - B + D \qquad (10)$$

where E is an error term, inseparable from M if only two censuses, five years apart, are considered. We have already shown how unreliable the series of census population is, and suggested that the completeness of enumeration varied a great deal. If these fluctuations are accepted as genuine, and treated as migration, or, in other words, allocated by age according to weights which give a disproportionate importance to the young adult ages, census errors will give rise alternatively to inflated and deflated cohorts which will be revealed in census year after census year in the R/E ratios. This was clearly unacceptable; a method to smooth the series of population totals had to be found. In most instances, in order to

[14] The "gradual" adjustment for migration consisted practically of allocating an increasing proportion of the intercensal migrants according to the weights $_5w_a$. Nine-tenths of the migrants of the period 1846-1850 were distributed proportionately to the size of the age group, and one-tenth according to the migration weights. In 1851-1856 the proportions were respectively eight-tenths and two-tenths, and so on until 1891-1896, when all the migrants were distributed according to the weights.

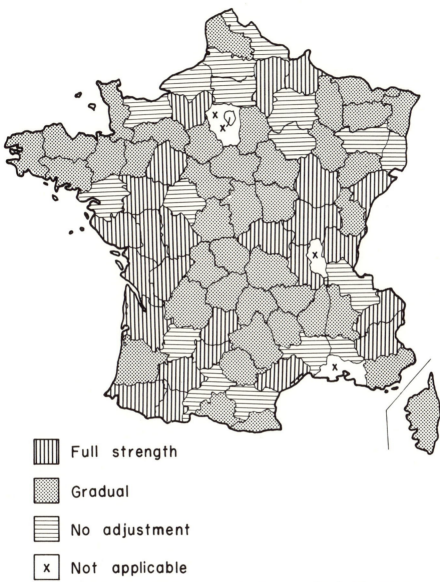

░░░ Full strength

▒▒▒ Gradual

≡≡≡ No adjustment

x̄ Not applicable

Map 3.2 Migration Adjustment, Type Used in Reconstruction, by Département

even out the effect of census errors, we fitted a trend line to the ratio of the reported population to the population estimated by the balance of birth and death starting in 1846 (R/CB). This trend line was presumed to express the relationship between the two totals better than the unadjusted series; and since the estimate based on the vital registration was supposed to diverge from the real population of the time only by the progressive action of migration in the intervening period since 1846, we presumed that the actual population total could be found by multiplying the balance estimate by the trend ratio. The procedure is illustrated in Table 3.5 by the example of Pyrénées (Hautes-).

TABLE 3.5

FEMALE POPULATION ESTIMATES BASED ON TREND OF THE RATIO OF REPORTED POPULATION TO COMPUTATION BASED ON BIRTHS AND DEATHS, PYRENEES (HAUTES-): 1851 TO 1906

Date	Reported total (R)	Computed total (CB)	R/CB ratio	Trend of R/CB ratio	Final population estimate (trend x CB)
1851	128,608	129,906	0.990	0.983	127,749
1856	127,598	131,670	0.969	0.968	127,468
1861	124,257	131,687	0.944	0.953	125,468
1866	123,515	132,226	0.934	0.937	123,958
1871	120,829	132,169	0.914	0.922	121,881
1876	121,172	132,232	0.916	0.907	119,915
1881	119,829	133,124	0.900	0.892	118,686
1886	117,840	133,409	0.883	0.876	116,898
1891	112,322	132,554	0.847	0.861	114,119
1896	109,645	130,104	0.843	0.846	110,018
1901	106,551	128,176	0.831	0.830	106,426
1906	103,996	127,099	0.818	0.815	103,586

NOTE: The computed total is derived from the balance of births and deaths over the 1846 reported population.

Figure 3.5 also allows us to compare the population reconstructions with and without the migration adjustment. By 1861, the action of migration was clearly influencing the age distribution (see the R/E ratios in 1861 and 1866). The relevance of the adjustment in 1851 is doubtful. By the end of the century, however, after a series of very bad censuses, the estimate with the migration adjustment is much closer to the recorded figures by age. If we take no account of migration, the R/E ratios exhibit the characteristic depression after 20, compensated under 20 and over 60 by ratios over 1.0. Note once again that whatever confidence we may have in the validity of the reconstruction rests on its conformity to a few selected censuses (prior to 1871 and after 1896). When the quality of enumeration breaks down from 1872 on (and no pattern of migration could explain the characteristics of age distributions such as that in the 1886 enumeration), we have little reliable indication that our estimation reflects the facts, except the satisfactory outcome of the adjustments just before and just after the bad censuses.

Another example is given in Figure 3.7: there was a substantial amount of migration in Côtes-du-Nord, but the early R/E ratios provide little indication that it had affected the age distribution much by midcentury. In this instance, we distributed gradually larger proportions of the migrants according to the migration weights of Table 3.4: 1/10 of the migrants during the period 1846–1851, 2/10 in 1851–1856, and so on, until all of them are allocated by age according to the migration weights in 1891–1896 and later. As in the previous instance of Pyrénées (Hautes-) the population size after 1846 was determined by the trend of R/CB.

The use of a trend line of R/CB clearly assumes that the migration streams were steady and represented a constant proportion of the population during 1846 to 1906. Such an assumption may seem far-fetched, and is tenable only when the trend line fits the successive values of R/CB in a satisfactory way. This appears to be the case in Pyrénées (Hautes-) and Côtes-du-Nord (see Figure 3.8). There are a few examples of départements, however, where the impact of migration appears to have varied greatly over time. In such cases, we have usually adopted ad hoc solutions. In most instances, we accepted the value of the reported populations, with an occasional correction when the R/CB ratios were clearly out of line; the correction was made by linear interpolation at the years in question—i.e. a line was run on a graph between the census years when the R/CB ratio appeared reliable, and the value for the desired year was read off on the R/CB scale. The process is illustrated graphically in the instance of Allier on Figure 3.8 (where all the data are the ones recorded by the census). Migrations in

[89]

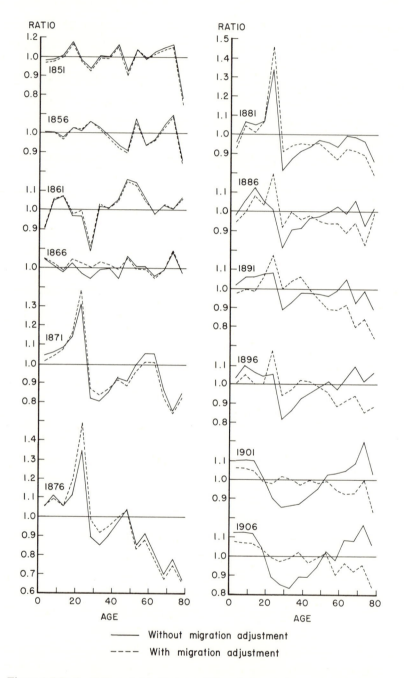

Figure 3.7 Ratio of Reported to Estimated Female Population, with and without Gradual Adjustment for Migration, by Age, Côtes-du-Nord: 1851 to 1906

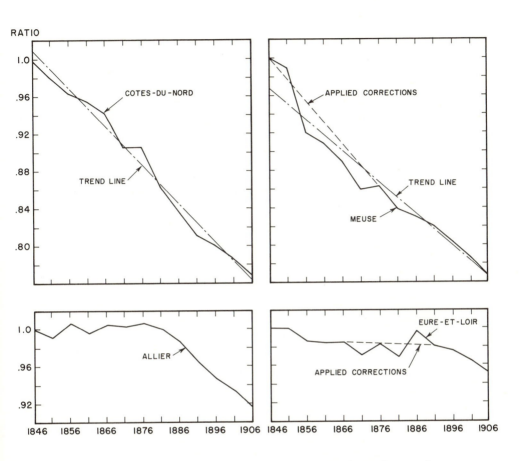

Figure 3.8 Examples of Ratios of Reported Female Population to Computation
Based on Female Births and Deaths, Trend Lines, and Applied
Corrections: 1846 to 1906

Allier appear to start decisively only after 1866. The trend line
would clearly misrepresent the series of R/CB. The instances
where R/CB do not appear to evolve linearly are few, however,
and the trend line usually works satisfactorily.

Another problem is illustrated by the instance of Meuse, also
plotted in Figure 3.8. The quality of the censuses appear somewhat
erratic, and the steep drop of the population in 1856 and the three
following censuses, followed by a recovery in 1876, will give birth
to large out- and in-migration cohorts. The linear interpolation

[91]

between 1846 and 1881 seemed to give satisfactory results, whereas a trend line based on the same data would have displaced the beginning of the series downward. (Both the trend line and the applied correction are plotted on the graph for Meuse.) As a final example, in Figure 3.8, Eure-et-Loir illustrates a combination of the characteristics of the two previous curves: an acceleration of migration in the last decade of the century, and erratic fluctuations of the enumerated population, corrected in this case by linear interpolation between the 1866 and 1891 censuses. In the presentation of the data in the second part of this book, we shall specify briefly how the migration adjustment was used, and we shall give the population total that has been accepted for each census date.

The corrections to the total population figures are generally rather small and are made for the sole purpose of the migration adjustment. These figures are not necessarily more accurate approximations to the real population at census date than the results of the enumeration itself, but they provide a series that is more consistent and that agrees with the population changes (mortality, fertility, and migration) in the reconstruction.

MIGRATION OF YOUNG CHILDREN

We must still deal with a special kind of migration, that of nurslings and orphans. The yearbook of Paris comments: "In general, out of 100 children born in Paris, at least 27 are sent to a nurse out of Paris [by their parents]; usually the departure to the province occurs in the first days after birth" (Seine, 1884, p. 127). For example, the number of births registered in Paris in 1884 was 63,840; of those, 16,718 were reported by their parents as having been sent out of Paris (although not necessarily out of the Seine département). Not included in these totals are the children sent to the countryside by the welfare services of the city. The latter were abandoned children, orphans, and foundlings. Their number is slightly over 4,000 a year, and, in 1891, 42 percent were aged less than one month when admitted in the service, and 59 percent were less than one year old. Only 3 percent were more than 13 years old (age at which they left the orphanage to learn a trade). The total number of children under 13 from Paris in province agencies was close to 21,000 (Seine, 1891, pp. 646ff.).

The yearbook of the city of Paris is full of interesting details on the subject for the end of the 19th century. We are less well informed about time trends prior to 1880. Parish registers from the Ile-de-France record numerous deaths of children from the capital for the 18th century (Ganiage, 1963, pp. 74-79; Galliano, 1966). The traffic had existed long before, but it seems to have been stimulated by the development of communication. Entire regions came to rely on the children from Paris as an important source of income, as far away as the Morvan, in the département of Côte-d'Or, 300 kilometers from Paris (Armengaud, 1964). The flows were significantly reduced only by the First World War; as late as 1913 15,354 nurslings were sent out of Paris, of whom 1,105 were breast-fed, and 14,249 received another kind of nourishment (Seine, 1923–1924, p. 39). There is an extensive bibliography on nurses, nurslings, and abandoned children (Delore, 1879; Lallemand, 1885), but the largest part discusses Paris rather than the whole of France. Less is known about the custom of using nurses and sending children away from home for other regions of France. The 1872 census gives a category of children nursed outside of their homes, and the numbers are fairly important in the regions around Paris, Lyon and Marseilles. But the data appear unreliable (the 1872 census in general grossly underestimates the number of children). Furthermore, we are interested only in children sent outside their département of birth. Many women, like Madame Bovary, sent their children to a nurse in the same village or close by (Flaubert, 1856, Chapter III).

We possess little information on the duration of the children's stay in the countryside. Presumably, in most cases, it was for a short duration only, a few years at most. Their presence in départements where they were not born would inflate the 0–4 age group, but not much in most cases—not enough to warrant an adjustment. In Eure-et-Loir, which was the most important outlet for Paris nurslings, about 1,600 to 1,700 children were sent every year between 1880 and 1910, of whom, say, half were girls. The total number of female children reported in the age group 0–4 was of the order of 12,000. At most, this would account for a few percent of the R/E ratios over 1.0, at an age where our estimate is very dependent on the accuracy of the mortality pattern, and where the R/E ratio is biased by the frequent underreporting of young children.

There exists a more subtle effect on our estimate of migration. The mortality of the nurslings and the welfare children was appalling. Bottle feeding and the poor hygiene of the country people who received the city children, as well as the hazards of transportation, contributed to the high risk of death. Deaths of persons who had not been registered at birth in the département biases the estimate of migration by the balance equation. In our regular migration adjustment, the excess of deaths would be assigned to in-migration, and apportioned by migration weights at the wrong ages. Of course, the passage of nurslings into the département is a form of migration, but it will be revealed only if they die; otherwise, in-migration will be soon compensated for by out-migration. In Eure-et-Loir at the end of the century, for example, there were about 800 girl nurslings every year. If a fourth of those died in the area, it would mean an excess of deaths of 1,000 every five years. This is enough to affect significantly the adjustment at the young adult age where the migration is normally concentrated. Nine départements were markedly affected by the migration of nurslings and orphans during the latter part of the 19th century: Cher, Eure-et-Loir, Loiret, Loir-et-Cher, Nièvre, Orne, Sarthe, Seine-et-Marne, and Yonne.[15] The location of these départements is indicated on Map 3.3.

A special adjustment was devised to cope with the problem. Two steps were taken: 1) correction of the number of deaths to eliminate deceased children foreign to the département; 2) subsidiary adjustment of the total population to account for the excessive number of temporary visitors. The first step accounted for the excessive number of deaths. We assumed that deaths over age

[15] The traffic of nurslings ranged much farther, but the numbers were less important, and no adjustment appears necessary. For an indication of the distribution of nurses by département, see the tables given each year in the Paris yearbook (Seine, 1882-1924).

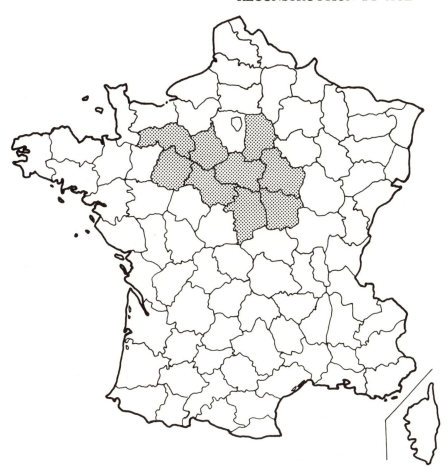

Map 3.3 Départements Requiring Adjustment for Migration of
Children from Paris

5 affected the regular inhabitants of the area, whereas deaths
under 5 were inflated. The published vital registration tabulates
(at least after 1860) deaths by age. The total number of deaths
recorded over age 5 in the vital registration determined the level of
the model life table used in the reconstruction of the population. For
the mortality level determined in that manner, the corresponding
mortality under age 5 determined the accepted number of deaths
of local children; the excess in the registration was assigned to the

migrant children, and therefore subtracted from the total of deaths.[16] Once a reasonable level of mortality has been derived on the basis of the deaths above age 5, it becomes clear that the recorded deaths show a very great inflation of infant deaths. In Figure 3.9 we plot by age the absolute number of deaths that were reported and the corrected number used in the projection for Eure-et-Loir.

A subsidiary adjustment of the population size attempts a rough estimate of the numbers of child migrants from the département's total. The nine départements discussed clearly all record too many children under age 5 at the time of the more reliable 1901 and 1906 censuses. Earlier enumerations do not give, however, such an obvious picture. The first age-group tends to be defective, and nurslings had probably a poorer chance of being fully counted than other children. Although the nursing industry in the region around Paris is ancient, the improvement of transportation as well as the population increase of Paris was leading to the recruitment of nurses in an ever-widening hinterland, and the movement had been less important at midcentury than in the last decades before 1900. As there is little numerical information available on trends, it is not possible to devise a completely satisfactory adjustment of the population figure that would exclude the child migrants.

This is how we proceeded. We looked at the R/E ratios at age 0-15 obtained in a first reconstruction made with the recorded

[16] Prior to 1861, when deaths were not published by age, we used a proportion of deaths under 5 based on the proportion after 1861. The proportions were as follows:

	Deaths under 5 in percent of all deaths
Cher	40
Eure-et-Loir	35
Loiret	36
Loir-et-Cher	36
Nièvre	38
Orne	23
Sarthe	23
Seine-et-Marne	35
Yonne	33

As for the mechanics of the reconstruction, we subtracted those deaths reported (and, before 1861, assumed) under 5 years of age from the total number of deaths and projected the population from one census year to the next, five years later, by using the mortality level that gave the same number of deaths over age 5.

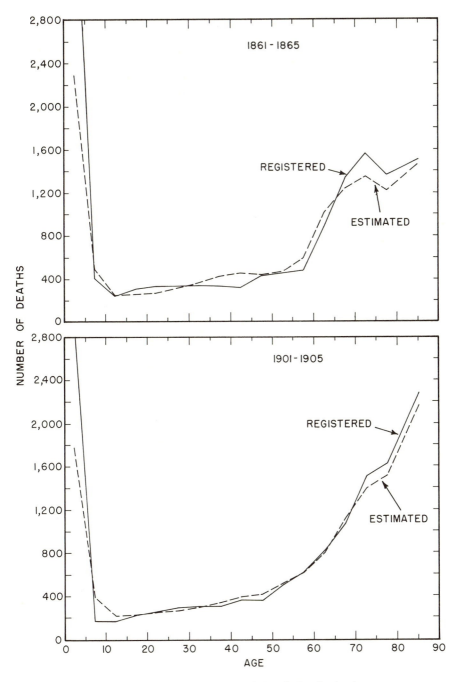

Figure 3.9 Registered and Estimated Female Deaths, by Age,
Eure-et-Loir: 1861-1865 to 1901-1905

population size. The excess of children in 1901 and 1906 over the expected number, related to the total population, gave the percentage of temporary migrants. A further look at the R/E ratios in earlier census years indicated when the apparent excess in the age-group had begun to be visible. Prior to that time, we assumed there were no young migrants, or at least that their presence was more than compensated for by underreporting in the age-group. In Eure-et-Loir, we accepted the enumerated population totals before 1841. Elsewhere, the last date when the enumerated total was accepted was much later; 1866 in most "nursling" départements, 1856 or 1861 in a few. The percentage correction in the intervening years was obtained by interpolation between 0 percent at that date, and the percentage calculated for 1901-1906.

The present chapter has introduced the methods used to reconstruct the female population of France by départements. An overall assessment of these methods, and of the extent of bias in the original data, will be postponed until Chapter 5, after Chapter 4 has explained how the population's marital status was reconstructed. The results of the application of the methods given in this chapter to the female population of the French départements are set out in the second part of this volume, département by département. We present these results in three tables for each département. Table 1 gives the total population, the extent to which it was corrected, and the R/CB ratios (ratios of the reported population over the population computed by the balance of the births and deaths over 1846). Table 2 presents the new estimates of the number of births and of the birth rate together with the extent of the correction of the registered births. Finally, Table 3 presents the population by age. The data cover the period 1801 to 1906. Additional information on the computations are given for each single département in a section of the second part.

CHAPTER 4: Reconstruction of the Female Population by Marital Status

I. *General description of the method*

In the preceding chapters we showed that the French population statistics revealed serious biases during the 19th century, and in particular that census age distributions were not reliable. It was possible, however, to reconstruct the population by age by relying extensively on the vital registration. In this chapter, we shall extend the reconstruction procedure to the marital status distribution. It was shown earlier that the censuses err also on the subject of marital status. Once the population has been reconstructed by age, we must find a way to allocate women within each age-group by marital status. This appears necessary a priori, since we have greatly modified the age distribution at the ages when at least some of the women were married at the time of the census or had been married earlier. Although the patterns of error may be related to marital state (e.g. young married women may be shifted to the age-group 20-24), there is no reason to assume that misreporting or underreporting at certain ages would be restricted to only one marital state.

As in the case of the population reconstruction, our strategy will rely as much as possible on the vital registration, which may not share the biases of the census. However, whereas we had a record of births and deaths extending back to the beginning of the century, we have no detailed information on marriages prior to 1861. From 1801 on, we possess information on the total number of marriages; from 1836 on, the spouses are distributed by marital status at the time of marriage and by sex (e.g. single girls with single men, with widowers, etc.). There is also information on the marital status of deceased persons after 1835. The most important data for our purpose are the ages at marriage by the previous marital state of the spouses, and, specifically, the age distribution of first marriages. The tabulations are available only from 1861 on by département (although the series goes back five more years for the whole of France). There are some gaps later in the century, notably in the 1890s, when the age distribution of marriages is un-accountably omitted from the yearly statistics. We filled the gap by distributing the total number of first marriages according to their distribution by age in the surrounding years. Once that was done, we had a series of first marriages by age of the women be-tween 1861 and 1906, in five-year intervals: 1861–1865, 1866–1870, . . . 1901–1905. Since the reconstruction of the population had been made for the beginning of 1861, 1866, . . . , and so on, we had the first marriages for the period between the dates when population data were available. We are interested in the proportion married at these dates. Diagram 1 indicates how first-marriage fre-quencies are computed from the recorded first marriages and the population data at the beginning and at the end of a five-year pe-riod. For instance, the first marriages in 1861–1865 of women aged 15–19 are related to the average population during the period, approximated by averaging the age-groups 15–19 estimated for the first of January of 1861 and 1866.

Our task now is to transform these rates into proportions ever-married. We shall later subtract the widowed and divorced from the ever-married women to get currently married women. We are pri-marily interested in the proportions married at the fecund ages, so that we need not be overly concerned with the widowed and di-vorced: they become numerous only after age 50. At this stage then, we must devise a way to derive the number of ever-married women by age from the first-marriage frequencies.

The relationship between first-marriage frequencies and the proportion ever-married in the population can be expressed as follows:

$$G(a) = \int_0^a g(x)dx \tag{11}$$

where
$$g(x) = \frac{M(x)}{W(x)} \tag{12}$$

$M(x)$ is the number of first marriages at age x; $W(x)$ is the female population at that age; $g(x)$ is the first-marriage frequency; and

[100]

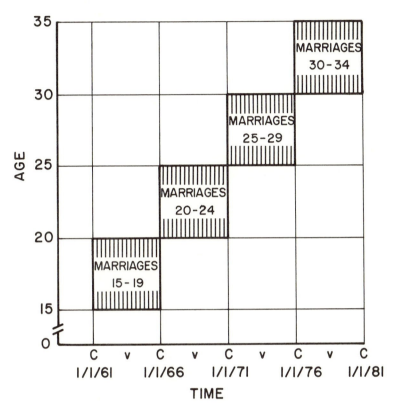

C: Population estimation date

v: Period of registration

$G(a)$ is the proportion of a *cohort* ever-married at age a. It is important to emphasize the word "cohort" at this stage. We are moving in time as we move in age, and must follow cohorts from census to census and from one five-year span of vital registration to the next five-year span. We determine the proportion ever-married in a certain age-group (say 30–34) at a certain census (say 1886) by

[101]

cumulating first-marriage frequencies in the cohort born in 1826–1850, and aged:

15–19	in	1866–1870
20–24	in	1871–1875
25–29	in	1876–1880
30–34	in	1881–1886

The analytical problem with which we have to cope is due to the fact that persons married between ages x and $x+5$ during any five-year period will have aged between the time of their marriage and the next census (or population estimate); some will still be in the x to $x+5$ age group, and some will have moved on to the $x+5$ to $x+10$ group. This simple fact, basic to demographic estimation, is illustrated by an example in Diagram 2. Some of the women

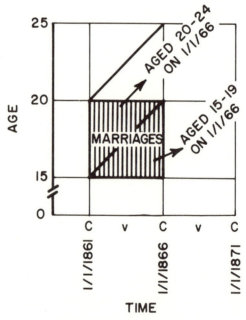

C: Population estimation date

v: Period of registration

married while aged 15 to 19 years between 1861 and 1865 will be aged 15–19 years on the first of January 1866, and some will be aged 20–24. There are two methods to cope with this difficulty. The first is the use of separation factors to apportion the women between the two age-groups. The separation factors would have to vary with age at marriage and in general with the shape of the first-marriage curve. The second method, used in this chapter, relies on the use of a model curve such that, for given first-marriage frequencies, we can read off the values of the proportions ever-married at various ages on the curve.

The use of a model curve has much to recommend it. The model has been described by A. J. Coale (1971) and uses three parameters to modify a standard curve:

a_0 the earliest age at which women get married; or the origin of the curve;

k the rate at which marriage increases, or the horizontal scale of the curve; and

C its level, or vertical scale.

In human populations over the world, the earliest age at which women marry varies according to customs and law. The proportion of women who never marry is extremely variable; it is typically high in Western Europe and very low in Asian populations. Finally, the time scale according to which nuptiality occurs can be short or long. Nevertheless, Coale has shown that there is an essential similarity of most patterns of first marriage by age, at least for cohorts that have not been subject to extraordinarily disturbing influences. The nuptiality of populations with widely varying marital customs and characteristics can be characterized by three parameters only.[1] At any age a the proportion ever-married $G(a)$ of those who will marry is equal to a proportion ever-married for a point of the standard scale, measured from the origin a_0, and

[1] The standard curve can be expressed in functional form, as a risk of first marriage among those who ever-marry that follows a double exponential. However, the tabulated "standard" is based on purely empirical data drawn from 19th-century Swedish experience (Coale, 1971).

expressed in a new time scale equal to the time scale of the standard curve times k. The curve must be scaled down vertically by C to account for the proportion who never marry. Finally, the expression for $G(a)$ is as follows:

$$G(a) = C \cdot G_s(\frac{a-a_0}{k}) \tag{13}$$

where the subscript s indicates the standard curve, k and a_0 are determined from the first-marriage frequencies computed by equation (12) above. The proportions ever-married under age 20 (EM_1), under age 25 (EM_2), and under age 30 (EM_3), are computed by cumulating the first marriage frequencies:

$$EM_1 = 5 \cdot g_1 \tag{14}$$
$$EM_2 = 5 \cdot (g_1 + g_2) \tag{15}$$
$$EM_3 = 5 \cdot (g_1 + g_2 + g_3) \tag{16}$$

We must convert those values, valid for the end of the age span, to the corresponding values for its middle; in other words, we are interested in the proportion married between 15–19 (or approximately at age 17.5), between 20–24 (age 22.5) and so on. But the EM_n's provide enough information to define a curve that can be approximated by a transformation of the standard curve. On the model curve thus defined, we can read off values for any age at which we want them, including the conventional 17.5, 22.5, . . . 47.5 in the middle of the age-group.

The model curve is identified for practical purposes by

$$RA_1 = \frac{EM_1}{EM_2}, \tag{17}$$

and

$$RA_2 = \frac{EM_2}{EM_3}. \tag{18}$$

RA_1 and RA_2 provide entries to a table of a_0 and k, given in appendix of Coale (1971).

In our reconstruction, successive EM's and RA's are computed by cohorts. The RA_1 and RA_2 provide parameters of the curve,

[104]

which enables us to find the value of a_0 and k.[2] Coale recommends the computation of C, the level of the curve (or the proportion eventually getting married in the cohort), by reference to EM_3 (p. 214), but in the French material this procedure does not yield very satisfactory results (a point to be discussed later). Once determined, the model curve indicates what proportions of the cohort were married at successive ages; and these proportions can be used to reconstruct the marital status distribution. At this stage, we again center the estimates on the census date by averaging the proportions married in the cohort age groups surrounding the population estimate date. For example, to get the number of ever-married women aged 15–19 on the first of January 1866, we multiply the average of the proportions married in the cohorts born in 1846–1850 and 1851–1855 by the number of women estimated at the ages 15–19 in 1866.

What is the impact of mortality and of migration on the estimation procedure? The question is relevant, since we are estimating ever-married women from the number of marriages occurring at home in the département. Some women will have died or departed between the time of the marriage and the time of the estimation. However, we have already accounted for migration and mortality in our estimate of the population, and they will influence the estimation only if there are strong differentials by marital status in the attrition due to these phenomena. In general, we know that mortality differentials by marital status are not considerable before age 50. Few data are available in France on internal migration by age, sex, and marital state, and the question must be settled empirically, by judging whether the estimates of proportions marrying appear to be affected or not by differential migration. This remains a potential source of bias, which we shall have to keep in mind and discuss later, when we present actual examples of estimations.

Before turning to a discussion of some of the underlying relation-

[2] Only occasionally have we determined a_0 and k by the relationship of RA_2 and RA_3. This was done for late-marrying areas of France (e.g. Brittany) in cohorts for which the combination of RA_1 and RA_2 fell out of the range of the table given in the appendix of Coale (1971).

ships, and to a description of some difficulties and problems encountered in the reconstruction (particularly when we attempt to go back in time prior to 1861, the date when first marriages start to be tabulated in the vital statistics publications), we must briefly explain how we subtract widowed and divorced women from the number ever-married to obtain the number of currently married women. If we were trying to estimate by age the number of all widowed and divorced women, it would be essential to obtain a close approximation; but we are actually concerned only with the widows and divorced under age 50, an age before which they represent, if not a negligible, at least a rather small proportion of the total number of women. We have taken the percentage of widows and divorced by age for France in 1896, as recorded in the census, and inflated (or deflated) these percentages at each age by a constant, so that the sum of the widows and divorced estimated (when multiplied by the age distribution) would be equal to the total number recorded in the census. In this instance, we rely exclusively on census data, but only because it does not matter very much. An indication of how close is the fit is given in Figure 4.1 for Calvados at various dates. Discrepancies between the estimates and the census figures must be explained by the uncertainty of the census figures, as much as by the inadequacy of the 1896 percentages for France to fit the experience of Calvados at all dates. Finally the impact of the approximation involved is rather small.

This section was devoted to a general discussion of the method of reconstruction of the marital status. The next section will discuss in more detail the procedures used for the cohorts marrying from 1861 on, when the first-marriage frequencies could be computed. In the third section of this chapter, we shall discuss the reconstruction of the cohorts for which information on first marriage was not yet available.

II. *Reconstruction of marital status for cohorts marrying after 1861*

Diagram 3 shows what cohorts we are able to reconstruct on the basis of the first marriages and reconstructed populations at the

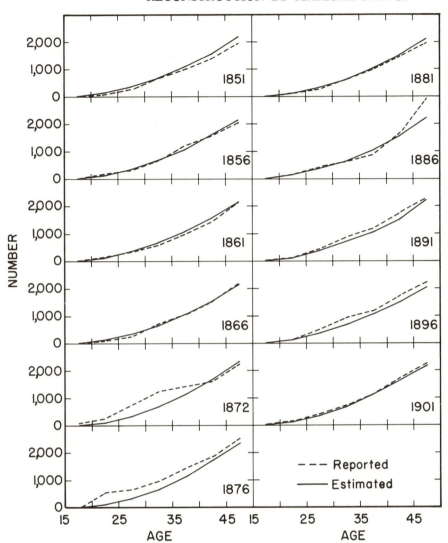

Figure 4.1 Reported and Estimated Widows and Divorcees, by Age,
Calvados: 1851 to 1901

time of a census. (We use the dates of birth to define the cohort.)
Enough data exist only for seven five-year cohorts, i.e. for cohorts
born from 1846 to 1880. We can extend the observation on both
sides without serious prejudice to the quality of the information. We
create one more cohort in the beginning (cohort 1841–1845), for

[107]

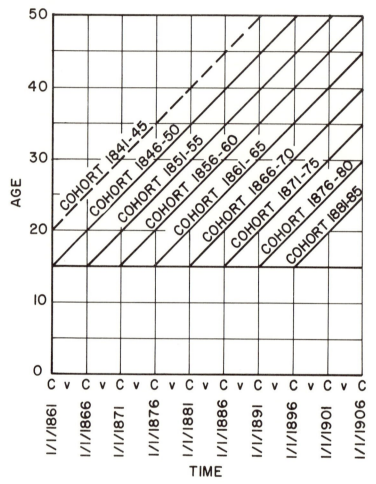

C: Population estimation date

v: Period of registration

which RA_2 and RA_3 are already known from the available data. RA_1 is assumed to have been equal to that of the next cohort, times a constant for France; the constant is the actual ratio of RA_1's for the entire country, known since there is a distribution of first marriages for France between 1856 and 1860. There are very few

[108]

married women aged 15–19 in general, so the bias will be small. At the other end, the cohort 1881–1885 is computed by using the recorded population (in the census of 1911) at ages 25–29 as part of the denominator of EM_3. This is acceptable because the censuses appear to be more reliable by the beginning of the 20th century.

It can be seen from Diagram 3 that the method up to now provides a series of proportions married at all ages after 1891 on a period basis (that is, when we abandon the cohort vantage); the only exception is the age-group 15–19 in 1901. Once again, we make use of the improvement in quality of the censuses of the 20th century, and of the relative insignificance of the 15–19 age-group. We accept the number of married women 15–19 reported in the 1901 census instead of an estimate. Diagram 3 makes it clear that the main problem that remains to be solved will concern the cohorts born before 1841. The question will be discussed in our next section. At this stage, we must cast a preliminary look at the results of the reconstruction of the proportions married in the cohorts born between 1841 and 1885.

Table 4.1 gives, for each of the nine cohorts, the values computed

TABLE 4.1

ORIGIN (a_o), ADJUSTED SCALE (k), AND PROPORTION WOMEN EVER-MARRIED (C),
CALVADOS: COHORTS BORN 1841-1845 TO 1881-1885

Cohort	Origin (a_o)	Adjusted scale (k)	Proportion ever-married (C)
1841-1845	15.2314	0.7665	0.8195
1846-1850	14.7387	0.8415	0.8039
1851-1855	15.5095	0.6871	0.8719
1856-1860	14.6334	0.8113	0.7613
1861-1865	14.5547	0.8424	0.7649
1866-1870	14.7967	0.8155	0.8021
1871-1875	15.0067	0.7955	0.8813
1876-1880	15.8226	0.7169	0.8645
1881-1885	15.6512	0.7489	0.8641

NOTE: Proportion ever-married is computed on basis of proportion ever-married under age 30 (EM_3).

for the parameters a_0, k, and C in Calvados. These figures tell us little in isolation. For each cohort, however, C, the level of the curve, can be compared with the proportions ever-married derived from the censuses. Age and marital status distributions in any particular census are liable to misreporting and biases of various sorts, but the proportions ever-married over age 50 in cohorts obtained from the summing up of successive age-groups in successive censuses are likely to be more reliable, since they will average data with age-specific biases as well as censuses of diverse completeness. Diagram 4 indicates how the cohorts are identified in the various

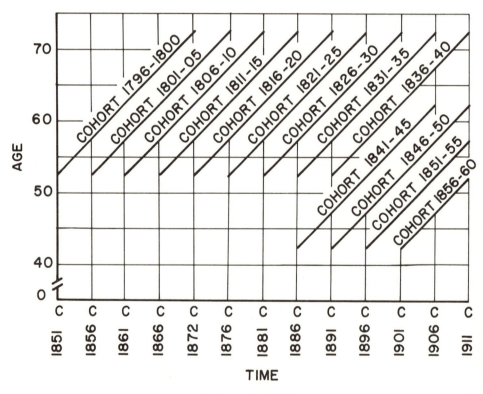

C: Census date

censuses, and for what dates an estimate of C can be obtained in this fashion. If we restrict ourselves to the ever-married in the age-group 50–75, and include the 1911 census and an estimate for the 1906 census,[3] we obtain estimates of C for the birth cohorts from 1796 to 1840 only. In other words, we stop short of the time when computed C's are obtained from the first-marriage registration (see Table 4.1). However, the ages 50–75 were selected arbitrarily. One may assert that, after age 40, very few women marry for the first time; the ages 40–65, or even 40–55, will yield an estimate of C which will be lower than that derived from 50–75, but can be adjusted upward by the ratio of

$$\frac{C_{50\text{-}75}}{C_{40\text{-}65}} \quad \text{or} \quad \frac{C_{50\text{-}75}}{C_{40\text{-}55}}$$

in the cohorts where both these estimates are known. In this way, we estimated the proportion ever-married in an additional number of cohorts, up to and including the birth cohort 1856–1860 (see Diagram 4). The four new C's calculated in this way, are the only ones that can be compared to the computed C's of Table 4.1. It is however possible to look beyond the World War, and to pick up various cohorts that were getting married before the war and had reached, after the war, the ages at which women normally do not marry any more for the first time: let us say they were over 40. We must balance the disadvantages of the procedure with its advantages. On the latter side, any upturn in C's after the cohort 1856–1860 would be missed if we did not use the additional information; that is, we could systematically underestimate the proportion married from 1881 on, at a time when there appears to have been an intensification of nuptiality. However, the disadvantages of the procedure must not be left unmentioned. The war may well have disrupted the situation, causing either differential mortality, or differential migration according to marital status. Furthermore, there is no census in 1916, and the censuses from 1921 on give the

---

[3] A full distribution by marital status and age is not given in 1906. The proportion ever-married at various ages was estimated by averaging the corresponding proportions in the censuses of 1901 and 1911.

marital status distribution only in ten-year age-groupings: 40–49, 50–59, 60–69, 70 and over. This confuses the cohorts. Diagram 5 shows how the age-groups straddle the cohorts. We used the averages of the proportions ever-married at ages

50–59	in	1921
60–69	in	1926
60–69	in	1931
70–79	in	1936

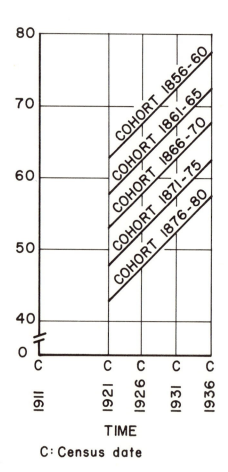

TIME

C: Census date

to estimate the proportion ever-married in the cohort born 1861–1865. Similar combinations were used for later cohorts. The results are plotted in Figure 4.2 together with the earlier C's for Calvados.

(Although they are of no use at this stage, the census C's for cohorts born between 1796 and 1840 will be used in the next section when we attempt to reconstruct the marital status in the cohorts where there is no information from the vital registration on first marriages by age.)

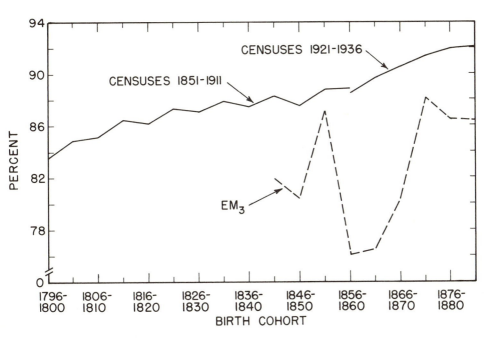

Figure 4.2 Proportion Women Ever-Married (C), Computations Based on Censuses 1851-1911 and 1921-1936 and on First Marriage Frequencies at Age 25-29 (EM_3), Calvados: Cohorts Born 1796 to 1886

The comparison of the proportions ever-married calculated from the registered data and recorded in the censuses for comparable cohorts is presented in Figure 4.2 for Calvados. The registered data on marriage provide a relatively reliable indication of the age structure of first marriages, and a relatively unreliable indication of the proportion ever-married in a given cohort. There are two conspicuous differences in the value of C from the two sources: one is the erratic nature of the values computed from the registered data, and the other is their different level. The level that is revealed by the census data on proportions ever-married among older women is not in itself free from biases, but its smooth trend is more plausible.

In order to avoid erroneous fluctuations in C, attributable to a systematic error in one or two censuses (and in the 1870s and 1880s for example, several censuses provide grossly misreported proportions ever-married above 50, as well as under 50), we used a trend line computed on the cohorts 1796–1860.[4] The continuation of the trend also provided values for the cohorts between 1861 and 1885 and, incidentally, for the cohorts between 1781 and 1795.

There are several reasons why the registration data fail to give a reliable image of the proportions ever-married in a cohort. They include the systematic misestimation of a cohort's size during the reconstruction of the population, the uncertainties of the averaging procedures used to relate the population and the registered marriages, the effect of differential migration and mortality by marital status, and the inadequacy of the model curve in abnormal times, such as those of the war of 1870, when many marriages were postponed.

In the end, the procedure utilized is to determine the age pattern of first marriages from the registered data, to determine the trend in the proportion ever-married by the end of life from the recorded proportions pertaining to each cohort from the series of censuses from 1851 to 1936, and then to make a final adjustment of the level through which the trend line passes by matching the aggregate number of married women recorded in the whole span of censuses from 1851 to 1901 with the aggregate number in the reconstructed population. This last adjustment will be described later, when the estimates derived by the methods explained in this section are joined

---

[4] In rare cases, when the distribution of marital status by age over age 50 in a census was very different from those in surrounding censuses, we have eliminated that census from the computation of the proportion ever-married by cohort.

with those of the next section. The procedures described until now reconstruct the proportions married by cohort on the basis of computed parameters, namely k, a_0, and C. We shall now turn to earlier cohorts, for which no values of k and a_0 can be computed directly.

III. *Reconstruction of marital status for cohorts marrying before 1861*

The estimation of the marriage curve for cohorts born prior to 1841 must rely on less information than thereafter, and the information available directly (namely an approximation of C) comes from the censuses, not from the more reliable vital registration. There is at least one fairly reliable hypothesis we can make on another parameter of the curve: a_0, the age at which women first marry, is subject to little change. Moreover, whatever changes there are in a_0 do not affect the marital distribution much. We shall estimate a_0 by the average of a_0 in cohorts marrying after 1861. In view of these estimates of C and of a_0, the brunt of the estimation will rest on k, the slope of the ever-married curve.

A provisional estimate of the proportions married can be obtained by assuming that k does not change and remains equal to the average of k's in the cohorts 1841–1845 and on. k determines the age at marriage, and C the proportion ever-marrying. Therefore, if we assume that k remains constant, changes in the number of married women that are reflected in the available census data must originate in C. But it can be shown that a constant k leads sometimes to impossible results. The censuses give the total enumerated number of ever-married women (i.e. married and widows at all ages). If we subtract from this number the number estimated under age 50 for each census year, we obtain an estimated number of ever-married women over 50. This number, of course, partakes of the unreliability of census results, but it should be reasonably satisfactory at least in certain years. When related to the number of women estimated over 50, it gives a proportion ever-married, which we shall hereafter call $EM50+$. The estimates of $EM50+$ are plotted for Calvados in Figure 4.3. On the same scale of percentage ever-married, we plot the proportions over age 50 at the

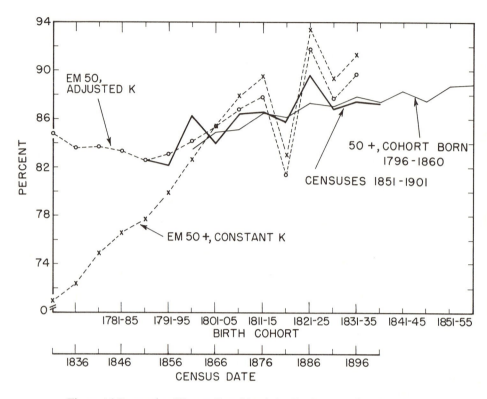

Figure 4.3 Proportion Women Ever-Married (*C*), Computations Based on Female Population Over 50 at Census Dates 1851 to 1901 and on Female Cohort Born 1781 to 1860, and Two Estimates of Proportion Women Ever-Married Over 50 (*EM*50+) from 1831 to 1896, Calvados

censuses from 1851 on, on a period basis, and the cohort estimates 50–75 (used as our estimates of *C*).[5] The *EM*50+ shows rather pronounced fluctuations due to the varying completeness of enumeration of the ever-married women, or to biases that may be present in the estimate of the population. For example, the sawteeth

[5] To identify the cohort on the period scale, we use the time when the center age of the cohort years covered is derived from the census on the time scale. For example, the 1796-1800 cohort is assigned to 1861, the time when the members of that cohort were aged 60-64 years. There is a rough correspondence on the time scale between period and cohort values of the proportions ever-married over age 50, although the cohort estimate of *C* is much more regular, since it averages censuses with particular misreporting problems.

around 1881 reproduce those in the total number of ever-married women enumerated in the census:

| 1876 | 128,372 | 1886 | 124,124 |
| 1881 | 120,502 | 1891 | 122,043 |

Figure 4.3 suggests that there is something wrong with the values taken by $EM50+$ when k is kept constant. The drop of the $EM50+$ back in time is much more precipitous than appears possible. The changes in the numbers married reflected in the census totals prior to 1861 are not compatible with a constant age at marriage by cohort (i.e. with a constant k) because all the recorded changes in the proportions married would have to imply changes in C which are unlikely. In the case of Calvados, for example, it is improbable that the proportion of ever-married women would have risen from 70 to 85 percent in the thirty-five years between 1831 and 1866. It is likely therefore that there was a change in k as well as a change in C, a change in the age at marriage as well as in the proportions ever-married.

The next step is to prepare another extreme estimate, where the proportion $EM50+$ coincides with the extension of the trend line of C's for the range of censuses studied, and where the change in k, and therefore in age at marriage, accounts for the change in the number of women ever-married under age 50. The difficulty is that our estimates of the proportion married are made by cohorts, while $EM50+$ is based on the censuses, and obtained for specific periods. Changing k, which is a cohort index, will require an approximation of the equivalence of cohort and period chronology. We shall presume that changes in k prior to the birth cohort 1841–1845 are progressive, and linear. We modify the value of k in each of the cohorts born between 1781–1840 by an amount proportional to the remoteness from the cohort 1841–1845, until $EM50+$ in 1846 is equal to the value of C in the cohort 1781–1785. The choice of 1846 is based on the fact that that census appears rather more reliable than most.[6] (For the purpose of the computations, we

[6] In the previous chapter, we also chose 1846 as the base of the balance equation when we were determining the cumulated extent of migration in the population.

add or subtract 0.01 at a time to the level of k computed on an average of the cohorts since the 1841–1845 one, to obtain a new value of k in the cohort 1836–1840; and to the previous cohorts, respectively, 1831–1835, 1826–1830, . . . 1791–1795, . . . 1781–1785, we add 0.02, 0.03, . . . 0.10, . . . 0.12 at a time, respectively. $EM50+$ is recomputed for these new values of k, and the final k's are obtained after several iterations by interpolation between values of k to provide in 1846 an $EM50+$ equal to the estimate of C in the cohort 1781–1785. The procedure is illustrated in Diagram 6.)

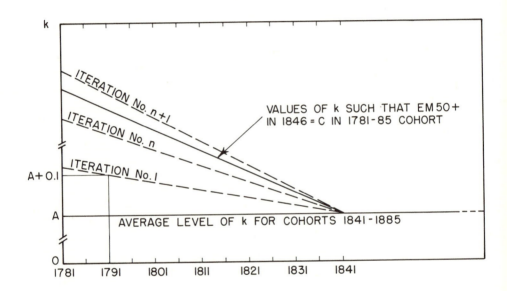

The new values of $EM50+$ before 1866 in Figure 4.3 are more in line with the proportions ever-married derived from later censuses. The new values of k imply new proportions married and new estimates of the age at first marriage.

We thus have two sets of estimates: a) one set relying on the assumption that there had been a constant age at marriage in the past, but changing proportions ever-married over age 50 (eventually diverging sharply from extrapolated values of C); b) another set where $EM50+$ are conforming to interpolated values of C's (and coming slowly down) but where age at marriage is changing.

If there were changes in nuptiality during the first half of the 19th century, it is likely that these changes influenced both the proportion married and the age at marriage. There is usually a rather close connection between the two variables, although it is not difficult to imagine conditions where the two would not move together. A shortage of men, resulting from war or migration, might result in a lower proportion of ever-married women without affecting the age at marriage of those who marry. However, the range of estimates covered by the two extreme sets of assumptions about k is rather wide, and, although it reflects the degree of approximation involved in the estimation procedure, it is impractical. Therefore we shall settle on an average of the two estimates and use this as our final estimate of the proportions ever-married.

The proportions ever-married by cohort can now be converted into numbers ever-married by multiplying the number of women estimated for an age-group in the beginning of a census year by the average of the proportions ever-married in the same age-group of the two surrounding cohorts. The estimated number of widows and divorced women is subtracted to yield the number of currently married women on January 1 of successive census years, i.e. 1831, 1836, . . . 1901.

The estimation of the married women before 1851, when we have no census data with which we can compare our estimates, remains the weakest link in our procedure, for several reasons already mentioned. First, estimation of the population is less and less reliable as we go back in time before 1851, because less and less birth cohorts can be used to estimate the population, and an increasing number of age-groups are made up of the survivors of the stable population assumed in 1801. Second, the determination of k depends increasingly on the adequacy of C (or at least of its extrapolation to the cohort most likely to be comparable to the proportion ever-married over age 50 in 1846) with the $EM50+$ in 1846. We know that $EM50+$ and C are not identical even after 1851 or 1866. The drop of $EM50+$ computed with constant k

in Calvados could be at least partly due to bad census enumeration of the total number of married women. The range between the two estimates of the ever-married population has only one valid boundary: what the marital status would have been had k remained constant at its average for the post-1841 cohorts. Its other boundary is subject to uncertainty, and depends on the accuracy of the enumeration of the married women in 1846. Although this is clearly a better census than the surrounding ones and appears to be exceptionally complete, the estimate of k on this basis is not foolproof. In some cases the procedure leads to absurdly abrupt changes in age at marriage, or an absurdly wide range of estimates. We shall indicate these instances with the results in the second part of the book. Using the average between our two estimating procedures for k, we may attempt to compare the number of married women enumerated in successive censuses after 1851 with our estimate. This may be conveniently done by R/E ratios, as we did earlier for the number of women in the population. The ratio of reported over estimated are given in Table 4.2 for Calvados.

One thing becomes apparent from Table 4.2. In general, the estimated number of married women is considerably higher than the reported number. If the differences between the two are averaged for the entire period covered by the censuses (i.e. 1851–1901), the discrepancy is in the neighborhood of 6 percent; i.e.

TABLE 4.2

UNADJUSTED RATIO OF REPORTED TO ESTIMATED MARRIED WOMEN, BY AGE,

CALVADOS: 1851 TO 1901

Age	1851	1856	1861	1866	1871	1876	1881	1886	1891	1896	1901
15-19	.741	.839	.826	.953	.607	.702	.708	.588	.760	.800	--
20-24	.857	.933	.890	.974	1.225	.930	.945	1.168	.986	.977	1.042
25-29	.881	.920	.951	.908	1.152	.947	.809	.754	.957	.971	1.002
30-34	.889	.905	.923	.950	.974	.908	.944	.714	.924	.901	.959
35-39	.972	.947	.892	.960	1.077	.916	.895	1.012	.960	.934	.935
40-44	.835	.941	.951	.916	1.088	.923	.871	1.034	.968	.962	.914
45-49	.956	.960	.969	.980	.977	.976	.951	.964	.980	.982	.934

SOURCE: France, passim.

the R/E ratio for the total married population 15–49 is 0.94. There are two possible conclusions: either our estimation procedure systematically overestimated the number married or the census systematically underestimated it. Although there is plenty of evidence that the censuses are unreliable, it is difficult to admit a systematic underreporting of this .nature, i.e. among fairly young women stabilized in the community by marriage. Ordinarily, either very old or very young people are missed, and unmarried ones, rather than married women in the fecund ages. The first explanation appears more likely: the estimation procedure is systematically in error. We have pointed out earlier the uncertainty of C. The systematic deviation from 1.0 of R/E ratios at all ages is, in fact, similar to the effect of a too high C in every cohort. Rather than attempting a further correction of C, we shall be content to multiply every estimate (including the estimates between 1831 and 1846) by the ratio of the total reported between 1851 and 1901 over the total estimated between these dates.[7]

The final results of the estimate of the number of married women in Calvados are given in Figure 4.4, which compares them with the census results. The total number of women, both reported and estimated, is also given in the graph. In this way the relationship between the two sets of estimates can be shown. It is evident, for example, that the same kinds of biases exist sometimes in the number of married women at age 20–24 as in the total number of women. We must once again resort to the ambiguous comparison of the recorded with the estimated data. In the final stretch of the analysis, the ultimate indication that the estimation method has worked resides in the fit of the estimated to at least certain features, or parts, of the reported series. It is only because the two agree at least in part that fluctuations of the reported data and areas of disagreement can be blamed on misreporting. In particular, agreement at the end of the century, in 1901 and 1906 when the censuses appear more reliable and in the 1850s and 1860s, is particularly valuable, since it suggests that the intervening years, although in disagreement, are fairly well represented by the estimates.

[7] This ratio is slightly different when the k's are kept constant and when they are adjusted before the 1841-1845 cohort.

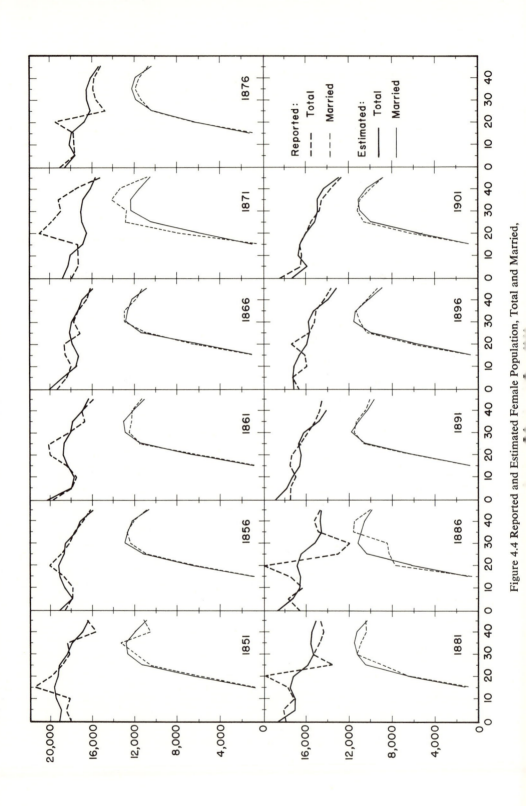

Figure 4.4 Reported and Estimated Female Population, Total and Married,

CHAPTER 5: The Total Female Population of France

The principles applied to the reconstruction of the population of the départements can also be used with the total population of France. One aim of this chapter is to present, for France as a whole, the method of reconstruction and its results in more detail than space allows for the départements, and to describe the format of five standard tables of results. Similar tables for each département are presented in the second part of the book, but the individual comments will be restricted to a few lines. All the population figures for France are expressed in hundreds. The two last digits have been omitted and the totals have been rounded.

Applying the methods described in the previous chapters to the population data for France as a whole yielded a first set of demographic estimates for the country; we shall call it hereafter the "aggregate set." Another set, called the "sum set," can be obtained by the addition of the reconstructed populations of the départements. The two sets will not, of course, give identical results. First, we have not reconstructed some départements that had intractable problems of border changes or very large urban populations.[1] They are part of the aggregate set, but not of the sum set. Second, many of the local biases and errors, adjusted for at the level of the départements, compensated at the national level; what looked like a large underregistration in one of the départements had only a trivial influence on the whole country, and no correction seemed warranted. Some comparisons between the two sets of national estimates can be made, and will be attempted in the course of this chapter.

I. *Reconstruction of the aggregate population of France*

After a preliminary run with uncorrected data, it became apparent that the population under age 15 was seriously underreported

---

[1] Namely: Alpes-Maritimes, Belfort (Territoire de), Bouches-du-Rhône, Meurthe-et-Moselle, Rhône, Savoie, Savoie (Haute-), Seine, and Seine-et-Oise.

in all censuses between 1851 and 1896. The extent of the under-reporting was estimated to be the difference between the population estimated in this preliminary run in the three first age-groups and the enumerated population under age 15. No age distribution was available before 1851, but a similar underreporting of children had probably existed before that date. The average underenumeration thus estimated for the censuses of 1851, 1856, 1861, and 1866 represented 1.2 percent of the total population at those dates. Accordingly, the census totals between 1801 and 1846 were inflated by this amount.

The first column of Table 5.1 gives the ratio of the reported population of successive censuses to a hypothetical closed population that would be equal to the population of 1846, plus the net balance of births and deaths between 1846 and the time of the censuses, under the heading R/CB (Reported/computed by balance).[2] Ratios differing systematically from 1.0—i.e. systematic difference between the enumerated population and the population computed by balance—might be due to the cumulated effect of migration over time, although the possible effect of uncorrected biases in the censuses and the vital registration must not be overlooked. For France as a whole, the R/CB ratios remain close to 1.0—i.e. there is little evidence of international migration before the end of the century.

The R/CB ratio drops steeply in 1801, and this is probably the effect of underenumeration in the census. We have discussed some of the reasons to be wary of the completeness of the census in Chapter 2. As a consequence, the population estimate for 1801 was inflated to make the ratio of the new total (146,447 instead of the enumerated 140,371) to the population computed by balance equal to the R/CB ratio in 1806.

The second column in Table 5.1 gives the extent of the correction applied to the enumerated population, and the third column gives the new estimated population of France at the beginning of each census year.

---

[2] Prior to 1846, births are subtracted and deaths added to the population enumerated in the 1846 census. After 1846, births are added and deaths subtracted.

The reconstructed population was compared by age to the enumerated one, and some underregistered birth cohorts became identifiable. The births were corrected between 1801 and 1820. The extent of the correction and the new estimate of the number of births make up columns 1 and 2 of Table 5.2. Column 3 presents new estimates of the crude birth rate covering the entire century.[3]

```
MORTALITY PATTERN: WEST                                              FRANCE
MIGRATION:  NO CORRECTION MADE FOR MIGRATION BY AGE
POPULATION IN HUNDREDS
```

TABLE 5.1 FEMALE POPULATION ESTIMATES: 1801 TO 1906

DATE	R/CB RATIO	% CORRECTION	FINAL POPULATION ESTIMATE	DATE	R/CB RATIO	% CORRECTION	FINAL POPULATION ESTIMATE
1801	0.981	4.3	146447	1856	0.998	1.0	183434
1806	1.011	1.2	149651	1861	0.993	0.8	188863
1811*	0.998	1.2	152587	1866	0.993	1.2	192741
1816*	0.985	1.2	155521	1871	0.964	1.4	183785
1821	0.975	1.2	158456	1876	0.980	1.1	187372
1826*	0.977	1.2	163281	1881	0.977	1.2	189647
1831	0.985	1.2	168106	1886	0.978	0.7	191688
1836	0.998	1.2	172770	1891	0.981	1.0	193928
1841	0.993	1.2	175189	1896	0.986	0.5	194416
1846	1.000	1.2	180642	1901	0.988	0.0	195339
1851	0.996	1.7	182863	1906	0.989	0.0	197449

```
NOTE:  R/CB RATIO REFERS TO THE POPULATION COMPUTED BY THE BALANCE OF BIRTHS
       AND DEATHS OVER THE REPORTED POPULATION
* INTERPOLATED VALUES
```

TABLE 5.2 FEMALE BIRTH ESTIMATES: 1801-1805 TO 1901-1905

DATE	% CORRECTION	FINAL BIRTH ESTIMATE	CRUDE BIRTH RATE	DATE	% CORRECTION	FINAL BIRTH ESTIMATE	CRUDE BIRTH RATE
1801-1805	6.6	23509	31.8	1856-1860	0.0	23579	25.6
1806-1810	5.2	23562	31.2	1861-1865	0.0	24496	25.7
1811-1815	5.5	23748	30.8	1866-1870	0.0	24353	25.3
1816-1820	1.1	23370	29.8	1871-1875	0.0	22651	24.4
1821-1825	0.0	23528	29.3	1876-1880	0.0	23011	24.4
1826-1830	0.0	23708	28.6	1881-1885	0.0	22803	23.9
1831-1835	0.0	23602	27.7	1886-1890	0.0	21587	22.4
1836-1840	0.0	23286	26.8	1891-1895	0.0	20979	21.6
1841-1845	0.0	23705	26.6	1896-1900	0.0	20779	21.3
1846-1850	0.0	23127	25.4	1901-1905	0.0	20369	20.7
1851-1855	0.0	22879	25.0				

[3] The births given for 1866-1870 were inflated to account for the absence of information on vital events in 1869 and 1870 in the territories of Alsace and Lorraine lost to Germany during the Franco-Prussian war. The crude birth rate is computed by relating these births to an estimate of the French population in the 1866 boundaries. Similarly, the birth rate in 1856-1860 relates the births of the period to the average population in the 1856 boundaries; i.e. without the two Savoies and Nice, which were added to France in 1860.

FRANCE

TABLE 5.3 FEMALE POPULATION ESTIMATES,
DISTRIBUTICN BY AGE: 1801 TO 1906

AGE	1801	1806	1811	1816	1821	1826	1831	1836	1841	1846	1851
0- 4	19067	17480	17729	17985	17874	18285	18377	18274	18173	19012	18215
5- 9	16358	16927	15536	15794	16105	16230	16634	16756	16560	16784	17350
10-14	15096	15711	16180	14852	15139	15634	15824	16285	16180	16226	16303
15-19	13913	14493	15012	15461	14229	14689	15237	15485	15718	15846	15753
20-24	12707	13216	13710	14204	14672	13677	14178	14764	14811	15261	15247
25-29	11509	11963	12397	12866	13372	13992	13095	13625	14014	14277	14575
30-34	10346	10756	11144	11556	12033	12670	13307	12498	12852	13429	13551
35-39	9248	9596	9948	10315	10734	11324	11967	12612	11713	12240	12665
40-44	8203	8521	8819	9150	9522	10039	10628	11269	11748	11090	11474
45-49	7239	7504	7775	8054	8388	8845	9357	9939	10426	11048	10325
50-54	6268	6507	6732	6984	7263	7665	8108	8605	9050	9653	10124
55-59	5274	5461	5666	5872	6118	6450	6824	7239	7619	8155	8604
60-64	4228	4359	4521	4702	4899	5176	5466	5796	6114	6560	6937
65-69	3129	3229	3344	3480	3643	3852	4072	4305	4557	4911	5197
70-74	2079	2131	2216	2306	2420	2572	2716	2872	3044	3300	3502
75-79	1160	1183	1228	1286	1352	1441	1527	1611	1718	1872	1993
80+	611	615	631	657	693	742	789	837	892	978	1048

AGE	1856	1861	1866	1871	1876	1881	1886	1891	1896	1901	1906
0- 4	17894	18953	19751	18292	18292	18758	18675	17857	17243	17364	17357
5- 9	16528	16650	17511	17103	16991	16911	17371	17435	16592	16109	16394
10-14	16768	16361	16277	16096	16843	16532	16457	17027	17022	16196	15816
15-19	15749	16591	15987	14954	15844	16380	16080	16122	16615	16606	15892
20-24	15081	15444	16077	14560	14595	15289	15811	15636	15613	16096	16190
25-29	14486	14679	14862	14536	14109	13993	14665	15278	15047	15039	15609
30-34	13762	14014	14045	13358	14003	13455	13352	14098	14627	14425	14520
35-39	12713	13229	13329	12546	12789	13280	12769	12767	13423	13951	13861
40-44	11810	12147	12509	11836	11941	12062	12534	12143	12089	12737	13339
45-49	10626	11208	11410	11033	11190	11188	11309	11841	11423	11397	12100
50-54	9411	9926	10368	9907	10270	10330	10338	10531	10979	10620	10683
55-59	8974	8552	8943	8762	8978	9245	9311	9392	9524	9968	9732
60-64	7277	7783	7368	7219	7588	7745	7991	8114	8145	8310	8794
65-69	5463	5880	6265	5548	5835	6131	6275	6530	6596	6681	6907
70-74	3682	3974	4273	4251	4044	4269	4502	4650	4812	4920	5062
75-79	2099	2269	2457	2461	2632	2528	2682	2856	2931	3084	3214
80+	1110	1205	1310	1322	1428	1552	1567	1650	1737	1837	1982

FRANCE

TABLE 5.4 MARRIED WOMEN ESTIMATES,
DISTRIBUTICN BY AGE: 1831 TO 1901

AGE	1831	1836	1841	1846	1851	1856	1861	1866
15-19	797	832	829	837	844	855	989	943
20-24	4777	4997	5053	5285	5340	5331	5513	5462
25-29	7901	8259	8554	8772	9006	8998	9170	9331
30-34	9486	8928	9236	9701	9826	10010	10233	10284
35-39	8830	9308	8702	9142	9489	9544	9965	10057
40-44	7799	8255	8674	8238	8547	8806	9086	9361
45-49	6461	6840	7259	7760	7278	7498	7942	8087

AGE	1871	1876	1881	1886	1891	1896	1901
15-19	894	998	1011	931	802	759	958
20-24	5127	5512	5872	5948	5708	5741	5839
25-29	8693	8657	9021	9531	9837	9599	9836
30-34	9766	9954	9722	9928	10528	10917	10711
35-39	9416	9615	9874	9586	9697	10247	10621
40-44	8769	8853	9012	9235	8943	8965	9396
45-49	7698	7811	7898	8038	8367	8055	7902

TABLE 5.5 DEMOGRAPHIC INDICES AND FEMALE SINGULATE MEAN AGE
AT MARRIAGE: 1831 TO 1901

DATE	IF OVERALL FERTILITY	IG MARITAL FERTILITY	IH ILLEGITIMATE FERTILITY	IM PROPORTION MARRIED	SINGULATE MEAN AGE AT MARRIAGE
1831	0.297	0.537	0.044	0.514	24.6
1836	0.288	0.518	0.044	0.514	24.6
1841	0.286	0.515	0.043	0.516	24.6
1846	0.279	0.498	0.041	0.520	24.5
1851	0.271	0.478	0.041	0.526	24.4
1856	0.273	0.478	0.043	0.530	24.4
1861	0.275	0.478	0.045	0.531	24.4
1866	0.276	0.481	0.045	0.530	24.5
1871	0.282	0.494	0.044	0.529	24.3
1876	0.270	0.471	0.041	0.533	24.1
1881	0.267	0.460	0.043	0.538	24.1
1886	0.256	0.435	0.046	0.541	24.3
1891	0.242	0.410	0.045	0.540	24.5
1896	0.235	0.396	0.045	0.541	24.4
1901	0.228	0.383	0.044	0.543	

METHODS

The reconstructed population itself is given by age in Table 5.3.

Table 5.4 presents the married population by age. This has been reconstructed in the standard fashion with the first-marriage frequencies computed from the vital registration and the estimated population by age. Finally, Table 5.5 gives three standardized fertility indices and two indices of nuptiality. The fertility indices are the ones used by the Princeton study of the fertility decline (Coale, 1969).

$$\text{Overall fertility index: } I_f = \frac{B}{\Sigma F_i w_i} \qquad (19)$$

$$\text{Legitimate fertility index: } I_g = \frac{B_L}{\Sigma F_i m_i} \qquad (20)$$

$$\text{Illegitimate fertility index: } I_h = \frac{B_I}{\Sigma F_i u_i} \qquad (21)$$

B are total births; B_L and B_I, legitimate and illegitimate births respectively. w_i, m_i, and u_i are, respectively, the total, the married, and the unmarried women in the ith fecund age-group ($i = 1$ for ages 15–19, and $i = 7$ for ages 45–49). F_i is the highest fertility pattern reliably recorded, that of the Hutterites.

The following indices of nuptiality are given in Table 5.5:

$$\text{Standardized proportion married: } I_m = \frac{\Sigma F_i m_i}{\Sigma F_i w_i} \qquad (22)$$

and singulate mean age at first marriage,

$$SMAM = 15 + \frac{(5 \Sigma S_i) - 50 S_{50}}{1 - S_{50}} \qquad (23)$$

where S_i is the proportion remaining single in age-group i in a synthetic cohort exposed to the nuptiality of the period, and S_{50} is the proportion never getting married in that cohort.[4]

The indices of fertility and nuptiality presented in Table 5.5 cover the period 1831 to 1901. Together with the crude birth rates, which

---

[4] S_i is obtained by relating the proportions single at two census years, five years apart. By age 50, first marriages become very rare, and S_{50} can be assumed to represent the final proportion of women who will never marry.

go back further in time until 1801, they represent the end product of this study. These results will be analyzed in a second book devoted to the determinants and correlates of the French fertility decline during the 19th century. At this stage, we want to test the validity of the methods used by examining the coherence of the results. The following sections of this chapter are devoted to this task for France as a whole. The next chapter attempts a similar analysis for the départements.

II. *Mortality pattern*

In a large area of the north of France, the use of the North pattern of mortality seemed to produce a better fit of the reconstructed to the enumerated population (i.e. the R/E ratios were closer to 1.0), particularly at the older ages. However, we used West in the greater number of départements. This pattern, on a priori grounds, seems more appropriate in general for the populations of Western Europe, and the official life tables of France conform to it. In the reconstruction of the whole of France we attempted a set of estimates based on North, in addition to those presented here based on the West pattern. This trial is worth mentioning, because the resulting estimated distribution of deaths was closer to the registered deaths by age than the distribution obtained with the West pattern. This shows mainly, we believe, that there was an inconsistency between the enumerated number of old people—too few if the North reconstruction was correct—and the registered deaths—too many at those ages. The tendency to exaggerate the age of the deceased is a well-recognized bias. There is also a tendency to underenumerate old people in censuses. Some combination of these two factors may have been present. To be consistent, we shall continue to accept the West pattern for the whole of France, on the basis of the criterion of better fit of the population reconstruction, since that criterion led to the choice of North or West in the instance of individual départements.

Figure 5.1 presents selected comparisons of reported distributions of deaths (in absolute numbers) and the estimated distributions according to both the West and the North patterns. The pop-

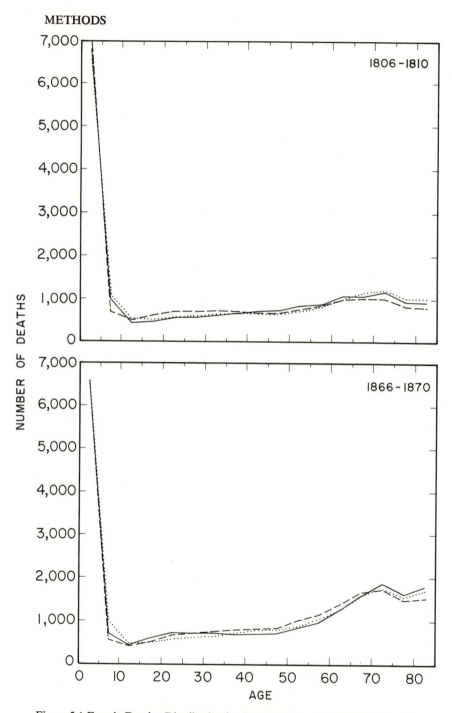

Figure 5.1 Female Deaths, Distribution by Age, according to Vital Registration and Two Reconstructions: 1806-1810 to 1896-1900

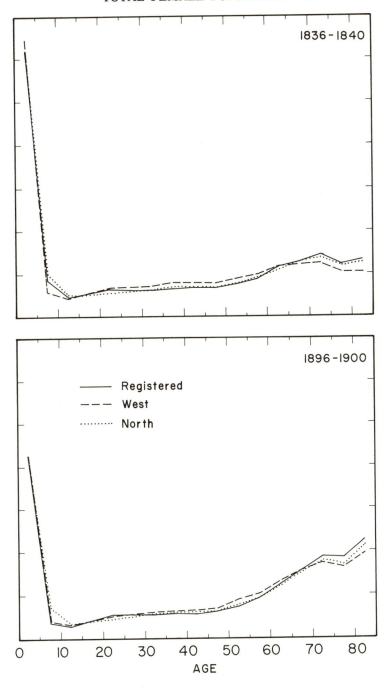

TOTAL FEMALE POPULATION OF FRANCE

1836 – 1840

1896 – 1900

——— Registered

– – – West

·········· North

AGE

ulation reconstruction is based on minimal information and the use of models. The reported mortality data, on the other hand, may not be reliable, and actually were suspected of serious biases at the time by statisticians such as Legoyt. In sum, the fit of both series is reassuring, and the West model, although slightly less satisfactory before the end of the century, is close enough. Finally, Figure 5.2 presents the comparison of the North and West reconstructions of the population by showing the R/E ratios between 1851 and 1906.

III. *A comparison of the sum of the départemental reconstructions to that of France as an aggregate*

We shall mostly compare percentages, or proportions, rather than absolute numbers, since the sum of the départemental estimates does not equal the aggregate set for France. The reason is that the population of several départements was not reconstructed. A major problem in comparing the sum and the aggregate sets is that the mostly urban populations of Bouches-du-Rhône (including Marseille), Rhône (including Lyon), and Seine (including Paris) had different population characteristics than the rest of France.

Table 5.6 compares the percentages of correction applied to the total population of the départements in the two sets. The extent of the correction should be different for various reasons. First, we have not bothered to correct many individual reconstructions, although there was some evidence of a slight underenumeration of children; at the level of the whole country, these small differences add up to a significant number of people. Second, we smoothed the population totals in individual départements to avoid large fluctuations in the migratory movements by age. Furthermore, in départements receiving large numbers of nurslings and very young children on temporary migration from Paris, we subtracted an estimate of the number of young migrants from the total population, since these children belonged logically to the population of the capital; since we did not reconstruct the population of Paris, there is no compensating amount in the sum of the départements. The last two factors explain why the aggregate set is consistently larger and why there are some negative corrections in the series for the

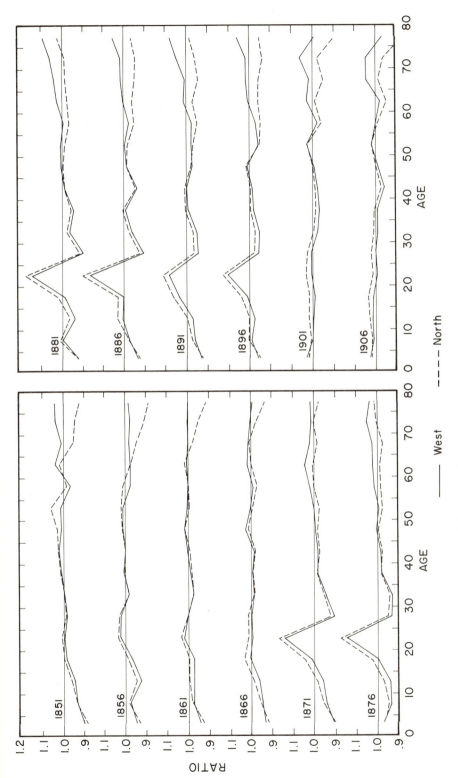

Figure 5.2 Ratio of Reported to Estimated Female Population, by Age, according to Two Reconstructions: 1851 to 1906

—— West   ---- North

METHODS

TABLE 5.6

CORRECTION PERCENTAGES APPLIED TO TWO SETS OF FEMALE
POPULATION ESTIMATES: 1801 TO 1906

Date	Aggregate	Sum
1801	4.3	3.5
1806	1.2	0.5
1811[a]	1.2	0.7
1816[a]	1.2	0.7
1821	1.2	0.9
1826[a]	1.2	0.7
1831	1.2	0.6
1836	1.2	0.5
1841	1.2	0.6
1846	1.2	0.6
1851	1.7	0.7
1856	1.0	0.9
1861	0.8	0.5
1866	1.2	0.5
1871	1.4	0.9
1876	1.1	-0.4
1881	1.2	0.2
1886	0.7	-0.1
1891	1.0	0.1
1896	0.5	-0.1
1901	0.0	-0.1
1906	0.0	-0.2

NOTES: Aggregate refers to reconstruction based on data for all
France.
Sum refers to total of figures from reconstructed
départements.

[a] Correction applied to interpolated values.

sum of the départements. The difference between the corrections in
Table 5.6 is in most cases rather small—less than one percentage
point. The largest difference occurs in 1801. The first national
census of France was obviously underenumerated, but it is difficult
to evaluate to what extent.

The correction of births is more interesting, and Table 5.7 shows

[134]

that the reconstruction of the aggregate of France and the sum of the départements agree fairly well on the order of magnitude of underregistration in the beginning of the century. After 1820, there were many small corrections of births, which were significant in particular départements but were swamped in the reconstruction of the whole country. Of course we do not know what extent of underregistration existed in the more urban départements, nor the extent to which births of children whose parents resided normally

TABLE 5.7

CORRECTION PERCENTAGES APPLIED TO TWO SETS OF FEMALE
BIRTH ESTIMATES: 1801-1805 TO 1901-1905

Date	Aggregate	Sum
1801-1805	6.6	6.1
1806-1810	5.2	4.3
1811-1815	5.5	4.9
1816-1820	1.1	1.4
1821-1825	0.0	0.6
1826-1830	0.0	0.9
1831-1835	0.0	0.8
1836-1840	0.0	0.6
1841-1845	0.0	0.2
1846-1850	0.0	1.7
1851-1855	0.0	0.7
1856-1860	0.0	0.3
1861-1865	0.0	-0.1
1866-1870	0.0	0.0
1871-1875	0.0	0.5
1876-1880	0.0	0.1
1881-1885	0.0	-0.3
1886-1890	0.0	-0.3
1891-1895	0.0	0.0
1896-1900	0.0	0.0
1901-1905	0.0	0.0

NOTES: Aggregate refers to reconstruction based on data for all France.
Sum refers to total of figures from reconstructed départements.

in the more rural départements occurred in the larger cities. On the whole, therefore, the comparison presented in Table 5.7 is satisfactory.

Table 5.8 offers a comparison of the proportionate age distributions, and Table 5.9 a comparison of the proportions married, according to both the aggregate reconstruction and the sum of the départemental reconstructions, at selected dates. Once again, the comparisons do not reveal any large inconsistency in the estimates. The two series of age distributions are quite close until the end of the century, when urban-rural differences might explain the shortage of adults and the relative excess of young and old people in the sum set. The differences in Table 5.9 between aggregates and sums must also, at least partly, be accounted for by the different nuptiality of the départements which were not reconstructed. These départements include large urban populations where the proportions married are less than in rural areas. We computed the proportions married according to the censuses in sets of départements comparable to those presented in Tables 5.8 and 5.9 (that is excluding the départements for which no reconstruction was made). The order of magnitude and the age distribution of the differences is the same as between the two sets of reconstructions. Table 5.10 shows the comparison for 1861 and 1901.

IV. *A comparison with Bourgeois-Pichat's reconstruction*

Jean Bourgeois-Pichat, in a well-known article (1951 and 1952 or 1965), has reconstructed the total French population by age and investigated the evolution of its characteristics. His reconstruction included both sexes and begins with 1776; it does not deal with marital status. If we restrict the comparison with our own reconstruction to females, during the 19th century, we can perhaps gain some insights into the respective merits of the methods followed, and into the reliability of the results. We must note that Bourgeois-Pichat assumed that the registration of deaths was complete, that ages at death were accurately recorded, and that migrations were negligible. He reconstructed the population on January first of

TABLE 5.8

FEMALE AGE DISTRIBUTION, COMPARISON BETWEEN TWO SETS OF ESTIMATES: 1801 TO 1901

Age	1801 Aggregate	1801 Sum	1821 Aggregate	1821 Sum	1841 Aggregate	1841 Sum	1861 Aggregate	1861 Sum	1881 Aggregate	1881 Sum	1901 Aggregate	1901 Sum
0-4	13.02	12.99	11.28	11.45	10.37	10.48	10.04	10.01	9.89	10.11	8.89	9.08
5-9	11.17	11.00	10.16	10.10	9.45	9.49	8.82	8.88	8.92	8.98	8.25	8.37
10-14	10.31	10.10	9.55	9.49	9.24	9.17	8.66	8.73	8.72	8.64	8.29	8.47
15-19	9.50	9.34	8.98	8.89	8.97	8.89	8.78	8.63	8.64	8.40	8.50	8.48
20-24	8.68	8.56	9.26	9.07	8.45	8.45	8.18	8.00	8.06	7.67	8.24	8.03
25-29	7.86	7.79	8.44	8.29	8.00	7.91	7.77	7.60	7.38	7.15	7.70	7.29
30-34	7.06	7.05	7.59	7.50	7.34	7.31	7.42	7.29	7.09	6.94	7.38	6.91
35-39	6.31	6.33	6.77	6.73	6.69	6.65	7.00	6.96	7.00	6.78	7.14	6.70
40-44	5.60	5.64	6.01	5.99	6.71	6.61	6.43	6.50	6.36	6.29	6.52	6.26
45-49	4.94	5.00	5.29	5.31	5.95	5.88	5.93	5.94	5.90	5.91	5.83	5.84
50-54	4.28	4.37	4.58	4.63	5.17	5.14	5.26	5.32	5.45	5.52	5.43	5.56
55-59	3.60	3.71	3.86	3.94	4.35	4.37	4.53	4.60	4.87	5.05	5.10	5.22
60-64	2.89	3.00	3.09	3.19	3.49	3.55	4.12	4.18	4.08	4.34	4.25	4.47
65-69	2.14	2.24	2.30	2.40	2.60	2.68	3.11	3.20	3.23	3.43	3.42	3.67
70-74	1.42	1.50	1.53	1.62	1.74	1.82	2.10	2.19	2.25	2.42	2.52	2.75
75-79	.79	.84	.85	.92	.98	1.04	1.20	1.28	1.33	1.45	1.58	1.78
80+	.42	.45	.44	.48	.51	.56	.64	.70	.82	.93	.94	1.12

NOTES: Aggregate refers to reconstruction based on data for all France.
Sum refers to total of figures from reconstructed départements.

TABLE 5.9

PERCENTAGE OF MARRIED WOMEN BY AGE GROUPS, COMPARISON BETWEEN

TWO SETS OF ESTIMATES: 1831 TO 1901

Age	1831 Aggregate	Sum	1841 Aggregate	Sum	1851 Aggregate	Sum	1861 Aggregate	Sum
15-19	5.23	5.00	5.27	5.08	5.36	5.26	5.96	5.93
20-24	33.69	33.81	34.12	34.65	35.02	35.55	35.70	36.69
25-29	60.34	59.94	61.04	61.28	61.79	62.43	62.47	63.61
30-34	71.29	71.14	71.86	72.10	72.51	73.23	73.02	74.08
35-39	73.79	73.94	74.29	74.68	74.92	75.78	75.33	76.47
40-44	73.38	74.46	73.83	74.99	74.49	75.61	74.80	76.15
45-49	69.05	70.11	69.62	70.76	70.49	71.51	70.86	72.19

Age	1871 Aggregate	Sum	1881 Aggregate	Sum	1891 Aggregate	Sum	1901 Aggregate	Sum
15-19	5.98	5.96	6.17	6.23	4.97	4.86	5.77	5.89
20-24	35.21	36.64	38.41	39.43	36.51	38.21	36.28	38.02
25-29	59.80	61.35	64.47	65.84	64.39	66.22	65.40	67.50
30-34	73.11	74.55	72.26	73.78	74.68	76.05	74.25	76.48
35-39	75.05	76.56	74.35	75.74	75.95	77.68	76.13	78.20
40-44	74.09	75.69	74.71	76.28	73.65	75.54	73.77	75.81
45-49	69.77	71.45	70.59	72.17	70.66	72.81	69.33	71.96

NOTES: Aggregate refers to reconstruction based on data for all France.
Sum refers to total of figures from reconstructed départements.

every fifth year, starting in 1806 and ending in 1901, by "rejuvenating" the deaths to their year of birth, and counting the individuals in all intervening census years between their births and their deaths. This procedure could be extended before 1806 by using additional assumptions concerning persons dying before 1806 on the basis of an interpolation of age-specific death rates between Duvillard's life table, assumed to be valid for 1770, and the values computed for 1806. These additional assumptions are not crucial for our purpose, which is to compare the estimates of the age distribution during the 19th century only. At this point, the main criticisms of the method are that (a) there *was* migration during the 19th century, mostly at the end, and this introduces a distortion by attributing, in effect, deaths of persons who were not born in the

TOTAL FEMALE POPULATION OF FRANCE

TABLE 5.10

PERCENTAGE OF MARRIED WOMEN BY AGE GROUPS, COMPARISON BETWEEN CENSUS
DATA FOR FRANCE AND FOR 78 DEPARTEMENTS: 1861 AND 1901

Age	1861		1901	
	France	78 départements	France	78 départements
15-19	5.36	5.64	6.17	6.16
20-24	34.30	35.19	40.35	41.18
25-29	60.67	61.70	67.69	69.63
30-34	72.38	72.95	76.42	78.54
35-39	76.34	77.08	77.87	80.01
40-44	76.11	76.06	75.89	77.99
45-49	73.81	75.49	72.43	74.48

SOURCE: France, 1864 and 1906, vol. 4.

country to the native population; (b) the registration of vital events was probably incomplete in the beginning of the century, and this may have been true for deaths as well as for births. It must be added that Bourgeois-Pichat is not very explicit about the details of his methods. Does he use a census to "close-off" his estimate? For instance, the population estimate for 1901 includes some persons who had not yet died at the time when the article was written (or even now). Also, how does he estimate fertility during the 19th century? Is the number of births used the registered number, or the lifetime cumulated number of deaths to the cohort born in the year in question? These points are not made explicit.

Figure 5.3 presents a comparison of Bourgeois-Pichat's and our estimates of the female age distribution, together with the recorded population when it becomes available from 1851 on. The graph was drawn for every fourth census year (or every twenty years), but the picture is much the same on other dates in between. This is illustrated by Figure 5.4, which presents age distributions for census years 1851 to 1866, the first four censuses with a recorded age distribution that appear to have less serious biases in reporting than later censuses before 1901. The reader may remember that we used the fit of successive cohorts at those dates to correct for underregistration of the births at the beginning of the century. It is

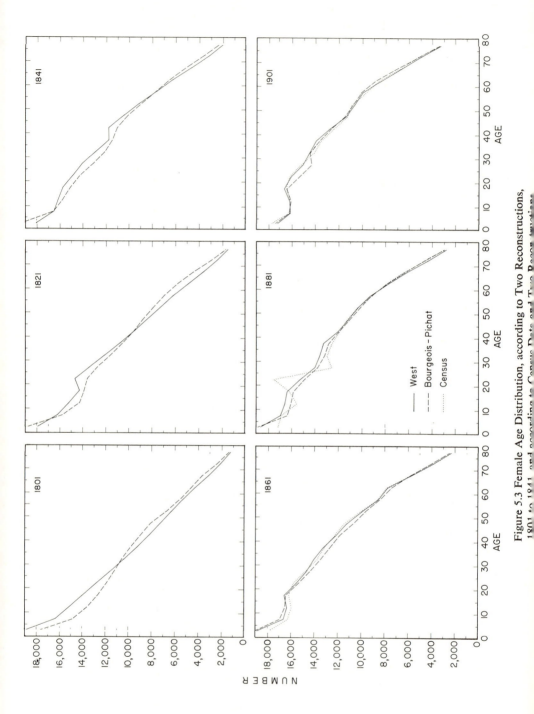

Figure 5.3 Female Age Distribution, according to Two Reconstructions,
1801 to 1841, and according to Census Data and Two Reconstructions,

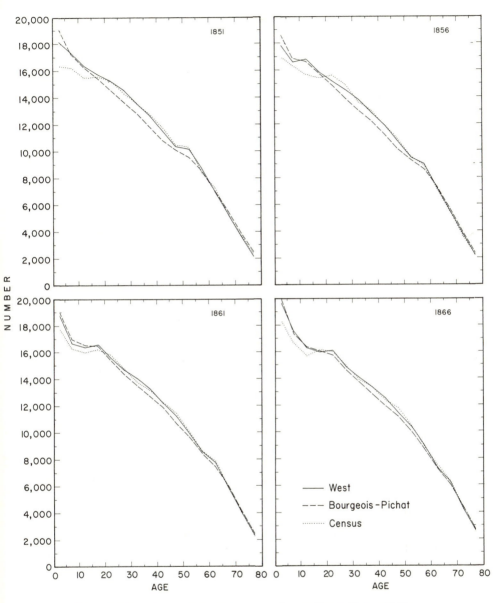

Figure 5.4 Female Age Distribution, according to Census Data and Two
Reconstructions: 1851 to 1866

therefore not surprising that our reconstructions are closer to the enumerated age distributions than are Bourgeois-Pichat's. The choice of assumptions in our reconstruction was determined by the criterion of closest possible fit with the series of recorded age groups. This is an ambiguous criterion, as was pointed out before, since we attempt to use the recorded figures as a standard, and to correct them at the same time. The methods used by Bourgeois-Pichat are subject to other constraints than the fit with the enumerated population, and it is difficult to find independent criteria to evaluate which method works best and gives the results closest to the real situation rather than to the recorded data. By hypothesis, Bourgeois-Pichat's age distribution of deaths is the registered one; our West model reconstruction of the death series deviates somewhat from the results of the vital registration (as we indicated in a previous section of this chapter).

Before 1851 (and to some extent also after that date) the two reconstructions have persistent differences: there are more teenagers and young adults in our reconstruction, more old people in Bourgeois-Pitchat's. The two distributions are quite different in 1801; we start with a rather steep stable population, whose survivors in 1851, 1856, 1861, and 1866 approximate closely the numbers in the tail of the recorded distributions. (In particular, the age-group 50–54 in 1851 is consistent with a stable population of substantially larger birth rate than that prevailing after the turn of the century. The cohort born in 1796–1800 appears to have been particularly large.)

Both reconstructions agree on several points. There was clearly a large underreporting of children in 1851 and in the following censuses. From 1872 on, the censuses inflated the age-group 20–24 at the expense of the neighboring age-groups.

Two further comparisons are possible between Bourgeois-Pichat's reconstruction and ours. The first is between the estimations of expectation of life at birth; the second is between the crude birth rates. The expectation of life at birth in our estimation is that of the model life table that has served to project the population between census years n and $n+5$. Bourgeois-Pichat computed expectations of life from an average of three years around the census year (i.e. for instance, from the years 1805, 1806, and 1807 related to the reconstructed population of 1806). The two estimates are thus not entirely comparable. Some years of high mortality influence our estimate, but fall outside of Bourgeois-Pichat's period: e.g. the cholera epidemics of 1849 and 1854. Furthermore, to the extent that Bourgeois-Pichat has more old people and less young adults in the early part of the century, he tends to produce an estimate of e_o^o which is higher than ours. Which estimate is the better will depend on what population is more accurate. On the whole, the expectation of life at birth moves up parallel in both sets (Figure 5.5).

The crude birth rates are presented in Figure 5.6. The comparison is between female crude birth rates in our reconstruction

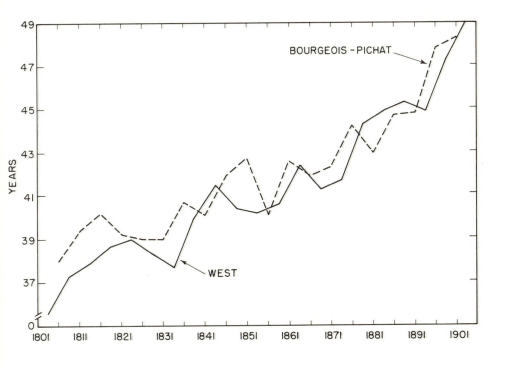

Figure 5.5 Female Expectation of Life at Birth, according to Two
Reconstructions: 1801-1805 to 1901-1905

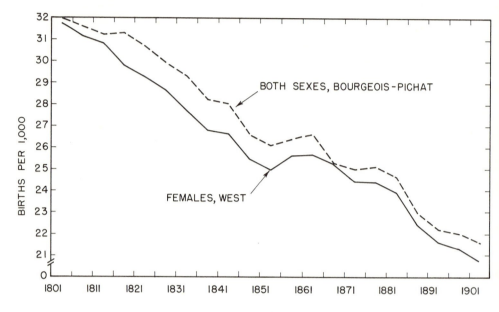

Figure 5.6 Crude Birth Rates, Reconstruction for Both Sexes and
Reconstruction for Females Only: 1801-1805 to 1901-1905

and crude birth rates for both sexes in Bourgeois-Pichat. Female
rates are expected to be lower. This explains the fact that both
series are roughly parallel, except in the beginning of the century,
when we corrected the births for underregistration.[5]

The evidence presented in this chapter indicates that the reconstruction of the départements is consistent with that of the whole
of France. Finally, although lack of clear criteria makes it difficult
to choose between our reconstruction and the classical work of
Bourgeois-Pichat, it is certain at least that we come closer to the
population characteristics recorded in the censuses of France.

A final check of the reconstruction, this time at the level of the
départements, will consist in a comparison of regional patterns in
the results. We devote the next chapter to that task.

[5] The two estimates appear incompatible in 1866-1870, when the two lines come
together. The official vital statistics do not give the number of births and deaths
for Alsace-Lorraine in 1868 and 1869. Perhaps a different adjustment for border
change in the two estimations is responsible for the inconsistency in the series.

CHAPTER 6: Patterns of Bias in the Départements

This chapter examines what, if anything, can be said about systematic defects of the data or of the reconstruction in the départements of France. We shall successively examine the registration of births, the population by age, and the population by marital status. In particular, we shall look for regional patterns and correlations.

I. *Births*

Reconstruction of the départements has yielded new numbers of female births and estimates of the extent of their deficiencies in the published statistics. The quality of the birth series varies with time; there was serious underestimation at the beginning of the century, but the errors were only occasional by 1821, with a serious relapse during the quinquennium 1846–1850. Figure 6.1 gives the number

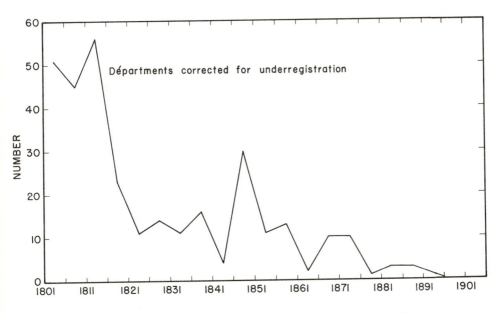

Figure 6.1 Number of Départements Adjusted for Deficiencies in Vital Statistics on Female Births: 1801-1805 to 1901-1905

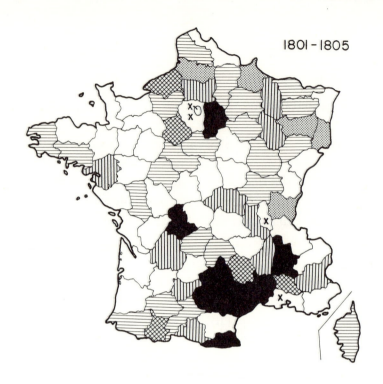

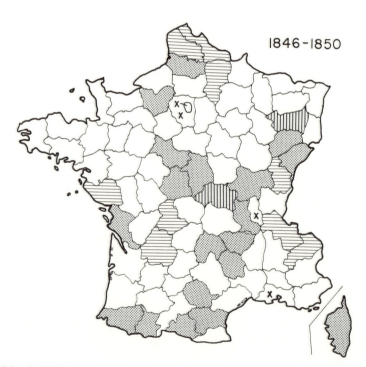

Map 6.1 Deficiencies in Vital Statistics on Female Births, by Département:
1801-1805, 1811-1815, and 1846-1850

PATTERNS OF BIAS IN DEPARTEMENTS

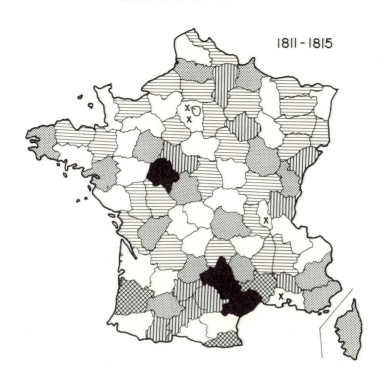

1811 - 1815

☐	No deficiency
▨	0 - 4 %
▤	5 - 9 %
▥	10 - 14 %
▨	15 - 19 %
■	20 + %
x	Not applicable

of corrections made in each five-year period over a total of 82 départements (78 départements after 1871). Most of the corrections are only by a few percentage points. They exceed 20 percent in eight départements in 1801–1805, in two départements in 1806–1810, and in three in 1811–1815. Map 6.1 presents the extent of understatement of births estimated by département in 1801–1805, 1811–1815, and 1846–1850. Whereas there are concentrations of heavy correction in some parts of France in the very beginning of the century (notably in the Languedoc area bordering on the Mediterranean Sea), by 1846–1850 they are generally moderate and characterize no region in particular.

The results shown on Map 6.1 have to be taken with caution, as they are based on evidence drawn from age distributions in censuses, compared to a reconstruction using the births of earlier times. There may well be instances where the deficiencies were so persistent that no clear pattern emerged in later censuses; or alternatively, sometimes the censuses were so erratic that no systematic deviation of the recorded over the estimated population could be legitimately interpreted as reflecting a shortage of recorded births. For example, the censuses of the Languedoc area were sometimes very bad (see for example the age distribution of Hérault in 1851, presented in Figure 2.5). It is therefore difficult to evaluate the extent of underregistration of births with great precision in that region. Figure 6.2 presents the new estimates of the crude birth rates at the beginning of the century in four départements of Languedoc where the birth series appears to have been especially deficient: Aveyron, Gard, Hérault, and Tarn. Our corrections in the first four quinquennia of the century are drastic, and they suggest a very steep drop of the birth rate at the time. In comparison, the rates based on recorded data were almost constant.[1] It is difficult to set one's mind completely at rest about the value of the corrections because they indicate very high birth rates at the start and a precipitous drop over a few years; this relies just on the evidence of rather poor censuses at midcentury. However, an interesting addi-

---

[1] The rates presented in Figure 6.1 relate five-year averages of births to the average of our estimated population figures at both ends of the interval.

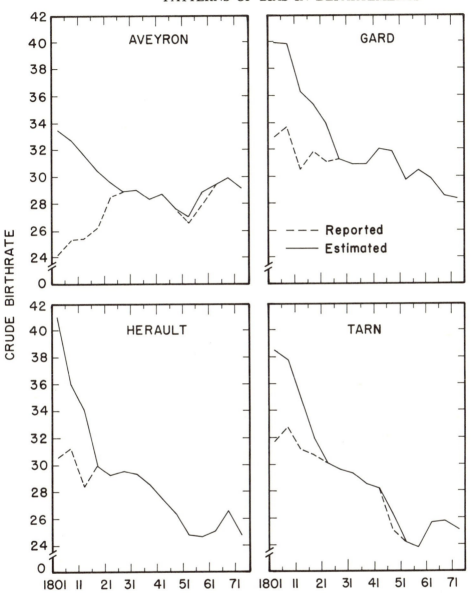

Figure 6.2 Female Crude Birth Rates, Based on Reported and Estimated Data,
Selected Départements of Languedoc: 1801-1805 to 1871-1875

tional piece of information exists. A census was taken in Languedoc
in 1788 by "thousands of vicars in thousands of parishes" (Le Roy
Ladurie, 1965). Although this was in most cases probably based

[149]

more on an informed estimate of the size of villages rather than a house-to-house count, Le Roy Ladurie thinks it gave reliable figures on the population and can be used to compute crude birth rates in conjunction with birth totals given perfunctorily by the parish priests to the civil authority. He finds birth rates of 38 per thousand in 1787–1788 for twelve dioceses of present départements of Gard, Hérault, and Aveyron.[2] Le Roy Ladurie postulates an earlier drop of the birth rate than we do, because he trusts the evidence of the official vital statistics. But he accepts a steep drop during the revolutionary period instead of the Napoleonic years.

The high rates estimated at the beginning of the century in Gard, Hérault, and Tarn, although not impossible, can be accepted only with some reservations. Equally high rates are found in neighboring Provence, as shown in Table 6.1. The corrections for underregistra-

TABLE 6.1

CORRECTED FEMALE CRUDE BIRTH RATES,

SELECTED DEPARTEMENTS IN PROVENCE:

1801-1805 TO 1826-1830

Date	Alpes (Basses-)		Var		Vaucluse	
	Crude birth rate	Correction (percent)	Crude birth rate	Correction (percent)	Crude birth rate	Correction (percent)
1801-1805	39.0	14.4	35.2	--	42.2	18.2
1806-1810	37.3	8.4	34.9	--	41.4	14.3
1811-1815	34.3	4.4	31.7	--	38.6	14.1
1816-1820	34.4	--	30.5	--	36.9	--
1821-1825	33.5	--	28.3	3.0	34.8	--
1826-1830	34.0	--	28.2	3.9	32.8	--

NOTE: Crude birth rate refers to number of female births per 1,000 women.

tion of births are less in Alpes (Basses-) and Vaucluse, and none was applied in Var, which nevertheless exhibits a very sharp decline in a few years. Although parish reconstitutions in the northern half of France point to somewhat lower birth rates before the French

[2] These rates, for both sexes together, are not strictly comparable to the female rates given in this book. The male birth rate is usually higher than the female one.

Revolution, it is possible that birth rates close to 40 per thousand were current in the South, where marriage was earlier. Le Roy Ladurie claims that "40% is a rate generally quoted as representative of French natality in the second half of the eighteenth century" (p. 389).

The example of Aveyron in Figure 6.2 is especially convincing, since the official statistics indicate a rising birth rate between 1801 and 1831, whereas our correction produces a moderate downward slope. But the correction may look more plausible in Aveyron only because fertility decline there was slower than among its neighbors. Figure 6.3 presents other examples of départements where a substantial correction of births was made. The new rates often present a downward slope that is more compatible with the expected trend, since these départements had already reached a level of birth rate suggesting control of fertility, and were to go on with the decline in later quinquennia.

II. *Age distribution*

In this section, we shall look at some of the more characteristic biases of recorded age distributions. As an illustration of patterns frequently encountered, we present R/E ratios by age in all the censuses of the Tarn département between 1851 and 1906 (Figure 6.4). The same patterns of R/E ratios do not appear for each département, nor do they characterize each census for a département. Nevertheless, the inflation of the 20–24 age-group is typical of censuses between 1871 and 1896 throughout France. The next age-group, 25–29, is often correspondingly deflated. This combination suggests misreporting of ages rather than overreporting in one group followed by omissions in the next. The underreporting of the 0–14 group is frequently encountered, and a special correction (by inflation of the total population) has been applied to the total population of several départements (including Tarn) which exhibited this tendency in a marked fashion at the censuses of 1851 to 1866. These départements are mapped on Map 6.2; the underreporting of young children is particularly apparent in the south of France.

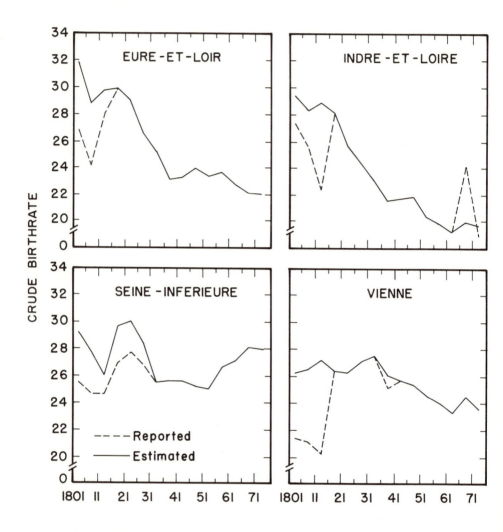

Figure 6.3 Female Crude Birth Rates, Based on Reported and Estimated Data, Selected Départements of France: 1801-1805 to 1871-1875

There is sometimes a large excess, and sometimes a large deficit, of old people. Both biases could be explained by misstatement of ages, and the second also by underreporting. In Tarn, the shape of the age distributions in 1881 and 1886 is certainly due to extraordinary and unaccountable misstatement of ages. Once again, it must be stated emphatically that no pattern of migration could

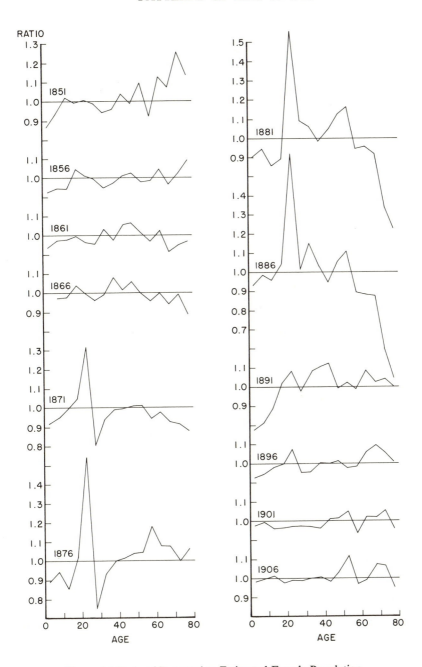

Figure 6.4 Ratio of Reported to Estimated Female Population,
by Age, Tarn: 1851 to 1906

Map 6.2 Départements Adjusted for Underreporting of Children

possibly explain such features of the age distributions which are encountered frequently in the census results of individual départements at the time.

Some of the same features are present in Allier (Figure 6.5): heaping in the 20–24 age-group, underreporting of old people (with a tendency, however, toward exaggerating very old ages, i.e. above 75 or 80).[3] There are unaccountable irregularities in some

[3] The R/E ratio for the ages above 80, not shown on the graph, is 1.22 in 1876 and 1881, 1.26 in 1891 and 1.37 in 1896.

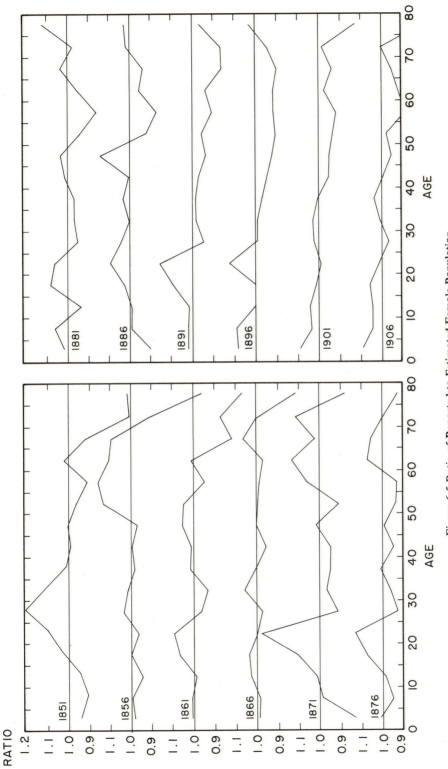

Figure 6.5 Ratio of Reported to Estimated Female Population, by Age, Allier: 1851 to 1906

censuses. The general shape, however, of the census age distribution in 1891 to 1901 exhibits a downward slope, with an excess of children and a shortage after age 40. It may be a pattern of misreporting—e.g. systematic understatement of age—or a failure of the estimating procedure. As Allier is not the only instance of the kind, the question deserves some elaboration.

The deficit of children in the reconstruction, when compared to the census results, cannot be due to the use of an inappropriate life table. The number of births in the five years preceding the census is clearly inconsistent with the number of children under five combined with the number of deaths recorded in the age-group; a similar observation applies to the children aged 5 to 9 and 10 to 15. This we illustrate with the instance of Allier for both 1901 and 1906. Children aged 0–14 in 1906 were born after 1890 and were subjected to the mortality of the period 1890 to 1906. Registered deaths by age for Allier, properly subtracted by age from the series of annual births, permit the computation of the number of survivors expected at census time. We used separation factors by single years of age between ages 0 and 5 (70 percent for the first years, and 50 percent for subsequent years) and by five years after age 5.[4] The results are presented in Table 6.2. Our reconstruction is consistently

TABLE 6.2

AGE GROUPS OF YOUNG FEMALES, BY THREE

DIFFERENT DATA SOURCES, ALLIER: 1901 AND 1906

| Data source | 1901 | | 1906 | | |
	0 - 4	5 - 9	0 - 4	5 - 9	10 - 14
Reported	19,201	18,100	18,153	17,442	17,720
Births - deaths	17,528	17,845	16,653	16,962	17,561
Estimated	17,543	17,469	16,575	16,683	17,001
Ratio					
Reported/estim.	1.09	1.04	1.10	1.05	1.04
Births - deaths/ estimated	.99	1.02	1.00	1.02	1.03

[4] The separation factor for the age-group 0-4 would have been .803 in 1891-1895 and .821 in 1896-1900. The data were not published in enough detail to compute it in 1901-1905; we used an average of the above figures, i.e. .812.

close to the number of surviving children obtained by subtracting deaths from births; the difference between the two figures is small and can be explained by various approximations involved in the computations. In comparison, there are clearly too many children enumerated in Allier, as well as in a number of other départements. If genuine, their presence must be explained by migration, not natural increase. We have mapped the départements characterized by this feature in 1901 and 1906, namely those where the R/E ratios in both census-years were above 1.05 under age 5 (Map 6.3). The same map shows the départements receiving a large number of nurslings and children from Paris, a feature discussed in Chapter 3. The excess of children is of course evident in the latter départements, and one must presume that a similar phenomenon existed in Allier and in other areas shaded in Map 6.3. In particular, the hinterland of Lyon may have received young, temporary migrants to a comparable extent to the region of Paris. And finally, at the time of the two last censuses (1901 and 1906), the region where nurses were recruited may have been extended beyond the areas where we adjusted the population to cope with this problem. At any rate, the presence of these children exerts a subtle distortion on our estimates of the age distribution. Fortunately, the bias appears somewhat less important at the adult ages which are the special concern of this study.

III. *Married population*

Figures 6.6 and 6.7 plot the R/E ratios for married women in Allier and Tarn. The age distribution of these départements was plotted in the previous section. The purpose of this choice is to suggest to what extent misreporting of the population and of the married population are related. There are clearly some common features: in Tarn, for instance, the accumulation of women in the 20–24 age-group at the censuses of 1872 to 1886 has clearly distorted the recording of the number of married women in the age-group. In Allier too, the curves often evolve in a parallel way. When this is the case, we may with confidence attribute the irregularities of the recorded series to biases in reporting. However, the answer is

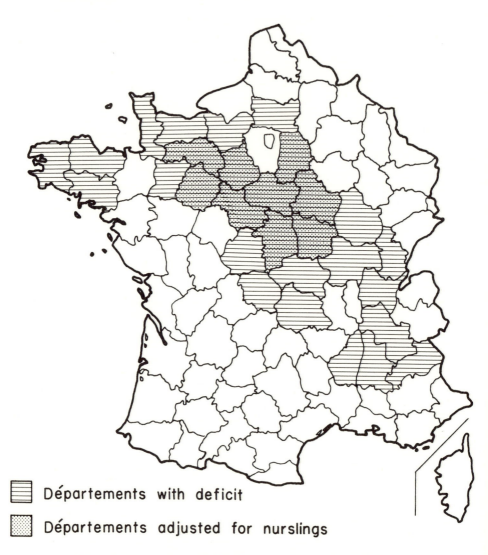

Départements with deficit

Départements adjusted for nurslings

Map 6.3 Départements with Significant and Consecutive Deficits in
Reconstructed Age-Group 0-4 for 1901 and 1906

less clear when we encounter features that are characteristic of the
distribution of married women only. The most persistent among
them is the low R/E ratios among younger married women (say
under 40) in the 1851, 1856, and (less often) 1861 censuses.

Two possible explanations must be discussed in turn: a priori,
the feature may be due either to a bias of the estimating procedure

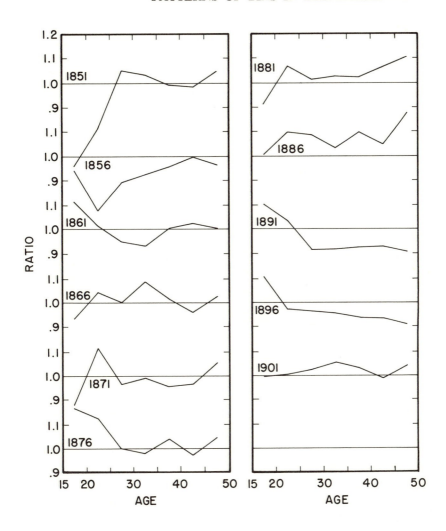

Figure 6.6 Ratio of Reported to Estimated Married Women, by Age,
Allier: 1851 to 1901

or to persistent underenumeration—or age misstatement—for
women in the young ages at those censuses. The explanation by a
defect in the estimation procedure would point to a faulty value of
k, the parameter indicating the pace at which women get married—
in fact, an underestimation of k in the cohorts aged 20–24 in 1851,
1856, and 1861. Since the k's for these cohorts—as well as earlier
ones—were estimated according to an indirect procedure (ex-

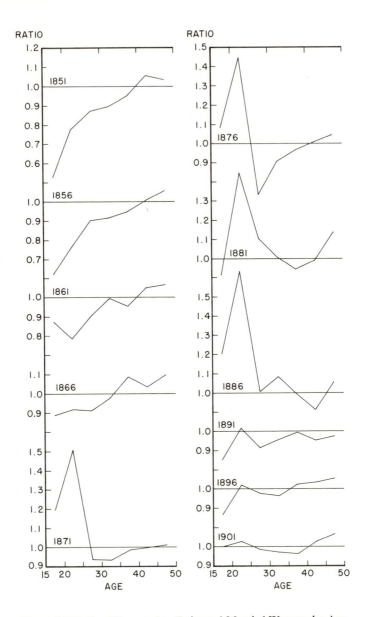

Figure 6.7 Ratio of Reported to Estimated Married Women, by Age,
Tarn: 1851 to 1901

plained in Chapter 4), the poor fit of the estimated population to the recorded one at those ages in those years could suggest that the procedure was not successful. The estimation started from a value of k equal to the average of k for the cohorts 1841 to 1895, inflated (or deflated) until the proportion ever-married over age 50 in 1846 was equal to C (the proportion ever-married according to later censuses). The average of an estimate of the marital status distribution with constant k and of another with constant C was finally accepted since it was improbable that k and the age of marriage were changing without concomitant change of C. The adjustment of k was proportional to the distance on the time scale between the birth date of the cohort whose k was being adjusted, and that born in 1841–1845. There is some room for an underestimation of k in all these assumptions.

Let us first examine the hypothesis that the average of k for the cohorts 1841 to 1895 was too low, since age at marriage was going slowly down during the period. We fail to find any relation between the speed of the decline of k, and the size of the gap between the estimated and the recorded proportion married.[5] A second crucial assumption was that changes of k and C were occurring simultaneously, and accounted for approximately equal parts of the changes in $EM50+$ (the proportion ever-married over 50) in 1846. This seems acceptable since the feature of an R/E at 20–25 under 1.0 is almost always encountered even in areas where we used both a constant k and C, and where there was very little difference between the alternative estimates.[6] Finally, it is possible that our assumption

[5] The correlations between the difference of the average of k in 1841 to 1895 or the average of k in 1841 to 1855, on the one hand, and the R/E ratios at 20-24 in 1851, 1856, and 1861, on the other, are not significant.

[6] In the départements where k for the cohort 1836-1840 has been increased by less than .01 (and earlier k's by less than .02 . . . .12 for cohorts 1831-1835 . . . 1881-1885) the R/E at 20-24 were as follows:

Alpes (Basses-)	.838	Garonne (Haute-)	.854	Pyrénées (Basses-)	.689
Alpes (Hautes-)	.889	Hérault	.442	Pyrénées (Hautes-)	.740
Ardèche	.895	Ille-et-Vilaine	.703	Pyrénées-Orientales	.087
Ariège	.725	Loire	.921	Saône (Haute-)	.673
Aube	.659	Loire-Inférieure	1.316	Seine-et-Marne	.923
Charente-Inférieure	1.074	Marne	.948	Vienne	.961
Creuse	.890	Meuse	.958	Vienne (Haute-)	.782

that changes of k in cohorts prior to 1841–1845 were linear does not reflect the facts. The cohorts that determine the number of young married women at the time of the 1851, 1856, and 1861 censuses may have had a rather different experience than the earlier ones. This is hard to prove. The crude marriage rates in Allier and Tarn evolve as indicated in Table 6.3. In both départements, there

TABLE 6.3

CRUDE MARRIAGE RATES, ALLIER AND TARN:

1831–1835 TO 1866–1870

Date	Allier	Tarn
1831-1835	18.9	15.3
1836-1840	19.0	15.2
1841-1845	19.2	14.8
1846-1850	17.7	14.5
1851-1855	18.5	14.1
1856-1860	19.1	15.6
1861-1865	19.8	16.5
1866-1870	19.6	15.4

NOTE: Crude marriage rate refers to the number of marriages per 1,000 women.

is a suggestion of a reversal of trend: between 1846 and 1850 in Allier, and between 1851 and 1855 in Tarn. But crude marriage rates are notoriously hard to interpret.

The estimation of the proportions married in cohorts marrying before 1861 remains a weak link of the procedure. A defective enumeration of young married women in the censuses between 1851 and 1861 still remains the most likely explanation of the level of the R/E ratios. If genuine, the process by which the enumeration yields a constant shortage of married women at 20–24 in the three first detailed censuses, and a large surplus at the same ages from 1872 on, would be worth investigating. The instructions to the interviewers, the schedules used, and the unit of interview (household or individual) might yield interesting clues. Table 6.4 presents the proportions married by age in Allier according to the census. Despite some quite implausible fluctuations, the figures

TABLE 6.4

PROPORTION WOMEN MARRIED, BY AGE

GROUP, ALLIER: 1851 TO 1866

Age	1851	1856	1861	1866
15-19	6.6	10.0	11.9	11.5
20-24	35.4	39.4	46.6	51.1
25-29	62.3	62.3	71.9	76.0
30-34	74.2	72.9	79.9	82.6
35-39	78.6	78.2	79.6	81.5
40-44	78.0	78.5	79.6	78.7
45-49	77.8	73.9	70.8	75.7
50-54	73.1	68.2	70.0	69.8
55-59	63.5	63.7	61.8	68.3
60-64	49.9	60.7	55.5	50.4
65+	34.8	48.8	37.9	34.6

SOURCE: France 1855, 1859, 1864, and 1869.

seem to indicate no clear trend of the proportions married over age 50. The most striking feature of the series is the extremely fast rise over time of the proportions married at 20–24 and, except for the irregularities in 1861 (compensated for by irregularities in the other direction at older ages), between 25–40. Such a fast rise at young ages is improbable a priori, and would only be explained by a process of making up for marriages delayed during the 1840s. One should remember that this is a remote possibility and that the percentage married in our 1851 estimate may well be overestimated at certain ages, in particular at 20–24.

IV. *Fertility and nuptiality indices*

The estimates of the population, together with the corrected number of births, were used to compute a series of indices of overall fertility (I_f), legitimate fertility (I_g), illegitimate fertility (I_h), and the proportion married (I_m), as well as the singulate mean age at marriage. These indices have been described in Chapter 5.

[163]

The fertility indices and I_m from our reconstruction can be compared to the indices computed directly from the unadjusted data from 1851 on. Of course, no such comparison is possible between 1831 and 1851. We can also compare estimates of the singulate mean age at marriage with the age at first marriage computed from the vital registration's data available from 1856 on. It is clear before any comparison is attempted that the estimated series should be much more regular, since the data are homogeneous and compatible from period to period. If there are biases, they will affect a series of estimates rather than one in particular.

Figure 6.8 presents the standardized indices for Allier and Tarn and similar indices computed from the recorded data. In those two départements, the reconstructed series tell the same story as the uncorrected indices, but they do so in a clearer way, because of their regularity. For example, a slight rise of fertility in the 1860s becomes apparent in both I_f and I_g. This is a widespread pattern among the French départements. So is the decline of I_m at the end of the century, following a long rise. Because of the fluctuation in the quality of the data and the patterns of error, the uncorrected indices offer a much more jagged, hard-to-read picture. In Allier, the apparent rise of the I_g index computed from the recorded data in 1856 appears to originate in an underreporting of the married, visible in Figure 6.6. The drop of I_m between 1886 and 1891, and the subsequent recovery in 1901, can be similarly explained by the inconsistency between the number of married women by age in the successive censuses, also illustrated in Figure 6.6. Remarks of the same kind can be made about Tarn: e.g. the dip in I_m in 1891 is the result of an underreporting of married women, the accumulation of women at 20–24 in 1871 to 1886 results in an underestimation of the three indices, and so on.

Before we turn to the age at marriage, we must point out that Allier and Tarn are instances where the recorded data do not collapse entirely and that there are other départements where the indices based on the reported and the estimated information vary to a considerably greater extent. We plot two "bad" cases in Figure 6.9: Finistère and Loire. The erratic age distribution of Finistère acts to hide the trend in marital fertility. In Loire, the underenumer-

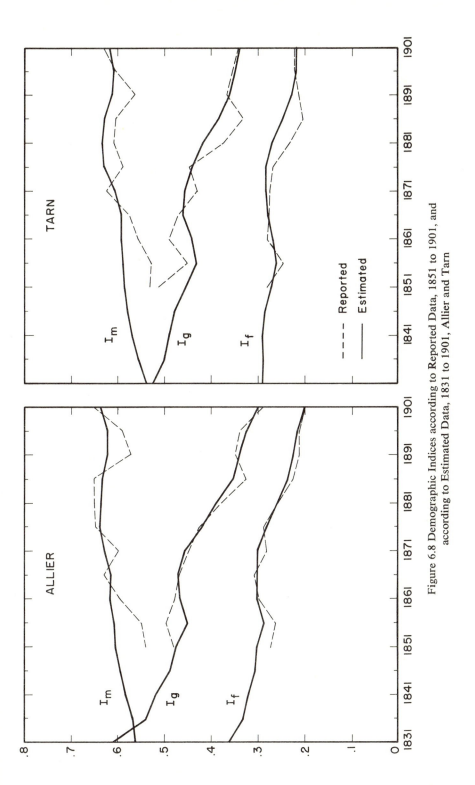

Figure 6.8 Demographic Indices according to Reported Data, 1851 to 1901, and
according to Estimated Data, 1831 to 1901, Allier and Tarn

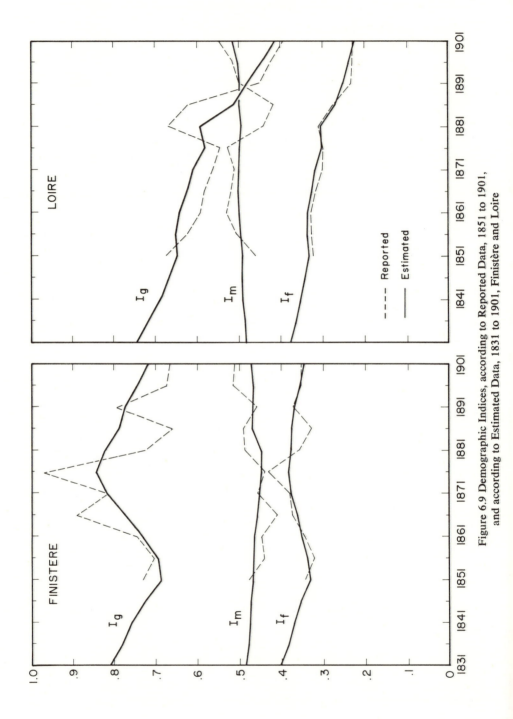

Figure 6.9 Demographic Indices, according to Reported Data, 1851 to 1901, and according to Estimated Data, 1831 to 1901, Finistère and Loire

ation of married women in 1851, 1881, and 1886 inflates I_g at these dates and deflates I_m; at other dates the heaping of married women in the age group 20–29 acts in the opposite direction.

Finally, Figure 6.10 presents a comparison between estimates of

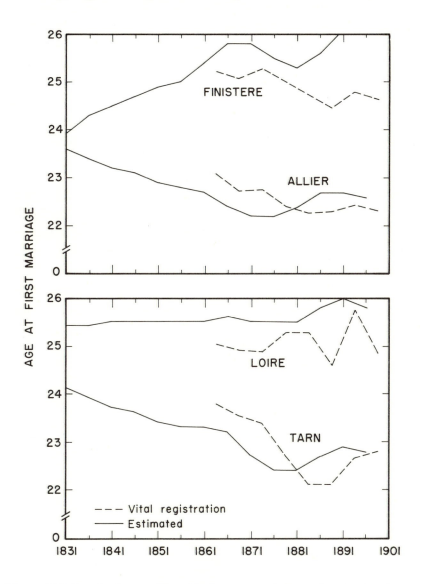

Figure 6.10 Female Age at First Marriage, according to Vital Registration, 1861-1865 to 1896-1901, and according to Estimated Data, 1831 to 1896, Selected Départements

the age at first marriage based on the reconstructed population by marital status and on the distribution of first marriages by age in the vital registration. The reconstructed index is based on the evolution of the proportion single in intercensal periods, and a moving average has been computed to find a value for the census year. The direct computation from vital registration data is for the intercensal period. Therefore the comparison is between different dates: e.g. the period 1861 to 1871 (centered on the census of 1866) and the vital registration for 1861 to 1866 or 1866 to 1871. Some further precision has been lost in the reconstruction of the proportions married by averaging period data to reconstitute cohorts. Finally, the two estimates of mean ages at first marriage are sufficiently close for any given date, as witnessed by high linear correlation coefficients (see Table 6.5). The main interest of the reconstructed series is that it allows estimates in time before 1861, and it seems to follow the long-term evolution of age of marriage in French départements. The results show, indeed, as illustrated by Figure 6.10, a wide range of behavior of nuptiality, from an almost continuous rise in Finistère to a persistent decline in Tarn.

The recorded data by département show very marked indications of bias and errors. Our reconstruction has used some parts of these

TABLE 6.5

FEMALE AGE AT FIRST MARRIAGE, LINEAR CORRELATION BETWEEN
RECONSTRUCTED ESTIMATES AND VITAL REGISTRATION FIGURES:
1866 AND 1896

	Vital registration date		
Reconstruction date	1861-1865	1866-1870	N
1866	r = .93	r = .95	78
	1891-1895	1896-1900	
1896	r = .95	r = .95	78

data, making assumptions which could not always be verified. The result is undoubtedly questionable at times, but we think it provides a more coherent picture of the evolution of the demography of French départements during the 19th century. The picture may be controversial, but the reconstruction would have not been needed if the published statistics themselves were complete and accurate. Under the existing conditions, it offers a way of filling in unknowns in the story of French fertility and nuptiality. In order to facilitate the use of estimates for individual départements, presented in the second part of this book, and to point out special characteristics of the reconstruction or of the results it yielded, we introduce the départemental results by individual comments, which are kept as brief as possible. In these comments, further indications of bias of either the recorded data, or of the reconstructed estimates, will be pointed out.

Before we turn to the second part of this book, the detailed results by département, two further tasks must be accomplished. In the next chapter, we shall briefly summarize the main trends in fertility and nuptiality by regions. Finally, we must present some results which were by-products of this study, but have their own interest. They pertain to migration and mortality, and are the subject of Chapter 8.

CHAPTER 7: Main Trends of Fertility and Nuptiality by Département

In this chapter, we attempt to summarize some of the fertility and nuptiality trends revealed in the study. At this stage, we abandon the critical approach followed in the previous chapters, and assume that the results reflect the changes that occurred in French départements during the 19th century. Of course, the regional coherence of the results, which were derived separately for individual départements, will reinforce their credibility. We shall consider in turn: the trends in the birth rate for the period before 1831 (when we have no separate evidence on marital status); and the trends in I_g and I_h (respectively, marital and illegitimate fertility indices); in I_m (the proportion married); and finally in I_f (the index of total fertility) after 1831.

We shall attempt to map the general evolution and to provide a few typical examples, rather than to follow each département individually. The results given in this section are drawn entirely from the tables given in the second part of the book.

I. *The female crude birth rate prior to 1831*

Map 7.1 presents the crude birth rates calculated for 1801–1805 and 1826–1830. The comparison of these results, twenty-five years apart, leaves no doubt that total fertility was declining in a large area of France well before the time that we can begin to trace the evolution of marital fertility. The first thirty years of the century are clearly crucially important for understanding the French fertility decline, and it is unfortunate that we do not have more refined indicators of it. The evolution of the crude birth rate reflects simultaneously the changes that may take place in the proportions married and in marital fertility. (Other factors, such as changes in the age distribution or in illegitimate fertility, are generally less important.) It is possible that changes in the birth rate early in the century reflected the evolution of nuptiality, perhaps as a result of male excess mortality and the large-scale drafting of men during the

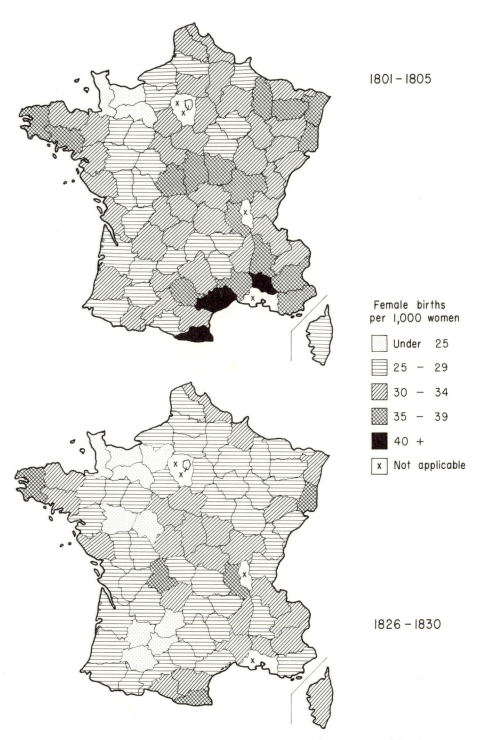

1801 – 1805

Female births
per 1,000 women

	Under 25
	25 – 29
	30 – 34
	35 – 39
	40 +
x	Not applicable

1826 – 1830

Map 7.1 Female Crude Birth Rate, by Département: 1801-1805 and 1826-1830

Napoleonic wars. The continued decline of the birth rate over time, however, cannot be interpreted as being primarily the result of later marriage or of larger proportions of spinsters, in view of the negative correlation between nuptiality (as measured by I_m) and marital fertility (the I_g index) later in the century. We may tentatively assume that the decline of the birth rate in the first thirty years of the century reflects primarily a drop of marital fertility.

Map 7.1 for 1801–1805 shows clearly the areas of high fertility (crude birth rates over 35 per thousand): Brittany, the eastern upper corner of France, the Mediterranean coast (with birth rates over 40 in three départements, perhaps in part the result of an excessive adjustment for understatement of births), and a strip of départements between the center of France and Lyon. The areas of low fertility (under 30 per thousand) include some areas of late decline in marital fertility, such as Corse and Lozère; but they are mostly départements where marital fertility has started to decrease. In 1826–1830, the area of low birth rates is enlarged considerably. By then we are able to look separately at marital fertility (see the next section).

When did the decline start? There are few conclusive indications in parish monographs that marital fertility had started to decline before the French Revolution. It is therefore remarkable that the birth rate was already low, and dropping, in a substantial number of départements as early as the first decade of the 19th century. Map 7.2 suggests the extent to which the birth rate had already started to drop at that time. The shaded départements are those where the birth rate dropped steadily after the first decade, never to reach the levels of 1801 to 1810 again. The intensity of the shadings varies with the level of the birth rate at that date. There are certainly départements where the birth rate was still over 30 per thousand in 1801–1810, but where the crude birth rate had been declining for a number of years from a higher level. There are perhaps also some départements where the birth rate was kept low by late marriage and celibacy, but where little change of levels had occurred. It becomes extremely likely, however, that birth rates under 25 per thousand represented the outcome of a prolonged drop

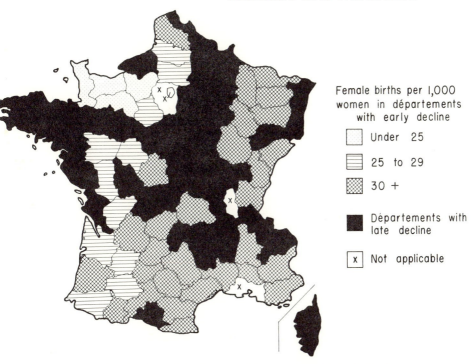

Female births per 1,000 women in départements with early decline

▢ Under 25

▤ 25 to 29

▨ 30 +

■ Départements with late decline

x Not applicable

Map 7.2 Female Crude Birth Rates in Départements with Early Decline,
by Rate in 1801-1810

in marital fertility; such birth rates are encountered in Normandy in 1801–1810. When the rates are between 25 and 30 per thousand at the time, and are continuously dropping, they are likely to signify that estimates of the birth rate in prior decades would show higher levels yet if they were available. Examples of birth rates belonging to the three categories shaded on Map 7.2 are plotted in Figure 7.1.

If we knew the predecline level of the birth rate, and could assume unchanging nuptiality, we could roughly estimate the date of decline of marital fertility. Unfortunately, proportions married were probably quite different in various regions of France under the Old Regime, and their differences could account for a range of levels of birth rates (leaving aside other factors of differential fertility). Furthermore, the proportions married may have changed over time, and changed in opposite directions and at a different pace in dif-

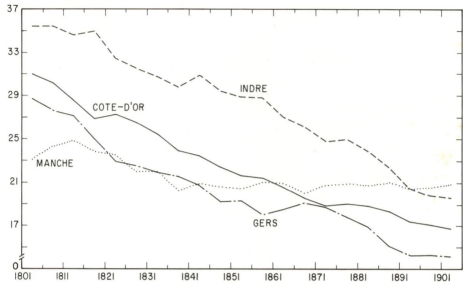

Figure 7.1 Decline in Female Crude Birth Rate, Selected Départements:
1801-1806 to 1901-1906

ferent départements. It is clear for instance that Manche, with a birth rate under 25 per thousand in 1801–1805, has rather low proportions of married women in the childbearing ages. On the contrary, marriage in Lot-et-Garonne occurs very early, so that the birth rate remains higher than in areas of Normandy where marital fertility may not have started to decline earlier.

The study of fertility before 1831 must omit the important marital component. The crude birth rate does not tell us all we want to know, but at least it is an effective index of the way reproduction is kept down by the joint effect of nuptiality and contraception. It is significant that areas of low and declining fertility are concentrated in the western half of the country. And it is important to know that there are many areas with birth rates over 30 per thousand at the beginning of the century where a continuous trend of decline is starting.

II. *Changes in marital fertility, 1831 to 1901*

Map 7.3 indicates the changes in I_g by showing the levels reached at the beginning and the end of the period of observation. As a

[174]

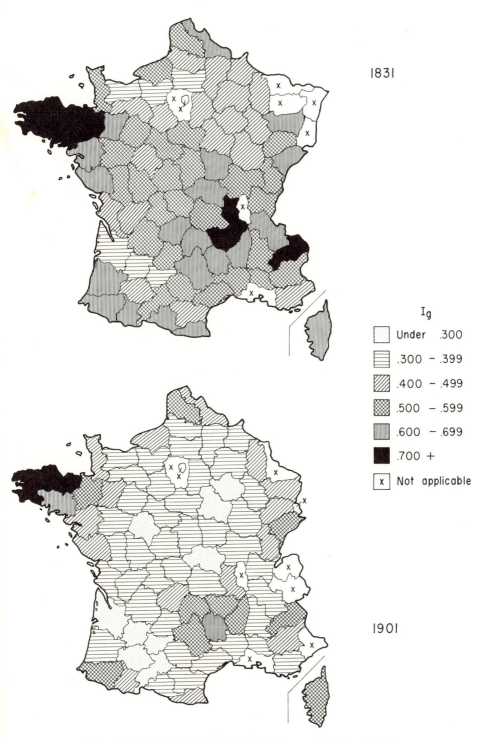

1831

I_g

☐ Under .300

▤ .300 – .399

▨ .400 – .499

▩ .500 – .599

▥ .600 – .699

■ .700 +

x̄ Not applicable

1901

Map 7.3 Marital Fertility (I_g), by Département: 1831 and 1901

rule of thumb, an I_g of less than .500 indicates with quasi-certainty the voluntary control of marital fertility, and an I_g of less than .600 the great probability of such control. Thus, there are wide areas of France where such control appears well established as early as 1831. The only sizable areas where high fertility has to some extent been maintained in 1901 are Brittany and one area of the Central Massif around Lozère.

Figure 7.2 distinguishes two different patterns of decline of marital fertility. With qualifications, we might characterize pattern I as "early decline" and pattern II as "late decline." Pattern II is characterized by a plateau of relatively high fertility, i.e. an I_g of at least .5 as its last high point, before it finally and unequivocally drops. Some early decline may have taken place, but the drop is halting, almost reluctant, with relapses into higher fertility. We distinguish between the late decline départements with I_g's over .6 before the decisive decline, and départements with I_g's between .5 and .6 at the time. Pattern I, however, is one of resolute and almost uninterrupted decline after 1831; three subpatterns are plotted, according to the level of I_g in 1831: under .5, from .5 to .6, and over .6.

The geographical distribution of the two patterns is presented separately on Map 7.4. We may now turn to a discussion of the significance of these patterns of decline of marital fertility. Although there are some doubtful instances which participate in some of the characteristics of both patterns, and although some of the results may be due to the unreliability of the basic data and of the reconstruction, we can be fairly certain that the two patterns correspond to two different courses of the fertility decline. In one case, the decline of I_g is progressive and continuous; in the other it appears to encounter some resistance.

We must pay special attention to the fact that the proportions married, and therefore total fertility, may be different for départements with approximately the same marital fertility—see, for example, Alpes (Basses-) and Manche. It is possible that marital fertility and proportions married are, in a way, complementary and that late age at marriage "explains" the survival of high marital

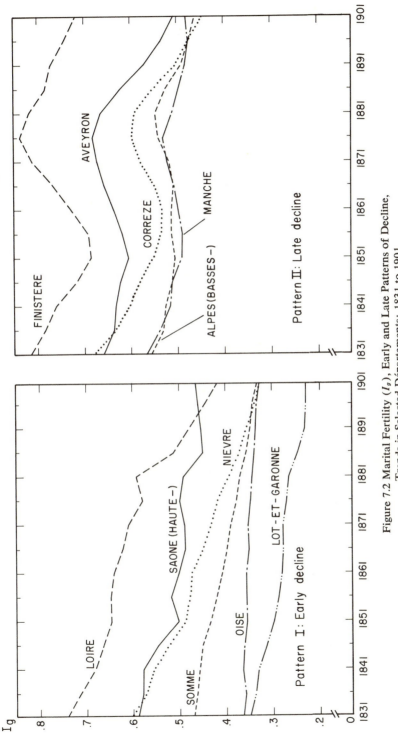

Figure 7.2 Marital Fertility (I_g), Early and Late Patterns of Decline, Trends in Selected Départements: 1831 to 1901

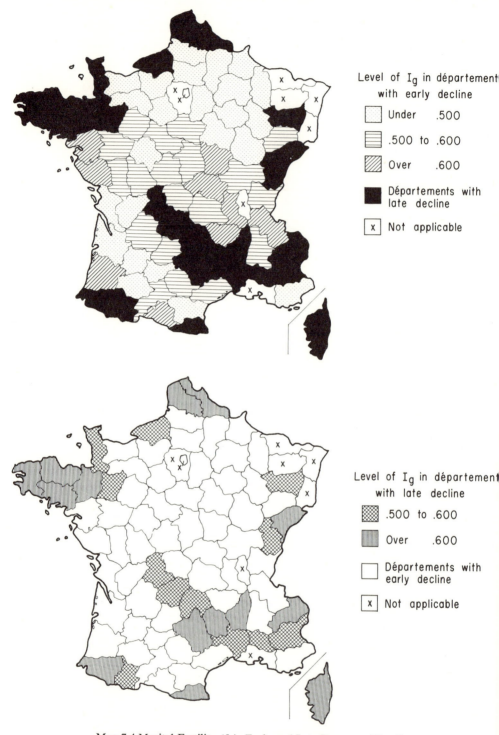

Level of I_g in département with early decline

▢ Under .500

▤ .500 to .600

▨ Over .600

■ Départements with late decline

[x] Not applicable

Level of I_g in département with late decline

▧ .500 to .600

▥ Over .600

▢ Départements with early decline

[x] Not applicable

Map 7.4 Marital Fertility (I_g), Early and Late Patterns of Decline,
Levels by Département

fertility in some départements. This question will be treated in more detail after we have analyzed the changes in I_m. Let us say here that the "resistance" to the decline of I_g, characteristic of our second pattern, is not invariably connected with a low proportion married, and that the two do not evolve in a related way through time.

Swings in I_g before a decisive decline are a characteristic feature of pattern II. It is as if fertility were going down in stages, as if high fertility départements in Brittany and elsewhere had followed the general trend of decline for a while, and then had hesitated, or even backtracked. This "ski jump" trend, as we might call it, seems to characterize the decline of marital fertility in several provinces of Europe, and even elsewhere. Its existence (rather than that of a plateau of predecline fertility) raises the question of the mechanism involved and suggests that similar declines, followed by rises, could have occurred in earlier times. Unfortunately, the data available do not provide answers to these questions in the case of the French départements. But there is undoubtedly, in France toward the middle of the 19th century, a slowing down of the fertility decline, due largely to the "ski jump" trends in certain départements—an intermediary rise or plateau at midcourse in the decline of I_g.

Some "ski jump" trends are plotted in Figure 7.3. They occur at different levels and dates, and have different intensities. In a few instances, the decline seems to have leveled off in 1831 at the very moment when we start recording it (see Cher). This suggests that some of the high plateaus of pattern II in Figure 7.2 may be intermediary stages of the same kind. We can suggest no explanation of these facts, but it may be analogous to the "baby boom" of the 1940s and 1950s in much of the Western world—a temporary reversal of long-term trends.

III. *Changes in illegitimate fertility, 1831 to 1901*

During the 19th century, France as a whole is characterized by a very constant level of illegitimate fertility as measured by I_h. The rate fluctuates between .041 and .046 during the period under review. But the absence of a trend characterizing the entire country really hides the evolution in opposite directions of its various areas.

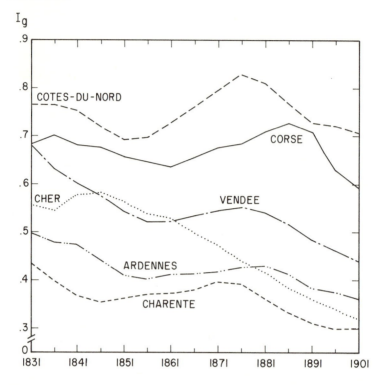

Figure 7.3 Marital Fertility (I_g), "Ski Jump" Trend, Selected Départements:
1831 to 1901

There is a great deal of variability in levels of I_h, both at the beginning and at the end of the century (Map. 7.5). In both periods, the high illegitimacy of a group of départements in the northern half of France stands out. In contrast, there are areas of consistently low illegitimate fertility in Brittany and the Massif Central. There are, however, clear regional trends toward more or toward less illegitimacy, and a number of départements show no marked change over the period. Some fluctuations may reflect the quality of the data, but, if we eliminate those that do not correspond to a trend, the picture that emerges is given by Map 7.6. (Changes in levels, either positive or negative, had to reach at least .01 over the period to be accepted as evidence of a trend—for example, from an I_h of .010 to .020 or from .060 to .070.)

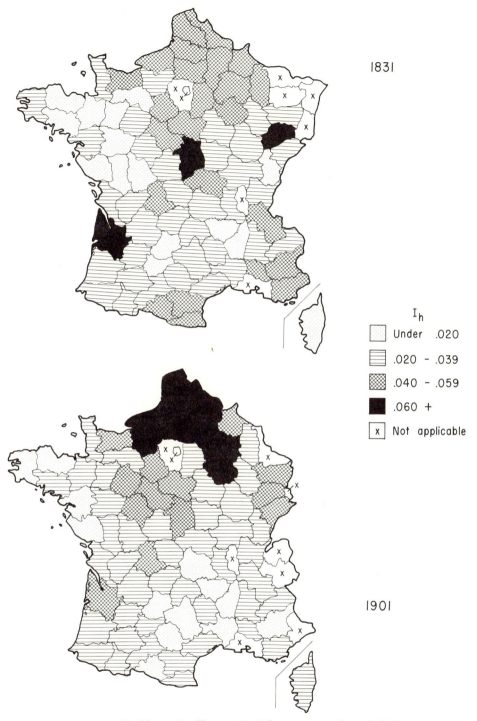

1831

I_h
Under .020
.020 – .039
.040 – .059
.060 +
x   Not applicable

1901

Map 7.5 Illegitimate Fertility (I_h), by Département: 1831 and 1901

[181]

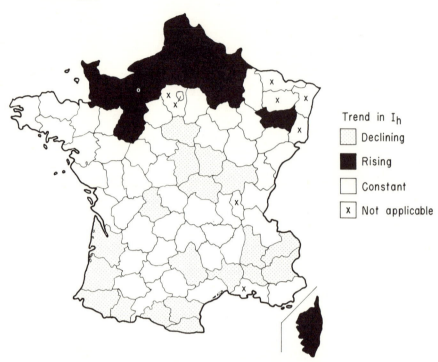

NOTE: Evidence of trend requires a minimum change of .01 in either direction.

Map 7.6 Trends in Illegitimate Fertility (I_h), by Département: 1831-1901

IV. *Changes in nuptiality, 1831 to 1901*

Map 7.7 presents, for 1831 and 1901, the geographical distribution of I_m, the standardized proportion married. One cannot fail to notice the marked increase over the century for France as a whole. Furthermore, it is remarkable that the maps of marital fertility and of the proportion married are strongly related: I_m is highly and negatively correlated with I_g in 1901. The départements that have preserved their low I_m's are, on the whole, those where marital fertility has lagged behind.

The départements either maintain the I_m reached by 1931 or increase it almost without exception. Only in Corse is there a clear, long-term decline. The increase is marked, in most instances, but there are a few low, and a few high, I_m départements where almost no change of levels is noticeable. We indicate on Map 7.8 which départements have a fairly constant I_m (i.e. with less than .05

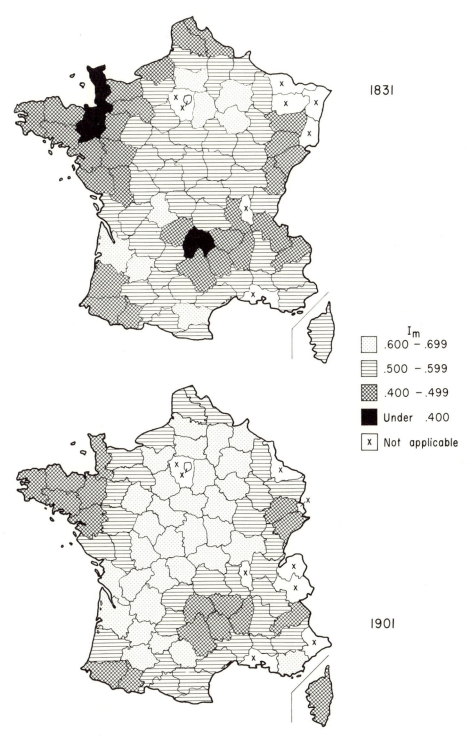

1831

I_m

☐ .600 – .699

▤ .500 – .599

▨ .400 – .499

■ Under .400

⊠ Not applicable

1901

Map 7.7 Proportion Married (I_m), by Département: 1831 and 1901

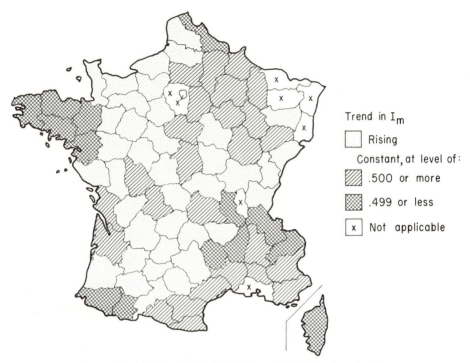

Map 7.8 Trends in Proportion Married (I_m), by Département: 1831-1901

change over the period) either at a level above or at a level under .5, and which départements undergo a marked rise (more than .05) of I_m. The pattern or rise may be continuous or may be followed by stabilization—or even a mild decline—before the end of the century. In Figure 7.4 we present a few types of evolution of I_m.

The evolution of I_m reflects in part—but only in part—the changes in the age at marriage that occurred during the period. There was at the same time an evolution in the proportion of women who ultimately got married. Although these two components of the proportions married often move together, there are at least some instances of compensatory movements in opposite directions. For example, in Finistère the I_m remains fairly constant with a high point of .483 in 1831, a mild decline until it reaches .445 in 1876, followed by a rise to .466 by 1901. Meanwhile, the singulate mean

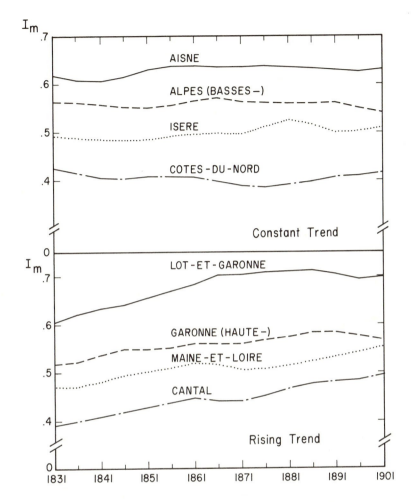

Figure 7.4 Proportion Married (I_m), Constant and Rising Trends,
Selected Départements: 1831 to 1901

age at marriage has increased by two years, from 24 to 26. There
has been a corresponding drop in the proportion of women who
were not married by the end of the childbearing years—from 17
percent of the women born in 1816–1820 to 10 percent of those
born in 1881–1885. The stability in I_m hides a rise in the age of
marriage, compensated for by an improved opportunity to get
married.

[185]

METHODS

V. *The evolution of overall fertility, 1831 to 1901*

I_f and the crude birth rate are related measures of total fertility since neither allows for the proportions married in the population. Therefore, the story told by Map 7.9 (I_f in 1831 and 1901) is the continuation of that told by Map 7.1 (birth rate in 1801–1805 and 1826–1830). Because of the high inverse correlation between marital fertility and proportions married in France, the geographical contrasts in I_f are much less marked than those in either I_g or I_m.

The evolution in time reflects the combined effect of changes in I_m and in I_g—that is, if we disregard the changes in I_h which have no more than a marginal importance. The formal relationship between the indices used in this study is as follows:

$$I_f = (I_g \times I_m) + I_h \times (1 - I_m) \qquad (24)$$

I_h is ordinarily low, so that we can write the approximation:

$$I_f \cong I_g \times I_m \qquad (25)$$

The three indices then can be presented in a single graph (see Figure 7.5). The locus of points of equal I_f, for various combinations of I_g and I_m, is presented by parallel segments of indifference curves. The evolution of I_g and I_m on the vertical and horizontal axes results in the evolution of I_f in relation to the indifference curves. We have selected four types of evolution of I_f for illustrations:

a) Gironde: the decline of I_f is entirely accounted for by declining marital fertility, with little or no change of I_m.

b) Pas-de-Calais: in the absence of a decline of I_g the rise in the proportions married actually accounts for a rise of I_f over the period.

c) Manche: the decline of I_g is compensated by a rise in I_m, with little drop of total fertility as a result.

d) Loir-et-Cher: dropping I_g more than compensates for the increasing I_m, so that I_f drops overall.

Patterns a) and d) predominate in France during the period under review. There are, however, a small number of départements

[186]

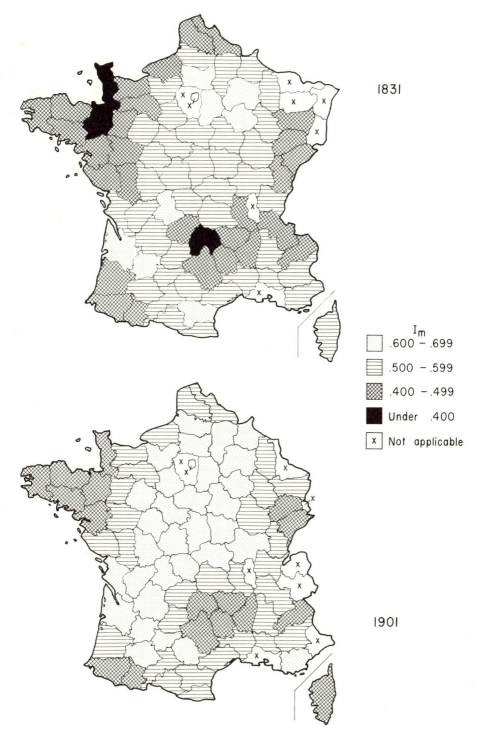

Map 7.9 Overall Fertility (I_f), by Département: 1831 and 1901

1831

1901

I_m
.600 – .699
.500 – .599
.400 – .499
Under .400
Not applicable

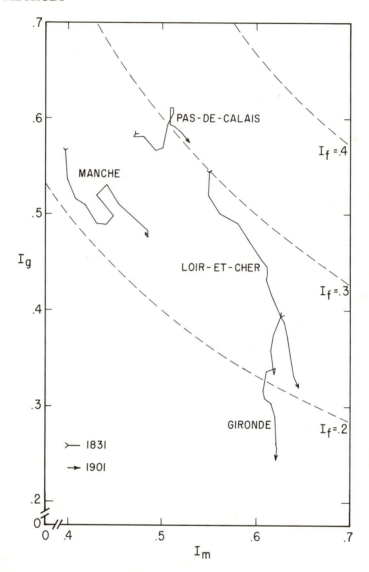

Figure 7.5 Trends in Overall Fertility (I_f) as a Function of Marital Fertility (I_g) and Proportion Married (I_m), Selected Départements: 1831-1901

with constant overall fertility, or even with an I_f that rises at least during a substantial part of the period. This happens at high levels of I_f (over .3) in areas where marital fertility starts to drop very late (as in the départements of Brittany, in Lozère, and in Doubs)

[188]

or at low levels (under .25) in Normandy, where the fertility decline was very early and, plausibly, was accompanied by a change of nuptiality earlier in the century. Manche combines low proportions married (as in Brittany) and early dropping, but still high marital fertility (as in Normandy); it is clearly an area of transition between two different cultural areas where strategies of family formation clash, and where a unique form of fertility control by late marriage prevails. Finally, there are areas of moderate and constant I_f's (.2 to .25) combining either low marital fertility and high proportions married (Somme or Oise) or low proportions married and high marital fertility (Pas-de-Calais, Aveyron). The evolution of total fertility is complex, and although special attention must be paid to marital fertility, it is well to remember that restrictions on marriage play an important complementary role in the control of overall fertility.

CHAPTER 8: Some Additional Results of the Reconstruction on Mortality and Migration

I. *Mortality*

In the process of reconstructing the population, the number of deaths of the period are used to determine a mortality level in the model life tables. When applied by age to the population at time t, the mortality rates $_5q_x$ at a level in the tables produce the number of deaths registered for the five-year intercensal period t to $t+5$. The survival factors chosen in the model life tables at this level of mortality are used in the population projection which yields the reconstructed population.

Estimates of the level of mortality (expressed in terms of expectation of life at birth e_0^o) thus become an interesting by-product of our study. They are available for most départements and are presented in Table 8.1. As an index of mortality, the expectation of life at birth is vastly preferable to the crude death rate, because it is free of the influence of the age distribution; the crude death rate reflects the proportions of children and old people in the population as well as the level of mortality itself.

The estimates cover the whole century in periods of five years. Their reliability is more doubtful in the beginning, when the slope of the stable population estimated for 1801 is an important factor in the allocation of deaths by age. It is also possible, of course, that the recording of deaths at the beginning of the century was incomplete, as in the case of the births. At least in a number of départements the evidence points in the opposite direction; the years 1801–1805 exhibit a very low expectation of life at birth, followed by a sharp rise in the next period. The initial low level, never reached again in the century, must be explained by extreme mortality conditions. Overreporting of deaths is unlikely, but could occur if deaths belonging to a period prior to the inception of the registration system were mistakenly included. Since the départements with a very low e_0^o are concentrated in the center and western part of France (see Map 8.1), it is plausible that exceptional mortality

TABLE 8.1

FEMALE EXPECTATION OF LIFE AT BIRTH (e^0_0), BY DEPARTEMENT: 1801-1805 TO 1901-1905

DEPARTEMENT	1801-1805	1806-1810	1811-1815	1816-1820	1821-1825	1826-1830	1831-1835	1836-1840	1841-1845	1846-1850	1851-1855
AIN	32.0	33.2	35.8	34.6	38.0	34.9	34.6	38.3	38.8	39.4	39.8
AISNE	37.4	34.5	33.7	37.4	39.0	38.5	36.8	41.8	42.2	39.7	40.2
ALLIER	28.6	34.9	37.2	39.9	33.4	33.5	36.5	36.0	40.9	37.3	42.8
ALPES (BASSES-)	35.4	33.0	32.7	32.2	31.7	32.3	30.7	33.6	33.3	33.1	33.2
ALPES (HAUTES-)	38.5	38.0	34.6	35.2	35.5	34.5	33.8	34.6	36.2	34.2	33.2
ARDECHE	41.9	41.9	41.0	38.8	43.1	39.3	37.5	37.8	38.9	39.0	37.1
ARDENNES	42.9	38.5	39.1	39.3	42.9	42.3	42.8	45.6	45.8	43.6	43.4
ARIEGE	45.2	45.2	43.0	40.9	43.7	42.4	42.3	43.6	44.4	42.3	43.8
AUBE	35.2	33.3	35.2	39.7	41.5	39.6	38.2	43.1	44.5	42.0	41.3
AUDE	38.1	40.7	37.7	35.8	38.0	38.9	37.3	39.2	40.5	39.7	40.0
AVEYRON	44.2	45.0	43.2	38.9	40.5	41.7	38.7	40.4	41.6	41.5	39.2
CALVADOS	47.8	47.7	47.5	47.8	46.1	46.4	47.0	49.0	49.1	47.5	44.1
CANTAL	44.1	41.9	45.7	43.7	44.6	44.9	41.6	44.3	46.2	44.9	44.1
CHARENTE	30.0	41.7	40.4	43.1	41.5	42.0	38.5	44.6	46.9	45.1	42.4
CHARENTE INFERIEURE	28.7	37.0	34.3	38.3	37.2	39.1	36.8	42.8	44.1	40.0	43.7
CHER	30.7	34.0	33.5	36.1	31.3	28.2	36.8	31.4	40.3	36.9	42.9
CORREZE	32.2	37.5	40.1	39.2	37.7	38.3	34.7	34.4	38.5	34.5	36.7
CORSE	38.6	39.4	38.4	38.6	41.7	43.1	46.2	48.7	45.7	45.4	41.2
COTE-D'OR	34.6	36.2	37.0	39.3	40.1	38.7	39.4	43.8	43.1	41.8	41.2
COTES-DU-NORD	36.5	39.3	36.4	33.8	38.4	35.3	35.6	38.0	40.7	39.8	38.7
CREUSE	31.2	39.3	45.2	45.9	40.4	42.5	43.6	41.6	48.2	45.2	44.9
DORDOGNE	28.6	40.1	40.1	39.2	39.5	40.6	34.7	39.4	40.4	40.2	42.1
DOUBS	36.2	43.0	40.4	39.4	41.2	41.3	41.1	43.0	42.2	42.6	39.7
DROME	36.0	38.7	39.1	38.2	37.6	39.2	36.6	37.8	38.9	39.1	37.8
EURE	41.1	40.2	40.9	41.4	40.4	41.3	41.6	43.4	44.4	43.8	43.7
EURE-ET-LOIR	28.6	31.6	35.2	39.6	39.7	39.3	40.3	42.9	45.8	44.8	46.0
FINISTERE	27.1	37.3	32.6	31.3	35.0	31.5	32.3	34.6	37.3	34.9	34.1
GARD	36.5	37.3	36.5	35.3	35.8	38.8	41.4	35.7	35.9	35.6	34.7
GARONNE (HAUTE-)	38.5	39.3	39.6	36.8	40.2	41.0	41.7	43.4	44.3	39.9	41.5

Département											
GERS	38.2	42.6	41.3	43.9	44.4	45.8	41.6	43.8	45.3	42.7	47.5
GIRONDE	34.8	40.6	41.4	46.9	46.2	44.9	39.5	44.6	44.6	43.1	45.7
HERAULT	38.2	37.5	36.6	35.8	36.9	35.8	35.0	37.0	38.3	38.1	36.2
ILLE-ET-VILAINE	29.2	35.7	38.7	34.4	36.1	32.7	33.0	38.5	39.7	41.1	39.3
INDRE	25.8	32.4	36.7	38.7	35.1	35.3	39.2	33.9	40.7	41.3	40.8
INDRE-ET-LOIRE	32.5	37.9	44.0	44.0	42.5	39.8	42.1	44.1	45.8	43.6	48.0
ISERE	36.7	39.1	39.5	37.6	37.5	37.6	38.6	39.3	40.5	41.3	39.1
JURA	37.0	38.0	38.3	36.3	39.7	37.6	37.2	38.5	38.2	38.1	36.2
LANDES	28.4	33.0	36.3	37.1	39.4	39.9	36.0	34.9	37.3	38.1	43.4
LOIR-ET-CHER	21.3	28.6	31.0	35.9	33.8	32.2	35.5	37.7	44.6	42.5	47.0
LOIRE (HAUTE-)	37.0	37.1	38.8	38.4	36.2	37.1	36.9	38.0	39.4	38.6	40.0
LOIRE	40.2	37.4	41.2	41.6	39.6	42.1	40.8	42.7	43.6	41.3	41.3
LOIRE-INFERIEURE	36.4	42.5	40.7	32.6	43.1	38.1	36.0	43.7	41.3	42.9	44.3
LOIRET	21.7	27.7	29.4	42.1	34.5	32.8	36.7	35.4	43.2	40.5	41.9
LOT	34.8	36.8	43.9	43.6	42.5	43.7	37.3	43.0	44.5	44.7	44.3
LOT-ET-GARONNE	40.5	42.7	40.3	37.1	45.2	46.3	42.6	44.6	41.4	45.0	48.0
LOZERE	45.3	45.4	42.1	44.6	39.6	42.0	38.7	39.7	44.1	40.8	39.1
MAINE-ET-LOIRE	34.8	44.0	41.1	46.4	43.2	40.2	40.1	44.3	48.0	43.9	47.2
MANCHE	47.8	39.2	45.1	44.3	45.4	44.3	40.7	47.9	45.7	46.0	45.8
MARNE	37.0	32.9	40.6	34.5	37.4	37.6	45.5	40.6	40.4	44.4	45.6
MARNE (HAUTE-)	33.5	36.1	31.5	41.4	42.1	38.6	34.5	42.3	45.2	40.3	37.8
MAYENNE	33.3	36.0	39.3	36.7	38.5	39.0	40.7	40.9	41.3	46.6	44.9
MEURTHE	36.1	34.6	34.2	36.0	38.2	40.5	38.1	42.0	42.5	41.0	36.7
MEUSE	36.0	33.3	32.8	40.1	36.1	43.2	41.6	37.3	41.4	41.4	43.7
MORBIHAN	35.4	39.3	34.6	34.0	45.5	42.6	34.5	41.7	43.6	38.9	37.6
MOSELLE	30.7	30.3	36.0	35.5	34.0	29.1	41.0	35.5	41.6	43.4	40.3
NIEVRE	39.1	36.5	32.6	38.2	36.0	35.0	34.7	37.2	43.0	37.3	43.9
NORD	23.5	34.2	36.5	46.7	39.0	39.4	33.0	41.4	38.3	35.4	38.8
OISE	36.0	39.1	33.7	40.7	48.5	48.4	38.4	42.0	42.2	39.3	39.4
ORNE	37.5	38.4	43.7	38.8	40.9	38.7	50.0	52.0	54.6	55.8	52.8
PAS-DE-CALAIS	39.2	37.9	39.5	47.7	39.2	39.2	35.9	40.9	41.4	39.4	41.6
PUY-DE-DOME	34.0	45.5	40.6	50.3	43.8	45.7	39.5	41.7	42.4	41.0	41.1
PYRENEES (BASSES-)	42.9	50.5	43.6	32.3	48.7	49.6	46.1	44.5	47.4	43.0	42.1
PYRENEES (HAUTES-)	42.5	50.5	48.5	37.6	32.3	31.0	47.2	46.0	48.3	45.8	47.5
PYRENEES-ORIENTALES	31.6	32.7	33.8	32.3	38.2	35.8	33.1	33.7	34.4	34.8	34.2
RHIN (BAS-)	39.1	35.1	34.2	37.6	38.2	35.8	34.9	36.0	37.4	37.5	36.4

DEPARTEMENT	1856-1860	1861-1865	1866-1870	1871-1875	1876-1880	1881-1885	1886-1890	1891-1895	1896-1900	1901-1905	
RHIN (HAUT-)	41.3	38.6	34.8	38.4	37.2	36.3	37.1	35.7	38.0	38.0	34.6
SAONE (HAUTE-)	34.4	35.3	36.8	37.4	43.8	41.0	41.1	42.9	42.6	42.8	40.4
SAONE-ET-LOIRE	32.4	33.3	35.3	37.6	35.0	33.0	35.9	39.0	39.8	39.3	41.9
SARTHE	30.2	34.6	39.3	45.7	43.3	39.2	45.7	48.7	49.9	50.9	52.1
SEINE-ET-MARNE	27.8	29.3	29.8	35.8	33.7	35.0	32.8	41.1	42.9	43.1	41.8
SEINE-INFERIEURE	43.7	44.4	42.5	41.1	40.6	40.1	39.5	40.3	40.6	40.1	40.6
SEVRES (DEUX-)	37.4	44.7	43.2	45.7	43.9	43.3	43.0	46.8	46.8	44.8	46.7
SOMME	42.1	39.9	37.5	39.5	42.0	41.3	38.7	41.5	40.8	39.9	41.1
TARN	39.7	39.5	36.3	35.2	38.0	37.8	35.9	39.2	40.8	40.8	40.1
TARN-ET-GARONNE	36.6	38.1	39.6	39.8	41.2	41.8	38.8	42.1	43.5	42.0	45.7
VAR	32.8	35.1	35.7	35.9	38.7	38.8	34.2	36.8	37.8	38.7	36.2
VAUCLUSE	32.7	34.1	32.7	31.6	31.6	33.2	32.6	32.4	34.5	36.7	34.8
VENDEE	33.6	39.6	40.4	37.9	38.8	37.3	38.2	42.6	43.5	41.0	44.2
VIENNE	43.8	48.3	49.5	50.6	45.9	45.4	43.2	43.2	47.0	44.5	46.0
VIENNE (HAUTE-)	24.5	34.6	38.4	37.9	31.2	33.9	33.5	32.6	38.9	35.7	36.3
VOSGES	37.6	39.0	40.0	41.4	42.7	41.4	40.1	42.4	43.8	42.8	42.3
YONNE	26.8	31.6	33.3	39.6	39.9	39.0	40.6	45.8	46.5	45.5	45.8
FRANCE	35.6	37.3	37.9	38.7	39.0	38.3	37.7	40.0	41.5	40.4	40.2
AIN	38.9	41.9	42.5	39.9	44.5	46.6	47.0	46.7	47.9	49.8	
AISNE	41.4	43.1	43.8	43.7	45.8	46.5	47.4	46.4	48.2	50.7	
ALLIER	39.9	45.0	45.4	45.6	51.2	52.4	52.4	52.2	54.7	56.8	
ALPES (BASSES-)	32.8	34.7	36.1	36.1	37.0	36.2	38.6	39.7	43.6	45.8	
ALPES (HAUTES-)	32.1	33.1	33.4	34.3	35.5	36.0	38.8	38.0	41.9	44.8	
ARDECHE	36.8	37.2	36.7	36.6	36.6	38.3	40.0	39.4	41.5	43.8	
ARDENNES	44.9	47.3	46.6	46.2	49.4	49.5	49.8	49.5	51.3	52.7	
ARIEGE	42.0	43.4	41.8	42.1	46.2	46.0	48.4	47.3	48.5	52.1	
AUBE	44.4	46.4	47.6	46.5	47.0	47.6	47.9	46.2	48.6	50.6	
AUDE	40.3	40.8	39.7	38.4	42.8	42.9	44.3	43.8	46.8	49.5	
AVEYRON	38.3	41.4	40.8	39.7	43.8	42.8	45.9	43.6	44.7	47.4	
CALVADOS	47.5	46.9	45.8	42.8	47.5	48.6	47.2	45.2	46.9	49.0	

CANTAL	43.0	43.7	43.3	45.0	48.1	49.0	48.1	48.9	49.6	52.4
CHARENTE	42.3	45.1	40.1	40.9	47.2	48.7	49.6	48.3	51.4	54.4
CHARENTE INFERIEURE	44.4	46.9	43.7	42.1	49.0	51.1	52.1	49.4	52.6	54.2
CHER	36.7	45.0	41.9	41.8	48.1	49.4	47.8	49.1	50.1	50.9
CORREZE	34.0	37.9	34.4	35.8	41.1	43.4	47.2	46.1	49.3	51.8
CORSE	41.6	46.7	39.3	39.2	37.6	37.5	41.9	42.1	45.0	49.1
COTE-D'OR	43.5	40.9	48.6	45.3	50.7	51.5	51.0	50.0	52.1	54.2
COTES-DU-NORD	37.8	47.4	39.5	38.4	43.4	44.3	43.2	42.8	45.0	47.2
CREUSE	40.3	40.9	43.3	47.2	52.8	55.0	55.2	53.7	56.4	59.2
DORDOGNE	38.6	43.7	39.1	41.2	46.2	48.1	47.4	46.4	49.9	52.4
DOUBS	43.8	39.2	40.7	39.1	43.0	44.5	45.2	44.4	44.5	47.8
DROME	37.8	38.1	39.1	39.1	40.2	41.0	42.6	41.9	44.9	46.7
EURE	44.3	46.1	45.2	47.3	47.8	50.8	47.7	44.4	48.1	49.6
EURE-ET-LOIR	45.9	49.6	47.0	46.0	49.7	50.4	50.6	46.6	49.2	50.6
FINISTERE	34.4	37.5	31.5	34.6	38.2	35.6	36.1	39.0	43.1	45.8
GARD	34.5	36.3	35.3	35.6	36.1	38.5	39.2	38.8	41.5	44.3
GARONNE (HAUTE-)	43.7	46.4	44.6	47.7	47.7	48.2	47.3	46.5	47.7	49.9
GERS	45.2	46.9	45.7	46.2	48.2	49.6	50.0	49.7	52.3	55.0
GIRONDE	45.0	44.9	46.3	46.3	46.5	45.9	47.8	47.9	50.2	52.2
HERAULT	37.6	40.5	38.6	39.1	41.5	40.9	41.6	40.5	42.4	44.9
ILLE-ET-VILAINE	40.6	41.4	40.8	39.0	42.9	42.7	43.8	43.1	45.7	48.3
INDRE	37.7	46.7	46.4	45.5	49.5	52.4	52.5	51.9	54.2	56.9
INDRE-ET-LOIRE	47.2	48.4	46.4	46.6	50.6	53.0	53.1	51.4	53.7	55.3
ISERE	32.7	37.9	39.7	39.3	42.0	46.3	43.8	43.4	46.8	48.3
JURA	39.5	39.1	40.6	42.4	45.0	46.3	46.1	44.9	46.4	48.2
LANDES	40.0	45.6	45.4	44.6	51.1	53.5	52.1	51.4	55.2	57.0
LOIR-ET-CHER	43.5	49.4	45.4	44.3	50.5	52.6	53.7	51.5	54.1	55.1
LOIRE	36.8	40.2	40.8	40.3	41.9	43.9	44.6	44.2	46.0	47.4
LOIRE (HAUTE-)	41.7	41.2	40.8	40.1	43.8	43.8	43.2	45.0	46.3	47.8
LOIRE-INFERIEURE	44.3	47.8	45.4	49.9	47.8	48.6	49.3	48.9	51.5	53.0
LOIRET	41.2	45.2	43.3	43.6	48.5	50.7	50.6	48.6	51.9	53.1
LOT	43.9	43.2	43.2	45.5	46.3	46.1	50.6	46.6	47.7	50.1
LOT-ET-GARONNE	45.8	46.4	44.9	46.9	48.1	50.6	51.8	50.6	53.5	54.7
LOZERE	38.7	40.6	39.9	41.0	41.2	40.4	45.5	45.6	47.3	49.4
MAINE-ET-LOIRE	45.0	46.9	46.2	43.9	47.6	49.6	48.4	48.1	51.3	52.4
MANCHE	45.9	47.2	45.4	44.6	47.6	47.0	46.9	45.8	48.8	51.3

MARNE	47.3	48.1	47.9	46.4	49.4	49.4	50.1	48.8	50.5	52.0
MARNE (HAUTE-)	42.8	44.4	44.8	42.8	45.6	44.6	45.3	44.4	46.4	47.9
MAYENNE	43.6	43.3	41.7	41.1	44.4	45.8	46.6	44.9	48.1	49.9
MEURTHE	43.0	44.4	41.7	47.1	48.1	49.4	48.3	46.2	49.4	51.6
MEUSE	45.6	47.5	44.8	38.0	44.0	44.2	44.6	44.4	49.0	49.6
MORBIHAN	36.3	42.2	36.7	0.0	0.0	0.0	0.0	0.0	0.0	0.0
MOSELLE	43.9	43.8	44.5	40.9	46.6	46.1	47.0	50.1	48.7	51.9
NIEVRE	39.9	43.2	41.1	41.0	42.7	44.2	44.8	44.3	46.4	48.4
NORD	39.8	41.1	40.3	43.0	46.0	47.0	46.3	44.7	46.6	49.6
OISE	40.8	42.7	43.1	46.4	48.9	51.6	49.7	45.9	49.4	49.5
ORNE	50.0	51.9	48.5	42.4	44.3	44.4	46.1	46.2	48.0	50.3
PAS-DE-CALAIS	42.2	43.1	42.0	42.8	45.5	46.9	47.5	47.4	49.8	52.2
PUY-DE-DOME	40.0	42.3	42.8	46.0	47.4	48.4	49.0	48.7	52.0	53.5
PYRENEES (BASSES-)	42.6	45.7	44.0	46.0	48.3	50.1	51.2	48.8	50.0	53.3
PYRENEES (HAUTES-)	44.2	46.0	45.8	46.0	48.3	50.1	49.0	48.7	50.0	53.3
PYRENEES-ORIENTALES	34.9	36.6	36.1	36.3	37.5	36.8	42.7	41.6	44.3	47.1
RHIN (BAS-)	38.6	38.8	39.7	—	—	—	—	—	—	—
RHIN (HAUT-)	39.1	37.5	38.7	—	—	—	—	—	—	—
SAONE (HAUTE-)	44.4	45.7	43.7	42.3	46.2	48.4	47.5	46.2	47.4	49.5
SAONE-ET-LOIRE	40.0	42.0	43.8	43.6	48.9	50.7	50.0	48.8	50.5	53.3
SARTHE	48.5	49.6	47.7	43.9	48.9	52.6	52.2	48.9	52.4	52.2
SEINE-ET-MARNE	45.9	47.6	36.9	47.5	50.0	42.7	50.2	48.2	49.3	50.5
SEINE-INFERIEURE	39.8	39.5	45.9	36.3	39.1	39.5	39.1	39.0	40.9	43.9
SEVRES (DEUX-)	43.6	46.2	40.8	44.2	49.7	51.5	51.1	50.6	53.3	56.3
SOMME	43.4	42.8	42.1	41.7	43.4	44.9	44.8	44.6	45.8	48.5
TARN	40.3	42.7	45.0	42.2	46.4	48.5	48.1	47.5	49.3	51.6
TARN-ET-GARONNE	43.5	45.3	40.3	46.1	48.6	49.8	49.4	49.4	50.0	52.2
VAR	38.2	39.3	37.5	41.5	41.8	39.2	41.9	43.2	43.9	45.3
VAUCLUSE	36.2	37.4	41.6	37.6	37.4	38.8	39.1	39.6	43.2	44.6
VENDEE	41.6	45.8	45.8	41.6	45.1	49.8	50.3	48.8	52.3	55.6
VIENNE	43.3	45.5	34.8	44.0	49.3	53.7	52.4	51.0	54.2	56.3
VIENNE (HAUTE-)	32.4	38.0	41.7	36.6	44.5	46.1	47.5	46.1	49.1	52.2
VOSGES	41.8	43.6	41.7	41.6	43.9	45.6	45.4	43.3	46.1	49.1
YONNE	48.4	51.4	51.3	50.1	52.2	53.6	54.7	49.7	51.8	52.2
FRANCE	40.6	42.4	41.3	41.7	44.3	44.9	45.3	44.9	47.2	49.1

NOTE: Evidence of trend requires a minimum change of .01 in either direction.

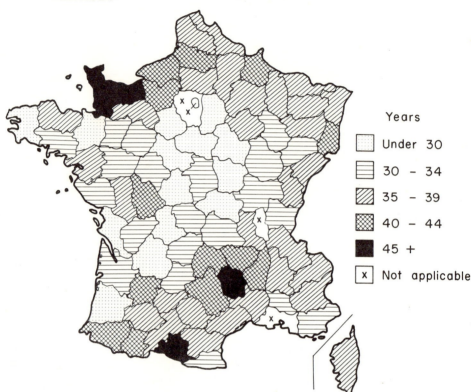

Map 8.1 Female Expectation of Life at Birth (e_0^f), by Département: 1801-1805

conditions prevailed in that region at the time. The literature is silent concerning these conditions. Reinhard and his colleagues do not mention any particular crisis at that time, although they present a graph of the absolute number of deaths which shows a clear maximum about that time in the years XI to XIII of the Republic (Reinhard, Armengaud, and Dupâquier, 1968, p. 295). A peak of mortality is clearly indicated for 1803 and 1804 (year XII of the Republic) in the INED sample of vital registration data for Brittany and Anjou (Blayo and Henry, 1967, pp. 100-105).

There are also a few instances of départements that had a high e_0^f in 1801–1805, but where the series suggests a downward trend, consistent with improving registration of deaths (see Map 8.2). Several of these départements fall in the Languedoc region, where

[196]

NOTE: Evidence of decline requires a lower average expectation of life in the period 1821-1835 than in the period 1801-1815.

Map 8.2 Départements with a Decline in Female Expectation of Life at Birth ($\overset{\circ}{e}_{\overset{\times}{0}}$) after 1801

we also identified marked deficiencies of the birth statistics in the beginning of the century.

Two qualifying remarks are still in order. First, the presence of a large number of nurslings and children from Paris in some rural départements disturbed the actual distribution of deaths. We adjusted the number of deaths for nine départements of the Paris region in order to eliminate this influence as much as possible. The $\overset{\circ}{e}_{\overset{\times}{0}}$ for these nine départements excludes the deaths of young migrants. Second, the influence of the cholera epidemic of 1854 on the expectation of life of Ariège, Marne (Haute-), Meuse, Savoie (Haute-), and Vosges has largely been eliminated in the reconstruction. The pattern of mortality of cholera is peculiar in that the disease primarily affects adults, while the model life tables concentrate deaths among children; the exceptional mortality of 1854 would have deflated some birth cohorts in the reconstruction, and appeared as overregistration of births. The result of our adjustment is an overestimation of the expectation of life for 1851–1855 in those départements.

We will not discuss the evolution of the expectation of life at birth by département at this point, since an analysis of the results of the reconstruction is postponed to another volume. It is sufficient to point out that the series of expectations of life is fairly irregular, and that the trend in general is one of steady increase. There are however, a certain number of départements where the e^0_x was high in the beginning and remains extraordinarily stable throughout the century. Calvados is a striking example. Overall, there is a convergence of mortality levels by the end of the century. In 1801–1805 the range is between an e^0_x of 21.3 years (Loir-et-Cher) and 47.8 (Calvados and Manche). This difference of 26.5 years is partly explained by the crisis mortality prevalent in the départements shaded in Map 8.1. In 1901–1905, one century later, the range is between 43.8 (in Ardèche) and 59.2 (in Creuse), a difference of only 15.4 years. Table 8.2 shows the trend of means and standard deviations of e^0_x in time. Although some of the evolution may be explained by changes in the quality of the data, the convergence of départemental e^0_x must correspond to real and pervasive changes. Another striking characteristic of the series is that the ranking of départements on the mortality scale does not remain stable for very long. Expectations of life at birth for any date are highly correlated with those of immediately adjacent years, but only very little with dates more remote in time. The 19th century obviously witnessed great changes in the distribution of mortality in France.

II. *Migration*

The balance equation provides the basis for our estimate of migration. We showed that intercensal balances of births and deaths provide an unreliable indicator of migration, because they do not account for differential misenumeration in censuses five

TABLE 8.2

FEMALE EXPECTATION OF LIFE AT BIRTH (e_o^o), MEAN, STANDARD DEVIATION, AND
CORRELATION WITH e_o^o IN 1801-1805, 1851-1855, AND 1901-1905:   1801-1805 TO 1901-1905

| Date | Expectation of life (e_o^o) | | Correlation coefficients | | |
	Mean	Standard deviation	e_o^o 1801-1805	e_o^o 1851-1855	e_o^o 1901-1905
1801-1805	35.5329	5.7960	1.000	0.023	-0.257
1806-1810	37.8853	4.5983	0.785	0.256	0.060
1811-1815	38.3171	4.2486	0.607	0.457	0.227
1816-1820	39.1878	4.3495	0.417	0.724	0.485
1821-1825	39.6390	4.0775	0.597	0.621	0.236
1826-1830	39.0524	4.3771	0.626	0.539	0.233
1831-1835	38.6146	3.9371	0.487	0.674	0.314
1836-1840	40.6756	4.2989	0.426	0.732	0.294
1841-1845	42.3134	3.8138	0.198	0.862	0.519
1846-1850	41.2292	3.7585	0.227	0.820	0.373
1851-1855	41.5268	4.1800	0.023	1.000	0.652
1856-1860	41.2780	4.0410	0.158	0.813	0.427
1861-1865	43.3890	3.9310	-0.111	0.855	0.670
1866-1870	42.3951	3.9307	-0.004	0.791	0.638
1871-1875	42.4013	3.6943	0.005	0.743	0.647
1876-1880	45.5077	4.1077	-0.195	0.767	0.829
1881-1885	46.5077	4.7440	-0.173	0.778	0.850
1886-1890	47.1487	4.0855	-0.232	0.764	0.900
1891-1895	46.2410	3.5690	-0.251	0.711	0.945
1896-1900	48.5807	3.5421	-0.298	0.699	0.974
1901-1905	50.6923	3.4338	-0.257	0.652	1.000

years apart. If, however, the balance equation is applied over a fairly long period, it will yield interesting results because then the errors in either census are likely to be small compared to the cumulated effect of migration on the intercensal increase. The first table presented for each département in Part Two of this book gives an index R/CB (reported population over population computed by the balance of births and deaths). The denominator was obtained as follows:

[199]

a) before 1846, by adding the deaths to, and subtracting the births from, the population recorded in 1846,

b) after 1846, by adding the births to, and subtracting the deaths from, the same 1846 population.

Some impression of the quality of enumeration can be gained on the basis of the fluctuations of this index. As discussed in previous chapters, we smoothed the R/CB ratios in order to correct the recorded population and eliminate the effect of a variation in the completeness of enumeration. Otherwise, intercensal changes would have been treated as migration, and would have left their marks on the age distribution. The correction was either the result of inter-polation between dates when the census appeared more reliable, or was computed from the trend line of the R/CB ratios. This new number of the population at the census date, divided by the popula-tion computed by balance, gives an estimate of the cumulated net migration during the period since the census of 1846 or (for dates prior to 1846) between these dates and 1846. Such estimates for 1806, 1831, 1856, 1881, and 1906 are presented in Table 8.3. Values under 1 before 1846, and over 1 after 1846 indicate net in-migration; the reverse is true for out-migration. Since the estimates are independent of the reconstruction by age, they can be computed for all départements that existed in 1846, including urban départe-ments such as Seine.

The resulting net values in 1906 are a cumulation over 60 years. Another index of net migration can be derived from the information published in the 1901 census on the place of birth and the place of residence of individuals. We computed such an index in the fol-lowing way: Net migration = (Population enumerated in the dé-partement − Population born in the département) / Population born in the département. It is given in the last column of Table 8.3. The sign indicates whether in- or out-migration prevails. The index refers this time to individuals of both sexes. Males are more mobile than females, and this index should therefore indicate more migra-tion than the previous index based on the cumulated balance of female births and deaths. The fact that the average age of the

TABLE 8.3   FEMALE NET MIGRATION INDEX, 1806 TO 1906, AND RATIO
OF NET MIGRANTS TO NATIVE-BORN POPULATION, 1901, BY DEPARTEMENT

DEPARTEMENT	1806	NET 1831	MIGRATION 1856	INDEX 1881	1906	RATIO 1901
AIN	1.013	0.992	0.988	0.963	0.918	-7.27
AISNE	1.026	0.994	0.983	0.936	0.890	-7.97
ALLIER	1.057	0.996	1.007	1.000	0.915	-7.04
ALPES (BASSES-)	1.162	1.025	0.967	0.853	0.739	-19.68
ALPES (HAUTES-)	1.164	1.051	0.959	0.859	0.739	-15.50
ARDECHE	1.130	1.007	0.962	0.861	0.759	-23.45
ARDENNES	1.124	0.988	0.968	0.910	0.852	-12.38
ARIEGE	1.139	1.056	0.901	0.787	0.652	-26.26
AUBE	1.077	0.997	1.006	1.003	1.045	3.37
AUDE	1.044	1.003	0.971	1.042	0.991	2.66
AVEYRON	1.225	1.025	0.987	0.898	0.760	-19.93
BOUCHES-DU-RHONE	0.803	0.937	1.104	1.416	1.708	20.69
CALVADOS	1.015	0.989	0.999	1.001	0.990	2.31
CANTAL	1.098	1.020	0.938	0.840	0.742	-20.55
CHARENTE	1.008	0.987	0.987	0.966	0.945	-2.58
CHARENTE INFERIEURE	1.008	0.993	0.992	0.965	0.938	0.96
CHER	1.047	0.985	0.984	0.907	0.815	-14.87
CORREZE	1.062	0.992	0.964	0.860	0.762	-20.76
CORSE	1.049	1.014	0.991	0.926	0.860	-12.93
COTE-D'OR	1.086	1.030	0.992	0.968	0.945	-2.09
COTES-DU-NORD	1.045	1.022	0.969	0.866	0.762	-17.49
CREUSE	1.025	1.010	0.958	0.867	0.776	-19.98
DORDOGNE	1.026	1.009	0.988	0.896	0.804	-15.03
DOUBS	0.987	0.989	0.971	0.920	0.870	-8.47
DROME	1.052	1.017	1.010	0.965	0.920	-3.22
EURE	1.003	0.986	0.987	0.972	0.956	-0.30
EURE-ET-LOIR	1.068	0.992	0.982	0.977	0.938	-7.66
FINISTERE	0.995	0.989	0.994	0.957	0.920	-5.19
GARD	1.252	1.048	1.039	0.954	0.999	1.78
GARONNE (HAUTE-)	0.999	0.985	1.027	0.957	0.994	3.17
GERS	0.977	0.996	0.997	0.961	0.925	-4.89
GIRONDE	0.963	0.939	1.037	1.224	1.412	17.48
HERAULT	1.088	1.035	1.119	1.099	1.305	16.82
ILLE-ET-VILAINE	1.000	0.995	1.000	0.966	0.932	-5.67
INDRE	1.013	1.017	0.965	0.876	0.808	-14.45
INDRE-ET-LOIRE	1.051	0.990	1.011	1.037	1.098	6.04
ISERE	1.052	1.008	0.933	0.929	0.918	-6.33
JURA	1.071	1.023	0.965	0.885	0.806	-11.36
LANDES	0.969	0.997	0.996	0.876	0.738	-17.27
LOIR-ET-CHER	1.010	0.988	0.988	0.936	0.884	-9.74
LOIRE	1.024	0.987	1.004	1.002	1.001	3.09
LOIRE (HAUTE-)	1.059	1.036	0.956	0.879	0.803	-17.34
LOIRE-INFERIEURE	1.001	0.997	1.041	1.000	0.990	0.26
LOIRET	1.049	1.000	0.995	0.960	0.893	-10.24
LOT	1.071	1.016	1.003	0.928	0.797	-17.76
LOT-ET-GARONNE	1.000	1.006	1.008	1.021	1.025	1.91
LOZERE	1.269	1.046	0.939	0.797	0.656	-36.01
MAINE-ET-LOIRE	0.946	0.967	1.014	1.023	1.051	2.05
MANCHE	1.049	1.011	0.978	0.905	0.832	-9.23
MARNE	0.984	0.970	1.021	1.064	1.062	5.17
MARNE (HAUTE-)	1.131	1.004	0.973	0.890	0.814	-10.86
MAYENNE	1.050	1.010	0.982	0.887	0.792	-15.38
MEURTHE	1.045	1.005	0.961	0.0	0.0	0.0
MEUSE	1.106	1.052	0.955	0.838	0.767	-7.30
MORBIHAN	1.058	1.014	0.992	0.938	0.884	-7.80
MOSELLE	1.235	1.045	0.946	0.0	0.0	0.0
NIEVRE	0.974	0.985	0.955	0.872	0.768	-19.80
NORD	0.995	0.975	1.005	1.038	1.013	-4.57
OISE	1.008	1.010	0.997	1.022	1.045	2.50
ORNE	1.025	1.019	0.975	0.901	0.843	-9.63
PAS-DE-CALAIS	1.026	1.010	0.965	0.947	0.928	-4.06
PUY-DE-DOME	1.074	1.010	0.968	0.927	0.886	-8.47
PYRENEES (BASSES-)	1.047	0.997	0.961	0.873	0.806	-7.66

PYRENEES (HAUTES-)	1.122	0.997	0.968	0.892	0.815	-9.01
PYRENEES-ORIENTALES	1.109	1.021	0.968	0.941	0.914	-4.24
RHIN (BAS-)	1.335	1.044	0.938	0.0	0.0	0.0
RHIN (HAUT-)	1.021	1.000	0.993	0.0	0.0	0.0
RHONE	0.802	0.880	1.088	1.286	1.575	22.69
SAONE (HAUTE-)	1.131	1.055	0.881	0.777	0.694	-21.27
SAONE-ET-LOIRE	1.066	1.019	0.980	0.924	0.829	-12.08
SARTHE	1.019	1.007	0.999	0.956	0.958	-3.79
SEINE	0.577	0.758	1.275	1.834	2.326	45.53
SEINE-ET-MARNE	1.087	1.011	0.994	1.006	1.001	-0.60
SEINE-ET-OISE	0.965	0.974	1.022	1.220	1.688	25.26
SEINE-INFERIEURE	1.100	1.017	1.095	1.004	1.001	1.99
SEVRES (DEUX-)	0.998	1.005	0.985	0.940	0.894	-8.18
SOMME	1.003	0.989	0.988	0.967	0.939	-5.11
TARN	1.112	1.018	0.981	0.907	0.833	-12.35
TARN-ET-GARONNE	1.125	1.019	1.013	0.978	0.944	-2.52
VAR	1.026	1.007	1.047	1.076	1.295	12.98
VAUCLUSE	1.083	1.013	1.014	0.898	0.960	-2.18
VENDEE	0.981	0.995	0.989	0.940	0.890	-8.54
VIENNE	1.118	1.007	0.996	0.944	0.892	-7.85
VIENNE (HAUTE-)	0.994	0.992	0.989	0.948	0.898	-6.70
VOSGES	1.074	1.019	0.932	0.931	0.913	-8.81
YONNE	1.029	1.004	0.969	0.928	0.858	-11.72

NOTES   NET MIGRATION INDEX SET AT 1846 = 1.000 BY COMPUTING THE RATIO OF
THE FINAL POPULATION ESTIMATE TO ESTIMATE COMPUTED BY BALANCE OF
BIRTHS AND DEATHS
RATIO CALCULATED FROM 1901 CENSUS DATA FOR BOTH SEXES

population in 1901 (and therefore the average period during which
the migration between the département of origin and the département of residence was recorded) was well below the 60 years over
which vital events are cumulated in the other index, may compensate for the sex difference. Finally, the two indices are highly
correlated ($r = .93$, with the slope of the regression line close to
45 degrees). Although the two indices were computed on an entirely independent basis, they clearly reflected the same phenomenon.

Conclusion

We have reached the end of our task in this book. We have described a systematic reconstruction of the female population of the French départements, based on the official statistics of the 19th century. We presented the methods of reconstruction, indicated the main defects of the data and described the main regional trends of fertility and nuptiality. Subsidiarily, we presented some estimates of mortality and migration for the départements. The detailed results of the study are presented in Part Two.

The production of a new set of demographic indicators only provides new material for a study of the fertility decline in France; the interpretation of the results remains to be attempted. We hope that our figures will be used for a variety of purposes by scholars who are not primarily interested in decline of fertility, or who reject our interpretations of the causes of the transition from high to low fertility rates. Therefore we present them separately, and will offer our interpretations in another volume. In this conclusion we want to map out the task ahead of us in our study of the vital revolution in France. Even at the descriptive level, there are clear gaps—both spatial and temporal—in our presentation. Some départements with special problems had to be left out of the estimation, either because they did not exist as recognizable administrative units during a part of the century or because they were predominantly urban and excessively affected by migration. We shall have to provide estimates of fertility and nuptiality for these areas too if we want to study the influence of particular cultural characters (as in the case of the German-speaking départements of Alsace and Lorraine detached from France in 1871) or the special impact of urbanization on fertility.

With respect to time, the story must be extended at both ends of our period, from demographic sources other than those presented here. Before 1800, the rich harvest gathered by the historical demographers in the baptism, burial, and marriage registers of the Old Regime throws some light on the beginnings of the fertility decline in selected parishes of France. On the other side, the official censuses and vital registration provide accurate and complete data which make it possible to follow the evolution of fertility and nuptiality in the 20th century without having to reconstruct the population. Although the fertility decline was almost spent by then, it is interesting to assess the extent to which contemporary differentials in fertility find their origin in past history.

The 19th century provides us a vantage point to discuss the long-term fertility decline, and to test at least some of the existing theories by means of the new indices provided in this book, in combination with the abundant statistical information collected by département throughout the century. This will be the main goal of the second part of this study. Some départements are well past the start of the long-term drop of fertility by 1801, when we can first compute crude birth rates by département, or by 1831, when it becomes possible to distinguish between overall and marital fertility. On the other hand, a few areas were lagging behind and were still clinging to the old reproductive regime which then also characterized the rest of Europe. In other terms, the mid-nineteenth century is a period of maximum contrast among French départements. Although we would like to be able to trace the beginning of the revolution in vital rates to some special circumstance before or around the political revolution, even in 1831 we are close enough to the crucial period to investigate the source of the geographical differentials at date of first decline. What distinguishes the départements where the birth rate is high and constant from those where it has started to drop? What characterizes départements with high marital fertility in contrast with those of low marital fertility?

The most important task ahead will consist in placing the decline of French fertility in its historical, social, and cultural context, and in attempting to explain its particular features in comparison to the rest of Europe. One basic limitation of départemental indices is that they hide some of the component variation for human groups that cannot be clearly identified with the population of départements. It is certain that there are strong social differentials in the date and speed of the fertility decline. The French upper classes are the forerunners of the movements, and most written testimony of the past—the literature and memoirs of the time—illuminates the motivations behind the diffusion of contraception in this group.[1] Beyond the evidence of literature, there is scanty statistical evidence in parish monographs or 20th-century censuses on fertility differences by socio-economic classes. These data have to be discussed, if only briefly.

Writers of the period considered, moralists as well as social scientists, have noticed the changes in French demographic trends and have tried to interpret them. Although these attempts often incorporated moral judgments and a preoccupation with restoring the normative order that gave rise to the earlier demographic regime, they provide us with a rich supply of explanations and hypotheses on the fertility decline. The student of an issue that has been so abundantly discussed cannot discard the insights of his predecessors, even if the decline of the French birthrate does not today elicit the passionate involvement of earlier times. Thus, the intellectual background must be presented before we turn to original interpretation.

Theory provides us with a number of hypotheses that can be tested at the ecological level and not, unfortunately (from the data at hand), at the level of individual behavior and motivation. Was the difference in fertility among geographical units related to their degree of urbanization or industrialization as transition theory suggests? Were there important contrasts in the level of living, the degree of literacy, or the access to means of communication of the populations concerned? Was the timing of the fertility decline different in areas distinguished by patterns of different land use or inheritance, language, religious fervor or indifference, political affiliations? And, finally, can combinations of demographic features of the areas be regrouped into characteristic growth strategies, into the multiphased responses suggested by recent schools of thought on the subject of the population transition (Davis, 1963)? The changes in nuptiality, as the data suggest, complement the changes in fertility. But, to go beyond this relationship, is the decline of the

---

[1] The best introduction to the subject is provided by Bergues et al. (1960) for the period prior to 1800.

birth rate related to the decline in mortality, as the population of an area reacts to pressures induced by population growth? Are the départements with abundant out-migration also those with lagging high levels of the birth rate? In other words, does leaving one's village in search of opportunities, or restricting one's family size at home, provide a real alternative that is reflected in the demographic statistics of the départements?

These questions will be discussed in detail in a subsequent volume. It is hoped that the provision of more detailed and, perhaps, more accurate indicators of the demographic history of the French départements in the present book can contribute to the solution of the historical puzzle: Why is France ahead of the rest of Europe in the fertility decline? Why are some départements ahead of the rest of France?

Part Two

RESULTS

1. Technical Notes on the Reconstruction of Individual Départements

AIN: The population in 1801 and 1806 and the births and deaths from 1801 to 1814 were inflated by the ratio of the total population (both sexes) of the Gex arrondissement to the total population of Ain in 1821 to account for a border change in 1815. Note a substantial discrepancy between the reported and the estimated population under 15 years of age both in 1901 and 1906; every reported age-group is almost 10 percent greater than in our estimate. The feature is discussed in Chapter 6, p. 156. Bad censuses: 1856, overreporting at adult ages, particularly at 35 to 39; 1876, implausibly large 20–24 age-group; 1881, underreporting of adults aged 15 to 49.

AISNE: The stable population estimated for 1801 seems too steep, and this results in a large discrepancy between the estimated and reported populations over age 70 after midcentury.

ALLIER: The total population was corrected in 1821, and by interpolation, in 1811, 1816, and 1826. Note a tendency to have too many reported children under age 5 in 1896–1906, in view of the reported number of births. The proportion single over 50 reported at the census in 1891 appears much too high.

ALPES (BASSES-): This is an area of heavy out-migration, and we are probably underestimating its impact on the age distribution at midcentury. Exceptionally, the birth cohort of 1866–1870 has been corrected downward. In general, the number of married women aged 20–24 appears grossly overreported. In 1891, the reported proportion single over 50 is unduly large, and the proportion married 15–49 appears much too low.

ALPES (HAUTES-): The estimated number of old people (65 and over) is consistently much larger than the reported; this may be due to a misestimation of migration. The censuses of 1876 and 1881 have a substantially larger reported number of married women than our estimate. This appears to originate in our deflation of the total population (see Table 1 of data). The census of 1851 had an irregular age distribution and underreported married women.

ALPES-MARITIMES: As the département was formed in 1860 at the annexation of Nice, reconstruction could not be performed.

ARDECHE: An unreliable set of data, and a heavy stream of out-migration. The results are questionable, most of all in 1901 and 1906 when the R/E ratios are under 1 at all ages between 15 and 65. The later censuses of 1872 and 1876 have erratic age distributions. There is clear overreporting of the age-group 20–24 in 1872, including the number of married women at that age (R/E = 2.9).

ARDENNES: Estimates for the ages over 65 from 1851 to 1866 are well below the reported numbers. It is possible that the stable population estimated for 1801 is responsible.

ARIEGE: This was the département hardest hit by the cholera epidemic in 1854, when the recorded crude death rate reached 66 per thousand (against 22 in neighboring years). Deaths were adjusted downward, to avoid a fictitiously small cohort of survivors, because cholera mortality does not conform to model life tables but spares children. This accounts for a discontinuity in the R/CB series between 1851 and 1856. The variation in the reported numbers of married women created sawteeth in the unadjusted fertility and nuptiality indices. Married R/E ratios are high in 1876, low in 1881, high in 1886, and low in 1891.

AUBE: The numbers between 1806 and 1836 were revised upward by linear interpolation between the censuses held at these dates, as the 1821 and 1831 censuses seemed to have underenumerated the population. As in neighboring Ardennes, the R/E ratios above 65 in 1851 are much above 1.0, and the excess of reported over estimated in these cohorts is carried over into the later censuses.

AUDE: One of the more unreliable reconstructions because of the inconsistency of the data. Although the R/CB ratios fluctuate a great deal, there is no conclusive indication of migration over the entire period, and the fluctuations are probably the result of mis-enumeration. Age distribution in the early censuses (1851 to 1866) is very irregular, and the irregularities cannot be safely traced to birth cohorts, but probably represent age misreporting at the census (few young adults, surplus from age 35 to 49). The differences between reported and estimated women by age are reproduced exaggeratedly by marital status until 1886. In 1871, 1876, and 1881, there is a collapse in the number of adults over 25 and under 40, and a considerable excess of persons over 50.

AVEYRON: (See Tarn-et-Garonne for general comment on border change.) The censuses from 1801 to 1866 were corrected for un-derenumeration of the children on the basis of the large difference between reported and estimated numbers under 15 years of age. The married R/E ratios tell an essentially inconsistent story, with low ratios among young adults (particularly at 20–24) until 1866, and high ratios among them between 1872 and 1896.

There may have been underreporting of young married women between 1851 and 1861, and severe misclassification by age in 1872 and 1876.

BELFORT (territoire de): Non-annexed part of Rhin (Haut-); exists only since 1871, and was not reconstructed.

BOUCHES-DU-RHONE: Département containing Marseilles and un-dergoing heavy in-migration. The reconstruction was unsatisfactory, and is not presented here.

CALVADOS: Was discussed extensively as an example in the text. A satisfactory reconstruction of a département without net migra-tion.

CANTAL: The population totals were corrected in 1801 and 1841. Persistent R/E ratios over 1.0 at ages 15–24 have not been elimi-nated, and they may be due to a characteristic migration pattern by age. In 1881 and 1886 the total number of married women is deficient.

CHARENTE: The 1896 population was corrected before computing the trend of R/CB. The censuses of 1851 to 1866 are unusually

[211]

irregular. The proportions ever-married in the 1896 census were corrected for absurdly high proportions single over age 50. Bad censuses: 1866, excessive number of women and married women, in particular at ages 20–24; 1896, reported numbers of women and married women highly irregular and inconsistent at all ages.

CHARENTE-INFERIEURE: The totals for 1801 and 1821 have been adjusted to bring the R/CB ratios in line with the rest of the series. In the process, interpolated values for 1811, 1816, and 1826 were also inflated. The results of the reconstruction by age do not fit the censuses well, although there is little evidence of consistent patterns of bias. In 1881 and 1886 the number of married women appears vastly underreported, and the age distribution by marital state extremely deficient.

CHER: Large numbers of child migrants (nurslings and orphans) from Paris upset the age distribution and the patterns of mortality and migration. The adjustment used is described in Chapter 3. Population totals were adjusted from 1871 on for the presence of immigrant children. Their number was estimated by assuming there were none in 1866, and that they represented 1.5 percent of the population in 1901 and 1906; at intervening censuses, the proportion was obtained by interpolation. Note, in 1886, the small reported number of married women aged 25–34.

CORREZE: As the age distribution of later years showed no evidence of exceptional migration, we reduced the recorded population totals substantially between 1876 and 1891. As the birth cohort 1836–1840 does not otherwise appear exceptionally large, we reduced the recorded number of births. The 1886 census reports too few married and widowed women at all ages, and too many single.

CORSE: A département with notoriously poor data. The match between the estimated and the enumerated population is only good in 1861; even the censuses of 1901 and 1906 have highly irregular R/E ratios. The enumerated distribution appears to have too few old people, except from 1876 to 1891, when it has too many. Every census is characterized by an overreporting of married women aged 20–24. Women and married women are heavily concentrated in the age group 20–24 in 1881, and the age distribution is highly irregular in 1896 and 1906.

COTE-D'OR: The totals for 1801 and for 1811 to 1831 were raised to get a series more consistent with that computed by the balance of births and deaths based on 1846. The totals between 1856 and 1891 were also adjusted, as the R/CB exhibited large fluctuations. The married R/E ratios are alternatively too high (in 1876, 1891, and 1901) and too low (1881). The census of 1881 seems to have greatly underestimated the number of married women.

CREUSE: The R/E at the oldest ages is dropping steeply in the censuses of 1851, 1856, and 1861. The cause may be an inappropriate mortality level (due to the underregistration of deaths) or an inadequate age distribution in the 1801 stable population. The married R/E ratios are usually low through all censuses except in 1876 and the three last ones, where they are too high. It is possible—even likely—that our estimate of the number married in 1891, 1896, and 1901 is too low, as it is pulled down by the general underenumeration of married women in earlier censuses, above all in 1886, when there is a substantial underreporting of married women and a collapse in the number of women over age 25.

DORDOGNE: The censuses of 1801 to 1866 were corrected for underenumeration of children under 15 years on the basis of the large difference between reported and estimated numbers at those ages. Exceptionally, the recorded total births for 1881–1885 and 1886–1890 were adjusted downward, as they created excessively large cohorts in the reconstructed population by age. Our estimate of the number of married women appears too low in 1866 and 1872. Bad censuses: in 1881 and 1886, excessive numbers of children were reported, as well as shortages of women and married women between ages 30 and 49.

DOUBS: The population size in 1876 and 1881 is reduced more than 2 percent by the use of the trend of R/CB. The series of married R/E is irregular, alternating years when the reported married women seem under-counted (1851 to 1861) and when they seem over-counted (1872 to 1881, 1901).

DROME: The censuses from 1801 to 1866 were corrected for underenumeration of children on the basis of the large difference between reported and enumerated numbers at young ages. The recorded age distributions are often patently unreliable (with gross over-counting of ages 20–24). Marital status is poorly reported. Both the reported age and marital distributions fall apart in 1856 and 1861. Women and married women between 25 and 49 years of age were underreported in 1891 and 1896.

EURE: Exceptionally, in 1816–1820 and 1821–1825, the births were adjusted downward. The R/E ratios are typically over 1.0 after age 60, and under 1.0 during the adult ages.

EURE-ET-LOIR: The département with the largest number of nurslings from Paris. A series of adjustments were used, as described in Chapter 3. The 1856 and 1861 censuses have a very irregular age distribution and, in the former instance, a serious underenumeration of young married women.

FINISTERE: The data appear unreliable. The married R/E ratios are characterized by an excess of the reported at ages 20–24 and a deficit over age 25.

GARD: The censuses from 1801 to 1866 were corrected for underenumeration of children under 15 years, on the basis of the large difference between reported and estimated number at those ages. The R/E ratios are very high over age 50 despite the use of the North pattern of mortality in the projections. Bad censuses: in 1872 note an over-large age group 20–24 for women and married women; in 1886 irregular age and marital status with underreporting between 25 and 45 years of age.

GARONNE (HAUTE-): (See Tarn-et-Garonne for general comment on border change.) The censuses from 1801 to 1866 were corrected for underenumeration of the children on the basis of the large difference between reported and estimated numbers under 15 years of age. There is a tendency toward underreporting the number of married women between 25 and 44 years. Note the excessive number of women and married women reported between 20 and 24 years in 1872 and 1876.

GERS: (See Tarn-et-Garonne for general comment on border change.) The censuses from 1801 to 1866 were corrected for underenumeration of the children on the basis of the large difference between reported and estimated numbers under 15 years of age. The enumerated population is exceptionally large in 1886. The married R/E ratios are exceptionally low in 1851, 1856, and 1866, and exceptionally high in 1876 and 1886.

GIRONDE: This is an area of fairly intensive in-migration (Bordeaux). The R/E ratios from 1886 on appear very low; it is possible that the married women were underenumerated. Note the excessive number of women and married women in 1856.

HERAULT: An unreliable set of estimates based on poor and inconsistent data. The censuses from 1801 to 1866 were corrected for underenumeration of the children on the basis of the large difference between reported and estimated numbers under 15 years of age. No satisfactory set of population figures could be found to produce a satisfactory migration adjustment. The age distribution is very erratic, so that it was difficult to correct the births for under-registration. In 1851 the age and marital distributions are totally unreliable; in 1886 underreporting of married women is obvious.

ILLE-ET-VILAINE: The very jagged age distribution in 1851, 1856, and 1861 allowed little leverage to correct the birth series. There is a close fit between the reported and estimated age distributions in 1866. The reporting of marital status was particularly bad, with inflation of the age group 20–24 except in 1851 and 1861, when there was considerable overreporting at most adult ages.

INDRE: A satisfactory reconstruction, except for a slight downward slope in the R/E ratios in 1901 and 1906.

INDRE-ET-LOIRE: The population total for 1851 was inflated to correct for underenumeration of the 0–15 age category. Births recorded for 1867 were clearly in excess.

ISERE: The data are poor in quality. The census of 1861 appears to be the most reliable. Vital registration also exhibits major inconsistencies between 1856 and 1865; the birth cohorts 1856–1860 and 1861–1865 were corrected on the basis of the R/E ratios in 1901 and 1906. The years 1881 and 1886 represent a total disruption of census-taking, for both the number of women and the number of married women.

JURA: The match of the enumerated and the estimated age distributions was not satisfactory in 1901 and 1906; the reconstitution gave too many young people and adults and too few persons over 55 years of age. It is possible that the migration adjustment was not wholly appropriate.

LANDES: An unsatisfactory reconstruction based on an inconsistent set of data. Landes loses approximately 8,500 people to Pyrénées (Basses-) in 1857; an adjustment was made for the border change. The censuses from 1801 to 1871 were corrected for underenumeration of children on the basis of the large difference between the reported and estimated numbers under 15 years of age.

LOIR-ET-CHER: A large number of child migrants (nurslings and orphans) from Paris upsets the age distribution and the patterns of mortality and migration. The adjustment used is described in Chapter 3. Population totals were adjusted from 1871 on for the temporary presence of children from outside the département. Their number was estimated by assuming there were none in 1866, and their number in 1901 and 1906 was derived from the excess in the ages 0–15 in the reported as against the estimated population; at censuses in between, the proportion was obtained by interpolation.

LOIRE: The population total for 1821 was inflated, resulting also in the inflation of the interpolated values for 1811, 1816, and 1826. The recorded number of births in 1881–1885 was reduced on the basis of the R/E ratios in 1901 and 1906. The reported number of married women appears too small in 1881 and 1886, probably because of misclassification of marital status.

LOIRE (HAUTE-): Compared to the estimated series the reported data are characterized by a shortage of people aged 60 and over, possibly due to underenumeration. There is a large excess of married women recorded in the age-group 20–24 in all the censuses after 1866.

LOIRE-INFERIEURE: The censuses from 1801 to 1866 were corrected for underenumeration of children on the basis of the large difference between reported and estimated numbers under 15 years of age. In view of its very poor quality, the age distribution of 1851 was omitted when making the correction of birth cohorts on the basis of the R/E ratios in the first censuses. The censuses of 1881 and 1886 have an excessive number of women 15–24 enumerated as married.

LOIRET: Large numbers of child migrants (nurslings and orphans) from Paris upset the age distribution and the patterns of mortality and migration. The adjustment used is described in Chapter 3. Population totals were adjusted from 1871 on for the presence of nurslings. Their number was estimated by assuming that there were none in 1866, and that they represented 1.3 percent of the population in 1901 and 1906; at censuses in between, the proportion was obtained by interpolation. The age group 60 to 64 in 1866 is obviously misreported.

LOT: (See Tarn-et-Garonne for general comment on border change.) The censuses from 1801 to 1866 were corrected for underenumeration of children on the basis of the large difference between reported and estimated numbers under 15 years of age. The reported figures on marital status are so erratic (with clearly absurd distributions in 1872, 1886, and 1896) that it is difficult to know if the reconstruction has been successful. In 1901 there appears to be a large discrepancy between the reported and estimated numbers of women married, and the estimation may well be an understatement. Note a very small age-group 25–29 in 1886, as well as the underenumeration of young married women at that date.

RESULTS

LOT-ET-GARONNE: (See Tarn-et-Garonne for general comment on border change.) The censuses 1801 to 1866 were corrected for underenumeration of children on the basis of the large difference between reported and estimated numbers under 15 years of age.

LOZERE: The data are of poor quality, which results in an unsatisfactory reconstruction. The deaths recorded for 1801–1805 would have corresponded to an implausibly low mortality, so that the number of deaths was arbitrarily increased. The 1801 stable population was computed with that higher mortality. The fit of the reconstructed population with the enumerated one is not satisfactory at any census. The reported marital status distribution was particularly poor in 1872.

MAINE-ET-LOIRE: An unorthodox handfitting procedure was used to smooth the series of population totals after 1866.

MANCHE: The reconstruction of the age distribution for 1901 and 1906 is not satisfactory; the estimated population is approximately 5 percent under the enumerated one for the first half of the age span, and approximately 5 percent above it for the second half. The estimates of the numbers married are consistently below the enumerated numbers between 1851 and 1861, and above them from 1886 on. In 1872 and 1876, the age distributions and the marital status are erratic, and there appears to have been an underenumeration of single women over 50 in all age groups. The estimates of the proportion ever married were inflated for the computations.

MARNE: The age distribution of the stable population in 1801 is very steep, as the result of a probably excessive birth rate. The censuses of 1801 to 1866 were corrected for underenumeration of the children on the basis of the large difference between reported and estimated numbers under 15 years of age. The census of 1881 has a substantial underreporting of married women.

MARNE (HAUTE-): The cholera epidemic of 1854 causes the same problems as in Ariège, and we adjusted the deaths downward in order to avoid a fictitiously small cohort. There are serious irregu-

[218]

larities and inconsistencies between 1851 and 1866 in the enumerated age distributions. The marital status distribution in 1866 is very irregular, with a shortage of young married women, and an excess between age 35 and 49.

MAYENNE: The R/E ratios in 1901 and 1906 show a downward slope with increasing age (i.e. too many children estimated and too few old people). The censuses 1891 and 1901 reported a substantially larger number of adult married women than we estimated.

MEURTHE: The non-annexed parts were joined to those of Moselle in 1871 to form Meurthe-et-Moselle. Our reconstruction stops after 1866 and does not include the estimation of marital status.

MEURTHE-ET-MOSELLE: No reconstruction of this département, created in 1871, was attempted here.

MEUSE: Affected, as were Ariège and Haute-Marne, by the cholera epidemic of 1854. A similar adjustment was made here, resulting in a sharp drop in the R/CB between 1851 and 1856. For the purposes of the migration adjustment, the irregularity was eliminated by extrapolating R/CB between 1846 and 1881. In part as a result of the above adjustment, the R/E ratios are under 1.0 at adult ages between 1851 and 1866.

MORBIHAN: Old people appear to be underenumerated in the censuses up to 1872. The census of 1856 has an erratic age distribution.

MOSELLE: The non-annexed parts were joined to those of Meurthe in 1871 to form Meurthe-et-Moselle. Our reconstruction stops after 1866, and does not include the estimation of marital status.

NIEVRE: Large numbers of child migrants (nurslings and orphans) from Paris upset the age distribution and the patterns of mortality and migration. The adjustment used is described in Chapter 3. Population totals were adjusted from 1856 on for the presence of young migrants from the city. Their number was estimated by assuming there were none in 1851, and that they represented 4.1 percent of the population of 1901 and 1906, as well as that of 1886,

1891, and 1896. Between 1856 and 1881, their proportion was obtained by interpolation. The inflation of the 0 to 15 age-group is clearer than in any other département, particularly in 1901 and 1906.

NORD: The stable age distribution estimated for 1801 appears to imply an excessive birth rate. Note the contrast between a shortage of ever-married women reported in 1886 and an excess in 1891.

OISE: As in Nord, the stable age distribution in 1801 is abnormally steep; and the implied birth rate seems too high. Population totals were inflated in 1871, 1886, and 1891 to bring the R/CB ratios in line with those of surrounding censuses.

ORNE: Large numbers of child migrants (nurslings and orphans) from Paris upset the age distribution and the patterns of mortality and migration. The adjustment used is described in Chapter 3. Population totals were adjusted from 1866 on for the presence of young migrants. Their number was estimated by assuming that there were none in 1861, and that they represented 2.6 percent of the population in 1901 and 1906. Between 1866 and 1896 the proportion was obtained by linear interpolation. The censuses from 1851 to 1872 appear to underreport the number of married women. This is especially true in 1866.

PAS-DE-CALAIS: A satisfactory reconstruction, except for a tendency to underreport (or overestimate) the numbers of young married women in 1851 and 1856.

PUY-DE-DOME: The estimated number of married women for 1896 and 1901 is consistently lower than the recorded.

PYRENEES (BASSES-): There was a border change in 1857, involving the addition of 8,500 persons from Landes. It was assumed that they had the same age and sex distribution as the rest of Pyrénées (Basses-). The enumerated proportions and numbers married vary a great deal from year to year. Our estimate ended up with a quite lower number than the reported figures at most ages in 1896 and 1901.

PYRENEES (HAUTES-): The 1841 population total was inflated by interpolation of R/CB between 1836 and 1846. There seems to have been a tendency to underenumerate the 65 and over age-group. The reporting of marital status was very irregular. There appears to have been an overreporting of married women in 1876 and 1881, followed by underreporting in 1886.

PYRENEES-ORIENTALES: An unreliable reconstruction based on poor data. The censuses from 1801 to 1866 were corrected for underenumeration of the children on the basis of the large difference between reported and estimated numbers under 15 years of age in the censuses of 1851 to 1866. The correction for underreporting of births based on the R/E ratios in the censuses of 1856, 1861, and 1866 (since 1851 was too unreliable to be used) may well be excessive. Note also that the stable population for 1801 appears much too steep. Both the age and marital distributions of 1851 are impossible.

RHIN (BAS-): Was annexed by Germany in 1871. Our reconstruction stops in 1866 and does not include the estimation of marital status.

RHIN (HAUT-): Was annexed by Germany in 1871 (except for the Territoire de Belfort). Our reconstruction stops in 1866 and does not include the estimation of marital status.

RHONE: Département containing Lyon and undergoing heavy in-migration. The reconstruction was unsatisfactory, and is not presented here.

SAONE (HAUTE-): Was hard hit by the 1854 cholera epidemic (see also Ariège, Marne (Haute-), and Meuse). We adjusted the number of deaths downward in order not to have to account for the peculiar age pattern of cholera mortality. The discontinuity in the R/CB series produced by the above adjustment would have affected the migration adjustment which, therefore, was applied only from 1856 on.

SAONE-ET-LOIRE: Incompatible deficit in 1886, and surplus in 1896, of married women in the reproductive ages.

SARTHE: Large numbers of child migrants (nurslings and orphans) from Paris upset the age distribution and the patterns of mortality and migration. The adjustment used is described in Chapter 3. Population totals were adjusted from 1871 on for the presence of young migrants from the city. Their number was estimated by assuming there were none in 1866, and that they represented 1.6 percent of the population in 1901 and 1906 (calculated from the difference between enumerated and estimated children). From 1871 to 1896 their proportion was obtained by interpolation. The earlier estimated age distributions exhibit a surplus of women in the cohorts born between 1816 and 1830, probably because of out-migration before 1846 for which we did not adjust.

SAVOIE: Became part of France only in 1860, and the reconstruction was not performed.

SAVOIE (HAUTE-): Became part of France only in 1860, and the reconstruction was not performed.

SEINE: Département containing Paris and undergoing heavy in-migration. The reconstruction was unsatisfactory, and is not presented here.

SEINE-ET-MARNE: Large numbers of child migrants (nurslings and orphans) from Paris upset the age distribution and the patterns of mortality and migration. The adjustment used is described in Chapter 3. Population totals were undergoing great fluctuations, and the series was smoothed by interpolation. They were adjusted from 1871 on for the presence of young migrants from the city. Their number was estimated by assuming that there were none in 1866, and that they represented 1.4 percent of the population in 1906. From 1871 to 1896, their proportion was obtained by interpolation. Apparent overestimation of the number of married women after 1866 may be due to underreporting.

SEINE-ET-OISE: Département undergoing heavy in-migration. The reconstruction was unsatisfactory, and is not presented here.

SEINE-INFERIEURE: An inconsistent set of records provided an unsatisfactory reconstruction. The censuses from 1801 to 1866 were corrected for underenumeration of the children on the basis of the large difference between reported and estimated numbers under 15 years of age in the censuses between 1851 and 1866. The correction was large, and disrupts the series of R/CB when interrupted abruptly in 1872. The age distribution of the early censuses is very irregular despite substantial corrections of the births in the beginning of the century. The reconstruction by marital status produces results which are systematically a few percentage points under the reported numbers in the censuses of 1886 to 1901. The censuses of 1856 to 1861 vastly underreported the number of married women aged 15 to 39 years.

SÈVRES (DEUX-): Underreporting (or overestimation) of the number of young married women in 1851, 1856, and to some extent 1861.

SOMME: The population totals were inflated in 1821 and, as a result, in 1811, 1816, and 1826 were obtained by interpolation between the R/CB of 1806 and 1831. The absence of a migration adjustment may account for an underestimation of the young adult women in the reconstruction. Although the married R/E ratios are regular, the reconstruction appears to have a shortage of young married women.

TARN: The censuses from 1801 to 1866 were corrected for underenumeration of the children on the basis of the large difference between reported and estimated numbers under 15 years of age in the censuses of 1851 to 1866. The censuses from 1851 to 1866 are characterized by a shortage of married women enumerated before age 35; those from 1872 to 1886 have an excess of married women, particularly in the age-group 20–24; those from 1891 to 1901 seem reasonable at most ages.

TARN-ET-GARONNE: The département was formed in 1808 from parts of Aveyron, Garonne (Haute-), Gers, Lot, and Lot-et-Garonne. For each of these départements, and for Tarn-et-Garonne, we start our projection from a fictitious population, estimated on the basis of the approximate size in 1801 of the distracted part, as given in the official statistics (France, 1923, pp. 31 and 72-75). The total numbers of women in 1801 and 1806, and the births and deaths between 1801 and 1808 have been adjusted by the same proportions. The population totals were corrected throughout for underenumeration of children. The correction for 1851 to 1906 was based on the difference between the reported and the estimated population under age 15, and prior to 1851 on the estimated underenumeration at those ages in 1851 to 1866.

VAR: In 1860, the arrondissement of Grasse was subtracted from Var and joined to the newly acquired Duchy of Nice to form the département of Alpes-Maritimes. In adjusting for the change of border, it was assumed that the population of Grasse had the same age distribution and vital characteristics as the remainder of the département. The population was adjusted for underreporting of children between 1801 and 1891. Exceptionally, gradual migration was started in 1881. Prior to that time, the ratios R/CB show little evidence of migration.

VAUCLUSE: The reconstruction is poor because the data appear unreliable. The censuses from 1801 to 1866 were corrected for underenumeration of the children on the basis of the large difference between reported and estimated numbers under 15 years of age in the censuses of 1851 to 1866. The correction of the birth series between 1801 and 1815 may well be excessive. No satisfactory adjustment for migration could be made. The R/CB ratios indicate that there may have been a reversal of migratory trends. The fit of the estimated to the reported age distribution is unsatisfactory in 1901 and 1906, perhaps because of the lack of migration adjustment. Contrary to the most frequent patterns, the estimated number of married women is lower than the reported number between 1856 and 1876, and higher from 1881 on.

VENDEE: The reconstruction is not very good, but the recorded data are erratic, and clear patterns of errors do not emerge.

VIENNE: There is obviously gross underenumeration of the population in 1856 (the totals in 1851, 1856, and 1861 are, respectively: 158,585, 146,120, and 161,184 women). The total was corrected by interpolation of R/CB between the neighboring censuses. The estimates of numbers married appear too small from 1876 on.

VIENNE (HAUTE-): The population of 1841 was inflated by interpolation between the R/CB of 1836 and 1846. The census of 1851 has an irregular age distribution and a shortage of young married women, followed by a large excess between ages 40 and 49 years.

VOSGES: Was hit by the 1854 cholera epidemic, and deaths were adjusted as in Ariège. A border change adjustment was necessary: in 1871 Vosges lost the population of the cantons of Schirmeck and Saales to Germany, estimated at 21,841 people. Despite the evidence of the R/CB no satisfactory adjustment for migration could be found, and the age distribution in 1901 and 1906 may be overestimated somewhat in the adult ages. The apparent overestimation of married women between 15 and 34 in 1851 and 1856 may have its explanation in the estimation procedure.

YONNE: Large numbers of child migrants (nurslings and orphans) from Paris upset the age distribution and the patterns of mortality and migration. The adjustment used is described in Chapter 3. Population totals were adjusted from 1871 on for the presence of nursling and immigrant children. Their number was estimated at 2.7 percent for 1906, from the excess of enumerated over estimated at that date; it was estimated that there were none in 1866, and that the censuses between 1866 and 1906 had the proportion estimated by interpolation. The fit of the reconstruction is not very satisfactory in 1901 and 1906, perhaps because the migration adjustment did not work well. There are also too many estimated married women in 1901.

2. The Data, by Département

AIN

MORTALITY PATTERN: WEST
MIGRATION: FULL STRENGTH, WITH UNCORRECTED POPULATION TOTALS EXCEPT FOR 1856,
1861, 1866, 1871, 1881, 1891 AND 1896, OBTAINED BY INTERPOLATION OF R/CB

TABLE 1   FEMALE POPULATION ESTIMATES: 1801 TO 1906

DATE	R/CB RATIO	% COR-RECTION	FINAL POPULATION ESTIMATE	DATE	R/CB RATIO	% COR-RECTION	FINAL POPULATION ESTIMATE
1801	1.006	0.0	160260	1856	0.978	1.1	184049
1806	1.013	0.0	162176	1861	0.974	1.1	182494
1811*	1.011	0.0	164092	1866	0.971	0.8	183339
1816*	0.997	0.0	166008	1871	0.953	2.3	182385
1821	0.994	0.0	167924	1876	0.970	0.0	180181
1826*	0.982	0.0	170936	1881	0.928	3.8	180415
1831	0.992	0.0	173948	1886	0.956	0.0	179632
1836	0.982	0.0	173543	1891	0.939	0.8	177698
1841	0.988	0.0	177733	1896	0.931	0.7	174570
1846	1.000	0.0	183314	1901	0.927	0.0	172548
1851	0.993	0.0	184393	1906	0.918	0.0	170781

NOTE: R/CB RATIO REFERS TO THE POPULATION COMPUTED BY THE BALANCE OF BIRTHS
       AND DEATHS OVER THE REPORTED POPULATION
* INTERPOLATED VALUES

TABLE 2   FEMALE BIRTH ESTIMATES: 1801-1805 TO 1901-1905

DATE	% COR-RECTION	FINAL BIRTH ESTIMATE	CRUDE BIRTH RATE	DATE	% COR-RECTION	FINAL BIRTH ESTIMATE	CRUDE BIRTH RATE
1801-1805	3.6	25918	32.2	1856-1860	0.0	21545	23.5
1806-1810	0.0	26121	32.0	1861-1865	0.0	22067	24.1
1811-1815	10.3	26201	31.7	1866-1870	3.8	20141	22.0
1816-1820	7.9	26103	31.3	1871-1875	0.0	20847	23.0
1821-1825	0.0	26129	30.8	1876-1880	0.0	20648	22.9
1826-1830	0.0	25741	29.9	1881-1885	0.0	18948	21.1
1831-1835	0.0	25867	29.8	1886-1890	0.0	18008	20.2
1836-1840	0.0	24665	28.1	1891-1895	0.0	16914	19.2
1841-1845	0.0	25415	28.2	1896-1900	0.0	17454	20.1
1846-1850	0.0	24538	26.7	1901-1905	0.0	16920	19.7
1851-1855	2.6	22548	24.5				

TABLE 3 FEMALE POPULATION ESTIMATES,
DISTRIBUTION BY AGE: 1801 TO 1906

AGE	1801	1806	1811	1816	1821	1826	1831	1836	1841	1846	1851
0- 4	19216	18540	18896	19384	19176	19843	19174	18880	19108	19905	19102
5- 9	16550	16848	16283	16667	17117	17123	17739	16823	17160	17505	17975
10-14	15628	15936	16162	15527	15984	16398	16609	16903	16385	16817	16880
15-19	14752	15044	15283	15406	14886	15306	15899	15821	16456	16050	16024
20-24	13751	14029	14261	14414	14607	14115	14679	14979	15254	15967	14845
25-29	12710	12946	13171	13332	13541	13738	13413	13702	14326	14684	14937
30-34	11641	11865	12056	12223	12430	12650	12957	12426	13018	13701	13818
35-39	10585	10774	10960	11105	11307	11530	11838	11909	11724	12366	12838
40-44	9553	9725	9881	10028	10202	10423	10717	10807	11166	11067	11546
45-49	8550	8712	8854	8977	9147	9339	9618	9713	10062	10468	10278
50-54	7529	7652	7787	7905	8043	8234	8466	8563	8895	9279	9579
55-59	6397	6511	6617	6740	6860	7031	7231	7300	7616	7970	8256
60-64	5135	5220	5323	5434	5541	5706	5851	5906	6181	6501	6740
65-69	3792	3843	3925	4041	4120	4276	4381	4407	4643	4901	5112
70-74	2474	2510	2563	2658	2726	2849	2923	2937	3106	3304	3462
75-79	1331	1351	1388	1452	1494	1586	1623	1632	1743	1864	1971
80+	667	668	683	715	743	792	827	835	892	963	1027

AGE	1856	1861	1866	1871	1876	1881	1886	1891	1896	1901	1906
0- 4	17623	16688	17612	16182	16324	16899	15789	15055	14100	14705	14466
5- 9	17290	15906	15270	16147	14672	15073	15697	14663	13969	13141	13792
10-14	17357	16695	15428	14806	15611	14251	14648	15249	14242	13586	12796
15-19	16132	16647	16111	14841	14201	15031	13651	13995	14604	13653	13025
20-24	14912	15144	15804	15197	13937	13344	14010	12571	12957	13600	12683
25-29	13918	14030	14374	14973	14334	13206	12594	13193	11826	12237	12883
30-34	14079	13110	13311	13643	14140	13650	12596	12003	12578	11295	11723
35-39	12966	13195	12376	12577	12817	13416	12992	11988	11417	11998	10805
40-44	12000	12094	12398	11646	11762	12115	12737	12343	11381	10868	11461
45-49	10732	11125	11293	11598	10826	11056	11443	12041	11660	10780	10332
50-54	9413	9796	10235	10414	10617	10038	10311	10686	11231	10908	10129
55-59	8530	8350	8775	9194	9271	9600	9141	9405	9733	10265	10021
60-64	6994	7197	7142	7528	7795	8021	8375	7987	8206	8534	9060
65-69	5313	5483	5746	5725	5941	6319	6574	6877	6547	6770	7102
70-74	3622	3739	3949	4159	4063	4363	4705	4907	5122	4916	5140
75-79	2074	2150	2298	2433	2497	2550	2788	3017	3137	3309	3222
80+	1094	1145	1229	1322	1372	1485	1582	1720	1858	1984	2141

TABLE 4   MARRIED WOMEN ESTIMATES,
DISTRIBUTION BY AGE: 1831 TO 1901

AGE	1831	1836	1841	1846	1851	1856	1861	1866
15-19	712	720	794	770	769	788	875	799
20-24	5201	5366	5539	5841	5515	5621	5780	5690
25-29	8523	8756	9238	9541	9774	9169	9304	9594
30-34	9562	9189	9704	10271	10405	10645	9952	10142
35-39	8943	8993	8935	9475	9872	10002	10209	9599
40-44	7947	7988	8350	8323	8711	9075	9165	9410
45-49	6706	6734	7094	7439	7333	7680	7980	8114

AGE	1871	1876	1881	1886	1891	1896	1901
15-19	693	818	781	641	607	715	778
20-24	5624	5589	5081	5392	4938	5288	5679
25-29	9489	9280	9104	8261	8823	8100	8632
30-34	10414	10448	10200	9771	9100	9644	8778
35-39	9752	9955	10252	9992	9430	8885	9371
40-44	8814	8905	9212	9578	9340	8729	8266
45-49	8290	7737	7947	8261	8756	8511	7830

TABLE 5   DEMOGRAPHIC INDICES AND FEMALE SINGULATE MEAN AGE
AT MARRIAGE: 1831 TO 1901

DATE	IF OVERALL FERTILITY	IG MARITAL FERTILITY	IH ILLEGITIMATE FERTILITY	IM PROPORTION MARRIED	SINGULATE MEAN AGE AT MARRIAGE
1831	0.319	0.582	0.028	0.526	24.3
1836	0.312	0.571	0.023	0.527	24.4
1841	0.300	0.543	0.025	0.532	24.2
1846	0.291	0.517	0.027	0.539	24.1
1851	0.275	0.479	0.029	0.548	24.1
1856	0.259	0.446	0.029	0.551	24.0
1861	0.256	0.443	0.027	0.550	24.0
1866	0.246	0.428	0.027	0.546	24.2
1871	0.241	0.417	0.026	0.550	24.0
1876	0.251	0.425	0.025	0.564	23.8
1881	0.243	0.413	0.022	0.565	24.0
1886	0.233	0.390	0.030	0.564	24.1
1891	0.228	0.377	0.032	0.567	24.0
1896	0.228	0.377	0.032	0.568	23.8
1901	0.229	0.375	0.030	0.577	

[228]

MORTALITY PATTERN: NORTH
MIGRATION: FULL STRENGTH, WITH POPULATION TOTALS OBTAINED BY TREND OF R/CB

TABLE 1 FEMALE POPULATION ESTIMATES: 1801 TO 1906

DATE	R/CB RATIO	% COR- RECTION	FINAL POPULATION ESTIMATE	DATE	R/CB RATIO	% COR- RECTION	FINAL POPULATION ESTIMATE
1801	1.021	1.3	219955	1856	0.978	0.5	282540
1806	1.026	0.0	226259	1861	0.978	-0.5	282606
1811*	1.026	0.0	232567	1866	0.967	-0.3	282496
1816*	1.015	0.0	238875	1871	0.947	0.8	280956
1821	0.992	0.0	245183	1876	0.956	-1.1	278655
1826*	0.986	0.0	255033	1881	0.932	0.4	278515
1831	0.994	0.0	264883	1886	0.945	-1.9	277342
1836	1.004	0.0	270573	1891	0.910	0.8	276093
1841	1.000	0.0	276701	1896	0.910	-0.2	273584
1846	1.000	0.0	282984	1901	0.894	0.6	272100
1851	0.986	0.6	284707	1906	0.886	0.4	271774

NOTE: R/CB RATIO REFERS TO THE POPULATION COMPUTED BY THE BALANCE OF BIRTHS
       AND DEATHS OVER THE REPORTED POPULATION
* INTERPOLATED VALUES

TABLE 2 FEMALE BIRTH ESTIMATES: 1801-1805 TO 1901-1905

DATE	% COR- RECTION	FINAL BIRTH ESTIMATE	CRUDE BIRTH RATE	DATE	% COR- RECTION	FINAL BIRTH ESTIMATE	CRUDE BIRTH RATE
1801-1805	9.9	36382	32.6	1856-1860	0.0	34796	24.6
1806-1810	9.9	36175	31.5	1861-1865	0.0	33940	24.0
1811-1815	10.1	39666	33.7	1866-1870	0.0	32416	23.0
1816-1820	0.0	40437	33.4	1871-1875	0.0	32037	22.9
1821-1825	0.0	39985	32.0	1876-1880	0.0	32392	23.3
1826-1830	0.0	38260	29.4	1881-1885	0.0	31125	22.4
1831-1835	0.0	36189	27.0	1886-1890	0.0	30245	21.9
1836-1840	0.0	34929	25.5	1891-1895	0.0	30083	21.9
1841-1845	0.0	34937	25.0	1896-1900	0.0	29686	21.8
1846-1850	5.6	36646	25.8	1901-1905	0.0	29111	21.4
1851-1855	0.0	33505	23.6				

TABLE 3 FEMALE POPULATION ESTIMATES,
DISTRIBUTION BY AGE: 1801 TO 1906

AGE	1801	1806	1811	1816	1821	1826	1831	1836	1841	1846	1851
0- 4	35413	27925	27282	29468	30871	31442	30292	28219	28275	28488	29170
5- 9	28274	30430	23856	23058	25206	27011	27757	26505	25161	25356	25054
10-14	24596	26459	23658	22315	21468	23874	25866	26514	25330	24149	24078
15-19	21756	23383	25373	27316	21107	20633	23208	25113	25663	24615	23025
20-24	19173	20610	22340	24094	25746	20217	19988	22452	24226	24857	23027
25-29	16794	18050	19556	21064	22567	24514	19466	19213	21542	23340	23486
30-34	14597	15689	16979	18276	19578	21332	23430	18565	18316	20623	22118
35-39	12595	13521	14618	15712	16842	18359	20223	22151	17572	17413	19427
40-44	10775	11582	12499	13418	14374	15683	17282	18978	20831	16599	16326
45-49	9173	9849	10640	11401	12202	13307	14676	16120	17747	19568	15493
50-54	7711	8288	8939	9585	10249	11171	12312	13531	14915	16495	18077
55-59	6335	6791	7315	7826	8398	9154	10081	11059	12237	13554	14879
60-64	4956	5328	5699	6082	6547	7178	7899	8639	9604	10684	11687
65-69	3607	3862	4117	4354	4714	5201	5751	6264	7009	7840	8574
70-74	2322	2489	2617	2750	2989	3333	3702	4031	4559	5138	5611
75-79	1257	1340	1392	1436	1579	1779	1993	2165	2497	2849	3105
80+	623	663	686	699	748	845	958	1054	1217	1417	1572

AGE	1856	1861	1866	1871	1876	1881	1886	1891	1896	1901	1906
0- 4	26797	28116	27836	26747	26404	27154	26224	25653	25335	25344	25302
5- 9	25669	23755	25132	24957	23960	23893	24621	23879	23266	23161	23422
10-14	23757	24437	22658	23998	23826	22955	22888	23637	22893	22364	22340
15-19	22787	22635	23275	21526	22833	22725	21806	21798	22537	21834	21320
20-24	21120	21189	20943	21501	19817	21146	20876	20079	20115	20834	20094
25-29	21563	19896	19943	19687	20227	18662	19877	19676	18912	18969	19670
30-34	22225	20470	18916	18972	18725	19309	17798	19004	18791	18098	18199
35-39	20834	21004	19398	17940	17990	17825	18394	16980	18109	17958	17353
40-44	18234	19608	19841	18351	16966	17087	16951	17522	17277	17277	17203
45-49	15266	17087	18448	18697	17290	16058	16197	16095	16604	15354	16499
50-54	14356	14174	15934	17233	17459	16226	15102	15259	15129	15665	14559
55-59	16347	13027	12937	14572	15749	16052	14955	13953	14059	14006	14586
60-64	12859	14198	11397	11352	12780	13928	14231	13303	12368	12541	12590
65-69	9410	10427	11632	9376	9331	10629	11625	11933	11099	10412	10667
70-74	6166	6836	7688	8627	6946	7031	8049	8862	9033	8509	8097
75-79	3414	3806	4308	4886	5474	4513	4601	5317	5796	6011	5773
80+	1736	1940	2212	2533	2877	3325	3146	3143	3393	3762	4102

TABLE 4   MARRIED WOMEN ESTIMATES,
DISTRIBUTION BY AGE: 1831 TO 1901

AGE	1831	1836	1841	1846	1851	1856	1861	1866
15-19	1725	1904	1987	1947	1863	1887	2246	2324
20-24	9472	10768	11773	12235	11476	10659	10828	10878
25-29	14302	14189	16021	17463	17661	16298	15108	15208
30-34	18859	14969	14847	16778	18030	18155	16748	15490
35-39	16345	17910	14296	14217	15877	17049	17196	15871
40-44	13590	14907	16498	13201	12986	14514	15601	15753
45-49	10926	11983	13360	14826	11743	11585	12961	13951

AGE	1871	1876	1881	1886	1891	1896	1901
15-19	2067	2286	2039	1708	1504	1506	1815
20-24	11355	10756	11321	10841	10283	10374	10623
25-29	14928	15443	14505	15326	15084	14598	14865
30-34	15523	15253	15791	14673	15594	15441	14982
35-39	14628	14650	14526	15012	13840	14735	14650
40-44	14478	13347	13488	13390	13743	12613	13467
45-49	14008	12900	12044	12174	11971	12266	11258

TABLE 5   DEMOGRAPHIC INDICES AND FEMALE SINGULATE MEAN AGE
AT MARRIAGE: 1831 TO 1901

DATE	IF OVERALL FERTILITY	IG MARITAL FERTILITY	IH ILLEGITIMATE FERTILITY	IM PROPORTION MARRIED	SINGULATE MEAN AGE AT MARRIAGE
1831	0.298	0.449	0.053	0.619	23.0
1836	0.280	0.428	0.052	0.608	22.9
1841	0.271	0.420	0.042	0.606	22.8
1846	0.272	0.414	0.046	0.615	22.7
1851	0.268	0.394	0.052	0.630	22.6
1856	0.266	0.381	0.064	0.638	22.5
1861	0.274	0.386	0.074	0.639	22.3
1866	0.270	0.383	0.072	0.636	22.3
1871	0.269	0.381	0.073	0.637	22.2
1876	0.273	0.386	0.073	0.638	22.2
1881	0.269	0.378	0.077	0.636	22.3
1886	0.261	0.364	0.083	0.634	22.5
1891	0.259	0.363	0.083	0.630	22.5
1896	0.257	0.361	0.082	0.628	22.5
1901	0.253	0.353	0.081	0.633	

MORTALITY PATTERN: WEST
MIGRATION: FULL STRENGTH, UNCORRECTED POPULATION TOTALS

TABLE 1 FEMALE POPULATION ESTIMATES: 1801 TO 1906

DATE	R/CB RATIO	% COR- RECTION	FINAL POPULATION ESTIMATE	DATE	R/CB RATIO	% COR- RECTION	FINAL POPULATION ESTIMATE
1801	1.008	3.2	130000	1856	1.007	0.0	174029
1806	1.057	0.0	131576	1861	0.996	0.0	176214
1811*	1.041	1.6	137371	1866	1.005	0.0	186005
1816*	1.024	3.1	143166	1871	1.003	0.0	193981
1821	0.994	4.6	148961	1876	1.007	0.0	201604
1826*	0.998	2.2	149231	1881	1.000	0.0	208715
1831	0.996	0.0	149502	1886	0.986	0.0	212761
1836	1.004	0.0	154659	1891	0.964	0.0	212570
1841	0.986	0.0	155365	1896	0.946	0.0	211884
1846	1.000	0.0	163691	1901	0.934	0.0	212038
1851	0.992	0.0	165763	1906	0.915	0.0	210179

NOTE: R/CB RATIO REFERS TO THE POPULATION COMPUTED BY THE BALANCE OF BIRTHS
       AND DEATHS OVER THE REPORTED POPULATION
* INTERPOLATED VALUES

TABLE 2 FEMALE BIRTH ESTIMATES: 1801-1805 TO 1901-1905

DATE	% COR- RECTION	FINAL BIRTH ESTIMATE	CRUDE BIRTH RATE	DATE	% COR- RECTION	FINAL BIRTH ESTIMATE	CRUDE BIRTH RATE
1801-1805	13.5	22745	34.8	1856-1860	0.0	24290	27.7
1806-1810	0.0	24006	35.7	1861-1865	0.0	25820	28.5
1811-1815	0.0	24184	34.5	1866-1870	0.0	27029	28.5
1816-1820	0.0	25138	34.4	1871-1875	0.0	26302	26.6
1821-1825	13.3	25639	34.4	1876-1880	0.0	24922	24.3
1826-1830	13.5	25844	34.6	1881-1885	0.0	23464	22.3
1831-1835	0.0	24038	31.6	1886-1890	0.0	21689	20.4
1836-1840	4.6	24010	31.0	1891-1895	0.0	21084	19.9
1841-1845	0.0	23716	29.7	1896-1900	0.0	19770	18.7
1846-1850	10.0	24363	29.6	1901-1905	0.0	18432	17.5
1851-1855	0.0	23485	27.6				

TABLE 3 FEMALE POPULATION ESTIMATES,
DISTRIBUTION BY AGE: 1801 TO 1906

AGE	1801	1806	1811	1816	1821	1826	1831	1836	1841	1846	1851
0- 4	15631	15614	17880	18393	19451	18252	18383	18239	17701	19027	18540
5- 9	13554	13520	13956	16069	16543	16793	15730	16555	16009	16405	17009
10-14	12741	13091	13111	13493	15408	15590	15790	15276	15697	15766	15768
15-19	11977	12303	12691	12671	12932	14516	14654	15328	14479	15452	14963
20-24	11136	11410	11798	12142	12034	12044	13489	14079	14377	14128	14217
25-29	10265	10486	10841	11192	11444	11100	11084	12849	13090	13925	13129
30-34	9381	9575	9889	10214	10483	10471	10134	10483	11860	12603	13039
35-39	8520	8665	8960	9250	9504	9514	9483	9515	9604	11346	11745
40-44	7683	7808	8054	8327	8555	8564	8556	8845	8659	9134	10537
45-49	6871	6987	7204	7432	7648	7653	7646	7924	7993	8179	8438
50-54	6043	6122	6334	6537	6718	6718	6709	6960	7037	7432	7444
55-59	5148	5186	5376	5577	5745	5709	5698	5924	5994	6367	6566
60-64	4158	4145	4316	4500	4675	4617	4580	4779	4842	5178	5328
65-69	3101	3046	3182	3347	3510	3456	3408	3554	3611	3899	4016
70-74	2053	1991	2082	2208	2347	2303	2264	2363	2398	2620	2706
75-79	1134	1072	1134	1213	1310	1277	1252	1316	1333	1475	1527
80+	581	553	565	603	656	654	642	670	683	756	792

AGE	1856	1861	1866	1871	1876	1881	1886	1891	1896	1901	1906
0- 4	18911	19013	21213	22283	21723	21554	20477	18939	18374	17543	16575
5- 9	17238	17087	17788	19717	20790	20542	20365	19217	17787	17469	16683
10-14	16710	16607	16795	17353	19299	20345	20032	19740	18655	17366	17001
15-19	15840	15851	16589	16352	17087	18700	19444	18759	18626	17841	16335
20-24	15491	14485	16170	15994	16162	16156	17109	17041	16701	17122	15833
25-29	14129	14416	14329	15528	15552	15442	15148	15694	15783	15749	15938
30-34	12651	13284	13905	13710	14916	14966	14796	14406	14974	15189	15128
35-39	12422	11855	12697	13236	13084	14323	14352	14136	13777	14421	14640
40-44	11068	11613	11225	12026	12545	12531	13740	13764	13553	13270	13935
45-49	9834	10297	10900	10563	11314	11953	11977	13149	13159	13003	12788
50-54	7727	9022	9504	10113	9788	10655	11309	11369	12451	12498	12422
55-59	6636	6899	8119	8603	9143	9022	9873	10511	10546	11589	11709
60-64	5639	5626	5980	7048	7474	8107	8028	8787	9348	9449	10445
65-69	4277	4449	4571	4869	5745	6257	6817	6752	7383	7930	8078
70-74	2912	3034	3277	3375	3600	4393	4811	5243	5187	5739	6224
75-79	1671	1747	1912	2072	2138	2382	2926	3206	3489	3503	3924
80+	874	930	1032	1139	1246	1387	1560	1858	2092	2358	2522

TABLE 4   MARRIED WOMEN ESTIMATES,
DISTRIBUTION BY AGE: 1831 TO 1901

AGE	1831	1836	1841	1846	1851	1856	1861	1866
15-19	1333	1436	1399	1544	1549	1704	1814	2120
20-24	5917	6304	6579	6610	6801	7581	7250	7903
25-29	7572	8877	9158	9864	9408	10243	10563	10610
30-34	7799	8112	9250	9905	10311	10071	10627	11178
35-39	7444	7482	7597	9025	9376	9962	9529	10232
40-44	6642	6847	6729	7124	8226	8663	9083	8780
45-49	5589	5765	5846	6014	6210	7263	7593	8034

AGE	1871	1876	1881	1886	1891	1896	1901
15-19	2293	2420	2311	1942	1602	1671	1983
20-24	8516	8801	8679	8825	8460	8592	8941
25-29	11257	11753	11768	11566	11757	11764	12170
30-34	11057	11928	12233	12315	11876	12206	12430
35-39	10668	10613	11634	12067	11736	11312	11864
40-44	9372	9840	9953	11336	11148	10771	10613
45-49	7740	8368	9006	9599	10214	9930	9866

TABLE 5   DEMOGRAPHIC INDICES AND FEMALE SINGULATE MEAN AGE
AT MARRIAGE: 1831 TO 1901

DATE	IF OVERALL FERTILITY	IG MARITAL FERTILITY	IH ILLEGITIMATE FERTILITY	IM PROPORTION MARRIED	SINGULATE MEAN AGE AT MARRIAGE
1831	0.364	0.610	0.049	0.561	23.6
1836	0.331	0.539	0.058	0.567	23.4
1841	0.321	0.519	0.047	0.582	23.2
1846	0.306	0.488	0.041	0.594	23.1
1851	0.303	0.476	0.039	0.604	22.9
1856	0.287	0.451	0.033	0.608	22.8
1861	0.303	0.467	0.038	0.617	22.7
1866	0.304	0.472	0.036	0.615	22.4
1871	0.301	0.456	0.037	0.629	22.2
1876	0.282	0.422	0.034	0.639	22.2
1881	0.259	0.389	0.033	0.636	22.4
1886	0.237	0.353	0.036	0.633	22.7
1891	0.225	0.341	0.035	0.622	22.7
1896	0.216	0.326	0.033	0.623	22.6
1901	0.201	0.297	0.031	0.639	

MORTALITY PATTERN: WEST
MIGRATION: GRADUAL, WITH POPULATION TOTALS OBTAINED BY TREND OF R/CB

TABLE 1 FEMALE POPULATION ESTIMATES: 1801 TO 1906

DATE	R/CB RATIO	% COR- RECTION	FINAL POPULATION ESTIMATE	DATE	R/CB RATIO	% COR- RECTION	FINAL POPULATION ESTIMATE
1801	1.109	8.1	71127	1856	0.963	0.5	72530
1806	1.162	0.0	73924	1861	0.943	0.2	70234
1811*	1.109	0.0	73987	1866	0.922	0.0	68296
1816*	1.076	0.0	74050	1871	0.903	-0.4	66296
1821	1.044	0.0	74113	1876	0.893	-2.0	64159
1826*	1.037	0.0	75242	1881	0.860	-0.8	62399
1831	1.025	0.0	76370	1886	0.841	-1.3	60100
1836	1.034	0.0	77440	1891	0.819	-1.5	57950
1841	1.005	0.0	75854	1896	0.780	0.6	55663
1846	1.000	0.0	75698	1901	0.739	3.1	53876
1851	0.977	1.4	74503	1906	0.736	0.4	52136

NOTE: R/CB RATIO REFERS TO THE POPULATION COMPUTED BY THE BALANCE OF BIRTHS
       AND DEATHS OVER THE REPORTED POPULATION
* INTERPOLATED VALUES

TABLE 2 FEMALE BIRTH ESTIMATES: 1801-1805 TO 1901-1905

DATE	% COR- RECTION	FINAL BIRTH ESTIMATE	CRUDE BIRTH RATE	DATE	% COR- RECTION	FINAL BIRTH ESTIMATE	CRUDE BIRTH RATE
1801-1805	14.4	14158	39.0	1856-1860	0.0	9926	27.8
1806-1810	8.4	13794	37.3	1861-1865	0.0	9518	27.5
1811-1815	4.4	12700	34.3	1866-1870	-7.3	8921	26.5
1816-1820	0.0	12729	34.4	1871-1875	0.0	8579	26.3
1821-1825	0.0	12492	33.5	1876-1880	0.0	8584	27.1
1826-1830	0.0	12870	34.0	1881-1885	0.0	8067	26.3
1831-1835	0.0	12346	32.1	1886-1890	0.0	7245	24.5
1836-1840	0.0	11177	29.2	1891-1895	0.0	6519	23.0
1841-1845	0.0	10737	28.3	1896-1900	0.0	6067	22.2
1846-1850	0.0	10159	27.1	1901-1905	0.0	5656	21.3
1851-1855	3.7	10152	27.6				

TABLE 3 FEMALE POPULATION ESTIMATES,
DISTRIBUTION BY AGE: 1801 TO 1906

AGE	1801	1806	1811	1816	1821	1826	1831	1836	1841	1846	1851
0- 4	10904	10319	9573	8878	8869	8819	9127	8689	7909	7746	7281
5- 9	8979	9501	9707	8159	7566	7689	7648	7953	7445	6927	6743
10-14	8026	8471	8765	8125	7627	7213	7313	7363	7431	7121	6591
15-19	7170	7569	7812	8176	7593	7269	6858	7039	6877	7106	6764
20-24	6342	6690	6899	7202	7550	7149	6829	6517	6500	6500	6655
25-29	5556	5864	6038	6237	6583	7035	6649	6421	5961	6084	6042
30-34	4827	5100	5251	5467	5709	6083	6489	6197	5826	5535	5619
35-39	4167	4396	4529	4714	4914	5229	5563	5994	5578	5366	5071
40-44	3571	3770	3876	4037	4207	4468	4748	5100	5357	5101	4883
45-49	3038	3208	3300	3430	3576	3797	4027	4320	4525	4864	4609
50-54	2541	2682	2756	2866	2981	3166	3358	3594	3764	4033	4315
55-59	2057	2173	2229	2315	2408	2551	2707	2892	3030	3245	3461
60-64	1579	1669	1707	1768	1836	1943	2059	2195	2307	2470	2631
65-69	1116	1183	1205	1244	1287	1358	1439	1527	1611	1729	1841
70-74	709	745	758	778	801	841	890	941	995	1072	1143
75-79	372	395	395	405	414	432	456	478	509	549	587
80+	179	188	189	191	194	201	210	220	231	249	267

AGE	1856	1861	1866	1871	1876	1881	1886	1891	1896	1901	1906
0- 4	7237	7047	6933	6616	6380	6463	6033	5578	5091	4924	4682
5- 9	6281	6226	6128	6069	5795	5615	5665	5349	4972	4605	4488
10-14	6355	5913	5879	5795	5744	5492	5313	5384	5095	4752	4404
15-19	6169	5920	5437	5449	5355	5298	5024	4853	4926	4668	4341
20-24	6194	5576	5310	4860	4770	4644	4512	4225	4048	4142	3897
25-29	6097	5641	5070	4809	4371	4278	4122	4002	3732	3588	3689
30-34	5527	5570	5177	4662	4423	4025	3928	3806	3706	3478	3354
35-39	5105	5018	5089	4748	4280	4073	3699	3636	3537	3474	3272
40-44	4582	4612	4567	4655	4353	3942	3750	3435	3394	3333	3290
45-49	4383	4114	4174	4157	4249	3994	3618	3475	3202	3195	3153
50-54	4065	3868	3664	3743	3739	3843	3615	3312	3202	2984	2995
55-59	3681	3469	3337	3187	3266	3283	3374	3215	2968	2908	2731
60-64	2789	2962	2827	2744	2627	2710	2719	2835	2722	2558	2529
65-69	1949	2061	2226	2149	2091	2019	2075	2122	2233	2195	2088
70-74	1210	1277	1379	1510	1462	1437	1381	1453	1502	1629	1626
75-79	623	656	712	783	860	843	823	815	870	935	1035
80+	285	301	326	359	396	441	448	457	463	507	561

[236]

TABLE 4 MARRIED WOMEN ESTIMATES,
DISTRIBUTION BY AGE: 1831 TO 1901

AGE	1831	1836	1841	1846	1851	1856	1861	1866
15-19	541	552	536	550	520	471	683	573
20-24	2664	2528	2512	2501	2550	2361	2116	2164
25-29	4325	4157	3854	3925	3890	3910	3608	3231
30-34	4919	4676	4400	4179	4240	4156	4184	3877
35-39	4357	4669	4360	4199	3973	3986	3919	3963
40-44	3720	3970	4198	4012	3853	3603	3633	3588
45-49	2977	3165	3352	3627	3457	3273	3084	3119

AGE	1871	1876	1881	1886	1891	1896	1901
15-19	520	474	334	308	289	288	278
20-24	1923	2051	1982	1814	1579	1412	1379
25-29	3050	2759	2901	2831	2762	2459	2279
30-34	3475	3245	2961	3021	2994	2950	2705
35-39	3679	3310	3129	2837	2885	2839	2828
40-44	3635	3395	3096	2859	2648	2629	2606
45-49	3082	3147	2993	2702	2637	2387	2343

TABLE 5 DEMOGRAPHIC INDICES AND FEMALE SINGULATE MEAN AGE
AT MARRIAGE: 1831 TO 1901

DATE	IF OVERALL FERTILITY	IG MARITAL FERTILITY	IH ILLEGITIMATE FERTILITY	IM PROPORTION MARRIED	SINGULATE MEAN AGE AT MARRIAGE
1831	0.331	0.556	0.043	0.562	24.3
1836	0.311	0.531	0.030	0.561	24.3
1841	0.300	0.526	0.015	0.558	24.3
1846	0.289	0.512	0.013	0.552	24.3
1851	0.284	0.505	0.012	0.552	24.3
1856	0.291	0.513	0.012	0.557	24.1
1861	0.296	0.513	0.012	0.567	24.0
1866	0.296	0.509	0.010	0.573	24.1
1871	0.298	0.518	0.014	0.565	24.1
1876	0.310	0.540	0.013	0.563	24.0
1881	0.314	0.547	0.015	0.563	24.0
1886	0.303	0.527	0.017	0.561	24.1
1891	0.284	0.491	0.017	0.563	24.5
1896	0.268	0.474	0.016	0.551	24.7
1901	0.256	0.462	0.014	0.540	

MORTALITY PATTERN: WEST
MIGRATION: FULL STRENGTH, WITH UNCORRECTED POPULATION TOTALS EXCEPT FOR 1876,
1881 AND 1886, OBTAINED BY LINEAR INTERPOLATION OF R/CB BETWEEN 1871 AND 1891

TABLE 1 FEMALE POPULATION ESTIMATES: 1801 TO 1906

DATE	R/CB RATIO	% COR- RECTION	FINAL POPULATION ESTIMATE	DATE	R/CB RATIO	% COR- RECTION	FINAL POPULATION ESTIMATE
1801	1.100	5.8	60723	1856	0.959	0.0	62413
1806	1.164	0.0	63085	1861	0.936	0.0	60619
1811*	1.120	0.0	62529	1866	0.922	0.0	59605
1816*	1.091	0.0	61972	1871	0.895	0.0	57745
1821	1.050	0.0	61416	1876	0.892	-1.7	56719
1826*	1.048	0.0	62910	1881	0.882	-2.6	56297
1831	1.051	0.0	64404	1886	0.873	-3.6	55407
1836	1.047	0.0	65172	1891	0.823	0.0	54639
1841	1.019	0.0	64548	1896	0.799	0.0	52804
1846	1.000	0.0	64394	1901	0.764	0.0	50751
1851	0.979	0.0	63877	1906	0.739	0.0	49578

NOTE: R/CB RATIO REFERS TO THE POPULATION COMPUTED BY THE BALANCE OF BIRTHS
AND DEATHS OVER THE REPORTED POPULATION
* INTERPOLATED VALUES

TABLE 2 FEMALE BIRTH ESTIMATES: 1801-1805 TO 1901-1905

DATE	% COR- RECTION	FINAL BIRTH ESTIMATE	CRUDE BIRTH RATE	DATE	% COR- RECTION	FINAL BIRTH ESTIMATE	CRUDE BIRTH RATE
1801-1805	0.0	9841	31.8	1856-1860	0.0	9155	29.8
1806-1810	3.5	9836	31.3	1861-1865	0.0	8926	29.7
1811-1815	2.7	10054	32.3	1866-1870	0.0	8633	29.4
1816-1820	0.0	10375	33.6	1871-1875	0.0	8639	30.2
1821-1825	0.0	10319	33.2	1876-1880	0.0	9040	32.0
1826-1830	0.0	10558	33.2	1881-1885	0.0	8493	30.4
1831-1835	0.0	10575	32.6	1886-1890	0.0	7764	28.2
1836-1840	0.0	10283	31.7	1891-1895	0.0	6946	25.9
1841-1845	0.0	9621	29.8	1896-1900	0.0	6476	25.0
1846-1850	7.8	9914	30.9	1901-1905	0.0	6138	24.5
1851-1855	0.0	9273	29.4				

TABLE 3 FEMALE POPULATION ESTIMATES,
DISTRIBUTION BY AGE: 1801 TO 1906

AGE	1801	1806	1811	1816	1821	1826	1831	1836	1841	1846	1851
0- 4	6864	7642	7299	7236	7466	7682	7790	7687	7391	7097	7270
5- 9	6052	6248	6666	6318	6233	6643	6821	6845	6643	6485	6193
10-14	5740	5900	5345	6269	5897	6004	6410	6530	6425	6292	6160
15-19	5438	5593	5517	5495	5848	5677	5791	6134	6127	6083	5804
20-24	5103	5248	5179	5130	5072	5571	5416	5480	5692	5740	5266
25-29	4752	4886	4821	4771	4691	4788	5265	5076	5038	5287	5158
30-34	4391	4519	4457	4407	4331	4396	4491	4896	4632	4646	4872
35-39	4033	4148	4094	4043	3970	4028	4091	4143	4433	4240	4273
40-44	3677	3785	3734	3688	3618	3667	3723	3748	3725	4031	3900
45-49	3333	3427	3384	3340	3277	3318	3365	3385	3345	3363	3696
50-54	2969	3056	3013	2973	2915	2953	2990	3005	2968	2969	3043
55-59	2568	2644	2609	2564	2514	2546	2577	2585	2552	2554	2603
60-64	2115	2177	2148	2103	2056	2083	2105	2108	2079	2085	2102
65-69	1613	1666	1641	1596	1557	1573	1587	1585	1564	1571	1581
70-74	1099	1139	1125	1085	1053	1062	1066	1062	1046	1055	1059
75-79	634	654	648	620	598	600	599	593	584	591	592
80+	339	353	348	335	320	319	317	311	303	305	307

AGE	1856	1861	1866	1871	1876	1881	1886	1891	1896	1901	1906
0- 4	6714	6533	6453	6264	6338	6732	6369	6004	5326	5170	5036
5- 9	6297	5769	5681	5571	5467	5569	5926	5678	5307	4730	4681
10-14	5859	5947	5485	5357	5291	5200	5292	5658	5392	5012	4504
15-19	5633	5328	5535	4946	4935	4878	4761	4865	5151	4770	4533
20-24	4915	4730	4690	4573	4248	4243	4123	4024	3988	3976	3872
25-29	4665	4318	4268	4085	4094	3792	3758	3662	3500	3341	3466
30-34	4729	4255	3975	3890	3757	3777	3489	3478	3363	3195	3096
35-39	4464	4318	3908	3631	3576	3464	3483	3237	3211	3112	2989
40-44	3918	4080	3960	3585	3340	3302	3203	3244	3008	3011	2938
45-49	3567	3572	3725	3625	3297	3075	3046	2978	3013	2828	2845
50-54	3334	3207	3211	3365	3276	2985	2802	2800	2737	2813	2653
55-59	2659	2897	2790	2810	2945	2882	2637	2503	2499	2491	2573
60-64	2130	2162	2369	2285	2313	2441	2396	2223	2102	2138	2158
65-69	1582	1589	1625	1785	1733	1771	1877	1877	1732	1678	1736
70-74	1055	1044	1059	1087	1204	1183	1215	1319	1310	1248	1235
75-79	586	575	577	587	610	686	679	720	775	802	785
80+	304	297	295	295	302	317	351	372	391	435	476

TABLE 4   MARRIED WOMEN ESTIMATES,
DISTRIBUTION BY AGE: 1831 TO 1901

AGE	1831	1836	1841	1846	1851	1856	1861	1866
15-19	291	311	319	305	281	271	270	289
20-24	1709	1719	1772	1768	1621	1512	1448	1272
25-29	3054	2941	2918	3063	2984	2698	2495	2465
30-34	3137	3423	3247	3267	3429	3337	3007	2814
35-39	2981	3024	3251	3126	3157	3312	3213	2918
40-44	2693	2719	2720	2967	2879	2910	3044	2970
45-49	2282	2300	2291	2328	2564	2494	2510	2633

AGE	1871	1876	1881	1886	1891	1896	1901
15-19	304	376	336	221	145	130	178
20-24	1387	1467	1417	1366	1315	1204	1104
25-29	2123	2288	2320	2177	2149	2156	2048
30-34	2756	2479	2605	2542	2449	2404	2370
35-39	2716	2679	2498	2561	2464	2410	2356
40-44	2695	2517	2522	2329	2388	2273	2250
45-49	2567	2332	2222	2198	2152	2198	2059

TABLE 5   DEMOGRAPHIC INDICES AND FEMALE SINGULATE MEAN AGE
AT MARRIAGE: 1831 TO 1901

DATE	IF OVERALL FERTILITY	IG MARITAL FERTILITY	IH ILLEGITIMATE FERTILITY	IM PROPORTION MARRIED	SINGULATE MEAN AGE AT MARRIAGE
1831	0.359	0.700	0.032	0.490	24.7
1836	0.347	0.679	0.030	0.489	24.9
1841	0.329	0.646	0.027	0.488	25.0
1846	0.320	0.634	0.019	0.489	25.0
1851	0.322	0.629	0.017	0.497	25.1
1856	0.322	0.624	0.016	0.502	25.1
1861	0.333	0.645	0.017	0.503	25.3
1866	0.332	0.664	0.016	0.487	25.4
1871	0.344	0.691	0.015	0.487	25.0
1876	0.364	0.713	0.017	0.499	24.8
1881	0.370	0.712	0.019	0.506	25.0
1886	0.353	0.682	0.021	0.501	25.5
1891	0.325	0.636	0.019	0.496	25.8
1896	0.301	0.596	0.018	0.489	25.6
1901	0.293	0.577	0.020	0.490	

MORTALITY PATTERN: WEST
MIGRATION: GRADUAL, WITH POPULATION TOTALS OBTAINED BY TREND OF R/CB

TABLE 1 FEMALE POPULATION ESTIMATES: 1801 TO 1906

DATE	R/CB RATIO	% COR- RECTION	FINAL POPULATION ESTIMATE	DATE	R/CB RATIO	% COR- RECTION	FINAL POPULATION ESTIMATE
1801	1.119	3.2	137922	1856	0.964	-0.2	191785
1806	1.130	0.0	143640	1861	0.948	-0.6	191324
1811*	1.076	0.0	146299	1866	0.923	-0.1	191321
1816*	1.033	0.0	148958	1871	0.894	0.8	189984
1821	1.007	0.0	151617	1876	0.885	-0.5	188176
1826*	0.999	0.0	160199	1881	0.856	0.5	185960
1831	1.007	0.0	168781	1886	0.838	0.3	184107
1836	1.004	0.0	174204	1891	0.824	-0.4	182142
1841	1.002	0.0	180234	1896	0.800	-0.0	178491
1846	1.000	0.0	187827	1901	0.780	0.0	174642
1851	0.979	0.4	191256	1906	0.760	-0.1	170634

NOTE: R/CB RATIO REFERS TO THE POPULATION COMPUTED BY THE BALANCE OF BIRTHS
       AND DEATHS OVER THE REPORTED POPULATION
* INTERPOLATED VALUES

TABLE 2 FEMALE BIRTH ESTIMATES: 1801-1805 TO 1901-1905

DATE	% COR- RECTION	FINAL BIRTH ESTIMATE	CRUDE BIRTH RATE	DATE	% COR- RECTION	FINAL BIRTH ESTIMATE	CRUDE BIRTH RATE
1801-1805	12.4	22954	32.6	1856-1860	0.0	28749	30.0
1806-1810	6.4	23875	32.9	1861-1865	0.0	29066	30.4
1811-1815	9.6	24074	32.6	1866-1870	0.0	28484	29.9
1816-1820	0.0	24022	32.0	1871-1875	3.0	28088	29.7
1821-1825	0.0	25286	32.4	1876-1880	0.0	27561	29.5
1826-1830	0.0	26783	32.6	1881-1885	0.0	26546	28.7
1831-1835	0.0	27427	32.0	1886-1890	0.0	25166	27.5
1836-1840	0.0	28153	31.8	1891-1895	0.0	23578	26.2
1841-1845	0.0	29991	32.6	1896-1900	0.0	21545	24.4
1846-1850	0.0	29794	31.4	1901-1905	0.0	19641	22.8
1851-1855	0.0	29441	30.7				

TABLE 3 FEMALE POPULATION ESTIMATES,
DISTRIBUTION BY AGE: 1801 TO 1906

AGE	1801	1806	1811	1816	1821	1826	1831	1836	1841	1846	1851
0- 4	19911	18031	18335	18412	18152	20328	20969	20857	21527	23216	22749
5- 9	16871	17973	15913	16197	16281	16658	18568	18809	18777	19486	20690
10-14	15143	16138	16809	14936	15325	15778	16255	17897	18178	18179	18565
15-19	13585	14479	15086	15770	14126	14844	15389	15661	17290	17592	17266
20-24	12089	12879	13420	14030	14773	13572	14344	14680	14981	16574	16475
25-29	10687	11380	11853	12389	13038	14098	13012	13569	13927	14247	15463
30-34	9389	10002	10412	10877	11439	12374	13430	12225	12786	13159	13245
35-39	8209	8733	9096	9494	9974	10792	11708	12529	11439	11999	12159
40-44	7127	7591	7895	8245	8652	9357	10149	10852	11648	10669	11026
45-49	6150	6546	6817	7108	7461	8063	8739	9341	10020	10789	9740
50-54	5234	5562	5788	6042	6328	6849	7409	7909	8481	9129	9693
55-59	4329	4608	4788	4992	5226	5660	6117	6509	6972	7509	7971
60-64	3430	3644	3792	3943	4112	4474	4817	5110	5458	5880	6242
65-69	2540	2695	2799	2911	3018	3292	3540	3731	3974	4277	4542
70-74	1701	1801	1868	1935	1999	2183	2339	2454	2599	2795	2966
75-79	971	1024	1060	1095	1121	1233	1310	1363	1438	1542	1636
80+	533	553	566	581	591	644	686	708	739	786	829

AGE	1856	1861	1866	1871	1876	1881	1886	1891	1896	1901	1906
0- 4	21982	21438	21825	21297	21005	20665	20322	19664	18361	17131	15964
5- 9	20033	19337	18911	19194	18719	18470	18316	18156	17534	16507	15534
10-14	19610	18987	18351	17918	18194	17747	17549	17447	17301	16748	15800
15-19	17473	18409	17788	17078	16605	16806	16333	16103	15961	15878	15403
20-24	15897	15939	16704	15888	15053	14429	14447	13828	13478	13424	13434
25-29	15199	14594	14599	15206	14374	13520	12888	12863	12220	11951	11969
30-34	14272	14020	13480	13454	14016	13242	12486	11932	11904	11350	11151
35-39	12152	13099	12898	12383	12365	12900	12243	11597	11080	11109	10642
40-44	11102	11107	12011	11824	11368	11376	11944	11411	10819	10389	10472
45-49	10006	10090	10131	10959	10810	10422	10504	11108	10628	10130	9781
50-54	8699	8954	9067	9112	9877	9774	9505	9661	10228	9845	9444
55-59	8401	7554	7811	7914	7973	8667	8661	8507	8656	9223	8946
60-64	6555	6911	6242	6446	6539	6603	7254	7326	7194	7391	7954
65-69	4754	4993	5291	4768	4929	5012	5130	5711	5762	5731	5966
70-74	3095	3238	3420	3613	3258	3376	3491	3632	4036	4138	4186
75-79	1696	1767	1862	1958	2069	1871	1980	2091	2168	2460	2579
80+	859	889	930	974	1023	1082	1054	1107	1162	1237	1408

TABLE 4 MARRIED WOMEN ESTIMATES,
DISTRIBUTION BY AGE: 1831 TO 1901

AGE	1831	1836	1841	1846	1851	1856	1861	1866
15-19	470	480	533	545	538	547	598	544
20-24	3849	3955	4058	4512	4503	4364	4394	3963
25-29	7244	7575	7811	8022	8731	8607	8289	8316
30-34	9393	8566	9002	9299	9377	10126	9969	9605
35-39	8713	9336	8573	9030	9161	9171	9903	9766
40-44	7677	8213	8880	8173	8451	8518	8533	9237
45-49	6257	6687	7247	7855	7090	7290	7361	7396

AGE	1871	1876	1881	1886	1891	1896	1901
15-19	658	667	577	601	491	341	471
20-24	4095	4478	4388	4300	4116	3927	3717
25-29	7668	7778	7948	7650	7644	7222	7161
30-34	9589	9272	9154	9068	8661	8686	8281
35-39	9364	9360	9391	9168	8876	8471	8539
40-44	9064	8715	8774	8882	8552	8220	7889
45-49	7955	7842	7623	7787	8178	7821	7474

TABLE 5 DEMOGRAPHIC INDICES AND FEMALE SINGULATE MEAN AGE
AT MARRIAGE: 1831 TO 1901

DATE	IF OVERALL FERTILITY	IG MARITAL FERTILITY	IH ILLEGITIMATE FERTILITY	IM PROPORTION MARRIED	SINGULATE MEAN AGE AT MARRIAGE
1831	0.341	0.688	0.018	0.482	25.8
1836	0.344	0.693	0.019	0.482	25.8
1841	0.351	0.709	0.023	0.478	25.8
1846	0.347	0.712	0.017	0.475	25.8
1851	0.338	0.685	0.018	0.480	25.7
1856	0.331	0.665	0.017	0.485	25.7
1861	0.327	0.657	0.016	0.484	25.9
1866	0.324	0.666	0.015	0.475	26.1
1871	0.324	0.674	0.012	0.471	25.8
1876	0.326	0.663	0.011	0.484	25.5
1881	0.325	0.642	0.014	0.496	25.4
1886	0.320	0.624	0.015	0.501	25.6
1891	0.311	0.607	0.012	0.501	25.9
1896	0.296	0.584	0.012	0.497	25.8
1901	0.275	0.546	0.011	0.494	

MORTALITY PATTERN: NORD
MIGRATION: FULL STRENGTH, WITH POPULATION TOTALS OBTAINED BY TREND OF R/CB

TABLE 1 FEMALE POPULATION ESTIMATES: 1801 TO 1906

DATE	R/CB RATIO	% COR-RECTION	FINAL POPULATION ESTIMATE	DATE	R/CB RATIO	% COR-RECTION	FINAL POPULATION ESTIMATE
1801	1.116	0.0	132166	1856	0.962	0.6	162585
1806	1.124	0.0	139115	1861	0.959	-0.2	162780
1811*	1.089	0.0	139238	1866	0.940	0.5	163767
1816*	1.053	0.0	139362	1871	0.921	1.3	163160
1821	1.010	0.0	139485	1876	0.928	-0.7	161798
1826*	0.997	0.0	144482	1881	0.914	-0.4	162366
1831	0.988	0.0	149479	1886	0.910	-1.3	162196
1836	1.012	0.0	157249	1891	0.885	0.1	160888
1841	1.001	0.0	160400	1896	0.869	0.7	158989
1846	1.000	0.0	164861	1901	0.860	0.4	157629
1851	0.987	-0.7	163516	1906	0.855	-0.3	156474

NOTE: R/CB RATIO REFERS TO THE POPULATION COMPUTED BY THE BALANCE OF BIRTHS
       AND DEATHS OVER THE REPORTED POPULATION
* INTERPOLATED VALUES

TABLE 2 FEMALE BIRTH ESTIMATES: 1801-1805 TO 1901-1905

DATE	% COR-RECTION	FINAL BIRTH ESTIMATE	CRUDE BIRTH RATE	DATE	% COR-RECTION	FINAL BIRTH ESTIMATE	CRUDE BIRTH RATE
1801-1805	1.8	19700	29.0	1856-1860	0.0	18986	23.3
1806-1810	0.0	20626	29.6	1861-1865	0.0	19090	23.4
1811-1815	3.2	20481	29.4	1866-1870	0.0	18448	22.6
1816-1820	0.0	21685	31.1	1871-1875	0.0	18045	22.2
1821-1825	0.0	21414	30.2	1876-1880	0.0	18559	22.9
1826-1830	0.0	22023	30.0	1881-1885	0.0	18133	22.3
1831-1835	0.0	20300	26.5	1886-1890	0.0	16790	20.8
1836-1840	0.0	20106	25.3	1891-1895	0.0	16253	20.3
1841-1845	0.0	20037	24.6	1896-1900	0.0	16092	20.3
1846-1850	0.0	19099	23.3	1901-1905	0.0	15885	20.2
1851-1855	0.0	18408	22.6				

TABLE 3 FEMALE POPULATION ESTIMATES,
DISTRIBUTION BY AGE: 1801 TO 1906

AGE	1801	1806	1811	1816	1821	1826	1831	1836	1841	1846	1851
0- 4	18397	16255	15788	15747	16603	17350	17803	16968	16595	16792	15733
5- 9	15382	16656	13872	13503	13399	14760	15423	16335	15260	15116	14924
10-14	13769	14872	15418	12840	12422	12721	14041	15118	15586	14715	14319
15-19	12488	13473	13975	14480	11984	11935	12252	13930	14580	15184	13650
20-24	11282	12180	12616	13079	13468	11477	11458	12116	13393	14160	13339
25-29	10141	10946	11337	11738	12094	12831	10959	11271	11592	12945	12990
30-34	9055	9779	10113	10472	10776	11451	12175	10714	10723	11143	12218
35-39	8031	8672	8961	9267	9538	10134	10790	11821	10130	10246	10512
40-44	7088	7643	7891	8155	8383	8914	9488	10411	11111	9623	9683
45-49	6215	6709	6914	7139	7334	7791	8299	9105	9732	10499	9083
50-54	5396	5821	6001	6186	6349	6745	7177	7880	8426	9105	9838
55-59	4580	4944	5078	5238	5369	5712	6076	6666	7142	7723	8355
60-64	3741	4035	4124	4242	4352	4644	4943	5424	5822	6315	6772
65-69	2847	3084	3125	3203	3278	3524	3758	4131	4450	4841	5189
70-74	1962	2112	2123	2160	2205	2388	2561	2824	3064	3352	3585
75-79	1139	1243	1221	1236	1254	1372	1479	1643	1802	1990	2126
80+	648	692	683	676	677	734	796	892	990	1111	1202

AGE	1856	1861	1866	1871	1876	1881	1886	1891	1896	1901	1906
0- 4	15131	15798	16190	15556	15169	15981	15628	14505	14009	14039	13984
5- 9	14046	13615	14372	14670	14066	13917	14661	14360	13308	12952	13049
10-14	14218	13421	13051	13755	14035	13523	13366	14099	13809	12827	12500
15-19	13550	13507	12739	12334	13016	13328	12779	12643	13387	13130	12158
20-24	12454	12447	12385	11556	11160	11854	12055	11550	11478	12233	11944
25-29	12485	11689	11693	11587	10781	10433	11058	11269	10806	10762	11488
30-34	12338	11892	11164	11145	11036	10305	9957	10569	10778	10356	10324
35-39	11571	11723	11345	10627	10602	10553	9845	9517	10105	10335	9945
40-44	9934	10970	11167	10790	10100	10133	10088	9416	9097	9688	9930
45-49	9122	9386	10416	10589	10224	9626	9662	9624	8978	8700	9285
50-54	8487	8549	8846	9800	9954	9673	9117	9155	9110	8527	8284
55-59	8990	7790	7903	8163	9030	9244	8991	8481	8508	8498	7980
60-64	7318	7921	6929	7010	7229	8085	8280	8061	7597	7659	7678
65-69	5556	6055	6641	5787	5841	6116	6844	7019	6825	6475	6561
70-74	3834	4155	4615	5034	4372	4509	4725	5297	5422	5322	5086
75-79	2266	2465	2744	3024	3283	2937	3032	3185	3562	3693	3659
80+	1285	1397	1567	1733	1902	2148	2110	2140	2209	2435	2619

TABLE 4 MARRIED WOMEN ESTIMATES,
DISTRIBUTION BY AGE: 1831 TO 1901

AGE	1831	1836	1841	1846	1851	1856	1861	1866
15-19	414	480	513	545	501	508	482	497
20-24	4186	4488	5035	5404	5167	4897	4969	4725
25-29	7535	7804	8094	9112	9214	8922	8415	8475
30-34	9702	8565	8620	9006	9919	10058	9733	9166
35-39	8796	9647	8310	8446	8696	9602	9757	9458
40-44	7602	8333	8943	7783	7856	8080	8943	9106
45-49	6320	6919	7453	8096	7033	7086	7311	8114

AGE	1871	1876	1881	1886	1891	1896	1901
15-19	504	604	615	494	439	501	809
20-24	4582	4769	4822	4798	4798	4791	5221
25-29	8184	7756	7807	7969	8090	8047	8095
30-34	9160	8967	8441	8290	8666	8836	8655
35-39	8846	8938	8756	8189	7986	8406	8596
40-44	8758	8200	8250	8182	7655	7384	7819
45-49	8187	7903	7469	7486	7474	6927	6658

TABLE 5 DEMOGRAPHIC INDICES AND FEMALE SINGULATE MEAN AGE
AT MARRIAGE: 1831 TO 1901

DATE	IF OVERALL FERTILITY	IG MARITAL FERTILITY	IH ILLEGITIMATE FERTILITY	IM PROPORTION MARRIED	SINGULATE MEAN AGE AT MARRIAGE
1831	0.311	0.498	0.052	0.580	24.2
1836	0.286	0.479	0.029	0.571	24.1
1841	0.279	0.474	0.026	0.564	24.1
1846	0.261	0.441	0.027	0.565	24.0
1851	0.253	0.411	0.030	0.584	23.9
1856	0.254	0.402	0.036	0.595	23.9
1861	0.262	0.411	0.039	0.598	23.9
1866	0.263	0.413	0.042	0.598	23.9
1871	0.265	0.417	0.038	0.599	23.7
1876	0.272	0.427	0.038	0.602	23.6
1881	0.274	0.430	0.044	0.596	23.7
1886	0.262	0.413	0.045	0.590	23.8
1891	0.250	0.388	0.048	0.595	23.7
1896	0.243	0.375	0.049	0.596	23.6
1901	0.238	0.362	0.047	0.605	

MORTALITY PATTERN: WEST
MIGRATION: GRADUAL, WITH UNCORRECTED POPULATION TOTALS EXCEPT FOR 1881, 1886,
  1891, 1896 AND 1901, OBTAINED BY INTERPOLATION OF R/CB BETWEEN 1876 AND 1906

TABLE 1 FEMALE POPULATION ESTIMATES: 1801 TO 1906

DATE	R/CB RATIO	% COR- RECTION	FINAL POPULATION ESTIMATE	DATE	R/CB RATIO	% COR- RECTION	FINAL POPULATION ESTIMATE
1801	1.086	5.4	104694	1856	0.901	0.0	127057
1806*	1.139	0.0	110037	1861	0.883	0.0	126530
1811*	1.112	0.0	112466	1866	0.854	0.0	125402
1816*	1.096	0.0	114896	1871	0.831	0.0	123443
1821	1.079	0.0	117325	1876	0.813	0.0	121943
1826*	1.068	0.0	121584	1881	0.764	3.0	119559
1831	1.056	0.0	125843	1886	0.748	1.6	116565
1836	1.038	0.0	129099	1891	0.709	3.3	112772
1841	1.021	0.0	132477	1896	0.692	2.1	107818
1846	1.000	0.0	135142	1901	0.667	1.8	103059
1851	0.971	0.0	133552	1906	0.652	0.0	98715

NOTE: R/CB RATIO REFERS TO THE POPULATION COMPUTED BY THE BALANCE OF BIRTHS
       AND DEATHS OVER THE REPORTED POPULATION
* INTERPOLATED VALUES

TABLE 2 FEMALE BIRTH ESTIMATES: 1801-1805 TO 1901-1905

DATE	% COR- RECTION	FINAL BIRTH ESTIMATE	CRUDE BIRTH RATE	DATE	% COR- RECTION	FINAL BIRTH ESTIMATE	CRUDE BIRTH RATE
1801-1805	10.1	15955	29.7	1856-1860	0.0	16445	25.9
1806-1810	3.7	15704	28.2	1861-1865	0.0	16985	27.0
1811-1815	0.0	15984	28.1	1866-1870	0.0	16195	26.0
1816-1820	5.2	17266	29.7	1871-1875	0.0	15456	25.2
1821-1825	2.3	17675	29.6	1876-1880	0.0	14030	23.2
1826-1830	0.0	19062	30.8	1881-1885	0.0	13595	23.0
1831-1835	0.0	19435	30.5	1886-1890	0.0	11639	20.3
1836-1840	5.3	19258	29.4	1891-1895	0.0	10232	18.6
1841-1845	0.0	19103	28.6	1896-1900	0.0	9807	18.6
1846-1850	1.8	17235	25.7	1901-1905	0.0	9370	18.6
1851-1855	0.0	16703	25.6				

TABLE 3 FEMALE POPULATION ESTIMATES,
DISTRIBUTION BY AGE: 1801 TO 1906

AGE	1801	1806	1811	1816	1821	1826	1831	1836	1841	1846	1851
0- 4	12396	13166	12700	12754	13506	14273	15191	15363	15410	15322	13447
5- 9	10993	11548	12017	11575	11529	12409	13029	13767	13991	14014	13675
10-14	10242	10753	11066	11571	11122	11167	11984	12497	13220	13389	13238
15-19	9538	10013	10299	10650	11112	10767	10779	11488	11995	12644	12584
20-24	8816	9255	9519	9831	10138	10673	10307	10248	10939	11384	11688
25-29	8100	8501	8743	9024	9289	9673	10146	9730	9693	10315	10522
30-34	7409	7770	7990	8243	8476	8815	9143	9523	9154	9092	9531
35-39	6736	7070	7264	7489	7693	7997	8282	8530	8908	8538	8359
40-44	6089	6393	6573	6769	6948	7218	7471	7683	7934	8263	7815
45-49	5468	5741	5905	6084	6238	6475	6698	6884	7099	7311	7517
50-54	4840	5081	5226	5384	5519	5728	5918	6078	6266	6446	6555
55-59	4180	4388	4513	4643	4752	4940	5098	5230	5392	5548	5629
60-64	3464	3640	3739	3837	3912	4073	4205	4308	4443	4576	4627
65-69	2689	2824	2908	2971	3014	3139	3239	3319	3426	3532	3565
70-74	1896	1988	2046	2089	2102	2187	2254	2308	2388	2466	2484
75-79	1140	1200	1233	1252	1253	1302	1337	1366	1417	1469	1475
80+	683	706	724	731	725	748	764	776	803	835	840

AGE	1856	1861	1866	1871	1876	1881	1886	1891	1896	1901	1906
0- 4	12833	12950	13492	12737	12256	11533	11190	9808	8577	8304	8159
5- 9	11626	11553	11607	12075	11480	11125	10450	10232	8939	7832	7660
10-14	12479	11090	10925	11006	11533	10923	10581	9963	9777	8535	7467
15-19	11813	11791	10243	10097	10268	10571	9916	9569	9000	8866	7640
20-24	10705	10880	10445	8956	8942	8638	8756	9027	7732	7267	7090
25-29	10227	9932	9888	9479	8158	7947	7583	7679	7001	6765	6309
30-34	9389	9542	9193	9164	8844	7580	7373	7060	7168	6541	6337
35-39	8498	8725	8824	8511	8542	8268	7080	6930	6643	6766	6197
40-44	7453	7870	8063	8167	7927	8015	7777	6713	6580	6323	6481
45-49	6943	6865	7244	7434	7575	7423	7530	7372	6376	6264	6061
50-54	6600	6307	6244	6597	6808	7024	6911	7080	6940	6025	5966
55-59	5613	5837	5592	5540	5885	6166	6384	6354	6510	6402	5618
60-64	4589	4734	4928	4713	4701	5074	5328	5587	5559	5721	5691
65-69	3531	3613	3739	3877	3735	3806	4116	4390	4595	4599	4805
70-74	2461	2508	2581	2654	2773	2746	2802	3088	3284	3463	3531
75-79	1464	1486	1528	1556	1614	1748	1733	1811	1986	2132	2303
80+	834	846	867	881	904	973	1052	1108	1152	1254	1398

[248]

TABLE 4   MARRIED WOMEN ESTIMATES,
DISTRIBUTION BY AGE: 1831 TO 1901

AGE	1831	1836	1841	1846	1851	1856	1861	1866
15-19	561	601	630	668	668	630	605	508
20-24	3447	3443	3695	3866	3989	3664	3747	3067
25-29	6025	5801	5811	6221	6376	6210	6071	6072
30-34	6389	6677	6456	6453	6796	6694	6857	6634
35-39	5977	6169	6482	6256	6153	6235	6462	6559
40-44	5296	5449	5665	5947	5648	5343	5710	5867
45-49	4480	4595	4774	4962	5120	4659	4678	4945

AGE	1871	1876	1881	1886	1891	1896	1901
15-19	593	658	689	646	507	444	512
20-24	2845	3214	3462	3457	2889	2880	2768
25-29	5202	4801	5033	5088	5118	4431	4502
30-34	6637	6000	5368	5470	5408	5516	4932
35-39	6345	6407	5993	5290	5308	5218	5361
40-44	5952	5817	5946	5681	4980	4977	4862
45-49	5073	5209	5176	5367	5285	4616	4539

TABLE 5   DEMOGRAPHIC INDICES AND FEMALE SINGULATE MEAN AGE
AT MARRIAGE: 1831 TO 1901

DATE	IF OVERALL FERTILITY	IG MARITAL FERTILITY	IH ILLEGITIMATE FERTILITY	IM PROPORTION MARRIED	SINGULATE MEAN AGE AT MARRIAGE
1831	0.336	0.628	0.040	0.503	24.1
1836	0.333	0.631	0.032	0.502	24.3
1841	0.323	0.611	0.034	0.501	24.3
1846	0.297	0.564	0.032	0.499	24.3
1851	0.275	0.517	0.031	0.501	24.4
1856	0.280	0.521	0.031	0.507	24.4
1861	0.280	0.521	0.028	0.512	24.6
1866	0.287	0.535	0.028	0.511	24.8
1871	0.288	0.541	0.022	0.512	24.5
1876	0.278	0.517	0.021	0.518	24.1
1881	0.271	0.489	0.024	0.532	23.9
1886	0.259	0.460	0.021	0.543	24.3
1891	0.235	0.417	0.021	0.541	24.6
1896	0.225	0.398	0.019	0.544	24.3
1901	0.225	0.391	0.019	0.552	

MORTALITY PATTERN: NORTH
MIGRATION: NO CORRECTION MADE FOR MIGRATION BY AGE

TABLE 1 FEMALE POPULATION ESTIMATES: 1801 TO 1906

DATE	R/CB RATIO	% COR- RECTION	FINAL POPULATION ESTIMATE	DATE	R/CB RATIO	% COR- RECTION	FINAL POPULATION ESTIMATE
1801	1.059	1.7	120917	1856	1.006	0.0	130940
1806	1.077	0.0	122144	1861	1.000	0.0	130644
1811*	1.061	1.5	123350	1866	0.998	0.0	129816
1816*	1.039	3.1	124600	1871	0.983	0.0	127359
1821	0.988	4.7	125950	1876	0.995	0.0	127025
1826*	0.979	3.1	127225	1881	1.003	0.0	126464
1831	0.982	1.5	128500	1886	1.025	0.0	127943
1836	1.006	0.0	129892	1891	1.038	0.0	128376
1841	0.996	0.0	130942	1896	1.042	0.0	126437
1846	1.000	0.0	132380	1901	1.043	0.0	124528
1851	1.007	0.0	132828	1906	1.045	0.0	123286

NOTE: R/CB RATIO REFERS TO THE POPULATION COMPUTED BY THE BALANCE OF BIRTHS
       AND DEATHS OVER THE REPORTED POPULATION
* INTERPOLATED VALUES

TABLE 2 FEMALE BIRTH ESTIMATES: 1801-1805 TO 1901-1905

DATE	% COR- RECTION	FINAL BIRTH ESTIMATE	CRUDE BIRTH RATE	DATE	% COR- RECTION	FINAL BIRTH ESTIMATE	CRUDE BIRTH RATE
1801-1805	6.0	18041	29.7	1856-1860	0.0	14363	22.0
1806-1810	0.0	17549	28.6	1861-1865	0.0	12904	19.8
1811-1815	12.0	17081	27.6	1866-1870	0.0	12492	19.4
1816-1820	0.0	18539	29.6	1871-1875	0.0	11822	18.6
1821-1825	0.0	17506	27.7	1876-1880	0.0	11924	18.8
1826-1830	0.0	17308	27.1	1881-1885	0.0	12180	19.2
1831-1835	0.0	15709	24.3	1886-1890	0.0	12256	19.1
1836-1840	0.0	15427	23.7	1891-1895	0.0	11884	18.7
1841-1845	0.0	13890	21.1	1896-1900	0.0	11238	17.9
1846-1850	0.0	13959	21.1	1901-1905	0.0	11003	17.8
1851-1855	0.0	13405	20.3				

TABLE 3 FEMALE POPULATION ESTIMATES,
DISTRIBUTION BY AGE: 1801 TO 1906

AGE	1801	1806	1811	1816	1821	1826	1831	1836	1841	1846	1851
0- 4	18481	13587	13060	12947	14385	13856	13616	12424	12558	11571	11436
5- 9	14803	15723	11515	11181	11148	12553	12100	12017	11089	11418	10434
10-14	13063	13843	14773	10835	10393	10437	11840	11593	11447	10715	11030
15-19	11728	12432	13259	14147	10215	9857	9985	11517	11175	11183	10482
20-24	10495	11120	11862	12650	13292	9656	9398	9679	11065	10883	10903
25-29	9337	9885	10535	11242	11816	12496	9153	9054	9251	10723	10554
30-34	8228	8720	9280	9901	10427	11037	11761	8753	8602	8913	10332
35-39	7184	7613	8105	8641	9112	9669	10307	11155	8259	8235	8528
40-44	6235	6596	7018	7488	7898	8395	8968	9706	10460	7859	7828
45-49	5371	5690	6043	6445	6806	7236	7741	8396	9052	9900	7430
50-54	4572	4842	5147	5482	5792	6168	6599	7165	7748	8480	9260
55-59	3786	4011	4256	4544	4810	5131	5491	5956	6469	7107	7754
60-64	2985	3162	3346	3576	3819	4090	4374	4738	5172	5715	6241
65-69	2169	2299	2421	2593	2798	3032	3244	3503	3852	4288	4691
70-74	1387	1468	1537	1650	1809	1991	2144	2307	2563	2884	3158
75-79	737	777	805	867	972	1094	1189	1280	1443	1648	1809
80+	360	376	388	412	460	528	591	648	737	857	959

AGE	1856	1861	1866	1871	1876	1881	1886	1891	1896	1901	1906
0- 4	10825	11872	10857	10483	10084	10169	10557	10567	10026	9632	9578
5- 9	10189	9770	10836	9846	9696	9314	9527	9830	9679	9262	8991
10-14	9981	9777	9425	10350	9621	9449	9190	9334	9521	9388	9025
15-19	10690	9685	9525	9085	10212	9466	9410	9086	9132	9314	9214
20-24	10125	10339	9406	9153	8937	10018	9399	9276	8862	8907	9113
25-29	10474	9744	9995	8999	8963	8726	9902	9223	9004	8605	8678
30-34	10071	10022	9370	9514	8765	8706	8582	9668	8906	8702	8348
35-39	9789	9575	9581	8870	9213	8466	8515	8334	9281	8561	8401
40-44	8027	9250	9101	9019	8540	8849	8234	8224	7954	8873	8222
45-49	7327	7544	8746	8524	8639	8159	8562	7911	7807	7565	8478
50-54	6879	6816	7063	8112	8084	8173	7819	8147	7436	7355	7161
55-59	8378	6265	6254	6425	7541	7498	7681	7297	7504	6874	6837
60-64	6732	7348	5548	5498	5765	6755	6809	6929	6486	6709	6191
65-69	5059	5541	6126	4599	4645	4865	5784	5795	5795	5475	5717
70-74	3406	3758	4190	4619	3526	3560	3789	4480	4394	4457	4265
75-79	1948	2172	2455	2740	3061	2339	2404	2546	2933	2937	3029
80+	1042	1166	1337	1524	1733	1952	1780	1729	1716	1913	2038

[251]

TABLE 4 MARRIED WOMEN ESTIMATES,
DISTRIBUTION BY AGE: 1831 TO 1901

AGE	1831	1836	1841	1846	1851	1856	1861	1866
15-19	607	709	696	706	670	692	763	758
20-24	4334	4501	5193	5154	5210	4880	5026	4824
25-29	6747	6711	6901	8050	7971	7951	7438	7667
30-34	9488	7091	7011	7308	8517	8335	8332	7817
35-39	8325	9046	6744	6772	7054	8127	7985	8013
40-44	6963	7568	8227	6236	6256	6438	7456	7354
45-49	5689	6200	6763	7485	5670	5613	5813	6754

AGE	1871	1876	1881	1886	1891	1896	1901
15-19	645	687	606	560	508	487	568
20-24	4630	4493	4811	4468	4421	4221	4067
25-29	6960	6897	6759	7479	6909	6816	6548
30-34	7944	7313	7260	7201	7957	7264	7134
35-39	7409	7713	7060	7122	6974	7651	6944
40-44	7257	6882	7142	6671	6643	6436	7014
45-49	6532	6626	6264	6607	6067	5992	5735

TABLE 5 DEMOGRAPHIC INDICES AND FEMALE SINGULATE MEAN AGE
AT MARRIAGE: 1831 TO 1901

DATE	IF OVERALL FERTILITY	IG MARITAL FERTILITY	IH ILLEGITIMATE FERTILITY	IM PROPORTION MARRIED	SINGULATE MEAN AGE AT MARRIAGE
1831	0.274	0.408	0.050	0.627	22.8
1836	0.261	0.384	0.068	0.612	22.9
1841	0.249	0.380	0.047	0.606	22.8
1846	0.234	0.357	0.039	0.613	22.8
1851	0.227	0.339	0.039	0.626	22.8
1856	0.230	0.339	0.042	0.634	22.7
1861	0.229	0.331	0.045	0.645	22.5
1866	0.220	0.315	0.039	0.655	22.5
1871	0.220	0.314	0.043	0.653	22.6
1876	0.216	0.313	0.042	0.642	22.7
1881	0.219	0.319	0.047	0.635	22.9
1886	0.222	0.316	0.057	0.636	23.0
1891	0.220	0.314	0.057	0.636	23.0
1896	0.214	0.302	0.062	0.634	23.0
1901	0.209	0.298	0.061	0.624	

AUDE

MORTALITY PATTERN: WEST
MIGRATION: NO CORRECTION MADE FOR MIGRATION BY AGE

TABLE 1 FEMALE POPULATION ESTIMATES: 1801 TO 1906

DATE	R/CB RATIO	% COR-RECTION	FINAL POPULATION ESTIMATE	DATE	R/CB RATIO	% COR-RECTION	FINAL POPULATION ESTIMATE
1801	1.014	2.9	113654	1856	0.971	0.0	142543
1806	1.044	0.0	118339	1861	0.942	1.3	142111
1811*	1.010	0.0	120679	1866	0.943	0.0	142475
1816*	0.999	0.0	123018	1871	0.935	0.0	141986
1821	1.000	0.0	125358	1876	0.977	0.0	147680
1826*	1.000	0.0	129573	1881	1.042	0.0	159857
1831	1.003	0.0	133788	1886	1.050	0.0	163002
1836	1.017	0.0	138653	1891	0.998	0.0	155302
1841	1.004	0.0	140398	1896	0.989	0.0	152909
1846	1.000	0.0	143354	1901	1.008	0.0	155577
1851	0.985	0.0	142891	1906	0.991	0.0	153462

NOTE: R/CB RATIO REFERS TO THE POPULATION COMPUTED BY THE BALANCE OF BIRTHS
       AND DEATHS OVER THE REPORTED POPULATION
* INTERPOLATED VALUES

TABLE 2 FEMALE BIRTH ESTIMATES: 1801-1805 TO 1901-1905

DATE	% COR-RECTION	FINAL BIRTH ESTIMATE	CRUDE BIRTH RATE	DATE	% COR-RECTION	FINAL BIRTH ESTIMATE	CRUDE BIRTH RATE
1801-1805	0.0	19141	33.0	1856-1860	6.2	18433	25.9
1806-1810	0.0	20039	33.5	1861-1865	0.0	18494	26.0
1811-1815	0.0	19465	31.9	1866-1870	0.0	18026	25.3
1816-1820	0.0	19271	31.0	1871-1875	0.0	17710	24.5
1821-1925	0.0	19978	31.3	1876-1880	0.0	19129	24.9
1826-1830	0.0	19894	30.2	1881-1885	0.0	19972	24.7
1831-1835	0.0	20455	30.0	1886-1890	0.0	17563	22.1
1836-1840	0.0	20188	28.9	1891-1895	0.0	15573	20.2
1841-1845	0.0	19593	27.6	1896-1900	0.0	14942	19.4
1846-1850	1.5	18452	25.8	1901-1905	0.0	14798	19.2
1851-1855	0.0	18126	25.4				

TABLE 3 FEMALE POPULATION ESTIMATES,
DISTRIBUTION BY AGE: 1801 TO 1906

AGE	1801	1806	1811	1816	1821	1826	1831	1836	1841	1846	1851
0- 4	13717	14736	15367	14715	14393	15347	15439	15772	15499	15383	14199
5- 9	11942	12410	13074	13681	13108	13002	13927	14054	14131	14091	13770
10-14	11189	11588	11709	12498	13179	12705	12620	13630	13454	13670	13453
15-19	10469	10851	10928	11189	12035	12768	12326	12346	13042	13008	13045
20-24	9704	10055	10143	10340	10660	11545	12270	11938	11704	12498	12300
25-29	8925	9244	9329	9519	9765	10144	11008	11785	11228	11132	11727
30-34	8146	8445	8525	8695	8923	9229	9608	10500	11013	10615	10380
35-39	7389	7654	7739	7890	8090	8375	8683	9100	9747	10345	9833
40-44	6653	6900	6972	7116	7292	7545	7831	8170	8395	9101	9524
45-49	5960	6169	6242	6367	6530	6753	7006	7317	7486	7785	8321
50-54	5241	5435	5494	5605	5742	5948	6169	6437	6595	6833	7005
55-59	4476	4641	4708	4790	4900	5078	5279	5501	5639	5856	5977
60-64	3644	3773	3838	3905	3973	4124	4293	4476	4592	4778	4885
65-69	2743	2850	2907	2952	2993	3101	3239	3373	3474	3625	3709
70-74	1846	1923	1977	2002	2019	2094	2187	2278	2351	2468	2529
75-79	1051	1089	1130	1145	1145	1188	1245	1291	1340	1415	1456
80+	557	577	597	609	611	629	658	685	708	751	778

AGE	1856	1861	1866	1871	1876	1881	1886	1891	1896	1901	1906
0- 4	14017	14268	14448	13963	14222	16404	16236	13650	12553	12711	12438
5- 9	12752	12578	12890	13019	13149	13946	15234	14311	12517	11966	11814
10-14	13179	12183	12083	12389	13133	13629	13683	14133	13832	12475	11555
15-19	12870	12584	11697	11607	12492	13605	13365	12687	13653	13777	12039
20-24	12366	12179	11976	11134	11591	12835	13233	12297	12160	13503	13212
25-29	11572	11615	11505	11312	11030	11828	12399	12096	11707	11956	12880
30-34	10964	10802	10906	10789	11132	11192	11363	11274	11455	11456	11355
35-39	9642	10169	10078	10169	10555	11229	10688	10274	10615	11151	10830
40-44	9078	8889	9431	9341	9876	10586	10663	9611	9620	10280	10490
45-49	8733	8312	8187	8681	9009	9839	9985	9525	8933	9255	9608
50-54	7509	7870	7536	7416	8235	8840	9142	8789	8729	8481	8536
55-59	6147	6581	6942	6637	6833	7872	8002	7846	7851	8085	7648
60-64	5003	5141	5543	5830	5822	6250	6819	6582	6713	6986	7023
65-69	3806	3897	4034	4330	4748	4977	5061	5253	5270	5613	5720
70-74	2599	2568	2754	2834	3163	3667	3642	3531	3807	4005	4191
75-79	1499	1542	1598	1635	1743	2080	2286	2171	2184	2484	2580
80+	806	833	867	891	946	1079	1202	1271	1300	1395	1542

[254]

TABLE 4 MARRIED WOMEN ESTIMATES,
DISTRIBUTICN BY AGE: 1831 TO 1901

AGE	1831	1836	1841	1846	1851	1856	1861	1866
15-19	1290	1214	1209	1140	1085	1019	992	926
20-24	6732	6384	6103	6352	6090	5970	5722	4864
25-29	8375	8892	8411	8271	8634	8450	8377	8207
30-34	7699	8375	8769	8426	8208	8655	8457	8494
35-39	6886	7183	7698	8162	7744	7610	7958	7863
40-44	6029	6251	6436	6975	7289	6982	6759	7154
45-49	5123	5306	5451	5672	6056	6410	6004	5898

AGE	1871	1876	1881	1886	1891	1896	1901
15-19	976	1187	1294	1196	867	746	956
20-24	5100	5662	6660	6840	6004	5686	6080
25-29	7398	7746	8530	9251	9020	8537	8721
30-34	8355	8269	8526	8885	8918	9110	9039
35-39	7893	8144	8408	8314	7983	8322	8802
40-44	7046	7403	7769	8035	7212	7193	7732
45-49	6208	6388	6764	7243	6807	6343	6514

TABLE 5 DEMOGRAPHIC INDICES AND FEMALE SINGULATE MEAN AGE
AT MARRIAGE: 1831 TO 1901

DATE	IF OVERALL FERTILITY	IG MARITAL FERTILITY	IH ILLEGITIMATE FERTILITY	IM PROPORTION MARRIED	SINGULATE MEAN AGE AT MARRIAGE
1831	0.319	0.485	0.043	0.623	22.1
1836	0.310	0.471	0.046	0.623	22.1
1841	0.300	0.462	0.039	0.616	22.3
1846	0.280	0.440	0.030	0.610	22.4
1851	0.270	0.428	0.027	0.604	22.5
1856	0.269	0.429	0.028	0.601	22.7
1861	0.273	0.439	0.028	0.596	23.0
1866	0.273	0.448	0.027	0.584	23.1
1871	0.273	0.450	0.024	0.585	22.8
1876	0.273	0.447	0.019	0.593	22.6
1881	0.271	0.439	0.021	0.598	22.5
1886	0.257	0.405	0.024	0.613	22.6
1891	0.238	0.376	0.024	0.607	22.9
1896	0.217	0.351	0.022	0.593	22.9
1901	0.203	0.330	0.020	0.590	

MORTALITY PATTERN: WEST
MIGRATION: GRADUAL, WITH POPULATION TOTALS OBTAINED BY INTERPOLATION OF R/CB
LINEARLY BETWEEN 1846 AND 1876, AND BETWEEN 1876 AND 1906

TABLE 1   FEMALE POPULATION ESTIMATES: 1801 TO 1906

DATE	R/CB RATIO	% COR-RECTION	FINAL POPULATION ESTIMATE	DATE	R/CB RATIO	% COR-RECTION	FINAL POPULATION ESTIMATE
1801	1.246	1.7	161800	1856	0.972	1.5	200421
1806	1.205	1.7	169845	1861	0.959	0.9	200331
1811*	1.119	1.7	170525	1866	0.936	1.8	203596
1816*	1.057	1.7	171205	1871	0.919	2.3	206542
1821	1.026	1.7	171885	1876	0.925	0.0	207134
1826*	1.017	1.7	177151	1881	0.891	0.8	208862
1831	1.008	1.7	182418	1886	0.877	-0.7	207058
1836	1.014	1.7	188309	1891	0.827	1.8	204374
1841	1.003	1.7	191845	1896	0.802	1.6	198010
1846	1.000	1.7	198193	1901	0.780	1.0	192250
1851	0.984	1.8	200724	1906	0.760	0.0	187138

NOTE: R/CB RATIO REFERS TO THE POPULATION COMPUTED BY THE BALANCE OF BIRTHS
        AND DEATHS OVER THE REPORTED POPULATION
* INTERPOLATED VALUES

TABLE 2   FEMALE BIRTH ESTIMATES: 1801-1805 TO 1901-1905

DATE	% COR-RECTION	FINAL BIRTH ESTIMATE	CRUDE BIRTH RATE	DATE	% COR-RECTION	FINAL BIRTH ESTIMATE	CRUDE BIRTH RATE
1801-1805	37.7	27652	33.4	1856-1860	3.5	28906	28.9
1806-1810	28.9	27849	32.7	1861-1865	0.0	29698	29.4
1811-1815	24.5	26988	31.6	1866-1870	0.0	30743	30.0
1816-1820	16.1	26099	30.4	1871-1875	0.0	30231	29.2
1821-1825	4.0	25807	29.6	1876-1880	0.0	31287	30.1
1826-1830	0.0	26013	28.9	1881-1885	0.0	29322	28.2
1831-1835	0.0	26834	29.0	1886-1890	0.0	26065	25.3
1836-1840	0.0	26918	28.3	1891-1895	0.0	22807	22.7
1841-1845	0.0	27981	28.7	1896-1900	0.0	21957	22.5
1846-1850	0.0	27537	27.6	1901-1905	0.0	21272	22.4
1851-1855	1.7	27058	27.0				

TABLE 3 FEMALE POPULATION ESTIMATES,
DISTRIBUTION BY AGE: 1801 TO 1906

AGE	1801	1806	1811	1816	1821	1826	1831	1836	1841	1846	1851
0- 4	21595	22211	21603	20805	19657	20211	20576	20865	20985	22270	21644
5- 9	18700	19685	19472	19003	18322	17827	18390	18734	18849	19220	20136
10-14	17015	17947	18132	18085	17900	17680	17198	17922	18014	18308	18434
15-19	15474	16322	16522	16832	17028	17264	17048	16754	17226	17488	17513
20-24	13968	14729	14913	15214	15638	16277	16505	16450	15959	16580	16523
25-29	12539	13208	13372	13639	14077	14894	15451	15799	15552	15251	15605
30-34	11198	11795	11930	12162	12538	13275	14055	14693	14845	14775	14304
35-39	9938	10473	10595	10787	11105	11748	12450	13275	13717	14017	13779
40-44	8777	9244	9357	9526	9788	10343	10954	11685	12319	12876	13002
45-49	7703	8110	8204	8357	8584	9054	9579	10210	10770	11485	11867
50-54	6666	7013	7094	7218	7408	7816	8257	8783	9262	9887	10425
55-59	5621	5917	5984	6081	6217	6561	6938	7355	7749	8277	8736
60-64	4555	4781	4842	4910	4990	5256	5567	5886	6193	6618	6984
65-69	3449	3628	3668	3715	3743	3929	4161	4386	4616	4935	5209
70-74	2377	2487	2523	2544	2542	2653	2806	2941	3095	3317	3502
75-79	1395	1464	1480	1491	1468	1526	1609	1672	1758	1889	1999
80+	815	832	836	836	818	836	873	901	936	1002	1062

AGE	1856	1861	1866	1871	1876	1881	1886	1891	1896	1901	1906
0- 4	20776	21981	23412	24123	23445	25212	23455	21505	18501	17997	17847
5- 9	19351	18475	19893	21139	21633	21192	22683	21327	19403	16727	16397
10-14	19236	18446	17739	19091	20224	20619	20133	21654	20343	18516	15928
15-19	17515	18190	17553	16808	17953	18644	18789	18236	19704	18523	16712
20-24	16342	16161	16915	16162	15142	15344	15481	15308	14713	16307	15056
25-29	15415	15146	15105	15749	14869	13519	13459	13497	13295	12821	14339
30-34	14547	14325	14215	14155	14690	13822	12473	12470	12488	12343	11926
35-39	13260	13449	13388	13272	13163	13696	12841	11654	11632	11687	11601
40-44	12709	12205	12522	12460	12316	12303	12796	12113	10974	10983	11097
45-49	11917	11629	11299	11592	11509	11487	11483	12071	11413	10370	10442
50-54	10708	10736	10612	10312	10558	10622	10621	10753	11275	10692	9797
55-59	9143	9370	9536	9423	9135	9503	9573	9712	9800	10300	9859
60-64	7293	7602	7935	8063	7926	7810	8107	8297	8369	8485	9014
65-69	5420	5628	6005	6253	6309	6343	6228	6595	6690	6790	6982
70-74	3631	3750	4008	4262	4398	4569	4569	4598	4810	4918	5082
75-79	2061	2116	2267	2411	2533	2718	2803	2891	2860	3024	3165
80+	1097	1120	1192	1268	1332	1459	1563	1692	1741	1769	1894

TABLE 4 MARRIED WOMEN ESTIMATES,
DISTRIBUTION BY AGE: 1831 TO 1901

AGE	1831	1836	1841	1846	1851	1856	1861	1866
15-19	624	635	676	713	743	774	1125	909
20-24	4197	4308	4315	4631	4768	4868	4976	4842
25-29	7664	8010	8081	8118	8503	8576	8613	8783
30-34	8682	9223	9509	9650	9514	9812	9813	9897
35-39	8176	8827	9295	9670	9660	9386	9636	9721
40-44	7323	7863	8431	8952	9161	8988	8702	9020
45-49	5959	6388	6885	7488	7863	7907	7780	7647

AGE	1871	1876	1881	1886	1891	1896	1901
15-19	746	903	1103	1031	678	609	688
20-24	4869	5032	5306	4977	4836	4909	5404
25-29	8390	8387	8359	8410	7868	7784	8104
30-34	9981	9716	9540	9155	9168	8793	8737
35-39	9715	9733	9773	9399	8841	8855	8657
40-44	8999	8950	9092	9180	8804	8212	8201
45-49	7844	7829	7985	8067	8492	8127	7407

TABLE 5 DEMOGRAPHIC INDICES AND FEMALE SINGULATE MEAN AGE
AT MARRIAGE: 1831 TO 1901

DATE	IF OVERALL FERTILITY	IG MARITAL FERTILITY	IH ILLEGITIMATE FERTILITY	IM PROPORTION MARRIED	SINGULATE MEAN AGE AT MARRIAGE
1831	0.298	0.660	0.028	0.428	25.6
1836	0.296	0.637	0.027	0.442	25.7
1841	0.301	0.633	0.026	0.454	25.5
1846	0.300	0.624	0.022	0.463	25.4
1851	0.296	0.605	0.021	0.471	25.2
1856	0.307	0.618	0.021	0.478	25.0
1861	0.323	0.638	0.024	0.486	25.0
1866	0.331	0.658	0.022	0.486	25.2
1871	0.338	0.673	0.020	0.486	25.0
1876	0.345	0.682	0.018	0.493	24.5
1881	0.345	0.665	0.019	0.505	24.6
1886	0.322	0.622	0.019	0.503	25.2
1891	0.291	0.570	0.020	0.493	25.4
1896	0.269	0.534	0.017	0.488	25.0
1901	0.258	0.508	0.015	0.494	

[258]

MORTALITY PATTERN: WEST
MIGRATION: NO CORRECTION MADE FOR MIGRATION BY AGE

TABLE 1   FEMALE POPULATION ESTIMATES: 1801 TO 1906

DATE	R/CB RATIO	% CORRECTION	FINAL POPULATION ESTIMATE	DATE	R/CB RATIO	% CORRECTION	FINAL POPULATION ESTIMATE
1801	0.941	7.1	257108	1856	0.999	0.0	252918
1806	1.015	0.0	262349	1861	1.008	0.0	251581
1811*	1.006	0.0	262766	1866	1.008	0.0	247287
1816*	0.997	0.0	263183	1871	0.990	0.0	237402
1821	0.992	0.0	263600	1876	1.013	0.0	234793
1826*	0.989	0.0	263340	1881	1.001	0.0	228574
1831	0.989	0.0	263080	1886	0.991	0.0	223997
1836	1.005	0.0	266323	1891	1.017	0.0	226129
1841	0.991	0.0	262399	1896	1.005	0.0	218026
1846	1.000	0.0	263032	1901	0.996	0.0	212559
1851	0.995	0.0	257629	1906	0.990	0.0	209678

NOTE: R/CB RATIO REFERS TO THE POPULATION COMPUTED BY THE BALANCE OF BIRTHS
        AND DEATHS OVER THE REPORTED POPULATION
* INTERPOLATED VALUES

TABLE 2   FEMALE BIRTH ESTIMATES: 1801-1805 TO 1901-1905

DATE	% CORRECTION	FINAL BIRTH ESTIMATE	CRUDE BIRTH RATE	DATE	% CORRECTION	FINAL BIRTH ESTIMATE	CRUDE BIRTH RATE
1801-1805	0.0	28163	21.7	1856-1860	0.0	23675	18.8
1806-1810	0.0	27516	21.0	1861-1865	0.0	23812	19.1
1811-1815	6.4	27782	21.1	1866-1870	0.0	22990	19.0
1816-1820	0.9	26952	20.5	1871-1875	0.0	22392	19.0
1821-1825	0.0	27318	20.7	1876-1880	0.0	22243	19.2
1826-1830	0.0	26295	20.0	1881-1885	0.0	22092	19.5
1831-1835	0.0	25838	19.5	1886-1890	0.0	21851	19.4
1836-1840	0.0	25006	18.9	1891-1895	0.0	21061	19.0
1841-1845	0.0	23656	18.0	1896-1900	0.0	20670	19.2
1846-1850	0.0	22879	17.6	1901-1905	0.0	20646	19.6
1851-1855	0.0	22869	17.9				

TABLE 3 FEMALE POPULATION ESTIMATES,
DISTRIBUTION BY AGE: 1801 TO 1906

AGE	1801	1806	1811	1816	1821	1826	1831	1836	1841	1846	1851
0- 4	27390	23833	22936	23137	22579	22620	21904	21938	20993	20318	19136
5- 9	24855	25837	22157	21325	21602	21010	21141	20806	20412	19978	18968
10-14	23557	24459	25066	21510	20770	21057	20555	20991	20137	20202	19470
15-19	22297	23169	23717	24321	20939	20236	20590	20397	20304	19918	19678
20-24	20380	21781	22312	22854	23514	20253	19646	20290	19601	19953	19268
25-29	19632	20380	20857	21377	21971	22607	19545	19246	19394	19160	19192
30-34	18298	18982	19425	19890	20457	21019	21710	19056	18316	18873	18343
35-39	16957	17604	18003	18431	18940	19468	20081	21060	18049	17740	17979
40-44	15637	16231	16610	16994	17461	17928	18501	19378	19848	17395	16813
45-49	14317	14870	15216	15578	15996	16420	16927	17738	18145	19006	16379
50-54	12952	13429	13749	14074	14463	14830	15286	16004	16387	17144	17650
55-59	11435	11869	12130	12422	12765	13088	13477	14113	14454	15137	15552
60-64	9712	10076	10308	10535	10835	11091	11422	11957	12270	12853	13200
65-69	7740	8051	8231	8419	8644	8837	9091	9525	9793	10280	10540
70-74	5621	5839	5984	6115	6286	6402	6580	6891	7110	7479	7669
75-79	3522	3648	3732	3822	3928	3992	4090	4285	4435	4682	4797
80+	2219	2290	2333	2380	2449	2482	2537	2649	2750	2917	2994

AGE	1856	1861	1866	1871	1876	1881	1886	1891	1896	1901	1906
0- 4	18993	20070	19902	18704	18425	18470	18530	18735	17127	17123	17458
5- 9	17899	17974	18779	18223	17597	17081	17208	17761	17200	15882	16050
10-14	18607	17686	17585	18027	18121	17033	16572	17234	17121	16676	15487
15-19	19089	18375	17294	16871	17917	17530	16516	16587	16605	16591	16252
20-24	19151	18722	17841	16470	16631	17213	16886	16417	15862	15977	16064
25-29	18638	18675	18072	16888	16125	15887	16490	16687	15601	15174	15387
30-34	18471	18090	17941	17021	16441	15331	15151	16219	15777	14852	14549
35-39	17560	17838	17289	16808	16473	15554	14551	14827	15251	14943	14173
40-44	17119	16871	16960	16111	16174	15504	14688	14166	13867	14370	14189
45-49	15903	16341	15936	15701	15400	15123	14546	14206	13161	12981	13557
50-54	15273	14972	15221	14544	14782	14202	13998	13875	13009	12149	12082
55-59	16060	14044	13618	13556	13338	13315	12847	13040	12396	11727	11055
60-64	13580	14197	12273	11641	11896	11550	11591	11502	11175	10735	10271
65-69	10815	11289	11659	9846	9548	9687	9467	9755	9242	9095	8858
70-74	7836	8178	8426	8488	7296	7072	7232	7244	7108	6837	6839
75-79	4885	5095	5242	5257	5356	4646	4548	4755	4518	4516	4432
80+	3040	3165	3249	3246	3274	3376	3177	3119	3005	2933	2976

TABLE 4 MARRIED WOMEN ESTIMATES,
DISTRIBUTION BY AGE: 1831 TO 1901

AGE	1831	1836	1841	1846	1851	1856	1861	1866
15-19	813	835	865	886	917	936	954	925
20-24	5652	6018	6007	6327	6327	6514	6610	6360
25-29	10498	10559	10882	10997	11261	11166	11435	11291
30-34	14105	12557	12263	12840	12668	12919	12836	12881
35-39	13702	14510	12592	12539	12853	12656	13001	12694
40-44	12815	13460	13892	12284	11957	12207	12127	12222
45-49	11001	11549	11925	12631	10977	10676	11079	10822

AGE	1871	1876	1881	1886	1891	1896	1901
15-19	982	1131	1053	928	778	662	781
20-24	6199	6513	6422	6208	6088	5850	5777
25-29	10501	10346	10416	10387	10507	10004	9936
30-34	12314	11829	11246	11197	11768	11497	10957
35-39	12356	12192	11510	10809	11084	11316	11085
40-44	11533	11823	11268	10530	10203	10050	10298
45-49	10530	10346	10333	9838	9623	8959	8750

TABLE 5 DEMOGRAPHIC INDICES AND FEMALE SINGULATE MEAN AGE
AT MARRIAGE: 1831 TO 1901

DATE	IF OVERALL FERTILITY	IG MARITAL FERTILITY	IH ILLEGITIMATE FERTILITY	IM PROPORTION MARRIED	SINGULATE MEAN AGE AT MARRIAGE
1831	0.215	0.397	0.045	0.482	25.3
1836	0.211	0.383	0.048	0.487	25.1
1841	0.209	0.381	0.043	0.492	25.0
1846	0.202	0.365	0.039	0.500	24.8
1851	0.202	0.355	0.044	0.509	24.6
1856	0.208	0.360	0.045	0.519	24.4
1861	0.215	0.365	0.045	0.531	24.3
1866	0.219	0.361	0.051	0.541	24.1
1871	0.224	0.365	0.054	0.546	23.9
1876	0.222	0.361	0.053	0.548	23.8
1881	0.226	0.367	0.058	0.545	23.9
1886	0.229	0.372	0.062	0.540	24.1
1891	0.222	0.361	0.058	0.541	24.2
1896	0.221	0.359	0.058	0.542	24.2
1901	0.222	0.364	0.055	0.542	

MORTALITY PATTERN: WEST
MIGRATION: GRADUAL, WITH POPULATION TOTALS OBTAINED BY TREND OF R/CB

TABLE 1 FEMALE POPULATION ESTIMATES: 1801 TO 1906

DATE	R/CB RATIO	% COR-RECTION	FINAL POPULATION ESTIMATE	DATE	R/CB RATIO	% COR-RECTION	FINAL POPULATION ESTIMATE
1801	0.994	11.9	131586	1856	0.944	-0.7	130917
1806	1.098	0.0	132396	1861	0.916	0.2	128042
1811*	1.086	0.0	132600	1866	0.893	0.6	126193
1816*	1.056	0.0	132804	1871	0.867	1.4	124061
1821	1.046	0.0	133008	1876	0.854	0.6	122501
1826*	1.034	0.0	134098	1881	0.834	0.6	121393
1831	1.020	0.0	135188	1886	0.815	0.6	120057
1836	1.034	0.0	137627	1891	0.803	-0.3	118263
1841	1.015	0.5	137433	1896	0.787	-0.8	115662
1846	1.000	0.0	137239	1901	0.769	-0.9	113432
1851	0.969	-1.2	132858	1906	0.743	-0.1	111535

NOTE: R/CB RATIO REFERS TO THE POPULATION COMPUTED BY THE BALANCE OF BIRTHS
       AND DEATHS OVER THE REPORTED POPULATION
* INTERPOLATED VALUES

TABLE 2 FEMALE BIRTH ESTIMATES: 1801-1805 TO 1901-1905

DATE	% COR-RECTION	FINAL BIRTH ESTIMATE	CRUDE BIRTH RATE	DATE	% COR-RECTION	FINAL BIRTH ESTIMATE	CRUDE BIRTH RATE
1801-1805	9.9	16550	25.1	1856-1860	0.6	14608	22.6
1806-1810	0.0	17029	25.7	1861-1865	0.0	15143	23.8
1811-1815	6.8	17201	25.9	1866-1870	2.1	15120	24.2
1816-1820	3.8	16194	24.4	1871-1875	0.0	14951	24.3
1821-1825	0.0	16752	25.1	1876-1880	0.0	14276	23.4
1826-1830	0.0	17179	25.5	1881-1885	0.0	13798	22.9
1831-1835	0.0	16827	24.7	1886-1890	0.0	13743	23.1
1836-1840	0.0	16464	23.9	1891-1895	0.0	12429	21.3
1841-1845	0.0	16423	23.9	1896-1900	0.0	12504	21.8
1846-1850	3.9	15956	23.6	1901-1905	0.0	12047	21.4
1851-1855	0.0	15254	23.1				

TABLE 3 FEMALE POPULATION ESTIMATES,
DISTRIBUTION BY AGE: 1801 TO 1906

AGE	1801	1806	1811	1816	1821	1826	1831	1836	1841	1846	1851
0- 4	13526	13359	13471	13904	13023	13590	13939	13559	13271	13389	12616
5- 9	12250	12394	12141	12260	12724	11964	12469	12928	12400	12155	11933
10-14	11745	11819	11936	11586	11829	12294	11536	12266	12445	11897	11386
15-19	11250	11326	11377	11384	11173	11423	11848	11343	11802	11934	11058
20-24	10696	10764	10810	10771	10891	10707	10925	11549	10829	11235	10882
25-29	10092	10168	10201	10172	10236	10370	10176	10573	10955	10247	10290
30-34	9476	9542	9580	9551	9615	9696	9804	9791	9976	10315	9408
35-39	8849	8910	8936	8922	8976	9057	9117	9375	9186	9344	9435
40-44	8213	8274	8295	8278	8338	8409	8469	8667	8747	8558	8514
45-49	7570	7628	7651	7634	7684	7759	7812	7997	8033	8097	7753
50-54	6877	6928	6946	6941	6982	7047	7104	7262	7304	7330	7235
55-59	6084	6136	6142	6149	6188	6244	6293	6429	6467	6506	6389
60-64	5155	5202	5200	5219	5250	5305	5347	5442	5486	5531	5429
65-69	4074	4127	4115	4146	4170	4217	4258	4314	4349	4405	4326
70-74	2906	2953	2946	2977	2997	3035	3068	3098	3122	3171	3123
75-79	1768	1799	1791	1826	1836	1865	1888	1896	1915	1952	1923
80+	1054	1068	1060	1083	1096	1115	1134	1138	1146	1173	1159

AGE	1856	1861	1866	1871	1876	1881	1886	1891	1896	1901	1906
0- 4	12243	11620	12155	12107	12180	11958	11669	11563	10554	10677	10520
5- 9	11459	11070	10544	11009	11036	11220	11050	10752	10693	9766	9974
10-14	11415	10948	10595	10077	10544	10599	10791	10624	10351	10300	9410
15-19	10812	10790	10332	9937	9410	9832	9850	9998	9815	9554	9499
20-24	10298	9952	9874	9309	8836	8214	8509	8423	8488	8317	8020
25-29	10179	9571	9233	9101	8540	8063	7426	7663	7556	7627	7454
30-34	9645	9520	8970	8638	8538	8042	7596	6975	7216	7121	7209
35-39	8781	8987	8900	8378	8100	8057	7605	7177	6602	6843	6778
40-44	8770	8154	8378	8299	7855	7655	7643	7218	6838	6299	6560
45-49	7868	8099	7563	7777	7749	7399	7244	7239	6868	6517	6037
50-54	7065	7166	7412	6930	7175	7222	6934	6796	6826	6489	6197
55-59	6428	6270	6393	6618	6239	6535	6615	6356	6265	6305	6040
60-64	5432	5448	5343	5445	5686	5435	5724	5789	5593	5527	5612
65-69	4322	4304	4344	4256	4386	4661	4485	4714	4798	4651	4649
70-74	3118	3094	3105	3129	3108	3273	3506	3362	3560	3639	3577
75-79	1922	1902	1905	1907	1955	1996	2122	2262	2189	2330	2425
80+	1159	1147	1146	1144	1166	1233	1290	1354	1450	1470	1574

TABLE 4   MARRIED WOMEN ESTIMATES,
DISTRIBUTION BY AGE: 1831 TO 1901

AGE	1831	1836	1841	1846	1851	1856	1861	1866
15-19	277	275	297	312	301	306	290	278
20-24	2408	2624	2543	2727	2728	2668	2668	2173
25-29	4631	4923	5232	5015	5152	5211	5018	4953
30-34	5551	5640	5868	6187	5738	5978	6009	5760
35-39	5447	5677	5671	5870	6005	5658	5883	5910
40-44	5022	5183	5325	5290	5310	5513	5198	5404
45-49	4320	4452	4568	4684	4519	4614	4824	4560

AGE	1871	1876	1881	1886	1891	1896	1901
15-19	304	323	353	355	305	280	414
20-24	2332	2530	2509	2731	2686	2662	2614
25-29	4254	4363	4512	4314	4618	4556	4638
30-34	5651	5128	5110	5110	4813	5129	5075
35-39	5658	5523	5266	5149	5013	4718	4999
40-44	5440	5175	5151	5058	4861	4707	4405
45-49	4778	4771	4678	4681	4701	4496	4263

TABLE 5   DEMOGRAPHIC INDICES AND FEMALE SINGULATE MEAN AGE
AT MARRIAGE: 1831 TO 1901

DATE	IF OVERALL FERTILITY	IG MARITAL FERTILITY	IH ILLEGITIMATE FERTILITY	IM PROPORTION MARRIED	SINGULATE MEAN AGE AT MARRIAGE
1831	0.278	0.663	0.031	0.390	25.3
1836	0.266	0.621	0.030	0.399	25.6
1841	0.263	0.600	0.029	0.410	25.4
1846	0.258	0.583	0.026	0.417	25.3
1851	0.257	0.564	0.028	0.428	25.2
1856	0.252	0.541	0.026	0.438	25.1
1861	0.257	0.540	0.029	0.447	25.3
1866	0.268	0.571	0.028	0.442	25.4
1871	0.277	0.592	0.028	0.442	25.1
1876	0.281	0.588	0.027	0.453	24.7
1881	0.280	0.565	0.030	0.468	24.6
1886	0.283	0.556	0.032	0.478	24.8
1891	0.274	0.533	0.033	0.483	25.0
1896	0.266	0.510	0.034	0.486	24.8
1901	0.265	0.500	0.033	0.495	

CHARENTE

MORTALITY PATTERN: WEST
MIGRATION: FULL STRENGTH, WITH POPULATION TOTALS OBTAINED BY TREND OF R/CB

TABLE 1 FEMALE POPULATION ESTIMATES: 1801 TO 1906

DATE	R/CB RATIO	% COR-RECTION	FINAL POPULATION ESTIMATE	DATE	R/CB RATIO	% COR-RECTION	FINAL POPULATION ESTIMATE
1801	0.903	6.0	160000	1856	0.984	0.2	188492
1806	1.008	0.0	164113	1861	0.981	0.1	186883
1811*	0.992	0.0	168111	1866	0.971	0.8	186370
1816*	0.993	0.0	172109	1871	0.966	0.8	182627
1821	0.980	0.0	176107	1876	0.991	-2.1	180265
1826*	0.982	0.0	179425	1881	0.974	-0.8	181408
1831	0.987	0.0	182743	1886	0.964	-0.2	181393
1836	1.000	0.0	184091	1891	0.952	0.7	179904
1841	0.992	0.0	184958	1896	0.974	-2.0	176667
1846	1.000	0.0	189128	1901	0.944	0.6	175424
1851	0.991	-0.0	189544	1906	0.948	-0.2	175249

NOTE: R/CB RATIO REFERS TO THE POPULATION COMPUTED BY THE BALANCE OF BIRTHS
AND DEATHS OVER THE REPORTED POPULATION
* INTERPOLATED VALUES

TABLE 2 FEMALE BIRTH ESTIMATES: 1801-1805 TO 1901-1905

DATE	% COR-RECTION	FINAL BIRTH ESTIMATE	CRUDE BIRTH RATE	DATE	% COR-RECTION	FINAL BIRTH ESTIMATE	CRUDE BIRTH RATE
1801-1805	0.0	23402	28.9	1856-1860	0.0	20880	22.2
1806-1810	0.0	24855	29.9	1861-1865	0.0	20080	21.5
1811-1815	3.8	24018	28.2	1866-1870	0.0	20324	22.0
1816-1820	0.0	25134	28.9	1871-1875	0.0	20855	23.0
1821-1825	0.0	23657	26.6	1876-1880	0.0	20488	22.7
1826-1830	0.0	22609	25.0	1881-1885	0.0	18985	20.9
1831-1835	0.0	21855	23.8	1886-1890	0.0	17033	18.9
1836-1840	0.0	20934	22.7	1891-1895	0.0	15858	17.8
1841-1845	0.0	20316	21.7	1896-1900	0.0	16129	18.3
1846-1850	0.0	21492	22.7	1901-1905	0.0	16007	18.3
1851-1855	0.0	21414	22.7				

TABLE 3 FEMALE POPULATION ESTIMATES,
DISTRIBUTION BY AGE: 1801 TO 1906

AGE	1801	1806	1811	1816	1821	1826	1831	1836	1841	1846	1851
0- 4	17807	16937	19589	18913	20066	18808	18153	17040	17019	17116	17687
5- 9	15745	16045	15351	17871	17238	18371	17337	16592	15691	16051	15809
10-14	14973	15727	15418	14905	17202	16744	17936	16972	16070	15473	15574
15-19	14227	14951	15105	14963	14340	16701	16340	17551	16430	15839	14803
20-24	13389	14023	14238	14528	14279	13803	16161	15836	16860	16079	14723
25-29	12502	13054	13259	13592	13770	13645	13262	15537	15115	16404	15176
30-34	11588	12080	12271	12580	12812	13082	13035	12666	14752	14636	15619
35-39	10672	11094	11285	11568	11788	12096	12421	12364	11959	14211	13890
40-44	9761	10139	10304	10575	10778	11064	11418	11707	11610	11461	13450
45-49	8874	9203	9353	9590	9788	10048	10374	10688	10921	11054	10792
50-54	7929	8204	8360	8568	8743	8984	9278	9552	9825	10254	10275
55-59	6880	7069	7254	7449	7610	7811	8077	8297	8563	9008	9299
60-64	5684	5769	5974	6169	6333	6497	6714	6878	7130	7543	7813
65-69	4348	4352	4550	4732	4904	5043	5214	5308	5537	5902	6135
70-74	2972	2930	3096	3244	3400	3521	3652	3697	3872	4166	4352
75-79	1718	1639	1770	1869	1986	2073	2168	2182	2305	2502	2629
80+	924	897	934	995	1070	1135	1204	1227	1299	1429	1518

AGE	1856	1861	1866	1871	1876	1881	1886	1891	1896	1901	1906
0- 4	17181	16734	16514	15946	16494	17166	16090	14541	13400	13967	14171
5- 9	16210	15740	15504	14990	14538	15411	16102	15142	13620	12697	13357
10-14	15331	15721	15319	14995	14525	14189	15050	15747	14787	13352	12471
15-19	14991	14759	15205	14712	14458	14098	13742	14614	15280	14421	13014
20-24	13955	14147	14019	14313	13954	13822	13396	13098	13930	14707	13843
25-29	13944	13213	13480	13225	13573	13366	13219	12840	12530	13426	14203
30-34	14405	13232	12608	12734	12527	13011	12830	12711	12321	12089	13005
35-39	14759	13608	12575	11850	11997	11960	12448	12297	12155	11849	11679
40-44	13067	13881	12880	11766	11110	11407	11402	11889	11716	11647	11411
45-49	12577	12216	13059	11977	10961	10501	10815	10829	11262	11160	11153
50-54	9948	11587	11334	11958	10989	10223	9830	10142	10126	10596	10563
55-59	9224	8927	10487	10095	10675	10009	9353	9015	9268	9323	9825
60-64	7972	7905	7741	8900	8598	9337	8799	8250	7915	8222	8345
65-69	6258	6381	6426	6116	7066	7070	7729	7316	6818	6630	6966
70-74	4436	4521	4703	4567	4374	5283	5332	5861	5506	5217	5146
75-79	2678	2726	2852	2828	2769	2811	3433	3489	3798	3645	3517
80+	1556	1587	1664	1654	1656	1746	1824	2123	2237	2477	2579

TABLE 4   MARRIED WOMEN ESTIMATES,
DISTRIBUTION BY AGE: 1831 TO 1901

AGE	1831	1836	1841	1846	1851	1856	1861	1866
15-19	1434	1591	1543	1546	1505	1592	1618	1719
20-24	6939	6960	7605	7447	7004	6817	7101	6506
25-29	8979	10658	10541	11623	10920	10172	9775	10107
30-34	10034	9807	11559	11594	12500	11614	10754	10323
35-39	9828	9788	9567	11474	11307	12065	11186	10391
40-44	9017	9186	9194	9146	10804	10504	11193	10415
45-49	7781	7930	8208	8397	8271	9641	9399	10080

AGE	1871	1876	1881	1886	1891	1896	1901
15-19	1820	2034	1921	1568	1367	1305	1494
20-24	7070	7511	7824	7459	6833	7117	7457
25-29	9372	9970	10300	10360	9977	9646	10217
30-34	10422	9973	10587	10683	10621	10465	9966
35-39	9723	9872	9763	10280	10247	10483	9820
40-44	9362	8840	9193	9169	9562	9979	9353
45-49	9015	9241	8042	8340	8310	9349	8509

TABLE 5   DEMOGRAPHIC INDICES AND FEMALE SINGULATE MEAN AGE
AT MARRIAGE: 1831 TO 1901

DATE	IF OVERALL FERTILITY	IG MARITAL FERTILITY	IH ILLEGITIMATE FERTILITY	IM PROPORTION MARRIED	SINGULATE MEAN AGE AT MARRIAGE
1831	0.264	0.437	0.034	0.571	23.7
1836	0.246	0.398	0.039	0.575	23.5
1841	0.232	0.367	0.037	0.590	23.3
1846	0.229	0.354	0.035	0.610	23.2
1851	0.241	0.363	0.036	0.628	23.0
1856	0.246	0.371	0.029	0.633	22.8
1861	0.246	0.372	0.026	0.636	22.8
1866	0.248	0.380	0.026	0.626	22.8
1871	0.258	0.398	0.027	0.622	22.5
1876	0.261	0.392	0.032	0.638	22.1
1881	0.250	0.360	0.039	0.657	22.2
1886	0.230	0.332	0.031	0.662	22.6
1891	0.211	0.311	0.027	0.647	22.7
1896	0.203	0.299	0.028	0.647	22.7
1901	0.202	0.303	0.027	0.635	

MORTALITY PATTERN: WEST
MIGRATION: FULL STRENGTH, WITH POPULATION TOTALS OBTAINED BY TREND OF R/CB

TABLE 1   FEMALE POPULATION ESTIMATES: 1801 TO 1906

DATE	R/CB RATIO	% COR- RECTION	FINAL POPULATION ESTIMATE	DATE	R/CB RATIO	% COR- RECTION	FINAL POPULATION ESTIMATE
1801	0.970	0.0	202547	1856	0.997	-0.5	234063
1806	1.008	0.0	204981	1861	0.996	-1.0	234019
1811*	0.984	1.0	208926	1866	0.984	-0.3	234988
1816*	0.975	2.1	212871	1871	0.963	1.3	232078
1821	0.955	3.1	216815	1876	0.979	-0.9	228557
1826*	0.976	-0.3	217474	1881	0.961	0.4	229740
1831	0.993	0.0	225953	1886	0.943	1.7	231323
1836	0.999	0.0	227701	1891	0.942	1.4	230119
1841	0.996	0.0	229816	1896	0.949	-0.1	225961
1846	1.000	0.0	234119	1901	0.949	-0.6	224023
1851	0.997	0.1	232685	1906	0.952	-1.5	222774

NOTE: R/CB RATIO REFERS TO THE POPULATION COMPUTED BY THE BALANCE OF BIRTHS
        AND DEATHS OVER THE REPORTED POPULATION
* INTERPOLATED VALUES

TABLE 2   FEMALE BIRTH ESTIMATES: 1801-1805 TO 1901-1905

DATE	% COR- RECTION	FINAL BIRTH ESTIMATE	CRUDE BIRTH RATE	DATE	% COR- RECTION	FINAL BIRTH ESTIMATE	CRUDE BIRTH RATE
1801-1805	0.0	30768	30.2	1856-1860	0.0	26281	22.5
1806-1810	0.0	31773	30.7	1861-1865	0.0	25704	21.9
1811-1815	7.8	32863	31.2	1866-1870	0.0	24806	21.2
1816-1820	0.0	32223	30.0	1871-1875	7.0	25337	22.0
1821-1825	0.0	30796	28.4	1876-1880	0.0	24728	21.6
1826-1830	0.0	30016	27.1	1881-1885	0.0	24315	21.1
1831-1835	7.0	29697	26.2	1886-1890	0.0	21144	18.3
1836-1840	0.0	26745	23.4	1891-1895	0.0	19832	17.4
1841-1845	0.0	26547	22.9	1896-1900	0.0	19991	17.8
1846-1850	2.0	268C2	23.0	1901-1905	0.0	20050	17.9
1851-1855	0.0	27368	23.5				

[268]

TABLE 3 FEMALE POPULATION ESTIMATES,
DISTRIBUTION BY AGE: 1801 TO 1906

AGE	1801	1806	1811	1816	1821	1826	1831	1836	1841	1846	1851
0- 4	26048	21409	23884	24174	24561	23125	23759	22565	21464	21756	21006
5- 9	22276	22809	19035	21169	21623	21792	21376	21391	20708	19976	19768
10-14	20662	21767	21827	18348	20291	20636	21530	20735	20749	20299	19343
15-19	19158	20186	20822	21032	17580	19357	20379	20875	20102	20328	19579
20-24	17581	18464	19115	19840	19957	16603	18938	19559	20072	19541	19321
25-29	15992	16751	17337	18044	18675	18690	16115	18020	18678	19385	18530
30-34	14430	15094	15619	16240	16872	17368	18025	15227	17112	17941	18338
35-39	12929	13490	13972	14515	15080	15579	16638	16907	14374	16344	16874
40-44	11516	11990	12407	12895	13394	13835	14831	15505	15869	13653	15290
45-49	10173	10599	10950	11368	11816	12202	13080	13724	14455	14974	12691
50-54	8828	9173	9516	9854	10246	10584	11350	11899	12603	13440	13702
55-59	7431	7669	7992	8292	8626	8906	9567	10016	10644	11423	11960
60-64	5930	6057	6350	6594	6910	7128	7671	8022	8573	9243	9690
65-69	4366	4399	4646	4828	5101	5290	5706	5955	6417	6971	7298
70-74	2861	2840	3018	3142	3348	3494	3803	3960	4304	4723	4950
75-79	1559	1515	1635	1698	1835	1926	2120	2213	2437	2705	2838
80+	795	770	801	837	901	958	1065	1129	1255	1418	1508

AGE	1856	1861	1866	1871	1876	1881	1886	1891	1896	1901	1906
0- 4	22221	21473	21464	20150	20268	21010	21012	18422	16912	17477	17727
5- 9	19363	20514	20012	19754	18433	19027	19860	19933	17309	16076	16688
10-14	19215	18810	19996	19419	19144	18003	18613	19450	19476	16972	15773
15-19	18694	18506	18184	19223	18670	18555	17430	18038	18844	18965	16496
20-24	18618	17616	17540	17042	18098	17758	17596	16497	17111	18034	18118
25-29	18399	17666	16794	16582	16103	17318	16993	16847	15760	16456	17361
30-34	17645	17521	16904	15959	15719	15461	16673	16379	16184	15214	15920
35-39	17381	16737	16706	16007	15063	15046	14846	16036	15689	15587	14687
40-44	15921	16424	15900	15763	15047	14370	14408	14241	15312	15063	15006
45-49	14339	14957	15512	14917	14730	14274	13687	13749	13523	14619	14422
50-54	11733	13286	13941	14351	13737	13796	13433	12909	12894	12758	13835
55-59	12346	10604	12094	12573	12870	12579	12704	12401	11837	11911	11831
60-64	10310	10674	9260	10428	10765	11327	11150	11297	10934	10540	10655
65-69	7817	8349	8758	7472	8336	8925	9478	9368	9387	9202	8924
70-74	5326	5732	6226	6394	5391	6299	6822	7280	7098	7225	7136
75-79	3082	3338	3671	3879	3922	3512	4164	4538	4759	4735	4865
80+	1653	1814	2025	2167	2261	2482	2454	2734	2933	3190	3333

[269]

TABLE 4 MARRIED WOMEN ESTIMATES,
DISTRIBUTICN BY AGE: 1831 TO 1901

AGE	1831	1836	1841	1846	1851	1856	1861	1866
15-19	1803	1805	1701	1684	1589	1488	1590	1573
20-24	9319	9530	9704	9368	9179	8769	8225	7431
25-29	11715	13074	13577	14099	13465	13366	12822	12168
30-34	14050	11868	13433	14154	14503	14006	13946	13474
35-39	12847	13053	11227	12870	13342	13828	13378	13387
40-44	10889	11363	11833	10301	11599	12184	12651	12288
45-49	8994	9394	10141	10677	9109	10411	10949	11393

AGE	1871	1876	1881	1886	1891	1896	1901
15-19	1537	1462	1695	1498	1295	1185	1483
20-24	7923	8581	8808	8930	8021	8148	8484
25-29	11149	11521	12646	12807	12765	11760	12298
30-34	12656	11985	12206	13337	13368	13312	12397
35-39	12725	11992	11739	11841	12911	12852	12766
40-44	12019	11493	11041	11051	11085	12037	11831
45-49	10717	10593	10341	10022	10157	10108	10768

TABLE 5 DEMOGRAPHIC INDICES AND FEMALE SINGULATE MEAN AGE
AT MARRIAGE: 1831 TO 1901

DATE	IF OVERALL FERTILITY	IG MARITAL FERTILITY	IH ILLEGITIMATE FERTILITY	IM PROPORTION MARRIED	SINGULATE MEAN AGE AT MARRIAGE
1831	0.281	0.449	0.032	0.598	22.2
1836	0.263	0.425	0.027	0.592	22.4
1841	0.246	0.386	0.039	0.597	22.5
1846	0.242	0.375	0.041	0.603	22.5
1851	0.247	0.388	0.029	0.607	22.6
1856	0.247	0.388	0.025	0.612	22.6
1861	0.246	0.387	0.022	0.614	22.8
1866	0.245	0.391	0.022	0.603	23.0
1871	0.248	0.404	0.021	0.592	22.9
1876	0.250	0.404	0.025	0.594	22.7
1881	0.245	0.389	0.021	0.608	22.6
1886	0.228	0.350	0.022	0.626	22.8
1891	0.206	0.315	0.024	0.626	23.0
1896	0.200	0.308	0.025	0.618	23.0
1901	0.199	0.309	0.025	0.613	

MORTALITY PATTERN: WEST
MIGRATION: GRADUAL, WITH CHILD MIGRANTS SUBTRACTED AFTER 1866, AND POPULATION
TOTALS OBTAINED AFTER 1881 BY INTERPOLATION OF R/CB BETWEEN 1886 AND 1906

TABLE 1   FEMALE POPULATION ESTIMATES: 1801 TO 1906

DATE	R/CB RATIO	% COR-RECTION	FINAL POPULATION ESTIMATE	DATE	R/CB RATIO	% COR-RECTION	FINAL POPULATION ESTIMATE
1801	1.070	0.0	109248	1856	0.984	0.0	155554
1806	1.047	0.0	110796	1861	0.976	0.0	158995
1811*	1.025	0.0	114375	1866	0.963	0.0	164844
1816*	0.999	0.0	117955	1871	0.934	-0.2	165091
1821	0.975	0.0	121534	1876	0.931	-0.4	168249
1826*	0.972	0.0	124625	1881	0.913	-0.6	171564
1831	0.985	0.0	127715	1886	0.893	-0.8	173042
1836	1.020	0.0	137913	1891	0.887	-2.1	173300
1841	0.990	0.0	135671	1896	0.851	-0.1	172082
1846	1.000	0.0	145123	1901	0.836	0.0	170832
1851	0.996	0.0	150215	1906	0.830	-1.8	167669

NOTE: R/CB RATIO REFERS TO THE POPULATION COMPUTED BY THE BALANCE OF BIRTHS
        AND DEATHS OVER THE REPORTED POPULATION
* INTERPOLATED VALUES

TABLE 2   FEMALE BIRTH ESTIMATES: 1801-1805 TO 1901-1905

DATE	% COR-RECTION	FINAL BIRTH ESTIMATE	CRUDE BIRTH RATE	DATE	% COR-RECTION	FINAL BIRTH ESTIMATE	CRUDE BIRTH RATE
1801-1805	0.0	19528	35.5	1856-1860	3.2	24011	30.5
1806-1810	0.0	20606	36.6	1861-1865	0.0	23990	29.6
1811-1815	6.8	21973	37.8	1866-1870	0.0	23245	28.2
1816-1820	0.0	21464	35.8	1871-1875	0.0	22133	26.6
1821-1825	0.0	21580	35.1	1876-1880	0.0	22419	26.4
1826-1830	2.5	21973	34.8	1881-1885	0.0	21114	24.5
1831-1835	0.0	22211	33.4	1886-1890	0.0	19364	22.4
1836-1840	5.2	22451	32.8	1891-1895	0.0	17770	20.6
1841-1845	0.0	24330	34.7	1896-1900	0.0	16612	19.4
1846-1850	3.1	24947	33.8	1901-1905	0.0	15793	18.7
1851-1855	0.0	24144	31.6				

TABLE 3 FEMALE POPULATION ESTIMATES,
DISTRIBUTION BY AGE: 1801 TO 1906

AGE	1801	1806	1811	1816	1821	1826	1831	1836	1841	1846	1851
0- 4	15705	13558	14902	15762	15835	15275	15090	17380	15451	19291	18843
5- 9	13117	13500	11843	12958	13841	13810	13256	13988	14726	14203	17249
10-14	11889	12459	12843	11238	12289	13299	13408	13237	13052	14413	13676
15-19	10769	11290	11848	12183	10654	11805	12908	13383	12348	12769	13867
20-24	9660	10097	10616	11111	11429	10108	11301	12754	12331	11971	12149
25-29	8584	8962	9405	9860	10332	10731	9564	11071	11629	11865	11302
30-34	7570	7894	8282	8666	9103	9618	10057	9304	10009	11121	11130
35-39	6625	6898	7237	7569	7941	8399	8926	9712	8338	9510	10358
40-44	5766	5992	6280	6567	6890	7273	7733	8564	8639	7875	8801
45-49	4979	5176	5416	5658	5936	6264	6644	7367	7561	8103	7237
50-54	4221	4384	4594	4790	5026	5293	5606	6223	6381	6981	7321
55-59	3472	3587	3766	3932	4127	4328	4561	5093	5205	5729	6119
60-64	2707	2778	2916	3048	3215	3350	3497	3938	4017	4460	4772
65-69	1945	1981	2080	2172	2305	2390	2460	2795	2844	3205	3440
70-74	1251	1255	1318	1375	1466	1513	1537	1758	1783	2042	2210
75-79	666	662	694	723	776	792	790	921	923	1084	1181
80+	332	325	333	344	367	379	378	426	434	502	559

AGE	1856	1861	1866	1871	1876	1881	1886	1891	1896	1901	1906
0- 4	19211	18141	19570	18301	17630	18795	17911	16273	15111	14236	13625
5- 9	17100	17207	16663	17551	16735	16277	17396	16597	15110	14117	13246
10-14	16541	16507	16607	15830	17013	16116	15647	16830	16056	14663	13623
15-19	13032	15960	15801	15448	15285	16018	14978	14744	15812	15231	13626
20-24	12993	12444	14964	14032	14707	13661	13975	13399	12931	14330	13249
25-29	11390	12303	11702	13647	13329	13596	12423	12937	12289	12018	13135
30-34	10603	10710	11632	10844	12938	12594	12835	11775	12276	11717	11397
35-39	10394	9897	10088	10777	10224	12233	11920	12184	11196	11722	11163
40-44	9630	9639	9293	9344	10111	9669	11612	11321	11618	10698	11212
45-49	8133	8868	9001	8576	8711	9532	9161	10989	10765	11061	10213
50-54	6594	7362	8171	8204	7877	8130	8948	8585	10345	10142	10460
55-59	6498	5790	6619	7253	7335	7186	7470	8190	7910	9533	9387
60-64	5190	5420	4981	5584	6193	6395	6303	6536	7211	6990	8444
65-69	3783	4008	4372	3922	4450	5081	5286	5188	5422	6010	5844
70-74	2464	2611	2930	3106	2820	3324	3830	3960	3923	4123	4589
75-79	1349	1426	1634	1769	1897	1813	2162	2468	2582	2577	2722
80+	648	704	815	901	994	1143	1186	1326	1525	1666	1734

TABLE 4 MARRIED WOMEN ESTIMATES,
DISTRIBUTION BY AGE: 1831 TO 1901

AGE	1831	1836	1841	1846	1851	1856	1861	1866
15-19	852	902	852	902	1005	969	1483	1343
20-24	4755	5447	5350	5281	5444	5917	5758	6901
25-29	6681	7795	8260	8511	8168	8299	9028	8655
30-34	7974	7407	8016	8975	9013	8628	8742	9538
35-39	7195	7846	6772	7788	8497	8561	8165	8356
40-44	6112	6773	6870	6326	7070	7765	7765	7523
45-49	4922	5462	5653	6151	5495	6210	6771	6914

AGE	1871	1876	1881	1886	1891	1896	1901
15-19	1159	1296	1362	1126	938	901	1037
20-24	6411	7015	6668	6740	6239	5988	6555
25-29	9824	9649	10219	9346	9607	9076	8991
30-34	8880	10446	10213	10672	9697	10033	9584
35-39	8878	8453	10046	9891	10170	9289	9645
40-44	7484	8127	7797	9432	9136	9449	8619
45-49	6480	6619	7277	7138	8474	8339	8557

TABLE 5 DEMOGRAPHIC INDICES AND FEMALE SINGULATE MEAN AGE
AT MARRIAGE: 1831 TO 1901

DATE	IF OVERALL FERTILITY	IG MARITAL FERTILITY	IH ILLEGITIMATE FERTILITY	IM PROPORTION MARRIED	SINGULATE MEAN AGE AT MARRIAGE
1831	0.360	0.555	0.100	0.572	23.9
1836	0.339	0.545	0.061	0.574	23.7
1841	0.361	0.577	0.057	0.585	23.6
1846	0.368	0.582	0.051	0.598	23.5
1851	0.358	0.563	0.055	0.597	23.4
1856	0.348	0.538	0.057	0.604	23.2
1861	0.336	0.528	0.051	0.598	23.2
1866	0.315	0.497	0.047	0.595	23.3
1871	0.300	0.472	0.048	0.594	23.2
1876	0.285	0.440	0.047	0.605	23.0
1881	0.275	0.417	0.047	0.617	23.0
1886	0.258	0.385	0.047	0.624	23.3
1891	0.240	0.361	0.046	0.617	23.4
1896	0.225	0.341	0.046	0.607	23.3
1901	0.211	0.321	0.042	0.605	

MORTALITY PATTERN: WEST
MIGRATION: GRADUAL, WITH UNCORRECTED POPULATION TOTALS EXCEPT FOR 1876, 1881,
  1886 AND 1891, OBTAINED BY LINEAR INTERPOLATION OF R/CB BETWEEN 1871 AND 1896

TABLE 1   FEMALE POPULATION ESTIMATES: 1801 TO 1906

DATE	R/CB RATIO	% COR-RECTION	FINAL POPULATION ESTIMATE	DATE	R/CB RATIO	% COR-RECTION	FINAL POPULATION ESTIMATE
1801	1.041	2.0	126947	1856	0.964	0.0	158013
1806	1.062	0.0	128654	1861	0.942	0.0	155112
1811*	1.035	0.0	131763	1866	0.924	0.0	155682
1816*	1.010	0.0	134872	1871	0.896	0.0	151774
1821	0.995	0.0	137981	1876	0.906	-3.1	150761
1826*	0.995	0.0	142571	1881	0.885	-2.8	153000
1831	0.992	0.0	147160	1886	0.886	-4.9	154594
1836	0.995	0.0	150303	1891	0.843	-2.2	156271
1841	1.001	0.0	153322	1896	0.807	0.0	155164
1846	1.000	0.0	158475	1901	0.787	0.0	154567
1851	0.995	0.0	160005	1906	0.762	0.0	152604

NOTE: R/CB RATIO REFERS TO THE POPULATION COMPUTED BY THE BALANCE OF BIRTHS
  AND DEATHS OVER THE REPORTED POPULATION
* INTERPOLATED VALUES

TABLE 2   FEMALE BIRTH ESTIMATES: 1801-1805 TO 1901-1905

DATE	% COR-RECTION	FINAL BIRTH ESTIMATE	CRUDE BIRTH RATE	DATE	% COR-RECTION	FINAL BIRTH ESTIMATE	CRUDE BIRTH RATE
1801-1805	7.2	21449	33.6	1856-1860	4.4	23083	29.5
1806-1810	0.0	22879	35.1	1861-1865	0.0	22944	29.5
1811-1815	0.0	22203	33.3	1866-1870	0.0	22951	29.9
1816-1820	0.0	22066	32.3	1871-1875	0.0	22974	30.4
1821-1825	0.0	22764	32.5	1876-1880	0.0	23685	31.2
1826-1830	0.0	23357	32.2	1881-1885	0.0	22638	29.4
1831-1835	0.0	23965	32.2	1886-1890	0.0	21119	27.2
1836-1840	-9.4	23858	31.4	1891-1895	0.0	18888	24.3
1841-1845	0.0	24293	31.2	1896-1900	0.0	18251	23.6
1846-1850	0.0	24921	31.3	1901-1905	0.0	17287	22.5
1851-1855	0.0	23715	29.8				

TABLE 3 FEMALE POPULATION ESTIMATES,
DISTRIBUTION BY AGE: 1801 TO 1906

AGE	1801	1806	1811	1816	1821	1826	1831	1836	1841	1846	1851
0- 4	14766	15344	17143	17051	16898	17403	17917	17716	17616	18735	18259
5- 9	12790	12924	13557	15281	15237	15215	15670	15916	15747	15927	16506
10-14	12149	12281	12269	12875	14591	14731	14683	15115	15377	15249	15246
15-19	11534	11661	11654	11646	12237	14100	14210	14157	14598	14884	14579
20-24	10816	10940	10957	10962	11011	11758	13470	13552	13522	13994	14054
25-29	10053	10155	10193	10228	10284	10449	11141	12728	12824	12859	13108
30-34	9262	9361	9398	9457	9534	9693	9836	10448	11952	12115	11965
35-39	8473	8552	8601	8662	8756	8923	9061	9152	9734	11214	11186
40-44	7691	7766	7807	7880	7970	8143	8289	8373	8468	9075	10285
45-49	6924	6998	7041	7104	7201	7361	7511	7605	7692	7840	8265
50-54	6133	6182	6238	6305	6387	6540	6678	6769	6861	7005	7014
55-59	5239	5292	5349	5432	5509	5631	5763	5830	5914	6070	6069
60-64	4233	4268	4355	4444	4523	4620	4723	4766	4824	4982	4980
65-69	3140	3164	3256	3369	3440	3518	3597	3602	3635	3772	3768
70-74	2063	2077	2161	2265	2342	2396	2456	2442	2444	2550	2539
75-79	1116	1127	1192	1272	1329	1371	1408	1389	1379	1444	1429
80+	563	562	590	639	683	718	748	744	735	761	754

AGE	1856	1861	1866	1871	1876	1881	1886	1891	1896	1901	1906
0- 4	17498	16611	17389	16626	17046	18641	18245	17649	15677	15547	15026
5- 9	15901	15132	14738	15005	14596	15333	16915	16793	16189	14494	14417
10-14	15490	14977	14411	13819	14248	13942	14666	16272	16152	15598	13893
15-19	14161	14434	14104	13180	12867	13282	12886	13561	15076	14957	14190
20-24	13176	12787	13204	12219	11735	11334	11462	10921	11436	12850	12221
25-29	12790	11987	11788	11779	11108	10674	10194	10288	9702	10197	11340
30-34	11975	11696	11122	10724	10869	10350	9957	9558	9633	9107	9546
35-39	10873	10889	10805	10096	9861	10125	9679	9387	8999	9118	8612
40-44	10122	9843	10022	9800	9264	9184	9492	9169	8893	8579	8728
45-49	9253	9110	9009	9052	8949	8597	8589	8378	8679	8476	8227
50-54	7321	8190	8212	8018	8142	8199	7953	8053	8420	8206	8081
55-59	6030	6277	7170	7081	6995	7261	7393	7285	7376	7783	7658
60-64	4943	4878	5213	5820	5834	5924	6222	6450	6344	6500	6915
65-69	3754	3682	3758	3901	4432	4607	4748	5103	5273	5268	5455
70-74	2540	2486	2542	2502	2650	3153	3339	3541	3788	3992	4041
75-79	1435	1397	1443	1408	1421	1599	1949	2140	2254	2474	2651
80+	751	735	754	743	745	796	904	1123	1273	1420	1605

TABLE 4   MARRIED WOMEN ESTIMATES,
DISTRIBUTION BY AGE: 1831 TO 1901

AGE	1831	1836	1841	1846	1851	1856	1861	1866
15-19	860	887	990	1006	1027	1043	970	979
20-24	4614	4770	4901	5188	5412	5231	5240	4632
25-29	6662	7748	7965	8150	8467	8410	8028	8051
30-34	7001	7518	8726	8975	8974	9077	8967	8645
35-39	6747	6856	7377	8600	8653	8460	8536	8569
40-44	6245	6298	6418	6936	7891	7766	7574	7788
45-49	5326	5366	5477	5639	5964	6661	6572	6580

AGE	1871	1876	1881	1886	1891	1896	1901
15-19	1027	1256	1525	1289	970	890	1251
20-24	4593	4851	4947	5676	5384	5164	5724
25-29	7261	7169	7294	7077	7631	7285	7483
30-34	8390	8049	7862	7855	7621	7925	7529
35-39	8009	7904	7865	7688	7656	7380	7564
40-44	7559	7207	7185	7366	7267	7144	6866
45-49	6521	6516	6297	6432	6868	6673	6454

TABLE 5   DEMOGRAPHIC INDICES AND FEMALE SINGULATE MEAN AGE
AT MARRIAGE: 1831 TO 1901

DATE	IF OVERALL FERTILITY	IG MARITAL FERTILITY	IH ILLEGITIMATE FERTILITY	IM PROPORTION MARRIED	SINGULATE MEAN AGE AT MARRIAGE
1831	0.351	0.680	0.026	0.496	24.7
1836	0.340	0.639	0.031	0.509	24.6
1841	0.330	0.602	0.032	0.523	24.5
1846	0.325	0.582	0.028	0.535	24.3
1851	0.318	0.552	0.034	0.548	24.1
1856	0.315	0.535	0.035	0.559	24.0
1861	0.317	0.533	0.038	0.563	24.2
1866	0.318	0.549	0.032	0.554	24.3
1871	0.334	0.580	0.030	0.552	23.9
1876	0.350	0.597	0.029	0.565	23.5
1881	0.353	0.593	0.025	0.578	23.3
1886	0.341	0.552	0.027	0.598	23.4
1891	0.317	0.504	0.031	0.603	23.7
1896	0.291	0.476	0.031	0.585	23.7
1901	0.271	0.448	0.025	0.582	

MORTALITY PATTERN: WEST
MIGRATION: GRADUAL, WITH POPULATICN TOTALS CBTAINFD BY TREND OF R/CB

TABLE 1   FEMALE POPULATION ESTIMATES: 1801 TO 1906

DATE	R/CB RATIO	% COR-RECTION	FINAL POPULATION ESTIMATE	DATE	R/CB RATIO	% COR-RECTION	FINAL POPULATION ESTIMATE
1801	1.016	4.3	87592	1856	0.986	0.5	122364
1806	1.049	0.0	88535	1861	0.991	-1.4	124535
1811*	1.034	0.0	88958	1866	0.992	-2.8	126311
1816*	1.024	0.0	89380	1871	0.944	0.8	129149
1821	1.001	0.0	89803	1876	0.937	0.2	130693
1826*	1.014	0.0	93966	1881	0.899	3.0	132264
1831	1.014	0.0	98128	1886	0.911	0.2	133072
1836	1.012	0.0	103862	1891	0.942	-4.5	136497
1841	1.005	0.0	109844	1896	0.883	0.3	137678
1846	1.000	0.0	114811	1901	0.875	-0.2	138673
1851	0.984	2.0	120694	1906	0.840	2.4	139863

NOTE: R/CB RATIO REFERS TO THE POPULATION CCMPUTED BY THE BALANCE OF BIRTHS
        AND DEATHS OVER THE REPORTED POPULATICN
* INTERPOLATED VALUES

TABLE 2   FEMALE BIRTH ESTIMATES: 1801-1805 TO 1901-1905

DATE	% COR-RECTION	FINAL BIRTH ESTIMATE	CRUDE BIRTH RATE	DATE	% COR-RECTION	FINAL BIRTH ESTIMATE	CRUDE BIRTH RATE
1801-1805	6.9	13044	29.6	1856-1860	0.0	17648	28.6
1806-1810	0.0	13009	29.3	1861-1865	0.0	18450	29.4
1811-1815	4.9	13016	29.2	1866-1870	0.0	20166	31.6
1816-1820	6.9	14066	31.4	1871-1875	0.0	19545	30.1
1821-1825	17.0	13781	30.0	1876-188C	0.0	20628	31.4
1826-1830	-7.4	14813	30.8	1881-1885	0.0	20336	30.7
1831-1835	0.0	16025	31.7	1886-1890	0.0	20918	31.0
1836-1840	2.8	16606	31.1	1891-1895	0.0	19161	28.0
1841-1845	0.0	16995	30.3	1896-1900	0.0	17490	25.3
1846-1850	2.9	17366	29.5	1901-1905	0.0	16113	23.1
1851-1855	0.0	17391	28.6				

TABLE 3 FEMALE POPULATION ESTIMATES,
DISTRIBUTION BY AGE: 1801 TO 1906

AGE	1801	1806	1811	1816	1821	1826	1831	1836	1841	1846	1851
0- 4	8908	10016	10001	9937	10656	11123	11988	13310	13989	13981	14364
5- 9	8015	8012	8975	8953	8817	9891	10274	11184	12449	12959	13044
10-14	7743	7717	7664	8607	8505	8676	9646	10038	10891	12094	12689
15-19	7480	7452	7379	7347	8172	8364	8457	9420	9769	10575	11841
20-24	7156	7130	7060	7006	6909	7969	8087	8199	9108	9416	10286
25-29	6788	6767	6703	6649	6536	6690	7653	7794	7884	8725	9096
30-34	6394	6377	6321	6271	6162	6291	6389	7339	7461	7515	8380
35-39	5983	5966	5917	5873	5772	5895	5973	6095	6992	7073	7178
40-44	5562	5547	5501	5463	5372	5490	5566	5668	5777	6593	6720
45-49	5133	5121	5080	5044	4963	5075	5149	5247	5338	5412	6222
50-54	4660	4649	4615	4582	4508	4616	4688	4785	4875	4930	5034
55-59	4108	4100	4072	4043	3977	4082	4155	4253	4346	4393	4473
60-64	3442	3442	3423	3396	3342	3442	3517	3620	3717	3758	3825
65-69	2672	2679	2673	2651	2607	2699	2773	2876	2979	3016	3069
70-74	1857	1865	1869	1856	1826	1900	1966	2060	2156	2193	2234
75-79	1086	1093	1099	1093	1077	1130	1179	1252	1330	1360	1391
80+	596	603	608	608	601	633	668	721	785	817	846

AGE	1856	1861	1866	1871	1876	1881	1886	1891	1896	1901	1906
0- 4	13634	13918	14301	15595	15088	15680	15442	16686	15325	14370	13700
5- 9	12965	12345	12506	12842	13968	13432	13941	14021	15149	14069	13377
10-14	12503	12455	11833	11993	12286	13363	12835	13413	13474	14628	13635
15-19	12108	11937	11841	11228	11293	11558	12534	12069	12526	12652	13838
20-24	11116	11349	11090	10952	10183	10204	10314	11250	10560	11099	11280
25-29	9644	10434	10593	10331	10109	9355	9310	9465	10252	9664	10247
30-34	8520	9056	9763	9914	9639	9411	8689	8733	8861	9671	9174
35-39	7809	7961	8432	9095	9219	8943	8726	8147	8185	8362	9205
40-44	6657	7266	7383	7824	8435	8531	8279	8184	7652	7739	7973
45-49	6194	6158	6699	6813	7220	7766	7862	7735	7665	7215	7360
50-54	5650	5646	5595	6091	6199	6552	7056	7253	7161	7149	6797
55-59	4449	5014	4988	4946	5389	5464	5782	6340	6541	6516	6582
60-64	3771	3766	4213	4191	4153	4497	4561	4940	5428	5669	5737
65-69	3007	2978	2945	3292	3271	3213	3479	3638	3949	4410	4702
70-74	2175	2141	2093	2067	2307	2266	2225	2504	2624	2908	3334
75-79	1343	1315	1272	1241	1223	1343	1318	1361	1536	1653	1896
80+	819	797	764	735	712	686	719	760	793	898	1025

[278]

TABLE 4   MARRIED WOMEN ESTIMATES,
DISTRIBUTION BY AGE: 1831 TO 1901

AGE	1831	1836	1841	1846	1851	1856	1861	1866
15-19	794	789	737	726	747	708	710	744
20-24	3204	3057	3203	3120	3217	3285	3182	3178
25-29	4652	4632	4588	4951	5026	5179	5455	5379
30-34	4383	4977	5032	5018	5535	5555	5844	6212
35-39	4175	4219	4847	4879	4928	5324	5422	5711
40-44	3870	3885	3977	4523	4603	4545	4997	5084
45-49	3334	3324	3406	3437	3943	3908	3930	4286

AGE	1871	1876	1881	1886	1891	1896	1901
15-19	477	557	819	911	798	626	705
20-24	3153	2795	2600	2862	3329	2985	2715
25-29	5389	5248	4959	4651	4746	5432	4914
30-34	6208	6144	6012	5749	5571	5660	6291
35-39	6114	6157	6096	6042	5766	5734	5697
40-44	5387	5823	5986	5770	5741	5496	5270
45-49	4360	4641	5121	5407	5385	5438	4771

TABLE 5   DEMOGRAPHIC INDICES AND FEMALE SINGULATE MEAN AGE
AT MARRIAGE: 1831 TO 1901

DATE	IF OVERALL FERTILITY	IG MARITAL FERTILITY	IH ILLEGITIMATE FERTILITY	IM PROPORTION MARRIED	SINGULATE MEAN AGE AT MARRIAGE
1831	0.358	0.683	0.016	0.513	23.8
1836	0.360	0.701	0.022	0.498	24.1
1841	0.350	0.681	0.035	0.488	24.4
1846	0.339	0.676	0.035	0.475	24.7
1851	0.319	0.656	0.033	0.460	25.0
1856	0.307	0.646	0.030	0.449	25.3
1861	0.304	0.636	0.036	0.447	25.4
1866	0.319	0.656	0.044	0.450	25.6
1871	0.328	0.676	0.037	0.455	25.8
1876	0.337	0.685	0.045	0.457	25.7
1881	0.350	0.710	0.047	0.457	25.4
1886	0.355	0.727	0.045	0.453	25.4
1891	0.341	0.710	0.037	0.453	25.9
1896	0.311	0.632	0.044	0.454	26.2
1901	0.280	0.593	0.037	0.437	

MORTALITY PATTERN: NORTH
MIGRATION: FULL STRENGTH, WITH POPULATION TOTALS BETWEEN 1856 AND 1891,
  OBTAINED BY LINEAR INTERPOLATICN OF R/CB BETWEEN 1851 AND 1896

TABLE 1 FEMALE POPULATION ESTIMATES: 1801 TO 1906

DATE	R/CB RATIO	% COR- RECTION	FINAL POPULATION ESTIMATE	DATE	R/CB RATIO	% COR- RECTION	FINAL POPULATION ESTIMATE
1801	1.057	4.3	182625	1856	0.972	2.0	198138
1806	1.086	0.0	182404	1861	0.965	2.3	196940
1811*	1.063	0.2	184534	1866	0.961	2.3	196299
1816*	1.045	0.8	187592	1871	0.945	3.5	195213
1821	1.028	1.8	191177	1876	0.964	0.9	190910
1826*	1.009	2.9	195626	1881	0.985	-1.7	190027
1831	1.004	2.6	197451	1886	0.972	-0.9	188959
1836	1.021	0.0	198237	1891	0.963	-0.4	187110
1841	1.010	0.0	200444	1896	0.954	0.0	183702
1846	1.000	0.0	201043	1901	0.950	0.0	180960
1851	0.997	0.0	200696	1906	0.945	0.0	178661

NOTE: R/CB RATIO REFERS TO THE POPULATICN CCMPUTED BY THE BALANCE CF BIRTHS
       AND DEATHS OVER THE REPORTED POPULATION
* INTERPOLATED VALUES

TABLE 2 FEMALE BIRTH ESTIMATES: 1801-1805 TO 1901-1905

DATE	% COR- RECTION	FINAL BIRTH ESTIMATE	CRUDE BIRTH RATE	DATE	% COR- RECTION	FINAL BIRTH ESTIMATE	CRUDE BIRTH RATE
1801-1805	9.8	28266	31.0	1856-1860	0.0	21117	21.4
1806-1810	7.7	27702	30.2	1861-1865	0.0	20176	20.5
1811-1815	1.5	26616	28.6	1866-1870	0.0	19054	19.5
1816-1820	0.0	25492	26.9	1871-1875	0.0	18175	18.8
1821-1825	0.0	26417	27.3	1876-1880	0.0	18139	19.0
1826-1830	0.0	26060	26.5	1881-1885	0.0	17845	18.8
1831-1835	0.0	25135	25.4	1886-1890	0.0	17161	18.3
1836-1840	0.0	23824	23.9	1891-1895	0.0	16098	17.4
1841-1845	0.0	23508	23.4	1896-1900	0.0	15589	17.1
1846-1850	0.0	22498	22.4	1901-1905	0.0	15003	16.7
1851-1855	0.0	21562	21.6				

TABLE 3 FEMALE POPULATION ESTIMATES,
DISTRIBUTION BY AGE: 1801 TO 1906

AGE	1801	1806	1811	1816	1821	1826	1831	1836	1841	1846	1851
0- 4	27689	20881	20955	20477	20098	21021	20413	19797	19497	19113	18254
5- 9	22217	23165	17769	18078	17946	17722	18343	17862	17725	17385	17053
10-14	19639	20487	21576	16723	17133	17060	16760	17348	17033	16871	16625
15-19	17663	18440	19404	20636	16079	16515	16376	16079	16733	16406	16288
20-24	15835	16523	17402	18492	19774	15446	15797	15656	15460	16065	15702
25-29	14111	14711	15491	16479	17615	18886	14686	15015	14977	14765	15370
30-34	12457	12997	13682	14556	15586	16709	17826	13860	14278	14217	14084
35-39	10897	11366	11980	12744	13658	14671	15644	16692	13094	13462	13474
40-44	9474	9864	10397	11077	11876	12770	13640	14547	15673	12269	12686
45-49	8175	8522	8969	9557	10263	11040	11803	12611	13585	14604	11501
50-54	6972	7265	7658	8148	8755	9436	10089	10791	11655	12527	13548
55-59	5785	6026	6357	6778	7285	7860	8412	9003	9761	10514	11360
60-64	4570	4755	5026	5370	5801	6267	6703	7187	7837	8467	9150
65-69	3328	3459	3665	3931	4274	4649	4964	5327	5865	6365	6885
70-74	2130	2209	2352	2535	2786	3058	3274	3516	3919	4286	4643
75-79	1134	1167	1250	1358	1515	1686	1811	1956	2216	2448	2661
80+	556	567	600	652	733	830	909	991	1135	1279	1412

AGE	1856	1861	1866	1871	1876	1881	1886	1891	1896	1901	1906
0- 4	17390	17379	17032	16315	15178	15763	15588	14938	13924	13673	13333
5- 9	16196	15645	15858	15673	14774	14100	14675	14497	13828	13009	12891
10-14	16257	15533	15072	15323	15049	14326	13669	14235	14036	13435	12683
15-19	15943	15719	15025	14592	14752	14613	13856	13261	13788	13634	13092
20-24	15378	15274	15023	14349	13807	14139	13888	13259	12636	13205	13126
25-29	14912	14739	14658	14434	13691	13298	13572	13377	12736	12174	12779
30-34	14618	14263	14156	14112	13819	13218	12834	13107	12897	12316	11809
35-39	13316	13899	13636	13574	13451	13295	12723	12351	12593	12433	11913
40-44	12676	12593	13229	13022	12884	12889	12756	12197	11821	12094	11981
45-49	11877	11927	11930	12576	12303	12289	12313	12172	11622	11392	11601
50-54	10661	11064	11195	11240	11771	11633	11641	11647	11498	11016	10748
55-59	12267	9718	10181	10350	10307	10932	10825	10816	10803	10708	10301
60-64	9858	10751	8624	9093	9136	9264	9846	9736	9703	9746	9715
65-69	7410	8095	8985	7272	7543	7770	7902	8382	8259	8295	8397
70-74	4992	5482	6142	6904	5459	5865	6066	6152	6494	6468	6567
75-79	2858	3161	3597	4101	4461	3703	4000	4122	4153	4447	4495
80+	1530	1699	1957	2283	2526	2932	2805	2862	2911	3003	3232

[281]

TABLE 4   MARRIED WOMEN ESTIMATES,
DISTRIBUTION BY AGE: 1831 TO 1901

AGE	1831	1836	1841	1846	1851	1856	1861	1866
15-19	649	647	694	713	689	684	723	727
20-24	5671	5673	5667	5947	5856	5826	5853	5762
25-29	9471	9718	9763	9686	10140	9889	9829	9818
30-34	13218	10276	10648	10653	10589	11021	10789	10724
35-39	11839	12595	9948	10279	10319	10218	10698	10496
40-44	10139	10746	11681	9201	9542	9548	9516	9982
45-49	8320	8804	9610	10427	8246	8533	8608	8589

AGE	1871	1876	1881	1886	1891	1896	1901
15-19	684	709	677	606	558	559	641
20-24	5733	5682	5749	5496	5000	4783	5027
25-29	9597	9261	9202	9321	9075	8519	8224
30-34	10681	10408	10063	9885	10015	9839	9393
35-39	10410	10306	10227	9849	9532	9688	9579
40-44	9756	9624	9726	9651	9121	8824	9006
45-49	8957	8721	8844	8933	8670	8234	7974

TABLE 5   DEMOGRAPHIC INDICES AND FEMALE SINGULATE MEAN AGE
AT MARRIAGE: 1831 TO 1901

DATE	IF OVERALL FERTILITY	IG MARITAL FERTILITY	IH ILLEGITIMATE FERTILITY	IM PROPORTION MARRIED	SINGULATE MEAN AGE AT MARRIAGE
1831	0.269	0.461	0.033	0.552	24.2
1836	0.265	0.450	0.038	0.549	24.1
1841	0.262	0.447	0.040	0.545	24.0
1846	0.258	0.439	0.040	0.545	24.0
1851	0.247	0.417	0.041	0.549	23.9
1856	0.242	0.405	0.039	0.555	23.8
1861	0.235	0.393	0.034	0.560	23.8
1866	0.226	0.373	0.035	0.564	23.8
1871	0.218	0.358	0.034	0.568	23.6
1876	0.218	0.359	0.031	0.571	23.6
1881	0.219	0.358	0.032	0.573	23.6
1886	0.217	0.349	0.039	0.574	23.7
1891	0.211	0.344	0.036	0.569	23.8
1896	0.205	0.335	0.037	0.564	23.8
1901	0.200	0.327	0.037	0.563	

MORTALITY PATTERN: WEST
MIGRATION: GRADUAL, WITH POPULATION TOTALS OBTAINED BY TREND OF R/CB

TABLE 1   FEMALE POPULATION ESTIMATES: 1801 TO 1906

DATE	R/CB RATIO	% COR-RECTION	FINAL POPULATION ESTIMATE	DATE	R/CB RATIO	% COR-RECTION	FINAL POPULATION ESTIMATE
1801	1.070	0.0	263860	1856	0.962	0.7	329961
1806	1.045	0.0	267762	1861	0.954	-0.6	327623
1811*	1.031	0.0	274316	1866	0.941	-1.4	329514
1816*	1.016	0.0	280871	1871	0.905	0.2	327105
1821	1.014	0.0	287425	1876	0.905	-2.1	323141
1826*	1.004	0.0	298637	1881	0.864	0.1	324923
1831	1.022	0.0	309849	1886	0.836	1.1	324850
1836	1.014	0.0	314077	1891	0.810	1.7	320877
1841	0.996	0.0	316697	1896	0.800	0.5	315927
1846	1.000	0.0	328027	1901	0.785	-0.3	313035
1851	0.980	1.0	332281	1906	0.767	-0.7	310656

NOTE: R/CB RATIO REFERS TO THE POPULATION COMPUTED BY THE BALANCE OF BIRTHS
       AND DEATHS OVER THE REPORTED POPULATION
* INTERPOLATED VALUES

TABLE 2   FEMALE BIRTH ESTIMATES: 1801-1805 TO 1901-1905

DATE	% COR-RECTION	FINAL BIRTH ESTIMATE	CRUDE BIRTH RATE	DATE	% COR-RECTION	FINAL BIRTH ESTIMATE	CRUDE BIRTH RATE
1801-1805	0.0	44838	33.7	1856-1860	0.0	46543	28.3
1806-1810	0.0	41085	30.3	1861-1865	0.0	47711	29.0
1811-1815	9.3	45416	32.7	1866-1870	0.0	46284	28.2
1816-1820	0.0	47421	33.4	1871-1875	0.0	46025	28.3
1821-1825	0.0	49409	33.7	1876-1880	0.0	46118	28.5
1826-1830	1.4	47774	31.4	1881-1885	0.0	44379	27.3
1831-1835	0.0	47987	30.8	1886-1890	0.0	41555	25.7
1836-1840	5.4	46701	29.6	1891-1895	0.0	40674	25.5
1841-1845	0.0	45890	28.5	1896-1900	0.0	40964	26.1
1846-1850	0.0	46111	27.9	1901-1905	0.0	40004	25.7
1851-1855	0.0	45156	27.3				

[283]

TABLE 3 FEMALE POPULATION ESTIMATES,
DISTRIBUTION BY AGE: 1801 TO 1906

AGE	1801	1806	1811	1816	1821	1826	1831	1836	1841	1846	1851
0- 4	35696	33042	31564	33863	34561	37799	36004	35559	35237	36382	35758
5- 9	30377	31225	29605	27952	29843	31009	34096	31857	31543	32318	32781
10-14	27813	28658	29383	28284	26846	28687	30305	32643	30315	30766	31049
15-19	25437	26228	27414	28537	27154	25794	28024	29002	31049	29554	29500
20-24	23049	23742	24856	25910	27089	25840	24928	26535	27317	30001	28006
25-29	20713	21327	22325	23290	24361	25570	24748	23394	24790	26201	28284
30-34	18478	19030	19926	20769	21726	22844	24308	23055	21709	23633	24584
35-39	16389	16853	17662	18401	19219	20233	21550	22474	21245	20564	22036
40-44	14423	14849	15545	16203	16909	17786	18958	19791	20579	23005	19065
45-49	12629	12976	13602	14160	14781	15539	16546	17287	17996	19245	18423
50-54	10852	11168	11695	12179	12685	13361	14204	14826	15459	16566	17445
55-59	9062	9308	9783	10156	10560	11137	11834	12336	12874	13844	14601
60-64	7207	7382	7771	8068	8332	8826	9353	9750	10193	11006	11632
65-69	5289	5432	5731	5930	6093	6466	6844	7119	7475	8120	8606
70-74	3491	3562	3788	3906	3978	4240	4468	4646	4891	5361	5708
75-79	1930	1970	2097	2162	2176	2332	2445	2534	2685	2972	3187
80+	1011	1011	1069	1101	1111	1173	1233	1272	1340	1490	1615

AGE	1856	1861	1866	1871	1876	1881	1886	1891	1896	1901	1906
0- 4	34332	35127	37257	35677	35120	37089	36046	33504	32748	33655	33511
5- 9	31738	30377	31518	33190	31628	31806	33696	32625	30284	29816	30867
10-14	31144	30154	28967	29958	31542	30226	30398	32222	31221	28988	28560
15-19	29296	29309	28366	26972	27806	29349	27872	27912	29652	28661	26407
20-24	27255	26846	26709	25296	23694	24273	25229	23485	23371	24942	23759
25-29	25932	25131	24776	24371	22903	21419	21756	22519	20794	20674	22124
30-34	26215	24008	23410	22962	22540	21369	19954	20238	20975	19389	19313
35-39	22658	24155	22291	21646	21200	21059	19991	18636	18924	19701	18254
40-44	20214	20786	22364	20579	19969	19832	19773	18770	17524	17882	18705
45-49	17383	18437	19145	20551	18906	18623	18581	18536	17633	16555	16980
50-54	16538	15614	16747	17355	18617	17430	17269	17244	17238	16508	15607
55-59	15214	14423	13805	14765	15281	16724	15764	15622	15628	15739	15194
60-64	12108	12592	12134	11549	12311	13064	14378	13526	13415	13545	13765
65-69	8960	9294	9873	9441	8940	9845	10519	11537	10856	10900	11136
70-74	5947	6160	6564	6904	6553	6466	7178	7631	8365	7995	8148
75-79	3325	3438	3688	3878	4036	4042	4028	4438	4711	5271	5137
80+	1704	1771	1900	2010	2096	2309	2418	2433	2588	2814	3189

TABLE 4   MARRIED WOMEN ESTIMATES,
DISTRIBUTICN BY AGE: 1831 TO 1901

AGE	1831	1836	1841	1846	1851	1856	1861	1866
15-19	682	669	683	621	595	569	631	622
20-24	5783	5916	5883	6250	5646	5314	5077	4342
25-29	12184	11323	11851	12364	13155	11858	11314	10982
30-34	15009	14141	13322	14495	15035	15923	14510	14072
35-39	14025	14570	13879	13525	14544	14925	15927	14708
40-44	12283	12778	13484	13288	12779	13568	14040	15205
45-49	9932	10297	10941	11921	11547	10893	11640	12182

AGE	1871	1876	1881	1886	1891	1896	1901
15-19	547	580	618	523	502	457	704
20-24	4387	4699	4876	5078	4636	4757	5165
25-29	9235	9124	9848	10128	10632	9861	10128
30-34	13661	12003	11847	12227	12668	13355	12446
35-39	14190	13855	12955	12561	12595	12989	13748
40-44	13940	13555	13764	12649	12280	11866	12207
45-49	12974	11949	12149	12222	12417	11714	10783

TABLE 5   DEMOGRAPHIC INDICES AND FEMALE SINGULATE MEAN AGE
AT MARRIAGE: 1831 TO 1901

DATE	IF OVERALL FERTILITY	IG MARITAL FERTILITY	Ih ILLEGITIMATE FERTILITY	IM PROPORTION MARRIED	SINGULATE MEAN AGE AT MARRIAGE
1831	0.331	0.765	0.010	0.425	25.6
1836	0.324	0.764	0.012	0.415	25.9
1841	0.312	0.753	0.012	0.405	26.1
1846	0.299	0.718	0.015	0.404	26.3
1851	0.294	0.693	0.017	0.409	26.5
1856	0.297	0.698	0.019	0.409	26.6
1861	0.3C9	0.729	0.021	0.407	26.9
1866	0.314	0.762	0.017	0.399	27.3
1871	0.320	0.797	0.017	0.389	27.3
1876	0.331	0.829	0.017	0.386	27.0
1881	0.328	0.810	0.018	0.392	26.7
1886	0.316	0.767	0.018	0.398	27.1
1891	0.309	0.728	0.019	0.409	27.5
1896	0.309	0.722	0.020	0.411	27.1
1901	0.305	0.708	0.018	0.417	

MORTALITY PATTERN: WEST
MIGRATION: GRADUAL, WITH POPULATION TOTALS OBTAINED BY TREND OF R/CB

TABLE 1   FEMALE POPULATION ESTIMATES: 1801 TO 1906

DATE	R/CB RATIO	% COR- RECTION	FINAL POPULATION ESTIMATE	DATE	R/CB RATIO	% COR- RECTION	FINAL POPULATION ESTIMATE
1801	0.976	3.7	115777	1856	0.958	-0.0	145295
1806	1.025	0.0	115619	1861	0.927	1.3	142293
1811*	1.027	0.0	119383	1866	0.917	0.4	142355
1816*	1.005	0.0	123146	1871	0.902	0.1	142471
1821	0.984	0.0	126910	1876	0.901	-1.7	141650
1826*	1.002	0.0	131265	1881	0.856	1.3	142173
1831	1.010	0.0	135619	1886	0.845	0.4	142201
1836	1.025	0.0	141782	1891	0.829	0.1	141469
1841	1.016	0.0	143403	1896	0.810	0.2	138715
1846	1.000	0.0	147380	1901	0.799	-0.7	136489
1851	0.987	-1.1	146389	1906	0.777	-0.2	134488

NOTE: R/CB RATIO REFERS TO THE POPULATION COMPUTED BY THE BALANCE OF BIRTHS
        AND DEATHS OVER THE REPORTED POPULATION
* INTERPOLATED VALUES

TABLE 2   FEMALE BIRTH ESTIMATES: 1801-1805 TO 1901-1905

DATE	% COR- RECTION	FINAL BIRTH ESTIMATE	CRUDE BIRTH RATE	DATE	% COR- RECTION	FINAL BIRTH ESTIMATE	CRUDE BIRTH RATE
1801-1805	0.0	17525	30.3	1856-1860	9.0	16511	23.0
1806-1810	0.0	18168	30.9	1861-1865	0.0	16094	22.6
1811-1815	0.0	19044	31.4	1866-1870	0.0	16281	22.9
1816-1820	0.0	19333	30.9	1871-1875	0.0	16229	22.8
1821-1825	0.0	18169	28.1	1876-1880	0.0	15754	22.2
1826-1830	1.5	18262	27.4	1881-1885	0.0	14990	21.1
1831-1835	0.0	19002	27.4	1886-1890	0.0	14628	20.6
1836-1840	5.8	19166	26.9	1891-1895	0.0	13230	18.9
1841-1845	0.0	19367	26.6	1896-1900	0.0	12915	18.8
1846-1850	0.0	17518	23.9	1901-1905	0.0	12409	18.3
1851-1855	0.0	16292	22.3				

TABLE 3 FEMALE POPULATICN ESTIMATES,
DISTRIBUTICN BY AGE: 1801 TO 1906

AGE	1801	1806	1811	1816	1821	1826	1831	1836	1841	1846	1851
0- 4	11775	12514	14214	15400	15711	14498	14776	15636	15129	16132	14103
5- 9	10594	10364	11416	12974	14078	14523	13430	13845	142C8	14021	14635
10-14	10235	1C277	10099	10942	12433	13850	14229	13272	13344	13724	13355
15-19	9887	9926	1C009	9674	10479	12226	13563	14055	12786	12883	13013
20-24	9459	9470	9577	9516	9197	10213	11873	13290	13424	12261	12036
25-29	8973	8966	9067	9049	8992	8896	9850	11557	12603	12802	11458
30-34	8452	8432	8529	8523	8508	8645	8532	9535	10895	11964	11959
35-39	7908	7873	7968	7974	7971	8127	8241	8212	8934	10292	11125
40-44	7352	7311	7394	7409	7418	7569	7704	7888	7649	8397	9526
45-49	6785	6747	6819	6830	6847	6995	7126	7324	7297	7142	7725
50-54	6159	6107	6191	6208	6223	6356	6487	6674	6671	6722	6481
55-59	5430	5354	5447	5499	5521	5618	5740	5921	5918	6005	5951
60-64	4550	4449	4552	4641	4694	4757	4854	5018	5017	5124	5094
65-69	3531	3413	3516	3637	3718	3767	3840	3970	3966	4088	4076
70-74	2454	2338	2423	2548	2644	2686	2746	2841	2830	2943	2949
75-79	1436	1337	1402	1503	1588	1617	1666	1733	1719	1807	1817
80+	787	743	760	820	887	922	961	1013	1013	1074	1C89

AGE	1856	1861	1866	1871	1876	1881	1886	1891	1896	1901	1906
0- 4	13183	12813	13357	13629	13484	13705	13269	12996	11655	11584	11323
5- 9	12862	11807	11803	12339	12542	12647	12946	12545	12239	11042	11044
10-14	14031	12271	11359	11359	11865	12127	12255	12560	12164	11889	10721
15-19	12717	13275	11655	10728	10669	11157	11383	11477	11752	11379	11C99
20-24	12172	11733	12303	10628	9602	9449	9808	9927	9951	10231	9823
25-29	11290	11303	10990	11495	9827	8842	8662	8973	9054	9102	9376
30-34	10767	10522	10683	10396	10857	9338	8415	8245	8535	8647	8719
35-39	11193	9989	9920	10093	9807	10348	8932	8054	7881	8196	8336
40-44	10369	10343	9396	9358	9515	9355	9927	8589	7739	7607	7948
45-49	8827	9526	9678	8823	8786	9044	8947	9520	8238	7460	7368
50-54	7061	7990	8802	8979	8187	8269	8571	8506	9045	7874	7176
55-59	5780	6219	7215	7982	8136	7547	7682	7987	7920	8470	7429
60-64	5080	4847	5384	6274	6924	7203	6737	6877	7134	7130	7686
65-69	4076	3967	3945	4407	5116	5795	6090	5714	5812	6090	6150
70-74	2956	2864	2937	2941	3268	3917	4491	4735	4420	4553	4833
75-79	1830	1759	1823	1885	1874	2169	2638	3036	3179	3015	3157
80+	1103	1063	1103	1156	1190	1265	1448	1730	1996	2219	2301

TABLE 4 MARRIED WOMEN ESTIMATES,
DISTRIBUTICN BY AGE: 1831 TO 1901

AGE	1831	1836	1841	1846	1851	1856	1861	1866
15-19	1016	1048	949	952	958	932	934	887
20-24	4947	5514	5551	5054	4941	4979	4782	4439
25-29	6393	7469	8125	8234	7343	7214	7200	6986
30-34	6126	6811	7768	8516	8478	7611	7416	7520
35-39	5965	5903	6413	7379	7937	7961	7081	7029
40-44	5447	5525	5352	5873	6621	7182	7137	6488
45-49	4762	4830	4810	4710	5051	5747	6174	6287

AGE	1871	1876	1881	1886	1891	1896	1901
15-19	860	886	1010	1068	924	846	1218
20-24	4091	3984	4317	4827	4831	4893	5076
25-29	6802	5997	5647	6023	6715	6735	6911
30-34	7299	7380	6460	5917	6291	7003	7079
35-39	7133	6928	7265	6264	5725	6058	6747
40-44	6444	6557	6526	6777	5910	5357	5642
45-49	5713	5702	5986	5831	6260	5428	4843

TABLE 5 DEMOGRAPHIC INDICES AND FEMALE SINGULATE MEAN AGE
AT MARRIAGE: 1831 TO 1901

DATE	IF OVERALL FERTILITY	IG MARITAL FERTILITY	IH ILLEGITIMATE FERTILITY	IM PROPORTION MARRIED	SINGULATE MEAN AGE AT MARRIAGE
1831	0.307	0.557	0.038	0.519	23.2
1836	0.288	0.523	0.037	0.518	23.2
1841	0.280	0.487	0.045	0.531	23.2
1846	0.262	0.454	0.036	0.540	23.2
1851	0.241	0.415	0.038	0.539	23.2
1856	0.237	0.414	0.033	0.536	23.2
1861	0.241	0.425	0.034	0.529	23.4
1866	0.243	0.439	0.030	0.523	23.4
1871	0.254	0.452	0.032	0.529	23.2
1876	0.263	0.466	0.028	0.537	22.9
1881	0.263	0.457	0.026	0.549	22.6
1886	0.261	0.442	0.030	0.560	22.5
1891	0.250	0.410	0.034	0.575	22.7
1896	0.235	0.373	0.037	0.590	22.7
1901	0.226	0.346	0.036	0.614	

DORDOGNE

MORTALITY PATTERN: WEST
MIGRATION: GRADUAL, WITH POPULATION TOTALS OBTAINED BY TREND OF R/CB

TABLE 1   FEMALE POPULATION ESTIMATES: 1801 TO 1906

DATE	R/CB RATIO	% COR- RECTION	FINAL POPULATION ESTIMATE	DATE	R/CB RATIO	% COR- RECTION	FINAL POPULATION ESTIMATE
1801	0.991	2.5	214595	1856	0.973	1.5	256708
1806*	1.013	1.3	215303	1861	0.964	0.6	251623
1811*	0.989	1.3	220810	1866	0.951	0.0	249913
1816*	0.974	1.3	226335	1871	0.911	2.3	245461
1821	0.979	3.6	237073	1876	0.921	-0.7	242154
1826*	0.992	1.3	238662	1881	0.899	-0.4	242577
1831	0.996	1.3	245464	1886	0.881	-0.4	240974
1836	1.005	1.3	247360	1891	0.861	-0.3	236604
1841	0.993	1.3	248733	1896	0.845	-0.5	230415
1846	1.000	1.3	254775	1901	0.817	0.7	226345
1851	0.987	2.0	257096	1906	0.801	0.4	222804

NOTE: R/CB RATIO REFERS TO THE POPULATION COMPUTED BY THE BALANCE OF BIRTHS
       AND DEATHS OVER THE REPORTED POPULATION
* INTERPOLATED VALUES

TABLE 2   FEMALE BIRTH ESTIMATES: 1801-1805 TO 1901-1905

DATE	% COR- RECTION	FINAL BIRTH ESTIMATE	CRUDE BIRTH RATE	DATE	% COR- RECTION	FINAL BIRTH ESTIMATE	CRUDE BIRTH RATE
1801-1805	12.8	37009	34.4	1856-1860	0.0	31779	25.0
1806-1810	0.0	35914	32.9	1861-1865	0.0	32398	25.8
1811-1815	8.7	35407	31.7	1866-1870	0.0	31834	25.7
1816-1820	3.1	32788	28.3	1871-1875	0.0	30693	25.2
1821-1825	0.0	31722	26.7	1876-1880	0.0	30710	25.3
1826-1830	0.0	32899	27.2	1881-1885	-9.6	27757	23.0
1831-1835	4.9	34450	28.0	1886-1890	-20.2	25210	21.1
1836-1840	0.0	33692	27.2	1891-1895	0.0	23485	20.1
1841-1845	0.0	33473	26.6	1896-1900	0.0	23068	20.2
1846-1850	5.4	34093	26.6	1901-1905	0.0	22295	19.9
1851-1855	0.0	32885	25.6				

TABLE 3 FEMALE POPULATION ESTIMATES,
DISTRIBUTION BY AGE: 1801 TO 1906

AGE	1801	1806	1811	1816	1821	1826	1831	1836	1841	1846	1851
0- 4	25279	25297	27643	27394	26059	24492	26077	25623	25971	26512	26639
5- 9	22117	21754	22598	24820	25414	23440	22474	23295	23022	23843	24020
10-14	20823	21245	20701	21613	24606	24403	22883	21794	22349	22499	23004
15-19	19578	19998	20207	19790	21418	23617	23812	22182	20899	21831	21678
20-24	18232	18548	18849	19143	19427	20366	22840	22831	21074	20233	20812
25-29	16847	17076	17351	17723	18646	18331	19550	21698	21522	20250	19170
30-34	15447	15630	15374	16213	17151	17482	17489	18433	20324	20553	19088
35-39	14074	14194	14436	14737	15585	15974	16573	16361	17151	19284	19254
40-44	12727	12829	13031	13321	14079	14427	15053	15398	15130	16176	17960
45-49	11449	11513	11697	11942	12639	12943	13502	13886	14142	14173	14963
50-54	10111	10148	10331	10551	11147	11433	11923	12235	12548	13038	12905
55-59	9672	8632	8856	9062	9571	9802	10245	10465	10746	11251	11545
60-64	7088	6947	7187	7411	7834	8023	8384	8520	8762	9196	9505
65-69	5361	5167	5385	5599	5955	6107	6393	6431	6634	6983	7233
70-74	3619	3426	3603	3774	4040	4171	4381	4365	4498	4757	4941
75-79	2070	1882	2021	2137	2299	2391	2535	2492	2579	2731	2849
80+	1098	1018	1042	1106	1203	1262	1352	1349	1382	1465	1531

AGE	1856	1861	1866	1871	1876	1881	1886	1891	1896	1901	1906
0- 4	25954	24209	25363	24486	24166	25345	23314	21099	19534	19739	19471
5- 9	24068	23068	21784	22624	22050	22180	23416	21493	19381	18134	18485
10-14	22982	22909	22069	20764	21639	21203	21357	22577	20708	18706	17518
15-19	21874	21668	21673	20711	19457	20324	19810	19933	21108	19330	17368
20-24	20230	20098	19923	19628	18623	17316	17884	17291	17345	18521	16743
25-29	19464	18699	18659	18321	18057	17151	15808	16316	15715	15828	16977
30-34	17940	18066	17476	17350	17116	17019	16190	14902	15384	14889	15040
35-39	17781	16571	16821	16197	16175	16131	16101	15316	14084	14637	14213
40-44	17854	16356	15377	15551	15077	15246	15287	15270	14525	13448	14036
45-49	16553	16327	15095	14144	14409	14158	14405	14457	14442	13838	12874
50-54	13591	14905	14850	13684	12933	13377	13240	13483	13531	13628	13130
55-59	11415	11893	13192	13082	12177	11724	12225	12109	12323	12490	12658
60-64	9751	9491	10028	11039	11075	10543	10241	10675	10555	10881	11116
65-69	7496	7530	7460	7800	8715	9002	9667	8408	8738	8788	9153
70-74	5148	5192	5330	5210	5549	6432	6737	6471	6252	6638	6760
75-79	2990	3005	3116	3142	3145	3512	4143	4324	4128	4101	4424
80+	1616	1637	1698	1728	1792	1915	2150	2481	2662	2750	2837

TABLE 4 MARRIED WOMEN ESTIMATES,
DISTRIBUTICN BY AGE: 1831 TO 1901

AGE	1831	1836	1841	1846	1851	1856	1861	1866
15-19	1624	1620	1550	1697	1774	1892	1588	1657
20-24	8743	9017	8573	8568	9135	9208	9493	8098
25-29	12376	14019	14243	13713	13272	13763	13495	13738
30-34	12779	13635	15313	15744	14846	14144	14425	14126
35-39	12491	12411	13226	15077	15237	14211	13362	13685
40-44	11299	11535	11495	12422	13913	13912	12807	12107
45-49	9525	9740	10106	10266	10953	12192	12082	11234

AGE	1871	1876	1881	1886	1891	1896	1901
15-19	1774	2116	2536	2313	1846	1800	2064
20-24	8759	9187	8864	9446	9162	8948	9471
25-29	12437	12952	12939	11926	12389	12056	12163
30-34	14127	13433	13608	13341	12291	12712	12320
35-39	13200	13336	12844	13054	12759	11774	12105
40-44	12177	11933	11889	11916	12211	11903	10875
45-49	10411	10751	10300	10606	10974	11260	10712

TABLE 5 DEMOGRAPHIC INDICES AND FEMALE SINGULATE MEAN AGE
AT MARRIAGE: 1831 TO 1901

DATE	IF OVERALL FERTILITY	IG MARITAL FERTILITY	IH ILLEGITIMATE FERTILITY	IM PROPORTION MARRIED	SINGULATE MEAN AGE AT MARRIAGE
1831	0.286	0.520	0.026	0.526	24.0
1836	0.284	0.496	0.031	0.544	24.0
1841	0.281	0.472	0.032	0.566	23.8
1846	0.281	0.461	0.031	0.581	23.5
1851	0.281	0.452	0.035	0.590	23.3
1856	0.278	0.447	0.027	0.597	23.2
1861	0.284	0.451	0.031	0.602	23.4
1866	0.287	0.468	0.027	0.591	23.4
1871	0.286	0.465	0.025	0.593	22.9
1876	0.289	0.453	0.023	0.617	22.5
1881	0.281	0.437	0.020	0.626	22.5
1886	0.260	0.398	0.022	0.633	22.7
1891	0.244	0.371	0.025	0.633	22.8
1896	0.236	0.361	0.027	0.625	22.7
1901	0.230	0.352	0.024	0.630	

MORTALITY PATTERN: WEST
MIGRATION: FULL STRENGTH, WITH POPULATION TOTALS OBTAINED BY TREND OF R/CB

TABLE 1   FEMALE POPULATION ESTIMATES: 1801 TO 1906

DATE	R/CB RATIO	% COR-RECTION	FINAL POPULATION ESTIMATE	DATE	R/CB RATIO	% COR-RECTION	FINAL POPULATION ESTIMATE
1801	0.967	2.1	113686	1856	0.959	1.2	146175
1806	0.987	0.0	116384	1861	0.957	0.4	147655
1811*	0.971	0.0	119483	1866	0.946	0.5	149329
1816*	0.968	0.0	122583	1871	0.917	2.6	148575
1821	0.971	0.0	125682	1876	0.951	-2.2	147518
1826*	0.980	0.0	130751	1881	0.941	-2.2	148703
1831	0.989	0.0	135819	1886	0.921	-1.1	149778
1836	1.006	0.0	141096	1891	0.897	0.4	149635
1841	1.024	0.0	147497	1896	0.894	-0.5	148618
1846	1.000	0.0	147183	1901	0.871	1.1	148427
1851	0.990	-0.9	147065	1906	0.862	0.9	148637

NOTE: R/CB RATIO REFERS TO THE POPULATION COMPUTED BY THE BALANCE OF BIRTHS
        AND DEATHS OVER THE REPORTED POPULATION
* INTERPOLATED VALUES

TABLE 2   FEMALE BIRTH ESTIMATES: 1801-1805 TO 1901-1905

DATE	% COR-RECTION	FINAL BIRTH ESTIMATE	CRUDE BIRTH RATE	DATE	% COR-RECTION	FINAL BIRTH ESTIMATE	CRUDE BIRTH RATE
1801-1805	0.0	18446	32.1	1856-1860	0.0	18593	25.3
1806-1810	8.3	17852	30.3	1861-1865	0.0	19483	26.2
1811-1815	10.5	18010	29.8	1866-1870	0.0	19042	25.6
1816-1820	0.0	17941	28.9	1871-1875	0.0	19215	26.0
1821-1825	0.0	18723	29.2	1876-1880	0.0	19931	26.9
1826-1830	0.0	19198	28.8	1881-1885	0.0	19589	26.3
1831-1835	0.0	18891	27.3	1886-1890	0.0	18036	24.1
1836-1840	0.0	19252	26.7	1891-1895	0.0	17384	23.3
1841-1845	0.0	19421	26.4	1896-1900	0.0	17649	23.8
1846-1850	2.8	18674	25.4	1901-1905	0.0	17047	23.0
1851-1855	6.2	18421	25.1				

TABLE 3 FEMALE POPULATION ESTIMATES,
DISTRIBUTION BY AGE: 1801 TO 1906

AGE	1801	1806	1811	1816	1821	1826	1831	1836	1841	1846	1851
0- 4	12826	13877	14186	14116	14000	14968	15370	15201	15809	15209	15015
5- 9	11254	11473	12596	12882	12342	12913	13815	14271	14253	14202	13814
10-14	10703	10866	11001	12172	12514	12580	12651	13624	14133	13555	13649
15-19	10180	10331	10414	10626	11820	12253	12319	12470	13484	13435	12640
20-24	9583	9724	9820	9969	10223	11472	11895	12037	12243	12711	11815
25-29	8938	9074	9181	9331	9516	9850	11057	11538	11737	11460	11627
30-34	8270	8403	8519	8670	8850	9115	9437	10661	11188	10923	10761
35-39	7600	7717	7843	7994	8169	8424	8678	9042	10277	10350	10264
40-44	6941	7045	7162	7315	7485	7729	7973	8266	8667	9452	9735
45-49	6286	6389	6495	6635	6803	7034	7266	7543	7870	7918	8863
50-54	5601	5687	5801	5922	6071	6294	6511	6767	7074	7081	7344
55-59	4835	4914	5031	5145	5267	5466	5669	5901	6184	6198	6401
60-64	3953	4027	4160	4258	4361	4529	4703	4907	5161	5181	5319
65-69	2989	3045	3188	3280	3356	3497	3635	3796	4013	4037	4154
70-74	2006	2056	2178	2262	2323	2425	2529	2643	2806	2834	2924
75-79	1125	1155	1253	1309	1353	1424	1489	1560	1665	1685	1747
80+	586	600	653	693	731	778	824	869	934	952	992

AGE	1856	1861	1866	1871	1876	1881	1886	1891	1896	1901	1906
0- 4	14393	15115	15820	15051	15034	16088	16022	14853	14204	14556	14351
5- 9	13542	13215	13870	14337	13586	13756	14792	14765	13640	13094	13529
10-14	13293	13110	12783	13359	13806	13131	13302	14316	14282	13205	12696
15-19	12910	12673	12474	12065	12642	13131	12440	12588	13589	13583	12533
20-24	11471	11899	11630	11283	10943	11564	11946	11229	11410	12419	12387
25-29	10938	10734	11124	10761	10444	10184	10751	11102	10423	10626	11610
30-34	10919	10365	10163	10461	10105	9870	9633	10181	10507	9880	10110
35-39	10077	10325	9794	9535	9799	9532	9330	9116	9623	9956	9399
40-44	9591	9507	9739	9177	8913	9229	9006	8829	8610	9110	9473
45-49	9053	9005	8925	9084	8537	8356	8683	8489	8305	8118	8635
50-54	8128	8389	8344	8213	8331	7899	7766	8087	7888	7737	7610
55-59	6552	7344	7578	7472	7326	7511	7161	7060	7328	7170	7087
60-64	5422	5651	6331	6452	6333	6299	6457	6213	6103	6362	6284
65-69	4192	4377	4559	5024	5089	5091	5104	5286	5031	4971	5246
70-74	2943	3062	3194	3259	3563	3698	3736	3766	3877	3716	3730
75-79	1751	1835	1907	1936	1954	2206	2319	2360	2360	2452	2399
80+	999	1047	1096	1109	1112	1158	1290	1395	1438	1471	1557

[293]

TABLE 4 MARRIED WOMEN ESTIMATES,
DISTRIBUTION BY AGE: 1831 TO 1901

AGE	1831	1836	1841	1846	1851	1856	1861	1866
15-19	301	310	342	347	332	346	325	302
20-24	2475	2543	2633	2777	2626	2592	2737	2419
25-29	5131	5416	5586	5514	5665	5392	5360	5617
30-34	5824	6634	7043	6928	6892	7053	6764	6681
35-39	5890	6176	7099	7188	7189	7106	7350	7008
40-44	5717	5947	6304	6889	7146	7071	7069	7258
45-49	4904	5106	5406	5445	6147	6308	6343	6296

AGE	1871	1876	1881	1886	1891	1896	1901
15-19	333	432	498	428	337	304	416
20-24	2355	2597	2987	3250	2945	2799	2991
25-29	5025	4935	5288	5745	6164	5718	5739
30-34	6924	6335	6325	6465	7020	7430	6935
35-39	6852	7044	6733	6569	6697	7183	7521
40-44	6847	6618	7027	6400	6404	6353	6721
45-49	6406	5965	6052	6153	6159	6018	5749

TABLE 5 DEMOGRAPHIC INDICES AND FEMALE SINGULATE MEAN AGE
AT MARRIAGE: 1831 TO 1901

DATE	IF OVERALL FERTILITY	IG MARITAL FERTILITY	IH ILLEGITIMATE FERTILITY	IM PROPORTION MARRIED	SINGULATE MEAN AGE AT MARRIAGE
1831	0.303	0.687	0.035	0.411	26.8
1836	0.291	0.643	0.035	0.421	26.9
1841	0.281	0.605	0.037	0.429	26.8
1846	0.275	0.587	0.037	0.432	26.7
1851	0.273	0.563	0.042	0.444	26.6
1856	0.278	0.559	0.050	0.447	26.6
1861	0.287	0.578	0.048	0.450	26.7
1866	0.293	0.592	0.050	0.448	26.8
1871	0.297	0.611	0.047	0.444	26.7
1876	0.308	0.639	0.044	0.444	26.3
1881	0.309	0.621	0.048	0.455	25.9
1886	0.293	0.584	0.044	0.462	26.1
1891	0.277	0.530	0.047	0.475	26.6
1896	0.270	0.524	0.044	0.470	26.5
1901	0.261	0.516	0.040	0.465	

MORTALITY PATTERN: WEST
MIGRATION: GRADUAL, WITH POPULATION TOTALS OBTAINED BY TREND OF R/CB

TABLE 1 FEMALE POPULATION ESTIMATES: 1801 TO 1906

DATE	R/CB RATIO	% COR- RECTION	FINAL POPULATION ESTIMATE	DATE	R/CB RATIO	% COR- RECTION	FINAL POPULATION ESTIMATE
1801	1.029	5.9	126287	1856	1.002	0.8	161935
1806	1.037	1.5	128562	1861	1.001	-0.0	160747
1811*	1.014	1.5	132491	1866	0.989	0.3	160354
1816*	0.996	1.5	136421	1871	0.976	0.7	158789
1821	0.986	1.5	140350	1876	0.978	-0.5	157434
1826*	0.994	1.5	146255	1881	0.921	4.8	155801
1831	1.002	1.5	152160	1886	0.933	2.5	153185
1836	1.002	1.5	154606	1891	0.946	0.1	151138
1841	0.999	1.5	157024	1896	0.933	0.5	147371
1846	1.000	1.5	160474	1901	0.942	-1.4	144835
1851	1.006	1.3	163075	1906	0.945	-2.7	142210

NOTE: R/CB RATIO REFERS TO THE POPULATION COMPUTED BY THE BALANCE OF BIRTHS
       AND DEATHS OVER THE REPORTED POPULATION
* INTERPOLATED VALUES

TABLE 2   FEMALE BIRTH ESTIMATES: 1801-1805 TO 1901-1905

DATE	% COR- RECTION	FINAL BIRTH ESTIMATE	CRUDE BIRTH RATE	DATE	% COR- RECTION	FINAL BIRTH ESTIMATE	CRUDE BIRTH RATE
1801-1805	20.4	23224	36.5	1856-1860	0.0	20542	25.5
1806-1810	9.5	22074	33.8	1861-1865	0.0	20569	25.6
1811-1815	9.4	21823	32.5	1866-1870	0.7	19784	24.8
1816-1820	0.0	21723	31.4	1871-1875	0.0	19998	25.3
1821-1825	0.0	22201	31.0	1876-1880	0.0	18661	23.8
1826-1830	0.0	21996	29.5	1881-1885	0.0	17193	22.3
1831-1835	0.0	21991	28.7	1886-1890	0.0	16776	22.1
1836-1840	0.0	21661	27.8	1891-1895	0.0	15283	20.5
1841-1845	0.0	21890	27.6	1896-1900	0.0	14624	20.0
1846-1850	0.0	21081	26.1	1901-1905	0.0	13672	19.1
1851-1855	0.0	20525	25.3				

TABLE 3 FEMALE POPULATION ESTIMATES,
DISTRIBUTION BY AGE: 1801 TO 1906

AGE	1801	1806	1811	1816	1821	1826	1831	1836	1841	1846	1851
0- 4	17563	16905	16729	16667	16556	17093	17210	16585	16547	16991	16421
5- 9	14781	15222	15000	14923	14916	15023	15612	15397	14914	15018	15457
10-14	13496	13839	14457	14303	14316	14538	14663	15058	14863	14477	14601
15-19	12311	12631	13138	13779	13715	13948	14184	14137	14529	14422	14078
20-24	11121	11402	11377	12404	13085	13231	13481	13535	13507	13965	13906
25-29	9951	10209	10636	11126	11684	12519	12688	12754	12825	12880	13348
30-34	8839	9070	9462	9899	10411	11102	11928	11919	12004	12151	12223
35-39	7786	7996	8348	8747	9198	9822	10507	11123	11139	11295	11453
40-44	6825	6997	7314	7670	8077	8623	9239	9734	10329	10416	10579
45-49	5933	6089	6356	6673	7033	7518	8055	8499	8976	9592	9688
50-54	5060	5203	5441	5705	6018	6438	6910	7283	7707	8201	8777
55-59	4190	4302	4516	4746	4997	5348	5750	6061	6413	6841	7292
60-64	3289	3382	3557	3754	3957	4223	4551	4791	5076	5423	5798
65-69	2379	2454	2597	2748	2904	3101	3341	3510	3722	3989	4271
70-74	1538	1585	1691	1801	1906	2038	2203	2302	2442	2625	2821
75-79	823	857	920	989	1052	1124	1222	1272	1347	1453	1567
80+	415	420	452	489	526	566	617	647	684	736	795

AGE	1856	1861	1866	1871	1876	1881	1886	1891	1896	1901	1906
0- 4	15600	15612	15310	15284	15464	14709	13624	13477	12205	12009	11401
5- 9	14672	13946	14063	14310	13757	14022	13361	12452	12277	11256	11146
10-14	14826	14089	13423	13521	13772	13259	13525	12920	12023	11907	10932
15-19	13960	14182	13492	12804	12904	13132	12624	12922	12291	11498	11404
20-24	13263	13138	13352	12596	11935	11965	12140	11701	11896	11419	10670
25-29	13053	12449	12358	12513	11802	11167	11184	11396	10928	11211	10780
30-34	12483	12219	11696	11595	11752	11115	10524	10581	10765	10391	10695
35-39	11357	11611	11416	10917	10834	11025	10441	9924	9965	10209	9888
40-44	10580	10505	10792	10607	10155	10127	10325	9818	9323	9426	9694
45-49	9708	9722	9702	9967	9807	9439	9432	9656	9177	8774	8905
50-54	8746	8777	8839	8823	9074	8983	8668	8701	8901	8523	8186
55-59	7693	7676	7756	7812	7806	8088	8029	7789	7811	8064	7764
60-64	6077	6417	6457	6520	6575	6629	6888	6885	6664	6768	7038
65-69	4481	4700	5018	5046	5100	5204	5265	5519	5498	5413	5549
70-74	2957	3103	3300	3520	3543	3636	3725	3811	3977	4048	4033
75-79	1642	1722	1840	1954	2086	2141	2209	2295	2333	2504	2589
80+	337	879	939	1002	1067	1161	1223	1289	1338	1414	1538

TABLE 4 MARRIED WOMEN ESTIMATES,
DISTRIBUTION BY AGE: 1831 TO 1901

AGE	1831	1836	1841	1846	1851	1856	1861	1866
15-19	850	849	859	862	851	853	982	947
20-24	4649	4669	4701	4921	4931	4733	4720	4775
25-29	7820	7873	7942	8009	8310	8137	7771	7725
30-34	8811	8796	8872	9008	9046	9224	9016	8617
35-39	8144	8601	8625	8781	8873	8771	8941	8766
40-44	7328	7690	8175	8290	8375	8337	8241	8431
45-49	6071	6380	6770	7310	7340	7318	7295	7250

AGE	1871	1876	1881	1886	1891	1896	1901
15-19	1000	1075	942	768	657	530	653
20-24	4737	4690	4580	4414	4321	4519	4132
25-29	7678	7451	7177	7062	7167	7073	7598
30-34	8506	8521	8147	7775	7869	8032	7886
35-39	8322	8216	8311	7912	7639	7664	7893
40-44	8197	7788	7707	7694	7481	7012	7048
45-49	7342	7157	6823	6809	7175	6672	6183

TABLE 5 DEMOGRAPHIC INDICES AND FEMALE SINGULATE MEAN AGE
AT MARRIAGE: 1831 TO 1901

DATE	IF OVERALL FERTILITY	IG MARITAL FERTILITY	IH ILLEGITIMATE FERTILITY	IM PROPORTION MARRIED	SINGULATE MEAN AGE AT MARRIAGE
1831	0.299	0.533	0.035	0.530	25.2
1836	0.292	0.520	0.033	0.532	25.0
1841	0.288	0.510	0.034	0.534	24.9
1846	0.281	0.497	0.029	0.537	24.9
1851	0.270	0.477	0.026	0.540	24.8
1856	0.270	0.472	0.030	0.543	24.7
1861	0.273	0.476	0.033	0.543	24.6
1866	0.272	0.477	0.028	0.542	24.5
1871	0.275	0.486	0.021	0.547	24.3
1876	0.275	0.478	0.023	0.553	24.3
1881	0.259	0.455	0.022	0.548	24.4
1886	0.250	0.441	0.026	0.538	24.4
1891	0.238	0.422	0.023	0.540	24.5
1896	0.225	0.393	0.023	0.546	24.4
1901	0.217	0.371	0.022	0.559	

MORTALITY PATTERN: WEST
MIGRATION: FULL STRENGTH, WITH POPULATION TOTALS OBTAINED BY TREND OF R/CB

TABLE 1   FEMALE POPULATION ESTIMATES: 1801 TO 1906

DATE	R/CB RATIO	% COR-RECTION	FINAL POPULATION ESTIMATE	DATE	R/CB RATIO	% COR-RECTION	FINAL POPULATION ESTIMATE
1801	0.984	3.0	214751	1856	0.982	0.6	205983
1806	1.003	0.0	216131	1861	0.984	0.0	200993
1811*	0.995	0.0	216677	1866	0.984	-0.3	197033
1816*	0.984	0.0	217222	1871	0.972	0.6	191697
1821	0.977	0.0	217768	1876	0.983	-0.8	186763
1826*	0.980	0.0	218935	1881	0.969	0.3	182109
1831	0.986	0.0	220102	1886	0.975	-0.6	179139
1836	0.996	0.0	220102	1891	0.966	-0.1	174851
1841	1.000	0.0	218763	1896	0.964	-0.2	169498
1846	1.000	0.0	216787	1901	0.955	0.5	166821
1851	0.992	-0.2	211018	1906	0.954	0.2	164765

NOTE: R/CB RATIO REFERS TO THE POPULATION COMPUTED BY THE BALANCE OF BIRTHS
        AND DEATHS OVER THE REPORTED POPULATION
* INTERPOLATED VALUES

TABLE 2   FEMALE BIRTH ESTIMATES: 1801-1805 TO 1901-1905

DATE	% COR-RECTION	FINAL BIRTH ESTIMATE	CRUDE BIRTH RATE	DATE	% COR-RECTION	FINAL BIRTH ESTIMATE	CRUDE BIRTH RATE
1801-1805	8.4	27893	25.9	1856-1860	0.0	19249	18.9
1806-1810	0.0	25721	23.8	1861-1865	0.0	19246	19.3
1811-1815	0.0	25588	23.6	1866-1870	0.0	18611	19.2
1816-1820	-3.6	24894	22.9	1871-1875	0.0	17235	18.2
1821-1825	-5.3	24478	22.4	1876-1880	0.0	16714	18.1
1826-1830	0.0	23730	21.6	1881-1885	0.0	16663	18.5
1831-1835	0.0	22005	20.0	1886-1890	0.0	16456	18.6
1836-1840	0.0	20679	18.8	1891-1895	0.0	16477	19.1
1841-1845	0.0	20536	18.9	1896-1900	0.0	16370	19.5
1846-1850	2.5	19771	18.5	1901-1905	0.0	16025	19.3
1851-1855	0.0	19443	18.7				

TABLE 3 FEMALE POPULATION ESTIMATES,
DISTRIBUTION BY AGE: 1801 TO 1906

AGE	1801	1806	1811	1816	1821	1826	1831	1836	1841	1846	1851
0- 4	28439	21755	20017	20050	19665	19339	18951	17677	16835	16831	16077
5- 9	24538	25595	19640	18120	18247	18001	17810	17525	16398	15638	15454
10-14	22425	23454	24608	18894	17499	17777	17601	17471	17152	16025	15137
15-19	20482	21424	22539	23662	18237	17040	17374	17257	17090	16754	15285
20-24	18558	19397	20403	21483	22643	17601	16509	16388	16746	16565	15511
25-29	16708	17448	18334	19304	20409	21690	16929	15933	16279	16127	15575
30-34	14954	15614	16390	17242	18231	19431	20737	16242	15274	15594	15305
35-39	13305	13887	14573	15316	16183	17246	18462	19773	15480	14550	14757
40-44	11773	12283	12883	13538	14291	15216	16290	17501	18740	14666	13731
45-49	10347	10795	11317	11887	12546	13346	14275	15337	16475	17637	13766
50-54	8963	9341	9789	10279	10846	11532	12327	13234	14224	15280	16325
55-59	7557	7874	8237	8651	9129	9697	10366	11123	11961	12864	13789
60-64	6095	6341	6625	6951	7340	7789	8326	8938	9626	10368	11097
65-69	4600	4769	4968	5211	5502	5833	6236	6698	7236	7816	8371
70-74	3136	3243	3361	3520	3718	3935	4209	4524	4904	5322	5711
75-79	1822	1876	1935	2019	2132	2252	2409	2593	2824	3082	3319
80+	1025	1037	1058	1096	1150	1211	1292	1390	1518	1669	1810

AGE	1856	1861	1866	1871	1876	1881	1886	1891	1896	1901	1906
0- 4	15791	15722	15969	15323	14444	14065	14270	13797	13472	13816	13681
5- 9	14845	14618	14651	14818	14320	13521	13257	13326	12752	12628	13010
10-14	15046	14465	14273	14276	14468	13989	13229	12933	12963	12461	12353
15-19	14705	14634	14095	13848	13869	14066	13604	12818	12504	12606	12117
20-24	14694	14161	14125	13490	13261	13293	13471	12964	12184	11988	12076
25-29	14850	14088	13615	13515	12934	12724	12772	12887	12355	11698	11516
30-34	14856	14183	13499	13012	12960	12413	12249	12239	12289	11866	11255
35-39	14520	14113	13522	12841	12426	12389	11909	11693	11618	11755	11378
40-44	13925	13721	13388	12803	12210	11827	11842	11325	11052	11067	11228
45-49	12873	13074	12932	12596	12100	11552	11240	11195	10639	10464	10509
50-54	12718	11911	12150	11997	11746	11296	10840	10486	10369	9940	9810
55-59	14699	11473	10804	10996	10926	10712	10367	9877	9470	9466	9113
60-64	11889	12705	9990	9374	9618	9575	9463	9070	8542	8310	8350
65-69	8953	9625	10385	8127	7709	7929	7976	7783	7348	7054	6910
70-74	6111	6564	7143	7661	6078	5783	6027	5967	5711	5524	5350
75-79	3557	3828	4177	4510	4924	3922	3796	3876	3742	3696	3616
80+	1951	2109	2315	2509	2770	3052	2827	2615	2488	2480	2494

TABLE 4 MARRIED WOMEN ESTIMATES,
DISTRIBUTION BY AGE: 1831 TO 1901

AGE	1831	1836	1841	1846	1851	1856	1861	1866
15-19	1098	1137	1180	1220	1181	1216	1353	1480
20-24	6511	6891	7093	7293	7108	7017	7053	7341
25-29	10973	10564	11065	11226	11094	10811	10469	10312
30-34	15395	12231	11707	12144	12094	11890	11478	11024
35-39	14110	15250	12118	11533	11825	11738	11489	11062
40-44	12499	13446	14560	11491	10834	11039	10905	10641
45-49	10316	11092	12105	13109	10329	9716	9895	9777

AGE	1871	1876	1881	1886	1891	1896	1901
15-19	1465	1425	1331	1171	965	888	1100
20-24	7074	7135	7129	6963	6647	6235	6040
25-29	10355	9869	9853	9886	9831	9464	9070
30-34	10692	10665	10208	10141	10105	10065	9780
35-39	10515	10209	10177	9779	9608	9487	9583
40-44	10121	9644	9373	9383	8939	8671	8675
45-49	9435	9041	8666	8425	8334	7834	7726

TABLE 5 DEMOGRAPHIC INDICES AND FEMALE SINGULATE MEAN AGE
AT MARRIAGE: 1831 TO 1901

DATE	IF OVERALL FERTILITY	IG MARITAL FERTILITY	IH ILLEGITIMATE FERTILITY	IM PROPORTION MARRIED	SINGULATE MEAN AGE AT MARRIAGE
1831	0.213	0.348	0.028	0.577	24.2
1836	0.206	0.328	0.036	0.581	23.9
1841	0.207	0.323	0.043	0.587	23.6
1846	0.209	0.323	0.043	0.595	23.4
1851	0.213	0.319	0.046	0.613	23.1
1856	0.218	0.318	0.050	0.626	22.8
1861	0.224	0.323	0.052	0.636	22.5
1866	0.227	0.320	0.059	0.646	22.4
1871	0.223	0.311	0.059	0.648	22.3
1876	0.216	0.304	0.054	0.649	22.3
1881	0.215	0.302	0.055	0.646	22.4
1886	0.215	0.303	0.058	0.642	22.6
1891	0.219	0.307	0.061	0.641	22.6
1896	0.225	0.315	0.064	0.641	22.6
1901	0.226	0.317	0.063	0.641	

MORTALITY PATTERN: NORTH
MIGRATION: GRADUAL, WITH CHILD MIGRANTS SUBTRACTED AFTER 1841, AND TOTALS FOR
1871 TO 1886 OBTAINED BY INTERPOLATION OF R/CB BETWEEN 1866 AND 1891

TABLE 1   FEMALE POPULATION ESTIMATES: 1801 TO 1906

DATE	R/CB RATIO	% COR-RECTION	FINAL POPULATION ESTIMATE	DATE	R/CB RATIO	% COR-RECTION	FINAL POPULATION ESTIMATE
1801	1.055	2.0	135000	1856	0.986	-0.4	147740
1806	1.068	0.0	136231	1861	0.984	-0.5	146396
1811*	1.061	0.0	136924	1866	0.985	-0.6	146191
1816*	1.035	0.0	137618	1871	0.971	1.1	145097
1821	0.996	0.0	138311	1876	0.983	-0.4	143218
1826*	0.985	0.0	141603	1881	0.969	0.8	142780
1831	0.992	0.0	144894	1886	0.997	-2.2	142103
1836	0.999	0.0	147303	1891	0.981	-1.3	141299
1841	0.997	0.0	147597	1896	0.976	-1.4	138760
1846	1.000	-0.1	149333	1901	0.965	-1.5	136062
1851	1.000	-0.3	149850	1906	0.952	-1.5	134175

NOTE: R/CB RATIO REFERS TO THE POPULATION COMPUTED BY THE BALANCE OF BIRTHS
        AND DEATHS OVER THE REPORTED POPULATION
* INTERPOLATED VALUES

TABLE 2   FEMALE BIRTH ESTIMATES: 1801-1805 TO 1901-1905

DATE	% COR-RECTION	FINAL BIRTH ESTIMATE	CRUDE BIRTH RATE	DATE	% COR-RECTION	FINAL BIRTH ESTIMATE	CRUDE BIRTH RATE
1801-1805	19.2	21562	31.8	1856-1860	0.0	17327	23.6
1806-1810	19.5	19612	28.7	1861-1865	0.0	16578	22.7
1811-1815	5.8	20360	29.7	1866-1870	0.0	16064	22.1
1816-1820	0.0	20578	29.8	1871-1875	0.0	15848	22.0
1821-1825	0.0	20193	28.9	1876-1880	0.0	16162	22.6
1826-1830	0.0	18997	26.5	1881-1885	0.0	15522	21.8
1831-1835	0.0	18364	25.1	1886-1890	0.0	15330	21.6
1836-1840	0.0	16952	23.0	1891-1895	0.0	14635	20.9
1841-1845	0.0	17221	23.2	1896-1900	0.0	14149	20.6
1846-1850	0.0	17876	23.9	1901-1905	0.0	13811	20.4
1851-1855	0.0	17327	23.3				

TABLE 3 FEMALE POPULATION ESTIMATES,
DISTRIBUTION BY AGE: 1801 TO 1906

AGE	1801	1806	1811	1816	1821	1826	1831	1836	1841	1846	1851
0- 4	20506	15297	14317	15211	15844	15940	15125	14718	13737	14314	14699
5- 9	16447	16950	12819	12089	13007	13884	14108	13427	13090	12412	12824
10-14	14533	15468	15888	11906	11171	12309	13289	13496	12757	12523	11809
15-19	13065	13997	14903	15019	11159	10722	11954	12890	12978	12331	12020
20-24	11708	12532	13343	13942	14029	10675	10377	11555	12354	12506	11756
25-29	10429	11136	11856	12482	12947	13342	10270	9973	11017	11848	11906
30-34	9203	9812	10434	10998	11510	12226	12744	9803	9451	10509	11240
35-39	8047	8555	9096	9589	10062	10785	11587	12073	9226	8960	9910
40-44	6993	7410	7862	8294	8712	9363	10150	10903	11291	8696	8403
45-49	6032	6396	6766	7125	7492	8061	8761	9496	10140	10586	8114
50-54	5143	5441	5764	6058	6365	6855	7459	8107	8740	9413	9779
55-59	4265	4487	4757	5021	5282	5685	6190	6740	7298	7948	8515
60-64	3368	3502	3712	3944	4192	4518	4914	5361	5833	6401	6924
65-69	2451	2506	2648	2837	3063	3337	3631	3964	4342	4811	5236
70-74	1569	1559	1642	1778	1964	2174	2389	2617	2888	3244	3556
75-79	835	793	829	912	1038	1177	1312	1456	1628	1860	2060
80+	409	391	388	414	473	552	636	725	829	969	1100

AGE	1856	1861	1866	1871	1876	1881	1886	1891	1896	1901	1906
0- 4	14226	14318	14125	13495	13212	13841	13404	13236	12291	12096	11926
5- 9	13058	12720	13054	12802	12161	12064	12694	12294	11971	11168	11091
10-14	12055	12363	12148	12491	12221	11638	11557	12183	11767	11442	10718
15-19	11099	11405	11758	11623	11903	11566	10955	10890	11571	11006	10796
20-24	11085	10257	10569	11032	10795	10859	10409	9824	9942	10237	9896
25-29	10960	10387	9645	10012	10401	10098	10114	9690	9194	9146	9540
30-34	11158	10341	9875	9191	9520	9909	9623	9652	9235	8734	8730
35-39	10492	10490	9809	9380	8711	9060	9450	9188	9185	8795	8345
40-44	9215	9828	9925	9285	8865	8284	8641	9026	8730	8762	8410
45-49	7782	8596	9262	9355	8742	8407	7884	8235	8549	8314	8360
50-54	7448	7197	8037	8653	8730	8228	7946	7464	7738	8089	7879
55-59	8792	6749	6607	7363	7913	8065	7636	7385	6875	7187	7525
60-64	7372	7666	5980	5833	6478	7049	7216	6839	6537	6137	6443
65-69	5639	6045	6418	4973	4826	5452	5965	6111	5695	5507	5201
70-74	3864	4188	4617	4846	3726	3705	4215	4613	4612	4371	4261
75-79	2263	2474	2784	3016	3130	2489	2497	2840	3005	3074	2945
80+	1233	1372	1577	1748	1885	2066	1897	1828	1864	1997	2109

TABLE 4 MARRIED WOMEN ESTIMATES,
DISTRIBUTION BY AGE: 1831 TO 1901

AGE	1831	1836	1841	1846	1851	1856	1861	1866
15-19	618	691	739	718	734	715	828	931
20-24	4275	4891	5384	5600	5440	5291	5051	5400
25-29	7124	7028	7897	8634	8806	8225	7900	7426
30-34	9999	7761	7567	8503	9166	9168	8547	8201
35-39	9245	9688	7477	7326	8146	8670	8699	8151
40-44	7983	8595	8985	6978	6764	7444	7948	8021
45-49	6476	7044	7629	8066	6211	5989	6627	7132

AGE	1871	1876	1881	1886	1891	1896	1901
15-19	889	864	805	710	662	702	832
20-24	5620	5582	5615	5389	4991	5093	5132
25-29	7767	8011	7859	7900	7603	7206	7240
30-34	7646	7930	8229	8033	8060	7735	7331
35-39	7773	7222	7512	7837	7620	7605	7284
40-44	7446	7093	6627	6924	7211	6955	6940
45-49	7120	6631	6375	5995	6234	6442	6213

TABLE 5 DEMOGRAPHIC INDICES AND FEMALE SINGULATE MEAN AGE
AT MARRIAGE: 1831 TO 1901

DATE	IF OVERALL FERTILITY	IG MARITAL FERTILITY	IH ILLEGITIMATE FERTILITY	IM PROPORTION MARRIED	SINGULATE MEAN AGE AT MARRIAGE
1831	0.277	0.432	0.047	0.597	24.0
1836	0.263	0.419	0.041	0.588	23.7
1841	0.256	0.413	0.034	0.587	23.5
1846	0.262	0.416	0.032	0.599	23.3
1851	0.263	0.406	0.033	0.616	23.1
1856	0.266	0.399	0.037	0.633	22.9
1861	0.269	0.399	0.038	0.638	22.7
1866	0.264	0.391	0.040	0.638	22.6
1871	0.260	0.387	0.042	0.633	22.6
1876	0.262	0.389	0.044	0.632	22.5
1881	0.260	0.383	0.046	0.635	22.5
1886	0.257	0.372	0.050	0.642	22.6
1891	0.255	0.370	0.050	0.641	22.6
1896	0.247	0.362	0.049	0.633	22.6
1901	0.244	0.358	0.048	0.634	

MORTALITY PATTERN: WEST
MIGRATION: GRADUAL, WITH POPULATION TOTALS OBTAINED BY TREND OF R/CB

TABLE 1   FEMALE POPULATION ESTIMATES: 1801 TO 1906

DATE	R/CB RATIO	% COR-RECTION	FINAL POPULATION ESTIMATE	DATE	R/CB RATIO	% COR-RECTION	FINAL POPULATION ESTIMATE
1801	0.966	4.0	231593	1856	0.992	0.2	308403
1806	0.995	0.0	229944	1861	0.988	-0.2	313987
1811*	0.991	0.0	235921	1866	0.989	-1.0	325520
1816*	0.980	0.0	241899	1871	0.960	1.3	326439
1821	0.982	0.0	247876	1876	0.964	0.0	333561
1826*	0.980	0.0	257672	1881	0.946	1.1	345231
1831	0.989	0.0	267468	1886	0.945	0.5	350521
1836	0.996	0.0	277553	1891	0.945	-0.3	357768
1841	1.001	0.0	286723	1896	0.934	0.1	367154
1846	1.000	0.0	299874	1901	0.937	-1.1	381371
1851	1.008	-0.7	305749	1906	0.920	-0.0	397482

NOTE: R/CB RATIO REFERS TO THE POPULATION COMPUTED BY THE BALANCE OF BIRTHS
        AND DEATHS OVER THE REPORTED POPULATION
* INTERPOLATED VALUES

TABLE 2   FEMALE BIRTH ESTIMATES: 1801-1805 TO 1901-1905

DATE	% COR-RECTION	FINAL BIRTH ESTIMATE	CRUDE BIRTH RATE	DATE	% COR-RECTION	FINAL BIRTH ESTIMATE	CRUDE BIRTH RATE
1801-1805	8.8	43457	37.7	1856-1860	0.0	51025	32.8
1806-1810	3.8	42676	36.6	1861-1865	0.0	54534	34.1
1811-1815	4.2	44156	37.0	1866-1870	0.0	56304	34.5
1816-1820	4.7	44529	36.4	1871-1875	0.0	56565	34.3
1821-1825	0.0	44799	35.4	1876-1880	0.0	57279	33.8
1826-1830	0.0	49255	37.5	1881-1885	0.0	57239	32.9
1831-1835	5.2	50234	36.9	1886-1890	0.0	58546	33.1
1836-1840	1.9	47600	33.7	1891-1895	0.0	57521	31.7
1841-1845	0.0	50140	34.2	1896-1900	0.0	58223	31.1
1846-1850	0.0	47667	31.5	1901-1905	0.0	59027	30.3
1851-1855	0.0	47948	31.2				

TABLE 3 FEMALE POPULATION ESTIMATES,
DISTRIBUTION BY AGE: 1801 TO 1906

AGE	1801	1806	1811	1816	1821	1826	1831	1836	1841	1846	1851
0- 4	30703	28357	30061	31441	31420	33181	35123	36173	35169	38210	35221
5- 9	25514	25578	24604	26112	27330	27901	29112	30914	32142	31652	33870
10-14	23797	23932	24447	23409	25006	26318	26948	28097	29842	31109	30437
15-19	22216	22317	22867	23251	22410	24071	25412	26000	27112	28871	29898
20-24	20437	20538	21062	21492	21986	21339	22957	24226	24813	25968	27436
25-29	18587	18665	19181	19600	20112	20745	20142	21668	22908	23568	24460
30-34	16750	16806	17283	17704	18134	18835	19414	18854	20332	21607	22037
35-39	14924	14992	15425	15819	16281	16898	17474	18019	17553	19042	20049
40-44	13205	13247	13658	14017	14440	15027	15561	16100	16661	16333	17549
45-49	11589	11630	11979	12320	12700	13232	13736	14233	14780	15394	14946
50-54	9970	9993	10317	10606	10950	11433	11865	12330	12834	13427	13839
55-59	8250	8267	8561	8831	9103	9551	9902	10295	10767	11316	11694
60-64	6388	6400	6676	6921	7145	7526	7799	8112	8516	9026	9339
65-69	4495	4491	4734	4957	5128	5451	5630	5864	6187	6615	6873
70-74	2757	2757	2933	3113	3243	3485	3602	3748	3980	4301	4486
75-79	1376	1365	1482	1595	1676	1838	1896	1981	2118	2323	2431
80+	607	610	652	710	762	843	895	940	1008	1111	1184

AGE	1856	1861	1866	1871	1876	1881	1886	1891	1896	1901	1906
0- 4	34910	37387	41459	39625	41592	43941	42520	43892	44600	47044	48832
5- 9	30913	30765	33488	35786	34933	37338	38842	37767	39537	40883	43531
10-14	32359	29615	29613	31812	34267	33611	35734	37272	36367	38267	39659
15-19	29006	30927	28408	27890	30255	32706	31754	33903	35407	34666	36500
20-24	28074	27305	29242	26055	25839	28156	29934	29171	31092	32653	31797
25-29	25600	26274	25704	26909	24227	24187	25976	27760	27073	29078	30585
30-34	22701	23833	24648	23644	25034	22710	22472	24224	26050	25607	27620
35-39	20299	20977	22214	22516	21853	23358	21007	20852	22648	24588	24283
40-44	18350	18639	19440	20179	20701	20301	21534	19426	19448	21335	23296
45-49	15951	16734	17160	17547	18434	19118	18615	19804	18032	18240	20131
50-54	13346	14292	15155	15213	15761	16765	17254	16854	18119	16699	17015
55-59	11964	11581	12565	12980	13238	13925	14668	15151	14993	16347	15205
60-64	9563	9825	9674	10125	10680	11106	11515	12188	12788	12896	14214
65-69	7035	7239	7607	7142	7683	8317	8482	8848	9561	10286	10522
70-74	4603	4737	5018	4962	4823	5363	5662	5818	6231	6951	7616
75-79	2498	2579	2759	2695	2791	2835	3049	3250	3457	3861	4411
80+	1229	1275	1367	1359	1392	1497	1502	1592	1752	1970	2266

TABLE 4 MARRIED WOMEN ESTIMATES,
DISTRIBUTION BY AGE: 1831 TO 1901

AGE	1831	1836	1841	1846	1851	1856	1861	1866
15-19	1583	1525	1505	1522	1503	1421	1706	1403
20-24	7996	8157	8093	8209	8399	8328	7845	7317
25-29	11821	12580	13179	13425	13751	14196	14394	13900
30-34	13110	12713	13742	14623	14859	15237	15967	16458
35-39	12021	12414	12191	13316	14015	14175	14705	15604
40-44	10351	10736	11262	11177	12028	12591	12906	13553
45-49	8422	8738	9244	9787	9502	10133	10755	11118

AGE	1871	1876	1881	1886	1891	1896	1901
15-19	1347	1659	1774	1598	1399	1123	1668
20-24	6758	7352	8229	9358	8736	8914	9383
25-29	12663	11891	12960	14211	15912	15226	16128
30-34	15743	14958	14117	15184	16096	17958	17458
35-39	15868	15196	15334	14609	14698	15952	17570
40-44	14196	14337	14288	15044	13189	13566	14702
45-49	11500	11764	12478	13201	13262	12114	12098

TABLE 5 DEMOGRAPHIC INDICES AND FEMALE SINGULATE MEAN AGE
AT MARRIAGE: 1831 TO 1901

DATE	IF OVERALL FERTILITY	IG MARITAL FERTILITY	IH ILLEGITIMATE FERTILITY	IM PROPORTION MARRIED	SINGULATE MEAN AGE AT MARRIAGE
1831	0.404	0.815	0.021	0.483	23.9
1836	0.384	0.783	0.020	0.477	24.3
1841	0.370	0.760	0.019	0.475	24.5
1846	0.353	0.727	0.021	0.471	24.7
1851	0.331	0.686	0.023	0.466	24.9
1856	0.336	0.691	0.026	0.465	25.0
1861	0.350	0.727	0.023	0.464	25.4
1866	0.361	0.767	0.019	0.458	25.8
1871	0.376	0.811	0.017	0.452	25.8
1876	0.381	0.838	0.014	0.445	25.5
1881	0.374	0.819	0.015	0.447	25.3
1886	0.374	0.784	0.015	0.466	25.6
1891	0.366	0.773	0.015	0.464	26.1
1896	0.351	0.744	0.016	0.461	26.0
1901	0.342	0.718	0.015	0.466	

MORTALITY PATTERN: NORTH
MIGRATION: NO CORRECTION MADE FOR MIGRATION BY AGE

TABLE 1   FEMALE POPULATION ESTIMATES: 1801 TO 1906

DATE	R/CB RATIO	% COR- RECTION	FINAL POPULATION ESTIMATE	DATE	R/CB RATIO	% COR- RECTION	FINAL POPULATION ESTIMATE
1801	1.249	5.5	158947	1856	1.005	3.4	211817
1806	1.204	3.9	164680	1861	1.006	4.1	216476
1811*	1.122	3.9	168076	1866	1.005	4.3	219641
1816*	1.077	3.9	171473	1871	0.990	0.0	208488
1821	1.045	3.9	174869	1876	0.993	0.0	210329
1826*	1.027	3.9	179760	1881	0.954	0.0	203739
1831	1.009	3.9	184650	1886	0.967	0.0	207942
1836	0.981	3.9	189355	1891	0.969	0.0	207833
1841	0.982	3.9	194289	1896	0.970	0.0	206615
1846	1.000	3.9	204276	1901	0.985	0.0	208788
1851	0.993	3.9	208247	1906	0.999	0.0	210935

NOTE: R/CB RATIO REFERS TO THE POPULATION COMPUTED BY THE BALANCE OF BIRTHS
       AND DEATHS OVER THE REPORTED POPULATION
* INTERPOLATED VALUES

TABLE 2   FEMALE BIRTH ESTIMATES: 1801-1805 TO 1901-1905

DATE	% COR- RECTION	FINAL BIRTH ESTIMATE	CRUDE BIRTH RATE	DATE	% COR- RECTION	FINAL BIRTH ESTIMATE	CRUDE BIRTH RATE
1801-1805	21.8	32303	39.9	1856-1860	0.0	32600	30.4
1806-1810	18.7	33146	39.8	1861-1865	0.0	31394	28.8
1811-1815	19.1	30763	36.2	1866-1870	0.8	30507	28.5
1816-1820	11.1	30562	35.3	1871-1875	1.2	29679	28.3
1821-1825	9.0	29933	33.8	1876-1880	0.0	29541	28.5
1826-1830	0.0	28392	31.2	1881-1885	0.0	27117	26.3
1831-1835	0.0	28814	30.8	1886-1890	0.0	24958	24.0
1836-1840	0.0	29542	30.8	1891-1895	0.0	23691	22.9
1841-1845	0.0	31925	32.0	1896-1900	0.0	22198	21.4
1846-1850	0.0	32803	31.8	1901-1905	0.0	20712	19.7
1851-1855	0.0	31239	29.7				

TABLE 3 FEMALE POPULATION ESTIMATES,
DISTRIBUTION BY AGE: 1801 TO 1906

AGE	1801	1806	1811	1816	1821	1826	1831	1836	1841	1846	1851
0- 4	25609	24143	24538	22972	22712	22627	22079	22770	22627	24959	24933
5- 9	20271	21505	20021	20587	19277	19344	19597	19245	19659	19923	21391
10-14	17680	18609	19433	18360	18981	18000	18153	18334	18223	18969	18734
15-19	15689	16500	17085	18118	17226	18028	17144	17205	17661	17886	18146
20-24	13876	14589	15095	15872	16936	16302	17111	16194	16513	17271	17047
25-29	12200	12820	13263	13933	14737	15922	15380	16075	15440	16042	16352
30-34	10624	11182	11565	12145	12829	13742	14912	14354	15201	14878	15064
35-39	9168	9652	10001	10497	11080	11854	12767	13917	13451	14515	13843
40-44	7862	8267	8570	9010	9502	10160	10936	11752	12848	12747	13403
45-49	6694	7047	7296	7674	8106	8661	9319	10010	10862	12102	11698
50-54	5629	5929	6148	6457	6822	7301	7854	8438	9142	10110	10974
55-59	4601	4856	5041	5299	5585	5981	6459	6950	7501	8284	8923
60-64	3583	3786	3942	4144	4364	4665	5061	5486	5885	6477	6964
65-69	2571	2727	2846	2997	3148	3366	3668	4013	4288	4693	5026
70-74	1625	1727	1815	1911	2002	2139	2353	2606	2763	3014	3207
75-79	854	909	961	1015	1057	1129	1258	1421	1489	1613	1708
80+	411	433	456	484	507	540	599	684	736	794	834

AGE	1856	1861	1866	1871	1876	1881	1886	1891	1896	1901	1906
0- 4	23757	24822	24211	22000	22752	21879	21604	19767	18718	18224	17396
5- 9	21466	20497	21529	19717	19022	18961	19431	19026	17394	16942	16718
10-14	20289	20423	19452	19267	18709	17356	18263	18512	18140	16891	16527
15-19	18092	19658	19708	17715	18600	17360	16969	17653	17913	17844	16662
20-24	17459	17463	18901	17883	17039	17195	16914	16345	17022	17562	17546
25-29	16290	16737	16682	17036	17087	15651	16653	16196	15667	16598	17183
30-34	15492	15481	15860	14910	16143	15567	15045	15832	15411	15177	16145
35-39	14137	14583	14540	14044	14000	14576	14844	14191	14944	14822	14669
40-44	12889	13202	13594	12776	13086	12546	13800	13904	13301	14279	14239
45-49	12402	11963	12232	11872	11832	11656	11809	12852	12956	12638	13643
50-54	10694	11371	10954	10554	10863	10415	10848	10875	11841	12178	11952
55-59	9757	9534	10139	9137	9400	9311	9454	9748	9774	10878	11275
60-64	7546	8272	8105	8103	7801	7679	8082	8131	8381	8620	9698
65-69	5425	5889	6499	5974	6344	5889	6190	6464	6495	6902	7209
70-74	3435	3712	4083	4213	4117	4223	4218	4408	4591	4794	5211
75-79	1810	1939	2141	2191	2407	2279	2542	2531	2634	2881	3106
80+	879	930	1011	1035	1128	1197	1277	1398	1433	1557	1759

[308]

TABLE 4   MARRIED WOMEN ESTIMATES,
DISTRIBUTION BY AGE: 1831 TO 1901

AGE	1831	1836	1841	1846	1851	1856	1861	1866
15-19	1128	1086	1072	1046	1024	987	1091	1147
20-24	7979	7405	7404	7594	7346	7379	7243	7327
25-29	11278	11726	11203	11570	11705	11581	11823	11690
30-34	11877	11436	12114	11853	11967	12292	12280	12544
35-39	10082	10949	10697	11575	11025	11276	11668	11623
40-44	8260	8931	9826	9801	10296	9939	10248	10555
45-49	6548	7101	7781	8742	8439	9000	8769	8970

AGE	1871	1876	1881	1886	1891	1896	1901
15-19	1082	1180	999	924	863	771	960
20-24	7112	7139	7355	7530	7044	7233	7081
25-29	11360	11505	10937	11779	11884	11397	12079
30-34	11688	12337	12060	11854	12539	12575	12305
35-39	11108	11053	11550	11783	11241	12019	12073
40-44	9775	10006	9843	10731	10639	10277	11018
45-49	8515	8479	8686	8811	9357	9505	9076

TABLE 5   DEMOGRAPHIC INDICES AND FEMALE SINGULATE MEAN AGE
AT MARRIAGE: 1831 TO 1901

DATE	IF OVERALL FERTILITY	IG MARITAL FERTILITY	IH ILLEGITIMATE FERTILITY	IM PROPORTION MARRIED	SINGULATE MEAN AGE AT MARRIAGE
1831	0.316	0.516	0.025	0.593	22.9
1836	0.320	0.520	0.026	0.595	23.0
1841	0.332	0.542	0.028	0.592	23.1
1846	0.340	0.549	0.039	0.589	23.2
1851	0.336	0.554	0.030	0.585	23.3
1856	0.331	0.549	0.028	0.582	23.4
1861	0.325	0.548	0.021	0.576	23.6
1866	0.306	0.526	0.020	0.566	23.7
1871	0.311	0.536	0.021	0.564	23.6
1876	0.303	0.520	0.016	0.569	23.5
1881	0.299	0.500	0.019	0.582	23.5
1886	0.272	0.447	0.015	0.594	23.5
1891	0.255	0.419	0.016	0.593	23.7
1896	0.239	0.393	0.016	0.593	23.7
1901	0.219	0.361	0.016	0.590	

GARONNE (HAUTE-)

MORTALITY PATTERN: WEST
MIGRATION: NO CORRECTION MADE FOR MIGRATION BY AGE

TABLE 1 FEMALE POPULATION ESTIMATES: 1801 TO 1906

DATE	R/CB RATIO	% COR- RECTION	FINAL POPULATION ESTIMATE	DATE	R/CB RATIO	% COR- RECTION	FINAL POPULATION ESTIMATE
1801	0.970	2.3	176735	1856	1.002	2.5	250929
1806	0.976	2.3	185819	1861	0.996	1.9	249467
1811*	0.953	2.3	191780	1866	1.011	2.8	257051
1816*	0.942	2.3	197740	1871	0.983	0.0	242493
1821	0.937	2.3	203701	1876	0.979	0.0	242744
1826*	0.953	2.3	212252	1881	0.957	0.0	237478
1831	0.963	2.3	220803	1886	0.985	0.0	243626
1836	0.997	2.3	235570	1891	0.983	0.0	239006
1841	0.980	2.3	238512	1896	0.987	0.0	233264
1846	1.000	2.3	248324	1901	0.987	0.0	228114
1851	0.992	2.2	247604	1906	0.994	0.0	224799

NOTE: R/CB RATIO REFERS TO THE POPULATION COMPUTED BY THE BALANCE OF BIRTHS
       AND DEATHS OVER THE REPORTED POPULATION
* INTERPOLATED VALUES

TABLE 2 FEMALE BIRTH ESTIMATES: 1801-1805 TO 1901-1905

DATE	% COR- RECTION	FINAL BIRTH ESTIMATE	CRUDE BIRTH RATE	DATE	% COR- RECTION	FINAL BIRTH ESTIMATE	CRUDE BIRTH RATE
1801-1805	8.5	30433	33.6	1856-1860	5.7	27107	21.7
1806-1810	11.5	33235	35.2	1861-1865	0.0	25606	20.2
1811-1815	11.6	31729	32.6	1866-1870	0.0	25343	20.3
1816-1820	16.2	33462	33.3	1871-1875	0.0	24488	20.2
1821-1825	0.0	29093	28.0	1876-1880	0.0	24009	20.0
1826-1830	0.0	29893	27.6	1881-1885	0.0	23402	19.5
1831-1835	0.0	31121	27.3	1886-1890	0.0	21278	17.6
1836-1840	6.2	30932	26.1	1891-1895	0.0	18974	16.1
1841-1845	0.0	28882	23.7	1896-1900	0.0	18985	16.5
1846-1850	0.0	30001	24.2	1901-1905	0.0	17783	15.7
1851-1855	0.0	27684	22.2				

TABLE 3 FEMALE POPULATION ESTIMATES,
DISTRIBUTION BY AGE: 1801 TO 1906

AGE	1801	1806	1811	1816	1821	1826	1831	1836	1841	1846	1851
0- 4	22636	23591	25311	24432	25167	23127	23890	25659	24678	24036	23297
5- 9	19480	20571	20955	22696	21771	23206	21345	22652	23323	23298	21694
10-14	18035	18962	19517	20052	21787	21379	22757	21456	21722	23178	22417
15-19	16676	17547	17982	18668	19242	21385	20954	22864	20565	21576	22291
20-24	15280	16070	16486	17041	17731	18716	20777	20874	21739	20268	20562
25-29	13886	14606	14981	15503	16048	17118	18052	20550	19714	21287	19168
30-34	12526	13186	13529	13998	14498	15397	16410	17750	19302	19202	20006
35-39	11235	11813	12133	12559	12995	13820	14668	16038	16576	18695	17929
40-44	9999	10529	10802	11194	11583	12313	13088	14252	14893	15966	17350
45-49	8854	9306	9561	9898	10251	10900	11581	12630	13146	14250	14716
50-54	7695	8105	8315	8621	8911	9494	10093	11005	11477	12395	12925
55-59	6498	6842	7039	7287	7529	8026	8554	9336	9746	10551	10931
60-64	5228	5501	5663	5882	6047	6471	6906	7563	7917	8586	8875
65-69	3886	4110	4234	4402	4519	4839	5190	5698	5999	6532	6721
70-74	2589	2739	2841	2957	3023	3254	3497	3862	4088	4482	4597
75-79	1452	1538	1599	1677	1703	1842	1993	2210	2363	2609	2668
80+	766	802	832	874	895	964	1048	1172	1264	1415	1459

AGE	1856	1861	1866	1871	1876	1881	1886	1891	1896	1901	1906
0- 4	22273	21799	21820	19696	20553	19792	20337	17807	15855	16003	15346
5- 9	21582	20377	20849	19203	18438	18892	19135	19014	16691	14902	15245
10-14	21321	20815	20404	19297	18761	17685	19035	18685	18653	16369	14736
15-19	22021	20552	20831	18875	18842	17985	17809	18578	18320	18282	16177
20-24	21709	21059	20421	19123	18305	17939	17990	17261	18085	17835	17955
25-29	19881	20624	20800	18626	18440	17329	17845	17336	16704	17506	17424
30-34	18425	18785	20270	18872	17878	17376	17160	17116	16695	16094	17031
35-39	19111	17310	18367	18290	18024	16763	17123	16376	16397	16006	15586
40-44	17027	17854	16835	16482	17379	16814	16435	16256	15606	15640	15424
45-49	16365	15801	17251	15008	15559	16107	16378	15502	15391	14789	14976
50-54	13667	14963	15053	15156	13973	14223	15477	15235	14471	14385	13975
55-59	11684	12180	13916	12897	13785	12479	13355	14062	13885	13214	13295
60-64	9442	9973	10878	11429	11278	11837	11271	11663	12308	12191	11765
65-69	7151	7542	8364	8371	9401	9110	10063	9254	9588	10165	10235
70-74	4883	5169	5745	5831	6265	6909	7051	7514	6911	7205	7787
75-79	2836	3012	3378	3424	3753	3960	4604	4526	4816	4468	4766
80+	1552	1653	1869	1912	2111	2279	2558	2823	2898	3061	3075

TABLE 4   MARRIED WOMEN ESTIMATES,
DISTRIBUTION BY AGE: 1831 TO 1901

AGE	1831	1836	1841	1846	1851	1856	1861	1866
15-19	1237	1361	1235	1306	1361	1356	1208	1285
20-24	7887	7981	8382	7884	8060	8579	8391	7338
25-29	11472	13140	12709	13845	12554	13121	13721	13946
30-34	11814	12845	14090	14155	14845	13780	14168	15413
35-39	10669	11713	12225	13949	13463	14474	13234	14169
40-44	9115	9951	10519	11444	12514	12401	13150	12530
45-49	7523	8208	8666	9574	9948	11190	10954	12111

AGE	1871	1876	1881	1886	1891	1896	1901
15-19	1265	1454	1339	1110	1023	971	1214
20-24	7278	7533	7609	7787	7130	7272	7011
25-29	11659	11925	11746	12202	12049	11360	11786
30-34	14384	13119	12939	13195	13298	13005	12217
35-39	14106	13997	12666	13154	12925	12987	12515
40-44	12215	12974	12551	12271	12419	12046	11930
45-49	10434	10900	11247	11653	11347	11296	10639

TABLE 5   DEMOGRAPHIC INDICES AND FEMALE SINGULATE MEAN AGE
AT MARRIAGE: 1831 TO 1901

DATE	IF OVERALL FERTILITY	IG MARITAL FERTILITY	IH ILLEGITIMATE FERTILITY	IM PROPORTION MARRIED	SINGULATE MEAN AGE AT MARRIAGE
1831	0.286	0.518	0.039	0.517	23.2
1836	0.270	0.478	0.043	0.523	23.5
1841	0.258	0.448	0.038	0.537	23.5
1846	0.247	0.423	0.033	0.548	23.5
1851	0.243	0.414	0.037	0.548	23.5
1856	0.228	0.385	0.035	0.551	23.5
1861	0.223	0.369	0.037	0.561	23.6
1866	0.212	0.352	0.034	0.560	23.7
1871	0.222	0.367	0.038	0.560	23.5
1876	0.220	0.361	0.035	0.569	23.3
1881	0.225	0.358	0.044	0.575	23.4
1886	0.211	0.332	0.040	0.585	23.7
1891	0.194	0.304	0.038	0.585	23.9
1896	0.184	0.288	0.041	0.577	23.9
1901	0.179	0.286	0.037	0.569	

MORTALITY PATTERN: WEST
MIGRATION: FULL STRENGTH, WITH POPULATION TOTALS OBTAINED BY TREND OF R/CB

TABLE 1 FEMALE POPULATION ESTIMATES: 1801 TO 1906

DATE	R/CB RATIO	% COR-RECTION	FINAL POPULATION ESTIMATE	DATE	R/CB RATIO	% COR-RECTION	FINAL POPULATION ESTIMATE
1801	0.919	6.3	138620	1856	0.989	0.8	153139
1806	0.971	0.7	140640	1861	0.982	0.8	149449
1811*	0.971	0.7	144478	1866	0.977	0.6	146789
1816*	0.979	0.7	148285	1871	0.957	2.0	143673
1821	0.986	0.7	152094	1876	0.972	-0.4	139753
1826*	0.989	0.7	154189	1881	0.973	-1.3	136421
1831	0.989	0.7	156284	1886	0.988	-3.5	132875
1836	0.997	0.7	156695	1891	0.947	-0.0	128249
1841	0.994	0.7	156229	1896	0.941	-0.1	123071
1846	1.000	0.7	157354	1901	0.919	1.5	118720
1851	0.991	1.3	154237	1906	0.914	1.3	115059

NOTE: R/CB RATIO REFERS TO THE POPULATION COMPUTED BY THE BALANCE OF BIRTHS
AND DEATHS OVER THE REPORTED POPULATION
* INTERPOLATED VALUES

TABLE 2 FEMALE BIRTH ESTIMATES: 1801-1805 TO 1901-1905

DATE	% COR-RECTION	FINAL BIRTH ESTIMATE	CRUDE BIRTH RATE	DATE	% COR-RECTION	FINAL BIRTH ESTIMATE	CRUDE BIRTH RATE
1801-1805	5.6	20034	28.7	1856-1860	0.0	13603	18.0
1806-1810	0.0	19660	27.6	1861-1865	0.0	13721	18.5
1811-1815	3.8	19808	27.1	1866-1870	0.0	13846	19.1
1816-1820	0.0	18794	25.0	1871-1875	0.0	13255	18.7
1821-1825	0.0	17509	22.9	1876-1880	0.0	12260	17.8
1826-1830	0.0	17461	22.5	1881-1885	0.0	11393	16.9
1831-1835	-5.8	17147	21.9	1886-1890	0.0	9879	15.1
1836-1840	0.0	16833	21.5	1891-1895	0.0	9012	14.3
1841-1845	0.0	16196	20.7	1896-1900	0.0	8634	14.3
1846-1850	0.0	14942	19.2	1901-1905	0.0	8303	14.2
1851-1855	0.0	14824	19.3				

TABLE 3 FEMALE POPULATION ESTIMATES,
DISTRIBUTION BY AGE: 1801 TO 1906

AGE	1801	1806	1811	1816	1821	1826	1831	1836	1841	1846	1851
0- 4	14808	15415	15823	15839	15383	14353	14454	13749	13639	13434	11983
5- 9	13195	13375	14196	14583	14735	14291	13376	13340	12671	12766	12322
10-14	12637	12775	13023	13888	14297	14404	13965	13093	12959	12450	12379
15-19	12098	12230	12433	12734	13608	13968	14067	13663	12712	12726	12059
20-24	11472	11595	11804	12052	12379	13193	13541	13646	13161	12391	12213
25-29	10790	10906	11115	11360	11639	11924	12712	13042	13057	12749	11821
30-34	10077	10190	10395	10633	10912	11152	11432	12170	12412	12584	12102
35-39	9349	9450	9655	9883	10156	10397	10635	10878	11517	11857	11877
40-44	8618	8713	8903	9125	9387	9623	9862	10060	10237	10980	11166
45-49	7891	7975	8153	8357	8609	8836	9068	9266	9404	9695	10236
50-54	7105	7183	7351	7535	7769	7986	8208	8389	8534	8779	8903
55-59	6213	6281	6448	6612	6828	7027	7240	7391	7531	7772	7853
60-64	5168	5228	5394	5541	5739	5920	6114	6230	6355	6580	6651
65-69	3982	4037	4196	4323	4502	4661	4833	4909	5013	5207	5262
70-74	2745	2788	2927	3031	3179	3312	3453	3499	3574	3725	3762
75-79	1596	1618	1721	1794	1903	1999	2103	2123	2174	2274	2291
80+	867	884	942	995	1070	1142	1222	1246	1279	1345	1358

AGE	1856	1861	1866	1871	1876	1881	1886	1891	1896	1901	1906
0- 4	12393	11144	11398	11420	10886	10333	9708	8456	7702	7529	7380
5- 9	11173	11442	10358	10559	10556	10173	9701	9128	7945	7304	7200
10-14	11996	10832	11130	10063	10250	10284	9928	9470	8914	7780	7168
15-19	12024	11582	10489	10756	9693	9905	9951	9598	9162	8653	7556
20-24	11596	11452	11073	9970	10179	9179	9391	9418	9096	8725	8250
25-29	11713	11039	10948	10554	9469	9714	8764	8967	9004	8732	8402
30-34	11306	11139	10543	10438	10050	9065	9325	8417	8616	8687	8460
35-39	11521	10702	10592	10009	9899	9592	8675	8935	8065	8292	8398
40-44	11252	10855	10131	10012	9453	9414	9150	8287	8536	7739	7994
45-49	10512	10535	10212	9518	9400	8938	8929	8693	7874	8145	7419
50-54	9506	9705	9776	9462	8813	8772	8372	8378	8156	7424	7718
55-59	8077	8562	8792	8839	8547	8036	8034	7683	7687	7527	6894
60-64	6846	6973	7446	7623	7650	7488	7079	7093	6780	6838	6748
65-69	5452	5542	5696	6058	6187	6308	6216	5894	5901	5699	5806
70-74	3924	4002	4113	4205	4458	4645	4776	4723	4473	4535	4435
75-79	2412	2465	2550	2602	2649	2881	3034	3133	3094	2978	3067
80+	1437	1480	1542	1585	1614	1695	1844	1976	2066	2134	2164

[314]

TABLE 4 MARRIED WOMEN ESTIMATES,
DISTRIBUTICN BY AGE: 1831 TO 1901

AGE	1831	1836	1841	1846	1851	1856	1861	1866
15-19	1153	1160	1122	1171	1159	1212	1273	1036
20-24	5013	5196	5171	5027	5115	5020	5124	4441
25-29	7704	8050	8239	8226	7787	7886	7583	7678
30-34	8108	8723	9048	9331	9106	8648	8638	8299
35-39	7856	8071	8669	9089	9177	9030	8476	8495
40-44	7344	7454	7665	8320	8519	8691	8439	7959
45-49	6363	6431	6610	6916	7353	7668	7734	7592

AGE	1871	1876	1881	1886	1891	1896	1901
15-19	1288	1356	1221	1067	877	749	923
20-24	4343	4717	4424	4820	4788	4540	4207
25-29	6741	6477	6867	6236	6797	6843	6673
30-34	8293	7533	7110	7434	6783	7149	7247
35-39	8059	8045	7597	7023	7396	6604	6936
40-44	7844	7451	7578	7209	6738	6840	6207
45-49	7025	6979	6828	6842	6872	6048	6257

TABLE 5 DEMOGRAPHIC INDICES AND FEMALE SINGULATE MEAN AGE
AT MARRIAGE: 1831 TO 1901

DATE	IF OVERALL FERTILITY	IG MARITAL FERTILITY	IH ILLEGITIMATE FERTILITY	IM PROPORTION MARRIED	SINGULATE MEAN AGE AT MARRIAGE
1831	0.235	0.421	0.031	0.523	24.1
1836	0.226	0.395	0.032	0.535	24.1
1841	0.221	0.380	0.023	0.554	23.9
1846	0.2C9	0.352	0.021	0.569	23.8
1851	0.206	0.338	0.023	0.581	23.6
1856	0.203	0.328	0.021	0.592	23.4
1861	0.202	0.321	0.023	0.601	23.5
1866	0.212	0.337	0.024	0.601	23.5
1871	0.218	0.346	0.025	0.599	23.1
1876	0.214	0.333	0.026	0.612	22.9
1881	0.207	0.316	0.027	0.622	23.0
1886	0.191	0.290	0.026	0.626	23.1
1891	0.174	0.259	0.022	0.639	23.3
1896	0.166	0.247	0.023	0.639	23.2
1901	0.163	0.241	0.022	0.648	

MORTALITY PATTERN: WEST
MIGRATION: FULL STRENGTH, WITH POPULATION TOTALS OBTAINED BY TREND OF R/CB

TABLE 1   FEMALE POPULATION ESTIMATES: 1801 TO 1906

DATE	R/CB RATIO	% COR- RECTION	FINAL POPULATION ESTIMATE	DATE	R/CB RATIO	% COR- RECTION	FINAL POPULATION ESTIMATE
1801	0.907	0.0	254201	1856	1.044	-0.7	320510
1806	0.963	0.0	264972	1861	1.074	-0.0	333109
1811*	0.954	0.0	266641	1866	1.114	-0.2	347421
1816*	0.955	0.0	268310	1871	1.130	1.7	362166
1821	0.930	0.0	269979	1876	1.186	0.1	372744
1826*	0.932	0.0	276733	1881	1.207	1.5	384390
1831	0.939	0.0	283487	1886	1.254	0.6	393558
1836	0.966	0.0	288917	1891	1.317	-1.3	404250
1841	0.963	0.0	292146	1896	1.364	-2.0	412080
1846	1.000	0.0	305893	1901	1.381	-0.4	423092
1851	1.004	-0.5	306629	1906	1.393	1.4	432740

NOTE: R/CB RATIO REFERS TO THE POPULATION COMPUTED BY THE BALANCE OF BIRTHS
        AND DEATHS OVER THE REPORTED POPULATION
* INTERPOLATED VALUES

TABLE 2   FEMALE BIRTH ESTIMATES: 1801-1805 TO 1901-1905

DATE	% COR- RECTION	FINAL BIRTH ESTIMATE	CRUDE BIRTH RATE	DATE	% COR- RECTION	FINAL BIRTH ESTIMATE	CRUDE BIRTH RATE
1801-1805	0.0	34396	26.5	1856-1860	0.0	34920	21.4
1806-1810	0.0	37514	28.2	1861-1865	0.0	37845	22.2
1811-1815	0.0	34490	25.8	1866-1870	0.0	38109	21.5
1816-1820	0.0	36082	26.8	1871-1875	0.0	35726	19.4
1821-1825	0.0	35160	25.7	1876-1880	0.0	37064	19.6
1826-1830	0.0	35434	25.3	1881-1885	0.0	37794	19.4
1831-1835	0.0	34305	24.0	1886-1890	0.0	37443	18.8
1836-1840	0.0	34934	24.0	1891-1895	0.0	36321	17.8
1841-1845	0.0	34331	23.0	1896-1900	0.0	36707	17.6
1846-1850	0.0	35252	23.0	1901-1905	0.0	34792	16.3
1851-1855	0.0	34182	21.8				

TABLE 3 FEMALE POPULATION ESTIMATES,
DISTRIBUTION BY AGE: 1801 TO 1906

AGE	1801	1806	1811	1816	1821	1826	1831	1836	1841	1846	1851
0- 4	24022	26923	29351	27379	29417	29210	29249	27383	28532	29133	28442
5- 9	22090	22574	24383	26838	24989	27448	27264	27200	25330	27413	26823
10-14	21505	22529	21749	23657	25612	24419	26924	27065	26462	25592	26651
15-19	20895	21924	21695	21091	22563	25014	23940	26715	26318	26722	24862
20-24	20158	21070	20925	20858	19975	21878	24338	23535	25778	26372	25740
25-29	19294	20141	19961	19974	19639	19252	21152	23741	22564	25667	25242
30-34	18379	19132	18965	18941	18716	18835	18517	20503	22643	22350	24437
35-39	17413	18084	17900	17884	17658	17857	18017	17830	19446	22303	21155
40-44	16371	17016	16818	16781	16585	16758	16988	17241	16818	19049	20993
45-49	15303	15883	15717	15659	15461	15637	15837	16145	16156	16366	17811
50-54	14108	14585	14440	14409	14228	14372	14565	14810	14909	15494	15075
55-59	12634	13025	12899	12885	12784	12910	13057	13240	13337	13944	13905
60-64	10854	11053	10996	10997	10983	11138	11246	11315	11429	11958	11977
65-69	8694	8760	8693	8745	8809	8985	9094	9064	9152	9602	9605
70-74	6279	6247	6202	6232	6367	6544	6649	6586	6642	6966	6972
75-79	3864	3760	3747	3775	3897	4057	4143	4068	4125	4322	4310
80+	2339	2266	2202	2207	2295	2419	2507	2477	2507	2639	2629

AGE	1856	1861	1866	1871	1876	1881	1886	1891	1896	1901	1906
0- 4	29080	29401	31726	32209	30044	31158	31398	31598	30592	31503	30337
5- 9	27396	27890	28184	30497	30857	28875	29766	30233	30357	29725	30760
10-14	27086	27591	28078	28372	30574	30962	28919	29870	30255	30523	29926
15-19	27206	27729	28413	29061	29364	31799	32183	30451	31332	32015	32209
20-24	25719	28387	29384	30494	31299	32223	34754	35738	34031	35470	35933
25-29	25949	26016	28823	29987	31079	32129	33012	35774	36662	35362	36710
30-34	25005	25623	25679	28443	29481	30570	31462	32427	35006	36062	34864
35-39	24021	24470	25025	25081	27654	28645	29553	30492	31339	33983	35089
40-44	20636	23297	23655	24167	24109	26531	27329	28246	29065	30009	32647
45-49	20317	19843	22316	22624	23001	22884	25041	25829	26626	27517	28519
50-54	16967	19221	18680	20982	21160	21440	21190	23231	23902	24753	25700
55-59	14008	15649	17648	17130	19151	19248	19366	19182	20990	21719	22617
60-64	12435	12439	13845	15637	15105	16860	16822	17020	16816	18557	19319
65-69	10051	10352	10315	11519	12947	12491	13823	13907	14039	14024	15597
70-74	7314	7585	7781	7794	8661	9726	9291	10399	10440	10686	10777
75-79	4549	4723	4877	5044	5027	5584	6197	6013	6717	6865	7113
80+	2773	2893	2995	3128	3231	3265	3453	3839	3912	4319	4624

TABLE 4   MARRIED WOMEN ESTIMATES,
DISTRIBUTICN BY AGE: 1831 TO 1901

AGE	1831	1836	1841	1846	1851	1856	1861	1866
15-19	3485	3777	3618	3574	3237	3451	4189	4264
20-24	13280	12640	13639	13750	13216	13011	14149	14689
25-29	15784	17557	16567	18718	18258	18634	18546	20374
30-34	14724	16173	17783	17493	19017	19384	19788	19719
35-39	14281	14004	15227	17440	16457	18649	18962	19298
40-44	13123	13158	12805	14509	15903	15627	17642	17831
45-49	11603	11633	11619	11796	12754	14564	14247	15939

AGE	1871	1876	1881	1886	1891	1896	1901
15-19	3575	3509	4379	4415	3339	3222	3496
20-24	15702	16031	16900	18098	17909	16941	17151
25-29	20923	22037	23053	24321	26239	26314	25770
30-34	21642	22277	23277	24127	25496	27682	28144
35-39	19140	20957	21735	22508	23311	24422	26673
40-44	17977	17798	19598	20124	20832	21272	22175
45-49	15864	15970	15930	17477	18061	18386	18541

TABLE 5   DEMOGRAPHIC INDICES AND FEMALE SINGULATE MEAN AGE
AT MARRIAGE: 1831 TO 1901

DATE	IF OVERALL FERTILITY	IG MARITAL FERTILITY	IH ILLEGITIMATE FERTILITY	IM PROPORTION MARRIED	SINGULATE MEAN AGE AT MARRIAGE
1831	0.278	0.393	0.083	0.626	22.1
1836	0.262	0.375	0.081	0.618	22.0
1841	0.253	0.358	0.085	0.616	22.1
1846	0.239	0.333	0.087	0.618	22.2
1851	0.239	0.341	0.072	0.620	22.3
1856	0.228	0.338	0.053	0.614	22.2
1861	0.230	0.336	0.063	0.613	22.2
1866	0.231	0.338	0.063	0.611	22.3
1871	0.216	0.316	0.060	0.607	22.4
1876	0.205	0.308	0.044	0.609	22.2
1881	0.202	0.303	0.040	0.615	22.1
1886	0.195	0.287	0.046	0.620	22.2
1891	0.186	0.265	0.055	0.621	22.4
1896	0.180	0.256	0.056	0.622	22.5
1901	0.172	0.245	0.053	0.621	

MORTALITY PATTERN: WEST
MIGRATION: NO CORRECTION MADE FOR MIGRATION BY AGE

TABLE 1 FEMALE POPULATION ESTIMATES: 1801 TO 1906

DATE	R/CB RATIO	% COR- RECTION	FINAL POPULATION ESTIMATE	DATE	R/CB RATIO	% COR- RECTION	FINAL POPULATION ESTIMATE
1801	1.033	6.9	148227	1856	1.031	8.6	214883
1806	1.017	6.9	159412	1861	1.060	5.6	215368
1811*	0.984	6.9	164180	1866	1.086	6.6	226034
1816*	0.962	6.9	168948	1871	1.084	0.0	213197
1821	0.962	6.9	173716	1876	1.131	0.0	220997
1826*	0.963	6.9	179515	1881	1.099	0.0	215875
1831	0.968	6.9	185314	1886	1.148	0.0	222676
1836	0.982	6.9	191844	1891	1.185	0.0	226783
1841	0.979	6.9	195523	1896	1.235	0.0	233910
1846	1.000	6.9	203881	1901	1.306	0.0	246048
1851	1.003	6.8	206780	1906	1.305	0.0	245191

NOTE: R/CB RATIO REFERS TO THE POPULATION COMPUTED BY THE BALANCE OF BIRTHS
       AND DEATHS OVER THE REPORTED POPULATION
* INTERPOLATED VALUES

TABLE 2 FEMALE BIRTH ESTIMATES: 1801-1805 TO 1901-1905

DATE	% COR- RECTION	FINAL BIRTH ESTIMATE	CRUDE BIRTH RATE	DATE	% COR- RECTION	FINAL BIRTH ESTIMATE	CRUDE BIRTH RATE
1801-1805	33.6	31339	40.7	1856-1860	0.0	26438	24.6
1806-1810	15.2	29085	36.0	1861-1865	0.0	27632	25.0
1811-1815	20.6	28375	34.1	1866-1870	0.0	29132	26.5
1816-1820	0.0	25605	29.9	1871-1875	0.0	26766	24.7
1821-1825	0.0	25787	29.2	1876-1880	0.0	26702	24.4
1826-1830	0.0	26914	29.5	1881-1885	0.0	24214	22.1
1831-1835	0.0	27633	29.3	1886-1890	0.0	22886	20.4
1836-1840	0.0	27596	28.5	1891-1895	0.0	24470	21.2
1841-1845	0.0	27318	27.4	1896-1900	0.0	24643	20.5
1846-1850	0.0	26999	26.3	1901-1905	0.0	23785	19.4
1851-1855	0.0	25994	24.7				

TABLE 3 FEMALE POPULATION ESTIMATES,
DISTRIBUTION BY AGE: 1801 TO 1906

AGE	1801	1806	1811	1816	1821	1826	1831	1836	1841	1846	1851
0- 4	22038	23952	21811	21263	19354	19790	20461	20978	21002	21566	20842
5- 9	18369	19776	21028	19245	19032	17482	17844	18526	18836	19411	19529
10-14	16485	17669	18582	19920	18552	18451	16991	17470	17879	18635	18834
15-19	14792	15851	16595	17595	19195	17979	17926	16628	16853	17680	18072
20-24	13127	14085	14746	15560	16783	18420	17288	17359	15881	16507	16982
25-29	11564	12399	12999	13712	14716	15973	17561	16593	16441	15432	15727
30-34	10117	10850	11368	12006	12877	13911	15121	16732	15608	15871	14605
35-39	8788	9427	9880	10426	11194	12088	13072	14299	15628	14965	14918
40-44	7576	8137	8531	9003	9657	10441	11285	12280	13269	14889	13977
45-49	6496	6966	7312	7720	8281	8945	9678	10525	11316	12555	13811
50-54	5474	5875	6158	6507	6980	7543	8151	8871	9537	10532	11454
55-59	4481	4808	5046	5320	5709	6173	6668	7242	7802	8624	9333
60-64	3486	3746	3933	4147	4435	4803	5183	5621	6057	6718	7275
65-69	2505	2705	2846	2958	3201	3461	3733	4039	4357	4844	5262
70-74	1626	1742	1844	1943	2069	2238	2404	2595	2802	3127	3402
75-79	381	952	1001	1058	1125	1216	1303	1397	1513	1695	1849
80+	448	474	499	524	558	602	645	690	741	830	910

AGE	1856	1861	1866	1871	1876	1881	1886	1891	1896	1901	1906
0- 4	20459	20409	22752	21250	21527	20708	19889	18911	20336	21307	19958
5- 9	19443	18517	19363	19406	19997	19217	19661	18812	18047	19890	19950
10-14	19631	18851	18644	17665	19540	18934	19395	19666	19018	18554	19440
15-19	18925	19024	18971	17002	17779	18493	19100	19390	19871	19542	18123
20-24	17975	18164	18981	17136	16949	16682	18491	18938	19427	20264	18958
25-29	16746	17114	17992	17010	16948	15790	16558	18208	18841	19685	19546
30-34	15400	15838	16851	16019	16713	15696	15577	16212	18010	18992	18900
35-39	14197	14465	15499	14902	15633	15383	15387	15161	15938	18054	18143
40-44	14406	13252	14072	13621	14453	14304	14991	14891	14819	15891	17159
45-49	13403	13354	12804	12282	13119	13135	13845	14410	14456	14677	15005
50-54	13019	12221	12704	10994	11636	11739	12515	13107	13776	14111	13669
55-59	10475	11530	11315	10598	10120	10136	10882	11540	12201	13115	12837
60-64	8108	8833	10199	8992	9292	8423	8971	9599	10269	11138	11471
65-69	5851	6348	7283	7531	7324	7216	6948	7394	7975	8786	9162
70-74	3783	4108	4721	4830	5504	5129	5361	5173	5543	6183	6575
75-79	2050	2237	2593	2639	2976	3273	3230	3397	3296	3676	3979
80+	1013	1103	1285	1320	1486	1617	1876	1973	2087	2183	2317

TABLE 4 MARRIED WOMEN ESTIMATES,
DISTRIBUTION BY AGE: 1831 TO 1901

AGE	1831	1836	1841	1846	1851	1856	1861	1866
15-19	1081	1019	1049	1119	1163	1239	1650	1482
20-24	6857	6968	6455	6796	7080	7593	7770	7711
25-29	11506	10959	10955	10379	10671	11474	11827	12536
30-34	11115	12373	11631	11929	11062	11773	12196	13064
35-39	9655	10618	11699	11310	11366	10935	11225	12110
40-44	7972	8716	9506	10791	10224	10685	9912	10603
45-49	6333	6922	7532	8488	9450	9346	9411	9105

AGE	1871	1876	1881	1886	1891	1896	1901
15-19	1250	1268	1261	1225	958	925	1337
20-24	7623	8082	7788	8143	7952	8122	8400
25-29	11140	11791	11610	12000	12775	13002	13846
30-34	12517	12467	12192	12389	12791	13997	14609
35-39	11745	12211	11880	12016	12025	12611	13983
40-44	10371	10811	10937	11255	11270	11386	11956
45-49	8855	9187	9490	9875	10298	10464	10420

TABLE 5 DEMOGRAPHIC INDICES AND FEMALE SINGULATE MEAN AGE
AT MARRIAGE: 1831 TO 1901

DATE	IF OVERALL FERTILITY	IG MARITAL FERTILITY	IH ILLEGITIMATE FERTILITY	IM PROPORTION MARRIED	SINGULATE MEAN AGE AT MARRIAGE
1831	0.288	0.508	0.031	0.538	23.3
1836	0.286	0.493	0.031	0.553	23.5
1841	0.289	0.490	0.031	0.561	23.4
1846	0.283	0.485	0.024	0.562	23.4
1851	0.277	0.472	0.028	0.562	23.3
1856	0.265	0.451	0.022	0.565	23.2
1861	0.270	0.452	0.027	0.573	23.2
1866	0.271	0.451	0.028	0.575	23.3
1871	0.286	0.467	0.032	0.583	23.1
1876	0.267	0.436	0.024	0.591	22.9
1881	0.262	0.421	0.027	0.596	23.1
1886	0.232	0.377	0.027	0.586	23.5
1891	0.226	0.372	0.027	0.577	23.6
1896	0.225	0.371	0.026	0.576	23.5
1901	0.211	0.342	0.027	0.583	

MORTALITY PATTERN: WEST
MIGRATION: GRADUAL, WITH POPULATION TOTALS OBTAINED BY TREND OF R/CB

TABLE 1   FEMALE POPULATION ESTIMATES: 1801 TO 1906

DATE	R/CB RATIO	% CORRECTION	FINAL POPULATION ESTIMATE	DATE	R/CB RATIO	% CORRECTION	FINAL POPULATION ESTIMATE
1801	0.965	3.7	266929	1856	1.005	-0.4	302343
1806	1.000	0.0	263220	1861	0.990	0.4	303446
1811*	1.000	0.0	268570	1866	0.987	-0.0	305641
1816*	0.989	0.0	273920	1871	0.972	0.8	307269
1821	0.992	0.0	279270	1876	0.990	-1.8	306042
1826*	0.984	0.0	281235	1881	0.979	-1.3	311378
1831	0.995	0.0	283200	1886	0.958	0.1	315592
1836	1.010	0.0	286938	1891	0.966	-1.4	318062
1841	0.997	0.0	286986	1896	0.949	-0.4	316508
1846	1.000	0.0	293999	1901	0.928	1.1	317293
1851	0.992	1.5	302336	1906	0.917	1.6	318994

NOTE: R/CB RATIO REFERS TO THE POPULATION COMPUTED BY THE BALANCE OF BIRTHS
         AND DEATHS OVER THE REPORTED POPULATION
* INTERPOLATED VALUES

TABLE 2   FEMALE BIRTH ESTIMATES: 1801-1805 TO 1901-1905

DATE	% CORRECTION	FINAL BIRTH ESTIMATE	CRUDE BIRTH RATE	DATE	% CORRECTION	FINAL BIRTH ESTIMATE	CRUDE BIRTH RATE
1801-1805	0.0	41886	31.6	1856-1860	0.0	38723	25.6
1806-1810	0.0	39779	29.9	1861-1865	0.0	39390	25.9
1811-1815	7.2	40973	30.2	1866-1870	0.0	40391	26.4
1816-1820	10.8	43761	31.6	1871-1875	0.0	40246	26.2
1821-1825	4.9	41752	29.8	1876-1880	0.0	42259	27.4
1826-1830	0.0	41635	29.5	1881-1885	0.0	42743	27.3
1831-1835	0.0	41701	29.3	1886-1890	0.0	40200	25.4
1836-1840	0.0	38590	26.9	1891-1895	0.0	36750	23.2
1841-1845	2.9	40361	27.8	1896-1900	0.0	35798	22.6
1846-1850	0.0	40437	27.1	1901-1905	0.0	34566	21.7
1851-1855	0.0	39394	26.1				

TABLE 3 FEMALE POPULATION ESTIMATES,
DISTRIBUTION BY AGE: 1801 TO 1906

AGE	1801	1806	1811	1816	1821	1826	1831	1836	1841	1846	1851
0- 4	32625	28481	29777	31285	32296	31098	30190	30521	29407	31666	32247
5- 9	27789	27794	25434	26669	27795	28623	27490	26880	27264	26848	29161
10-14	26240	26347	26843	24406	25756	26603	27702	26766	25718	26554	26263
15-19	24779	24872	25436	25746	23562	24641	25739	26963	25597	25037	25993
20-24	23101	23176	23759	24162	24582	22308	23561	24761	25539	24691	24347
25-29	21297	21366	21943	22388	22855	23070	21119	22445	23265	24446	23789
30-34	19475	19516	20081	20540	21015	21295	21663	19956	20950	22129	23380
35-39	17647	17679	18205	18668	19129	19436	19830	20301	18500	19795	21027
40-44	15864	15893	16381	16817	17265	17574	17968	18451	18701	17374	18693
45-49	14158	14179	14621	15027	15442	15750	16128	16596	16879	17443	16292
50-54	12392	12402	12819	13193	13553	13845	14187	14624	14934	15491	16101
55-59	10458	10462	10869	11235	11522	11783	12059	12442	12782	13325	13914
60-64	8301	8294	8699	9069	9292	9509	9695	9994	10354	10875	11434
65-69	6029	5999	6373	6738	6914	7092	7187	7384	7722	8196	8700
70-74	3846	3826	4112	4426	4570	4711	4749	4853	5117	5494	5908
75-79	2007	1991	2192	2406	2438	2606	2610	2656	2834	3077	3359
80+	952	945	1025	1146	1224	1294	1322	1345	1423	1559	1727

AGE	1856	1861	1866	1871	1876	1881	1886	1891	1896	1901	1906
0- 4	30458	30398	31202	31801	31102	34007	34351	32653	29677	29602	29210
5- 9	29053	27638	27694	28343	28633	28525	31134	31571	29921	27486	27662
10-14	28065	28047	26720	26745	27288	27751	27601	30163	30567	29080	26768
15-19	25200	27005	27009	25662	25552	26270	26579	26382	28808	29389	27986
20-24	24611	23902	25623	25505	23980	24123	24518	24658	24323	26976	27573
25-29	22956	23282	22631	24200	23928	22708	22700	23033	23091	22973	25601
30-34	22347	21655	22009	21357	22734	22699	21495	21517	21805	21997	21975
35-39	21829	20960	20360	20663	19956	21469	21411	20318	20315	20715	20999
40-44	19521	20365	19609	19023	19221	18765	20180	20187	19139	19249	19733
45-49	17240	18094	18931	18208	17589	17966	17542	18928	18921	18042	18246
50-54	14789	15735	16568	17314	16576	16207	16562	16237	17504	17606	16896
55-59	14204	13132	14025	14743	15316	14880	14556	14944	14636	15896	16111
60-64	11693	12030	11173	11902	12407	13138	12757	12545	12850	12724	13957
65-69	8934	9227	9548	8836	9307	9948	10527	10290	10086	10482	10516
70-74	6106	6346	6601	6800	6203	6743	7201	7684	7478	7466	7888
75-79	3500	3674	3854	3985	4027	3828	4156	4486	4758	4743	4838
80+	1835	1956	2084	2184	2225	2354	2324	2466	2627	2869	3035

TABLE 4 MARRIED WOMEN ESTIMATES,
DISTRIBUTION BY AGE: 1831 TO 1901

AGE	1831	1836	1841	1846	1851	1856	1861	1866
15-19	360	378	360	354	369	358	249	317
20-24	3913	4118	4273	4154	4118	4165	4067	3547
25-29	8890	9456	9859	10412	10183	9826	10016	9751
30-34	12624	11627	12291	13058	13875	13243	12907	13130
35-39	12839	13125	12069	13010	13920	14404	13932	13536
40-44	12316	12607	12932	12131	13174	13679	14407	13862
45-49	10340	10581	10952	11476	10863	11387	12116	12652

AGE	1871	1876	1881	1886	1891	1896	1901
15-19	491	462	490	477	401	388	662
20-24	3779	4247	4557	4699	4612	4560	5022
25-29	9692	9857	9645	10350	10542	10564	10695
30-34	12696	13182	13394	12725	13264	13715	13677
35-39	13650	13215	14143	14392	13383	14023	14251
40-44	13311	13484	13311	13855	13669	13099	13148
45-49	11972	11601	12042	12113	12757	13068	11944

TABLE 5   DEMOGRAPHIC INDICES AND FEMALE SINGULATE MEAN AGE
AT MARRIAGE: 1831 TO 1901

DATE	IF OVERALL FERTILITY	IG MARITAL FERTILITY	IH ILLEGITIMATE FERTILITY	IM PROPORTION MARRIED	SINGULATE MEAN AGE AT MARRIAGE
1831	0.316	0.790	0.017	0.388	27.6
1836	0.298	0.751	0.018	0.382	27.6
1841	0.292	0.733	0.016	0.385	27.6
1846	0.295	0.722	0.017	0.394	27.6
1851	0.286	0.693	0.014	0.400	27.6
1856	0.282	0.680	0.014	0.402	27.6
1861	0.282	0.682	0.016	0.400	27.8
1866	0.286	0.714	0.015	0.388	27.8
1871	0.289	0.726	0.016	0.385	27.6
1876	0.300	0.731	0.016	0.396	27.4
1881	0.307	0.729	0.022	0.404	27.1
1886	0.300	0.701	0.021	0.410	27.2
1891	0.279	0.649	0.023	0.409	27.6
1896	0.261	0.601	0.023	0.411	27.5
1901	0.245	0.575	0.020	0.406	

MORTALITY PATTERN: WEST
MIGRATION: GRADUAL, WITH POPULATICN TOTALS CBTAINED BY INTERPOLATION OF R/CB
 LINEARLY BETWEEN 1851 AND 1876, ANE BETWEEN 1881 AND 1906

TABLE 1 FEMALE POPUIATION ESTIMATES: 1801 TO 1906

DATE	R/CB RATIO	% COR-RECTION	FINAL POPULATION ESTIMATE	DATE	R/CB RATIO	% COR-RECTION	FINAL POPULATION ESTIMATE
1801	1.008	0.0	103529	1856	0.957	0.8	135968
1806	1.013	0.0	101909	1861	0.934	1.4	135434
1811*	1.026	0.0	106755	1866	0.920	1.1	138407
1816*	1.024	0.0	111601	1871	0.900	1.3	139646
1821	1.010	0.0	116447	1876	0.894	0.0	139928
1826*	1.014	0.0	119648	1881	0.876	0.0	141820
1831	1.017	0.0	122849	1886	0.876	-1.6	144153
1836	1.027	0.0	128949	1891	0.843	0.7	145428
1841	1.006	0.0	127049	1896	0.831	0.5	144843
1846	1.000	0.0	132111	1901	0.818	0.5	144614
1851	0.983	0.0	134382	1906	0.808	0.C	144533

NOTE: R/CB RATIO REFERS TO THE ECPULATICN CCMPUTED BY THE BALANCE OF BIRTHS
       AND DEATHS OVER THE REPORTED POPULATICN
* INTERPOLATED VALUES

TABLE 2 FEMALE BIRTH ESTIMATES: 1801-1805 TO 1901-1905

DATE	% COR-RECTION	FINAL BIRTH ESTIMATE	CRUDE BIRTH RATE	CATE	% COR-RECTION	FINAL BIRTH ESTIMATE	CRUDE BIRTH RATE
1801-1805	0.0	18172	35.4	1856-1860	5.8	19525	28.8
1806-1810	0.0	18481	35.4	1861-1865	0.0	18467	27.0
1811-1815	1.4	18863	34.6	1866-1870	0.0	18118	26.1
1816-1820	0.0	19969	35.0	1871-1875	0.0	17340	24.8
1821-1325	0.0	19155	32.5	1876-1880	0.0	17644	25.0
1826-1830	0.0	19079	31.5	1881-1885	0.0	17C91	23.9
1831-1835	0.0	19394	30.8	1886-1890	0.0	16186	22.4
1836-1840	5.7	19096	29.8	1891-1895	0.0	14823	20.4
1841-1845	0.0	20001	30.9	1896-1900	0.0	14342	19.8
1846-1850	2.5	19554	29.4	1901-1905	0.0	14153	19.6
1851-1855	0.0	19555	28.9				

TABLE 3 FEMALE POPULATION ESTIMATES,
DISTRIBUTION BY AGE: 1801 TO 1906

AGE	1801	1806	1811	1816	1821	1826	1831	1836	1841	1846	1851
0- 4	13812	11689	13455	14260	15284	14220	14227	15241	13649	15763	15292
5- 9	11644	11479	10399	12062	12775	13595	12686	13048	13161	12441	14195
10-14	10760	10981	11196	10047	11564	12318	13137	12432	12273	12756	11892
15-19	9946	10145	10706	10813	9628	11146	11899	12869	11689	11889	12156
20-24	9079	9238	9775	10234	10264	9180	10652	11547	11964	11224	11179
25-29	8211	8326	8811	9264	9638	9698	8694	10256	10634	11403	10521
30-34	7362	7452	7876	8292	8667	9038	9116	8317	9371	10073	10658
35-39	6554	6611	6990	7358	7705	8065	8431	8663	7539	8821	9362
40-44	5791	5834	6156	6487	6794	7121	7473	7963	7797	7054	8155
45-49	5073	5114	5393	5673	5949	6235	6551	7009	7116	7246	6480
50-54	4371	4384	4640	4885	5117	5363	5636	6046	6151	6509	6556
55-59	3640	3626	3845	4077	4282	4470	4698	5054	5135	5474	5731
60-64	2357	2819	3003	3209	3403	3545	3713	4015	4063	4363	4601
65-69	2068	1998	2143	2320	2488	2601	2719	2950	2972	3217	3420
70-74	1319	1256	1344	1480	1614	1694	1778	1940	1940	2119	2273
75-79	699	642	699	778	868	917	967	1071	1060	1172	1270
80+	339	315	326	361	407	442	473	523	534	587	643

AGE	1856	1861	1866	1871	1876	1881	1886	1891	1896	1901	1906
0- 4	15236	14725	15242	14790	14192	14962	14867	14114	12891	12679	12733
5- 9	13742	13486	13548	13936	13529	13165	14059	13197	13256	12196	12061
10-14	13563	13064	12980	13000	13392	13046	12755	13657	13593	12905	11864
15-19	11286	12781	12425	12244	12225	12598	12311	12042	12882	12886	12159
20-24	11331	10332	11842	11298	11014	10919	11290	11013	10635	11569	11442
25-29	10430	10457	9655	10987	10427	10164	10108	10479	10161	9864	10734
30-34	9820	9659	9872	9068	10334	9869	9674	9638	9989	9727	9455
35-39	9899	9048	9096	9264	8515	9795	9415	9245	9210	9592	9367
40-44	8654	9083	8500	8524	8699	8076	9360	9016	8860	8862	9269
45-49	7492	7864	8489	7931	7972	8224	7695	8335	8617	8499	8542
50-54	5866	6729	7286	7822	7331	7460	7759	7280	8458	8190	8126
55-59	5774	5118	6067	6553	7054	6709	6894	7185	6753	7874	7678
60-64	4812	4778	4419	5214	5645	6182	5948	6125	6385	6041	7098
65-69	3630	3693	3877	3562	4213	4663	5179	4995	5142	5406	5165
70-74	2410	2474	2723	2834	2611	3174	3573	3977	3832	3987	4244
75-79	1358	1392	1566	1705	1778	1697	2107	2377	2642	2580	2727
80+	696	723	821	915	1007	1117	1161	1352	1537	1758	1868

[326]

TABLE 4 MARRIED WOMEN ESTIMATES,
DISTRIBUTION BY AGE: 1831 TO 1901

AGE	1831	1836	1841	1846	1851	1856	1861	1866
15-19	820	906	850	895	949	916	1283	1218
20-24	4352	4814	5107	4905	5002	5194	4851	5544
25-29	5864	7004	7350	7987	7458	7485	7587	7086
30-34	7033	6461	7326	7942	8457	7847	7756	7973
35-39	6670	6880	6007	7078	7541	8015	7341	7410
40-44	5879	6267	6135	5584	6464	6885	7220	6773
45-49	4862	5205	5281	5427	4863	5653	5948	6420

AGE	1871	1876	1881	1886	1891	1896	1901
15-19	1027	1113	1247	1093	836	838	1048
20-24	5345	5417	5545	5659	5364	5148	5492
25-29	7883	7552	7645	7698	7878	7605	7506
30-34	7336	8259	7951	7952	7969	8224	7998
35-39	7530	6945	7979	7702	7636	7646	7938
40-44	6744	6897	6466	7483	7209	7122	7119
45-49	5933	5983	6264	5892	6838	6607	6477

TABLE 5 DEMOGRAPHIC INDICES AND FEMALE SINGULATE MEAN AGE
AT MARRIAGE: 1831 TO 1901

DATE	IF OVERALL FERTILITY	IG MARITAL FERTILITY	IH ILLEGITIMATE FERTILITY	IM PROPORTION MARRIED	SINGULATE MEAN AGE AT MARRIAGE
1831	0.338	0.577	0.035	0.558	24.1
1836	0.318	0.537	0.043	0.558	23.8
1841	0.323	0.529	0.050	0.570	23.7
1846	0.317	0.512	0.043	0.586	23.5
1851	0.310	0.493	0.042	0.594	23.4
1856	0.312	0.488	0.043	0.605	23.1
1861	0.308	0.482	0.042	0.605	23.0
1866	0.293	0.458	0.042	0.603	23.1
1871	0.284	0.444	0.043	0.602	23.0
1876	0.282	0.437	0.039	0.609	22.7
1881	0.278	0.425	0.038	0.621	22.7
1886	0.266	0.402	0.040	0.624	22.9
1891	0.249	0.376	0.041	0.620	23.1
1896	0.234	0.358	0.038	0.614	23.0
1901	0.225	0.345	0.037	0.613	

MORTALITY PATTERN: WEST
MIGRATION: NO CORRECTION MADE FOR MIGRATION BY AGE

TABLE 1 FEMALE POPULATION ESTIMATES: 1801 TO 1906

DATE	R/CB RATIO	% COR-RECTION	FINAL POPULATION ESTIMATE	DATE	R/CB RATIO	% COR-RECTION	FINAL POPULATION ESTIMATE
1801	1.020	3.9	142936	1856	1.011	0.0	163197
1806	1.051	0.0	141119	1861	1.016	0.0	164133
1811*	1.035	0.0	142855	1866	1.016	0.0	163977
1816*	1.001	0.0	144590	1871	1.003	0.0	160828
1821	0.971	0.0	146326	1876	1.033	0.0	163935
1826*	0.973	0.0	149954	1881	1.037	0.0	165174
1831	0.990	0.0	153581	1886	1.065	0.0	170903
1836	1.009	0.0	157997	1891	1.065	0.0	171016
1841	1.001	0.0	157924	1896	1.080	0.0	171308
1846	1.000	0.0	159803	1901	1.081	0.0	169933
1851	1.002	1.9	163537	1906	1.098	0.0	172109

NOTE: R/CB RATIO REFERS TO THE POPULATION COMPUTED BY THE BALANCE OF BIRTHS
       AND DEATHS OVER THE REPORTED POPULATION
* INTERPOLATED VALUES

TABLE 2 FEMALE BIRTH ESTIMATES: 1801-1805 TO 1901-1905

DATE	% COR-RECTION	FINAL BIRTH ESTIMATE	CRUDE BIRTH RATE	DATE	% COR-RECTION	FINAL BIRTH ESTIMATE	CRUDE BIRTH RATE
1801-1805	7.2	20883	29.4	1856-1860	0.0	16317	19.9
1806-1810	10.3	20075	28.3	1861-1865	0.7	15840	19.3
1811-1815	28.9	20794	28.9	1866-1870	-17.4	16264	20.0
1816-1820	0.0	20446	28.1	1871-1875	3.8	15975	19.7
1821-1825	0.0	18968	25.6	1876-1880	0.0	16277	19.8
1826-1830	0.0	18540	24.4	1881-1885	0.0	16446	19.6
1831-1835	0.0	17977	23.1	1886-1890	0.0	15676	18.3
1836-1840	0.0	17074	21.6	1891-1895	0.0	14716	17.2
1841-1845	0.0	17238	21.7	1896-1900	0.0	14257	16.7
1846-1850	0.0	17739	21.9	1901-1905	0.0	14585	17.1
1851-1855	0.0	16664	20.4				

TABLE 3 FEMALE POPULATION ESTIMATES,
DISTRIBUTION BY AGE: 1801 TO 1906

AGE	1801	1806	1811	1816	1821	1826	1831	1836	1841	1846	1851
0- 4	19123	14730	15205	16206	16193	15235	14717	14651	13814	14281	14694
5- 9	16112	16465	13122	13591	14582	14901	14065	13766	13460	12884	13470
10-14	14870	15200	15739	12418	12884	14198	14672	13933	13321	13163	12816
15-19	13746	14033	14524	14887	11765	12538	13973	14527	13475	13020	13087
20-24	12541	12811	13277	13623	13994	11355	12227	13719	13940	13075	12842
25-29	11335	11571	12022	12367	12722	13412	10988	11920	13078	13443	12810
30-34	10158	10373	10786	11133	11487	12123	12897	10551	11303	12549	13099
35-39	9037	9218	9602	9928	10283	10881	11581	12426	10042	10788	12158
40-44	7980	8142	8478	8787	9119	9684	10331	11094	11651	9533	10393
45-49	6989	7137	7436	7707	8017	8531	9132	9830	10333	10988	9123
50-54	6016	6133	6411	6657	6328	7387	7916	8556	9021	9607	10360
55-59	5008	5105	5349	5588	5834	6217	6664	7222	7656	8185	8827
60-64	3929	4014	4236	4459	4692	5007	5349	5813	6191	6666	7202
65-69	2841	2891	3090	3298	3505	3762	4008	4356	4666	5359	5488
70-74	1811	1852	1994	2171	2346	2537	2707	2946	3165	3460	3767
75-79	959	976	1074	1192	1319	1445	1544	1692	1828	2011	2198
80+	465	470	511	573	657	742	810	897	982	1093	1204

AGE	1856	1861	1866	1871	1876	1881	1886	1891	1896	1901	1906
0- 4	13935	13750	13417	13377	13684	14083	14800	13764	12913	12568	13198
5- 9	13684	13128	12944	12384	12849	13033	13808	14154	13245	12370	12283
10-14	13079	13469	12974	12509	12448	12682	13164	13601	14085	13052	12393
15-19	12437	12867	13201	12434	12566	12278	12799	12956	13525	13868	13065
20-24	12615	12150	12527	12658	12402	12318	12318	12522	12804	13240	13810
25-29	12309	12253	11764	11941	12551	12095	12299	11995	12314	12477	13128
30-34	12223	11900	11811	11159	11782	12190	12032	11932	11749	11956	12329
35-39	12437	11756	11414	11145	10954	11393	12078	11626	11637	11362	11769
40-44	11485	11900	11220	10714	10882	10541	11236	11617	11285	11202	11134
45-49	9754	10918	11284	10462	10393	10405	10330	10739	11205	10795	10908
50-54	8446	9144	10212	10375	10008	9808	10069	9749	10225	10585	10383
55-59	9371	7733	8359	9166	9689	9239	9295	9306	9084	9461	9978
60-64	7679	8245	6801	7205	8222	8621	8454	8295	8363	8120	8625
65-69	5896	6352	6827	5505	6071	6903	7458	7134	7039	7072	7012
70-74	4089	4434	4790	5019	4214	4653	5464	5759	5531	5449	5600
75-79	2416	2643	2880	3022	3297	2792	3194	3658	3863	3716	3752
80+	1342	1491	1653	1753	1924	2139	2107	2210	2440	2641	2742

TABLE 4 MARRIED WOMEN ESTIMATES,
DISTRIBUTION BY AGE: 1831 TO 1901

AGE	1831	1836	1841	1846	1851	1856	1861	1866
15-19	798	878	823	825	864	857	989	1033
20-24	4899	5626	5848	5650	5697	5748	5690	5676
25-29	7478	8217	9164	9560	9238	8996	9074	8820
30-34	10066	8362	8982	10066	10594	9957	9763	9748
35-39	9267	9957	8141	8811	9990	10269	9755	9506
40-44	8198	8768	9322	7674	8402	9309	9675	9136
45-49	6846	7320	7835	8405	7020	7532	8466	8765

AGE	1871	1876	1881	1886	1891	1896	1901
15-19	916	976	999	953	817	832	1028
20-24	5925	6046	6196	6173	6148	6387	6433
25-29	8669	9283	9215	9489	9210	9431	9764
30-34	9208	9588	10017	10029	10000	9814	9995
35-39	9227	9108	9425	10037	9737	9741	9494
40-44	8608	8770	8540	9086	9418	9134	9045
45-49	7961	7941	8010	7968	8301	8610	8260

TABLE 5 DEMOGRAPHIC INDICES AND FEMALE SINGULATE MEAN AGE
AT MARRIAGE: 1831 TO 1901

DATE	IF OVERALL FERTILITY	IG MARITAL FERTILITY	IH ILLEGITIMATE FERTILITY	IM PROPORTION MARRIED	SINGULATE MEAN AGE AT MARRIAGE
1831	0.252	0.408	0.037	0.578	24.1
1836	0.234	0.376	0.041	0.574	23.9
1841	0.230	0.360	0.045	0.586	23.7
1846	0.234	0.364	0.037	0.602	23.5
1851	0.227	0.347	0.035	0.615	23.4
1856	0.222	0.335	0.032	0.625	23.2
1861	0.219	0.328	0.033	0.630	23.1
1866	0.220	0.333	0.033	0.624	23.2
1871	0.226	0.345	0.032	0.621	23.0
1876	0.223	0.335	0.031	0.630	22.8
1881	0.227	0.332	0.037	0.643	22.8
1886	0.218	0.316	0.039	0.646	22.9
1891	0.207	0.303	0.037	0.641	22.9
1896	0.195	0.285	0.037	0.637	22.9
1901	0.192	0.279	0.040	0.636	

[330]

MORTALITY PATTERN: WEST
MIGRATION: NO CORRECTION MADE FOR MIGRATION BY AGE

TABLE 1 FEMALE POPULATION ESTIMATES: 1801 TO 1906

DATE	R/CB RATIO	% COR- RECTION	FINAL POPULATION ESTIMATE	DATE	R/CB RATIO	% COR- RECTION	FINAL POPULATION ESTIMATE
1801	1.017	3.4	228770	1856	0.933	0.0	292504
1806	1.052	0.0	237187	1861	0.943	0.0	290931
1811*	1.032	0.0	244053	1866	0.949	0.0	292292
1816*	1.015	0.0	250919	1871	0.931	0.0	287232
1821	1.001	0.0	257785	1876	0.947	0.0	291513
1826*	1.003	0.0	268026	1881	0.929	0.0	288030
1831	1.008	0.0	278266	1886	0.921	0.0	288659
1836	1.012	0.0	289368	1891	0.905	0.0	282764
1841	1.008	0.0	296269	1896	0.918	0.0	284227
1846	1.000	0.0	301520	1901	0.919	0.0	283323
1851	0.981	0.0	302580	1906	0.918	0.0	281710

NOTE: R/CB RATIO REFERS TO THE POPULATION COMPUTED BY THE BALANCE OF BIRTHS
       AND DEATHS OVER THE REPORTED POPULATION
* INTERPOLATED VALUES

TABLE 2 FEMALE BIRTH ESTIMATES: 1801-1805 TO 1901-1905

DATE	% COR- RECTION	FINAL BIRTH ESTIMATE	CRUDE BIRTH RATE	DATE	% COR- RECTION	FINAL BIRTH ESTIMATE	CRUDE BIRTH RATE
1801-1805	0.0	38454	33.0	1856-1860	-6.4	39251	26.9
1806-1810	0.0	38406	31.9	1861-1865	-6.8	36599	25.1
1811-1815	0.0	38433	31.1	1866-1870	3.0	35136	24.3
1816-1820	0.0	40947	32.2	1871-1875	0.0	34189	23.6
1821-1825	0.0	42042	32.0	1876-1880	0.0	34640	23.9
1826-1830	0.0	42879	31.4	1881-1885	0.0	31912	22.1
1831-1835	0.0	43897	30.9	1886-1890	0.0	29920	20.9
1836-1840	0.0	42368	28.9	1891-1895	0.0	28481	20.1
1841-1845	0.0	41030	27.5	1896-1900	0.0	27353	19.3
1846-1850	7.9	39970	26.5	1901-1905	0.0	26092	18.5
1851-1855	13.9	40329	27.1				

TABLE 3 FEMALE POPULATION ESTIMATES,
DISTRIBUTION BY AGE: 1801 TO 1906

AGE	1801	1806	1811	1816	1821	1826	1831	1836	1841	1846	1851
0- 4	32584	28959	29342	29553	30944	32173	32825	34042	32813	32091	31176
5- 9	27411	29097	25832	26278	26319	27920	29073	29817	30757	29714	28850
10-14	24823	26383	27739	24691	25136	25513	27124	28274	28778	29633	28355
15-19	22468	23882	25141	26501	23608	24356	24776	26366	27277	27713	28263
20-24	20131	21396	22545	23797	25090	22649	23417	23854	25200	26034	26204
25-29	17899	19006	20039	21176	22344	23871	21594	22366	22621	23873	24438
30-34	15804	16780	17687	18703	19747	21114	22603	20490	21074	21299	22277
35-39	13865	14708	15511	16399	17318	18528	19849	21300	19177	19716	19752
40-44	12072	12819	13512	14293	15087	16145	17307	18589	19814	17834	18176
45-49	10457	11082	11695	12365	13058	13967	14975	16095	17172	18300	16330
50-54	8897	9437	9947	10531	11109	11837	12738	13700	14629	15612	16498
55-59	7355	7789	8231	8708	9185	9816	10522	11321	12102	12937	13697
60-64	5785	6116	6474	6870	7223	7719	8262	8905	9531	10215	10844
65-69	4202	4453	4725	5025	5284	5628	6021	6494	6970	7494	7986
70-74	2751	2891	3089	3296	3461	3686	3929	4245	4565	4934	5281
75-79	1506	1586	1693	1821	1908	2029	2161	2334	2520	2737	2950
80+	778	803	852	913	964	1025	1090	1177	1269	1384	1502

AGE	1856	1861	1866	1871	1876	1881	1886	1891	1896	1901	1906
0- 4	29900	28499	28066	26934	27057	27215	26248	23924	23425	22881	22077
5- 9	26984	26460	25788	25034	24863	24405	25160	23873	22420	21944	21528
10-14	26686	26142	25735	24538	24684	23754	23639	24122	23603	21964	21512
15-19	26216	25845	25415	24477	24184	23571	22995	22652	23837	23110	21520
20-24	25887	25092	24877	23951	23900	22899	22654	21861	22206	23176	22492
25-29	23813	24533	23951	23264	23204	22471	21875	21394	21287	21463	22431
30-34	22066	22384	23257	22257	22394	21691	21360	20547	20719	20476	20680
35-39	19980	20569	21069	21470	21282	20807	20510	19949	19783	19827	19633
40-44	17606	18490	19236	19332	20403	19659	19570	19048	19099	18833	18915
45-49	16089	16174	17171	17529	18245	18720	18369	18054	18116	18064	17851
50-54	14222	14508	14769	15397	16277	16485	17245	16697	16915	16895	16890
55-59	13963	12401	12859	12875	13896	14320	14822	15279	15245	15404	15437
60-64	11047	11501	10451	10689	11075	11688	12361	12579	13357	13338	13541
65-69	8129	8359	8984	8082	8548	8697	9471	9817	10287	10981	11036
70-74	5376	5450	5844	6245	5806	6058	6398	6806	7261	7685	8273
75-79	3000	2982	3201	3434	3788	3438	3821	3923	4293	4658	4986
80+	1540	1541	1618	1724	1905	2091	2161	2241	2374	2625	2908

[332]

TABLE 4 MARRIED WOMEN ESTIMATES,
DISTRIBUTION BY AGE: 1831 TO 1901

AGE	1831	1836	1841	1846	1851	1856	1861	1866
15-19	1021	1100	1152	1186	1226	1153	1243	1328
20-24	6753	6935	7400	7717	7838	7824	7640	7400
25-29	12046	12516	12728	13493	13863	13579	13999	13704
30-34	15619	14156	14610	14792	15481	15379	15535	16124
35-39	14606	15636	14123	14531	14541	14747	15054	15367
40-44	13189	14092	15070	13561	13780	13384	13864	14333
45-49	10838	11576	12430	13263	11801	11692	11532	12147

AGE	1871	1876	1881	1886	1891	1896	1901
15-19	1368	1592	1450	947	733	657	1010
20-24	7206	8631	7939	7074	6750	6849	7077
25-29	12898	12779	14080	13086	12073	12651	13113
30-34	15396	15163	14790	15590	14413	14378	14764
35-39	15576	15414	15214	14976	14746	14551	14570
40-44	14278	15017	14886	14452	13551	13889	13592
45-49	12255	12710	13630	13450	12564	12648	12370

TABLE 5 DEMOGRAPHIC INDICES AND FEMALE SINGULATE MEAN AGE
AT MARRIAGE: 1831 TO 1901

DATE	IF OVERALL FERTILITY	IG MARITAL FERTILITY	IH ILLEGITIMATE FERTILITY	IM PROPORTION MARRIED	SINGULATE MEAN AGE AT MARRIAGE
1831	0.329	0.614	0.054	0.491	25.9
1836	0.321	0.608	0.046	0.488	25.7
1841	0.305	0.597	0.030	0.485	25.6
1846	0.290	0.571	0.027	0.484	25.5
1851	0.283	0.549	0.032	0.486	25.5
1856	0.287	0.563	0.019	0.492	25.4
1861	0.271	0.526	0.020	0.496	25.3
1866	0.255	0.492	0.020	0.499	25.3
1871	0.253	0.487	0.021	0.498	25.0
1876	0.250	0.472	0.019	0.511	24.6
1881	0.250	0.453	0.023	0.527	24.8
1886	0.236	0.436	0.021	0.518	25.3
1891	0.229	0.432	0.025	0.502	25.4
1896	0.217	0.409	0.023	0.503	25.2
1901	0.207	0.385	0.021	0.511	

MORTALITY PATTERN: WEST
MIGRATION: GRADUAL, WITH POPULATION TOTALS OBTAINED BY TREND OF R/CB

TABLE 1   FEMALE POPULATION ESTIMATES: 1801 TO 1906

DATE	R/CB RATIO	% COR-RECTION	FINAL POPULATION ESTIMATE	DATE	R/CB RATIO	% COR-RECTION	FINAL POPULATION ESTIMATE
1801	1.095	0.0	147799	1856	0.948	1.8	152532
1806	1.071	0.0	150740	1861	0.946	0.3	149079
1811*	1.053	0.0	152740	1866	0.947	-1.5	146237
1816*	1.035	0.0	154740	1871	0.921	-0.4	142909
1821	1.041	0.0	156740	1876	0.917	-1.7	140501
1826*	1.023	0.0	158561	1881	0.886	-0.1	139312
1831	1.023	0.0	160381	1886	0.870	-0.0	137920
1836	1.021	0.0	161052	1891	0.839	1.8	135291
1841	1.011	0.0	161374	1896	0.833	0.6	131439
1846	1.000	0.0	160249	1901	0.823	-0.1	128670
1851	0.982	-0.2	157292	1906	0.810	-0.5	126281

NOTE: R/CB RATIO REFERS TO THE POPULATION COMPUTED BY THE BALANCE OF BIRTHS
       AND DEATHS OVER THE REPORTED POPULATION
* INTERPOLATED VALUES

TABLE 2   FEMALE BIRTH ESTIMATES: 1801-1805 TO 1901-1905

DATE	% COR-RECTION	FINAL BIRTH ESTIMATE	CRUDE BIRTH RATE	DATE	% COR-RECTION	FINAL BIRTH ESTIMATE	CRUDE BIRTH RATE
1801-1805	0.0	25147	33.7	1856-1860	0.0	17320	23.0
1806-1810	1.7	22964	30.3	1861-1865	0.0	18160	24.6
1811-1815	2.4	22672	29.5	1866-1870	0.0	16923	23.4
1816-1820	0.8	21025	27.0	1871-1875	0.0	16693	23.6
1821-1825	0.0	21870	27.7	1876-1880	0.0	16826	24.1
1826-1830	0.0	21524	27.0	1881-1885	0.0	16220	23.4
1831-1835	0.0	21178	26.4	1886-1890	0.0	14825	21.7
1836-1840	0.0	21419	26.6	1891-1895	0.0	13605	20.4
1841-1845	0.0	20496	25.5	1896-1900	0.0	13793	21.2
1846-1850	5.9	19565	24.6	1901-1905	0.0	13543	21.2
1851-1855	8.4	18659	24.1				

TABLE 3 FEMALE POPULATION ESTIMATES,
DISTRIBUTION BY AGE: 1801 TO 1906

AGE	1801	1806	1811	1816	1821	1826	1831	1836	1841	1846	1851
0- 4	19493	18715	17317	17189	15873	16863	16433	16064	16376	15605	14895
5- 9	16683	17163	16597	15410	15421	14245	15173	14732	14398	14637	13875
10-14	15357	15812	16331	15829	14918	14765	13768	14635	14144	13794	13923
15-19	14117	14549	15039	15569	15318	14277	14265	13274	14044	13544	13074
20-24	12860	13240	13703	14199	14910	14525	13657	13615	12616	13318	12649
25-29	11616	11959	12368	12833	13481	14030	13779	12925	12836	11867	12401
30-34	10415	10727	11097	11506	12097	12604	13219	12951	12106	11994	11014
35-39	9285	9548	9884	10252	10766	11236	11792	12335	12046	11234	11065
40-44	8212	8457	8742	9074	9529	9939	10445	10933	11402	11108	10306
45-49	7226	7428	7689	7970	8375	8737	9175	9616	10035	10441	10124
50-54	6239	6426	6641	6895	7230	7556	7931	8304	8682	9039	9364
55-59	5234	5383	5579	5784	6066	6342	6658	6966	7283	7595	7877
60-64	4183	4292	4447	4625	4832	5073	5315	5559	5817	6064	6300
65-69	3086	3177	3290	3422	3574	3759	3942	4111	4310	4496	4674
70-74	2044	2096	2182	2269	2362	2499	2616	2728	2859	2986	3110
75-79	1136	1165	1211	1267	1312	1396	1462	1520	1598	1668	1742
80+	598	602	622	648	675	715	752	783	821	860	898

AGE	1856	1861	1866	1871	1876	1881	1886	1891	1896	1901	1906
0- 4	13844	13359	13980	13231	13312	13761	13430	12281	11168	11477	11431
5- 9	13114	12397	11957	12578	12002	12196	12659	12350	11248	10280	10626
10-14	13192	12540	11863	11443	12079	11552	11747	12203	11905	10854	9920
15-19	13166	12519	11885	11191	10795	11398	10838	10994	11441	11186	10158
20-24	12123	12232	11577	10860	10173	9715	10161	9528	9676	10164	9897
25-29	11723	11296	11387	10733	10071	9409	8922	9313	8699	8881	9356
30-34	11478	10944	10550	10652	10082	9497	8877	8409	8779	8220	8414
35-39	10129	10662	10174	9832	9981	9500	8970	8385	7934	8314	7804
40-44	10120	9365	9869	9453	9191	9396	8977	8487	7927	7525	7914
45-49	9365	9301	8619	9121	8793	8614	8845	8466	7998	7496	7144
50-54	9047	8476	8429	7853	8369	8139	8017	8247	7886	7479	7042
55-59	8115	7959	7466	7471	7020	7557	7395	7299	7492	7199	6865
60-64	6474	6796	6667	6299	6367	6056	6561	6427	6324	6532	6317
65-69	4789	5042	5291	5240	5014	5149	4937	5354	5220	5178	5395
70-74	3172	3351	3525	3744	3766	3676	3812	3658	3940	3882	3893
75-79	1766	1875	1977	2112	2289	2362	2334	2422	2303	2515	2513
80+	914	965	1020	1094	1196	1337	1440	1470	1499	1488	1594

TABLE 4   MARRIED WOMEN ESTIMATES,
DISTRIBUTION BY AGE: 1831 TO 1901

AGE	1831	1836	1841	1846	1851	1856	1861	1866
15-19	357	344	378	380	385	408	498	463
20-24	2987	3070	2948	3226	3183	3174	3343	3440
25-29	6518	6254	6379	6048	6478	6276	6202	6400
30-34	8210	8164	7787	7848	7318	7740	7493	7310
35-39	8036	8486	8432	7964	7924	7322	7787	7471
40-44	7788	8139	8574	8387	7791	7654	7104	7459
45-49	6435	6727	7128	7460	7247	6708	6691	6165

AGE	1871	1876	1881	1886	1891	1896	1901
15-19	399	398	390	319	306	319	470
20-24	2939	2840	2925	3084	2774	2753	2931
25-29	6173	5445	5267	5270	5606	5225	5296
30-34	7451	7101	6478	6211	6060	6454	6072
35-39	7233	7396	7061	6595	6231	6019	6375
40-44	7086	6896	7073	6665	6228	5885	5611
45-49	6443	6220	6123	6371	6079	5780	5353

TABLE 5   DEMOGRAPHIC INDICES AND FEMALE SINGULATE MEAN AGE
AT MARRIAGE: 1831 TO 1901

DATE	IF OVERALL FERTILITY	IG MARITAL FERTILITY	IH ILLEGITIMATE FERTILITY	IM PROPORTION MARRIED	SINGULATE MEAN AGE AT MARRIAGE
1831	0.271	0.597	0.019	0.436	27.3
1836	0.275	0.584	0.023	0.448	26.9
1841	0.277	0.582	0.020	0.457	26.7
1846	0.270	0.560	0.024	0.460	26.5
1851	0.266	0.539	0.026	0.468	26.3
1856	0.258	0.513	0.028	0.475	26.0
1861	0.260	0.506	0.027	0.485	25.7
1866	0.264	0.503	0.026	0.499	25.7
1871	0.264	0.499	0.028	0.500	25.8
1876	0.275	0.526	0.024	0.500	25.6
1881	0.280	0.535	0.026	0.499	25.3
1886	0.271	0.513	0.029	0.501	25.3
1891	0.256	0.481	0.030	0.502	25.6
1896	0.249	0.473	0.027	0.498	25.6
1901	0.248	0.471	0.026	0.500	

MORTALITY PATTERN: WEST
MIGRATION: GRADUAL FROM 1876 ON, WITH POPULATION TOTALS OBTAINED BY LINEAR
INTERPOLATION OF R/CB BETWEEN 1866 AND 1906

TABLE 1 FEMALE POPULATION ESTIMATES: 1801 TO 1906

DATE	R/CB RATIO	% COR- RECTION	FINAL POPULATION ESTIMATE	DATE	R/CB RATIO	% COR- RECTION	FINAL POPULATION ESTIMATE
1801	0.911	6.4	121728	1856	0.953	4.5	158075
1806	0.952	1.8	120329	1861	0.966	1.8	153382
1811*	0.958	1.8	123993	1866	0.945	1.8	155348
1816*	0.957	1.8	127657	1871	0.906	3.1	155416
1821	0.958	1.8	131322	1876	0.892	1.5	154521
1826*	0.967	1.8	137299	1881	0.850	3.1	155665
1831	0.979	1.8	143274	1886	0.822	3.2	155975
1836	0.982	1.8	144610	1891	0.797	2.8	154265
1841	0.989	1.8	146603	1896	0.773	2.3	150480
1846	1.000	1.8	151909	1901	0.756	0.8	147965
1851	0.991	1.8	153385	1906	0.738	0.0	146295

NOTE: R/CB RATIO REFERS TO THE POPULATION COMPUTED BY THE BALANCE OF BIRTHS
AND DEATHS OVER THE REPORTED POPULATION
* INTERPOLATED VALUES

TABLE 2 FEMALE BIRTH ESTIMATES: 1801-1805 TO 1901-1905

DATE	% COR- RECTION	FINAL BIRTH ESTIMATE	CRUDE BIRTH RATE	DATE	% COR- RECTION	FINAL BIRTH ESTIMATE	CRUDE BIRTH RATE
1801-1805	0.0	20136	33.3	1856-1860	0.0	20813	26.4
1806-1810	0.0	21036	34.4	1861-1865	0.0	20190	26.2
1811-1815	15.5	20878	33.2	1866-1870	0.0	20257	26.1
1816-1820	2.0	20955	32.4	1871-1875	0.0	20263	26.2
1821-1825	0.0	20951	31.2	1876-1880	0.0	19819	25.6
1826-1830	0.0	20975	29.9	1881-1885	0.0	18140	23.3
1831-1835	0.0	20450	28.4	1886-1890	0.0	17462	22.5
1836-1840	0.0	21036	28.9	1891-1895	0.0	15209	20.0
1841-1845	0.0	22558	30.2	1896-1900	0.0	15354	20.6
1846-1850	0.0	22226	29.1	1901-1905	0.0	15334	20.8
1851-1855	0.0	22858	29.4				

TABLE 3 FEMALE POPULATION ESTIMATES,
DISTRIBUTION BY AGE: 1801 TO 1906

AGE	1801	1806	1811	1816	1821	1826	1831	1836	1841	1846	1851
0- 4	14239	13578	15323	15683	15824	16462	16596	15340	15679	17398	16903
5- 9	12320	12112	12030	13684	14046	14490	15136	14822	13713	14277	15548
10-14	11690	11712	11735	11596	13212	13732	14202	14604	14372	13426	13684
15-19	11087	11110	11343	11307	11191	12911	13453	13697	14155	14066	12863
20-24	10385	10394	10635	10817	10800	10835	12533	12840	13133	13716	13344
25-29	9642	9624	9852	10054	10244	10376	10439	11857	12198	12618	12906
30-34	8374	8851	9049	9247	9454	9778	9934	9804	11180	11640	11794
35-39	8109	8067	8254	8430	8632	8965	9301	9260	9173	10593	10805
40-44	7353	7313	7469	7638	7818	8135	8475	8613	8606	8635	9770
45-49	6613	6580	6721	6863	7034	7317	7638	7792	7946	8044	7909
50-54	5851	5797	5937	6070	6213	6477	6761	6902	7063	7304	7246
55-59	4994	4940	5059	5200	5330	5561	5820	5924	6061	6301	6389
60-64	4030	3955	4074	4207	4337	4548	4765	4840	4930	5140	5245
65-69	2397	2903	2998	3134	3248	3442	3627	3664	3717	3875	3971
70-74	1960	1884	1951	2059	2162	2315	2468	2490	2506	2614	2683
75-79	1059	1005	1049	1122	1191	1302	1404	1417	1420	1480	1523
80+	534	505	514	548	538	652	722	744	752	781	802

AGE	1856	1861	1866	1871	1876	1881	1886	1891	1896	1901	1906
0- 4	18335	15610	16358	16238	16039	16610	15532	14319	12887	13402	13606
5- 9	15451	15971	14253	14788	14599	14771	15393	14292	13626	11961	12549
10-14	14996	14343	15299	13523	13933	13872	14085	14631	13601	12996	11436
15-19	13191	13915	13732	14507	12780	13200	13062	13122	13609	12557	11981
20-24	12300	12129	13223	12925	13605	11860	12105	11672	11587	11844	10765
25-29	12676	11224	11455	12369	12044	12695	11016	11097	10636	10497	10753
30-34	12192	11495	10547	10661	11465	11259	11922	11285	10373	9981	9903
35-39	11078	10985	10743	9763	9827	10685	10554	11143	9626	9774	9463
40-44	10091	9920	10212	9891	8950	9127	9997	9959	10442	9099	9309
45-49	9064	8974	9161	9340	9008	8266	8498	9301	9207	9843	8649
50-54	7228	7933	8170	8259	8383	8218	7612	7926	8598	8605	9276
55-59	6454	6152	7047	7186	7229	7483	7411	5865	7085	7877	7959
60-64	5448	5240	5244	5947	6030	6214	6501	6419	5960	6234	7001
65-69	4184	4117	4190	4151	4675	4893	5107	5320	5262	4967	5256
70-74	2864	2844	2987	3008	2956	3465	3681	3821	3984	4020	3845
75-79	1650	1647	1767	1836	1832	1895	2262	2385	2475	2646	2712
80+	873	884	963	1027	1066	1151	1239	1409	1523	1663	1831

TABLE 4 MARRIED WOMEN ESTIMATES,
DISTRIBUTION BY AGE: 1831 TO 1901

AGE	1831	1836	1841	1846	1851	1856	1861	1866
15-19	644	665	696	701	650	676	1048	809
20-24	3722	3848	3978	4204	4136	3859	3848	4397
25-29	5877	6707	6947	7246	7466	7396	6593	6780
30-34	6872	6790	7777	8151	8304	8646	8187	7555
35-39	6809	6764	6721	7812	8006	8268	8222	8084
40-44	6309	6370	6374	6439	7313	7614	7495	7756
45-49	5344	5393	5506	5627	5560	6443	6387	6565

AGE	1871	1876	1881	1886	1891	1896	1901
15-19	619	579	542	557	625	831	1243
20-24	3824	4040	3405	3172	3617	4639	5264
25-29	7102	6661	7320	6201	5921	6388	7353
30-34	7643	7968	7741	8595	7308	7244	7287
35-39	7328	7407	7886	7923	8589	7470	7294
40-44	7461	6775	6945	7582	7512	8218	6840
45-49	6618	6411	5924	6384	7053	7171	7160

TABLE 5 DEMOGRAPHIC INDICES AND FEMALE SINGULATE MEAN AGE
AT MARRIAGE: 1831 TO 1901

DATE	IF OVERALL FERTILITY	IG MARITAL FERTILITY	IH ILLEGITIMATE FERTILITY	IM PROPORTION MARRIED	SINGULATE MEAN AGE AT MARRIAGE
1831	0.318	0.624	0.038	0.477	25.4
1836	0.308	0.592	0.047	0.478	25.4
1841	0.311	0.585	0.056	0.482	25.4
1846	0.306	0.556	0.064	0.491	25.3
1851	0.308	0.562	0.050	0.505	25.3
1856	0.300	0.528	0.059	0.514	25.1
1861	0.288	0.511	0.053	0.513	25.0
1866	0.285	0.513	0.048	0.511	25.4
1871	0.285	0.534	0.045	0.490	25.6
1876	0.283	0.530	0.046	0.490	25.5
1881	0.271	0.506	0.039	0.496	25.6
1886	0.256	0.475	0.040	0.497	25.7
1891	0.241	0.440	0.039	0.504	25.2
1896	0.230	0.403	0.032	0.534	24.3
1901	0.236	0.392	0.032	0.569	

MORTALITY PATTERN: NORTH
MIGRATION: GRADUAL, WITH CHILD MIGRANTS SUBTRACTED AFTER 1866, AND POPULATION
TOTALS OBTAINED BY TREND OF R/CB

TABLE 1   FEMALE POPULATION ESTIMATES: 1801 TO 1906

DATE	R/CB RATIO	% COR-RECTION	FINAL POPULATION ESTIMATE	DATE	R/CB RATIO	% COR-RECTION	FINAL POPULATION ESTIMATE
1801	0.994	0.0	108350	1856	0.981	0.7	134895
1806	1.010	0.0	108311	1861	0.979	-0.1	134646
1811*	1.018	0.0	111516	1866	0.982	-1.5	136082
1816*	1.009	0.0	114720	1871	0.956	0.1	136200
1821	0.990	0.0	117925	1876	0.956	-1.0	135965
1826*	0.981	0.0	119641	1881	0.937	-0.1	136907
1831	0.988	0.0	121356	1886	0.941	-1.7	137728
1836	1.000	0.0	124954	1891	0.929	-1.5	138449
1841	1.002	0.0	126629	1896	0.916	-1.2	137682
1846	1.000	0.0	130445	1901	0.906	-1.3	136899
1851	0.993	0.6	133092	1906	0.898	-1.7	136316

NOTE: R/CB RATIO REFERS TO THE POPULATION COMPUTED BY THE BALANCE OF BIRTHS
        AND DEATHS OVER THE REPORTED POPULATION
* INTERPOLATED VALUES

TABLE 2   FEMALE BIRTH ESTIMATES: 1801-1805 TO 1901-1905

DATE	% COR-RECTION	FINAL BIRTH ESTIMATE	CRUDE BIRTH RATE	DATE	% COR-RECTION	FINAL BIRTH ESTIMATE	CRUDE BIRTH RATE
1801-1805	7.3	18530	34.2	1856-1860	0.0	17020	25.3
1806-1810	9.0	18347	33.4	1861-1865	0.0	17006	25.1
1811-1815	13.3	19507	34.5	1866-1870	0.0	16921	24.9
1816-1820	0.0	18634	32.0	1871-1875	4.1	16582	24.4
1821-1825	0.0	18445	31.1	1876-1880	0.0	15694	23.0
1826-1830	0.0	18060	30.0	1881-1885	0.0	15200	22.1
1831-1835	0.0	18272	29.7	1886-1890	0.0	14689	21.3
1836-1840	0.0	17183	27.3	1891-1895	0.0	13849	20.1
1841-1845	0.0	17411	27.1	1896-1900	0.0	13118	19.1
1846-1850	2.8	18153	27.6	1901-1905	0.0	12857	18.8
1851-1855	0.0	17260	25.8				

TABLE 3 FEMALE POPULATION ESTIMATES,
DISTRIBUTION BY AGE: 1801 TO 1906

AGE	1801	1806	1811	1816	1821	1826	1831	1836	1841	1846	1851
0- 4	16194	11989	13132	14203	14320	13778	13403	14111	13408	14366	14718
5- 9	12916	12722	9992	11006	12235	12157	11704	11678	12312	12070	12792
10-14	11478	12191	12057	9396	10339	11493	11515	11195	11083	11773	11492
15-19	10403	11197	11831	11582	8969	9896	11108	11206	10791	10714	11334
20-24	9392	10099	10321	11320	11016	8553	9527	10770	10764	10399	10257
25-29	8422	9022	9679	10274	10699	10431	8173	9176	10282	10322	9923
30-34	7483	7974	8553	9099	9635	10041	9874	7807	8694	9803	9802
35-39	6574	6971	7469	7953	8460	8954	9406	9345	7334	8236	9247
40-44	5736	6052	6469	6884	7340	7798	8317	8834	8716	6907	7722
45-49	4968	5240	5578	5923	6316	6724	7197	7764	8191	8164	6441
50-54	4251	4465	4763	5041	5371	5714	6126	6638	7116	7594	7535
55-59	3536	3664	3926	4173	4454	4723	5053	5499	5931	6460	6854
60-64	2778	2820	3033	3252	3519	3720	3957	4320	4694	5187	5602
65-69	2012	1954	2115	2292	2540	2701	2853	3121	3418	3854	4208
70-74	1263	1158	1254	1383	1584	1705	1800	1980	2190	2535	2809
75-79	646	537	591	663	798	873	925	1036	1164	1395	1577
80+	301	255	251	275	330	332	419	473	541	665	782

AGE	1856	1861	1866	1871	1876	1881	1886	1891	1896	1901	1906
0- 4	14387	13838	14453	14023	13666	13550	13322	12995	12096	11653	11491
5- 9	13249	12761	12569	12962	12551	12540	12533	12405	12017	11289	10930
10-14	12147	12528	12143	11947	12339	12027	12045	12086	11954	11611	10932
15-19	10944	11519	11849	11510	11348	11670	11315	11374	11451	11315	11038
20-24	10646	10172	10572	10946	10655	10288	10445	10142	10284	10310	10292
25-29	9681	9991	9501	9909	10291	9952	9541	9732	9472	9602	9689
30-34	9388	9121	9460	8993	9396	9809	9497	9134	9319	9089	9242
35-39	9235	8806	8620	8930	8497	8951	9377	9113	8753	8963	8760
40-44	8675	8626	8307	8115	8414	8092	8565	9009	8738	8429	8645
45-49	7213	8068	8110	7792	7617	7993	7728	8211	8618	8396	8110
50-54	5963	6647	7527	7543	7250	7187	7585	7365	7803	8227	7734
55-59	6837	5379	6090	6858	6870	6719	6706	7107	6879	7328	7734
60-64	5999	5920	4753	5334	5999	6139	6046	6066	6401	6240	6665
65-69	4619	4866	4943	3913	4378	5071	5237	5191	5174	5513	5395
70-74	3152	3376	3708	3682	2898	3383	3966	4129	4052	4095	4385
75-79	1822	1972	2239	2378	2341	1953	2315	2742	2816	2814	2864
80+	939	1055	1238	1365	1456	1582	1504	1647	1855	2025	2119

TABLE 4   MARRIED WOMEN ESTIMATES,
DISTRIBUTION BY AGE: 1831 TO 1901

AGE	1831	1836	1841	1846	1851	1856	1861	1866
15-19	421	442	445	466	524	542	595	692
20-24	3263	3821	3969	3995	4111	4466	4474	4649
25-29	5199	5988	6888	7098	6987	6983	7372	7162
30-34	7489	6026	6834	7840	7941	7711	7576	7936
35-39	7462	7514	5985	6813	7704	7764	7449	7327
40-44	6782	7248	7216	5767	6448	7273	7236	6967
45-49	5521	6013	6432	6494	5124	5774	6465	6496

AGE	1871	1876	1881	1886	1891	1896	1901
15-19	645	626	671	654	606	571	794
20-24	4818	4850	4869	4923	4799	5023	5033
25-29	7425	7639	7570	7420	7561	7382	7670
30-34	7568	7896	8231	8032	7839	8007	7826
35-39	7557	7221	7648	7968	7812	7552	7743
40-44	6711	6961	6759	7108	7522	7295	7043
45-49	6112	5979	6365	6113	6562	6875	6659

TABLE 5   DEMOGRAPHIC INDICES AND FEMALE SINGULATE MEAN AGE
AT MARRIAGE: 1831 TO 1901

DATE	IF OVERALL FERTILITY	IG MARITAL FERTILITY	IH ILLEGITIMATE FERTILITY	IM PROPORTION MARRIED	SINGULATE MEAN AGE AT MARRIAGE
1831	0.321	0.545	0.048	0.550	25.3
1836	0.308	0.521	0.048	0.549	24.9
1841	0.300	0.501	0.043	0.561	24.6
1846	0.305	0.491	0.050	0.580	24.3
1851	0.299	0.474	0.046	0.591	24.1
1856	0.289	0.453	0.039	0.604	23.8
1861	0.289	0.446	0.042	0.611	23.6
1866	0.287	0.442	0.042	0.612	23.5
1871	0.282	0.434	0.043	0.611	23.5
1876	0.271	0.413	0.042	0.617	23.3
1881	0.259	0.388	0.042	0.628	23.1
1886	0.252	0.371	0.046	0.633	23.2
1891	0.242	0.354	0.047	0.636	23.1
1896	0.230	0.334	0.046	0.638	23.0
1901	0.222	0.320	0.044	0.645	

MORTALITY PATTERN: WEST
MIGRATION: FULL STRENGTH, WITH POPULATION TOTALS OBTAINED BY TREND OF R/CB

TABLE 1 FEMALE POPULATION ESTIMATES: 1801 TO 1906

DATE	R/CB RATIO	% COR- RECTION	FINAL POPULATION ESTIMATE	DATE	R/CB RATIO	% COR- RECTION	FINAL POPULATION ESTIMATE
1801	1.022	0.0	153801	1856	1.022	-1.7	248180
1806	1.024	0.0	161705	1861	1.009	-0.5	256556
1811*	1.000	1.1	168364	1866	1.003	0.1	266968
1816*	0.971	2.2	175023	1871	0.988	1.5	277419
1821	0.959	3.2	181681	1876	1.023	-2.0	285841
1826*	0.978	1.5	189891	1881	1.007	-0.4	296316
1831	0.987	0.0	198101	1886	0.978	2.5	304676
1836	0.994	0.0	208002	1891	0.999	0.3	311790
1841	0.998	0.0	217760	1896	0.999	0.2	316357
1846	1.000	0.0	228206	1901	1.011	-1.0	321300
1851	0.991	1.4	237991	1906	1.002	-0.1	325847

NOTE: R/CB RATIO REFERS TO THE POPULATION COMPUTED BY THE BALANCE OF BIRTHS
       AND DEATHS OVER THE REPORTED POPULATION
* INTERPOLATED VALUES

TABLE 2 FEMALE BIRTH ESTIMATES: 1801-1805 TO 1901-1905

DATE	% COR- RECTION	FINAL BIRTH ESTIMATE	CRUDE BIRTH RATE	DATE	% COR- RECTION	FINAL BIRTH ESTIMATE	CRUDE BIRTH RATE
1801-1805	14.3	27917	35.4	1856-1860	0.0	41045	32.5
1806-1810	10.9	29949	36.3	1861-1865	0.0	40401	30.9
1811-1815	6.2	30894	36.0	1866-1870	0.0	41115	30.2
1816-1820	0.0	31455	35.3	1871-1875	0.0	40778	29.0
1821-1825	0.0	32369	34.8	1876-1880	0.0	41921	28.8
1826-1830	0.0	34211	35.3	1881-1885	-6.3	39042	26.0
1831-1835	0.0	35006	34.5	1886-1890	4.9	37626	24.4
1836-1840	0.0	35396	33.3	1891-1895	0.0	36275	23.1
1841-1845	0.0	36027	32.3	1896-1900	0.0	35355	22.2
1846-1850	3.4	36816	31.6	1901-1905	0.0	34467	21.3
1851-1855	0.0	37848	31.1				

TABLE 3 FEMALE POPULATION ESTIMATES,
DISTRIBUTION BY AGE: 1801 TO 1906

AGE	1801	1806	1811	1816	1821	1826	1831	1836	1841	1846	1851
0- 4	20120	21244	22533	23515	23468	24391	25866	26577	27225	28120	28419
5- 9	17246	18119	18894	20060	20909	21031	21803	23331	24129	24771	25494
10-14	15300	16720	17339	17994	19279	20228	20228	21174	22640	23443	24043
15-19	14640	15409	15393	16505	17287	18644	19448	19637	20538	21987	22889
20-24	13358	14045	14591	15081	15690	16544	17746	18689	18862	19761	21505
25-29	12387	12707	13188	13650	14210	14886	15614	16908	17805	18007	18995
30-34	10855	11417	11849	12257	12769	13385	13951	14774	16000	16890	17065
35-39	9694	10180	10570	10938	11380	11938	12455	13105	13883	15077	15873
40-44	8589	9032	9363	9697	10087	10569	11037	11623	12237	13001	14057
45-49	7572	7946	8249	8530	8879	9302	9703	10228	10777	11381	12026
50-54	6550	6887	7136	7393	7677	8048	8396	8839	9327	9863	10344
55-59	5505	5780	6001	6214	6450	6748	7049	7422	7827	8296	8706
60-64	4408	4617	4788	4978	5145	5383	5618	5921	6253	6636	6988
65-69	3259	3424	3543	3690	3810	3971	4151	4370	4629	4930	5192
70-74	2163	2264	2351	2450	2520	2626	2739	2888	3061	3278	3460
75-79	1205	1260	1304	1371	1399	1454	1520	1599	1702	1831	1939
80+	635	653	672	702	722	746	776	816	867	936	996

AGE	1856	1861	1866	1871	1876	1881	1886	1891	1896	1901	1906
0- 4	29667	31041	31730	32463	32056	33487	31760	30813	29602	29315	28912
5- 9	25881	26600	28281	29976	29574	29434	30949	29451	28528	27607	27477
10-14	24739	25002	25809	27460	28104	28771	28665	30183	28707	27879	27022
15-19	23350	23917	24256	25059	26600	27367	27969	27936	29397	28061	27301
20-24	22276	22392	23310	23364	24023	25752	26334	27042	26984	28563	27336
25-29	20545	20951	21369	21984	22257	23042	24668	25305	25962	26029	27619
30-34	18009	19334	19862	20281	20833	21187	21985	23583	24173	24897	25025
35-39	16070	16821	18209	18730	19099	19704	20106	20903	22404	23055	23811
40-44	14351	14907	15745	17067	17536	17952	18601	19013	19749	21250	21931
45-49	13060	13677	13858	14656	15871	16368	16838	17474	17845	18608	20081
50-54	10994	11822	12513	12697	13416	14585	15129	15588	16161	16575	17339
55-59	9195	9654	10518	11154	11304	12003	13142	13659	14057	14650	15085
60-64	7385	7674	8196	8952	9474	9672	10356	11374	11802	12235	12820
65-69	5518	5706	6067	6501	7081	7567	7812	8398	9203	9643	10067
70-74	3687	3811	4059	4333	4627	5103	5531	5733	6153	6826	7216
75-79	2079	2135	2295	2457	2611	2834	3184	3474	3592	3913	4391
80+	1074	1112	1191	1285	1374	1488	1647	1855	2038	2194	2413

TABLE 4 MARRIED WOMEN ESTIMATES,
DISTRIBUTION BY AGE: 1831 TO 1901

AGE	1831	1836	1841	1846	1851	1856	1861	1866
15-19	677	683	714	764	795	810	849	933
20-24	5123	5388	5442	5705	6213	6378	6474	6446
25-29	9105	9851	10397	10534	11135	12057	12320	12559
30-34	10084	10664	11591	12270	12438	13148	14161	14536
35-39	9497	9965	10609	11565	12230	12407	13044	14094
40-44	8451	8856	9388	10024	10903	11546	11659	12270
45-49	6983	7296	7759	8246	8783	9561	10091	10157

AGE	1871	1876	1881	1886	1891	1896	1901
15-19	1122	1300	993	868	746	740	1114
20-24	6619	7689	7177	7672	7445	7779	8615
25-29	12538	13144	12855	14360	14869	15055	15893
30-34	14822	15226	14768	16025	17080	17781	18212
35-39	14456	15309	14381	15578	16184	17332	17938
40-44	13234	14052	13383	14418	14616	15226	16230
45-49	10648	12049	11225	12745	13082	13378	13774

TABLE 5 DEMOGRAPHIC INDICES AND FEMALE SINGULATE MEAN AGE
AT MARRIAGE: 1831 TO 1901

DATE	IF OVERALL FERTILITY	IG MARITAL FERTILITY	IH ILLEGITIMATE FERTILITY	IM PROPORTION MARRIED	SINGULATE MEAN AGE AT MARRIAGE
1831	0.376	0.743	0.032	0.483	25.3
1836	0.363	0.714	0.031	0.486	25.4
1841	0.352	0.684	0.030	0.492	25.5
1846	0.341	0.665	0.027	0.493	25.5
1851	0.332	0.646	0.027	0.492	25.5
1856	0.336	0.649	0.028	0.496	25.5
1861	0.336	0.642	0.030	0.500	25.5
1866	0.326	0.622	0.028	0.501	25.5
1871	0.318	0.610	0.027	0.500	25.5
1876	0.301	0.579	0.025	0.498	25.5
1881	0.306	0.592	0.027	0.494	25.5
1886	0.269	0.512	0.027	0.499	25.8
1891	0.251	0.478	0.026	0.498	26.0
1896	0.237	0.445	0.025	0.503	25.8
1901	0.225	0.414	0.023	0.518	

LOIRE (HAUTE-)

MORTALITY PATTERN: WEST
MIGRATION: GRADUAL, WITH POPULATION TOTALS OBTAINED BY TREND OF R/CB

TABLE 1 FEMALE POPULATION ESTIMATES: 1801 TO 1906

DATE	R/CB RATIO	% COR-RECTION	FINAL POPULATION ESTIMATE	DATE	R/CB RATIO	% COR-RECTION	FINAL POPULATION ESTIMATE
1801	0.934	12.4	134353	1856	0.953	0.3	156413
1806	1.059	0.0	138122	1861	0.935	0.6	157762
1811*	1.061	0.0	139594	1866	0.939	-1.5	158214
1816*	1.047	0.0	141067	1871	0.907	0.4	158957
1821	1.044	0.0	142539	1876	0.903	-0.9	159441
1826*	1.047	0.0	145835	1881	0.875	0.6	160757
1831	1.036	0.0	149131	1886	0.863	0.1	160806
1836	1.022	0.0	150613	1891	0.837	1.4	160366
1841	1.007	0.0	152835	1896	0.834	-0.0	159388
1846	1.000	0.0	157568	1901	0.815	0.4	158550
1851	0.972	-0.1	155866	1906	0.812	-1.2	157280

NOTE: R/CB RATIO REFERS TO THE POPULATION COMPUTED BY THE BALANCE OF BIRTHS
       AND DEATHS OVER THE REPORTED POPULATION
* INTERPOLATED VALUES

TABLE 2 FEMALE BIRTH ESTIMATES: 1801-1805 TO 1901-1905

DATE	% COR-RECTION	FINAL BIRTH ESTIMATE	CRUDE BIRTH RATE	DATE	% COR-RECTION	FINAL BIRTH ESTIMATE	CRUDE BIRTH RATE
1801-1805	0.0	18697	27.4	1856-1860	6.0	22000	28.0
1806-1810	6.9	19578	28.2	1861-1865	0.0	21761	27.5
1811-1815	0.0	19476	27.8	1866-1870	0.0	22495	28.4
1816-1820	0.0	20116	28.4	1871-1875	3.4	22999	28.9
1821-1825	0.0	20692	28.7	1876-1880	0.0	21929	27.4
1826-1830	0.0	21517	29.2	1881-1885	0.0	20755	25.8
1831-1835	0.0	21441	28.6	1886-1890	0.0	20635	25.7
1836-1840	0.0	21373	28.2	1891-1895	0.0	19133	23.9
1841-1845	0.0	22697	29.2	1896-1900	0.0	18723	23.6
1846-1850	3.2	21485	27.4	1901-1905	0.0	17654	22.4
1851-1855	5.1	21200	27.2				

[346]

TABLE 3 FEMALE POPULATION ESTIMATES,
DISTRIBUTION BY AGE: 1801 TO 1906

AGE	1801	1806	1811	1816	1821	1826	1831	1836	1841	1846	1851
0- 4	14215	14330	14952	15291	15458	16206	17090	16733	16971	18311	16608
5- 9	12629	13076	13365	13538	13789	14107	14770	15416	15201	15590	16287
10-14	12159	12372	12667	12848	13078	13420	13614	14163	14806	14727	14718
15-19	11702	11906	11980	12172	12406	12723	12946	13048	13595	14337	13831
20-24	11151	11356	11414	11411	11640	11958	12170	12298	12423	13060	13241
25-29	10520	10740	10736	10794	10826	11133	11358	11476	11628	11854	12059
30-34	9848	10069	10140	10148	10172	10289	10514	10646	10790	11036	10939
35-39	9149	9365	9440	9473	9498	9603	9658	9793	9950	10181	10132
40-44	8451	8649	8723	8766	8810	8913	8962	8942	9100	9336	9303
45-49	7739	7934	7999	8046	8096	8210	8261	8241	8253	8482	8479
50-54	6973	7150	7215	7264	7310	7424	7495	7478	7493	7579	7589
55-59	6086	6266	6312	6376	6410	6516	6599	6601	6623	6706	6600
60-64	5025	5218	5260	5328	5357	5448	5538	5549	5592	5676	5571
65-69	3842	4012	4060	4140	4156	4235	4323	4340	4394	4484	4398
70-74	2606	2760	2794	2880	2896	2952	3033	3051	3104	3187	3132
75-79	1478	1585	1615	1682	1697	1738	1798	1815	1858	1921	1889
80+	779	836	862	909	929	960	1002	1021	1053	1100	1091

AGE	1856	1861	1866	1871	1876	1881	1886	1891	1896	1901	1906
0- 4	16627	17348	17086	17615	17912	17715	16807	16652	15727	15561	14865
5- 9	14979	15029	15635	15379	15810	16313	16140	15284	15252	14462	14385
10-14	15594	14356	14380	14966	14704	15176	15670	15509	14712	14703	13952
15-19	14015	14837	13575	13564	14063	13793	14202	14657	14480	13729	13734
20-24	12940	13040	13671	12374	12216	12576	12181	12498	12828	12695	11973
25-29	12397	12092	12110	12667	11368	11209	11498	11089	11369	11719	11610
30-34	11286	11617	11305	11318	11821	10663	10511	10784	10428	10723	11086
35-39	10185	10528	10322	10531	10531	11091	10006	9865	10169	9856	10168
40-44	9390	9463	9774	10054	9780	9875	10420	9406	9327	9641	9375
45-49	8569	8674	8739	9035	9293	9136	9246	9764	8873	8822	9149
50-54	7694	7802	7898	7967	8238	8577	8456	8566	9109	8309	8293
55-59	6703	6821	6915	7006	7067	7414	7739	7636	7801	8323	7632
60-64	5562	5668	5758	5837	5903	6059	6370	6646	6620	6797	7296
65-69	4379	4389	4463	4529	4578	4737	4872	5115	5402	5416	5606
70-74	3116	3117	3114	3161	3196	3324	3447	3537	3769	4014	4065
75-79	1883	1884	1876	1869	1887	1980	2064	2133	2230	2402	2592
80+	1092	1097	1094	1086	1075	1121	1176	1224	1295	1377	1500

TABLE 4 MARRIED WOMEN ESTIMATES,
DISTRIBUTION BY AGE: 1831 TO 1901

AGE	1831	1836	1841	1846	1851	1856	1861	1866
15-19	304	315	338	368	367	384	431	347
20-24	2630	2718	2820	3044	3169	3184	3301	3297
25-29	5377	5515	5700	5920	6129	6418	6376	6501
30-34	6499	6636	6828	7076	7094	7411	7724	7604
35-39	6509	6618	6812	7042	7059	7162	7472	7742
40-44	6333	6284	6457	6665	6653	6749	6837	7087
45-49	5542	5468	5541	5731	5729	5818	5918	5979

AGE	1871	1876	1881	1886	1891	1896	1901
15-19	391	479	471	460	400	355	501
20-24	3265	3649	3957	3518	3232	3341	3074
25-29	6485	6307	6732	6977	6394	6159	6550
30-34	7692	7787	7380	7543	7875	7426	7426
35-39	7581	7646	7924	7235	7419	7739	7416
40-44	7300	7137	7286	7307	6853	6954	7219
45-49	6177	6385	6366	6267	6867	6333	6294

TABLE 5 DEMOGRAPHIC INDICES AND FEMALE SINGULATE MEAN AGE
AT MARRIAGE: 1831 TO 1901

DATE	IF OVERALL FERTILITY	IG MARITAL FERTILITY	IH ILLEGITIMATE FERTILITY	IM PROPORTION MARRIED	SINGULATE MEAN AGE AT MARRIAGE
1831	0.321	0.741	0.017	0.421	26.4
1836	0.317	0.721	0.020	0.424	26.4
1841	0.321	0.722	0.018	0.430	26.3
1846	0.311	0.698	0.016	0.433	26.2
1851	0.301	0.658	0.020	0.440	26.1
1856	0.302	0.650	0.018	0.449	25.9
1861	0.301	0.640	0.020	0.454	25.9
1866	0.304	0.640	0.020	0.458	25.9
1871	0.318	0.658	0.020	0.466	25.5
1876	0.318	0.644	0.018	0.479	25.1
1881	0.305	0.599	0.016	0.495	25.0
1886	0.299	0.592	0.018	0.490	25.5
1891	0.288	0.581	0.018	0.479	25.9
1896	0.272	0.559	0.017	0.471	25.8
1901	0.262	0.537	0.016	0.473	

[348]

MORTALITY PATTERN: WEST
MIGRATION: NO CORRECTION MADE FOR MIGRATION BY AGE

TABLE 1 FEMALE POPULATION ESTIMATES: 1801 TO 1906

DATE	R/CB RATIO	% COR- RECTION	FINAL POPULATION ESTIMATE	DATE	R/CB RATIO	% COR- RECTION	FINAL POPULATION ESTIMATE
1801	0.928	9.5	214944	1856	1.022	1.9	289057
1806	0.986	1.6	216247	1861	1.034	1.3	297105
1811*	0.967	1.6	220421	1866	1.030	1.5	307454
1816*	0.954	1.6	224594	1871	1.020	0.0	305455
1821	0.933	1.6	228768	1876	1.018	0.0	313345
1826*	0.948	1.6	238659	1881	1.000	0.0	316531
1831	0.981	1.6	248551	1886	1.004	0.0	326112
1836	0.978	1.6	248856	1891	0.993	0.0	329581
1841	0.974	1.6	255722	1896	0.997	0.0	334587
1846	1.000	1.6	268806	1901	0.986	0.0	336268
1851	1.007	1.6	276759	1906	0.990	0.0	343182

NOTE: R/CB RATIO REFERS TO THE POPULATION COMPUTED BY THE BALANCE OF BIRTHS
       AND DEATHS OVER THE REPORTED POPULATION
* INTERPOLATED VALUES

TABLE 2 FEMALE BIRTH ESTIMATES: 1801-1805 TO 1901-1905

DATE	% COR- RECTION	FINAL BIRTH ESTIMATE	CRUDE BIRTH RATE	DATE	% COR- RECTION	FINAL BIRTH ESTIMATE	CRUDE BIRTH RATE
1801-1805	10.6	33240	30.8	1856-1860	0.0	36940	25.2
1806-1810	3.8	31547	28.9	1861-1865	0.0	38392	25.4
1811-1815	2.3	32866	29.5	1866-1870	0.0	36985	24.1
1816-1820	0.0	33244	29.3	1871-1875	1.5	35519	23.0
1821-1825	0.0	31426	26.9	1876-1880	3.0	38829	24.7
1826-1830	2.7	32362	26.6	1881-1885	0.0	38860	24.2
1831-1835	7.2	34637	27.9	1886-1890	0.0	37676	23.0
1836-1840	1.8	34036	27.0	1891-1895	0.0	35150	21.2
1841-1845	0.0	36243	27.6	1896-1900	0.0	34587	20.4
1846-1850	0.0	35842	26.3	1901-1905	0.0	33594	19.8
1851-1855	0.0	36266	25.6				

TABLE 3 FEMALE POPULATION ESTIMATES,
DISTRIBUTION BY AGE: 1801 TO 1906

AGE	1801	1806	1811	1816	1821	1826	1831	1836	1841	1846	1851
0- 4	25443	24679	24905	25615	26406	25729	25637	25895	27573	29526	29091
5- 9	22124	22439	22313	22450	23163	24673	23947	22826	23867	25889	27378
10-14	20857	21053	21462	21388	21409	22853	24625	23035	22180	23785	25362
15-19	19664	19838	20125	20562	20386	21112	22799	23678	22372	22093	23290
20-24	18338	18511	18807	19111	19443	19940	20858	21693	22814	22092	21457
25-29	16955	17114	17427	17728	17951	18890	19540	19672	20764	22366	21310
30-34	15542	15710	16021	16328	16561	17344	18387	18296	18728	20235	21453
35-39	14158	14295	14619	14915	15165	15907	16765	17088	17318	18138	19296
40-44	12809	12936	13226	13528	13775	14485	15279	15478	16084	16674	17197
45-49	11492	11621	11888	12156	12412	13069	13816	14006	14471	15381	15704
50-54	10142	10248	10519	10756	10988	11600	12260	12447	12902	13625	14269
55-59	8670	8772	9034	9253	9475	10006	10567	10709	11175	11823	12314
60-64	7026	7121	7397	7591	7811	8259	8675	8761	9209	9783	10226
65-69	5259	5338	5610	5792	5992	6366	6645	6649	7050	7910	7910
70-74	3494	3569	3798	3955	4136	4415	4590	4546	4841	5189	5494
75-79	1938	1986	2161	2269	2409	2597	2680	2627	2824	3024	3229
80+	998	1017	1109	1190	1287	1417	1483	1452	1548	1664	1781

AGE	1856	1861	1866	1871	1876	1881	1886	1891	1896	1901	1906
0- 4	30176	30347	32369	29806	30390	32199	33052	31756	29935	29384	29584
5- 9	27455	28124	28521	29415	28150	28089	30417	30838	29992	28170	28198
10-14	27196	26935	27576	27200	28835	27144	27630	29500	30305	29181	27852
15-19	25181	26668	26396	26284	26647	27789	26685	26782	28974	29464	28827
20-24	22944	24500	25957	24973	25590	25507	27140	25700	26133	27997	28934
25-29	21002	22179	23712	24406	24187	24356	24774	25999	24942	25126	27362
30-34	20747	20194	21367	22182	23538	22915	23551	23630	25121	23886	24465
35-39	20770	19837	19358	19881	21295	22189	22051	22358	22723	23954	23164
40-44	18578	19750	18919	17915	18992	19973	21245	20830	21392	21566	23124
45-49	16448	17548	18714	17393	17005	17698	19000	19941	19803	20174	20687
50-54	14800	15310	16401	16959	16293	15630	16609	17596	18703	18436	19110
55-59	13113	13432	13978	14501	15537	14630	14336	15039	16133	17040	17100
60-64	10845	11404	11793	11858	12799	13416	12913	12499	13272	14177	15260
65-69	8434	8833	9419	9383	9870	10397	11149	10609	10390	11013	12004
70-74	5908	6220	6638	6798	7126	7296	7870	8352	8037	7877	8531
75-79	3506	3722	4022	4103	4458	4532	4758	5086	5453	5273	5291
80+	1954	2103	2315	2398	2633	2772	2933	3065	3279	3552	3689

TABLE 4 MARRIED WOMEN ESTIMATES,
DISTRIBUTION BY AGE: 1831 TO 1901

AGE	1831	1836	1841	1846	1851	1856	1861	1866
15-19	467	487	463	460	487	530	687	685
20-24	4309	4492	4762	4644	4534	4878	5239	5529
25-29	9350	9424	10027	10872	10407	10316	10950	11764
30-34	11674	11609	11993	13052	13897	13521	13228	14064
35-39	11602	11788	12087	12769	13643	14787	14200	13927
40-44	10938	11006	11613	12169	12607	13731	14687	14147
45-49	9259	9274	9791	10560	10837	11473	12333	13241

AGE	1871	1876	1881	1886	1891	1896	1901
15-19	649	573	534	588	514	452	837
20-24	5361	4983	5168	6122	5847	6220	6768
25-29	11620	11626	10825	11798	13702	13053	13888
30-34	14568	15006	14635	14543	15170	17404	16433
35-39	14225	15309	15506	15791	15530	16211	17871
40-44	13263	14130	14753	15413	15119	15324	15515
45-49	12100	11900	12228	13738	14386	14379	14435

TABLE 5 DEMOGRAPHIC INDICES AND FEMALE SINGULATE MEAN AGE
AT MARRIAGE: 1831 TO 1901

DATE	IF OVERALL FERTILITY	IG MARITAL FERTILITY	IH ILLEGITIMATE FERTILITY	IM PROPORTION MARRIED	SINGULATE MEAN AGE AT MARRIAGE
1831	0.290	0.649	0.025	0.425	26.7
1836	0.291	0.658	0.025	0.421	26.8
1841	0.291	0.645	0.025	0.429	26.8
1846	0.289	0.624	0.025	0.441	26.7
1851	0.286	0.613	0.022	0.446	26.7
1856	0.280	0.602	0.023	0.445	26.7
1861	0.280	0.608	0.023	0.440	26.7
1866	0.272	0.589	0.022	0.440	26.8
1871	0.261	0.570	0.020	0.438	27.0
1876	0.260	0.567	0.023	0.436	27.1
1881	0.268	0.603	0.020	0.426	26.8
1886	0.258	0.563	0.021	0.439	26.6
1891	0.246	0.515	0.022	0.454	26.8
1896	0.229	0.471	0.021	0.464	26.8
1901	0.220	0.444	0.019	0.472	

MORTALITY PATTERN: NORTH
MIGRATION: GRADUAL, WITH CHILD MIGRANTS SUBTRACTED AFTER 1866, AND POPULATION
TOTAL FOR 1866 AND 1871 OBTAINED BY INTERPOLATION OF R/CB BETWEEN 1861 AND 1876

TABLE 1   FEMALE POPULATION ESTIMATES: 1801 TO 1906

DATE	R/CB RATIO	% COR- RECTION	FINAL POPULATION ESTIMATE	DATE	R/CB RATIO	% COR- RECTION	FINAL POPULATION ESTIMATE
1801	1.039	0.0	147105	1856	0.995	0.0	174741
1806	1.049	0.0	145525	1861	0.995	0.0	176871
1811*	1.048	0.0	147725	1866	0.992	-0.3	179431
1816*	1.027	0.0	149924	1871	0.974	0.8	180178
1821	1.008	0.0	152124	1876	0.979	-1.0	180334
1826*	0.996	0.0	155022	1881	0.972	-1.3	182915
1831	1.000	0.0	157920	1886	0.959	-1.3	184430
1836	1.009	0.0	162443	1891	0.957	-1.3	187174
1841	1.003	0.0	162495	1896	0.937	-1.3	184312
1846	1.000	0.0	167815	1901	0.918	-1.2	182128
1851	1.000	0.0	171610	1906	0.906	-1.4	180609

NOTE: R/CB RATIO REFERS TO THE POPULATION COMPUTED BY THE BALANCE OF BIRTHS
        AND DEATHS OVER THE REPORTED POPULATION
* INTERPOLATED VALUES

TABLE 2   FEMALE BIRTH ESTIMATES: 1801-1805 TO 1901-1905

DATE	% COR- RECTION	FINAL BIRTH ESTIMATE	CRUDE BIRTH RATE	DATE	% COR- RECTION	FINAL BIRTH ESTIMATE	CRUDE BIRTH RATE
1801-1805	5.2	24170	33.0	1856-1860	0.0	24021	27.3
1806-1810	9.0	24742	33.7	1861-1865	0.0	23680	26.6
1811-1815	0.0	26571	35.7	1866-1870	0.0	22872	25.4
1816-1820	0.0	24961	33.1	1871-1875	2.7	22961	25.5
1821-1825	0.0	24748	32.2	1876-1880	0.0	22782	25.1
1826-1830	2.0	24193	30.9	1881-1885	0.0	21855	23.8
1831-1835	0.0	23510	29.4	1886-1890	0.0	20838	22.4
1836-1840	0.0	22999	28.3	1891-1895	0.0	19353	20.8
1841-1845	0.0	23793	28.8	1896-1900	0.0	17791	19.4
1846-1850	0.0	24555	28.9	1901-1905	0.0	17043	18.8
1851-1855	0.0	24782	28.6				

TABLE 3 FEMALE POPULATION ESTIMATES,
DISTRIBUTION BY AGE: 1801 TO 1906

AGE	1801	1806	1811	1816	1821	1826	1831	1836	1841	1846	1851
0- 4	21336	15648	17346	18824	18347	18602	18089	18327	17424	19417	19632
5- 9	16736	16715	12829	14247	15804	15619	15868	15830	15666	15581	17168
10-14	15044	15674	15661	11918	13303	14829	14800	15166	14856	14943	14827
15-19	13859	14552	15051	14885	11351	12710	14329	14379	14482	14338	14404
20-24	12725	13342	13915	14247	14122	10805	12234	13871	13680	13932	13758
25-29	11573	12122	12649	13065	13418	13350	10325	11768	13109	13093	13307
30-34	10416	10870	11364	11752	12191	12577	12641	9853	11029	12470	12430
35-39	9255	9630	10065	10437	10854	11318	11788	11958	9150	10422	11753
40-44	8146	8458	8831	9159	9559	9997	10520	11068	11019	8592	9758
45-49	7119	7387	7703	7983	8335	8750	9234	9819	10137	10291	8000
50-54	6129	6352	6633	6869	7173	7537	7981	8518	8886	9369	9479
55-59	5114	5249	5514	5727	5993	6308	6677	7171	7502	8035	8429
60-64	3995	4058	4281	4489	4738	5012	5300	5723	6015	6525	6930
65-69	2825	2804	2993	3168	3403	3649	3862	4203	4429	4900	5247
70-74	1693	1627	1762	1902	2091	2299	2451	2707	2862	3249	3523
75-79	808	726	808	896	1026	1166	1263	1432	1528	1798	1979
80+	339	312	321	356	415	492	560	651	719	862	988

AGE	1856	1861	1866	1871	1876	1881	1886	1891	1896	1901	1906
0- 4	19972	19302	19594	18685	18828	19399	18919	18066	16577	15598	15048
5- 9	17389	17682	17314	17459	16624	17132	17772	17509	16390	15281	14503
10-14	16287	16530	16818	16451	16543	15884	16372	17180	16699	15733	14744
15-19	14191	15632	15735	16007	15494	15633	14802	15759	15931	15613	14898
20-24	13656	13482	14580	14655	14587	14071	13754	13893	13545	13971	14129
25-29	13046	12978	12687	13726	13641	13622	12929	13098	12609	12420	13069
30-34	12589	12368	12295	12009	12955	12972	12935	12429	12402	12012	11908
35-39	11686	11858	11673	11590	11301	12311	12345	12410	11813	11863	11537
40-44	10987	10944	11152	10964	10888	10730	11737	11813	11841	11334	11406
45-49	9076	10236	10250	10431	10267	10312	10217	11189	11264	11348	10873
50-54	7366	8369	9503	9501	9688	9654	9762	9664	10613	10735	10814
55-59	8530	6639	7613	8619	8639	8940	8979	9069	9002	9940	10057
60-64	7280	7371	5807	6627	7513	7675	8001	8059	8101	8120	8993
65-69	5595	5872	6058	4735	5416	6301	6500	6794	6797	6924	6969
70-74	3801	4042	4367	4449	4139	4139	4880	5044	5222	5321	5452
75-79	2174	2333	2588	2744	2811	2317	2797	3302	3369	3575	3671
80+	1117	1233	1398	1530	1651	1824	1731	1895	2137	2340	2540

TABLE 4   MARRIED WOMEN ESTIMATES,
DISTRIBUTICN BY AGE: 1831 TO 1901

AGE	1831	1836	1841	1846	1851	1856	1861	1866
15-19	505	523	544	559	584	627	700	709
20-24	4324	5020	5080	5314	5387	5497	5557	5937
25-29	6864	7930	8968	9093	9361	9304	9374	9276
30-34	9886	7761	8771	10012	10038	10240	1C119	10110
35-39	9526	9697	7478	8585	9703	9695	9867	9736
40-44	8487	8925	8943	7023	7966	8997	8966	9134
45-49	7043	7484	7803	8008	6213	7083	7995	8CO2

AGE	1871	1876	1881	1886	1891	1896	1901
15-19	677	795	858	727	697	613	781
20-24	5953	6257	6179	6065	6201	5987	6029
25-29	9936	9797	10145	9661	9802	9510	9427
30-34	9893	10624	10610	10746	10431	10388	10074
35-39	9642	9417	10252	10259	10449	9962	10065
40-44	8912	8843	E736	9520	9666	9590	9308
45-49	8052	7916	7980	7898	E768	8662	8753

TABLE 5   DEMOGRAPHIC INDICES AND FEMALE SINGULATE MEAN AGE
AT MAFRIAGE: 1831 TO 1901

DATE	IF OVERALL FERTILITY	IG MARITAL FERTILITY	IH ILLEGITIMATE FERTILITY	IM PROPCRTION MARRIED	SINGULATE MEAN AGE AT MARRIAGE
1831	0.331	0.546	0.056	0.561	24.8
1836	0.316	0.515	0.068	0.555	24.5
1841	0.318	0.514	0.070	0.560	24.3
1846	0.321	0.513	0.064	0.572	24.2
1851	0.321	0.513	0.052	0.584	24.0
1856	0.316	0.485	0.067	0.594	23.9
1861	0.305	0.479	0.053	0.593	23.8
1866	0.294	0.461	0.054	0.589	23.8
1871	0.286	0.450	0.054	0.586	23.7
1876	0.285	0.441	0.054	0.595	23.5
1881	0.277	0.421	0.053	0.607	23.4
1886	0.269	0.402	0.057	0.614	23.4
1891	0.251	0.377	0.052	0.613	23.5
1896	0.236	0.356	0.050	0.608	23.5
1901	0.223	0.336	0.048	0.609	

MORTALITY PATTERN: WEST
MIGRATION: FULL STRENGTH, WITH POPULATION TOTALS OBTAINED BY LINEAR INTERPOL-
ATION OF R/CB BETWEEN 1876 AND 1891

TABLE 1 FEMALE POPULATION ESTIMATES: 1801 TO 1906

DATE	R/CB RATIO	% COR- RECTION	FINAL POPULATION ESTIMATE	DATE	R/CB RATIO	% COR- RECTION	FINAL POPULATION ESTIMATE
1801	1.031	2.0	133829	1856	0.986	1.8	151508
1806	1.050	2.0	137369	1861	0.982	1.2	150458
1811*	1.037	2.0	138940	1866	0.960	2.1	148272
1816*	1.013	2.0	140510	1871	0.942	2.7	145705
1821	1.005	2.0	142081	1876	0.926	3.0	143493
1826*	1.001	2.0	144184	1881	0.924	0.4	139209
1831	0.996	2.0	146288	1886	0.908	-0.7	133188
1836	1.011	2.0	147643	1891	0.873	0.0	127420
1841	0.997	2.0	148285	1896	0.844	0.0	119943
1846	1.000	2.0	151645	1901	0.820	0.0	113799
1851	0.995	2.1	152512	1906	0.797	0.0	108336

NOTE: R/CB RATIO REFERS TO THE POPULATION COMPUTED BY THE BALANCE OF BIRTHS
       AND DEATHS OVER THE REPORTED POPULATION
* INTERPOLATED VALUES

TABLE 2 FEMALE BIRTH ESTIMATES: 1801-1805 TO 1901-1905

DATE	% COR- RECTION	FINAL BIRTH ESTIMATE	CRUDE BIRTH RATE	DATE	% COR- RECTION	FINAL BIRTH ESTIMATE	CRUDE BIRTH RATE
1801-1805	0.0	20290	29.9	1856-1860	0.0	16705	22.1
1806-1810	-5.8	21154	30.6	1861-1865	0.0	16865	22.6
1811-1815	4.8	18983	27.2	1866-1870	0.0	16083	21.9
1816-1820	0.0	18043	25.5	1871-1875	0.0	15235	21.1
1821-1825	0.0	17977	25.1	1876-1880	0.0	14660	20.7
1826-1830	0.0	17801	24.5	1881-1885	-7.0	12558	18.4
1831-1835	0.0	18561	25.3	1886-1890	-10.3	10661	16.4
1836-1840	0.0	18474	25.0	1891-1895	0.0	10015	16.2
1841-1845	0.0	18265	24.4	1896-1900	0.0	9664	16.5
1846-1850	0.0	17386	22.9	1901-1905	0.0	8921	16.1
1851-1855	0.0	17036	22.4				

TABLE 3 FEMALE POPULATION ESTIMATES,
DISTRIBUTION BY AGE: 1801 TO 1906

AGE	1801	1806	1811	1816	1821	1826	1831	1836	1841	1846	1851
0- 4	15454	15231	15858	15125	14327	14396	14409	14307	14743	15057	14200
5- 9	13500	13932	13531	14362	13785	13141	13261	13115	13042	13741	13915
10-14	12785	13210	13335	12913	13862	13375	12763	12980	12630	12773	13352
15-19	12108	12505	12639	12720	12458	13443	12984	12487	12493	12364	12396
20-24	11346	11714	11843	11961	12168	11981	12946	12576	11921	12137	11893
25-29	10538	10877	10999	11134	11362	11621	11462	12435	11925	11508	11614
30-34	9707	10026	10141	10285	10516	10790	11057	10934	11725	11452	10962
35-39	8884	9164	9280	9429	9655	9927	10208	10473	10249	11199	10851
40-44	8077	8329	8427	8581	8800	9062	9338	9605	9761	9736	10554
45-49	7283	7518	7605	7740	7954	8204	8468	8726	8893	9211	9115
50-54	6460	6659	6749	6882	7065	7304	7553	7780	7958	8271	8500
55-59	5551	5722	5799	5953	6118	6318	6554	6735	6913	7219	7444
60-64	4520	4659	4734	4900	5060	5233	5430	5556	5727	6013	6228
65-69	3402	3499	3568	3745	3889	4043	4208	4266	4417	4670	4862
70-74	2273	2344	2395	2554	2682	2806	2942	2959	3065	3264	3421
75-79	1268	1305	1346	1464	1555	1647	1742	1737	1811	1938	2045
80+	657	674	692	761	826	892	963	972	1012	1092	1160

AGE	1856	1861	1866	1871	1876	1881	1886	1891	1896	1901	1906
0- 4	13791	13517	13527	12928	12516	12086	10361	9153	8346	8125	7651
5- 9	13012	12661	12316	12346	11897	11414	11011	9562	8316	7654	7531
10-14	13421	12590	12192	11868	11925	11372	10905	10566	9126	7975	7365
15-19	12822	12932	11993	11613	11303	11036	10453	9990	9618	8408	7360
20-24	11729	12177	12053	11151	10731	9782	9396	8734	8207	8252	7224
25-29	11251	11129	11424	11315	10459	9738	8777	8403	7711	7403	7535
30-34	10977	10665	10433	10781	10721	9806	9118	8262	7864	7266	7016
35-39	10312	10355	10008	9856	10187	10074	9216	8646	7786	7448	6916
40-44	10160	9683	9682	9376	9288	9585	9496	8785	8200	7402	7116
45-49	9821	9480	9002	9021	8792	8712	9011	9035	8320	7777	7055
50-54	8362	9033	8691	8272	8349	8158	8107	8498	8472	7809	7337
55-59	7604	7498	8069	7781	7471	7564	7411	7484	7782	7765	7204
60-64	6376	6525	6400	6902	6726	6458	6549	6541	6530	6817	6863
65-69	4997	5122	5209	5120	5596	5459	5250	5455	5361	5380	5683
70-74	3532	3633	3696	3767	3766	4125	4029	3992	4062	4019	4093
75-79	2124	2192	2234	2279	2374	2381	2610	2648	2552	2619	2641
80+	1216	1266	1298	1329	1392	1460	1489	1667	1692	1681	1746

TABLE 4   MARRIED WOMEN ESTIMATES,
DISTRIBUTION BY AGE: 1831 TO 1901

AGE	1831	1836	1841	1846	1851	1856	1861	1866
15-19	722	717	743	796	797	861	1002	851
20-24	4117	4100	3997	4190	4199	4299	4605	4292
25-29	6537	7204	7041	6926	7120	7018	7064	7371
30-34	7654	7631	8293	8210	7953	8046	7899	7832
35-39	7489	7703	7620	8419	8231	7870	7958	7726
40-44	7118	7276	7442	7477	8142	7847	7499	7494
45-49	6110	6233	6410	6708	6680	7205	6979	6617

AGE	1871	1876	1881	1886	1891	1896	1901
15-19	785	808	791	884	755	614	614
20-24	3873	4034	4248	4352	3758	3309	3331
25-29	6850	6321	6279	6181	6165	5371	4988
30-34	8104	7735	7116	6955	6510	6419	5734
35-39	7613	7911	7682	7161	6782	6303	6061
40-44	7213	7158	7466	7401	6720	6447	5744
45-49	6567	6413	6454	6939	6762	6355	5710

TABLE 5   DEMOGRAPHIC INDICES AND FEMALE SINGULATE MEAN AGE
AT MARRIAGE: 1831 TO 1901

DATE	IF OVERALL FERTILITY	IG MARITAL FERTILITY	IH ILLEGITIMATE FERTILITY	IM PROPORTION MARRIED	SINGULATE MEAN AGE AT MARRIAGE
1831	0.262	0.509	0.017	0.498	25.5
1836	0.264	0.493	0.028	0.509	25.2
1841	0.265	0.486	0.025	0.521	25.0
1846	0.256	0.465	0.019	0.532	24.8
1851	0.249	0.446	0.020	0.538	24.7
1856	0.249	0.446	0.014	0.542	24.4
1861	0.247	0.437	0.018	0.547	24.4
1866	0.246	0.435	0.017	0.548	24.7
1871	0.240	0.429	0.015	0.543	24.6
1876	0.235	0.418	0.013	0.548	24.1
1881	0.226	0.385	0.015	0.570	23.5
1886	0.205	0.331	0.019	0.597	23.6
1891	0.195	0.319	0.013	0.596	24.1
1896	0.199	0.329	0.013	0.589	24.1
1901	0.199	0.333	0.011	0.583	

MORTALITY PATTERN: WEST
MIGRATION: NO CORRECTION MADE FOR MIGRATION BY AGE

TABLE 1 FEMALE POPULATION ESTIMATES: 1801 TO 1906

DATE	R/CB RATIO	% COR-RECTION	FINAL POPULATION ESTIMATE	DATE	R/CB RATIO	% COR-RECTION	FINAL POPULATION ESTIMATE
1801	0.925	8.2	163792	1856	0.999	0.9	172115
1806	0.985	1.5	166731	1861	0.992	1.2	167967
1811*	0.972	1.5	168515	1866	0.994	1.4	165722
1816*	0.980	1.5	170299	1871	0.992	0.7	159982
1821	0.983	1.5	172082	1876	1.013	1.4	160717
1826*	0.989	1.5	174994	1881	1.015	0.5	156090
1831	0.992	1.5	177905	1886	1.014	0.4	152319
1836	1.001	1.5	178242	1891	1.011	0.7	148338
1841	0.998	1.5	177415	1896	1.028	0.0	144910
1846	1.000	1.5	176528	1901	1.017	0.0	139713
1851	0.996	2.3	174955	1906	1.025	0.0	137391

NOTE: R/CB RATIO REFERS TO THE POPULATION COMPUTED BY THE BALANCE OF BIRTHS
       AND DEATHS OVER THE REPORTED POPULATION
* INTERPOLATED VALUES

TABLE 2 FEMALE BIRTH ESTIMATES: 1801-1805 TO 1901-1905

DATE	% COR-RECTION	FINAL BIRTH ESTIMATE	CRUDE BIRTH RATE	DATE	% COR-RECTION	FINAL BIRTH ESTIMATE	CRUDE BIRTH RATE
1801-1805	0.0	22679	27.4	1856-1860	0.0	14966	17.6
1806-1810	0.0	22456	26.8	1861-1865	0.0	14993	18.0
1811-1815	0.0	20556	24.3	1866-1870	0.0	14655	18.0
1816-1820	0.0	19045	22.3	1871-1875	0.0	13921	17.4
1821-1825	0.0	19187	22.1	1876-1880	0.0	13719	17.3
1826-1830	0.0	19484	22.1	1881-1885	0.0	12493	16.2
1831-1835	0.0	18739	21.0	1886-1890	0.0	11161	14.8
1836-1840	0.0	18280	20.6	1891-1895	0.0	10477	14.3
1841-1845	0.0	17665	20.0	1896-1900	0.0	10335	14.5
1846-1850	0.0	16390	18.7	1901-1905	0.0	10050	14.5
1851-1855	0.0	15926	18.4				

TABLE 3 FEMALE POPULATION ESTIMATES,
DISTRIBUTION BY AGE: 1801 TO 1906

AGE	1801	1806	1811	1816	1821	1826	1831	1836	1841	1846	1851
0- 4	18124	17848	17843	16250	15500	15872	16263	15184	14945	14489	13531
5- 9	16132	16514	16220	16354	15057	14491	14873	15082	14056	13887	13515
10-14	15309	15639	15864	15829	15980	14789	14219	14586	14682	13739	13607
15-19	14516	14834	15016	15475	15459	15688	14504	13937	14191	14343	13454
20-24	13651	13940	14126	14516	14993	15062	15275	14099	13457	13757	13940
25-29	12732	13012	13185	13553	13971	14516	14578	14746	13526	12962	13287
30-34	11809	12062	12238	12572	12973	13456	13980	13994	14073	12960	12454
35-39	10879	11116	11277	11594	11965	12427	12892	13340	13281	13410	12385
40-44	9961	10180	10333	10620	10972	11399	11844	12232	12592	12585	12745
45-49	9054	9257	9399	9665	9983	10385	10793	11162	11469	11853	11882
50-54	8106	8282	8419	8652	8951	9313	9694	10018	10314	10640	11030
55-59	7067	7213	7337	7537	7810	8145	8486	8765	9028	9330	9658
60-64	5869	6002	6114	6268	6515	6815	7127	7340	7572	7829	8123
65-69	4531	4644	4754	4864	5070	5330	5600	5760	5942	6151	6390
70-74	3146	3227	3323	3403	3559	3759	3977	4088	4224	4373	4552
75-79	1851	1898	1966	2014	2124	2258	2407	2471	2563	2657	2769
80+	1042	1063	1101	1132	1199	1290	1392	1440	1500	1563	1635

AGE	1856	1861	1866	1871	1876	1881	1886	1891	1895	1901	1906
0- 4	13315	12337	12544	11935	11957	11504	10724	9697	9107	9004	8992
5- 9	12595	12355	11582	11550	11479	11159	10869	10200	9276	8628	8722
10-14	13117	12255	12142	11205	11615	11167	10925	10680	10110	9043	8578
15-19	13199	12755	12037	11741	11262	11294	10926	10727	10578	9848	8983
20-24	12963	12741	12439	11551	11718	10877	10981	10663	10559	10245	9730
25-29	13356	12437	12351	11862	11461	11254	10522	10663	10442	10178	10077
30-34	12672	12750	11998	11717	11713	10957	10842	10178	10400	10029	9977
35-39	11820	12033	12236	11319	11511	11144	10509	10443	9882	9949	9793
40-44	11694	11164	11487	11481	11062	10895	10637	10075	10092	9411	9671
45-49	11956	10973	10587	10707	11148	10403	10334	10133	9674	9549	9089
50-54	10996	11059	10261	9727	10252	10341	9739	9719	9603	9040	9109
55-59	9973	9925	10096	9194	9093	9293	9471	8965	9011	8789	8450
60-64	8399	8640	8701	8675	8258	7928	8203	8411	8012	7965	7941
65-69	6647	6828	7114	7009	7322	6776	6603	6881	7092	6699	6814
70-74	4760	4904	5106	5194	5376	5469	5153	5063	5298	5428	5251
75-79	2918	3009	3147	3190	3421	3457	3595	3420	3369	3518	3697
80+	1736	1802	1893	1926	2068	2171	2288	2423	2405	2391	2517

TABLE 4   MARRIED WOMEN ESTIMATES,
DISTRIBUTION BY AGE: 1831 TO 1901

AGE	1831	1836	1841	1846	1851	1856	1861	1866
15-19	1538	1543	1650	1763	1762	1857	1938	2129
20-24	7210	6925	6861	7284	7678	7432	7607	7781
25-29	10178	10510	9874	9670	10129	10391	9862	9965
30-34	10833	10964	11210	10456	10181	10479	10651	10113
35-39	10194	10589	10686	10877	10141	9755	10002	10233
40-44	9381	9627	10006	10022	10205	9400	9004	9290
45-49	8104	8293	8638	8948	9037	9138	8422	8152

AGE	1871	1876	1881	1886	1891	1896	1901
15-19	2086	1866	1798	1669	1541	1463	1512
20-24	7393	7616	7225	7071	6665	6375	6053
25-29	9708	9410	9316	8892	8912	8628	8331
30-34	9903	9952	9335	9326	8805	8960	8678
35-39	9434	9635	9350	8914	8782	8293	8488
40-44	9182	8865	8780	8717	8130	8014	7649
45-49	8098	8452	7946	8087	7742	7207	7285

TABLE 5   DEMOGRAPHIC INDICES AND FEMALE SINGULATE MEAN AGE
AT MARRIAGE: 1831 TO 1901

DATE	IF OVERALL FERTILITY	IG MARITAL FERTILITY	IH ILLEGITIMATE FERTILITY	IM PROPORTION MARRIED	SINGULATE MEAN AGE AT MARRIAGE
1831	0.225	0.351	0.031	0.605	23.3
1836	0.221	0.339	0.026	0.622	22.9
1841	0.219	0.333	0.022	0.634	22.6
1846	0.211	0.315	0.025	0.641	22.3
1851	0.204	0.298	0.024	0.656	22.0
1856	0.201	0.290	0.019	0.670	21.7
1861	0.199	0.282	0.021	0.683	21.3
1866	0.201	0.279	0.020	0.701	21.1
1871	0.203	0.280	0.019	0.705	21.0
1876	0.198	0.271	0.019	0.710	20.9
1881	0.195	0.266	0.020	0.713	20.9
1886	0.182	0.246	0.022	0.714	21.1
1891	0.170	0.232	0.023	0.705	21.3
1896	0.166	0.230	0.021	0.695	21.5
1901	0.168	0.230	0.023	0.700	

[360]

MORTALITY PATTERN: WEST
MIGRATION: GRADUAL, WITH POPULATION TOTALS OBTAINED BY TREND OF R/CB

TABLE 1   FEMALE POPULATION ESTIMATES: 1801 TO 1906

DATE	R/CB RATIO	% COR- RECTION	FINAL POPULATION ESTIMATE	DATE	R/CB RATIO	% COR- RECTION	FINAL POPULATION ESTIMATE
1801	1.220	4.4	68132	1856	0.940	-0.2	70126
1806	1.269	0.0	71287	1861	0.896	1.7	69457
1811*	1.176	0.0	69651	1866	0.872	1.2	68982
1816*	1.105	0.0	68014	1871	0.836	2.2	68701
1821	1.064	0.0	66378	1876	0.834	-1.0	68122
1826*	1.063	0.0	67811	1881	0.814	-2.0	68110
1831	1.046	0.0	69243	1886	0.791	-2.8	67713
1836	1.033	0.0	69705	1891	0.726	2.1	67466
1841	1.009	0.0	69655	1896	0.742	-4.0	66069
1846	1.000	0.0	71346	1901	0.663	3.1	64818
1851	0.978	-1.1	70784	1906	0.646	1.5	63327

NOTE: R/CB RATIO REFERS TO THE POPULATION COMPUTED BY THE BALANCE OF BIRTHS
        AND DEATHS OVER THE REPORTED POPULATION
* INTERPOLATED VALUES

TABLE 2   FEMALE BIRTH ESTIMATES: 1801-1805 TO 1901-1905

DATE	% COR- RECTION	FINAL BIRTH ESTIMATE	CRUDE BIRTH RATE	DATE	% COR- RECTION	FINAL BIRTH ESTIMATE	CRUDE BIRTH RATE
1801-1805	16.8	9667	27.7	1856-1860	0.0	10424	29.9
1806-1810	7.7	10114	28.7	1861-1865	0.0	10177	29.4
1811-1815	4.1	9894	28.7	1866-1870	0.0	10766	31.3
1816-1820	6.6	9858	29.3	1871-1875	0.0	10352	30.3
1821-1825	0.0	9520	28.4	1876-1880	0.0	11116	32.6
1826-1830	0.0	10013	29.2	1881-1885	0.0	11255	33.1
1831-1835	0.0	10171	29.3	1886-1890	0.0	10259	30.4
1836-1840	0.0	9977	28.6	1891-1895	0.0	8802	26.4
1841-1845	0.0	10370	29.4	1896-1900	0.0	8526	26.1
1846-1850	1.0	10222	28.8	1901-1905	0.0	7922	24.7
1851-1855	0.0	10274	29.2				

TABLE 3 FEMALE POPULATION ESTIMATES,
DISTRIBUTION BY AGE: 1801 TO 1906

AGE	1801	1806	1811	1816	1821	1826	1831	1836	1841	1846	1851
0- 4	7782	8022	7842	7557	7225	7434	7913	7760	7626	8179	7843
5- 9	6913	7286	7015	6845	6548	6569	6746	7069	6904	6933	7242
10-14	6503	6794	6688	6470	6382	6353	6314	6450	6709	6661	6525
15-19	6113	6387	6233	6165	6030	6189	6104	6034	6119	6470	6234
20-24	5702	5959	5816	5699	5688	5794	5896	5778	5672	5851	5950
25-29	5280	5525	5393	5282	5213	5423	5481	5537	5390	5384	5381
30-34	4865	5090	4974	4870	4798	4939	5100	5113	5132	5085	4951
35-39	4454	4664	4558	4465	4392	4516	4617	4726	4708	4812	4653
40-44	4059	4247	4154	4068	4001	4109	4197	4252	4325	4389	4382
45-49	3671	3845	3758	3683	3620	3717	3793	3838	3864	4004	3972
50-54	3269	3428	3354	3282	3222	3309	3379	3412	3433	3523	3570
55-59	2840	2978	2917	2853	2786	2863	2929	2953	2967	3045	3056
60-64	2358	2482	2431	2375	2302	2361	2423	2438	2448	2514	2519
65-69	1829	1933	1900	1850	1775	1815	1865	1873	1880	1935	1938
70-74	1282	1360	1342	1307	1237	1257	1294	1293	1298	1340	1343
75-79	766	816	809	786	733	741	762	756	758	785	788
80+	445	472	469	456	425	422	430	424	421	435	437

AGE	1856	1861	1866	1871	1876	1881	1886	1891	1896	1901	1906
0- 4	7796	7891	7870	8286	8071	8716	8783	8426	7270	7147	6752
5- 9	6921	6867	7004	6964	7360	7175	7725	7940	7633	6598	6526
10-14	6831	6525	6482	6608	6568	6950	6758	7325	7555	7269	6267
15-19	6094	6350	6030	5949	6014	5931	6219	5982	6519	6757	6477
20-24	5673	5457	5611	5209	4994	4935	4672	4771	4471	5305	5220
25-29	5453	5158	4928	5026	4592	4339	4198	3889	3958	3680	4195
30-34	4950	5010	4749	4525	4615	4206	3948	3837	3546	3624	3365
35-39	4534	4532	4607	4362	4163	4253	3863	3660	3565	3299	3385
40-44	4244	4139	4163	4235	4027	3856	3943	3634	3459	3381	3141
45-49	3975	3855	3787	3814	3901	3727	3578	3720	3449	3296	3237
50-54	3549	3558	3481	3427	3475	3574	3428	3359	3512	3274	3147
55-59	3100	3088	3127	3064	3040	3101	3198	3141	3098	3252	3054
60-64	2523	2560	2576	2607	2572	2564	2614	2764	2729	2710	2867
65-69	1933	1935	1990	1999	2040	2023	2012	2119	2253	2244	2251
70-74	1335	1330	1354	1388	1409	1445	1429	1480	1567	1685	1700
75-79	781	775	788	799	830	847	865	900	938	1008	1101
80+	434	429	435	439	451	469	480	518	550	587	643

[362]

TABLE 4 MARRIED WOMEN ESTIMATES,
DISTRIBUTION BY AGE: 1831 TO 1901

AGE	1831	1836	1841	1846	1851	1856	1861	1866
15-19	195	197	206	224	222	223	197	186
20-24	1441	1442	1450	1531	1594	1557	1536	1493
25-29	2756	2824	2800	2845	2890	2976	2865	2784
30-34	3269	3305	3367	3380	3328	3365	3451	3314
35-39	3184	3272	3304	3414	3329	3271	3307	3399
40-44	2979	3010	3098	3169	3178	3093	3044	3089
45-49	2526	2537	2593	2710	2698	2711	2657	2637

AGE	1871	1876	1881	1886	1891	1896	1901
15-19	239	356	402	321	186	156	205
20-24	1434	1348	1519	1677	1612	1319	1338
25-29	2777	2607	2331	2352	2450	2488	2236
30-34	3187	3210	2948	2675	2684	2667	2751
35-39	3236	3109	3098	2862	2711	2678	2602
40-44	3145	2999	2819	2842	2734	2582	2559
45-49	2651	2714	2512	2453	2698	2527	2439

TABLE 5 DEMOGRAPHIC INDICES AND FEMALE SINGULATE MEAN AGE
AT MARRIAGE: 1831 TO 1901

DATE	IF OVERALL FERTILITY	IG MARITAL FERTILITY	IH ILLEGITIMATE FERTILITY	IM PROPORTION MARRIED	SINGULATE MEAN AGE AT MARRIAGE
1831	0.315	0.682	0.024	0.442	25.9
1836	0.314	0.668	0.026	0.449	26.0
1841	0.319	0.671	0.024	0.456	25.9
1846	0.317	0.672	0.017	0.459	25.8
1851	0.319	0.665	0.020	0.464	25.7
1856	0.328	0.665	0.027	0.472	25.6
1861	0.332	0.663	0.030	0.476	25.6
1866	0.343	0.688	0.027	0.478	25.6
1871	0.357	0.713	0.025	0.482	25.4
1876	0.375	0.745	0.028	0.484	25.2
1881	0.404	0.806	0.029	0.482	24.9
1886	0.402	0.799	0.026	0.487	25.0
1891	0.368	0.715	0.030	0.494	25.4
1896	0.341	0.678	0.026	0.483	25.8
1901	0.320	0.656	0.025	0.467	

MORTALITY PATTERN: WEST
MIGRATION: FULL STRENGTH, WITH UNCORRECTED POPULATION TOTALS UNTIL 1866, AND
A HANDFITTED TREND OF R/CB FROM 1871 ON

TABLE 1 FEMALE POPULATION ESTIMATES: 1801 TO 1906

DATE	R/CB RATIO	% COR- RECTION	FINAL POPULATION ESTIMATE	DATE	R/CB RATIO	% COR- RECTION	FINAL POPULATION ESTIMATE
1801	0.882	6.1	209336	1856	1.014	0.0	265369
1806	0.946	0.0	212789	1861	1.015	0.0	265148
1811*	0.950	0.0	219377	1866	1.017	0.0	266908
1816*	0.953	0.0	225965	1871	1.003	1.4	266672
1821	0.948	0.0	232553	1876	1.015	0.2	262968
1826*	0.953	0.0	237554	1881	1.011	1.1	263788
1831	0.967	0.0	242555	1886	1.028	0.0	265195
1836	0.981	0.0	246683	1891	1.024	0.9	264488
1841	0.982	0.0	249601	1896	1.027	1.3	261707
1846	1.000	0.0	256630	1901	1.041	0.4	261000
1851	1.037	0.0	260393	1906	1.054	-0.3	260879

NOTE: R/CB RATIO REFERS TO THE POPULATION COMPUTED BY THE BALANCE OF BIRTHS
        AND DEATHS OVER THE REPORTED POPULATION
* INTERPOLATED VALUES

TABLE 2 FEMALE BIRTH ESTIMATES: 1801-1805 TO 1901-1905

DATE	% COR- RECTION	FINAL BIRTH ESTIMATE	CRUDE BIRTH RATE	DATE	% COR- RECTION	FINAL BIRTH ESTIMATE	CRUDE BIRTH RATE
1801-1805	-4.5	30976	29.4	1856-1860	0.0	27620	20.8
1806-1810	0.0	29002	26.8	1861-1865	0.0	27829	20.9
1811-1815	0.0	30891	27.7	1866-1870	0.0	27457	20.6
1816-1820	0.0	30892	26.9	1871-1875	0.0	26390	19.9
1821-1825	0.0	29161	24.8	1876-1880	0.0	25794	19.6
1826-1830	6.0	29667	24.7	1881-1885	0.0	25434	19.2
1831-1835	4.0	29335	24.0	1886-1890	0.0	24471	18.5
1836-1840	0.0	27999	22.6	1891-1895	0.0	22904	17.4
1841-1845	0.0	28893	22.8	1896-1900	0.0	22563	17.3
1846-1950	0.0	29564	22.9	1901-1905	0.0	22582	17.3
1851-1855	0.0	28570	21.7				

TABLE 3 FEMALE POPULATION ESTIMATES,
DISTRIBUTION BY AGE: 1801 TO 1906

AGE	1801	1806	1811	1816	1821	1826	1831	1836	1841	1846	1851
0- 4	24865	23052	23263	24548	25178	23632	23608	23333	22907	23980	24053
5- 9	21608	22223	21223	21338	22654	23278	21817	21794	21649	21591	22314
10-14	20357	20964	21669	20679	20708	22113	22889	21455	21282	21493	21170
15-19	19181	19743	20431	21103	20058	20203	21733	22498	20940	21117	21346
20-24	17375	18399	19079	19723	20313	19411	19677	21169	21788	20616	21274
25-29	16516	16990	17656	18284	18864	19525	18763	19022	20369	21311	20207
30-34	15130	15579	16209	16819	17396	18032	18757	18026	18206	19816	20465
35-39	13773	14161	14774	15345	15913	16532	17211	17903	17156	17612	18673
40-44	12452	12803	13351	13903	14439	15037	15684	16329	16946	16504	16634
45-49	11164	11492	11989	12479	12996	13553	14169	14779	15353	16194	15460
50-54	9846	10121	10598	11032	11495	12017	12568	13139	13693	14457	14925
55-59	8410	8646	9088	9489	9911	10357	10837	11334	11870	12569	12985
60-64	6810	6998	7423	7772	8172	8548	8912	9324	9813	10440	10846
65-69	5093	5227	5610	5918	6272	6592	6848	7138	7561	8081	8432
70-74	3382	3480	3781	4030	4327	4573	4751	4934	5242	5636	5907
75-79	1874	1925	2140	2304	2519	2689	2790	2897	3096	3337	3517
80+	964	986	1092	1200	1339	1464	1543	1609	1728	1876	1987

AGE	1856	1861	1866	1871	1876	1881	1886	1891	1896	1901	1906
0- 4	23919	22691	23246	22795	21467	21668	21726	20699	19319	19535	19707
5- 9	22651	22224	21271	21697	21069	20240	20553	20532	19529	18449	18731
10-14	21953	22112	21780	20796	21134	20727	19938	20229	20189	19279	18247
15-19	21102	21446	21765	21312	20225	21021	20600	19835	20072	20116	19270
20-24	21580	20502	21138	21193	20532	20386	21073	20701	19863	20207	20330
25-29	20944	20792	19936	20413	20314	20185	20038	20699	20289	19582	19968
30-34	19526	20049	20006	19129	19482	19627	19552	19380	19993	19702	19053
35-39	19617	18585	19174	19089	18155	18685	18986	18776	18594	19292	19045
40-44	17949	18565	17662	18192	18021	17281	17856	18006	17888	17822	18523
45-49	15694	16873	17520	16646	17062	17021	16392	16895	17027	17019	16984
50-54	14363	14538	15693	16277	15334	15876	15918	15284	15745	15977	15997
55-59	13541	12978	13202	14231	14663	13980	14518	14504	13915	14456	14701
60-64	11353	11736	11334	11497	12278	12840	12335	12752	12724	12344	12863
65-69	8914	9224	9632	9268	9285	10111	10680	10200	10527	10657	10379
70-74	6301	6564	6880	7151	6773	6956	7671	8043	7665	8055	8194
75-79	3793	3970	4205	4381	4461	4364	4555	4975	5202	5075	5366
80+	2170	2298	2464	2603	2662	2819	2903	2977	3164	3432	3521

TABLE 4   MARRIED WOMEN ESTIMATES,
DISTRIBUTION BY AGE: 1831 TO 1901

AGE	1831	1836	1841	1846	1851	1856	1861	1866
15-19	695	741	711	742	778	800	1019	1047
20-24	4973	5478	5799	5644	5988	6260	6133	5943
25-29	9788	10076	11009	11738	11319	11949	12076	11779
30-34	12546	12153	12463	13743	14329	13831	14354	14460
35-39	12485	13021	12648	13121	14134	14816	14137	14665
40-44	12092	12514	13122	12858	12944	14024	14542	13842
45-49	10347	10692	11279	12004	11436	11677	12599	13088

AGE	1871	1876	1881	1886	1891	1896	1901
15-19	934	794	766	782	689	649	1024
20-24	6019	6283	6468	6734	6463	6611	7016
25-29	11086	11124	11888	12257	12855	12416	12618
30-34	13872	13374	13555	14167	14351	15011	14648
35-39	14542	13924	13892	14075	14410	14474	15007
40-44	14071	13987	13479	13376	13515	13747	13586
45-49	12188	12554	12614	12155	12544	12762	12520

TABLE 5   DEMOGRAPHIC INDICES AND FEMALE SINGULATE MEAN AGE
AT MARRIAGE: 1831 TO 1901

DATE	IF OVERALL FERTILITY	IG MARITAL FERTILITY	IH ILLEGITIMATE FERTILITY	IM PROPORTION MARRIED	SINGULATE MEAN AGE AT MARRIAGE
1831	0.260	0.532	0.019	0.470	26.6
1836	0.246	0.492	0.028	0.470	26.3
1841	0.242	0.499	0.002	0.481	26.1
1846	0.244	0.467	0.026	0.495	26.0
1851	0.240	0.451	0.027	0.502	25.8
1856	0.229	0.427	0.022	0.511	25.6
1861	0.228	0.418	0.022	0.520	25.5
1866	0.227	0.419	0.022	0.517	25.7
1871	0.222	0.416	0.023	0.506	25.7
1876	0.220	0.409	0.023	0.509	25.5
1881	0.215	0.394	0.024	0.516	25.2
1886	0.208	0.372	0.027	0.525	25.3
1891	0.198	0.349	0.024	0.535	25.5
1896	0.192	0.329	0.027	0.545	25.1
1901	0.190	0.324	0.025	0.554	

[366]

MORTALITY PATTERN: WEST
MIGRATION: GRADUAL, WITH POPULATION TOTALS OBTAINED BY TREND OF R/CB

TABLE 1 FEMALE POPULATION ESTIMATES: 1801 TO 1906

DATE	R/CB RATIO	% COR- RECTION	FINAL POPULATION ESTIMATE	DATE	R/CB RATIO	% COR- RECTION	FINAL POPULATION ESTIMATE
1801	0.997	5.2	292137	1856	0.982	-0.5	305920
1806	1.049	0.0	298364	1861	0.967	-0.5	300579
1811*	1.048	0.0	302967	1866	0.945	0.4	295911
1816*	1.041	0.0	307570	1871	0.911	2.5	287816
1821	1.035	0.0	312173	1876	0.913	0.7	279851
1826*	1.014	0.0	311671	1881	0.880	2.9	274832
1831	1.011	0.0	311169	1886	0.891	-0.0	268611
1836	1.011	0.0	313686	1891	0.877	-0.1	262562
1841	1.006	0.0	313993	1896	0.858	0.4	254766
1846	1.000	0.0	314912	1901	0.847	-0.0	249455
1851	0.994	-0.2	311860	1906	0.840	-0.9	245906

NOTE: R/CB RATIO REFERS TO THE POPULATION COMPUTED BY THE BALANCE OF BIRTHS
       AND DEATHS OVER THE REPORTED POPULATION
* INTERPOLATED VALUES

TABLE 2 FEMALE BIRTH ESTIMATES: 1801-1805 TO 1901-1905

DATE	% COR- RECTION	FINAL BIRTH ESTIMATE	CRUDE BIRTH RATE	DATE	% COR- RECTION	FINAL BIRTH ESTIMATE	CRUDE BIRTH RATE
1801-1805	0.0	34074	23.1	1856-1860	0.0	31775	21.0
1806-1810	0.0	36581	24.3	1861-1865	0.0	31179	20.9
1811-1815	0.0	37788	24.8	1866-1870	0.0	29199	20.0
1816-1820	0.0	36839	23.8	1871-1875	0.0	29306	20.7
1821-1825	0.0	36595	23.5	1876-1880	0.0	29043	20.9
1826-1830	0.0	34240	22.0	1881-1885	0.0	28141	20.7
1831-1835	0.0	34306	22.0	1886-1890	0.0	27885	21.0
1836-1840	0.0	31645	20.2	1891-1895	0.0	26442	20.4
1841-1845	0.0	32785	20.9	1896-1900	0.0	25816	20.5
1846-1850	0.0	32274	20.6	1901-1905	0.0	25743	20.8
1851-1855	0.0	31477	20.4				

TABLE 3 FEMALE POPULATION ESTIMATES,
DISTRIBUTION BY AGE: 1801 TO 1906

AGE	1801	1806	1811	1816	1821	1826	1831	1836	1841	1846	1851
0- 4	31935	28649	29806	30926	30504	29880	27722	28372	26541	27533	26580
5- 9	28835	29935	26514	27556	28734	27954	27521	25820	26512	24819	25484
10-14	27205	28202	29182	25747	26802	27567	27142	26883	25166	25851	24074
15-19	25629	26592	27478	28323	25029	25699	26752	26498	26187	24524	25030
20-24	24005	24882	25707	26469	27336	23827	24742	25926	25637	25347	23520
25-29	22361	23174	23897	24608	25394	25869	22789	23831	24943	24677	24215
30-34	20742	21487	22137	22757	23494	23914	24607	21839	22822	23899	23489
35-39	19134	19833	20409	20966	21614	22009	22618	23456	20812	21760	22634
40-44	17564	18201	18734	19225	19808	20141	20700	21445	22238	19741	20504
45-49	16016	16599	17078	17531	18045	18338	18817	19497	20200	20959	18483
50-54	14423	14930	15347	15752	16224	16471	16880	17473	18115	18779	19348
55-59	12677	13135	13457	13809	14231	14457	14778	15294	15861	16455	16919
60-64	10719	11101	11342	11612	11980	12178	12423	12850	13351	13856	14228
65-69	8505	8830	8975	9176	9462	9627	9793	10135	10554	10976	11246
70-74	6151	6375	6462	6583	6792	7005	7250	7576	7897	8086	
75-79	3836	3966	3984	4056	4130	4253	4288	4443	4663	4879	4988
80+	2404	2473	2459	2474	2543	2582	2592	2673	2814	2961	3035

AGE	1856	1861	1866	1871	1876	1881	1886	1891	1896	1901	1906
0- 4	25773	26082	25906	23917	23860	24301	23460	23265	21879	21909	22287
5- 9	24439	23719	24113	23786	21901	22091	22447	21674	21414	20339	20532
10-14	24570	23579	22910	23233	22927	21169	21333	21697	20927	20738	19720
15-19	23030	23528	22536	21770	22066	21779	19971	20114	20413	19713	19523
20-24	23643	21661	21368	20780	19970	20186	19691	17871	17878	18218	17477
25-29	22241	22325	20408	20565	19396	18651	18756	18258	16437	16512	16843
30-34	22908	21054	21180	19282	19424	18411	17671	17783	17278	15613	15729
35-39	22125	21607	19914	19967	18166	18422	17443	16754	16838	16452	14911
40-44	21227	20786	20374	18723	18770	17206	17447	16541	15872	16051	15752
45-49	19113	19826	19492	19055	17512	17696	16228	16479	15613	15078	15320
50-54	16994	17612	18352	17992	17586	16313	16491	15153	15372	14673	14251
55-59	17359	15284	15924	16529	16195	16001	14848	15034	13798	14120	13571
60-64	14557	14965	13258	13729	14225	14123	13940	12951	13073	12138	12525
65-69	11488	11778	12203	10722	11070	11667	11563	11425	11568	10832	10166
70-74	8240	8437	8734	8952	7832	8260	8684	8615	8461	7978	8288
75-79	5078	5188	5376	5487	5590	5026	5281	5556	5467	5505	5282
80+	3086	3149	3262	3322	3363	3530	3358	3393	3479	3586	3730

[368]

TABLE 4 MARRIED WOMEN ESTIMATES,
DISTRIBUTION BY AGE: 1831 TO 1901

AGE	1831	1836	1841	1846	1851	1856	1861	1866
15-19	597	611	626	609	647	622	570	549
20-24	4749	5112	5224	5339	5126	5337	5075	4044
25-29	9705	10341	11100	11250	11307	10629	10934	10236
30-34	13960	12521	13342	14217	14209	14072	13154	13440
35-39	14154	14731	13293	14090	14846	14670	14518	13532
40-44	13982	14370	15070	13473	14082	14631	14439	14228
45-49	11923	12174	12800	13393	11896	12340	12923	12777

AGE	1871	1876	1881	1886	1891	1896	1901
15-19	679	844	844	711	561	464	665
20-24	4212	5004	5641	5735	5094	4939	4964
25-29	8598	8750	9707	10252	10334	9320	9447
30-34	12379	11148	11158	11626	12023	11999	10859
35-39	13642	12537	12024	11669	11793	12067	11911
40-44	13037	13128	12302	11663	11246	11138	11226
45-49	12406	11452	11940	10940	11155	10619	10031

TABLE 5 DEMOGRAPHIC INDICES AND FEMALE SINGULATE MEAN AGE
AT MARRIAGE: 1831 TO 1901

DATE	IF OVERALL FERTILITY	IG MARITAL FERTILITY	IH ILLEGITIMATE FERTILITY	IM PROPORTION MARRIED	SINGULATE MEAN AGE AT MARRIAGE
1831	0.238	0.567	0.021	0.398	27.3
1836	0.228	0.537	0.022	0.399	27.1
1841	0.223	0.516	0.022	0.407	27.0
1846	0.227	0.511	0.021	0.419	26.8
1851	0.225	0.491	0.025	0.430	26.6
1856	0.231	0.490	0.027	0.440	26.5
1861	0.238	0.498	0.028	0.447	26.6
1866	0.236	0.507	0.025	0.439	26.9
1871	0.238	0.520	0.027	0.428	26.5
1876	0.246	0.532	0.027	0.434	25.9
1881	0.246	0.511	0.027	0.453	25.6
1886	0.249	0.496	0.029	0.471	25.8
1891	0.251	0.483	0.033	0.484	26.2
1896	0.248	0.476	0.034	0.484	25.9
1901	0.249	0.480	0.034	0.483	

MORTALITY PATTERN: NORTH
MIGRATION: NO CORRECTION MADE FOR MIGRATION BY AGE

TABLE 1 FEMALE POPULATION ESTIMATES: 1801 TO 1906

DATE	R/CB RATIO	% COR-RECTION	FINAL POPULATION ESTIMATE	DATE	R/CB RATIO	% COR-RECTION	FINAL POPULATION ESTIMATE
1801	0.962	2.6	161056	1856	1.009	1.2	191180
1806	0.973	1.2	161695	1861	1.016	0.2	193487
1811*	0.961	1.2	162622	1866	1.015	1.9	197908
1816*	0.952	1.2	163547	1871	1.015	0.0	196210
1821	0.935	1.2	164474	1876	1.050	0.0	203772
1826*	0.945	1.2	170504	1881	1.064	0.0	209235
1831	0.959	1.2	176534	1886	1.067	0.0	211924
1836	0.980	1.2	179982	1891	1.082	0.0	217195
1841	0.988	1.2	184399	1896	1.085	0.0	218416
1846	1.000	1.2	189019	1901	1.065	0.0	215176
1851	1.004	1.3	191578	1906	1.062	0.0	216197

NOTE: R/CB RATIO REFERS TO THE POPULATION COMPUTED BY THE BALANCE OF BIRTHS
       AND DEATHS OVER THE REPORTED POPULATION
* INTERPOLATED VALUES

TABLE 2 FEMALE BIRTH ESTIMATES: 1801-1805 TO 1901-1905

DATE	% COR-RECTION	FINAL BIRTH ESTIMATE	CRUDE BIRTH RATE	DATE	% COR-RECTION	FINAL BIRTH ESTIMATE	CRUDE BIRTH RATE
1801-1805	6.8	24872	30.8	1856-1860	0.0	23728	24.7
1806-1810	10.3	25338	31.3	1861-1865	0.0	22208	22.7
1811-1815	5.7	26129	32.0	1866-1870	0.0	22970	23.3
1816-1820	0.0	25745	31.4	1971-1875	0.0	24001	24.0
1821-1825	0.0	24683	29.5	1876-1880	0.0	24637	23.9
1826-1830	0.0	24641	28.4	1881-1885	0.0	25203	23.9
1831-1835	3.5	24112	27.1	1886-1890	0.0	25050	23.4
1836-1840	0.0	22815	25.0	1891-1895	0.0	24795	22.8
1841-1845	0.0	23238	24.9	1896-1900	0.0	23232	21.4
1846-1850	0.0	23459	24.7	1901-1905	0.0	22914	21.2
1851-1855	0.0	23435	24.5				

TABLE 3 FEMALE POPULATION ESTIMATES,
DISTRIBUTION BY AGE: 1801 TO 1906

AGE	1801	1806	1811	1816	1821	1826	1831	1836	1841	1846	1851
0- 4	23870	18339	18569	18915	19122	19402	19489	18546	18471	18863	18890
5- 9	19076	20026	15332	15430	15914	16826	17164	16982	16609	16596	16823
10-14	16984	17728	18537	14251	14313	15250	16198	16490	16367	16070	15948
15-19	15421	16086	16788	17648	13460	13934	14911	15846	16109	16053	15656
20-24	13949	14550	15174	15868	16607	13057	13576	14533	15428	15747	15587
25-29	12531	13068	13627	14235	14830	16009	12643	13141	14070	14996	15203
30-34	11152	11634	12126	12660	13190	14137	15384	12133	12636	13583	14378
35-39	9815	10252	10687	11146	11619	12510	13518	14623	11580	12107	12925
40-44	8578	8949	9340	9738	10148	10940	11834	12748	13863	11021	11443
45-49	7443	7772	8101	8456	8812	9499	10288	11091	12017	13119	10357
50-54	6378	6660	6948	7240	7558	8153	8830	9525	10342	11248	12194
55-59	5315	5546	5782	6023	6293	6816	7388	7950	8675	9454	10209
60-64	4181	4388	4567	4743	4979	5419	5900	6325	6943	7602	8224
65-69	3034	3170	3314	3424	3610	3973	4348	4650	5150	5670	6162
70-74	1908	2010	2087	2154	2286	2551	2825	3006	3385	3759	4106
75-79	977	1037	1082	1101	1186	1351	1519	1611	1854	2092	2303
80+	456	478	501	515	545	625	718	782	900	1038	1170

AGE	1856	1861	1866	1871	1876	1881	1886	1891	1896	1901	1906
0- 4	18390	19416	18702	18793	20295	20896	20990	21224	20607	19222	19471
5- 9	16570	16518	17850	16685	17442	18722	18986	19359	19259	18497	17642
10-14	16046	15900	16141	16909	16542	17044	18071	18564	18674	18269	17866
15-19	15450	15585	15710	15456	16966	16332	16632	17856	18107	17891	17806
20-24	15114	14956	15349	14996	15459	16700	15888	16382	17361	17294	17384
25-29	14954	14554	14657	14580	14920	15143	16165	15574	15849	16504	16729
30-34	14475	14312	14181	13844	14416	14535	14574	15758	14980	14988	15887
35-39	13576	13759	13856	13310	13595	13959	13901	14120	15060	14083	14348
40-44	12116	12823	13241	12928	12989	13088	13270	13389	13414	14078	13407
45-49	10664	11381	12273	12287	12547	12438	12375	12713	12651	12473	13333
50-54	9541	9912	10783	11274	11800	11894	11641	11736	11890	11647	11699
55-59	10952	8675	9194	9699	10591	10959	10900	10814	10746	10729	10716
60-64	8760	9572	7749	7968	8759	9485	9675	9762	9536	9359	9541
65-69	6544	7166	8024	6306	6735	7375	7859	8142	8077	7817	7850
70-74	4347	4814	5424	5901	4794	5134	5520	5985	6083	6007	5968
75-79	2427	2731	3128	3428	3831	3149	3301	3619	3838	3908	3978
80+	1253	1412	1647	1847	2091	2383	2176	2199	2282	2411	2573

[371]

TABLE 4 MARRIED WOMEN ESTIMATES,
DISTRIBUTICN BY AGE: 1831 TO 1901

AGE	1831	1836	1841	1846	1851	1856	1861	1866
15-19	890	955	981	989	975	973	1059	1013
20-24	6047	6509	6960	7149	7118	6942	6911	6883
25-29	9098	9472	10185	10885	11056	10893	10621	10715
30-34	12215	9631	10075	10848	11486	11562	11434	11332
35-39	10795	11664	9298	9740	10397	10912	11055	11131
40-44	9200	9890	10864	8662	8990	9506	10054	10378
45-49	7582	8152	8973	9843	7770	7988	8521	9189

AGE	1871	1876	1881	1886	1891	1896	1901
15-19	1252	1497	1077	1031	1013	930	1150
20-24	6947	7803	8514	7500	7613	8184	7892
25-29	10412	10869	11442	12163	11531	11746	12425
30-34	11023	11363	11646	11721	12664	12068	12099
35-39	10622	10827	11240	11074	11208	12010	11270
40-44	10028	10042	10342	10252	10208	10198	10694
45-49	9061	9212	9440	9107	9172	9075	8816

TABLE 5 DEMOGRAPHIC INDICES AND FEMALE SINGULATE MEAN AGE
AT MARRIAGE: 1831 TO 1901

DATE	IF OVERALL FERTILITY	IG MARITAL FERTILITY	IH ILLEGITIMATE FERTILITY	IM PROPORTION MARRIED	SINGULATE MEAN AGE AT MARRIAGE
1831	0.295	0.450	0.057	0.605	23.3
1836	0.281	0.437	0.053	0.595	23.2
1841	0.273	0.426	0.052	0.593	23.1
1846	0.272	0.422	0.049	0.596	23.1
1851	0.269	0.407	0.058	0.604	23.0
1856	0.270	0.405	0.061	0.609	23.0
1861	0.264	0.392	0.062	0.610	23.0
1866	0.256	0.380	0.066	0.606	23.0
1871	0.272	0.397	0.081	C.605	22.7
1876	0.272	0.399	0.071	0.612	22.6
1881	0.272	0.394	0.071	0.624	22.8
1886	0.273	0.401	0.071	0.613	22.9
1891	0.264	0.393	0.068	0.602	22.9
1896	0.249	0.370	0.066	0.602	23.0
1901	0.240	0.357	0.060	0.604	

MORTALITY PATTERN: NORTH
MIGRATION: GRADUAL, WITH UNCORRECTED POPULATION TOTALS EXCEPT FOR 1851, 1856, 1861, 1866, 1871, 1891 AND 1896, OBTAINED BY INTERPOLATION OF R/CB

TABLE 1   FEMALE POPULATION ESTIMATES: 1801 TO 1906

DATE	R/CB RATIO	% COR- RECTION	FINAL POPULATION ESTIMATE	DATE	R/CB RATIO	% COR- RECTION	FINAL POPULATION ESTIMATE
1801	1.102	0.0	116096	1856	0.942	3.3	132388
1806	1.131	0.0	122575	1861	0.938	2.2	132672
1811*	1.085	0.0	122349	1866	0.932	1.4	131839
1816*	1.054	0.0	122123	1871	0.905	2.9	130368
1821	1.015	0.0	121897	1876	C.910	0.0	126638
1826*	1.005	0.0	125567	1881	0.890	0.0	124395
1831	1.004	C.0	129236	1886	0.874	0.0	122220
1836	1.019	0.0	131884	1891	0.866	-0.8	119593
1841	1.005	0.0	132715	1896	0.842	0.3	115829
1846	1.000	0.0	133926	1901	0.829	0.0	112639
1851	1.002	-1.6	133464	1906	0.814	0.0	109563

NOTE: R/CB RATIO REFERS TO THE POPULATION COMPUTED BY THE BALANCE CF BIRTHS
AND DEATHS OVER THE REPORTED POPULATION
* INTERPOLATED VALUES

TABLE 2   FEMALE BIRTH ESTIMATES: 1801-1805 TO 1901-1905

DATE	% COR- RECTION	FINAL BIRTH ESTIMATE	CRUDE BIRTH RATE	DATE	% COR- RECTION	FINAL BIRTH ESTIMATE	CRUDE BIRTH RATE
1801-1805	10.9	18721	31.4	1856-1860	0.0	15026	22.7
1806-1810	14.9	19022	31.1	1861-1865	0.0	14034	21.2
1811-1815	0.0	16827	27.5	1866-1870	0.0	13442	20.5
1816-1820	0.0	16167	26.5	1871-1875	9.7	12892	20.1
1821-1825	0.0	16645	26.9	1876-1880	0.0	13065	20.8
1826-1830	0.0	16643	26.1	1881-1885	0.0	12532	20.3
1831-1835	0.0	15925	24.4	1886-1890	0.0	11635	19.2
1836-1840	0.0	15544	23.5	1891-1895	C.0	10548	17.9
1841-1845	1.4	14878	22.3	1896-1900	0.0	10251	17.9
1846-1850	0.0	14965	22.4	1901-1905	0.0	9933	17.9
1851-1855	0.0	14049	21.1				

TABLE 3 FEMALE POPULATION ESTIMATES,
DISTRIBUTION BY AGE: 1801 TO 1906

AGE	1801	1806	1811	1816	1821	1826	1831	1836	1841	1846	1851
0- 4	14876	14881	14548	13157	12944	13791	13782	12929	12794	12402	12314
5- 9	12470	13262	12654	12581	11505	11677	12473	12382	11599	11597	11113
10-14	11389	12130	12197	11776	11698	11006	11231	12066	11789	11134	11032
15-19	10566	11259	11319	11505	11072	11310	10704	11013	11612	11434	10684
20-24	9767	10408	10470	10640	10783	10671	10965	10461	10566	11227	10901
25-29	8975	9559	9621	9787	9923	10342	10294	10655	9987	10167	10686
30-34	8190	8716	8774	8933	9074	9464	9919	9935	10115	9557	9643
35-39	7407	7885	7937	8086	8230	8602	9019	9501	9373	9621	9013
40-44	6654	7079	7131	7265	7404	7755	8147	8582	8910	8864	9023
45-49	5943	6321	6364	6490	6617	6940	7306	7708	8004	8382	8270
50-54	5244	5580	5620	5730	5851	6140	6471	6837	7117	7454	7743
55-59	4512	4797	4841	4942	5057	5318	5604	5914	6182	6494	6744
60-64	3712	3939	3984	4082	4200	4430	4674	4911	5154	5440	5658
65-69	2826	3000	3042	3132	3255	3457	3653	3817	4019	4263	4451
70-74	1907	2020	2063	2138	2254	2424	2573	2667	2824	3011	3153
75-79	1077	1138	1170	1229	1321	1445	1548	1591	1696	1824	1914
80+	575	602	615	649	709	796	875	914	975	1057	1121

AGE	1856	1861	1866	1871	1876	1881	1886	1891	1896	1901	1906
0- 4	11647	12634	11874	11374	10766	11179	10753	10052	9045	8893	8705
5- 9	11080	10562	11488	10795	10192	9785	10210	9858	9167	8310	8216
10-14	10591	10593	10096	10995	10229	9711	9361	9792	9444	8808	7987
15-19	10578	10155	10115	9630	10296	9571	9140	8796	9215	8922	8289
20-24	10138	10006	9498	9434	8580	9197	8616	8166	7823	8312	7989
25-29	10368	9642	9473	8979	8713	7904	8571	8004	7564	7276	7741
30-34	10154	9982	9184	9031	8473	8262	7521	8177	7623	7228	6957
35-39	9115	9636	9383	8729	8519	8042	7871	7176	7804	7299	6927
40-44	8477	8613	9118	8892	8229	8090	7661	7518	6851	7471	7005
45-49	8446	7974	8116	8606	8358	7796	7686	7301	7162	6544	7154
50-54	7667	7872	7450	7596	8026	7862	7354	7274	6907	6793	6227
55-59	7033	7008	7215	6839	6946	7412	7278	6834	6752	6434	6349
60-64	5903	6203	6199	6399	6011	6180	6614	6520	6108	6065	5802
65-69	4656	4907	5176	5177	5285	5054	5211	5603	5503	5190	5182
70-74	3317	3519	3728	3935	4054	4054	3888	4032	4311	4273	4062
75-79	2025	2171	2321	2458	2552	2594	2714	2621	2696	2919	2924
80+	1194	1294	1406	1511	1579	1700	1773	1868	1849	1903	2048

[374]

TABLE 4 MARRIED WOMEN ESTIMATES,
DISTRIBUTION BY AGE: 1831 TO 1901

AGE	1831	1836	1841	1846	1851	1856	1861	1866
15-19	379	401	436	444	430	442	567	601
20-24	3449	3364	3486	3802	3790	3621	3678	3856
25-29	6353	6658	6341	6554	6987	6874	6488	6463
30-34	7436	7485	7703	7345	7467	7919	7772	7274
35-39	7117	7494	7458	7705	7248	7357	7826	7652
40-44	6555	6854	7164	7153	7286	6846	6986	7408
45-49	5607	5849	6134	6459	6378	6514	6189	6314

AGE	1871	1876	1881	1886	1891	1896	1901
15-19	435	409	406	345	309	316	446
20-24	3541	3304	3709	3355	3052	2939	3111
25-29	6265	5756	5469	6202	5640	5312	5185
30-34	7178	6762	6438	6043	6670	6201	5918
35-39	7110	6951	6589	6430	5849	6446	6051
40-44	7178	6632	6556	6262	5974	5460	5990
45-49	6631	6423	6040	6088	5589	5463	4964

TABLE 5 DEMOGRAPHIC INDICES AND FEMALE SINGULATE MEAN AGE
AT MARRIAGE: 1831 TO 1901

DATE	IF OVERALL FERTILITY	IG MARITAL FERTILITY	IH ILLEGITIMATE FERTILITY	IM PROPORTION MARRIED	SINGULATE MEAN AGE AT MARRIAGE
1831	0.270	0.480	0.029	0.534	25.3
1836	0.257	0.454	0.025	0.541	25.1
1841	0.248	0.436	0.025	0.544	24.9
1846	0.241	0.421	0.023	0.548	24.8
1851	0.238	0.404	0.026	0.559	24.6
1856	0.242	0.401	0.032	0.570	24.4
1861	0.247	0.406	0.027	0.582	24.1
1866	0.240	0.386	0.026	0.594	24.1
1871	0.238	0.387	0.026	0.588	24.3
1876	0.244	0.403	0.029	0.576	24.1
1881	0.248	0.408	0.027	0.581	23.9
1886	0.242	0.385	0.033	0.592	24.1
1891	0.229	0.367	0.034	0.586	24.2
1896	0.220	0.355	0.031	0.583	24.2
1901	0.216	0.347	0.032	0.584	

MORTALITY PATTERN: WEST
MIGRATION: GRADUAL, WITH POPULATION TOTALS OBTAINED BY TREND OF R/CB

TABLE 1 FEMALE POPULATION ESTIMATES: 1801 TO 1906

DATE	R/CB RATIO	% COR- RECTION	FINAL POPULATION ESTIMATE	DATE	R/CB RATIO	% COR- RECTION	FINAL POPULATION ESTIMATE
1801	0.982	1.8	164665	1856	0.982	0.0	189988
1806	1.050	0.0	171116	1861	0.973	-1.0	186922
1811*	1.060	0.0	173549	1866	0.950	-0.6	184105
1816*	1.050	0.0	175983	1871	0.914	1.2	180044
1821	1.032	0.0	178416	1876	0.920	-1.4	175461
1826*	1.010	0.0	179672	1881	0.890	-0.2	173067
1831	1.010	0.0	180928	1886	0.869	-0.0	170184
1836	1.021	0.0	185009	1891	0.851	-0.2	167087
1841	1.011	0.0	185265	1896	0.831	-0.0	161980
1846	1.000	0.0	187428	1901	0.806	0.6	158292
1851	0.989	1.3	191387	1906	0.789	0.5	154923

NOTE: R/CB RATIO REFERS TO THE POPULATION COMPUTED BY THE BALANCE OF BIRTHS
       AND DEATHS OVER THE REPORTED POPULATION
* INTERPOLATED VALUES

TABLE 2 FEMALE BIRTH ESTIMATES: 1801-1805 TO 1901-1905

DATE	% COR- RECTION	FINAL BIRTH ESTIMATE	CRUDE BIRTH RATE	DATE	% COR- RECTION	FINAL BIRTH ESTIMATE	CRUDE BIRTH RATE
1801-1805	0.0	23355	27.8	1856-1860	0.0	21542	22.9
1806-1810	0.0	23023	26.7	1861-1865	0.0	21830	23.5
1811-1815	0.0	24221	27.7	1866-1870	0.0	21513	23.6
1816-1820	0.0	25103	28.3	1871-1875	0.0	20964	23.6
1821-1825	0.0	24881	27.8	1876-1880	0.0	20784	23.9
1826-1830	0.0	23937	26.6	1881-1885	0.0	19445	22.7
1831-1835	0.0	23390	25.6	1886-1890	0.0	18685	22.2
1836-1840	0.0	22562	24.4	1891-1895	0.0	17211	20.9
1841-1845	0.0	22842	24.5	1896-1900	0.0	16728	20.9
1846-1850	0.0	22242	23.5	1901-1905	0.0	16260	20.8
1851-1855	0.0	22289	23.4				

TABLE 3 FEMALE POPULATION ESTIMATES,
DISTRIBUTION BY AGE: 1801 TO 1906

AGE	1801	1806	1811	1816	1821	1826	1831	1836	1841	1846	1851
0- 4	19297	17624	17442	18739	19675	19539	18468	18652	17914	18654	18567
5- 9	16691	17675	15893	15739	16324	17728	17657	17034	16981	16512	17461
10-14	15831	16696	17216	15319	15086	16147	17152	17319	16416	16434	16173
15-19	15009	15831	16256	16586	14675	14386	15615	16815	16683	15879	16093
20-24	14054	14836	15253	15516	15753	13877	13780	15173	16062	16016	15448
25-29	13045	13758	14170	14445	14630	14792	13186	13291	14393	15324	15480
30-34	12001	12668	13045	13334	13540	13659	13963	12642	12535	13661	14735
35-39	10963	11560	11923	12193	12421	12564	12806	13301	11851	11834	13067
40-44	9937	10485	10807	11076	11292	11459	11706	12126	12393	11127	11259
45-49	8933	9435	9733	9971	10187	10348	10602	11009	11226	11564	10517
50-54	7902	8327	8608	8835	9029	9194	9418	9815	10037	10321	10777
55-59	6742	7125	7366	7594	7787	7934	8128	8482	8715	9003	9391
60-64	5439	5748	5983	6194	6394	6543	6680	6989	7202	7498	7868
65-69	4330	4265	4463	4678	4865	5017	5116	5352	5542	5811	6156
70-74	2644	2803	2956	3134	3312	3445	3519	3691	3831	4055	4334
75-79	1428	1525	1626	1753	1883	1994	2037	2151	2247	2400	2596
80+	720	757	807	878	964	1045	1094	1166	1232	1333	1466

AGE	1856	1861	1866	1871	1876	1881	1886	1891	1896	1901	1906
0- 4	18048	17250	17465	16984	16471	16884	16028	15530	14131	14117	13920
5- 9	16950	16384	15649	15740	15265	15006	15463	14721	14190	13045	13103
10-14	16752	16231	15694	14953	15034	14641	14406	14877	14148	13680	12572
15-19	15411	15887	15351	14745	13981	14073	13633	13390	13823	13162	12696
20-24	15065	14245	14594	13898	13193	12404	12320	11820	11519	11999	11318
25-29	14507	14053	13234	13465	12747	12104	11292	11194	10676	10445	10907
30-34	14562	13604	13178	12361	12565	11971	11380	10627	10515	10079	9877
35-39	13802	13606	12718	12281	11511	11800	11276	10745	10011	9969	9579
40-44	12189	12849	12684	11827	11423	10808	11131	10675	10157	9527	9519
45-49	10440	11284	11914	11737	10951	10683	10163	10507	10064	9644	9081
50-54	9620	9535	10323	10875	10719	10118	9934	9495	9799	9461	9108
55-59	9614	8563	8502	9176	9666	9657	9183	9060	8641	9000	8737
60-64	8023	8177	7289	7198	7759	8308	8363	7992	7851	7582	7949
65-69	6302	6385	6510	5759	5674	6246	6752	6837	6491	6483	6315
70-74	4469	4537	4596	4639	4090	4137	4607	5015	5033	4880	4927
75-79	2692	2744	2783	2782	2794	2548	2616	2937	3158	3257	3202
80+	1543	1588	1623	1626	1618	1680	1638	1663	1772	1962	2115

TABLE 4 MARRIED WOMEN ESTIMATES,
DISTRIBUTION BY AGE: 1831 TO 1901

AGE	1831	1836	1841	1846	1851	1856	1861	1866
15-19	369	414	431	433	466	476	423	443
20-24	2896	3317	3672	3836	3889	3992	3985	3526
25-29	5913	6150	6901	7610	7966	7721	7736	7529
30-34	8134	7537	7685	8600	9523	9623	9188	9082
35-39	8123	8581	7834	7996	9024	9684	9693	9180
40-44	8003	8322	8640	7852	8049	8762	9288	9199
45-49	6767	7044	7327	7667	7088	7071	7682	8125

AGE	1871	1876	1881	1886	1891	1896	1901
15-19	466	588	663	565	461	406	602
20-24	3755	4128	4113	4001	3673	3583	3744
25-29	6997	7094	7477	6953	6738	6341	6374
30-34	8650	8372	8396	8312	7774	7576	7255
35-39	8917	8474	8637	8235	8136	7559	7470
40-44	8521	8287	8163	7923	7768	7525	7040
45-49	7898	7423	7673	6975	7343	7055	6785

TABLE 5 DEMOGRAPHIC INDICES AND FEMALE SINGULATE MEAN AGE
AT MARRIAGE: 1831 TO 1901

DATE	IF OVERALL FERTILITY	IG MARITAL FERTILITY	IH ILLEGITIMATE FERTILITY	IM PROPORTION MARRIED	SINGULATE MEAN AGE AT MARRIAGE
1831	0.289	0.677	0.018	0.411	26.9
1836	0.273	0.640	0.018	0.411	26.7
1841	0.267	0.610	0.020	0.418	26.5
1846	0.261	0.575	0.021	0.435	26.2
1851	0.253	0.531	0.021	0.454	25.9
1856	0.252	0.508	0.023	0.472	25.7
1861	0.255	0.505	0.023	0.482	25.7
1866	0.262	0.525	0.023	0.478	25.7
1871	0.266	0.533	0.024	0.477	25.3
1876	0.273	0.529	0.024	0.494	24.8
1881	0.272	0.503	0.022	0.520	24.7
1886	0.267	0.496	0.022	0.516	25.1
1891	0.260	0.487	0.022	0.513	25.3
1896	0.253	0.480	0.023	0.503	25.1
1901	0.250	0.474	0.021	0.506	

MEURTHE

MORTALITY PATTERN: NORTH
MIGRATION: GRADUAL, WITH UNCORRECTED POPULATION TOTALS

TABLE 1   FEMALE POPULATION ESTIMATES: 1801 TO 1866

DATE	R/CB RATIO	% COR- RECTION	FINAL POPULATION ESTIMATE	DATE	R/CB RATIO	% COR- RECTION	FINAL POPULATION ESTIMATE
1801	1.021	4.1	182146	1856	0.961	0.0	219944
1806	1.045	0.0	188539	1861	0.954	0.0	220787
1811*	1.017	0.0	191943	1866	0.939	0.0	220363
1816*	1.001	0.0	195346				
1821	0.991	0.0	198750				
1826*	0.996	0.0	207287				
1831	1.005	0.0	215825				
1836	1.002	0.0	219706				
1841	1.013	0.0	227974				
1846	1.000	0.0	230353				
1851	0.989	0.0	229611				

NOTE: R/CB RATIO REFERS TO THE POPULATION COMPUTED BY THE BALANCE OF BIRTHS
       AND DEATHS OVER THE REPORTED POPULATION
* INTERPOLATED VALUES

TABLE 2   FEMALE BIRTH ESTIMATES: 1801-1805 TO 1861-1865

DATE	% COR- RECTION	FINAL BIRTH ESTIMATE	CRUDE BIRTH RATE	DATE	% COR- RECTION	FINAL BIRTH ESTIMATE	CRUDE BIRTH RATE
1801-1805	9.1	33862	36.5	1856-1860	0.0	25218	22.9
1806-1810	2.6	33598	35.3	1861-1865	0.0	25787	23.4
1811-1815	6.4	33373	34.5				
1816-1820	0.0	30293	30.7				
1821-1825	0.0	31185	30.7				
1826-1830	0.0	31243	29.5				
1831-1835	0.0	30690	28.2				
1836-1840	0.0	30197	27.0				
1841-1845	0.0	30008	26.2				
1846-1850	0.0	27275	23.7				
1851-1855	0.0	25448	22.6				

TABLE 3 FEMALE POPULATION ESTIMATES,
DISTRIBUTION BY AGE: 1801 TO 1866

AGE	1801	1806	1811	1816	1821	1826	1831	1836	1841	1846	1851
0- 4	26049	25645	25143	24757	23146	24687	24918	23981	24554	23975	21752
5- 9	21171	22200	21608	21155	21241	20424	21905	21742	21550	21643	21099
10-14	18953	19755	20492	20071	19830	20324	19615	20763	21010	20392	20469
15-19	17263	17985	18546	19388	19125	19259	19806	18879	20334	20142	19506
20-24	15675	16322	16823	17481	18407	18510	18704	18996	18426	19428	19143
25-29	14137	14724	15168	15747	16490	17708	17869	17829	18437	17509	18415
30-34	12642	13172	13572	14074	14738	15748	16972	16906	17189	17405	16519
35-39	11195	11674	12032	12472	13057	13960	14974	15925	16179	16109	16307
40-44	9847	10260	10583	10970	11485	12281	13181	13949	15139	15063	15000
45-49	8598	8970	9245	9589	10040	10739	11528	12207	13186	14016	13950
50-54	7425	7739	7987	8273	8674	9283	9968	10555	11414	12076	12843
55-59	6241	6508	6709	6950	7290	7822	8407	8899	9641	10216	10812
60-64	4993	5214	5377	5549	5841	6287	6779	7174	7797	8281	8770
65-69	3681	3855	3979	4091	4314	4678	5065	5367	5862	6252	6633
70-74	2378	2506	2593	2810	2810	3071	3355	3559	3924	4211	4483
75-79	1276	1346	1401	1424	1519	1681	1854	1977	2206	2394	2562
80+	636	662	686	702	744	826	924	999	1126	1241	1350

AGE	1856	1861	1866
0- 4	19244	20600	21209
5- 9	18382	17223	18417
10-14	19482	17565	16362
15-19	19040	18799	16710
20-24	17793	18243	17578
25-29	17609	17017	17219
30-34	16975	16783	16127
35-39	15120	16077	15335
40-44	14847	14238	15108
45-49	13590	13908	13322
50-54	12505	12601	12892
55-59	11216	11342	11437
60-64	8990	9777	9396
65-69	6747	7337	8005
70-74	4510	4955	5424
75-79	2541	2830	3144
80+	1355	1493	1678

MORTALITY PATTERN: NORTH
MIGRATION: GRADUAL, WITH UNCORRECTED POPULATION TOTALS EXCEPT FOR 1851, 1856, 1861, 1866, 1871 AND 1876, OBTAINED BY LINEAR INTERPOLATION OF R/CB

TABLE 1   FEMALE POPULATION ESTIMATES: 1801 TO 1906

DATE	R/CB RATIO	% COR- RECTION	FINAL POPULATION ESTIMATE	DATE	R/CB RATIO	% COR- RECTION	FINAL POPULATION ESTIMATE
1801	1.096	3.0	142276	1856	0.920	3.8	160878
1806	1.106	0.0	145965	1861	0.908	2.6	158502
1811*	1.082	0.0	148196	1866	0.889	2.2	155587
1816*	1.076	0.0	150426	1871	0.859	2.7	149931
1821	1.062	0.0	152657	1876	0.863	-0.4	146086
1826*	1.053	0.0	157962	1881	0.838	0.0	142791
1831	1.052	0.0	163267	1886	0.830	0.0	141657
1836	1.031	0.0	163592	1891	0.820	0.0	139471
1841	1.015	0.0	165041	1896	0.803	0.0	134972
1846	1.000	0.0	166002	1901	0.786	0.0	131708
1851	0.989	-1.1	163537	1906	0.767	0.0	128631

NOTE: R/CB RATIO REFERS TO THE POPULATION COMPUTED BY THE BALANCE OF BIRTHS
       AND DEATHS OVER THE REPORTED POPULATION
* INTERPOLATED VALUES

TABLE 2   FEMALE BIRTH ESTIMATES: 1801-1805 TO 1901-1905

DATE	% COR- RECTION	FINAL BIRTH ESTIMATE	CRUDE BIRTH RATE	DATE	% COR- RECTION	FINAL BIRTH ESTIMATE	CRUDE BIRTH RATE
1801-1805	10.3	25609	35.5	1856-1860	0.0	17422	21.8
1806-1810	8.7	24815	33.7	1861-1865	0.0	16170	20.6
1811-1815	0.0	24080	32.3	1866-1870	4.3	15331	20.1
1816-1820	0.0	22728	30.0	1871-1875	0.0	15305	20.7
1821-1825	0.0	22761	29.3	1876-1880	0.0	15378	21.3
1826-1830	0.0	22471	28.0	1881-1885	0.0	14877	20.9
1831-1835	0.0	20668	25.3	1886-1890	0.0	14366	20.4
1836-1840	0.0	20848	25.4	1891-1895	0.0	13890	20.2
1841-1845	0.0	20618	24.9	1896-1900	0.0	13570	20.4
1846-1850	0.0	19421	23.6	1901-1905	0.0	13245	20.4
1851-1855	0.0	18002	22.2				

TABLE 3 FEMALE POPULATION ESTIMATES,
DISTRIBUTION BY AGE: 1801 TO 1906

AGE	1801	1806	1811	1816	1821	1826	1831	1836	1841	1846	1851
0- 4	21642	19181	18408	17730	17257	18136	18045	16418	16737	16616	15410
5- 9	17353	18293	16111	15468	15156	15230	16117	15802	14505	14820	14517
10-14	15329	16107	16934	15045	14484	14414	14573	15139	14951	13734	13896
15-19	13776	14477	15181	16126	14329	13966	13981	13866	14505	14331	12997
20-24	12341	12963	13594	14401	15302	13769	13501	13258	13242	13858	13443
25-29	10990	11536	12090	12802	13576	14621	13235	12733	12593	12584	12999
30-34	9695	10187	10666	11281	11971	12883	13958	12402	12017	11893	11770
35-39	8475	8905	9330	9852	10454	11274	12207	12986	11622	11271	11052
40-44	7362	7724	8091	8547	9060	9779	10611	11283	12092	10832	10414
45-49	6349	6669	6975	7365	7813	8427	9151	9752	10447	11207	9956
50-54	5411	5682	5949	6269	6653	7187	7800	8321	8935	9581	10194
55-59	4486	4713	4930	5193	5513	5976	6497	6932	7453	8013	8517
60-64	3541	3720	3889	4081	4352	4747	5180	5543	5964	6424	6832
65-69	2576	2710	2827	2952	3160	3491	3835	4127	4457	4808	5114
70-74	1648	1734	1806	1870	2015	2264	2521	2739	2978	3229	3430
75-79	877	920	954	977	1061	1221	1384	1531	1684	1841	1958
80+	429	446	460	470	502	578	671	762	860	960	1036

AGE	1856	1861	1866	1871	1876	1881	1886	1891	1896	1901	1906
0- 4	14578	14356	13544	12583	12839	13027	12789	12256	11676	11686	11580
5- 9	13610	12996	12903	11986	11287	11582	11971	11684	11017	10641	10730
10-14	13664	12856	12307	12134	11348	10705	11147	11499	11118	10526	10173
15-19	13132	12897	12089	11416	11315	10536	10228	10617	10705	10350	9713
20-24	12075	12114	11771	10723	10128	9950	9787	9399	9258	9336	8843
25-29	12591	11280	11285	13807	9868	9275	9417	9215	8583	8460	8477
30-34	12200	11859	10644	10576	10198	9321	8884	9004	8723	8146	8029
35-39	10990	11448	11172	9963	9979	9650	8913	8480	8538	8311	7772
40-44	10274	10277	10761	10449	9337	9450	9208	8495	8056	8158	7968
45-49	9636	9568	9627	10035	9830	8881	8984	8746	8058	7688	7816
50-54	9125	8896	8891	8909	9370	9223	8375	8466	8239	7644	7330
55-59	9142	8253	8108	8059	8159	8625	8537	7743	7815	7669	7158
60-64	7340	7955	7245	7049	7096	7225	7709	7608	6857	6997	6910
65-69	5518	6004	6585	5914	5849	5930	6103	6484	6340	5802	5971
70-74	3723	4087	4520	4858	4459	4450	4570	4674	4899	4895	4532
75-79	2138	2375	2667	2866	3171	2945	2984	3039	3049	3291	3341
80+	1141	1282	1466	1604	1792	2016	2052	2061	2040	2108	2286

TABLE 4 MARRIED WOMEN ESTIMATES,
DISTRIBUTION BY AGE: 1831 TO 1901

AGE	1831	1836	1841	1846	1851	1856	1861	1866
15-19	553	553	582	579	529	541	517	479
20-24	4825	4758	4778	5022	4892	4415	4448	4255
25-29	8788	8466	8397	8404	8691	8432	7570	7585
30-34	10794	9591	9317	9225	9127	9466	9215	8274
35-39	9675	10289	9242	8966	8786	8741	9124	8907
40-44	8315	8836	9524	8538	8200	8097	8126	8514
45-49	6796	7241	7831	8415	7471	7247	7236	7293

AGE	1871	1876	1881	1886	1891	1896	1901
15-19	442	532	536	476	438	372	521
20-24	3792	3675	3740	3806	3634	3640	3688
25-29	7176	6449	6178	6316	6336	5970	6013
30-34	8194	7850	7129	6849	6979	6897	6518
35-39	7900	7892	7629	7006	6674	6763	6694
40-44	8199	7344	7391	7128	6536	6185	6295
45-49	7515	7323	6629	6673	6450	5906	5584

TABLE 5 DEMOGRAPHIC INDICES AND FEMALE SINGULATE MEAN AGE
AT MARRIAGE: 1831 TO 1901

DATE	IF OVERALL FERTILITY	IG MARITAL FERTILITY	IH ILLEGITIMATE FERTILITY	IM PROPORTION MARRIED	SINGULATE MEAN AGE AT MARRIAGE
1831	0.273	0.453	0.041	0.564	24.5
1836	0.268	0.452	0.031	0.564	24.4
1841	0.271	0.460	0.031	0.559	24.3
1846	0.263	0.448	0.032	0.555	24.3
1851	0.252	0.425	0.029	0.562	24.3
1856	0.245	0.411	0.027	0.567	24.2
1861	0.237	0.398	0.026	0.568	24.3
1866	0.230	0.383	0.029	0.569	24.3
1871	0.237	0.397	0.029	0.566	24.3
1876	0.249	0.422	0.027	0.564	24.1
1881	0.258	0.433	0.029	0.568	24.0
1886	0.257	0.426	0.033	0.569	24.0
1891	0.253	0.418	0.037	0.568	24.0
1896	0.253	0.416	0.037	0.569	24.0
1901	0.252	0.410	0.037	0.577	

MORTALITY PATTERN: WEST
MIGRATION: GRADUAL, WITH POPULATION TOTALS OBTAINED BY TREND OF R/CB

TABLE 1 FEMALE POPULATION ESTIMATES: 1801 TO 1906

DATE	R/CB RATIO	% COR- RECTION	FINAL POPULATION ESTIMATE	DATE	R/CB RATIO	% COR- RECTION	FINAL POPULATION ESTIMATE
1801	1.097	0.0	212570	1856	0.983	0.9	248565
1806	1.058	0.0	208133	1861	0.986	-0.5	247960
1811*	1.043	0.0	211323	1866	0.972	-0.1	254955
1816*	1.028	0.0	214512	1871	0.955	0.5	253992
1821	1.028	0.0	217702	1876	0.959	-1.0	257333
1826*	1.014	0.0	221704	1881	0.958	-2.1	265376
1831	1.014	0.0	225706	1886	0.930	-0.2	272141
1836	1.022	0.0	232950	1891	0.919	-0.2	277820
1841	0.984	0.0	229889	1896	0.904	0.2	281779
1846	1.000	0.0	242344	1901	0.892	0.3	288503
1851	0.995	0.8	248567	1906	0.872	1.4	294751

NOTE: R/CB RATIO REFERS TO THE POPULATION COMPUTED BY THE BALANCE OF BIRTHS
       AND DEATHS OVER THE REPORTED POPULATION
* INTERPOLATED VALUES

TABLE 2 FEMALE BIRTH ESTIMATES: 1801-1805 TO 1901-1905

DATE	% COR- RECTION	FINAL BIRTH ESTIMATE	CRUDE BIRTH RATE	DATE	% COR- RECTION	FINAL BIRTH ESTIMATE	CRUDE BIRTH RATE
1801-1805	8.1	36790	35.0	1856-1860	0.0	34834	28.1
1806-1810	0.0	36205	34.5	1861-1865	0.0	37109	29.5
1811-1815	0.0	35855	33.7	1866-1870	0.0	36638	28.8
1816-1820	4.9	36376	33.7	1871-1875	7.4	39236	30.7
1821-1825	0.0	35999	32.8	1876-1880	0.0	39324	30.1
1826-1830	7.3	37290	33.3	1881-1885	0.0	39367	29.3
1831-1835	4.7	37733	32.9	1886-1890	0.0	38845	28.3
1836-1840	10.2	35338	30.5	1891-1895	0.0	38003	27.2
1841-1845	0.0	34371	29.1	1896-1900	0.0	37295	26.2
1846-1850	0.0	35259	28.7	1901-1905	0.0	37432	25.7
1851-1855	0.0	34235	27.5				

TABLE 3 FEMALE POPULATION ESTIMATES,
DISTRIBUTION BY AGE: 1801 TO 1906

AGE	1801	1806	1811	1816	1821	1826	1831	1836	1841	1846	1851
0- 4	26423	24961	26014	26127	25978	26713	26983	28006	25926	27775	27379
5- 9	22429	22147	21752	22784	22825	22943	23479	24099	24267	24134	25214
10-14	21110	20744	21069	20690	21836	21773	22032	22787	22455	23968	23428
15-19	19871	19519	19727	20032	19823	20821	20901	21375	21224	22168	23265
20-24	18464	18144	18350	18551	18964	18705	19757	20054	19710	20772	21330
25-29	16966	16682	16893	17097	17386	17738	17577	18782	18337	19152	19818
30-34	15461	15196	15409	15620	15891	16145	16535	16581	17055	17713	18146
35-39	13963	13726	13921	14137	14395	14647	14926	15476	14950	16373	16668
40-44	12512	12302	12486	12685	12933	13180	13445	13875	13864	14268	15310
45-49	11128	10942	11109	11295	11519	11758	12011	12408	12342	13141	13248
50-54	9707	9545	9702	9872	10066	10293	10519	10887	10852	11518	12004
55-59	8165	8038	8188	8350	8504	8721	8908	9234	9242	9858	10223
60-64	6461	6369	6521	6676	6789	6993	7135	7406	7452	8021	8336
65-69	4677	4612	4753	4903	4981	5163	5261	5469	5538	6033	6303
70-74	2973	2946	3054	3181	3238	3382	3445	3588	3660	4042	4256
75-79	1547	1538	1618	1702	1735	1839	1870	1956	2016	2267	2405
80+	730	724	760	809	839	891	923	968	1001	1139	1234

AGE	1856	1861	1866	1871	1876	1881	1886	1891	1896	1901	1906
0- 4	25896	26023	29571	27511	29387	31926	32046	31763	31052	31682	31963
5- 9	24377	22945	23736	26213	24618	27508	29293	29445	29162	28969	29609
10-14	24120	23315	22158	22666	25170	23777	26564	28313	28460	28314	28126
15-19	22323	22958	22392	20919	21543	24003	22524	25166	26794	27034	26854
20-24	21822	20853	21681	20562	19342	19841	21919	20301	22656	24307	24444
25-29	19943	20360	19700	20070	19160	18073	18420	20340	18698	21080	22642
30-34	18476	18567	19237	18314	18779	18114	17057	17391	19212	17778	20078
35-39	16810	17091	17455	17737	17049	17710	17081	16096	16412	18302	16939
40-44	15356	15465	15995	16081	16499	16040	16681	16119	15200	15647	17471
45-49	14012	14035	14385	14651	14821	15445	15041	15679	15169	14448	14893
50-54	11930	12596	12865	12971	13296	13694	14302	13970	14581	14267	13617
55-59	10494	10402	11245	11256	11433	11979	12368	12955	12674	13406	13148
60-64	8492	8677	8868	9322	9420	9837	10324	10689	11201	11154	11827
65-69	6420	6495	6908	6805	7238	7588	7940	8360	8656	9286	9276
70-74	4346	4385	4667	4738	4735	5278	5546	5824	6131	6540	7043
75-79	2466	2485	2680	2683	2774	2948	3295	3478	3650	3993	4281
80+	1284	1307	1413	1434	1468	1614	1741	1931	2072	2296	2540

[385]

TABLE 4 MARRIED WOMEN ESTIMATES, DISTRIBUTION BY AGE: 1831 TO 1901

AGE	1831	1836	1841	1846	1851	1856	1861	1866
15-19	712	700	670	675	686	638	891	734
20-24	5023	4985	4776	4912	4915	4906	4608	4242
25-29	8965	9473	9161	9482	9693	9639	9803	9313
30-34	10443	10446	10746	11169	11394	11558	11711	11968
35-39	9897	10278	9988	11018	11216	11320	11730	11814
40-44	8865	9193	9296	9701	10443	10526	10950	11141
45-49	7293	7576	7662	8319	8414	8950	9402	9383

AGE	1871	1876	1881	1886	1891	1896	1901
15-19	649	713	654	554	592	504	768
20-24	4222	4421	4708	5224	4614	5480	5504
25-29	8041	8283	8730	9073	10508	9492	11270
30-34	11275	10206	10478	10663	11116	12836	11770
35-39	11939	11422	11011	10956	11016	11432	13094
40-44	11107	11433	11335	10683	10685	10499	10811
45-49	9416	9556	10244	9942	10588	10317	9632

TABLE 5 DEMOGRAPHIC INDICES AND FEMALE SINGULATE MEAN AGE AT MARRIAGE: 1831 TO 1901

DATE	IF OVERALL FERTILITY	IG MARITAL FERTILITY	IH ILLEGITIMATE FERTILITY	IM PROPORTION MARRIED	SINGULATE MEAN AGE AT MARRIAGE
1831	0.357	0.810	0.013	0.431	25.5
1836	0.337	0.766	0.015	0.429	25.8
1841	0.325	0.737	0.017	0.428	25.9
1846	0.309	0.700	0.016	0.428	26.0
1851	0.298	0.682	0.016	0.424	26.2
1856	0.295	0.675	0.015	0.424	26.2
1861	0.307	0.689	0.017	0.431	26.5
1866	0.311	0.716	0.018	0.420	26.9
1871	0.327	0.773	0.018	0.410	26.9
1876	0.346	0.817	0.018	0.410	26.6
1881	0.343	0.802	0.019	0.414	26.3
1886	0.339	0.779	0.023	0.419	26.7
1891	0.330	0.739	0.024	0.428	27.0
1896	0.312	0.697	0.021	0.430	26.7
1901	0.296	0.652	0.023	0.434	

MORTALITY PATTERN: NORTH
MIGRATION: GRADUAL, WITH UNCORRECTED POPULATION TOTALS

TABLE 1 FEMALE POPULATION ESTIMATES: 1801 TO 1866

DATE	R/CB RATIO	% COR- RECTION	FINAL POPULATION ESTIMATE	DATE	R/CB RATIO	% COR- RECTION	FINAL POPULATION ESTIMATE
1801	1.177	5.0	188801	1856	0.946	0.0	222398
1806	1.235	0.0	199943	1861	0.924	0.0	223425
1811*	1.164	2.9	203873	1866	0.912	0.0	226101
1816*	1.121	3.5	203150				
1821	1.059	5.6	205246				
1826*	1.045	3.4	211072				
1831	1.045	0.0	213842				
1836	1.040	0.0	220387				
1841	1.015	0.0	221941				
1846	1.000	0.0	226251				
1851	0.984	0.0	229145				

NOTE: R/CB RATIO REFERS TO THE POPULATION COMPUTED BY THE BALANCE OF BIRTHS
       AND DEATHS OVER THE REPORTED POPULATION
* INTERPOLATED VALUES

TABLE 2 FEMALE BIRTH ESTIMATES: 1801-1805 TO 1861-1865

DATE	% COR- RECTION	FINAL BIRTH ESTIMATE	CRUDE BIRTH RATE	DATE	% COR- RECTION	FINAL BIRTH ESTIMATE	CRUDE BIRTH RATE
1801-1805	0.0	32465	33.4	1856-1860	0.0	29588	26.5
1806-1810	0.0	32265	32.0	1861-1865	0.0	30212	26.9
1811-1815	0.0	31705	31.2				
1816-1820	3.0	31250	30.6				
1821-1825	0.0	31136	29.9				
1826-1830	0.0	31618	29.8				
1831-1835	0.0	31833	29.3				
1836-1840	0.0	30899	27.9				
1841-1845	0.0	31102	27.8				
1846-1850	0.0	30323	26.6				
1851-1855	0.0	28795	25.5				

TABLE 3 FEMALE POPULATION ESTIMATES,
DISTRIBUTION BY AGE: 1801 TO 1866

AGE	1801	1806	1811	1816	1821	1826	1831	1836	1841	1846	1851
0- 4	25738	25933	25042	23671	24279	25391	25129	25551	24511	25163	24604
5- 9	21323	22868	22371	21053	20383	21540	22163	22282	22332	21751	22343
10-14	19242	20501	21332	20607	19547	19160	20095	21123	20880	21156	20595
15-19	17639	18772	19401	19985	19400	18566	18093	19409	20049	20019	20221
20-24	16095	17148	17704	18110	18751	18369	17476	17417	18360	19159	18993
25-29	14610	15555	16078	16418	16894	17669	17199	16729	16386	17455	18151
30-34	13166	14019	14480	14789	15210	15833	16441	16354	15638	15483	16480
35-39	11761	12532	12947	13199	13596	14167	14631	15519	15179	14676	14528
40-44	10434	11118	11494	11713	12053	12590	13010	13719	14310	14156	13694
45-49	9203	9806	10138	10335	10634	11102	11498	12130	12580	13273	13141
50-54	8012	8553	8842	9008	9281	9697	10032	10604	11004	11546	12196
55-59	6804	7265	7526	7649	7898	8291	8570	9039	9403	9880	10382
60-64	5522	5905	6120	6204	6426	6803	7043	7408	7696	8118	8541
65-69	4149	4455	4626	4660	4855	5203	5407	5679	5891	6221	6574
70-74	2758	2980	3109	3105	3256	3558	3718	3902	4050	4285	4537
75-79	1538	1668	1753	1734	1834	2056	2170	2276	2368	2517	2674
80+	805	865	909	908	952	1077	1167	1247	1305	1394	1492

AGE	1856	1861	1866
0- 4	22343	24061	24722
5- 9	21024	19775	21456
10-14	20575	19819	18776
15-19	18977	19417	18865
20-24	18172	17508	18146
25-29	17308	16969	16495
30-34	16667	16263	16063
35-39	15057	15595	15325
40-44	13224	14036	14636
45-49	12414	12277	13116
50-54	11801	11422	11368
55-59	10698	10627	10352
60-64	8702	9250	9249
65-69	6671	7055	7547
70-74	4587	4876	5189
75-79	2679	2873	3073
80+	1500	1601	1723

[388]

MORTALITY PATTERN: WEST
MIGRATION: GRADUAL, WITH CHILD MIGRANTS SUBTRACTED AFTER 1851, AND TOTALS
  OBTAINED IN 1871, 1876 AND 1881 BY LINEAR INTERPOLATION BETWEEN 1866 AND 1886

TABLE 1 FEMALE POPULATION ESTIMATES: 1801 TO 1906

DATE	R/CB RATIO	% COR-RECTION	FINAL POPULATION ESTIMATE	DATE	R/CB RATIO	% COR-RECTION	FINAL POPULATION ESTIMATE
1801	0.952	0.0	117369	1856	0.960	-0.6	159752
1806	0.974	0.0	119253	1861	0.959	-1.2	161432
1811*	0.970	0.0	122436	1866	0.949	-1.7	164582
1816*	0.957	0.0	125619	1871	0.929	-1.4	164534
1821	0.941	0.0	128802	1876	0.934	-4.1	163452
1826*	0.951	0.0	134384	1881	0.900	-3.1	163909
1831	0.985	0.0	139966	1886	0.889	-4.1	162727
1836	1.001	0.0	146667	1891	0.870	-4.1	161262
1841	0.999	0.0	150808	1896	0.844	-4.1	157583
1846	1.000	0.0	158370	1901	0.821	-4.0	153243
1851	0.990	0.0	160255	1906	0.801	-4.1	149421

NOTE: R/CB RATIO REFERS TO THE POPULATION COMPUTED BY THE BALANCE OF BIRTHS
       AND DEATHS OVER THE REPORTED POPULATION
* INTERPOLATED VALUES

TABLE 2 FEMALE BIRTH ESTIMATES: 1801-1805 TO 1901-1905

DATE	% COR-RECTION	FINAL BIRTH ESTIMATE	CRUDE BIRTH RATE	DATE	% COR-RECTION	FINAL BIRTH ESTIMATE	CRUDE BIRTH RATE
1801-1805	0.0	20968	35.4	1856-1860	0.0	22789	28.4
1806-1810	0.0	21795	36.1	1861-1865	0.0	23425	28.7
1811-1815	0.0	22374	36.1	1866-1870	0.0	21826	26.5
1816-1820	0.0	22764	35.8	1871-1875	0.0	21002	25.6
1821-1825	0.0	22382	34.0	1876-1880	0.0	20446	25.0
1826-1830	0.0	22863	33.3	1881-1885	0.0	18774	23.0
1831-1835	0.0	23912	33.4	1886-1890	0.0	17893	22.1
1836-1840	4.5	24293	32.7	1891-1895	0.0	16085	20.2
1841-1845	0.0	24728	32.0	1896-1900	0.0	14692	18.9
1846-1850	0.0	24109	30.3	1901-1905	0.0	13786	18.2
1851-1855	0.0	22788	28.5				

TABLE 3 FEMALE POPULATION ESTIMATES,
DISTRIBUTION BY AGE: 1801 TO 1906

AGE	1801	1806	1811	1816	1821	1826	1831	1836	1841	1846	1851
0- 4	15233	13505	15249	16011	16507	16617	16249	17961	18101	19687	18190
5- 9	12714	12969	11732	13307	14016	14793	14807	14665	15999	16585	17510
10-14	11909	12468	12470	11211	12683	13675	14677	14511	14144	15546	15852
15-19	11165	11678	11985	11912	10681	12369	13564	14378	13990	13737	14827
20-24	10317	10771	11083	11314	11222	10300	12106	13142	13714	13471	12925
25-29	9424	9816	10112	10359	10558	10720	9968	11622	12423	13111	12608
30-34	8528	8865	9134	9375	9592	10008	10278	9497	10905	11807	12213
35-39	7633	7930	8174	8397	8612	9020	9505	9716	8844	10301	10925
40-44	6782	7033	7256	7460	7660	8042	8499	8924	8987	8305	9474
45-49	5979	6198	6387	6574	6756	7101	7520	7922	8195	8382	7587
50-54	5167	5340	5519	5680	5847	6151	6508	6886	7149	7526	7532
55-59	4293	4418	4588	4746	4890	5153	5433	5772	6021	6391	6565
60-64	3340	3410	3573	3726	3868	4080	4274	4565	4787	5144	5298
65-69	2359	2377	2519	2665	2797	2972	3083	3312	3496	3816	3953
70-74	1456	1447	1547	1665	1778	1910	1972	2126	2262	2513	2625
75-79	730	707	772	846	923	1009	1033	1133	1213	1381	1452
80+	324	322	337	371	412	463	491	535	580	667	721

AGE	1856	1861	1866	1871	1876	1881	1886	1891	1896	1901	1906
0- 4	17942	17683	18753	17140	16477	16904	15507	14924	13794	12458	11992
5- 9	16184	16131	16073	16891	15411	15083	15493	14273	13766	12730	11611
10-14	16421	15511	15480	15373	16155	14770	14482	14928	13676	13250	12282
15-19	14663	15642	14721	14585	14422	15085	13758	13515	13591	12635	12272
20-24	13285	13683	14478	13394	13118	12664	13296	12043	10968	11632	10771
25-29	11729	12418	12763	13397	12305	11969	11541	12187	10618	9848	10549
30-34	11569	10971	11660	11923	12510	11556	11254	10887	11468	10012	9319
35-39	11178	10769	10265	10859	11104	11770	10885	10641	10311	10883	9541
40-44	9975	10358	10048	9537	10097	10458	11106	10314	10160	9823	10428
45-49	8608	9187	9613	9290	8830	9481	9839	10492	9848	9662	9396
50-54	6808	7810	8411	8766	8487	8208	8827	9200	9938	9277	9162
55-59	6588	6009	6970	7467	7793	7703	7464	8064	8532	9149	8612
60-64	5480	5535	5118	5888	6311	6747	6676	6508	7127	7503	8130
65-69	4140	4286	4410	4032	4638	5132	5490	5470	5425	5902	6298
70-74	2796	2911	3087	3130	2860	3427	3791	4089	4162	4093	4529
75-79	1585	1663	1787	1858	1882	1814	2171	2425	2687	2706	2719
80+	802	864	947	1003	1049	1140	1147	1303	1513	1682	1809

TABLE 4 MARRIED WOMEN ESTIMATES,
DISTRIBUTION BY AGE: 1831 TO 1901

AGE	1831	1836	1841	1846	1851	1856	1861	1866
15-19	966	1057	1064	1084	1218	1258	1791	1693
20-24	5270	5871	6276	6320	6214	6549	6921	7381
25-29	7034	8300	8992	9620	9360	8809	9437	9844
30-34	8182	7601	8798	9609	9991	9516	9076	9760
35-39	7711	7893	7226	8476	9007	9242	8936	8638
40-44	6813	7128	7206	6701	7632	8036	8359	8259
45-49	5692	5963	6203	6404	5782	6560	7018	7547

AGE	1871	1876	1881	1886	1891	1896	1901
15-19	1428	1301	1296	1142	1010	958	1016
20-24	6808	7115	6947	7052	6258	5693	5879
25-29	10048	9229	9446	9223	9588	8318	7777
30-34	9921	10264	9516	9516	9214	9683	8443
35-39	9006	9231	9760	9065	8903	8676	9133
40-44	7634	8089	8456	9006	8273	8229	7936
45-49	7007	6667	7259	7608	7980	7558	7387

TABLE 5 DEMOGRAPHIC INDICES AND FEMALE SINGULATE MEAN AGE
AT MARRIAGE: 1831 TO 1901

DATE	IF OVERALL FERTILITY	IG MARITAL FERTILITY	IH ILLEGITIMATE FERTILITY	IM PROPORTION MARRIED	SINGULATE MEAN AGE AT MARRIAGE
1831	0.361	0.605	0.026	0.579	23.7
1836	0.353	0.574	0.047	0.580	23.5
1841	0.347	0.557	0.044	0.592	23.3
1846	0.335	0.524	0.039	0.610	23.2
1851	0.317	0.488	0.045	0.615	23.0
1856	0.311	0.479	0.039	0.619	22.7
1861	0.310	0.474	0.039	0.623	22.5
1866	0.299	0.449	0.039	0.635	22.7
1871	0.284	0.432	0.034	0.629	22.7
1876	0.278	0.418	0.032	0.636	22.4
1881	0.265	0.394	0.033	0.642	22.5
1886	0.253	0.371	0.035	0.647	22.6
1891	0.241	0.357	0.032	0.644	22.7
1896	0.229	0.339	0.030	0.642	22.6
1901	0.218	0.325	0.028	0.640	

MORTALITY PATTERN: NORTH
MIGRATION: NO CORRECTION MADE FOR MIGRATION BY AGE

TABLE 1 FEMALE POPULATION ESTIMATES: 1801 TO 1906

DATE	R/CB RATIO	% COR- RECTION	FINAL POPULATION ESTIMATE	DATE	R/CB RATIO	% COR- RECTION	FINAL POPULATION ESTIMATE
1801	0.955	4.2	412013	1856	1.005	0.0	601482
1806	0.995	0.0	426760	1861	1.019	0.0	640295
1811*	0.982	0.0	439978	1866	1.038	0.0	683304
1816*	0.971	0.0	453197	1871	1.033	0.0	712143
1821	0.964	0.0	466415	1876	1.042	0.0	752341
1826*	0.961	0.0	485803	1881	1.038	0.0	788930
1831	0.975	0.0	505191	1886	1.037	0.0	830629
1836	0.988	0.0	521812	1891	1.037	0.0	868576
1841	0.988	0.0	541323	1896	1.049	0.0	914054
1846	1.000	0.0	566408	1901	1.034	0.0	941899
1851	0.997	0.0	576631	1906	1.013	0.0	960166

NOTE: R/CB RATIO REFERS TO THE POPULATION COMPUTED BY THE BALANCE OF BIRTHS
       AND DEATHS OVER THE REPORTED POPULATION
* INTERPOLATED VALUES

TABLE 2 FEMALE BIRTH ESTIMATES: 1801-1805 TO 1901-1905

DATE	% COR- RECTION	FINAL BIRTH ESTIMATE	CRUDE BIRTH RATE	DATE	% COR- RECTION	FINAL BIRTH ESTIMATE	CRUDE BIRTH RATE
1801-1805	0.0	71586	34.1	1856-1860	0.0	103355	33.3
1806-1810	9.8	72613	33.5	1861-1865	0.0	108027	32.6
1811-1815	8.1	73717	33.0	1866-1870	0.0	115754	33.2
1816-1820	0.0	76571	33.3	1871-1875	0.0	118529	32.4
1821-1825	0.0	82434	34.6	1876-1880	0.0	123259	32.0
1826-1830	0.0	79732	32.2	1881-1885	0.0	124343	30.7
1831-1835	3.0	84097	32.8	1886-1890	0.0	122040	28.7
1836-1840	0.0	85402	32.1	1891-1895	0.0	124213	27.9
1841-1845	0.0	85681	30.9	1896-1900	0.0	126257	27.2
1846-1850	6.5	89602	31.4	1901-1905	0.0	119524	25.1
1851-1855	0.0	91734	31.1				

TABLE 3 FEMALE POPULATION ESTIMATES,
DISTRIBUTION BY AGE: 1801 TO 1906

AGE	1801	1806	1811	1816	1821	1826	1831	1836	1841	1846	1851
0- 4	63996	54524	55305	56242	57994	63145	61243	63200	66441	68100	68146
5- 9	51085	54889	46664	47414	48066	50005	54825	52475	55098	58905	58458
10-14	44925	48007	51359	43739	44492	45392	47754	52149	49872	53010	55535
15-19	40193	42940	45669	48942	41762	42731	44122	46313	50361	48712	50854
20-24	35839	38277	40701	43363	46558	39963	41382	42627	44566	49018	46559
25-29	31773	33907	36048	38397	40976	44263	38441	39693	40761	43115	46540
30-34	27893	29816	31678	33737	35983	38641	42218	36536	37661	39142	40595
35-39	24267	25940	27611	29386	31326	33628	36512	39722	34369	35870	36515
40-44	20984	22397	23842	25422	27076	29054	31529	34071	37092	32502	33206
45-49	18011	19250	20461	21819	23281	24961	27074	29235	31626	34872	29904
50-54	15271	16327	17380	18507	19743	21209	22980	24790	26823	29397	31701
55-59	12593	13477	14357	15310	16297	17512	18996	20438	22164	24316	26007
60-64	9887	10590	11302	12061	12838	13777	14927	16028	17443	19209	20482
65-69	7154	7680	8212	8779	9331	10027	10825	11555	12668	14034	14928
70-74	4559	4898	5259	5633	5977	6425	6922	7308	8082	9053	9594
75-79	2417	2593	2793	3004	3178	3421	3670	3825	4271	4850	5128
80+	1174	1249	1339	1442	1535	1649	1772	1847	2024	2306	2480

AGE	1856	1861	1866	1871	1876	1881	1886	1891	1896	1901	1906
0- 4	72990	83741	88680	92396	96458	100565	103041	101549	104094	105111	100327
5- 9	60391	65611	75913	78393	83049	86414	91041	93501	92955	94002	95149
10-14	56133	58593	63909	72306	75727	79509	83205	87720	91019	88702	89400
15-19	54123	55234	57831	61715	70778	73384	77418	81045	86350	87718	85091
20-24	49388	53074	54334	55656	60208	68364	71227	75171	79526	82963	83891
25-29	44947	48151	51920	51993	53996	57849	66022	68819	73393	76051	78995
30-34	44601	43515	46792	49343	50107	51560	55543	63429	66802	69816	72065
35-39	38591	42847	41978	44133	47204	47518	49186	53027	61176	63176	65804
40-44	34469	36821	41061	39326	41942	44483	45057	46678	50834	57525	59221
45-49	31163	32700	35087	38248	37163	39306	41951	42530	44506	47549	53645
50-54	27749	29237	30824	32326	35754	34463	36690	39197	40137	41220	43918
55-59	28697	25415	26927	27732	29523	32428	31491	33569	36213	36435	37355
60-64	22520	25176	22457	23220	24298	25739	28532	27759	29864	31728	31930
65-69	16477	18392	20757	18043	18981	19822	21244	23614	23167	24631	26245
70-74	10679	12003	13574	14897	13202	13922	14765	15889	17788	17336	18559
75-79	5773	6571	7519	8244	9249	8266	8897	9490	10269	11500	11345
80+	2793	3216	3741	4172	4704	5335	5316	5589	5961	6436	7224

TABLE 4   MARRIED WOMEN ESTIMATES,
DISTRIBUTION BY AGE: 1831 TO 1901

AGE	1831	1836	1841	1846	1851	1856	1861	1866
15-19	1085	1164	1295	1284	1376	1504	1705	1815
20-24	10492	11010	11751	13190	12774	13838	15195	14676
25-29	20810	21740	22634	24247	26457	25870	28057	30601
30-34	28789	25093	26132	27395	28568	31638	31108	33666
35-39	26462	28928	25273	26566	27109	28833	32212	31692
40-44	23343	25272	27773	24478	24982	26063	27981	31272
45-49	18821	20376	22356	24862	21282	22343	23618	25421

AGE	1871	1876	1881	1886	1891	1896	1901
15-19	2048	2540	2422	2081	1821	1973	3301
20-24	16632	19627	21215	20591	21472	23805	25642
25-29	28984	32114	36336	40093	40249	43790	47693
30-34	35590	35040	37246	41569	46528	48345	51154
35-39	33258	35704	35378	37563	40808	46810	48021
40-44	29747	31784	33761	33933	35052	38319	43057
45-49	27422	26712	28313	30933	30871	32097	33763

TABLE 5   DEMOGRAPHIC INDICES AND FEMALE SINGULATE MEAN AGE
AT MARRIAGE: 1831 TO 1901

DATE	IF OVERALL FERTILITY	IG MARITAL FERTILITY	IH ILLEGITIMATE FERTILITY	IM PROPORTION MARRIED	SINGULATE MEAN AGE AT MARRIAGE
1831	0.344	0.658	0.059	0.476	26.0
1836	0.351	0.672	0.059	0.476	25.9
1841	0.347	0.676	0.054	0.472	25.8
1846	0.343	0.660	0.056	0.476	25.7
1851	0.349	0.664	0.056	0.483	25.6
1856	0.360	0.674	0.063	0.486	25.5
1861	0.371	0.684	0.066	0.492	25.4
1866	0.374	0.684	0.073	0.493	25.4
1871	0.380	0.698	0.074	0.491	25.1
1876	0.368	0.670	0.074	0.494	25.0
1881	0.354	0.640	0.074	0.495	25.1
1886	0.330	0.595	0.074	0.493	25.4
1891	0.310	0.561	0.070	0.488	25.4
1896	0.293	0.520	0.071	0.495	25.1
1901	0.276	0.478	0.066	0.509	

MORTALITY PATTERN: NORTH
MIGRATION: NO CORRECTION MADE FOR MIGRATION BY AGE

TABLE 1   FEMALE POPULATION ESTIMATES: 1801 TO 1906

DATE	R/CB RATIO	% COR-RECTION	FINAL POPULATION ESTIMATE	DATE	R/CB RATIO	% COR-RECTION	FINAL POPULATION ESTIMATE
1801	0.988	2.9	184797	1856	0.997	0.0	201497
1806	1.008	0.0	187733	1861	1.003	0.0	201672
1811*	1.010	0.0	190083	1866	1.007	0.0	201426
1816*	1.006	0.0	192432	1871	1.003	0.0	199651
1821	0.995	0.0	194782	1876	1.018	0.0	201177
1826*	0.998	0.0	199774	1881	1.022	0.0	201891
1831	1.010	0.0	204765	1886	1.019	0.0	201748
1836	1.006	0.0	204144	1891	1.027	0.0	202484
1841	0.997	0.0	204050	1896	1.043	0.0	204026
1846	1.000	0.0	206365	1901	1.043	0.0	203759
1851	0.998	0.0	204207	1906	1.045	0.0	205428

NOTE: R/CB RATIO REFERS TO THE POPULATION COMPUTED BY THE BALANCE OF BIRTHS
       AND DEATHS OVER THE REPORTED POPULATION
* INTERPOLATED VALUES

TABLE 2   FEMALE BIRTH ESTIMATES: 1801-1805 TO 1901-1905

DATE	% COR-RECTION	FINAL BIRTH ESTIMATE	CRUDE BIRTH RATE	DATE	% COR-RECTION	FINAL BIRTH ESTIMATE	CRUDE BIRTH RATE
1801-1805	14.8	28197	30.3	1856-1860	0.0	23118	22.9
1806-1810	7.2	27243	28.8	1861-1865	0.0	22431	22.3
1811-1815	5.8	28478	29.8	1866-1870	0.0	22361	22.3
1816-1820	0.0	26751	27.6	1871-1875	0.0	21813	21.8
1821-1825	0.0	26603	27.0	1876-1880	0.0	21762	21.6
1826-1830	0.0	25375	25.1	1881-1885	0.0	21671	21.5
1831-1835	0.0	24344	23.8	1886-1890	0.0	20858	20.6
1836-1840	0.0	23393	22.9	1891-1895	0.0	21708	21.4
1841-1845	0.0	23547	22.9	1896-1900	0.0	21556	21.1
1846-1850	0.0	23194	22.6	1901-1905	0.0	21203	20.7
1851-1855	0.0	22338	22.0				

TABLE 3 FEMALE POPULATION ESTIMATES,
DISTRIBUTION BY AGE: 1801 TO 1906

AGE	1801	1806	1811	1816	1821	1826	1831	1836	1841	1846	1851
0- 4	27148	21663	20491	21270	20782	21113	20371	19062	18778	19253	18367
5- 9	22129	23341	18483	17396	18439	18354	18833	17786	16879	16888	16945
10-14	19646	20711	21987	17363	16372	17631	17696	17837	16905	16250	16073
15-19	17734	18679	19872	21047	16590	15885	17245	17015	17175	16479	15689
20-24	15937	16801	17855	18950	20040	16042	15484	16523	16329	16687	15856
25-29	14243	15005	15949	16907	17934	19263	15545	14746	15770	15780	15962
30-34	12635	13308	14120	14968	15892	17114	18534	14695	13982	15143	14987
35-39	11123	11705	12402	13122	13945	15035	16338	17378	13833	13333	14269
40-44	9710	10230	10822	11433	12138	13109	14254	15210	16252	13107	12477
45-49	8436	8877	9399	9913	10514	11344	12357	13193	14145	15313	12194
50-54	7236	7624	8057	8504	9013	9716	10574	11307	12137	13186	14088
55-59	6065	6374	6728	7084	7540	8127	8839	9438	10166	11063	11839
60-64	4845	5103	5346	5618	6004	6505	7078	7543	8143	8902	9508
65-69	3592	3777	3937	4103	4419	4815	5270	5609	6076	6666	7115
70-74	2356	2481	2553	2642	2866	3154	3475	3710	4048	4467	4747
75-79	1299	1362	1381	1408	1549	1721	1920	2055	2275	2536	2681
80+	663	692	701	704	756	845	953	1037	1157	1313	1409

AGE	1856	1861	1866	1871	1876	1881	1886	1891	1896	1901	1906
0- 4	17735	18729	18424	18300	18261	18349	18282	17686	18301	18188	18338
5- 9	16203	15885	16889	16534	16756	16724	16760	16820	16261	16742	16909
10-14	16160	15610	15306	16176	16120	16236	16115	16299	16423	15714	16296
15-19	15549	15778	15224	14835	15953	15778	15795	15829	16088	16026	15415
20-24	15126	15131	15338	14703	14583	15566	15303	15467	15574	15651	15673
25-29	15198	14637	14632	14741	14385	14162	15029	14915	15143	15081	15241
30-34	15191	14608	14067	13977	14332	13895	13603	14570	14520	14587	14619
35-39	14151	14493	13942	13346	13500	13762	13271	13111	14095	13906	14069
40-44	13380	13411	13745	13146	12913	12888	13070	12717	12608	13422	13340
45-49	11632	12609	12649	12889	12552	12167	12176	12458	12164	11942	12810
50-54	11242	10842	11768	11738	12190	11801	11383	11492	11795	11409	11291
55-59	12675	10236	9898	10683	10856	11222	10825	10530	10655	10844	10589
60-64	10198	11069	8383	8641	9510	9649	9941	9663	9405	9456	9744
65-69	7619	8305	9090	7343	7211	7952	8054	8353	8104	7859	8030
70-74	5379	5549	6133	6687	5526	5465	6029	6138	6329	6146	6091
75-79	2857	3137	3499	3857	4312	3613	3587	3969	3997	4149	4147
80+	1502	1643	1840	2051	2329	2662	2528	2468	2565	2638	2826

TABLE 4 MARRIED WOMEN ESTIMATES,
DISTRIBUTICN BY AGE: 1831 TO 1901

AGE	1831	1836	1841	1846	1851	1856	1861	1866
15-19	1407	1420	1467	1443	1410	1435	1825	1768
20-24	7898	8543	8564	8879	8555	8276	8397	8901
25-29	11861	11321	12193	12286	12500	11969	11593	11638
30-34	15240	12119	11587	12607	12513	12716	12266	11818
35-39	13393	14275	11421	11063	11865	11788	12105	11629
40-44	11294	12069	12977	10532	10044	10787	1C844	11077
45-49	9248	9894	10709	11703	9345	8934	9727	9708

AGE	1871	1876	1881	1886	1891	1896	1901
15-19	1609	1714	1574	1325	1136	1182	1501
20-24	8702	8605	8981	8525	8338	8442	8461
25-29	11794	11601	11450	12047	11805	11964	12091
30-34	11729	12032	11698	11486	12228	12122	12227
35-39	11085	11203	11416	11042	10870	11631	11479
40-44	10514	10225	10276	10462	10114	9970	10610
45-49	9779	9490	9188	9248	9371	9069	8907

TABLE 5 DEMOGRAPHIC INDICES AND FEMALE SINGULATE MEAN AGE
AT MARRIAGE: 1831 TO 1901

DATE	IF OVERALL FERTILITY	IG MARITAL FERTILITY	IH ILLEGITIMATE FERTILITY	IM PROPORTION MARRIED	SINGULATE MEAN AGE AT MARRIAGE
1831	0.253	0.365	0.049	0.646	22.6
1836	0.248	0.359	0.049	0.642	22.5
1841	0.251	0.365	0.046	0.641	22.4
1846	0.252	0.363	0.046	0.648	22.3
1851	0.249	0.355	0.047	0.657	22.2
1856	0.253	0.357	0.049	0.663	22.0
1861	0.255	0.357	0.053	0.667	21.8
1866	0.254	0.350	0.057	0.673	21.8
1871	0.256	0.352	0.057	0.676	21.7
1876	0.251	0.348	0.055	0.671	21.8
1881	0.249	0.344	0.058	0.667	21.9
1886	0.243	0.339	0.057	0.660	22.1
1891	0.241	0.337	0.063	0.651	22.2
1896	0.241	0.335	0.066	0.651	22.2
1901	0.238	0.329	0.064	0.656	

MORTALITY PATTERN: WEST
MIGRATION: GRADUAL, WITH CHILD MIGRANTS SUBTRACTED AFTER 1861, AND TOTALS
OBTAINED IN 1871 AND 1876 BY LINEAR INTERPOLATION BETWEEN 1866 AND 1881

TABLE 1 FEMALE POPULATION ESTIMATES: 1801 TO 1906

DATE	R/CB RATIO	% COR- RECTION	FINAL POPULATION ESTIMATE	DATE	R/CB RATIO	% COR- RECTION	FINAL POPULATION ESTIMATE
1801	0.980	4.6	215268	1856	C.975	0.0	224215
1806	1.025	0.0	217218	1861	0.963	0.0	219297
1811*	1.031	0.0	218342	1866	0.953	-0.4	213092
1816*	1.021	0.0	219467	1871	0.935	-0.5	205109
1821	1.004	0.0	220591	1876	0.946	-3.2	196245
1826*	1.007	0.0	225714	1881	0.916	-1.7	189359
1831	1.019	0.0	230837	1886	0.903	-2.2	182908
1836	1.016	0.0	231890	1891	0.899	-2.6	177315
1841	1.006	0.0	231527	1896	0.887	-2.6	168834
1846	1.000	0.0	231146	1901	C.876	-2.5	162799
1851	0.986	0.0	228268	1906	0.866	-2.7	157072

NOTE: R/CB RATIO REFERS TO THE POPULATION COMPUTED BY THE BALANCE OF BIRTHS
       AND DEATHS OVER THE REPORTED POPULATION
* INTERPOLATED VALUES

TABLE 2 FEMALE BIRTH ESTIMATES: 1801-1805 TO 1901-1905

DATE	% COR- RECTION	FINAL BIRTH ESTIMATE	CRUDE BIRTH RATE	DATE	% COR- RECTION	FINAL BIRTH ESTIMATE	CRUDE BIRTH RATE
1801-1805	0.0	26807	24.8	1856-1860	0.0	19934	18.0
1806-1810	0.0	24903	22.9	1861-1865	0.0	19415	18.0
1811-1815	0.0	25630	23.4	1866-1870	0.0	18921	18.1
1816-1820	0.0	25567	23.2	1871-1875	0.0	18135	18.1
1821-1825	0.0	24817	22.2	1876-1880	0.0	17590	18.2
1826-1830	0.0	23954	21.0	1881-1885	0.0	17230	18.5
1831-1835	0.0	23217	20.1	1886-1890	0.0	15623	17.3
1836-1840	4.5	22706	19.6	1891-1895	0.0	14416	16.7
1841-1845	0.0	21232	18.4	1896-190C	0.0	14287	17.2
1846-1850	0.0	20574	17.9	1901-1905	0.0	13862	17.3
1851-1855	0.0	20570	18.2				

TABLE 3 FEMALE POPULATION ESTIMATES,
DISTRIBUTION BY AGE: 1801 TO 1906

AGE	1801	1806	1811	1816	1821	1826	1831	1836	1841	1846	1851
0- 4	22804	21015	19577	20712	21066	21112	20499	19798	19519	18610	18044
5- 9	20544	20864	19289	18001	19120	19911	20079	19285	18622	18528	17569
10-14	19594	20085	20467	18699	17382	18823	19725	19601	18734	18149	17919
15-19	18673	19147	19694	19831	18046	17102	18637	19245	19026	18243	17472
20-24	17661	18077	18599	18930	19004	17638	16821	18069	18567	18427	17368
25-29	16575	16963	17421	17760	18034	18472	17252	16225	17346	17902	17574
30-34	15480	15818	16243	16545	16837	17450	17987	16571	15515	16666	17083
35-39	14375	14674	15045	15338	15605	16214	16910	17198	15780	14849	15855
40-44	13273	13543	13871	14127	14391	14952	15632	16089	16300	15034	14074
45-49	12167	12419	12713	12938	13169	13700	14323	14779	15154	15432	14164
50-54	10986	11200	11470	11683	11892	12367	12946	13363	13742	14169	14367
55-59	9673	9829	10052	10274	10485	10915	11421	11814	12163	12590	12932
60-64	8147	8244	8406	8624	8857	9259	9698	10042	10375	10771	11107
65-69	6401	6456	6554	6748	6985	7364	7746	8042	8331	8698	9005
70-74	4542	4556	4609	4760	4967	5289	5610	5861	6098	6399	6670
75-79	2749	2728	2745	2856	3008	3240	3471	3667	3849	4069	4269
80+	1626	1601	1588	1640	1743	1908	2079	2240	2407	2610	2796

AGE	1856	1861	1866	1871	1876	1881	1886	1891	1896	1901	1906
0- 4	17763	17040	16672	15865	14979	14863	14880	13335	11942	12181	11829
5- 9	16939	16627	15896	15393	14565	13877	13824	13949	12318	11159	11400
10-14	17003	16419	16030	15292	14805	14051	13347	13463	13522	11975	10851
15-19	17221	16345	15568	15132	14408	13954	13012	12805	12816	12927	11448
20-24	16515	16252	15002	14135	13681	12956	12038	12103	11722	11798	11982
25-29	16504	15689	15229	13957	13103	12695	11794	11384	11328	11026	11137
30-34	16752	15747	14891	14405	13174	12425	12018	11292	10819	10832	10552
35-39	16238	15939	14934	14072	13589	12499	11807	11491	10719	10336	10356
40-44	15021	15399	15093	14093	13257	12891	11915	11267	10892	10231	9869
45-49	13258	14165	14511	14176	13216	12523	12254	11314	10623	10350	9723
50-54	13183	12351	13197	13467	13129	12341	11789	11495	10538	9983	9720
55-59	13092	12016	11267	11973	12176	11983	11370	10815	10448	9677	9167
60-64	11364	11489	10544	9805	10363	10659	10588	10024	9409	9211	8534
65-69	9228	9413	9524	8640	7970	8546	8895	8800	8185	7818	7657
70-74	6843	6980	7132	7108	6379	5990	6517	6743	6522	6201	5927
75-79	4394	4476	4579	4585	4503	4132	3953	4264	4284	4263	4057
80+	2895	2952	3024	3010	2950	2975	2909	2771	2739	2831	2863

TABLE 4   MARRIED WOMEN ESTIMATES,
DISTRIBUTICN BY AGE: 1831 TO 1901

AGE	1831	1836	1841	1846	1851	1856	1861	1866
15-19	714	769	799	813	834	923	1065	973
20-24	4516	5048	5425	5654	5620	5657	5889	5397
25-29	8752	8504	9419	10074	10250	9969	9814	9849
30-34	11368	10729	10316	11368	11939	11970	11495	11074
35-39	11520	11927	11180	10729	11666	12129	12077	11438
40-44	11697	12063	12319	11438	10769	11525	11852	11615
45-49	10123	10465	10850	11148	10310	9679	10380	10620

AGE	1871	1876	1881	1886	1891	1896	1901
15-19	945	835	748	699	670	671	821
20-24	5368	5424	5240	4919	4916	4833	4795
25-29	8693	8503	8484	8056	7929	7897	7808
30-34	10865	9682	9335	9188	8766	8505	8566
35-39	10831	10532	9524	9120	8996	8433	8204
40-44	10769	10107	9811	8946	8578	8296	7792
45-49	10254	9516	8984	8818	8233	7683	7430

TABLE 5   DEMOGRAPHIC INDICES AND FEMALE SINGULATE MEAN AGE
AT MARRIAGE: 1831 TO 1901

DATE	IF OVERALL FERTILITY	IG MARITAL FERTILITY	IH ILLEGITIMATE FERTILITY	IM PROPORTION MARRIED	SINGULATE MEAN AGE AT MARRIAGE
1831	0.226	0.475	0.007	0.469	26.6
1836	0.220	0.455	0.009	0.474	26.1
1841	0.212	0.429	0.010	0.482	25.8
1846	0.202	0.394	0.013	0.497	25.4
1851	0.202	0.376	0.016	0.518	25.1
1856	0.204	0.364	0.019	0.535	24.7
1861	0.204	0.352	0.022	0.552	24.4
1866	0.209	0.357	0.021	0.560	24.4
1871	0.214	0.366	0.021	0.560	24.2
1876	0.218	0.369	0.023	0.564	24.0
1881	0.223	0.376	0.023	0.568	23.8
1886	0.224	0.372	0.024	0.576	23.8
1891	0.211	0.346	0.027	0.579	23.8
1896	0.208	0.340	0.028	0.579	23.7
1901	0.207	0.338	0.026	0.580	

MORTALITY PATTERN: NORTH
MIGRATION: GRADUAL, WITH POPULATION TOTALS OBTAINED BY TREND OF R/CB

TABLE 1   FEMALE POPULATION ESTIMATES: 1801 TO 1906

DATE	R/CB RATIO	% COR-RECTION	FINAL POPULATION ESTIMATE	DATE	R/CB RATIO	% COR-RECTION	FINAL POPULATION ESTIMATE
1801	0.947	9.5	283555	1856	0.964	0.1	353312
1806	1.026	0.0	288718	1861	0.959	0.2	363440
1811*	1.034	0.0	300157	1866	0.956	0.1	373426
1816*	1.035	0.0	311596	1871	0.948	0.7	381660
1821	1.033	0.0	323035	1876	0.960	-1.0	391091
1826*	1.012	0.0	329499	1881	0.945	0.2	404958
1831	1.010	0.0	335962	1886	0.944	-0.1	419241
1836	1.014	0.0	339976	1891	0.943	-0.4	435261
1841	1.009	0.0	347595	1896	0.931	0.4	453197
1846	1.000	0.0	354024	1901	0.919	1.4	474819
1851	0.972	-0.4	348657	1906	0.939	-1.1	499694

NOTE: R/CB RATIO REFERS TO THE POPULATION COMPUTED BY THE BALANCE OF BIRTHS
       AND DEATHS OVER THE REPORTED POPULATION
* INTERPOLATED VALUES

TABLE 2   FEMALE BIRTH ESTIMATES: 1801-1805 TO 1901-1905

DATE	% COR-RECTION	FINAL BIRTH ESTIMATE	CRUDE BIRTH RATE	DATE	% COR-RECTION	FINAL BIRTH ESTIMATE	CRUDE BIRTH RATE
1801-1805	7.2	44396	31.0	1856-1860	0.0	52142	29.1
1806-1810	1.5	42984	29.2	1861-1865	0.0	53438	29.0
1811-1815	0.0	44595	29.2	1866-1870	0.0	54932	29.1
1816-1820	0.0	45778	28.9	1871-1875	0.0	56576	29.3
1821-1825	0.0	48302	29.6	1876-1880	0.0	59539	29.9
1826-1830	0.0	46770	28.1	1881-1885	0.0	61666	29.9
1831-1835	0.0	47240	28.0	1886-1890	0.0	62226	29.1
1836-1840	0.0	47200	27.5	1891-1895	0.0	65713	29.6
1841-1845	4.5	48178	27.5	1896-1900	0.0	69055	29.8
1846-1850	6.7	48494	27.6	1901-1905	0.0	71418	29.3
1851-1855	0.0	45857	26.1				

TABLE 3 FEMALE POPULATION ESTIMATES,
DISTRIBUTION BY AGE: 1801 TO 1906

AGE	1801	1806	1811	1816	1821	1826	1831	1836	1841	1846	1851
0- 4	40908	34151	34047	35551	36782	38221	36805	36317	37861	38685	37466
5- 9	33473	35185	30172	30141	31589	32157	33505	31876	32190	33533	33141
10-14	29835	31316	33733	28856	28817	29690	30549	31807	30376	30600	31055
15-19	27031	28350	30480	32724	27963	27447	28627	29499	30716	29253	28600
20-24	24384	25595	27497	29468	31604	26545	26372	27543	28391	29482	27005
25-29	21877	22945	24675	26428	28299	29834	25353	25207	26361	27101	27288
30-34	19483	20431	21957	23549	25210	26536	28287	24034	23964	24999	25040
35-39	17216	18043	19391	20792	22296	23465	24957	26574	22681	22562	22940
40-44	15091	15829	17003	18236	19554	20616	21914	23268	24912	21214	20585
45-49	13164	13793	14829	15898	17053	17979	19141	20306	21689	23170	19257
50-54	11335	11893	12776	13712	14706	15510	16505	17527	18724	19956	20808
55-59	9534	9984	10744	11530	12389	13066	13889	14712	15788	16836	17493
60-64	7648	8022	8623	9285	9990	10559	11193	11796	12712	13625	14113
65-69	5691	5967	6432	6934	7501	7943	8402	8779	9508	10242	10624
70-74	3747	3936	4249	4610	5009	5337	5620	5807	6331	6864	7115
75-79	2372	2170	2354	2570	2823	3023	3175	3225	3552	3884	4020
80+	1065	1109	1197	1310	1450	1573	1669	1700	1838	2018	2109

AGE	1856	1861	1866	1871	1876	1881	1886	1891	1896	1901	1906
0- 4	37038	42388	43733	44528	46042	49256	51047	52239	55265	58854	61906
5- 9	33334	33111	37999	38962	39756	41505	44384	46371	47503	50648	54502
10-14	31623	31901	31675	36263	37211	38103	39754	42644	44583	45788	48990
15-19	29980	30621	30802	30482	34903	35868	36610	38227	41025	42924	44096
20-24	27461	28899	29339	29346	28958	33214	33874	34508	36002	38643	40360
25-29	25835	26357	27656	27973	27957	27620	31594	32238	32828	34275	36821
30-34	25973	24661	25143	26317	26634	26700	26348	30231	30863	31491	32957
35-39	23669	24623	23380	23776	24910	25309	25361	25107	28836	29520	30216
40-44	21549	22299	23214	21988	22388	23561	23944	24088	23868	27504	28263
45-49	19231	20191	20914	21720	20603	21077	22194	22651	22811	22683	26240
50-54	17801	17831	18746	19370	20149	19214	19675	20815	21268	21502	21481
55-59	14799	16136	16196	16975	17573	18395	17561	18086	19155	19667	19998
60-64	15169	16368	14087	14073	14781	15429	16157	15536	16020	17075	17659
65-69	11431	12348	13380	11439	11461	12176	12716	13449	12950	13472	14502
70-74	7715	8354	9084	9751	8370	8522	9060	9595	10166	9914	10455
75-79	4394	4804	5254	5638	6084	5341	5443	5900	6262	6753	6707
80+	2311	2549	2825	3061	3313	3668	3519	3578	3793	4107	4541

TABLE 4 MARRIED WOMEN ESTIMATES,
DISTRIBUTION BY AGE: 1831 TO 1901

AGE	1831	1836	1841	1846	1851	1856	1861	1866
15-19	642	685	741	736	753	830	824	868
20-24	6758	7277	7754	8331	7896	8326	9097	8828
25-29	13554	13762	14724	15475	15902	15379	16021	17149
30-34	18673	16088	16306	17270	17508	18405	17700	18251
35-39	17349	18658	16147	16257	16654	17352	18219	17425
40-44	15413	16435	17789	15278	14858	15651	16291	17017
45-49	12635	13466	14596	15767	13124	13207	13965	14513

AGE	1871	1876	1881	1886	1891	1896	1901
15-19	914	1191	1323	1207	1041	1065	1954
20-24	9408	9699	10963	10968	11645	12822	13871
25-29	16878	17456	17647	19804	19995	21126	23236
30-34	19277	19226	19592	19528	22478	22793	23695
35-39	17794	18756	18882	19027	19238	22036	22470
40-44	16103	16435	17343	17432	18021	17836	20448
45-49	15023	14276	14639	15331	16216	16228	15937

TABLE 5 DEMOGRAPHIC INDICES AND FEMALE SINGULATE MEAN AGE
AT MARRIAGE: 1831 TO 1901

DATE	IF OVERALL FERTILITY	IG MARITAL FERTILITY	IH ILLEGITIMATE FERTILITY	IM PROPORTION MARRIED	SINGULATE MEAN AGE AT MARRIAGE
1831	0.298	0.582	0.048	0.469	25.6
1836	0.300	0.581	0.051	0.470	25.5
1841	0.302	0.583	0.051	0.471	25.3
1846	0.305	0.582	0.048	0.480	25.2
1851	0.305	0.567	0.050	0.493	25.0
1856	0.313	0.569	0.056	0.500	24.8
1861	0.330	0.593	0.063	0.505	24.8
1866	0.334	0.597	0.066	0.506	24.7
1871	0.341	0.607	0.064	0.512	24.5
1876	0.347	0.611	0.069	0.512	24.4
1881	0.347	0.611	0.073	0.509	24.5
1886	0.342	0.593	0.085	0.507	24.5
1891	0.340	0.591	0.076	0.514	24.4
1896	0.342	0.586	0.077	0.521	24.3
1901	0.339	0.573	0.075	0.531	

MORTALITY PATTERN: WEST
MIGRATION: GRADUAL, WITH POPULATION TOTALS OBTAINED BY TREND OF R/CB

TABLE 1   FEMALE POPULATION ESTIMATES: 1801 TO 1906

DATE	R/CB RATIO	% COR- RECTION	FINAL POPULATION ESTIMATE	DATE	R/CB RATIO	% COR- RECTION	FINAL POPULATION ESTIMATE
1801	1.029	4.4	272641	1856	0.977	-0.8	297636
1806	1.074	0.0	276158	1861	0.955	0.5	293654
1811*	1.054	0.0	278967	1866	0.944	0.9	291561
1816*	1.035	0.0	281775	1871	0.936	0.8	289464
1821	1.020	0.0	284584	1876	0.944	-0.9	286154
1826*	1.015	0.0	288835	1881	0.916	1.3	284613
1831	1.010	0.0	293086	1886	0.918	0.2	282424
1836	1.021	0.0	301647	1891	0.911	-0.0	278824
1841	1.003	0.0	301199	1896	0.911	-0.9	272919
1846	1.000	0.0	306262	1901	0.892	0.2	268585
1851	0.984	-0.7	300087	1906	0.890	-0.4	264532

NOTE: R/CB RATIO REFERS TO THE POPULATION COMPUTED BY THE BALANCE OF BIRTHS
        AND DEATHS OVER THE REPORTED POPULATION
* INTERPOLATED VALUES

TABLE 2   FEMALE BIRTH ESTIMATES: 1801-1805 TO 1901-1905

DATE	% COR- RECTION	FINAL BIRTH ESTIMATE	CRUDE BIRTH RATE	DATE	% COR- RECTION	FINAL BIRTH ESTIMATE	CRUDE BIRTH RATE
1801-1805	0.0	43157	31.5	1856-1860	0.0	34052	23.0
1806-1810	0.0	41684	30.0	1861-1865	0.0	33369	22.8
1811-1815	2.6	39319	28.0	1866-1870	0.0	33207	22.9
1816-1820	0.0	40765	28.8	1871-1875	0.0	32129	22.3
1821-1825	0.0	39923	27.8	1876-1880	0.0	31200	21.9
1826-1830	0.0	40487	27.8	1881-1885	0.0	29476	20.8
1831-1835	0.0	40776	27.4	1886-1890	0.0	27431	19.5
1836-1840	0.0	38601	25.6	1891-1895	0.0	24898	18.1
1841-1845	0.0	38924	25.6	1896-1900	0.0	24317	18.0
1846-1850	0.0	36117	23.8	1901-1905	0.0	23037	17.3
1851-1855	0.0	34328	23.0				

TABLE 3 FEMALE POPULATION ESTIMATES,
DISTRIBUTION BY AGE: 1801 TO 1906

AGE	1801	1806	1811	1816	1821	1826	1831	1836	1841	1846	1851
0- 4	33106	31541	31468	30477	31157	30888	31353	32145	30224	31177	27998
5- 9	28652	29205	28304	28238	27256	28132	27909	28790	28958	27744	27854
10-14	26883	27516	27822	26735	27021	26295	27157	27353	27502	28129	26333
15-19	25226	25808	26202	26548	25571	26056	25372	26604	26117	26702	25587
20-24	23498	23946	24335	24780	25152	24429	24907	24625	25185	25146	24850
25-29	21538	22011	22395	22844	23291	23840	23170	23988	23146	24080	23369
30-34	19644	20096	20447	20894	21331	21935	22467	22173	22415	22004	22342
35-39	17807	18183	18538	18956	19378	19955	20533	21358	20591	21182	20304
40-44	16027	16368	16667	17083	17471	18016	18565	19401	19719	19347	19448
45-49	14304	14626	14898	15254	15636	16131	16645	17420	17790	18403	17651
50-54	12556	12819	13093	13421	13735	14204	14663	15369	15729	16351	16536
55-59	10675	10893	11143	11473	11741	12126	12549	13161	13509	14079	14298
60-64	8606	8766	9009	9320	9560	9878	10209	10737	11055	11564	11747
65-69	6403	6509	6726	7020	7214	7477	7732	8125	8416	8840	8995
70-74	4231	4305	4475	4718	4876	5067	5256	5529	5743	6076	6195
75-79	2331	2364	2490	2659	2763	2891	3007	3176	3320	3528	3611
80+	1192	1203	1256	1356	1432	1515	1592	1692	1782	1911	1970

AGE	1856	1861	1866	1871	1876	1881	1886	1891	1896	1901	1906
0- 4	27039	26533	26637	26649	25804	25703	24589	23019	20882	20792	20087
5- 9	25415	24433	24224	24367	24374	23854	23874	22893	21425	19604	19688
10-14	26857	24480	23610	23421	23554	23644	23168	23214	22266	20899	19160
15-19	25312	25769	23529	22667	22437	22619	22691	22233	22281	21464	20159
20-24	25232	23914	24384	22163	21222	21025	21119	21166	20711	20942	20169
25-29	23500	23797	22627	23061	20893	20067	19869	19968	20014	19703	19972
30-34	22029	22110	22508	21419	21826	19876	19129	18968	19070	19207	18968
35-39	20940	20607	20806	21210	20185	20700	18901	18222	18076	18262	18464
40-44	18929	19486	19300	19520	19909	19077	19633	17964	17326	17268	17520
45-49	18012	17501	18137	17998	18217	18711	17998	18563	16995	16468	16485
50-54	16100	16396	16052	16671	16559	16894	17428	16806	17340	15959	15541
55-59	14678	14251	14646	14375	14943	14986	15367	15896	15336	15922	14744
60-64	12115	12382	12162	12533	12309	12952	13068	13444	13909	13537	14163
65-69	9280	9513	9370	9727	10031	10009	10614	10752	11061	11576	11378
70-74	6404	6553	6845	7132	7035	7400	7455	7944	8046	8398	8896
75-79	3741	3825	4011	4213	4393	4445	4734	4798	5110	5273	5590
80+	2054	2108	2214	2338	2462	2652	2786	2974	3070	3310	3549

[405]

TABLE 4 MARRIED WOMEN ESTIMATES,
DISTRIBUTION BY AGE: 1831 TO 1901

AGE	1831	1836	1841	1846	1851	1856	1861	1866
15-19	1087	1162	1163	1249	1262	1198	1063	1087
20-24	8294	8309	8627	8741	8728	8999	8683	8091
25-29	14063	14666	14291	15001	14675	14880	15192	14556
30-34	16044	15888	16185	15988	16310	16164	16306	16670
35-39	15135	15754	15303	15827	15216	15750	15557	15746
40-44	13543	14119	14468	14265	14356	14007	14456	14326
45-49	11478	11955	12347	12853	12336	12620	12295	12739

AGE	1871	1876	1881	1886	1891	1896	1901
15-19	1158	1190	1279	1263	1092	1034	1268
20-24	7626	7896	8207	8357	8186	8010	8083
25-29	14175	12999	13017	13236	13386	13286	13279
30-34	15886	15851	14540	14270	14378	14519	14594
35-39	16020	15297	15562	14249	13922	13919	14108
40-44	14400	14719	14203	14486	13348	12929	12918
45-49	12509	12689	13157	12669	13181	12059	11642

TABLE 5 DEMOGRAPHIC INDICES AND FEMALE SINGULATE MEAN AGE
AT MARRIAGE: 1831 TO 1901

DATE	IF OVERALL FERTILITY	IG MARITAL FERTILITY	IH ILLEGITIMATE FERTILITY	IM PROPORTION MARRIED	SINGULATE MEAN AGE AT MARRIAGE
1831	0.295	0.553	0.024	0.513	24.5
1836	0.283	0.527	0.023	0.515	24.5
1841	0.278	0.517	0.020	0.519	24.4
1846	0.266	0.492	0.018	0.523	24.3
1851	0.253	0.466	0.018	0.526	24.3
1856	0.246	0.447	0.018	0.532	24.2
1861	0.245	0.442	0.016	0.536	24.3
1866	0.245	0.444	0.015	0.536	24.3
1871	0.247	0.445	0.016	0.539	24.2
1876	0.248	0.440	0.018	0.545	24.0
1881	0.243	0.428	0.016	0.552	23.8
1886	0.233	0.407	0.016	0.555	24.0
1891	0.217	0.377	0.018	0.555	24.1
1896	0.206	0.357	0.019	0.555	24.0
1901	0.199	0.341	0.019	0.561	

PYRENEES (BASSES-)

MORTALITY PATTERN: WEST
MIGRATION: FULL STRENGTH, WITH UNCORRECTED POPULATION TOTALS EXCEPT FOR 1871,
 OBTAINED BY LINEAR INTERPOLATION OF R/CB BETWEEN 1866 AND 1876

TABLE 1   FEMALE POPULATION ESTIMATES: 1801 TO 1906

DATE	R/CB RATIO	% COR-RECTION	FINAL POPULATION ESTIMATE	DATE	R/CB RATIO	% COR-RECTION	FINAL POPULATION ESTIMATE
1801	1.007	3.9	190038	1856	0.961	0.0	227677
1806	1.047	0.0	196217	1861	0.931	0.0	226823
1811*	1.024	0.0	199073	1866	0.913	0.0	225614
1816*	1.010	0.0	201928	1871	0.888	1.7	224744
1821	0.987	0.0	204784	1876	0.892	0.0	223858
1826*	0.996	0.0	211658	1881	0.873	0.0	223219
1831	0.997	0.0	218532	1886	0.850	0.0	220963
1836	1.014	0.0	228019	1891	0.834	0.0	219015
1841	1.014	0.0	232294	1896	0.825	0.0	217755
1846	1.000	0.0	235169	1901	0.822	0.0	219907
1851	0.980	0.0	231565	1906	0.806	0.0	219186

NOTE: R/CB RATIO REFERS TO THE POPULATION COMPUTED BY THE BALANCE OF BIRTHS
        AND DEATHS OVER THE REPORTED POPULATION
* INTERPOLATED VALUES

TABLE 2   FEMALE BIRTH ESTIMATES: 1801-1805 TO 1901-1905

DATE	% COR-RECTION	FINAL BIRTH ESTIMATE	CRUDE BIRTH RATE	DATE	% COR-RECTION	FINAL BIRTH ESTIMATE	CRUDE BIRTH RATE
1801-1805	7.2	27028	28.0	1856-1860	8.7	27873	24.8
1806-1810	0.0	26358	26.7	1861-1865	0.0	26997	23.9
1811-1815	0.0	26481	26.4	1866-1870	0.0	27213	24.2
1816-1820	0.0	25856	25.4	1871-1875	0.0	27157	24.2
1821-1825	0.0	26892	25.8	1876-1880	0.0	27391	24.5
1826-1830	0.0	28141	26.2	1881-1885	0.0	26592	23.9
1831-1835	0.0	27706	24.8	1886-1890	0.0	24669	22.4
1836-1840	0.0	28249	24.5	1891-1895	0.0	23417	21.4
1841-1845	0.0	28083	24.0	1896-1900	0.0	23448	21.4
1846-1850	3.9	27021	23.2	1901-1905	0.0	23822	21.7
1851-1855	2.4	26928	23.5				

TABLE 3 FEMALE POPULATION ESTIMATES,
DISTRIBUTION BY AGE: 1801 TO 1906

AGE	1801	1806	1811	1816	1821	1826	1831	1836	1841	1846	1851
0- 4	22269	21764	21334	21219	21300	22054	23286	23360	23108	23282	21416
5- 9	19685	20510	19854	19466	19495	19867	20557	22066	21657	21393	21045
10-14	18428	19166	19630	19107	18663	19166	19423	20408	21524	20936	20429
15-19	17238	17933	18334	18881	18309	18339	18728	19272	19897	20796	19918
20-24	16003	16638	17028	17494	17769	17849	17788	18448	18645	19092	19520
25-29	14749	15339	15700	16140	16555	17403	17206	17416	17733	17787	17883
30-34	13526	14058	14402	14801	15203	15946	16691	16764	16653	16838	16629
35-39	12322	12816	13129	13499	13872	14560	15213	16177	15939	15734	15661
40-44	11177	11609	11904	12236	12587	13211	13816	14666	15297	14982	14562
45-49	10062	10459	10712	11021	11336	11908	12454	13232	13776	14285	13778
50-54	8919	9274	9514	9771	10070	10566	11065	11759	12249	12688	12946
55-59	7711	8008	8231	8457	8721	9149	9581	10198	10615	11019	11203
60-64	6372	6624	6820	7007	7258	7590	7961	8477	8823	9179	9304
65-69	4921	5115	5292	5432	5656	5912	6196	6613	6870	7174	7246
70-74	3433	3569	3707	3812	3990	4168	4379	4673	4854	5081	5118
75-79	2042	2120	2215	2278	2409	2509	2645	2832	2932	3086	3088
80+	1181	1214	1267	1307	1392	1460	1543	1660	1723	1818	1819

AGE	1856	1861	1866	1871	1876	1881	1886	1891	1896	1901	1906
0- 4	21224	22361	22080	22036	22028	22829	22376	20915	19860	20413	20954
5- 9	19315	19351	20477	20222	20196	20276	21007	20756	19514	18840	19213
10-14	20107	18628	18579	19758	19524	19417	19428	20282	20173	19119	18253
15-19	19389	19099	17635	17727	18851	18281	17880	18155	19342	19604	17861
20-24	18549	17783	17574	16387	16406	16744	15530	15608	16572	18436	17181
25-29	18230	17311	16585	16508	15352	15045	15071	14157	14578	15885	16991
30-34	16715	17212	16303	15672	15608	14463	14114	14255	13489	14049	15139
35-39	15469	15735	16170	15354	14772	14729	13632	13386	13590	12970	13436
40-44	14505	14529	14744	15178	14431	13951	13946	12968	12759	13035	12460
45-49	13406	13556	13544	13763	14189	13581	13185	13232	12312	12173	12499
50-54	12501	12363	12477	12472	12695	13205	12715	12386	12419	11608	11578
55-59	11437	11230	11105	11201	11217	11544	12082	11676	11365	11461	10814
60-64	9450	9796	9655	9531	9628	9753	10085	10612	10269	10103	10231
65-69	7329	7563	7902	7758	7671	7871	8021	8344	8789	8624	8539
70-74	5151	5297	5536	5748	5652	5704	5896	6048	6296	6747	6665
75-79	3093	3169	3323	3438	3575	3613	3680	3833	3933	4186	4524
80+	1808	1839	1924	1991	2064	2214	2314	2401	2497	2654	2859

[408]

TABLE 4 MARRIED WOMEN ESTIMATES,
DISTRIBUTION BY AGE: 1831 TO 1901

AGE	1831	1836	1841	1846	1851	1856	1861	1866
15-19	650	668	689	719	688	669	1225	1035
20-24	4144	4297	4346	4454	4552	4325	4147	4874
25-29	7900	8068	8238	8284	8339	8509	8095	7767
30-34	9714	9702	9756	9908	9805	9873	10198	9683
35-39	9460	10077	9916	9921	9902	9803	10014	10323
40-44	8757	9308	9785	9588	9421	9412	9479	9657
45-49	7396	7862	8266	8657	8314	8173	8323	8352

AGE	1871	1876	1881	1886	1891	1896	1901
15-19	642	716	652	557	421	421	605
20-24	4771	4104	4180	3690	3472	3549	3857
25-29	8007	7955	7395	7406	6813	6866	7590
30-34	9306	9279	9037	8678	8823	8330	8616
35-39	9791	9437	9367	9005	8810	9034	8629
40-44	9919	9450	9196	8962	8548	8394	8566
45-49	8444	8719	8415	8331	8459	7900	7672

TABLE 5 DEMOGRAPHIC INDICES AND FEMALE SINGULATE MEAN AGE
AT MARRIAGE: 1831 TO 1901

DATE	IF OVERALL FERTILITY	IG MARITAL FERTILITY	IH ILLEGITIMATE FERTILITY	IM PROPORTION MARRIED	SINGULATE MEAN AGE AT MARRIAGE
1831	0.276	0.621	0.036	0.411	25.9
1836	0.268	0.595	0.040	0.411	26.0
1841	0.267	0.597	0.036	0.411	26.0
1846	0.258	0.576	0.038	0.410	26.1
1851	0.254	0.563	0.038	0.411	26.1
1856	0.261	0.577	0.038	0.415	25.9
1861	0.268	0.580	0.039	0.424	25.6
1866	0.269	0.566	0.038	0.438	25.7
1871	0.278	0.589	0.033	0.441	25.8
1876	0.284	0.614	0.032	0.433	25.9
1881	0.287	0.622	0.034	0.430	25.8
1886	0.282	0.620	0.029	0.429	26.1
1891	0.269	0.601	0.028	0.420	26.5
1896	0.257	0.591	0.027	0.408	26.5
1901	0.247	0.576	0.024	0.404	

MORTALITY PATTERN: WEST
MIGRATION: FULL STRENGTH, WITH POPULATION TOTALS OBTAINED BY TREND OF R/CB

TABLE 1 FEMALE POPULATION ESTIMATES: 1801 TO 1906

DATE	R/CB RATIO	% COR- RECTION	FINAL POPULATION ESTIMATE	DATE	R/CB RATIO	% COR- RECTION	FINAL POPULATION ESTIMATE
1801	1.036	11.1	98659	1856	0.969	-0.1	127468
1806	1.122	0.0	100877	1861	0.944	1.0	125468
1811*	1.067	0.0	102902	1866	0.934	0.4	123958
1816*	1.032	0.0	104927	1871	0.914	0.9	121881
1821	0.999	0.0	106952	1876	0.916	-1.0	119915
1826*	1.000	0.0	111877	1881	0.900	-1.0	118686
1831	0.997	0.0	116801	1886	0.883	-0.8	116898
1836	1.016	0.0	123022	1891	0.847	1.6	114119
1841	0.997	1.0	125116	1896	0.843	0.3	11CC18
1846	1.000	0.0	128121	1901	0.831	-0.1	106426
1851	0.990	-0.7	127749	1906	0.818	-0.4	103586

NOTE: R/CB RATIO REFERS TO THE POPULATION CCMPUTEC BY THE BALANCE OF BIRTHS
       AND DEATHS OVER THE REPORTED POPULATION
* INTERPOLATED VALUES

TABLE 2 FEMALE BIRTH ESTIMATES: 1801-1805 TO 1901-1905

DATE	% COR- RECTION	FINAL BIRTH ESTIMATE	CRUDE BIRTH RATE	DATE	% COR- RECTION	FINAL BIRTH ESTIMATE	CRUDE BIRTH RATE
1801-1805	17.1	15293	30.7	1856-1860	0.0	13441	21.3
1806-1810	7.6	14971	29.4	1861-1865	0.0	13192	21.2
1811-1815	11.8	14637	28.2	1866-1870	0.0	12851	20.9
1816-1820	3.1	14254	26.9	1871-1875	0.0	12965	21.4
1821-1825	0.0	14548	26.6	1876-1880	0.0	13089	21.9
1826-1830	0.0	15267	26.7	1881-1885	0.0	12035	20.4
1831-1835	0.0	15363	25.6	1886-1890	0.0	10505	18.2
1836-1840	0.0	15352	24.7	1891-1895	0.0	9561	17.1
1841-1845	0.0	15229	24.1	1896-1900	0.0	9362	17.3
1846-1850	1.7	14456	22.6	1901-1905	0.0	9061	17.3
1851-1855	0.0	13714	21.5				

TABLE 3 FEMALE POPULATION ESTIMATES,
DISTRIBUTION BY AGE: 1801 TO 1906

AGE	1801	1806	1811	1816	1821	1826	1831	1836	1841	1846	1851
0- 4	11432	12064	12370	12036	11387	12356	12997	13091	12616	12801	11960
5- 9	10127	10328	10977	11300	11062	11206	11630	12380	12099	11790	11778
10-14	9500	9679	9741	10443	10771	10856	10959	11575	11991	11779	11377
15-19	8906	9075	9122	9262	9948	10564	10610	10901	11206	11668	11061
20-24	8285	8437	8500	8617	8768	9693	10259	10480	10476	10831	10389
25-29	7652	7794	7862	7985	8115	8496	9363	10075	10011	10070	9990
30-34	7032	7158	7234	7353	7489	7829	8172	9152	9576	9579	9525
35-39	6420	6539	6613	6732	6855	7190	7495	7948	8653	9119	9067
40-44	5836	5936	6012	6124	6255	6558	6850	7252	7474	8198	8638
45-49	5264	5359	5423	5531	5653	5937	6207	6584	6775	7036	7740
50-54	4676	4761	4832	4922	5040	5294	5545	5884	6064	6291	6573
55-59	4051	4119	4200	4286	4387	4612	4835	5134	5289	5503	5739
60-64	3355	3414	3502	3584	3681	3864	4057	4302	4430	4618	4785
65-69	2596	2641	2733	2814	2904	3054	3204	3393	3484	3641	3768
70-74	1815	1846	1934	2004	2081	2195	2309	2436	2495	2608	2696
75-79	1082	1098	1168	1219	1280	1355	1432	1509	1536	1608	1655
80+	627	630	676	716	764	820	876	926	940	982	1007

AGE	1856	1861	1866	1871	1876	1881	1886	1891	1896	1901	1906
0- 4	11509	10971	10935	10632	10750	11060	10315	9087	8114	8017	7962
5- 9	11077	10529	10102	10061	9793	9979	10328	9670	8446	7566	7557
10-14	11401	10677	10168	9750	9716	9473	9669	10029	9372	8188	7346
15-19	10735	10719	10053	9554	9161	9138	8900	9119	9492	8880	7728
20-24	9921	9559	9610	8960	8507	8126	8087	7899	8180	8599	7998
25-29	9637	9137	8835	8880	8271	7850	7485	7474	7312	7616	8040
30-34	9491	9097	8653	8360	8411	7855	7468	7131	7107	6969	7294
35-39	9052	8961	8621	8193	7921	8002	7492	7135	6789	6783	6684
40-44	8620	8547	8493	8167	7766	7542	7646	7172	6801	6486	6516
45-49	8182	8108	8070	8015	7712	7369	7183	7295	6812	6474	6211
50-54	7252	7604	7566	7527	7480	7237	6947	6785	6853	6415	6139
55-59	6020	6575	6927	6888	6857	6860	6672	6421	6231	6311	5956
60-64	5023	5202	5722	6023	5996	6020	6062	5917	5649	5504	5631
65-69	3939	4065	4249	4669	4921	4955	5017	5075	4902	4705	4645
70-74	2821	2886	3014	3147	3463	3703	3768	3837	3831	3726	3634
75-79	1735	1766	1835	1913	2001	2244	2433	2493	2497	2515	2496
80+	1052	1066	1103	1142	1190	1272	1427	1582	1633	1674	1748

TABLE 4 MARRIED WOMEN ESTIMATES,
DISTRIBUTION BY AGE: 1831 TO 1901

AGE	1831	1836	1841	1846	1851	1856	1861	1866
15-19	286	295	305	318	303	295	211	201
20-24	2268	2321	2329	2417	2326	2231	2158	1761
25-29	4451	4792	4781	4826	4802	4651	4427	4296
30-34	5048	5649	5936	5958	5940	5946	5721	5463
35-39	5032	5321	5822	6156	6136	6158	6122	5914
40-44	4775	5026	5210	5734	6055	6080	6057	6048
45-49	4101	4307	4463	4653	5128	5464	5446	5452

AGE	1871	1876	1881	1886	1891	1896	1901
15-19	277	361	398	358	264	242	341
20-24	1869	2180	2381	2242	1912	1952	2102
25-29	3849	3946	4204	4287	4019	3646	3973
30-34	5284	5000	4982	5094	4957	4833	4565
35-39	5622	5446	5391	5320	5078	4985	4960
40-44	5809	5531	5492	5473	4992	4817	4693
45-49	5397	5197	5127	5252	5009	4679	4392

TABLE 5 DEMOGRAPHIC INDICES AND FEMALE SINGULATE MEAN AGE
AT MARRIAGE: 1831 TO 1901

DATE	IF OVERALL FERTILITY	IG MARITAL FERTILITY	IH ILLEGITIMATE FERTILITY	IM PROPORTION MARRIED	SINGULATE MEAN AGE AT MARRIAGE
1831	0.284	0.630	0.038	0.415	26.3
1836	0.269	0.587	0.038	0.420	26.4
1841	0.261	0.563	0.038	0.425	26.4
1846	0.246	0.536	0.030	0.427	26.4
1851	0.237	0.500	0.035	0.434	26.4
1856	0.233	0.489	0.033	0.440	26.4
1861	0.236	0.491	0.035	0.440	26.7
1866	0.237	0.510	0.031	0.432	26.8
1871	0.245	0.531	0.028	0.431	26.3
1876	0.257	0.541	0.028	0.447	25.7
1881	0.257	0.509	0.031	0.474	25.4
1886	0.238	0.458	0.029	0.488	26.0
1891	0.217	0.433	0.028	0.466	26.5
1896	0.206	0.426	0.024	0.451	26.3
1901	0.200	0.411	0.023	0.455	

MORTALITY PATTERN: WEST
MIGRATION: GRADUAL, WITH POPULATION TOTALS OBTAINED BY TREND OF R/CB

TABLE 1   FEMALE POPULATION ESTIMATES: 1801 TO 1906

DATE	R/CB RATIO	% COR- RECTION	FINAL POPULATION ESTIMATE	DATE	R/CB RATIO	% COR- RECTION	FINAL POPULATION ESTIMATE
1801	1.065	7.6	59425	1856	0.954	1.5	91521
1806	1.087	2.0	63805	1861	0.936	2.9	92517
1811*	1.044	2.0	66848	1866	0.938	2.0	94965
1816*	1.001	2.0	69890	1871	0.930	2.3	96340
1821	0.986	2.0	72933	1876	0.942	0.5	98215
1826*	0.993	2.0	76359	1881	0.962	-2.2	100440
1831	1.001	2.0	79786	1886	0.926	1.1	101778
1836	1.000	2.0	83115	1891	0.939	-0.9	103540
1841	0.996	2.0	86106	1896	0.918	0.7	103902
1846	1.000	2.0	90046	1901	0.925	-0.6	105103
1851	0.967	0.7	89888	1906	0.914	0.0	106336

NOTE: R/CB RATIO REFERS TO THE POPULATION COMPUTED BY THE BALANCE OF BIRTHS
       AND DEATHS OVER THE REPORTED POPULATION
* INTERPOLATED VALUES

TABLE 2   FEMALE BIRTH ESTIMATES: 1801-1805 TO 1901-1905

DATE	% COR- RECTION	FINAL BIRTH ESTIMATE	CRUDE BIRTH RATE	DATE	% COR- RECTION	FINAL BIRTH ESTIMATE	CRUDE BIRTH RATE
1801-1805	26.8	15666	50.9	1856-1860	2.9	13938	30.3
1806-1810	16.9	15021	46.0	1861-1865	0.0	14935	31.9
1811-1815	18.5	15146	44.3	1866-1870	3.0	14811	31.0
1816-1820	14.6	14552	40.8	1871-1875	0.0	15535	31.9
1821-1825	0.0	13452	36.0	1876-1880	0.0	15884	32.0
1826-1830	0.0	14130	36.2	1881-1885	0.0	15660	31.0
1831-1835	0.0	14372	35.3	1886-1890	0.0	13596	26.5
1836-1840	0.0	14728	34.8	1891-1895	0.0	12489	24.1
1841-1845	0.0	15237	34.6	1896-1900	0.0	12380	23.7
1846-1850	0.0	16009	35.6	1901-1905	0.0	11768	22.3
1851-1855	5.0	14859	32.8				

[413]

TABLE 3 FEMALE POPULATION ESTIMATES,
DISTRIBUTION BY AGE: 1801 TO 1906

AGE	1801	1806	1811	1816	1821	1826	1831	1836	1841	1846	1851
0- 4	10815	10875	10453	10680	10251	9670	10019	10409	10704	11267	11408
5- 9	8415	9226	9227	8913	9195	9005	8464	8818	9155	9532	9612
10-14	7274	7896	8570	8574	8415	8856	8695	8141	8456	8864	8824
15-19	6287	6823	7332	7961	8092	8102	8549	8360	7804	8184	8149
20-24	5360	5826	6262	6734	7424	7699	7723	8124	7923	7470	7353
25-29	4522	4916	5294	5696	6217	6993	7262	7269	7626	7513	6717
30-34	3779	4112	4430	4778	5216	5808	6539	6780	6770	7176	6759
35-39	3132	3407	3675	3967	4338	4831	5383	6055	6264	6320	6416
40-44	2573	2802	3023	3268	3575	3989	4444	4949	5554	5807	5620
45-49	2104	2286	2468	2668	2924	3264	3642	4056	4507	5113	5131
50-54	1682	1833	1976	2140	2343	2619	2923	3263	3627	4075	4442
55-59	1295	1416	1533	1658	1816	2029	2265	2533	2824	3175	3431
60-64	939	1029	1118	1216	1328	1485	1653	1855	2074	2341	2529
65-69	624	683	746	817	895	997	1107	1245	1398	1585	1720
70-74	362	401	439	484	532	595	656	740	833	950	1037
75-79	172	192	213	237	261	292	322	363	411	471	518
80+	77	81	89	100	111	125	138	156	176	203	224

AGE	1856	1861	1866	1871	1876	1881	1886	1891	1896	1901	1906
0- 4	10834	10265	11256	11076	11665	12095	11832	10933	9947	10108	9845
5- 9	10019	9560	9168	10001	9866	10447	10785	10830	9967	9172	9412
10-14	9184	9592	9204	8798	9614	9493	10034	10436	10476	9679	8927
15-19	8409	8763	9216	8789	8414	9189	9026	9592	9980	10085	9322
20-24	7648	7892	8305	8643	8256	7858	8507	8363	8908	9392	9499
25-29	6859	7145	7436	7772	8107	7734	7308	7982	7839	8433	8924
30-34	6234	6383	6699	6944	7272	7601	7229	6911	7543	7455	8060
35-39	6228	5761	5943	6216	6456	6779	7069	6817	6507	7149	7104
40-44	5874	5720	5332	5485	5747	5989	6278	6649	6401	6146	6794
45-49	5110	5358	5258	4889	5038	5299	5515	5874	6209	6013	5811
50-54	4583	4581	4843	4742	4417	4573	4803	5091	5410	5755	5614
55-59	3942	3981	4017	4235	4155	3892	4023	4321	4566	4890	5246
60-64	2807	3160	3314	3330	3519	3475	3244	3451	3692	3946	4274
65-69	1907	2131	2435	2540	2560	2729	2682	2601	2752	2989	3242
70-74	1153	1289	1467	1666	1744	1777	1883	1942	1870	2017	2232
75-79	578	650	744	840	958	1017	1028	1161	1186	1171	1294
80+	253	286	329	374	425	491	532	587	651	703	738

TABLE 4   MARRIED WOMEN ESTIMATES,
DISTRIBUTION BY AGE: 1831 TO 1901

AGE	1831	1836	1841	1846	1851	1856	1861	1866
15-19	316	310	290	305	305	315	291	294
20-24	2649	2793	2735	2589	2556	2665	2761	2365
25-29	4667	4682	4935	4883	4379	4480	4687	4888
30-34	4891	5083	5110	5447	5150	4759	4902	5155
35-39	4084	4606	4813	4895	4995	4859	4534	4687
40-44	3254	3636	4142	4383	4271	4477	4415	4126
45-49	2455	2747	3122	3605	3654	3652	3902	3842

AGE	1871	1876	1881	1886	1891	1896	1901
15-19	315	399	553	539	354	261	436
20-24	2595	3061	3239	3558	3234	3247	3298
25-29	4483	4846	5303	5192	5607	5312	5804
30-34	5336	5193	5548	5689	5509	5994	5826
35-39	4888	5065	5156	5430	5426	5242	5743
40-44	4221	4404	4643	4752	5022	4959	4773
45-49	3539	3621	3874	4049	4277	4546	4371

TABLE 5   DEMOGRAPHIC INDICES AND FEMALE SINGULATE MEAN AGE
AT MARRIAGE: 1831 TO 1901

DATE	IF OVERALL FERTILITY	IG MARITAL FERTILITY	IH ILLEGITIMATE FERTILITY	IM PROPORTION MARRIED	SINGULATE MEAN AGE AT MARRIAGE
1831	0.348	0.630	0.051	0.513	24.4
1836	0.342	0.594	0.067	0.521	24.5
1841	0.349	0.603	0.056	0.535	24.4
1846	0.362	0.624	0.052	0.541	24.4
1851	0.371	0.646	0.049	0.539	24.4
1856	0.345	0.614	0.038	0.534	24.4
1861	0.341	0.609	0.039	0.531	24.7
1866	0.339	0.627	0.038	0.512	25.0
1871	0.337	0.634	0.036	0.504	24.7
1876	0.346	0.631	0.028	0.528	24.0
1881	0.345	0.594	0.031	0.557	23.8
1886	0.318	0.534	0.030	0.570	24.2
1891	0.279	0.475	0.029	0.560	24.6
1896	0.260	0.454	0.026	0.546	24.5
1901	0.243	0.427	0.022	0.545	

MORTALITY PATTERN: WEST
MIGRATION: GRADUAL, WITH UNCORRECTED POPULATION TOTALS

TABLE 1   FEMALE POPULATION ESTIMATES: 1801 TO 1866

DATE	R/CB RATIO	% CORRECTION	FINAL POPULATION ESTIMATE	DATE	R/CB RATIO	% CORRECTION	FINAL POPULATION ESTIMATE
1801	1.339	0.0	234147	1856	0.938	0.0	293136
1806	1.335	0.0	257102	1861	0.922	0.0	297816
1811*	1.218	0.0	258217	1866	0.912	0.0	304381
1816*	1.149	0.0	259333				
1821	1.080	0.0	260448				
1826*	1.056	0.0	268870				
1831	1.044	0.0	277292				
1836	1.048	0.0	288632				
1841	1.014	0.0	290299				
1846	1.000	0.0	299761				
1851	0.981	0.0	302044				

NOTE: R/CB RATIO REFERS TO THE PCPULATION CCMPUTED BY THE BALANCE OF BIRTHS
       AND DEATHS OVER THE REPORTED FOPULATICN
* INTERPOLATED VALUES

TABLE 2   FEMALE BIRTH ESTIMATES: 1801-1805 TO 1861-1865

DATE	% CORRECTION	FINAL BIRTH ESTIMATE	CRUDE BIRTH RATE	DATE	% CORRECTION	FINAL BIRTH ESTIMATE	CRUDE BIRTH RATE
1801-1805	0.0	46866	38.2	1856-1860	0.0	45038	30.5
1806-1810	11.0	54685	42.4	1861-1865	0.0	47645	31.6
1811-1815	0.0	50805	39.3				
1816-1820	5.5	47086	36.2				
1821-1825	0.0	44807	33.9				
1826-1830	0.0	45975	33.7				
1831-1835	0.0	47480	33.6				
1836-1840	0.0	47913	33.1				
1841-1845	0.0	49618	33.6				
1846-1850	0.0	45762	30.4				
1851-1855	0.0	42412	28.5				

TABLE 3 FEMALE POPULATION ESTIMATES,
DISTRIBUTION BY AGE: 1801 TO 1866

AGE	1801	1806	1811	1816	1821	1826	1831	1836	1841	1846	1851
0- 4	34928	37087	38116	35553	34168	33825	34112	35326	34906	37409	34271
5- 9	29092	32276	30972	32157	30409	30282	29924	30449	30649	31058	32996
10-14	26091	28733	29220	28426	29546	28889	28963	28976	28542	29316	29434
15-19	23395	25757	26002	26808	26107	28057	27620	28035	27151	27289	27682
20-24	20746	22879	23058	23591	24378	24552	26542	26445	25995	25701	25365
25-29	18262	20130	20297	20724	21275	22740	23022	25182	24305	24401	23811
30-34	15966	17606	17725	18102	18562	19714	21168	21678	22977	22659	22536
35-39	13858	15289	15383	15683	16099	17082	18213	19778	19633	21269	20794
40-44	11937	13188	13268	13517	13858	14721	15676	16901	17793	18056	19408
45-49	10227	11292	11363	11574	11861	12585	13414	14443	15098	16250	16368
50-54	8612	9510	9550	9735	9937	10593	11269	12142	12680	13557	14492
55-59	7043	7782	7300	7922	8155	8663	9196	9881	10335	11051	11738
60-64	5475	6064	6050	6126	6311	6733	7136	7642	7983	8565	9091
65-69	3930	4382	4352	4378	4525	4836	5126	5472	5708	6132	6531
70-74	2550	2824	2801	2800	2896	3108	3285	3500	3648	3924	4186
75-79	1380	1546	1506	1499	1556	1675	1765	1870	1952	2106	2251
80+	702	769	753	738	757	815	862	912	946	1019	1092

AGE	1856	1861	1866
0- 4	30843	34414	36589
5- 9	29435	27521	30333
10-14	30595	28127	26377
15-19	26905	29048	26754
20-24	24430	24980	27064
25-29	22662	22731	23311
30-34	21465	21116	21250
35-39	20231	19896	19640
40-44	18605	18666	18423
45-49	17273	17062	17181
50-54	14349	15596	15464
55-59	12326	12589	13735
60-64	9444	10278	10540
65-69	6766	7314	7994
70-74	4342	4701	5105
75-79	2331	2542	2766
80+	1134	1235	1354

MORTALITY PATTERN: WEST
MIGRATION: NO ADJUSTMENT MADE FOR MIGRATION BY AGE

TABLE 1   FEMALE POPULATION ESTIMATES: 1801 TO 1866

DATE	R/CB RATIO	% COR- RECTION	FINAL POPULATION ESTIMATE	DATE	R/CB RATIO	% COR- RECTION	FINAL POPULATION ESTIMATE
1801	0.996	3.3	160512	1856	0.993	0.0	255673
1806	1.021	0.0	170980	1861	0.976	0.0	262323
1811*	0.995	0.0	177392	1866	0.968	0.0	271033
1816*	0.991	0.0	183805				
1821	0.973	0.0	190217				
1826*	0.989	0.0	203528				
1831	1.000	0.0	216840				
1836	1.005	0.0	227607				
1841	1.000	0.0	237236				
1846	1.000	0.0	248637				
1851	0.981	0.0	250617				

NOTE: R/CB RATIO REFERS TO THE POPULATION COMPUTED BY THE BALANCE OF BIRTHS
       AND DEATHS OVER THE REPORTED POPULATION
* INTERPOLATED VALUES

TABLE 2   FEMALE BIRTH ESTIMATES: 1801-1805 TO 1861-1865

DATE	% COR- RECTION	FINAL BIRTH ESTIMATE	CRUDE BIRTH RATE	DATE	% COR- RECTION	FINAL BIRTH ESTIMATE	CRUDE BIRTH RATE
1801-1805	2.8	29721	35.9	1856-1860	0.0	40343	31.2
1806-1810	6.8	32651	37.5	1861-1865	0.0	44589	33.4
1811-1815	5.3	33184	36.7				
1816-1820	5.1	32919	35.2				
1821-1825	0.0	35676	36.2				
1826-1830	0.0	39125	37.2				
1831-1835	0.0	38422	34.6				
1836-1840	0.0	41989	36.1				
1841-1845	0.0	41483	34.2				
1846-1850	0.0	37679	30.2				
1851-1855	0.0	35939	28.4				

TABLE 3 FEMALE POPULATION ESTIMATES,
DISTRIBUTION BY AGE: 1801 TO 1866

AGE	1801	1806	1311	1816	1821	1826	1831	1836	1841	1846	1851
0- 4	20960	23533	24646	24390	24928	27532	29766	29280	31263	31800	28261
5- 9	17972	19135	20806	21745	21663	22730	24894	26816	26011	28180	28050
10-14	16575	17417	18111	19921	20693	21247	22179	24132	25764	25154	26669
15-19	15268	16056	16478	17335	18949	20287	20724	21491	23176	24905	23795
20-24	13936	14661	15046	15600	16331	18391	19583	19880	20422	22185	23330
25-29	12614	13286	13629	14114	14578	15717	17600	18627	18724	19389	20612
30-34	11333	11954	12269	12689	13102	13934	14933	16624	17416	17658	17893
35-39	10124	10673	10965	11334	11698	12433	13141	14005	15427	16310	16182
40-44	8974	9479	9728	10060	10384	11029	11649	12244	12909	14355	14852
45-49	7914	8345	8580	8862	9152	9721	10260	10778	11206	11928	12981
50-54	6849	7246	7430	7678	7930	8425	8889	9333	9693	10184	10608
55-59	5759	6102	6267	6441	6673	7084	7471	7847	8137	8553	8794
60-64	4614	4902	5026	5148	5329	5667	5965	6268	6490	6832	7028
65-69	3412	3662	3750	3809	3955	4193	4414	4636	4791	5056	5208
70-74	2265	2441	2513	2530	2623	2784	2917	3069	3161	3344	3453
75-79	1263	1375	1412	1413	1468	1551	1622	1703	1749	1857	1922
80+	665	713	736	737	760	802	835	873	895	946	980

AGE	1856	1861	1866
0- 4	26751	30920	33805
5- 9	25286	23949	27645
10-14	27257	24201	23008
15-19	25907	26076	23240
20-24	22861	24551	24792
25-29	22208	21495	23149
30-34	19472	20746	20129
35-39	16772	18068	19290
40-44	15063	15466	16692
45-49	13726	13795	14189
50-54	11785	12367	12444
55-59	9327	10318	10829
60-64	7325	7781	8592
65-69	5398	5679	6007
70-74	3560	3758	3925
75-79	1966	2091	2182
80+	1008	1064	1116

MORTALITY PATTERN: WEST
MIGRATION: GRADUAL STARTING IN 1856, WITH UNCORRECTED POPULATION TOTALS EXCEPT
FOR 1871 AND FOR 1891 AND 1896, OBTAINED BY INTERPOLATION OF R/CB

TABLE 1 FEMALE POPULATION ESTIMATES: 1801 TO 1906

DATE	R/CB RATIO	% COR- RECTION	FINAL POPULATION ESTIMATE	DATE	R/CB RATIO	% COR- RECTION	FINAL POPULATION ESTIMATE
1801	1.127	0.0	150151	1856	0.881	0.0	161071
1806	1.131	0.0	153655	1861	0.865	0.0	161596
1811*	1.116	0.0	156476	1866	0.846	0.0	161114
1816*	1.106	0.0	159296	1871	0.809	2.1	157966
1821	1.091	0.0	162117	1876	0.806	0.0	153840
1826*	1.067	0.0	168032	1881	0.777	0.0	149627
1831	1.055	0.0	173946	1886	0.759	0.0	146934
1836	1.044	0.0	176355	1891	0.726	2.0	143389
1841	1.025	0.0	178929	1896	0.709	1.6	138717
1846	1.000	0.0	178595	1901	0.701	0.0	134484
1851	0.980	0.0	178015	1906	0.694	0.0	133482

NOTE: R/CB RATIO REFERS TO THE POPULATION COMPUTED BY THE BALANCE OF BIRTHS
       AND DEATHS OVER THE REPORTED POPULATION
* INTERPOLATED VALUES

TABLE 2 FEMALE BIRTH ESTIMATES: 1801-1805 TO 1901-1905

DATE	% COR- RECTION	FINAL BIRTH ESTIMATE	CRUDE BIRTH RATE	DATE	% COR- RECTION	FINAL BIRTH ESTIMATE	CRUDE BIRTH RATE
1801-1805	9.1	24169	31.8	1856-1860	0.0	20381	25.3
1806-1810	4.5	24821	32.0	1861-1865	0.0	19803	24.5
1811-1815	6.7	23702	30.0	1866-1870	0.0	18181	22.8
1816-1820	0.0	24335	30.3	1871-1875	0.0	17478	22.4
1821-1825	0.0	25129	30.4	1876-1880	0.0	17041	22.5
1826-1830	0.0	26650	31.2	1881-1885	0.0	15323	20.7
1831-1835	0.0	23985	27.4	1886-1890	0.0	14899	20.5
1836-1840	0.0	24065	27.1	1891-1895	4.4	14263	20.2
1841-1845	0.0	23086	25.8	1896-1900	0.0	13929	20.4
1846-1850	2.7	21903	24.6	1901-1905	0.0	14352	21.4
1851-1855	9.4	20974	24.7				

TABLE 3 FEMALE POPULATION ESTIMATES,
DISTRIBUTION BY AGE: 1801 TO 1906

AGE	1801	1806	1811	1816	1821	1826	1831	1836	1841	1846	1851
0- 4	19777	17800	18298	17824	18381	20144	20949	18792	19109	18133	17315
5- 9	16832	17531	15704	16300	15883	16758	18287	18941	17054	17182	16389
10-14	15539	16217	16756	15068	15610	15262	16164	17561	18163	16217	16413
15-19	14336	14966	15494	16071	14425	14992	14715	15515	16832	17263	15483
20-24	13094	13655	14145	14710	15232	13744	14328	14000	14749	15865	16348
25-29	11852	12356	12791	13315	13826	14418	13040	13533	13219	13806	14921
30-34	10645	11099	11488	11956	12430	13016	13596	12243	12706	12304	12912
35-39	9488	9890	10240	10661	11081	11635	12197	12686	11427	11756	11439
40-44	8412	8755	9064	9441	9818	10315	10838	11313	11773	10512	10868
45-49	7395	7706	7966	8297	8633	9078	9544	9984	10429	10758	9652
50-54	6384	6654	6889	7169	7461	7865	8268	8655	9066	9386	9730
55-59	5348	5563	5764	6015	6257	6625	6970	7297	7656	7947	8269
60-64	4247	4413	4569	4782	4992	5322	5607	5875	6177	6420	6700
65-69	3111	3231	3347	3510	3679	3974	4199	4407	4649	4840	5059
70-74	2031	2106	2184	2299	2417	2650	2824	2973	3151	3290	3445
75-79	1100	1144	1188	1258	1330	1486	1597	1697	1811	1898	1994
80+	569	571	590	624	663	748	820	885	959	1018	1078

AGE	1856	1861	1866	1871	1876	1881	1886	1891	1896	1901	1906
0- 4	14899	16400	16078	14522	13820	13900	12841	12423	11791	11659	12244
5- 9	14254	13570	14945	14536	13065	12481	12804	11789	11354	10830	10924
10-14	14363	13662	12965	14248	13852	12369	11976	12287	11294	10902	10546
15-19	14377	13719	12944	12186	13369	12741	11566	11142	11401	10443	10452
20-24	13441	13563	12737	11813	10973	11580	11374	10132	9611	9836	9682
25-29	14085	12653	12673	11788	10859	9835	10661	10415	9170	8678	9293
30-34	12777	13234	11861	11830	10984	10074	9257	10037	9787	8629	8304
35-39	10986	11945	12362	11037	10997	10214	9499	8721	9452	9253	8250
40-44	9674	10220	11115	11470	10235	10243	9638	8967	8228	8961	8835
45-49	9128	8943	9456	10258	10583	9503	9628	9068	8437	7784	8515
50-54	7980	8319	8166	8611	9337	9714	8835	8959	8439	7900	7311
55-59	7824	7092	7413	7250	7637	8370	8824	8033	8138	7717	7255
60-64	6345	6659	6053	6285	6128	6534	7283	7671	6964	7105	6805
65-69	4788	5059	5334	4803	4962	4923	5353	5954	6244	5718	5906
70-74	3253	3458	3677	3829	3424	3620	3673	3981	4401	4663	4334
75-79	1876	2008	2153	2252	2322	2142	2326	2349	2524	2825	3049
80+	1019	1092	1182	1248	1294	1386	1396	1462	1481	1579	1777

TABLE 4 MARRIED WOMEN ESTIMATES,
DISTRIBUTION BY AGE: 1831 TO 1901

AGE	1831	1836	1841	1846	1851	1856	1861	1866
15-19	407	428	463	474	425	393	358	324
20-24	3756	3664	3854	4139	4261	3489	3520	2878
25-29	7168	7431	7254	7572	8183	7694	6918	6924
30-34	9369	8429	8749	8472	8897	8758	9093	8148
35-39	8925	9275	8359	8604	8386	7992	8726	9032
40-44	8058	8404	8755	7826	8113	7140	7593	8262
45-49	6743	7044	7369	7614	6859	6377	6310	6676

AGE	1871	1876	1881	1886	1891	1896	1901
15-19	328	446	435	350	298	285	410
20-24	2886	3191	3321	3131	2650	2550	2842
25-29	5810	5670	5817	6166	5823	5056	4919
30-34	8098	7075	6703	6718	7117	6875	6035
35-39	8024	7986	7195	6947	6557	7063	6889
40-44	8465	7544	7589	7094	6529	6100	6568
45-49	7164	7376	6676	7114	6525	6030	5444

TABLE 5 DEMOGRAPHIC INDICES AND FEMALE SINGULATE MEAN AGE
AT MARRIAGE: 1831 TO 1901

DATE	IF OVERALL FERTILITY	IG MARITAL FERTILITY	IH ILLEGITIMATE FERTILITY	IM PROPORTION MARRIED	SINGULATE MEAN AGE AT MARRIAGE
1831	0.316	0.591	0.061	0.481	25.8
1836	0.299	0.579	C.044	0.477	25.8
1841	0.290	0.578	0.036	0.467	25.8
1846	0.270	0.546	0.035	0.461	25.8
1851	0.254	0.501	0.037	0.468	25.8
1856	0.268	0.518	0.041	0.475	25.8
1861	0.261	0.501	0.038	0.482	26.0
1866	0.254	0.487	0.039	0.480	26.2
1871	0.252	0.490	0.C37	0.476	25.8
1876	0.255	0.499	0.031	0.477	25.5
1881	0.249	0.480	0.033	0.484	25.4
1886	0.240	0.449	0.036	0.494	25.8
1891	0.242	0.453	0.C38	0.492	26.1
1896	0.242	0.458	0.035	0.490	25.7
1901	0.252	0.465	0.041	0.498	

MORTALITY PATTERN: WEST
MIGRATION: FULL STRENGTH, WITH UNCORRECTED POPULATION TOTALS EXCEPT FOR 1856,
   1861, 1866, 1871, 1881, 1886 AND 1891, OBTAINED BY INTERPOLATION OF R/CB

TABLE 1 FEMALE POPULATION ESTIMATES: 1801 TO 1906

DATE	R/CB RATIO	% COR-RECTION	FINAL POPULATION ESTIMATE	DATE	R/CB RATIO	% COR-RECTION	FINAL POPULATION ESTIMATE
1801	1.061	1.7	236328	1856	0.974	0.7	293632
1806	1.066	0.0	239379	1861	0.962	0.9	295368
1811*	1.058	0.0	245077	1866	0.959	0.4	300423
1816*	1.034	0.0	250774	1871	0.937	1.7	305934
1821	1.017	0.0	256472	1876	0.943	0.0	308474
1826*	1.010	0.0	261871	1881	0.919	0.6	312812
1831	1.019	0.0	267270	1886	0.898	0.7	314607
1836	1.018	0.0	274086	1891	0.870	1.7	313278
1841	1.010	0.0	280208	1896	0.865	0.0	309182
1846	1.000	0.0	285864	1901	0.849	0.0	308269
1851	0.990	0.0	288915	1906	0.829	0.0	305489

NOTE: R/CB RATIO REFERS TO THE POPULATION COMPUTED BY THE BALANCE OF BIRTHS
       AND DEATHS OVER THE REPORTED POPULATION
* INTERPOLATED VALUES

TABLE 2 FEMALE BIRTH ESTIMATES: 1801-1805 TO 1901-1905

DATE	% COR-RECTION	FINAL BIRTH ESTIMATE	CRUDE BIRTH RATE	DATE	% COR-RECTION	FINAL BIRTH ESTIMATE	CRUDE BIRTH RATE
1801-1805	7.3	41904	35.2	1856-1860	0.0	39768	27.0
1806-1810	3.1	40921	33.8	1861-1865	0.0	41642	28.0
1811-1815	6.1	42696	34.4	1866-1870	0.0	41626	27.5
1816-1820	0.0	40481	31.9	1871-1875	0.0	40058	26.1
1821-1825	0.0	41489	32.0	1876-1880	0.0	40128	25.8
1826-1830	0.0	41033	31.0	1881-1885	0.0	37355	23.8
1831-1835	0.0	41708	30.8	1886-1890	0.0	34810	22.2
1836-1840	0.0	40844	29.5	1891-1895	0.0	33705	21.7
1841-1845	0.0	40811	28.8	1896-1900	0.0	34106	22.1
1846-1850	1.5	40114	27.9	1901-1905	0.0	32132	20.9
1851-1855	0.0	39556	27.2				

TABLE 3 FEMALE POPULATION ESTIMATES,
DISTRIBUTION BY AGE: 1801 TO 1906

AGE	1801	1806	1811	1816	1821	1826	1831	1836	1841	1846	1851
0- 4	33906	29550	29494	31244	30452	30583	29863	31277	31453	31664	31197
5- 9	28154	29203	25850	25818	27699	26904	27066	26684	28139	28377	28539
10-14	25618	26577	27899	24508	24585	26534	26031	26138	25666	27073	27323
15-19	23329	24175	25381	26440	23328	23542	25664	25129	25129	24683	25670
20-24	20983	21754	22822	23797	24919	22097	22506	24515	23932	23946	22526
25-29	18673	19372	20338	21206	22243	23390	20919	21309	23164	22631	22242
30-34	16489	17098	17967	18758	19686	20722	21965	19663	20005	21767	21251
35-39	14456	14971	15728	16445	17291	18199	19299	20492	18335	18676	20374
40-44	12573	13030	13674	14298	15061	15876	16828	17885	18990	17013	17432
45-49	10841	11249	11815	12343	13004	13730	14574	15485	16460	17499	15802
50-54	9185	9520	10014	10478	11039	11647	12373	13179	14020	14926	16020
55-59	7533	7797	8199	8607	9037	9579	10151	10848	11595	12361	13287
60-64	5820	6038	6349	6682	7107	7483	7891	8446	9093	9749	10448
65-69	4137	4283	4522	4778	5116	5395	5666	6069	6580	7114	7662
70-74	2600	2696	2846	3033	3276	3460	3623	3889	4245	4628	5022
75-79	1366	1400	1485	1594	1748	1848	1924	2079	2295	2524	2758
80+	647	664	695	745	820	884	929	998	1106	1232	1363

AGE	1856	1861	1866	1871	1876	1881	1886	1891	1896	1901	1906
0- 4	31592	31149	33286	33852	32501	34072	32173	29817	28606	29336	28234
5- 9	28454	28573	28437	30586	31037	30171	31784	29933	27577	26696	27518
10-14	27585	27431	27636	27530	29576	30003	29147	30729	28862	26697	25779
15-19	26039	26220	26196	26343	26107	27658	27925	27138	28602	27128	24660
20-24	23660	23919	24295	24108	23978	22650	23788	24182	23268	25392	23159
25-29	21035	22029	22421	22743	22427	21883	20446	21605	21894	21371	23097
30-34	21010	19779	20826	21243	21505	21236	20712	19327	20390	20811	20270
35-39	20016	19699	18635	19687	20055	20431	20207	19692	18314	19435	19869
40-44	19141	18716	18511	17583	18564	19113	19533	19297	18762	17507	18662
45-49	16296	17806	17496	17384	16510	17655	18246	18620	18357	17892	16797
50-54	14575	14948	16416	16220	16117	15564	16717	17242	17553	17339	17032
55-59	14383	13004	13424	14835	14658	14851	14430	15457	15893	16220	16164
60-64	11367	12197	11130	11581	12785	12898	13147	12747	13598	14063	14473
65-69	8345	8972	9746	8987	9338	10596	10775	10954	10562	11352	11867
70-74	5521	5923	6469	7122	6555	7052	8082	8192	8270	8050	8767
75-79	3075	3315	3630	4035	4431	4268	4650	5307	5330	5447	5393
80+	1539	1687	1869	2095	2330	2712	2847	3040	3346	3534	3748

[424]

TABLE 4 MARRIED WOMEN ESTIMATES,
DISTRIBUTION BY AGE: 1831 TO 1901

AGE	1831	1836	1841	1846	1851	1856	1861	1866
15-19	1261	1283	1339	1424	1513	1629	1849	2083
20-24	8257	9283	9380	9724	9447	10352	10880	11725
25-29	13471	14011	15581	15553	15601	15057	16070	16658
30-34	16492	14959	15467	17065	16863	16875	16044	17049
35-39	14967	16033	14544	14973	16467	16320	16158	15371
40-44	13100	13958	14982	13517	13903	15352	15040	14904
45-49	10620	11320	12226	13128	11916	12386	13565	13359

AGE	1871	1876	1881	1886	1891	1896	1901
15-19	2188	2027	1960	1757	1471	1507	1943
20-24	11862	12011	11368	11065	10677	10716	12026
25-29	17238	17033	16861	15828	16123	16136	16276
30-34	17462	17811	17843	17433	16250	17001	17190
35-39	16212	16589	17330	17115	16566	15543	16253
40-44	14032	14835	15853	16159	15764	15484	14226
45-49	13089	12450	14070	14489	14505	14508	13781

TABLE 5 DEMOGRAPHIC INDICES AND FEMALE SINGULATE MEAN AGE
AT MARRIAGE: 1831 TO 1901

DATE	IF OVERALL FERTILITY	IG MARITAL FERTILITY	IH ILLEGITIMATE FERTILITY	IM PROPORTION MARRIED	SINGULATE MEAN AGE AT MARRIAGE
1831	0.321	0.562	0.035	0.543	24.7
1836	0.315	0.541	0.040	0.549	24.3
1841	0.310	0.520	0.043	0.561	24.1
1846	0.307	0.504	0.040	0.575	23.9
1851	0.303	0.490	0.040	0.585	23.7
1856	0.300	0.477	0.044	0.592	23.4
1861	0.308	0.490	0.035	0.600	23.1
1866	0.313	0.488	0.036	0.613	22.9
1871	0.304	0.470	0.034	0.620	22.8
1876	0.298	0.457	0.033	0.626	22.8
1881	0.290	0.438	0.034	0.633	22.9
1886	0.271	0.418	0.033	0.618	23.2
1891	0.258	0.407	0.032	0.603	23.3
1896	0.256	0.405	0.032	0.603	23.1
1901	0.247	0.385	0.029	0.612	

MORTALITY PATTERN: WEST
MIGRATION: FULL STRENGTH. CHILD MIGRANTS SUBTRACTED AFTER 1866, AND POPULATION
TOTALS INTERPOLATED BETWEEN 1846 AND 1876, 1876 AND 1896, AND 1896 AND 1906

TABLE 1   FEMALE POPULATION ESTIMATES: 1801 TO 1906

DATE	R/CB RATIO	% COR-RECTION	FINAL POPULATION ESTIMATE	DATE	R/CB RATIO	% COR-RECTION	FINAL POPULATION ESTIMATE
1801	0.983	3.8	207695	1856	0.974	2.5	247469
1806	1.019	0.0	208506	1861	0.970	2.0	244761
1811*	1.033	0.0	212719	1866	0.966	1.8	241911
1816*	1.021	0.0	216932	1871	0.946	3.0	237134
1821	0.991	0.0	221145	1876	0.965	-0.4	228620
1826*	0.990	0.0	228712	1881	0.957	-0.2	225104
1831	1.007	0.0	236279	1886	0.955	-0.2	223061
1836	1.009	0.0	241362	1891	0.950	-0.0	220029
1841	1.001	0.0	243001	1896	0.964	-1.5	215830
1846	1.000	0.0	245469	1901	0.964	-0.7	215341
1851	0.987	1.3	246752	1906	0.974	-1.6	213812

NOTE: R/CB RATIO REFERS TO THE POPULATION COMPUTED BY THE BALANCE OF BIRTHS
        AND DEATHS OVER THE REPORTED POPULATION
* INTERPOLATED VALUES

TABLE 2   FEMALE BIRTH ESTIMATES: 1801-1805 TO 1901-1905

DATE	% COR-RECTION	FINAL BIRTH ESTIMATE	CRUDE BIRTH RATE	DATE	% COR-RECTION	FINAL BIRTH ESTIMATE	CRUDE BIRTH RATE
1801-1805	0.0	30010	28.8	1856-1860	0.0	24388	19.8
1806-1810	0.0	27413	26.0	1861-1865	0.0	23856	19.6
1811-1815	3.7	30052	28.0	1866-1870	0.0	23281	19.4
1816-1820	0.0	30691	28.0	1871-1875	0.0	22600	19.4
1821-1825	0.0	30986	27.6	1876-1880	0.0	21875	19.3
1826-1830	0.0	31049	26.7	1881-1885	0.0	21557	19.2
1831-1835	0.0	28052	23.5	1886-1890	0.0	20850	18.8
1836-1840	0.0	26140	21.6	1891-1895	0.0	20380	18.7
1841-1845	0.0	25712	21.1	1896-1900	0.0	20597	19.1
1846-1850	0.0	25020	20.3	1901-1905	0.0	20838	19.4
1851-1855	0.0	24854	20.1				

TABLE 3 FEMALE POPULATION ESTIMATES,
DISTRIBUTION BY AGE: 1801 TO 1906

AGE	1801	1806	1811	1816	1821	1826	1831	1836	1841	1846	1851
0- 4	25944	21167	20614	23283	24782	25106	24591	23199	21879	21830	21594
5- 9	22320	22748	19140	18625	21172	22900	23209	22905	21558	20507	20542
10-14	20823	21676	22346	18470	17760	20650	22622	22673	22161	20975	19984
15-19	19425	20217	21284	21553	17603	17314	20390	22087	21923	21548	20091
20-24	17927	18618	19634	20338	20391	17023	16937	19762	21216	21184	19979
25-29	16403	16997	17914	18615	19124	19586	16521	16314	18879	20394	20059
30-34	14883	15413	16230	16876	17416	18268	18887	15834	15516	18071	19570
35-39	13416	13858	14602	15188	15705	16540	17498	18005	14987	14784	17317
40-44	12015	12396	13039	13581	14058	14831	15745	16592	16956	14210	14150
45-49	10671	11018	11580	12044	12489	13187	14021	14832	15525	15974	13543
50-54	9316	9595	10110	10524	10917	11540	12266	13019	13692	14434	15050
55-59	7883	8081	8527	8930	9309	9831	10432	11114	11747	12449	13309
60-64	6325	6433	6803	7179	7581	8024	8468	9071	9650	10290	11030
65-69	4683	4715	4994	5325	5718	6112	6425	6909	7416	7971	8605
70-74	3083	3074	3257	3511	3849	4168	4395	4757	5146	5590	6088
75-79	1690	1657	1768	1934	2175	2392	2530	2787	3053	3349	3692
80+	863	844	878	957	1096	1241	1343	1504	1696	1908	2149

AGE	1856	1861	1866	1871	1876	1881	1886	1891	1896	1901	1906
0- 4	21643	20642	20364	19579	18395	18577	18846	18170	17309	17984	18167
5- 9	20381	20178	19298	18920	17897	17206	17565	17811	17072	16544	17089
10-14	20024	19798	19612	18719	18238	17426	16778	17137	17415	16828	16224
15-19	19078	19077	18846	18649	17595	17507	16653	16055	16660	17232	16392
20-24	18450	17448	17407	17185	16680	16374	16103	15359	15363	16522	16528
25-29	18852	17313	16340	16275	15855	15784	15439	15214	14739	15052	15912
30-34	19257	18002	16540	15559	15360	15175	15153	14824	14623	14306	14531
35-39	18783	18375	17201	15747	14681	14677	14570	14546	14197	14120	13772
40-44	16606	17898	17545	16364	14859	14001	14087	13974	13877	13630	13548
45-49	13515	15752	17013	16615	15377	14101	13381	13451	13253	13232	13004
50-54	12800	12677	14806	15918	15415	14415	13331	12638	12592	12471	12472
55-59	13917	11735	11660	13538	14398	14124	13340	12324	11566	11601	11508
60-64	11832	12228	10351	10215	11684	12670	12577	11863	10845	10293	10319
65-69	9265	9788	10166	8530	8253	9684	10663	10568	9834	9122	8650
70-74	6607	6980	7422	7623	6237	6234	7454	8191	7983	7563	7009
75-79	4048	4288	4568	4787	4758	4061	4158	4960	5334	5319	5034
80+	2412	2581	2773	2910	2935	3087	2964	2943	3171	3522	3655

TABLE 4 MARRIED WOMEN ESTIMATES,
DISTRIBUTION BY AGE: 1831 TO 1901

AGE	1831	1836	1841	1846	1851	1856	1861	1866
15-19	734	829	864	899	896	920	975	944
20-24	5213	6317	7077	7395	7324	7126	7120	6877
25-29	9488	9639	11507	12811	12984	12569	11873	11504
30-34	13112	11201	11223	13332	14713	14736	13992	13022
35-39	12854	13393	11349	11355	13477	14794	14611	13763
40-44	12137	12793	13196	11116	11123	13115	14168	13872
45-49	10252	10841	11499	11915	10168	10210	11933	12855

AGE	1871	1876	1881	1886	1891	1896	1901
15-19	924	929	1022	971	860	910	1150
20-24	7142	7174	7199	7187	6940	7164	7571
25-29	11153	11219	11410	11247	11111	10848	11353
30-34	12346	12030	12067	12178	11965	11789	11586
35-39	12595	11805	11723	11737	11799	11483	11402
40-44	12805	11622	10971	11019	10994	10856	10607
45-49	12353	11416	10490	9984	10084	9826	9719

TABLE 5 DEMOGRAPHIC INDICES AND FEMALE SINGULATE MEAN AGE
AT MARRIAGE: 1831 TO 1901

DATE	IF OVERALL FERTILITY	IG MARITAL FERTILITY	IH ILLEGITIMATE FERTILITY	IM PROPORTION MARRIED	SINGULATE MEAN AGE AT MARRIAGE
1831	0.278	0.516	0.030	0.510	25.7
1836	0.249	0.465	0.029	0.504	25.3
1841	0.234	0.429	0.031	0.510	24.9
1846	0.223	0.395	0.033	0.527	24.6
1851	0.218	0.364	0.037	0.554	24.3
1856	0.219	0.355	0.033	0.578	24.0
1861	0.222	0.352	0.037	0.590	23.9
1866	0.226	0.357	0.039	0.588	23.8
1871	0.228	0.366	0.036	0.583	23.6
1876	0.231	0.364	0.039	0.590	23.4
1881	0.229	0.358	0.038	0.597	23.3
1886	0.227	0.347	0.043	0.606	23.3
1891	0.226	0.341	0.045	0.612	23.2
1896	0.227	0.342	0.047	0.610	23.1
1901	0.225	0.340	0.046	0.608	

MORTALITY PATTERN: NORTH
MIGRATION: GRADUAL, WITH CHILD MIGRANTS SUBTRACTED AFTER 1866, AND POPULATION
  TOTALS OBTAINED IN 1856, 1871 TO 1881, 1891 AND 1901 BY INTERPOLATION OF R/CB

TABLE 1 FEMALE POPULATION ESTIMATES: 1801 TO 1906

DATE	R/CB RATIO	% CORRECTION	FINAL POPULATION ESTIMATE	DATE	R/CB RATIO	% CORRECTION	FINAL POPULATION ESTIMATE
1801	1.087	3.5	155737	1856	0.983	1.1	170247
1806	1.087	0.0	153855	1861	0.997	0.0	172198
1811*	1.073	0.0	154809	1866	0.999	0.0	174005
1816*	1.047	0.0	155762	1871	0.974	3.1	174774
1821	1.003	0.0	156716	1876	0.991	1.6	174821
1826*	1.002	0.0	161114	1881	0.988	1.9	175772
1831	1.011	0.0	165512	1886	1.011	-0.6	176644
1836	1.015	0.0	165800	1891	1.000	0.6	177534
1841	1.006	0.0	167088	1896	1.013	-0.9	176782
1846	1.000	0.0	169222	1901	1.003	0.5	177189
1851	0.992	0.0	170124	1906	1.015	-1.4	176047

NOTE: R/CB RATIO REFERS TO THE POPULATION COMPUTED BY THE BALANCE OF BIRTHS
        AND DEATHS OVER THE REPORTED POPULATION
* INTERPOLATED VALUES

TABLE 2 FEMALE BIRTH ESTIMATES: 1801-1805 TO 1901-1905

DATE	% CORRECTION	FINAL BIRTH ESTIMATE	CRUDE BIRTH RATE	DATE	% CORRECTION	FINAL BIRTH ESTIMATE	CRUDE BIRTH RATE
1801-1805	24.0	24786	32.0	1856-1860	0.0	21451	25.1
1806-1810	5.0	24037	31.1	1861-1865	0.0	20934	24.2
1811-1815	5.3	25545	32.9	1866-1870	0.0	19563	22.4
1816-1820	0.0	25288	32.4	1871-1875	0.0	18925	21.7
1821-1825	0.0	24520	30.9	1876-1880	0.0	19189	21.9
1826-1830	0.0	23486	28.8	1881-1885	0.0	19100	21.7
1831-1835	0.0	22693	27.4	1886-1890	0.0	18621	21.0
1836-1840	0.0	21119	25.4	1891-1895	0.0	18080	20.4
1841-1845	0.0	21398	25.5	1896-1900	0.0	17706	20.0
1846-1850	0.0	21727	25.6	1901-1905	0.0	17115	19.4
1851-1855	0.0	20893	24.6				

TABLE 3 FEMALE POPULATION ESTIMATES,
DISTRIBUTION BY AGE: 1801 TO 1906

AGE	1801	1806	1811	1816	1821	1826	1831	1836	1841	1846	1851
0- 4	25033	17077	17060	18101	18812	18507	18055	16889	16819	17344	17581
5- 9	19827	20168	14055	13988	15174	16144	16084	15336	14853	14958	15374
10-14	17302	18254	18781	13007	12858	14413	15434	15183	14493	14107	14152
15-19	15362	16326	17391	17775	12162	12445	14025	14858	14539	13931	13471
20-24	13594	14435	15491	16393	16559	11727	12065	13450	14180	13930	13203
25-29	11958	12664	13586	14485	15171	15855	11292	11487	12765	13515	13188
30-34	10419	11017	11794	12573	13296	14397	15139	10652	10830	12092	12752
35-39	8995	9480	10141	10791	11436	12494	13618	14135	9969	10189	11338
40-44	7718	8106	8647	9195	9741	10659	11726	12610	13142	9321	9500
45-49	6575	6907	7344	7788	8250	9022	9943	10789	11658	12219	8646
50-54	5531	5802	6174	6526	6904	7546	8314	9034	9867	10727	11218
55-59	4523	4718	5021	5314	5632	6138	6766	7336	8072	8880	9634
60-64	3524	3626	3849	4077	4369	4755	5237	5661	6289	6985	7666
65-69	2530	2554	2688	2844	3095	3389	3740	4018	4528	5094	5646
70-74	1600	1562	1626	1709	1902	2099	2342	2500	2877	3300	3706
75-79	841	781	796	830	949	1059	1200	1280	1519	1791	2052
80+	405	379	366	367	406	463	532	582	690	840	999

AGE	1856	1861	1866	1871	1876	1881	1886	1891	1896	1901	1906
0- 4	16848	17862	17682	16517	16027	16550	16510	16115	15427	15237	14852
5- 9	15601	15209	15258	16131	15077	14765	15259	15272	14779	14289	14088
10-14	14624	14907	14577	15644	15517	14527	14226	14754	14730	14343	13800
15-19	13600	14042	14320	14096	15093	14904	13901	13719	14230	14423	13757
20-24	12847	12893	13279	13704	13391	14182	13904	13141	12976	13911	13474
25-29	12573	12225	12270	12735	13103	12732	13461	13303	12557	12615	13233
30-34	12513	11974	11673	11765	12205	12569	12210	12958	12783	12139	12127
35-39	12020	11860	11390	11140	11229	11678	12033	11718	12408	12292	11649
40-44	10623	11340	11237	10820	10590	10715	11156	11513	11181	11865	11772
45-49	8854	9975	10697	10625	10241	10068	10201	10630	10939	10635	11321
50-54	7974	8237	9327	10020	9966	9657	9510	9639	10013	10306	10069
55-59	10113	7270	7555	8567	9218	9228	8958	8826	8909	9259	9582
60-64	8335	8881	6433	6697	7605	8245	8266	8035	7871	7974	8317
65-69	6197	6885	7411	5373	5615	6433	6986	7012	6762	6657	6777
70-74	4093	4638	5226	5624	4090	4330	4979	5414	5373	5217	5171
75-79	2286	2642	3052	3434	3711	2753	2921	3363	3601	3607	3534
80+	1149	1359	1618	1884	2155	2438	2164	2122	2244	2420	2524

[430]

TABLE 4 MARRIED WOMEN ESTIMATES,
DISTRIBUTION BY AGE: 1831 TO 1901

AGE	1831	1836	1841	1846	1851	1856	1861	1866
15-19	1001	1068	1054	1018	992	1010	1424	1411
20-24	6304	7043	7457	7354	6994	6828	6874	7512
25-29	8870	9006	10029	10628	10376	9891	9616	9643
30-34	12693	8892	9065	10131	10684	10473	10012	9736
35-39	11337	11689	8286	8486	9450	10007	9863	9442
40-44	9446	10061	10579	7536	7696	8599	9173	9053
45-49	7584	8119	8902	9402	6681	6841	7708	8224

AGE	1871	1876	1881	1886	1891	1896	1901
15-19	1153	1186	1073	900	823	825	1031
20-24	7646	7363	7589	7375	6923	6867	7144
25-29	10085	10318	10060	10526	10457	9932	10069
30-34	9767	10149	10432	10113	10711	10615	10145
35-39	9169	9205	9611	9831	9564	10106	10058
40-44	8629	8402	8507	8768	9029	8710	9232
45-49	8054	7711	7599	7591	7894	8049	7776

TABLE 5 DEMOGRAPHIC INDICES AND FEMALE SINGULATE MEAN AGE
AT MARRIAGE: 1831 TO 1901

DATE	IF OVERALL FERTILITY	IG MARITAL FERTILITY	IH ILLEGITIMATE FERTILITY	IM PROPORTION MARRIED	SINGULATE MEAN AGE AT MARRIAGE
1831	0.296	0.426	0.046	0.658	22.6
1836	0.284	0.421	0.043	0.639	22.5
1841	0.280	0.421	0.035	0.636	22.4
1846	0.285	0.427	0.031	0.642	22.4
1851	0.283	0.416	0.036	0.651	22.4
1856	0.282	0.409	0.043	0.652	22.2
1861	0.283	0.411	0.044	0.651	22.0
1866	0.270	0.390	0.044	0.653	22.1
1871	0.255	0.370	0.041	0.649	22.2
1876	0.248	0.366	0.037	0.642	22.2
1881	0.245	0.361	0.040	0.639	22.3
1886	0.242	0.353	0.042	0.641	22.3
1891	0.237	0.345	0.041	0.644	22.3
1896	0.232	0.339	0.041	0.642	22.4
1901	0.223	0.327	0.039	0.638	

[431]

MORTALITY PATTERN: NORTH
MIGRATION: NO CORRECTION MADE FOR MIGRATION BY AGE

TABLE 1   FEMALE POPULATION ESTIMATES: 1801 TO 1906

DATE	R/CB RATIO	% COR- RECTION	FINAL POPULATION ESTIMATE	DATE	R/CB RATIO	% COR- RECTION	FINAL POPULATION ESTIMATE
1801	1.036	6.6	336085	1856	1.012	8.2	431559
1806	1.032	6.6	350257	1861	1.009	4.7	421456
1811*	1.004	6.6	355045	1866	1.002	5.0	424416
1816*	0.993	6.6	359834	1871	0.996	0.0	402758
1821	0.968	6.6	364621	1876	1.007	0.0	406935
1826*	0.956	6.6	372587	1881	1.004	0.0	411807
1831	0.955	6.6	380552	1886	1.004	0.0	419377
1836	0.990	6.6	397350	1891	1.013	0.0	429663
1841	0.993	6.6	403949	1896	1.008	0.0	428909
1846	1.000	6.6	412696	1901	1.009	0.0	436345
1851	0.994	8.3	420457	1906	1.001	0.0	442285

NOTE: R/CB RATIO REFERS TO THE POPULATION COMPUTED BY THE BALANCE OF BIRTHS
        AND DEATHS OVER THE REPORTED POPULATION
* INTERPOLATED VALUES

TABLE 2   FEMALE BIRTH ESTIMATES: 1801-1805 TO 1901-1905

DATE	% COR- RECTION	FINAL BIRTH ESTIMATE	CRUDE BIRTH RATE	DATE	% COR- RECTION	FINAL BIRTH ESTIMATE	CRUDE BIRTH RATE
1801-1805	15.2	50150	29.2	1856-1860	0.0	56720	26.6
1806-1810	12.4	48815	27.7	1861-1865	0.0	57333	27.1
1811-1815	5.7	46498	26.0	1866-1870	0.0	58144	28.1
1816-1820	10.4	53862	29.7	1871-1875	0.0	56706	28.0
1821-1825	8.5	55325	30.0	1876-1880	0.0	58131	28.4
1826-1830	6.2	53515	28.4	1881-1885	0.0	59963	28.9
1831-1835	0.0	49624	25.5	1886-1890	0.0	61121	28.8
1836-1840	0.0	51189	25.6	1891-1895	0.0	56800	26.5
1841-1845	0.0	52186	25.6	1896-1900	0.0	57752	26.7
1846-1850	0.0	52393	25.2	1901-1905	0.0	56852	25.9
1851-1855	0.0	53264	25.0				

TABLE 3 FEMALE POPULATION ESTIMATES,
DISTRIBUTION BY AGE: 1801 TO 1906

AGE	1801	1806	1811	1816	1821	1826	1831	1836	1841	1846	1851
0- 4	41828	41303	39565	37570	42574	43943	42663	40730	41122	42247	42311
5- 9	35771	37703	36545	35131	32791	37411	38820	38883	36239	36819	37801
10-14	32749	34354	35458	34705	32945	31016	35629	38221	37278	34917	35513
15-19	30368	31817	32668	34089	32977	31586	29950	35582	37150	36406	34147
20-24	28048	29409	30159	31304	32284	31510	30397	29808	34468	36159	35482
25-29	25774	27024	27738	28747	29482	30674	30151	30077	28711	33360	35040
30-34	23551	24685	25342	26273	26894	27822	29148	29623	28771	27600	32105
35-39	21351	22408	23001	23838	24400	25190	26237	28415	28122	27452	26360
40-44	19259	20190	20754	21499	21993	22702	23595	25402	26794	26655	26042
45-49	17262	18112	18599	19291	19724	20346	21143	22712	23816	25252	25141
50-54	15317	16067	16515	17106	17507	18048	18741	20126	21062	22201	23557
55-59	13288	13951	14343	14854	15168	15647	16233	17413	18226	19177	20224
60-64	11093	11647	11995	12397	12636	12998	13486	14443	15113	15913	16741
65-69	8646	9113	9397	9697	9841	10095	10435	11165	11679	12303	12940
70-74	6072	6401	6639	6826	6892	7028	7236	7701	8064	8501	8933
75-79	3617	3850	4004	4113	4118	4169	4260	4506	4707	4974	5221
80+	2118	2222	2323	2393	2395	2404	2431	2542	2628	2760	2898

AGE	1856	1861	1866	1871	1876	1881	1886	1891	1896	1901	1906
0- 4	43490	43763	45425	42768	44096	45927	47692	48789	44617	46615	46582
5- 9	38221	37232	38513	37478	37392	38749	40564	42342	42637	39787	41771
10-14	36757	35322	35407	34674	35845	35556	36974	38966	40050	40873	37960
15-19	35003	34451	34074	32397	33720	34585	34414	36038	37400	38906	39443
20-24	33543	32695	33120	31066	31392	32422	33359	33427	34470	36210	37425
25-29	34658	31150	31248	30005	29907	30005	31091	32211	31783	33187	34655
30-34	33995	31961	29561	28083	28654	28381	28570	29806	30407	30397	31575
35-39	30915	31107	30093	26341	26586	26977	26813	27173	27912	28866	28732
40-44	25214	28096	29088	26618	24746	24855	25311	25324	25269	26323	27119
45-49	24768	22783	26121	25576	24856	23001	23187	23768	23414	23696	24595
50-54	23651	22133	20946	22700	23601	22845	21220	21530	21729	21719	21913
55-59	21644	20632	19861	17735	20400	21167	20571	19226	19206	19692	19658
60-64	17816	18086	17727	16046	15196	17509	18251	17838	16412	16695	17155
65-69	13748	13857	14457	13257	12710	12126	14048	14714	14155	13309	13636
70-74	9500	9537	9871	9560	9267	9029	8671	10082	10392	10272	9802
75-79	5555	5566	5732	5448	5562	5545	5448	5243	5996	6397	6483
80+	3080	3087	3172	3002	3005	3128	3193	3188	3059	3402	3781

[433]

TABLE 4 MARRIED WOMEN ESTIMATES,
DISTRIBUTION BY AGE: 1831 TO 1901

AGE	1831	1836	1841	1846	1851	1856	1861	1866
15-19	820	1007	1090	1112	1091	1176	1265	1213
20-24	7390	7448	8889	9640	9795	9603	9721	9605
25-29	15296	15545	15169	18009	19318	19503	17874	18281
30-34	18933	19442	19165	18638	21948	23496	22295	20801
35-39	18469	20096	20116	19830	19189	22638	22856	22176
40-44	17866	19126	20266	20220	19768	19114	21206	21864
45-49	15169	16172	17092	18220	18177	17889	16364	18663

AGE	1871	1876	1881	1886	1891	1896	1901
15-19	1171	1246	1374	1395	1270	1201	1604
20-24	9282	9724	10320	10893	10860	11451	12064
25-29	17008	17377	17879	18840	19836	19505	21013
30-34	19791	19870	20028	20301	21473	22207	22153
35-39	19252	19471	19766	19625	19921	20679	21584
40-44	19607	18156	18400	18145	18113	18002	18802
45-49	17741	17155	16109	15966	16224	15814	15695

TABLE 5 DEMOGRAPHIC INDICES AND FEMALE SINGULATE MEAN AGE
AT MARRIAGE: 1831 TO 1901

DATE	IF OVERALL FERTILITY	IG MARITAL FERTILITY	IH ILLEGITIMATE FERTILITY	IM PROPORTION MARRIED	SINGULATE MEAN AGE AT MARRIAGE
1831	0.298	0.580	0.054	0.462	26.8
1836	0.279	0.538	0.056	0.463	26.4
1841	0.278	0.540	0.054	0.461	26.2
1846	0.273	0.521	0.056	0.467	26.0
1851	0.272	0.499	0.059	0.483	25.8
1856	0.278	0.491	0.066	0.498	25.6
1861	0.298	0.519	0.072	0.505	25.5
1866	0.305	0.531	0.075	0.504	25.4
1871	0.324	0.573	0.079	0.497	25.3
1876	0.322	0.569	0.079	0.497	25.0
1881	0.328	0.574	0.080	0.503	24.8
1886	0.331	0.572	0.085	0.506	24.8
1891	0.315	0.539	0.083	0.508	24.9
1896	0.301	0.514	0.080	0.509	24.8
1901	0.291	0.494	0.076	0.513	

MORTALITY PATTERN: WEST
MIGRATION: FULL STRENGTH, WITH POPULATION TOTALS OBTAINED BY TREND OF R/CB

TABLE 1 FEMALE POPULATION ESTIMATES: 1801 TO 1906

DATE	R/CB RATIO	% COR- RECTION	FINAL POPULATION ESTIMATE	DATE	R/CB RATIO	% COR- RECTION	FINAL POPULATION ESTIMATE
1801	0.959	4.0	126701	1856	0.984	0.1	164313
1806	0.998	0.0	128181	1861	0.972	0.4	163625
1811*	0.997	0.0	132644	1866	0.965	0.2	164942
1816*	0.999	0.0	137107	1871	0.948	1.0	166070
1821	0.994	0.0	141570	1876	0.951	-0.2	165893
1826*	1.001	0.0	145254	1881	0.952	-1.3	168480
1831	1.005	0.0	148938	1886	0.953	-2.4	170907
1836	1.009	0.0	153190	1891	0.937	-1.7	171932
1841	0.995	0.0	155414	1896	0.912	-0.0	171209
1846	1.000	0.0	160660	1901	0.893	1.1	171459
1851	0.987	0.7	162597	1906	0.874	2.3	172086

NOTE: R/CB RATIO REFERS TO THE POPULATION COMPUTED BY THE BALANCE OF BIRTHS
       AND DEATHS OVER THE REPORTED POPULATION
* INTERPOLATED VALUES

TABLE 2 FEMALE BIRTH ESTIMATES: 1801-1805 TO 1901-1905

DATE	% COR- RECTION	FINAL BIRTH ESTIMATE	CRUDE BIRTH RATE	DATE	% COR- RECTION	FINAL BIRTH ESTIMATE	CRUDE BIRTH RATE
1801-1805	6.4	18313	28.7	1856-1860	3.4	18932	23.1
1806-1810	0.0	17770	27.3	1861-1865	0.0	19506	23.7
1811-1815	5.5	18772	27.8	1866-1870	0.0	20076	24.3
1816-1820	0.0	19152	27.5	1871-1875	0.0	20107	24.2
1821-1825	0.0	17994	25.1	1876-1880	0.0	20081	24.0
1826-1830	4.1	18953	25.8	1881-1885	0.0	19659	23.2
1831-1835	8.5	20155	26.7	1886-1890	0.0	18794	21.9
1836-1840	2.8	19219	24.9	1891-1895	0.0	17274	20.1
1841-1845	0.0	19772	25.0	1896-1900	0.0	17024	19.9
1846-1850	0.0	19825	24.5	1901-1905	0.0	16338	19.0
1851-1855	0.0	19308	23.6				

TABLE 3 FEMALE POPULATION ESTIMATES,
DISTRIBUTION BY AGE: 1801 TO 1906

AGE	1801	1806	1811	1816	1821	1826	1831	1836	1841	1846	1851
0- 4	14057	13946	14573	15219	15767	14725	15402	16347	15843	16594	16270
5- 9	12506	12635	12944	13479	14107	14662	13644	14266	15091	14892	15339
10-14	11863	12085	12330	12640	13103	13822	14338	13348	13773	14836	14468
15-19	11243	11458	11787	12034	12280	12831	13510	14020	12880	13532	14273
20-24	10568	10751	11090	11411	11606	11931	12441	13103	13433	12566	12690
25-29	9852	10022	10340	10664	10937	11202	11491	11984	12480	13028	11888
30-34	9133	9278	9588	9888	10171	10500	10729	11007	11360	12046	12408
35-39	8409	8540	9828	9115	9380	9708	9998	10217	10381	10909	11432
40-44	7696	7813	8081	8345	8601	8904	9193	9468	9585	9916	10318
45-49	6991	7100	7344	7588	7823	8110	8375	8647	8825	9097	9329
50-54	6256	6342	6577	6794	7012	7268	7515	7759	7947	8258	8445
55-59	5451	5508	5730	5928	6126	6351	6562	6784	6964	7262	7478
60-64	4525	4563	4771	4944	5130	5315	5490	5670	5849	6113	6291
65-69	3491	3511	3704	3850	4015	4167	4297	4434	4593	4824	4964
70-74	2423	2424	2582	2702	2837	2951	3046	3137	3265	3443	3550
75-79	1425	1413	1525	1605	1706	1780	1839	1895	1983	2101	2167
80+	801	791	848	900	969	1026	1068	1103	1163	1243	1287

AGE	1856	1861	1866	1871	1876	1881	1886	1891	1896	1901	1906
0- 4	16105	15362	16204	16627	16404	17163	17041	16240	14870	14956	14645
5- 9	15110	14772	14243	15001	15288	15385	16192	16048	15264	14102	14304
10-14	14905	14621	14349	13819	14523	14893	15006	15787	15639	14917	13802
15-19	13848	14197	14010	13713	13144	13916	14266	14357	15122	15034	14335
20-24	13241	12712	13200	12956	12582	12132	12829	13136	13228	14053	13958
25-29	11948	12386	11981	12416	12120	11868	11419	12076	12372	12522	13354
30-34	11329	11312	11802	11398	11771	11602	11377	10933	11562	11898	12093
35-39	11806	10703	10753	11209	10782	11258	11121	10896	10461	11116	11495
40-44	10855	11135	10153	10192	10585	10298	10785	10647	10423	10052	10737
45-49	9750	10187	10509	9577	9579	10064	9824	10281	10141	9973	9669
50-54	8708	9033	9494	9788	8887	9005	9496	9265	9685	9600	9496
55-59	7699	7865	8219	8631	8853	8171	8318	8763	8540	8979	8963
60-64	6527	6635	6852	7150	7457	7813	7252	7373	7756	7620	8081
65-69	5159	5263	5427	5594	5735	6205	6548	6068	6158	6544	6502
70-74	3698	3763	3910	4022	4098	4391	4751	5004	4627	4755	5125
75-79	2271	2302	2398	2483	2516	2685	2909	3141	3298	3099	3242
80+	1356	1378	1437	1492	1520	1632	1773	1917	2062	2237	2286

[436]

TABLE 4   MARRIED WOMEN ESTIMATES,
DISTRIBUTION BY AGE: 1831 TO 1901

AGE	1831	1836	1841	1846	1851	1856	1861	1866
15-19	442	477	458	507	567	589	590	611
20-24	3499	3818	4074	3982	4213	4619	4673	4386
25-29	6521	6983	7491	8063	7581	7847	8371	8328
30-34	7680	8013	8445	9148	9606	8929	9062	9600
35-39	7728	7977	8235	8799	9348	9769	8943	9063
40-44	7662	7863	8004	8345	8721	9201	9447	8620
45-49	6647	6820	7014	7310	7540	7909	8269	8535

AGE	1871	1876	1881	1886	1891	1896	1901
15-19	716	768	722	706	640	573	729
20-24	4612	5207	5298	5390	5310	5309	5603
25-29	8046	8181	8686	8539	8983	9050	9177
30-34	9371	9340	9441	9614	9320	9827	10043
35-39	9472	9184	9490	9479	9453	9072	9634
40-44	8590	8941	8814	9092	9021	8847	8535
45-49	7687	7709	8255	8086	8463	8262	8107

TABLE 5   DEMOGRAPHIC INDICES AND FEMALE SINGULATE MEAN AGE
AT MARRIAGE: 1831 TO 1901

DATE	IF OVERALL FERTILITY	IG MARITAL FERTILITY	IH ILLEGITIMATE FERTILITY	IM PROPORTION MARRIED	SINGULATE MEAN AGE AT MARRIAGE
1831	0.286	0.560	0.012	0.499	26.5
1836	0.277	0.528	0.020	0.506	26.0
1841	0.271	0.498	0.020	0.525	25.7
1846	0.270	0.475	0.026	0.544	25.4
1851	0.265	0.455	0.029	0.554	25.1
1856	0.259	0.433	0.032	0.566	24.9
1861	0.263	0.431	0.036	0.575	24.8
1866	0.270	0.452	0.027	0.572	24.8
1871	0.275	0.460	0.025	0.574	24.4
1876	0.279	0.453	0.024	0.595	24.0
1881	0.277	0.436	0.026	0.612	23.9
1886	0.266	0.417	0.028	0.611	24.1
1891	0.247	0.390	0.027	0.607	24.3
1896	0.232	0.368	0.028	0.599	24.2
1901	0.219	0.349	0.025	0.599	

MORTALITY PATTERN: NORTH
MIGRATION: NO CORRECTION MADE FOR MIGRATION BY AGE

TABLE 1 FEMALE POPULATION ESTIMATES: 1801 TO 1906

DATE	R/CB RATIO	% COR-RECTION	FINAL POPULATION ESTIMATE	DATE	R/CB RATIO	% COR-RECTION	FINAL POPULATION ESTIMATE
1801	0.970	4.1	245876	1856	0.988	0.0	289904
1806	1.003	0.0	253586	1861	0.980	0.0	290838
1811*	0.992	0.8	258797	1866	0.976	0.0	289638
1816*	0.983	1.1	262790	1871	0.961	1.1	285969
1821	0.971	2.2	268906	1876	0.967	0.0	282684
1826*	0.974	1.0	274612	1881	0.954	1.3	282068
1831	0.989	0.0	280319	1886	0.951	1.3	281758
1836	0.998	0.0	284621	1891	0.954	0.6	279532
1841	0.995	0.0	287759	1896	0.955	0.0	276625
1846	1.000	0.0	291971	1901	0.947	0.0	273517
1851	0.992	0.0	290956	1906	0.939	0.0	271585

NOTE: R/CB RATIO REFERS TO THE POPULATION COMPUTED BY THE BALANCE OF BIRTHS
       AND DEATHS OVER THE REPORTED POPULATION
* INTERPOLATED VALUES

TABLE 2 FEMALE BIRTH ESTIMATES: 1801-1805 TO 1901-1905

DATE	% COR-RECTION	FINAL BIRTH ESTIMATE	CRUDE BIRTH RATE	DATE	% COR-RECTION	FINAL BIRTH ESTIMATE	CRUDE BIRTH RATE
1801-1805	4.4	36853	29.5	1856-1860	0.0	34539	23.8
1806-1810	1.6	36128	28.2	1861-1865	0.0	32891	22.7
1811-1815	2.5	38137	29.2	1866-1870	0.0	32600	22.7
1816-1820	0.0	37809	28.4	1871-1875	0.0	31621	22.2
1821-1825	0.0	37283	27.4	1876-1880	0.0	31337	22.2
1826-1830	0.0	35244	25.4	1881-1885	0.0	31253	22.2
1831-1835	0.0	35728	25.3	1886-1890	0.0	29703	21.2
1836-1840	0.0	35528	24.8	1891-1895	0.0	29214	21.0
1841-1845	0.0	35912	24.8	1896-1900	0.0	28703	20.9
1846-1850	4.3	36229	24.9	1901-1905	0.0	27413	20.1
1851-1855	0.0	33911	23.4				

TABLE 3 FEMALE POPULATION ESTIMATES,
DISTRIBUTION BY AGE: 1801 TO 1906

AGE	1801	1806	1811	1816	1821	1826	1831	1836	1841	1846	1851
0- 4	31423	29743	28669	29580	29989	30060	28559	28421	28685	29027	28682
5- 9	26736	27909	26178	24884	26056	26614	26879	25310	25298	25631	25486
10-14	24356	25430	26504	24735	23683	24771	25554	25819	24168	24314	24282
15-19	22477	23459	24491	25441	23880	22800	24097	24914	24974	23542	23359
20-24	20653	21578	22516	23425	24477	22913	22106	23411	24019	24245	22540
25-29	18882	19720	20591	21402	22406	23359	22093	21348	22447	23187	23080
30-34	17164	17915	18687	19423	20326	21247	22376	21180	20336	21525	21919
35-39	15477	16170	16846	17478	18303	19139	20204	21278	20031	19356	20191
40-44	13892	14487	15103	15642	16357	17123	18081	19078	19992	18939	18033
45-49	12384	12931	13453	13940	14554	15217	16085	16973	17825	18795	17544
50-54	10928	11405	11876	12275	12827	13397	14141	14930	15689	16576	17219
55-59	9427	9840	10226	10561	11024	11542	12165	12804	13487	14252	14826
60-64	7831	8153	8452	8685	9083	9528	10058	10536	11104	11750	12212
65-69	6068	6331	6520	6653	6949	7336	7750	8091	8532	9021	9374
70-74	4237	4403	4517	4547	4744	5037	5345	5543	5873	6200	6422
75-79	2505	2619	2654	2636	2736	2928	3117	3214	3421	3619	3729
80+	1458	1495	1513	1485	1513	1601	1710	1772	1878	1992	2059

AGE	1856	1861	1866	1871	1876	1881	1886	1891	1896	1901	1906
0- 4	27218	28232	26805	26105	25541	25783	25940	24614	24164	23892	23275
5- 9	25423	24374	25253	23729	23229	23016	23328	23437	22214	21859	21875
10-14	24275	24280	23289	24045	22636	22318	22105	22376	22471	21270	21024
15-19	23436	23456	23480	22475	23232	22003	21667	21434	21691	21738	20634
20-24	22469	22572	22610	22583	21643	22510	21295	20943	20712	20918	21024
25-29	21561	21530	21644	21624	21629	20862	21678	20482	20137	19879	20142
30-34	21931	20536	20518	20562	20578	20724	19978	20733	19581	19223	19050
35-39	20676	20749	19437	19347	19427	19586	19722	18988	19696	18580	18323
40-44	18920	19440	19515	18206	18161	18376	18528	18632	17930	18581	17614
45-49	16803	17692	18184	18176	16995	17085	17291	17410	17500	16825	17523
50-54	16171	15549	16376	16753	16786	15823	15913	16083	16186	16258	15716
55-59	15507	14641	14077	14738	15122	15292	14432	14495	14640	14734	14901
60-64	12809	13506	12744	12150	12774	13253	13440	12666	12710	12855	13059
65-69	9844	10451	11003	10257	9838	10488	10938	11076	10425	10496	10755
70-74	6765	7234	7657	7921	7449	7276	7825	8147	8234	7800	7999
75-79	3933	4252	4526	4674	4894	4714	4667	5009	5203	5313	5163
80+	2163	2342	2520	2624	2752	2958	3011	3008	3132	3295	3507

TABLE 4   MARRIED WOMEN ESTIMATES,
DISTRIBUTION BY AGE: 1831 TO 1901

AGE	1831	1836	1841	1846	1851	1856	1861	1866
15-19	905	967	1004	983	1066	1067	1064	1149
20-24	7655	8309	8755	9079	8675	8848	9202	8674
25-29	13936	13656	14588	15294	15440	14627	14816	15095
30-34	16439	15672	15199	16223	16641	16770	15826	15914
35-39	15290	16150	15322	14885	15588	16029	16175	15210
40-44	13594	14315	15089	14330	13653	14343	14792	14868
45-49	11462	12049	12757	13492	12596	12080	12781	13152

AGE	1871	1876	1881	1886	1891	1896	1901
15-19	1128	1249	1273	1103	925	985	1428
20-24	9168	9405	9916	9358	9064	9138	9339
25-29	14538	14896	14913	15609	14733	14561	14740
30-34	15994	15742	15982	15683	16416	15565	15379
35-39	15116	15219	15171	15356	14932	15586	14826
40-44	13777	13745	13865	13958	14087	13553	14169
45-49	13003	12151	12150	12328	12459	12461	11978

TABLE 5   DEMOGRAPHIC INDICES AND FEMALE SINGULATE MEAN AGE
AT MARRIAGE: 1831 TO 1901

DATE	IF OVERALL FERTILITY	IG MARITAL FERTILITY	IH ILLEGITIMATE FERTILITY	IM PROPORTION MARRIED	SINGULATE MEAN AGE AT MARRIAGE
1831	0.271	0.471	0.040	0.536	24.4
1836	0.268	0.463	0.044	0.536	24.3
1841	0.268	0.458	0.044	0.541	24.1
1846	0.270	0.450	0.047	0.552	24.0
1851	0.266	0.434	0.050	0.562	23.8
1856	0.262	0.420	0.054	0.568	23.7
1861	0.260	0.409	0.058	0.573	23.7
1866	0.254	0.398	0.064	0.569	23.6
1871	0.252	0.390	0.068	0.571	23.4
1876	0.249	0.379	0.069	0.579	23.2
1881	0.248	0.371	0.072	0.588	23.2
1886	0.244	0.357	0.079	0.594	23.3
1891	0.240	0.349	0.080	0.594	23.3
1896	0.238	0.344	0.083	0.596	23.2
1901	0.233	0.331	0.085	0.603	

MORTALITY PATTERN: WEST
MIGRATION: GRADUAL, WITH POPULATION TOTALS OBTAINED BY TREND OF R/CB

TABLE 1 FEMALE POPULATION ESTIMATES: 1801 TO 1906

DATE	R/CB RATIO	% COR-RECTION	FINAL POPULATION ESTIMATE	DATE	R/CB RATIO	% COR-RECTION	FINAL POPULATION ESTIMATE
1801	1.109	1.0	136414	1856	0.969	1.3	179702
1806	1.101	1.0	147275	1861	0.956	1.1	177890
1811*	1.044	1.0	150824	1866	0.940	1.2	178689
1816*	1.021	1.0	154373	1871	0.924	1.4	178150
1821	1.016	1.0	157923	1876	0.932	-1.2	176751
1826*	1.010	1.0	162660	1881	0.912	-0.6	176672
1831	1.008	1.0	167398	1886	0.910	-2.0	175810
1836	1.019	1.0	172613	1891	0.865	1.4	172881
1841	1.007	1.0	175706	1896	0.860	0.2	168932
1846	1.000	1.0	180181	1901	0.838	1.2	165819
1851	0.987	0.9	181248	1906	0.838	-0.7	163391

NOTE: R/CB RATIO REFERS TO THE POPULATION COMPUTED BY THE BALANCE OF BIRTHS
       AND DEATHS OVER THE REPORTED POPULATION
* INTERPOLATED VALUES

TABLE 2 FEMALE BIRTH ESTIMATES: 1801-1805 TO 1901-1905

DATE	% COR-RECTION	FINAL BIRTH ESTIMATE	CRUDE BIRTH RATE	DATE	% COR-RECTION	FINAL BIRTH ESTIMATE	CRUDE BIRTH RATE
1801-1805	21.5	27238	38.4	1856-1860	0.0	21191	23.7
1806-1810	15.1	28079	37.7	1861-1865	0.0	22825	25.6
1811-1815	12.2	26549	34.8	1866-1870	0.0	22896	25.7
1816-1820	7.6	24865	31.8	1871-1875	0.0	22252	25.1
1821-1825	0.0	24044	30.0	1876-1880	0.0	21180	24.0
1826-1830	0.0	24378	29.5	1881-1885	0.0	19441	22.1
1831-1835	0.0	24841	29.2	1886-1890	0.0	17358	19.9
1836-1840	0.0	24750	28.4	1891-1895	0.0	16258	19.0
1841-1845	0.0	24982	28.1	1896-1900	0.0	16076	19.2
1846-1850	4.6	23633	26.2	1901-1905	0.0	15925	19.3
1851-1855	0.0	21724	24.1				

TABLE 3 FEMALE POPULATION ESTIMATES,
DISTRIBUTION BY AGE: 1801 TO 1906

AGE	1801	1806	1811	1816	1821	1826	1831	1836	1841	1846	1851
0- 4	19943	21314	20949	19560	18341	18367	18635	18805	19053	19645	18440
5- 9	16779	18159	18526	18339	17274	16472	16530	16814	16895	17318	17707
10-14	15056	16298	16849	17500	17549	16642	15914	16120	16140	16323	16595
15-19	13518	14618	15115	15910	16740	16899	16072	15514	15467	15586	15600
20-24	12016	13005	13432	14126	15055	15963	16161	15503	14747	14805	14708
25-29	10613	11471	11857	12444	13246	14240	15140	15452	14621	14012	13916
30-34	9301	10068	10392	10907	11582	12445	13414	14371	14479	13809	13123
35-39	8115	8766	9061	9489	10074	10806	11641	12637	13376	13588	12857
40-44	7029	7601	7841	8219	8705	9339	10043	10894	11690	12479	12583
45-49	6044	6539	6752	7061	7486	8014	8620	9332	10008	10831	11480
50-54	5115	5532	5715	5977	6320	6778	7274	7871	8435	9128	9811
55-59	4216	4552	4700	4907	5183	5556	5973	6439	6914	7485	8045
60-64	3309	3577	3687	3832	4034	4336	4658	5018	5391	5858	6295
65-69	2416	2612	2695	2780	2909	3131	3371	3617	3905	4257	4591
70-74	1594	1714	1768	1815		2023	2181	2336	2528	2777	3004
75-79	883	956	980	997	1025	1101	1185	1264	1378	1524	1661
80+	467	493	505	510	519	550	589	626	679	756	831

AGE	1856	1861	1866	1871	1876	1881	1886	1891	1896	1901	1906
0- 4	16840	16507	18231	18183	17716	17537	16402	14626	13646	13692	13813
5- 9	16556	15158	15026	16531	16494	16326	16277	15206	13528	12694	12836
10-14	16939	15869	14589	14424	15877	15917	15787	15746	13097	12304	12304
15-19	15792	16132	15148	13816	13607	15033	15047	14897	14864	13891	12320
20-24	14585	14735	15081	13945	12546	12289	13556	13496	13345	13373	12418
25-29	13750	13639	13837	14064	12935	11632	11359	12551	12493	12395	12440
30-34	13001	12875	12849	12997	13211	12236	11025	10763	11911	11896	11836
35-39	12194	12112	12078	12026	12173	12489	11615	10463	10215	11354	11379
40-44	11889	11309	11319	11271	11237	11494	11859	11039	9946	9745	10876
45-49	11562	10959	10508	10507	10480	10565	10873	11229	10458	9458	9307
50-54	10387	10497	10039	9619	9639	9736	9885	10184	10519	9838	8945
55-59	8634	9174	9367	8948	8595	8744	8905	9050	9321	9673	9102
60-64	6747	7267	7818	7962	7620	7457	7657	7801	7921	8213	8586
65-69	4915	5288	5787	6205	6332	6209	6149	6313	6421	6577	6885
70-74	3224	3466	3804	4145	4454	4686	4663	4615	4727	4861	5039
75-79	1785	1925	2123	2317	2531	2829	3031	3013	2971	3086	3223
80+	902	977	1085	1191	1306	1494	1721	1889	1938	1977	2081

TABLE 4   MARRIED WOMEN ESTIMATES,
DISTRIBUTION BY AGE: 1831 TO 1901

AGE	1831	1836	1841	1846	1851	1856	1861	1866
15-19	894	894	926	972	1018	1082	963	940
20-24	6169	6079	5956	6159	6305	6445	6718	6322
25-29	9811	10180	9817	9577	9671	9704	9779	10075
30-34	9975	10794	11029	10646	10222	10211	10204	10274
35-39	8862	9681	10381	10654	10159	9682	9681	9723
40-44	7555	8209	8922	9609	9741	9218	8808	8866
45-49	6070	6582	7190	7880	8412	8483	8088	7814

AGE	1871	1876	1881	1886	1891	1896	1901
15-19	1038	1235	1455	1362	1085	958	1117
20-24	6340	6380	6567	6935	6427	6309	6372
25-29	9862	9443	8926	8860	9536	9213	9286
30-34	10448	10450	9863	9108	8948	9830	9711
35-39	9697	9850	10052	9489	8600	8450	9378
40-44	8806	8785	9045	9421	8745	7893	7752
45-49	7776	7757	7889	8268	8480	7887	7087

TABLE 5   DEMOGRAPHIC INDICES AND FEMALE SINGULATE MEAN AGE
AT MARRIAGE: 1831 TO 1901

DATE	IF OVERALL FERTILITY	IG MARITAL FERTILITY	IH ILLEGITIMATE FERTILITY	IM PROPORTION MARRIED	SINGULATE MEAN AGE AT MARRIAGE
1831	0.290	0.523	0.020	0.537	24.1
1836	0.287	0.499	0.021	0.555	23.9
1841	0.290	0.489	0.025	0.569	23.7
1846	0.285	0.478	0.021	0.577	23.6
1851	0.271	0.452	0.019	0.582	23.4
1856	0.261	0.431	0.019	0.586	23.3
1861	0.268	0.441	0.020	0.590	23.3
1866	0.279	0.461	0.018	0.590	23.2
1871	0.283	0.456	0.019	0.605	22.7
1876	0.283	0.441	0.018	0.627	22.4
1881	0.270	0.417	0.018	0.632	22.4
1886	0.246	0.383	0.016	0.627	22.7
1891	0.227	0.361	0.016	0.612	22.8
1896	0.218	0.349	0.016	0.607	22.8
1901	0.216	0.339	0.016	0.618	

MORTALITY PATTERN: WEST
MIGRATION: FULL STRENGTH, WITH POPULATION TOTALS OBTAINED BY TREND OF R/CB

TABLE 1 FEMALE POPULATION ESTIMATES: 1801 TO 1906

DATE	R/CB RATIO	% COR- RECTION	FINAL POPULATION ESTIMATE	DATE	R/CB RATIO	% COR- RECTION	FINAL POPULATION ESTIMATE
1801	1.090	2.4	117829	1856	0.988	2.6	122430
1806	1.099	2.4	122973	1861	0.991	1.6	119807
1811*	1.048	2.4	122962	1866	0.979	2.1	117764
1816*	1.023	2.4	122951	1871	0.964	2.9	115111
1821	1.011	2.4	122941	1876	0.979	0.7	112226
1826*	1.004	2.4	123800	1881	0.960	1.9	109927
1831	0.995	2.4	124659	1886	0.957	1.6	107199
1836	1.001	2.4	125360	1891	0.951	1.4	103970
1841	0.993	2.4	124311	1896	0.953	0.5	100557
1846	1.000	2.4	125810	1901	0.953	-0.2	97596
1851	0.994	2.7	123532	1906	0.940	0.5	95032

NOTE: R/CB RATIO REFERS TO THE POPULATION COMPUTED BY THE BALANCE OF BIRTHS
       AND DEATHS OVER THE REPORTED POPULATION
* INTERPOLATED VALUES

TABLE 2 FEMALE BIRTH ESTIMATES: 1801-1805 TO 1901-1905

DATE	% COR- RECTION	FINAL BIRTH ESTIMATE	CRUDE BIRTH RATE	DATE	% COR- RECTION	FINAL BIRTH ESTIMATE	CRUDE BIRTH RATE
1801-1805	10.2	19638	32.6	1856-1860	0.0	11827	19.5
1806-1810	8.4	20266	33.0	1861-1865	0.0	11683	19.7
1811-1815	11.9	17098	27.8	1866-1870	0.0	11335	19.5
1816-1820	0.0	15117	24.6	1871-1875	0.0	10622	18.7
1821-1825	0.0	14613	23.7	1876-1880	0.0	10184	18.3
1826-1830	0.0	14948	24.1	1881-1885	0.0	9286	17.1
1831-1835	0.0	14819	23.7	1886-1890	0.0	8671	16.4
1836-1840	0.0	13423	21.5	1891-1895	0.0	8157	16.0
1841-1845	0.0	13456	21.5	1896-1900	0.0	8176	16.5
1846-1850	0.0	12123	19.4	1901-1905	0.0	7775	16.1
1851-1855	0.0	12072	19.6				

TABLE 3 FEMALE POPULATION ESTIMATES,
DISTRIBUTION BY AGE: 1801 TO 1906

AGE	1801	1806	1811	1816	1821	1826	1831	1836	1841	1846	1851
0- 4	15376	14958	14957	13008	11664	11519	11836	11532	10648	11007	9654
5- 9	13186	13891	12977	13255	11680	1C610	1C491	1C777	10500	9920	10063
10-14	12163	12841	12928	12275	12696	11284	10245	10220	10392	1C319	9609
15-19	11205	11840	11945	12222	11752	12259	1C890	9976	9851	10208	9984
20-24	10229	10796	10907	11189	11594	11249	11731	10504	9535	9599	9782
25-29	9260	9771	9864	10138	10533	11018	10687	11225	9969	9229	9143
30-34	8321	8783	8868	9110	9483	9949	10406	10160	10592	9596	8746
35-39	7434	7835	7916	8136	8466	8902	9340	9826	9529	10138	9040
40-44	6590	6954	7016	7218	7514	7900	8308	8764	9162	9069	9496
45-49	5813	6122	6184	6354	6621	6964	7323	7741	8117	8662	8438
50-54	5031	5308	5354	5511	5735	6041	6357	6713	7061	7560	7937
55-59	4231	4456	4508	4638	4836	5092	5368	5661	5961	6409	6745
60-64	3390	3560	3601	3722	3881	4101	4324	4553	4807	5181	5466
65-69	2508	2640	2669	2766	2898	3068	3250	3408	3610	3909	4125
70-74	1665	1745	1774	1842	1935	2065	2193	2298	2438	2655	2808
75-79	928	971	987	1034	1090	1170	1253	1308	1398	1529	1621
80+	489	504	508	531	564	609	658	694	742	820	875

AGE	1856	1861	1866	1871	1876	1881	1886	1891	1896	1901	1906
0- 4	9936	9538	9592	9285	8786	8607	7923	7380	6949	6993	6774
5- 9	8946	9121	8825	8862	8609	8222	8082	7430	6920	6530	6627
10-14	9784	8666	8862	8567	8612	8393	8020	7883	7247	6754	6389
15-19	9322	9447	8384	8556	8268	8333	8109	7744	7604	6998	6534
20-24	9590	8883	9024	7959	8110	7850	7882	7660	7287	7186	6620
25-29	9362	9123	8476	8591	7572	7746	7489	7517	7297	6955	6880
30-34	8720	8884	8694	8069	8195	7255	7433	7184	7213	7011	6703
35-39	8300	8232	8427	8241	7665	7827	6942	7112	6876	6913	6743
40-44	8536	7796	7771	7952	7797	7295	7468	6622	6789	6570	6632
45-49	8909	7967	7314	7289	7479	7378	6921	7085	6283	6452	6269
50-54	7305	8193	7370	6764	6763	6985	6913	6485	6643	5902	6083
55-59	7163	6995	7393	6648	6126	6173	6401	6332	5946	6097	5448
60-64	5840	6143	6052	6390	5773	5374	5441	5637	5580	5249	5422
65-69	4440	4685	4984	4903	5209	4768	4465	4515	4681	4645	4410
70-74	3040	3220	3446	3660	3628	3919	3613	3378	3418	3555	3568
75-79	1773	1880	2028	2165	2322	2351	2563	2358	2206	2241	2365
80+	965	1034	1123	1211	1312	1450	1534	1649	1614	1546	1564

TABLE 4 MARRIED WOMEN ESTIMATES,
DISTRIBUTICN BY AGE: 1831 TO 1901

AGE	1831	1836	1841	1846	1851	1856	1861	1866
15-19	910	867	894	970	997	983	1171	1006
20-24	5393	4964	4648	4827	5075	5136	4910	4977
25-29	7432	7925	7179	6769	6823	7108	7034	6638
30-34	7952	7815	8272	7590	6995	7057	7255	7170
35-39	7185	7559	7440	8004	7203	6685	6676	6893
40-44	6200	6487	6889	6889	7268	6602	6057	6087
45-49	5140	5354	5737	6203	6099	6528	5865	5438

AGE	1871	1876	1881	1886	1891	1896	1901
15-19	955	1095	1074	888	729	700	876
20-24	4521	4841	4836	4656	4346	4042	3878
25-29	6624	5949	6271	6077	5980	5780	5503
30-34	6689	6722	6021	6266	6029	6007	5837
35-39	6748	6304	6409	5726	5893	5685	5663
40-44	6206	6099	5754	5928	5254	5425	5186
45-49	5378	5526	5507	5206	5315	4757	4843

TABLE 5 DEMOGRAPHIC INDICES AND FEMALE SINGULATE MEAN AGE
AT MARRIAGE: 1831 TO 1901

DATE	IF OVERALL FERTILITY	IG MARITAL FERTILITY	IH ILLEGITIMATE FERTILITY	IM PROPORTION MARRIED	SINGULATE MEAN AGE AT MARRIAGE
1831	0.236	0.390	0.019	0.586	22.8
1836	0.228	0.364	0.022	0.603	22.8
1841	0.226	0.351	0.025	0.617	22.5
1846	0.219	0.337	0.024	0.623	22.4
1851	0.214	0.329	0.020	0.628	22.2
1856	0.218	0.330	0.018	0.642	21.9
1861	0.221	0.328	0.020	0.652	21.8
1866	0.222	0.328	0.016	0.663	21.8
1871	0.220	0.325	0.016	0.663	21.6
1876	0.216	0.316	0.014	0.672	21.4
1881	0.208	0.299	0.014	0.679	21.5
1886	0.196	0.283	0.016	0.674	21.8
1891	0.188	0.274	0.018	0.666	21.9
1896	0.187	0.273	0.019	0.662	22.0
1901	0.189	0.274	0.020	0.664	

MORTALITY PATTERN: NORTH
MIGRATION: GRADUAL FROM 1881 ON, WITH UNCORRECTED POPULATION TOTALS

TABLE 1   FEMALE POPULATION ESTIMATES: 1801 TO 1906

DATE	R/CB RATIO	% COR- RECTION	FINAL POPULATION ESTIMATE	DATE	R/CB RATIO	% COR- RECTION	FINAL POPULATION ESTIMATE
1801	0.930	10.3	144974	1856	1.019	2.8	171662
1806	0.998	2.8	148477	1861	1.069	2.8	143061
1811*	0.984	2.8	151627	1866	1.076	2.8	144985
1816*	0.984	2.8	154777	1871	1.049	2.9	142532
1821	0.985	2.8	157927	1876	1.055	2.8	142778
1826*	0.983	2.8	161122	1881	1.046	2.8	140575
1831	0.980	2.8	164317	1886	1.049	2.8	137385
1836	0.988	2.8	165176	1891	1.083	2.8	140240
1841	0.970	2.8	163514	1896	1.180	0.0	146203
1846	1.000	2.8	170293	1901	1.251	0.0	152788
1851	1.003	2.8	171126	1906	1.295	0.0	157711

NOTE: R/CB RATIO REFERS TO THE POPULATION COMPUTED BY THE BALANCE OF BIRTHS
        AND DEATHS OVER THE REPORTED POPULATION
* INTERPOLATED VALUES

TABLE 2   FEMALE BIRTH ESTIMATES: 1801-1805 TO 1901-1905

DATE	% COR- RECTION	FINAL BIRTH ESTIMATE	CRUDE BIRTH RATE	DATE	% COR- RECTION	FINAL BIRTH ESTIMATE	CRUDE BIRTH RATE
1801-1805	0.0	25792	35.2	1856-1860	0.0	21864	25.4
1806-1810	0.0	26194	34.9	1861-1865	0.0	18505	25.7
1811-1815	0.0	24281	31.7	1866-1870	0.0	18282	25.4
1816-1820	0.0	23879	30.5	1871-1875	0.0	16231	22.8
1821-1825	3.0	22555	28.3	1876-1880	0.0	15557	22.0
1826-1830	3.9	22945	28.2	1881-1885	0.0	14401	20.7
1831-1835	0.0	22843	27.7	1886-1890	0.0	14715	21.2
1836-1840	0.0	22254	27.1	1891-1895	0.0	14115	19.7
1841-1845	0.0	22367	26.8	1896-1900	0.0	14677	19.6
1846-1850	0.0	21182	24.8	1901-1905	0.0	16026	20.6
1851-1855	0.0	20732	24.2				

TABLE 3 FEMALE POPULATION ESTIMATES,
DISTRIBUTION BY AGE: 1801 TO 1906

AGE	1801	1806	1811	1816	1821	1826	1831	1836	1841	1846	1851
0- 4	18256	19114	19679	18518	18301	17749	18075	17291	16932	18013	16728
5- 9	15227	15442	16225	16922	15988	16041	15571	15521	14764	15240	15848
10-14	13986	14316	14412	15306	16014	15187	15247	14764	14471	14448	14530
15-19	13073	13409	13598	13831	14733	15439	14650	14726	13991	14382	13981
20-24	12180	12486	12690	13002	13265	14155	14842	14096	13905	13856	13869
25-29	11264	11549	11736	12054	12389	12668	13526	14181	13226	13686	13282
30-34	10326	10582	10765	11057	11391	11745	12017	12812	13201	12919	13023
35-39	9340	9602	9772	10049	10355	10712	11052	11273	11822	12787	12194
40-44	8462	8659	8798	9053	9339	9669	10010	10285	10325	11370	11985
45-49	7593	7754	7836	8101	8363	8670	8982	9257	9364	9872	10595
50-54	6717	6870	6976	7175	7394	7676	7964	8205	8330	8850	9095
55-59	5788	5902	6014	6178	6375	6621	6878	7073	7193	7676	7954
60-64	4748	4823	4918	5073	5231	5461	5676	5806	5915	6332	6599
65-69	3586	3628	3705	3829	3966	4162	4349	4408	4493	4830	5057
70-74	2385	2387	2450	2540	2638	2806	2948	2958	3015	3253	3429
75-79	1304	1298	1334	1393	1453	1570	1672	1651	1688	1829	1943
80+	665	653	669	697	731	793	859	869	878	950	1013

AGE	1856	1861	1866	1871	1876	1881	1886	1891	1896	1901	1906
0- 4	16143	14279	14792	14318	13190	12510	11412	12243	12033	12521	13607
5- 9	14660	11764	12687	12830	12828	11683	11021	10512	11594	11443	11748
10-14	15209	11598	11304	11857	12332	12179	11132	10874	10625	11720	11378
15-19	14180	12216	11306	10710	11544	11858	11775	11240	11430	11323	12131
20-24	13595	11350	11867	10676	10393	11064	11425	12029	12271	12811	12281
25-29	13398	10816	10962	11142	10303	9907	10597	11434	12499	12881	13116
30-34	12727	10580	10371	10221	10683	9758	9421	10426	11500	12565	12735
35-39	12367	9968	10065	9598	9730	10046	9206	9185	10365	11411	12277
40-44	11493	9617	9417	9252	9077	9091	9412	8897	9023	10148	11024
45-49	11228	8985	9033	8607	8701	8433	8468	9035	8664	8749	9721
50-54	9808	8581	8253	8166	8008	7998	7768	8033	8685	8281	8267
55-59	8198	7310	7778	7285	7425	7195	7189	7202	7551	8126	7664
60-64	6833	5841	6343	6581	6359	6406	6190	6415	6547	6849	7294
65-69	5238	4519	4713	5000	5365	5125	5125	5161	5461	5567	5776
70-74	3540	3075	3248	3319	3653	3878	3652	3834	3955	4188	4249
75-79	1996	1745	1863	1935	2062	2247	2329	2325	2512	2599	2751
80+	1052	917	984	1035	1126	1197	1262	1395	1490	1608	1692

[448]

TABLE 4 MARRIED WOMEN ESTIMATES,
DISTRIBUTION BY AGE: 1831 TO 1901

AGE	1831	1836	1841	1846	1851	1856	1861	1866
15-19	1222	1211	1134	1150	1103	1104	1108	974
20-24	6623	6230	6093	6018	5970	5801	4804	4894
25-29	9520	9920	9212	9486	9161	9195	7396	7455
30-34	9446	10021	10306	10057	10109	9851	8183	7991
35-39	8786	8914	9346	10092	9606	9725	7852	7904
40-44	7795	7960	8006	8812	9282	8897	7481	7307
45-49	6595	6743	6848	7224	7754	8221	6562	6654

AGE	1871	1876	1881	1886	1891	1896	1901
15-19	803	861	914	1043	917	746	1038
20-24	4454	4569	4867	5108	5367	5261	5323
25-29	7308	6840	6907	7450	8182	8823	8939
30-34	7822	8005	7356	7288	8198	9207	9936
35-39	7476	7560	7741	7076	7185	8240	9158
40-44	7105	6959	6978	7070	6711	6850	7720
45-49	6250	6310	6134	6094	6538	6250	6140

TABLE 5 DEMOGRAPHIC INDICES AND FEMALE SINGULATE MEAN AGE
AT MARRIAGE: 1831 TO 1901

DATE	IF OVERALL FERTILITY	IG MARITAL FERTILITY	IH ILLEGITIMATE FERTILITY	IM PROPORTION MARRIED	SINGULATE MEAN AGE AT MARRIAGE
1831	0.294	0.470	0.044	0.585	23.4
1836	0.285	0.459	0.037	0.587	23.4
1841	0.285	0.458	0.037	0.590	23.4
1846	0.271	0.437	0.033	0.590	23.5
1851	0.264	0.427	0.031	0.588	23.5
1856	0.269	0.442	0.026	0.585	23.5
1861	0.276	0.456	0.026	0.582	23.5
1866	0.282	0.460	0.035	0.580	23.7
1871	0.275	0.454	0.031	0.577	23.6
1876	0.254	0.421	0.027	0.577	23.4
1881	0.240	0.398	0.024	0.577	23.3
1886	0.232	0.378	0.030	0.581	23.2
1891	0.222	0.352	0.033	0.593	23.5
1896	0.208	0.325	0.035	0.597	23.6
1901	0.210	0.324	0.039	0.600	

VAUCLUSE

MORTALITY PATTERN: NORTH
MIGRATION: NO CORRECTION MADE FOR MIGRATION BY AGE

TABLE 1   FEMALE POPULATION ESTIMATES: 1801 TO 1906

DATE	R/CB RATIO	% COR- RECTION	FINAL POPULATION ESTIMATE	DATE	R/CB RATIO	% COR- RECTION	FINAL POPULATION ESTIMATE
1801	1.050	7.1	102883	1856	0.995	1.9	134382
1806	1.060	2.1	105501	1861	0.980	2.2	134584
1811*	1.013	2.1	108529	1866	0.963	2.9	134414
1816*	0.991	2.1	111558	1871	0.948	0.0	129032
1821	0.981	2.1	114586	1876	0.926	0.0	126193
1826*	0.987	2.1	118470	1881	0.898	0.0	120651
1831	0.992	2.1	122354	1886	0.902	0.0	119580
1836	0.995	2.1	125028	1891	0.900	0.0	116911
1841	0.998	2.1	127084	1896	0.922	0.0	117171
1846	1.000	2.1	130581	1901	0.932	0.0	117259
1851	0.995	2.2	133303	1906	0.960	0.0	119535

NOTE: R/CB RATIO REFERS TO THE POPULATION COMPUTED BY THE BALANCE OF BIRTHS
        AND DEATHS OVER THE REPORTED POPULATION
* INTERPOLATED VALUES

TABLE 2   FEMALE BIRTH ESTIMATES: 1801-1805 TO 1901-1905

DATE	% COR- RECTION	FINAL BIRTH ESTIMATE	CRUDE BIRTH RATE	DATE	% COR- RECTION	FINAL BIRTH ESTIMATE	CRUDE BIRTH RATE
1801-1805	18.2	21973	42.2	1856-1860	0.0	19425	28.9
1806-1810	14.3	22136	41.4	1861-1865	0.0	18213	27.1
1811-1815	14.1	21234	38.6	1866-1870	0.0	17292	26.3
1816-1820	0.0	20885	36.9	1871-1875	0.0	16580	26.0
1821-1825	0.0	20300	34.8	1876-1880	0.0	14201	23.0
1826-1830	0.0	19745	32.8	1881-1885	0.0	12847	21.4
1831-1835	0.0	19514	31.6	1886-1890	0.0	11654	19.7
1836-1840	0.0	19465	30.9	1891-1895	0.0	11224	19.2
1841-1845	0.0	20172	31.3	1896-1900	0.0	11329	19.3
1846-1850	0.0	19799	30.0	1901-1905	0.0	11222	19.0
1851-1855	0.0	19595	29.3				

[450]

TABLE 3 FEMALE POPULATION ESTIMATES,
DISTRIBUTION BY AGE: 1801 TO 1906

AGE	1801	1806	1811	1816	1821	1826	1831	1836	1841	1846	1851
0- 4	17783	15691	16032	15389	15094	14874	14756	14458	14390	15295	15252
5- 9	13563	14502	12899	13265	12761	12693	12663	12491	12221	12363	13230
10-14	11694	12301	13171	11865	12297	12001	11986	11926	11756	11578	11682
15-19	10303	10817	11381	12356	11228	11807	11552	11514	11451	11342	11121
20-24	9045	9494	9970	10635	11647	10739	11322	11054	11013	11006	10855
25-29	7878	8274	8690	9249	9950	11055	10224	10755	10496	10512	10466
30-34	6790	7140	7507	7988	8570	9353	10431	9622	10116	9933	9918
35-39	5789	6091	6415	6830	7322	7970	8736	9716	8957	9482	9289
40-44	4889	5150	5430	5788	6207	6752	7384	8070	8969	8330	8802
45-49	4105	4322	4562	4868	5227	5686	6215	6777	7402	8289	7686
50-54	3396	3582	3781	4039	4339	4726	5169	5633	6137	6757	7559
55-59	2730	2878	3047	3250	3493	3806	4174	4549	4952	5449	6003
60-64	2069	2194	2326	2484	2660	2899	3190	3482	3790	4180	4617
65-69	1424	1524	1631	1738	1859	2019	2231	2439	2658	2945	3277
70-74	849	913	992	1062	1128	1223	1356	1485	1619	1811	2040
75-79	400	445	489	528	559	602	673	737	804	910	1045
80+	170	183	206	227	245	265	293	322	353	398	462

AGE	1856	1861	1866	1871	1876	1881	1886	1891	1896	1901	1906
0- 4	14812	14780	14057	12922	12653	10729	10196	9222	9156	9420	9609
5- 9	13047	12678	12769	11757	11032	10702	9484	8974	8352	8346	8800
10-14	12463	12222	11927	11627	10923	10163	9878	9032	8777	8124	8282
15-19	11203	11872	11680	11032	10973	10223	9905	9905	8960	8640	8150
20-24	10626	10633	11305	10766	10374	10233	9902	9513	9792	8791	8640
25-29	10302	10020	10063	10356	10061	9615	9853	9479	9350	9557	9456
30-34	9848	9636	9410	9147	9604	9253	9190	9365	9252	9071	9456
35-39	9244	9130	8973	8481	8412	8758	8773	8666	9069	8915	8918
40-44	8590	8505	8439	8029	7743	7615	8245	8215	8334	8684	8713
45-49	8089	7856	7816	7507	7286	6968	7128	7676	7855	7937	8442
50-54	6978	7311	7136	6872	6735	6481	6449	6561	7253	7403	7637
55-59	6676	6141	6473	6115	6010	5838	5852	5793	6057	6693	6975
60-64	5043	5600	5192	5297	5108	4975	5043	5031	5121	5371	6074
65-69	3573	3910	4388	3938	4101	3918	3992	4030	4138	4252	4576
70-74	2226	2444	2713	2948	2702	2786	2796	2840	2956	3094	3273
75-79	1145	1267	1419	1525	1693	1535	1672	1676	1758	1889	2045
80+	518	578	654	711	784	859	877	932	985	1071	1198

TABLE 4 MARRIED WOMEN ESTIMATES,
DISTRIBUTION BY AGE: 1831 TO 1901

AGE	1831	1836	1841	1846	1851	1856	1861	1866
15-19	857	809	764	720	674	650	796	764
20-24	5006	4740	4593	4460	4276	4068	3960	4161
25-29	7119	7383	7133	7057	6940	6738	6467	6399
30-34	8043	7348	7712	7532	7485	7382	7182	6958
35-39	6779	7469	6912	7303	7149	7087	6987	6830
40-44	5620	6071	6810	6331	6709	6537	6484	6413
45-49	4462	4790	5318	5975	5576	5865	5725	5679

AGE	1871	1876	1881	1886	1891	1896	1901
15-19	683	711	604	480	459	441	688
20-24	3902	3815	3570	3468	3581	3932	3571
25-29	6417	6182	6009	5936	5861	6251	6673
30-34	6678	6904	6636	6617	6672	6833	6967
35-39	6376	6273	6525	6464	6397	6808	6804
40-44	6019	5765	5687	5990	5936	6141	6362
45-49	5355	5154	4963	4983	5336	5599	5489

TABLE 5 DEMOGRAPHIC INDICES AND FEMALE SINGULATE MEAN AGE
AT MARRIAGE: 1831 TO 1901

DATE	IF OVERALL FERTILITY	IG MARITAL FERTILITY	IH ILLEGITIMATE FERTILITY	IM PROPORTION MARRIED	SINGULATE MEAN AGE AT MARRIAGE
1831	0.321	0.527	0.041	0.577	23.5
1836	0.315	0.519	0.042	0.572	23.5
1841	0.320	0.532	0.042	0.569	23.6
1846	0.323	0.546	0.035	0.564	23.7
1851	0.321	0.546	0.034	0.560	23.9
1856	0.321	0.555	0.030	0.554	23.9
1861	0.311	0.547	0.029	0.544	24.0
1866	0.291	0.520	0.028	0.536	24.2
1871	0.287	0.518	0.027	0.529	24.2
1876	0.264	0.477	0.025	0.529	24.3
1881	0.238	0.428	0.024	0.529	24.4
1886	0.216	0.392	0.020	0.526	24.3
1891	0.204	0.365	0.020	0.535	24.1
1896	0.202	0.340	0.021	0.565	23.9
1901	0.207	0.333	0.026	0.589	

MORTALITY PATTERN: WEST
MIGRATION: FULL STRENGTH, WITH POPULATION TOTALS OBTAINED BY TREND OF R/CB

TABLE 1 FEMALE POPULATION ESTIMATES: 1801 TO 1906

DATE	R/CB RATIO	% COR- RECTION	FINAL POPULATION ESTIMATE	DATE	R/CB RATIO	% COR- RECTION	FINAL POPULATION ESTIMATE
1801	0.925	0.0	129006	1856	0.985	0.4	196721
1806	0.981	0.0	138317	1861	0.978	0.1	198210
1811*	0.990	0.0	145989	1866	0.965	0.4	202945
1816*	0.990	0.0	153661	1871	0.953	0.7	204273
1821	1.017	0.0	161333	1876	0.959	-1.0	205435
1826*	1.008	0.0	163866	1881	0.947	-0.8	209887
1831	0.995	0.0	166398	1886	0.946	-1.7	215356
1836	0.998	0.0	171345	1891	0.926	-0.7	219474
1841	0.996	0.0	178505	1896	0.914	-0.4	220773
1846	1.000	0.0	187875	1901	0.893	0.8	223671
1851	0.993	0.6	192472	1906	0.874	1.9	227630

NOTE: R/CB RATIO REFERS TO THE POPULATION COMPUTED BY THE BALANCE OF BIRTHS
       AND DEATHS OVER THE REPORTED POPULATION
* INTERPOLATED VALUES

TABLE 2 FEMALE BIRTH ESTIMATES: 1801-1805 TO 1901-1905

DATE	% COR- RECTION	FINAL BIRTH ESTIMATE	CRUDE BIRTH RATE	DATE	% COR- RECTION	FINAL BIRTH ESTIMATE	CRUDE BIRTH RATE
1801-1805	0.0	21720	32.5	1856-1860	0.0	25324	25.6
1806-1810	0.0	24183	34.0	1861-1865	0.0	26013	25.9
1811-1815	0.0	26136	34.9	1866-1870	0.0	26646	26.2
1816-1820	0.0	24741	31.4	1871-1875	0.0	26888	26.3
1821-1825	9.4	24329	29.9	1876-1880	0.0	28380	27.3
1826-1830	17.7	25965	31.4	1881-1885	0.0	27410	25.8
1831-1835	8.0	25837	30.6	1886-1890	0.0	26656	24.5
1836-1840	0.0	26196	30.0	1891-1895	0.0	25178	22.9
1841-1845	0.0	27810	30.4	1896-1900	0.0	24810	22.3
1846-1850	5.2	26845	28.2	1901-1905	0.0	24653	21.9
1851-1855	0.0	25754	26.5				

TABLE 3 FEMALE POPULATION ESTIMATES,
DISTRIBUTION BY AGE: 1801 TO 1906

AGE	1801	1806	1811	1816	1821	1826	1831	1836	1841	1846	1851
0- 4	14132	16726	19057	20575	19345	18639	19548	19902	21046	22656	21237
5- 9	12533	13177	15347	17387	18931	17338	16574	17680	18300	19525	20659
10-14	11951	12745	12902	14905	17170	18153	16581	16070	17192	17907	18917
15-19	11388	12149	12473	12525	14712	16457	17353	16069	15618	16814	17246
20-24	10749	11446	11780	12000	12242	13968	15575	16655	15489	15153	15895
25-29	10065	10700	11013	11249	11633	11530	13108	14827	15943	14928	14337
30-34	9357	9941	10230	10451	10831	10885	10746	12396	14113	15282	14133
35-39	8642	9166	9442	9646	9993	10066	10073	10092	11729	13450	14396
40-44	7929	8407	8653	8849	9165	9230	9255	9400	9495	11115	12610
45-49	7229	7657	7881	8054	8349	8406	8426	8577	8784	8938	10358
50-54	6478	6855	7063	7221	7473	7533	7546	7680	7894	8146	8207
55-59	5639	5945	6147	6294	6505	6551	6563	6679	6885	7135	7279
60-64	4672	4894	5083	5228	5395	5432	5426	5529	5728	5959	6078
65-69	3584	3732	3893	4026	4156	4185	4169	4243	4431	4639	4732
70-74	2458	2542	2667	2774	2867	2893	2874	2922	3071	3246	3318
75-79	1424	1447	1535	1610	1662	1683	1668	1696	1800	1919	1968
80+	769	789	823	867	903	917	913	928	986	1063	1102

AGE	1856	1861	1866	1871	1876	1881	1886	1891	1896	1901	1906
0- 4	21008	20160	21519	21210	21403	23343	23444	22881	21367	21645	21995
5- 9	19534	19109	19657	19576	19298	19753	21887	22005	21359	20181	20640
10-14	20018	18851	18550	17998	18896	18707	19219	21310	21388	20832	19722
15-19	18047	19024	18044	17597	17076	18032	17843	18316	20317	20461	19935
20-24	15864	16497	17684	16491	16091	15693	16524	16270	16659	18673	18803
25-29	14879	14744	15527	16483	15357	15077	14707	15484	15186	15629	17628
30-34	13588	14023	14027	14639	15552	14584	14407	14049	14759	14546	15040
35-39	13370	12775	13313	13189	13770	14745	13935	13771	13389	14151	14016
40-44	13594	12550	12105	12496	12380	13029	14084	13321	13128	12843	13649
45-49	11851	12699	11835	11310	11674	11660	12395	13410	12650	12546	12343
50-54	9614	10924	11823	10909	10425	10858	10974	11676	12591	11965	11942
55-59	7433	8633	9929	10607	9789	9462	9995	10116	10722	11658	11164
60-64	6288	6350	7506	8482	9061	8489	8353	8837	8899	9539	10469
65-69	4917	5012	5181	5983	6760	7367	7066	6967	7322	7482	8117
70-74	3466	3534	3711	3724	4300	4983	5595	5379	5259	5629	5838
75-79	2076	2116	2242	2265	2273	2713	3267	3680	3500	3503	3820
80+	1174	1209	1292	1315	1332	1391	1661	2003	2278	2390	2508

TABLE 4 MARRIED WOMEN ESTIMATES,
DISTRIBUTION BY AGE: 1831 TO 1901

AGE	1831	1836	1841	1846	1851	1856	1861	1866
15-19	392	371	370	409	431	464	375	397
20-24	4219	4591	4363	4362	4673	4769	5072	4455
25-29	7732	8830	9633	9143	8890	9348	9383	10002
30-34	7948	9198	10587	11573	10782	10456	10879	10957
35-39	7879	7881	9255	10700	11510	10765	10354	10839
40-44	7326	7383	7535	8886	10109	10964	10177	9841
45-49	6273	6305	6555	6741	7839	9045	9765	9130

AGE	1871	1876	1881	1886	1891	1896	1901
15-19	441	538	645	578	535	555	795
20-24	4392	4997	5316	5781	5672	5817	6487
25-29	9538	9115	9795	9815	10500	10387	10816
30-34	11442	11564	10990	11283	11267	11893	11799
35-39	10684	11203	11745	11043	11376	11133	11771
40-44	10037	9971	10560	10981	10739	10747	10499
45-49	8562	8867	8936	9281	10510	9972	9852

TABLE 5 DEMOGRAPHIC INDICES AND FEMALE SINGULATE MEAN AGE
AT MARRIAGE: 1831 TO 1901

DATE	IF OVERALL FERTILITY	IG MARITAL FERTILITY	IH ILLEGITIMATE FERTILITY	IM PROPORTION MARRIED	SINGULATE MEAN AGE AT MARRIAGE
1831	0.334	0.685	0.018	0.474	25.8
1836	0.317	0.630	0.019	0.487	25.7
1841	0.317	0.601	0.018	0.513	25.6
1846	0.310	0.575	0.016	0.526	25.4
1851	0.294	0.543	0.015	0.528	25.3
1856	0.284	0.521	0.018	0.529	25.3
1861	0.283	0.523	0.017	0.525	25.4
1866	0.284	0.534	0.017	).516	25.7
1871	0.289	0.545	0.018	0.514	25.4
1876	0.301	0.552	0.017	0.530	25.0
1881	0.303	0.540	0.019	0.546	24.7
1886	0.293	0.516	0.021	0.550	24.8
1891	0.281	0.483	0.022	0.561	24.9
1896	0.265	0.462	0.021	0.555	24.8
1901	0.253	0.441	0.019	0.554	

MORTALITY PATTERN: WEST
MIGRATION: FULL STRENGTH, WITH POPULATION TOTALS OBTAINED BY TREND OF R/CB

TABLE 1 FEMALE POPULATION ESTIMATES: 1801 TO 1906

DATE	R/CB RATIO	% COR-RECTION	FINAL POPULATION ESTIMATE	DATE	R/CB RATIO	% COR-RECTION	FINAL POPULATION ESTIMATE
1801	1.113	0.0	124865	1856	0.900	10.6	161636
1806	1.118	0.0	128990	1861	0.983	0.2	161527
1811*	1.079	0.0	130700	1866	0.975	0.0	162137
1816*	1.038	0.0	132411	1871	0.950	1.5	163629
1821	1.001	0.0	134121	1876	0.967	-1.3	162996
1826*	1.006	0.0	139045	1881	0.966	-2.3	165120
1831	1.007	0.0	143969	1886	0.941	-0.8	168124
1836	0.997	0.0	146594	1891	0.927	-0.4	169460
1841	0.992	0.0	148810	1896	0.917	-0.4	168523
1846	1.000	0.0	155063	1901	0.894	0.9	168410
1851	1.000	0.6	159495	1906	0.878	1.6	168165

NOTE: R/CB RATIO REFERS TO THE POPULATION COMPUTED BY THE BALANCE OF BIRTHS
       AND DEATHS OVER THE REPORTED POPULATION
* INTERPOLATED VALUES

TABLE 2 FEMALE BIRTH ESTIMATES: 1801-1805 TO 1901-1905

DATE	% COR-RECTION	FINAL BIRTH ESTIMATE	CRUDE BIRTH RATE	DATE	% COR-RECTION	FINAL BIRTH ESTIMATE	CRUDE BIRTH RATE
1801-1805	21.9	16598	26.2	1856-1860	0.0	19370	24.0
1806-1810	25.7	17213	26.5	1861-1865	0.0	18869	23.3
1811-1815	9.3	17876	27.2	1866-1870	0.0	19929	24.5
1816-1820	0.0	17606	26.4	1871-1875	0.0	19302	23.6
1821-1825	0.0	17977	26.3	1876-1880	0.0	19304	23.5
1826-1830	0.0	19160	27.1	1881-1885	0.0	18815	22.6
1831-1835	0.0	20011	27.5	1886-1890	0.0	18245	21.6
1836-1840	4.1	19261	26.1	1891-1895	0.0	16805	19.9
1841-1845	0.0	19556	25.7	1896-1900	0.0	16277	19.3
1846-1850	0.0	19992	25.4	1901-1905	0.0	15517	18.4
1851-1855	0.0	19751	24.6				

TABLE 3 FEMALE POPULATION ESTIMATES,
DISTRIBUTION BY AGE: 1801 TO 1906

AGE	1801	1806	1811	1816	1821	1826	1831	1836	1841	1846	1851
0- 4	14393	13569	14147	14754	14673	14955	15835	16040	15478	16487	16362
5- 9	12764	13381	12403	12916	13534	13734	13936	14480	14706	14599	15345
10-14	11385	12507	12745	11767	12277	13280	13431	13454	14017	14499	14293
15-19	11247	11738	11906	12085	11177	12040	12979	12959	13017	13812	14312
20-24	10473	10927	11099	11217	11408	10881	11680	12422	12437	12737	13738
25-29	9682	10109	10276	10402	10535	11039	10491	11104	11842	12099	12422
30-34	8906	9295	9463	9589	9729	10143	10589	9918	10526	11465	11618
35-39	8139	8501	8659	8789	8929	9317	9677	9953	9348	10139	10925
40-44	7405	7726	7879	8002	8145	8505	8842	9044	9327	8957	9589
45-49	6686	6983	7115	7235	7368	7708	8018	8209	8419	8879	8405
50-54	5945	6212	6343	6447	6575	6874	7162	7333	7527	7904	8202
55-59	5156	5383	5514	5620	5732	5987	6233	6383	6552	6901	7118
60-64	4274	4472	4597	4705	4816	5009	5208	5317	5459	5772	5971
65-69	3310	3470	3595	3697	3804	3950	4087	4154	4252	4520	4679
70-74	2316	2432	2540	2636	2729	2832	2924	2948	3004	3201	3319
75-79	1382	1452	1532	1607	1682	1741	1795	1797	1816	1942	2009
80+	802	836	887	944	1007	1051	1084	1080	1082	1150	1187

AGE	1856	1861	1866	1871	1876	1881	1886	1891	1896	1901	1906
0- 4	16367	15670	15569	16497	15717	16448	16573	15933	14513	14392	13912
5- 9	15146	14984	14469	14401	15138	14709	15617	15672	14987	13791	13757
10-14	14892	14640	14526	14035	13920	14733	14364	15237	15269	14648	13492
15-19	13644	14146	13958	13870	13302	13297	14111	13721	14562	14653	14057
20-24	13218	12439	13013	12875	12628	12232	12196	12951	12559	13459	13558
25-29	12921	12324	11644	12221	11989	11884	11522	11456	12172	11857	12761
30-34	11819	12223	11709	11070	11566	11462	11421	11045	10961	11714	11442
35-39	11032	11156	11595	11117	10459	11049	11022	10958	10572	10549	11314
40-44	10357	10398	10564	10989	10492	9981	10624	10575	10489	10175	10188
45-49	9048	9715	9798	9964	10325	9969	9559	10153	10082	10053	9788
50-54	7836	8381	9043	9127	9244	9697	9448	9041	9574	9563	9574
55-59	7463	7075	7615	8222	8257	8491	9002	8748	8345	8898	8930
60-64	6194	6422	6145	6623	7097	7277	7584	8012	7753	7466	8009
65-69	4877	4986	5232	5015	5352	5894	6149	6379	6702	6564	6371
70-74	3469	3549	3684	3875	3668	4053	4560	4730	4874	5197	5141
75-79	2109	2152	2246	2339	2420	2396	2721	3039	3125	3282	3544
80+	1245	1270	1326	1389	1422	1548	1651	1811	1984	2149	2328

[457]

TABLE 4 MARRIED WOMEN ESTIMATES,
DISTRIBUTION BY AGE: 1831 TO 1901

AGE	1831	1836	1841	1846	1851	1856	1861	1866
15-19	873	866	893	975	1041	1024	1234	1308
20-24	4541	4887	5020	5248	5775	5681	5450	5444
25-29	6960	7430	8026	8303	8621	9093	8746	8350
30-34	8197	7693	8241	9055	9237	9504	9849	9486
35-39	7765	7960	7539	8240	8917	9113	9192	9584
40-44	7113	7201	7485	7239	7766	8507	8470	8612
45-49	6141	6186	6414	6831	6482	7122	7548	7614

AGE	1871	1876	1881	1886	1891	1896	1901
15-19	1362	1214	1117	1080	791	723	946
20-24	5446	5670	5740	5745	6041	5869	6067
25-29	8343	8180	8423	8540	8476	9085	9079
30-34	8990	9120	9065	9373	9081	9069	9737
35-39	9175	8644	9035	9274	9082	8854	8836
40-44	8903	8486	8152	8962	8582	8585	8314
45-49	7664	7915	7750	7935	7966	7947	7870

TABLE 5 DEMOGRAPHIC INDICES AND FEMALE SINGULATE MEAN AGE
AT MARRIAGE: 1831 TO 1901

DATE	IF OVERALL FERTILITY	IG MARITAL FERTILITY	IH ILLEGITIMATE FERTILITY	IM PROPORTION MARRIED	SINGULATE MEAN AGE AT MARRIAGE
1831	0.301	0.525	0.012	0.563	24.2
1836	0.295	0.507	0.024	0.562	24.1
1841	0.287	0.480	0.029	0.571	24.0
1846	0.280	0.459	0.033	0.578	23.9
1851	0.268	0.435	0.036	0.583	23.8
1856	0.263	0.418	0.031	0.600	23.6
1861	0.260	0.409	0.032	0.604	23.5
1866	0.264	0.420	0.031	0.601	23.6
1871	0.269	0.429	0.034	0.595	23.6
1876	0.270	0.429	0.034	0.598	23.4
1881	0.268	0.422	0.029	0.609	23.3
1886	0.260	0.400	0.029	0.622	23.5
1891	0.245	0.382	0.028	0.612	23.7
1896	0.230	0.358	0.028	0.611	23.5
1901	0.216	0.337	0.025	0.612	

MORTALITY PATTERN: WEST
MIGRATION: GRADUAL, WITH UNCORRECTED POPULATION TOTALS EXCEPT FOR 1851, 1856,
 1876 AND 1881, OBTAINED BY LINEAR INTERPOLATION OF R/CB

TABLE 1 FEMALE POPULATION ESTIMATES: 1801 TO 1906

DATE	R/CB RATIO	% COR-RECTION	FINAL POPULATION ESTIMATE	DATE	R/CB RATIO	% COR-RECTION	FINAL POPULATION ESTIMATE
1801	0.974	0.0	123564	1856	0.982	0.7	160734
1806	0.994	0.0	121851	1861	0.984	0.0	158945
1811*	1.001	0.0	127018	1866	0.973	0.0	162379
1816*	0.996	0.0	132185	1871	0.959	0.0	161978
1821	0.984	0.0	137352	1876	0.966	-1.3	165605
1826*	1.003	0.0	140143	1881	0.951	-0.3	172722
1831	0.992	0.0	142933	1886	0.943	0.0	179149
1836	0.995	0.0	146260	1891	0.937	0.0	184447
1841	0.979	1.9	148616	1896	0.927	0.0	186526
1846	1.000	0.0	156590	1901	0.916	0.0	189345
1851	0.987	0.8	159377	1906	0.898	0.0	191663

NOTE: R/CB RATIO REFERS TO THE POPULATION COMPUTED BY THE BALANCE OF BIRTHS
       AND DEATHS OVER THE REPORTED POPULATION
* INTERPOLATED VALUES

TABLE 2 FEMALE BIRTH ESTIMATES: 1801-1805 TO 1901-1905

DATE	% COR-RECTION	FINAL BIRTH ESTIMATE	CRUDE BIRTH RATE	DATE	% COR-RECTION	FINAL BIRTH ESTIMATE	CRUDE BIRTH RATE
1801-1805	0.0	21262	34.7	1856-1860	0.0	22757	28.5
1806-1810	0.0	21767	35.0	1861-1865	0.0	24305	30.3
1811-1815	0.0	22340	34.5	1866-1870	0.0	24775	30.6
1816-1820	0.0	24514	36.4	1871-1875	0.0	26086	31.9
1821-1825	0.0	23757	34.2	1876-1880	0.0	25609	30.3
1826-1830	7.2	24980	35.3	1881-1885	0.0	24863	28.3
1831-1835	0.0	24584	34.0	1886-1890	0.0	23840	26.2
1836-1840	0.0	24415	33.1	1891-1895	0.0	22655	24.4
1841-1845	0.0	25872	33.9	1896-1900	0.0	22363	23.8
1846-1850	7.1	25451	32.2	1901-1905	0.0	22151	23.3
1851-1855	0.0	23385	29.2				

TABLE 3 FEMALE POPULATION ESTIMATES,
DISTRIBUTION BY AGE: 1801 TO 1906

AGE	1801	1806	1811	1816	1821	1826	1831	1836	1841	1846	1851
0- 4	13928	13639	16223	17151	18608	16931	18101	17894	17565	20142	18885
5- 9	12137	11695	12225	14608	15312	16348	14827	15362	15697	15987	17826
10-14	11599	11662	11387	11793	13993	14825	15595	14264	15333	15280	15303
15-19	11080	11145	11351	10980	11291	13544	14137	14999	13697	14918	14604
20-24	10452	10479	10728	10840	10411	10794	12770	13442	14233	13202	14081
25-29	9771	9754	9994	10163	10194	9849	10081	12026	12630	13610	12370
30-34	9056	9018	9233	9405	9493	9561	9127	9419	11207	11998	12677
35-39	8334	8266	8463	8629	8724	8826	8789	8458	8704	10575	11094
40-44	7608	7539	7739	7865	7953	8050	8056	8087	7760	8162	9716
45-49	6886	6827	6981	7110	7199	7284	7295	7359	7366	7226	7447
50-54	6134	6042	6209	6333	6400	6468	6482	6543	6579	6748	6480
55-59	5267	5159	5322	5471	5535	5552	5571	5626	5656	5857	5866
60-64	4282	4123	4305	4465	4550	4526	4526	4573	4594	4796	4828
65-69	3189	3014	3172	3353	3444	3406	3397	3418	3430	3620	3654
70-74	2110	1941	2064	2215	2317	2277	2272	2278	2271	2426	2460
75-79	1147	1022	1107	1214	1288	1260	1261	1264	1252	1355	1378
80+	583	526	538	589	639	643	644	648	643	688	708

AGE	1856	1861	1866	1871	1876	1881	1886	1891	1896	1901	1906
0- 4	17482	16211	19562	18159	19655	20912	20609	20001	18798	19014	19308
5- 9	16759	15191	14532	16258	16215	18133	19410	19210	19503	17548	17854
10-14	17072	15966	14611	13808	15653	15733	17629	18893	18628	17979	17009
15-19	14611	16209	15294	13711	13244	15072	15141	16958	18002	17752	16879
20-24	13738	13618	15286	13933	12946	12456	14169	14131	15501	16479	15680
25-29	13184	12745	12798	14061	13112	12259	11784	13402	13166	14505	15220
30-34	11531	12180	11951	11820	13184	12465	11682	11241	12723	12547	13819
35-39	11738	10570	11352	10981	11008	12486	11844	11124	10657	12131	11983
40-44	10211	10692	9799	10389	10167	10384	11827	11256	10547	10163	11630
45-49	8882	9236	9847	8918	9555	9537	9783	11183	10628	10023	9726
50-54	6695	7889	8371	8816	8065	8840	8869	9139	10433	9990	9511
55-59	5651	5750	6343	7262	7734	7279	8025	8094	8328	9586	9278
60-64	4853	4577	4810	5690	6046	6677	6330	7020	7047	7332	8526
65-69	3695	3609	3552	3636	4384	4891	5452	5207	5738	5846	6162
70-74	2497	2433	2509	2391	2503	3213	3625	4079	3864	4338	4491
75-79	1408	1359	1423	1407	1379	1568	2042	2333	2596	2519	2887
80+	727	711	738	739	755	817	929	1175	1368	1593	1699

TABLE 4 MARRIED WOMEN ESTIMATES,
DISTRIBUTION BY AGE: 1831 TO 1901

AGE	1831	1836	1841	1846	1851	1856	1861	1866
15-19	1803	1902	1727	1871	1822	1813	1943	1817
20-24	6914	7259	7680	7116	7577	7380	7303	7250
25-29	7628	9089	9567	10328	9392	10017	9689	9750
30-34	7348	7565	9037	9706	10265	9348	9882	9735
35-39	7020	6722	6955	8483	8904	9428	8492	9169
40-44	6137	6102	5897	6233	7415	7791	8150	7523
45-49	5225	5186	5239	5170	5314	6326	6557	7057

AGE	1871	1876	1881	1886	1891	1896	1901
15-19	1749	1944	2075	1983	2079	1937	2225
20-24	7270	7308	7214	8068	7711	8327	8859
25-29	9931	9825	9604	9261	10472	10092	11083
30-34	9595	10352	10104	9698	9329	10518	10278
35-39	8808	8890	9953	9625	9159	8761	9922
40-44	7877	7782	8059	9214	8847	8335	7997
45-49	6259	6795	6916	7200	8282	7888	7425

TABLE 5 DEMOGRAPHIC INDICES AND FEMALE SINGULATE MEAN AGE
AT MARRIAGE: 1831 TO 1901

DATE	IF OVERALL FERTILITY	IG MARITAL FERTILITY	IH ILLEGITIMATE FERTILITY	IM PROPORTION MARRIED	SINGULATE MEAN AGE AT MARRIAGE
1831	0.388	0.598	0.059	0.610	21.7
1836	0.361	0.557	0.058	0.608	21.9
1841	0.356	0.537	0.057	0.622	21.9
1846	0.345	0.518	0.054	0.628	22.0
1851	0.322	0.480	0.053	0.630	22.0
1856	0.302	0.450	0.049	0.631	22.0
1861	0.307	0.464	0.050	0.622	22.3
1866	0.313	0.485	0.044	0.610	22.4
1871	0.332	0.509	0.041	0.621	22.0
1876	0.343	0.509	0.042	0.645	21.8
1881	0.333	0.491	0.040	0.650	21.9
1886	0.317	0.466	0.042	0.648	22.2
1891	0.295	0.441	0.042	0.634	22.3
1896	0.275	0.416	0.044	0.621	22.3
1901	0.260	0.391	0.042	0.626	

MORTALITY PATTERN: WEST
MIGRATION: NO CORRECTION MADE FOR MIGRATION BY AGE

TABLE 1 FEMALE POPULATION ESTIMATES: 1801 TO 1906

DATE	R/CB RATIO	% COR- RECTION	FINAL POPULATION ESTIMATE	DATE	R/CB RATIO	% COR- RECTION	FINAL POPULATION ESTIMATE
1801	1.050	3.1	166755	1856	0.932	0.0	213232
1806	1.074	0.0	173879	1861	0.928	0.0	215548
1811*	1.050	0.0	178733	1866	0.912	0.0	216478
1816*	1.023	0.0	183586	1871	0.934	0.0	203894
1821	1.018	0.0	188440	1876	0.950	0.0	208082
1826*	1.015	0.0	197671	1881	0.931	0.0	206824
1831	1.019	0.0	206901	1886	0.923	0.0	207447
1836	1.022	0.0	212953	1891	0.912	0.0	206952
1841	1.014	0.0	218214	1896	0.924	0.0	210059
1846	1.000	0.0	222037	1901	0.913	0.0	211280
1851	0.978	0.0	221389	1906	0.913	0.0	215842

NOTE: R/CB RATIO REFERS TO THE POPULATION COMPUTED BY THE BALANCE OF BIRTHS
       AND DEATHS OVER THE REPORTED POPULATION
* INTERPOLATED VALUES

TABLE 2 FEMALE BIRTH ESTIMATES: 1801-1805 TO 1901-1905

DATE	% COR- RECTION	FINAL BIRTH ESTIMATE	CRUDE BIRTH RATE	DATE	% COR- RECTION	FINAL BIRTH ESTIMATE	CRUDE BIRTH RATE
1801-1805	3.5	29318	34.4	1856-1860	0.0	27228	25.4
1806-1810	2.7	29114	33.0	1861-1865	0.0	28347	26.2
1811-1815	8.9	29534	32.6	1866-1870	4.2	27818	25.8
1816-1820	0.0	25635	27.6	1871-1875	0.0	25640	24.9
1821-1825	0.0	28812	29.8	1876-1880	0.0	26096	25.2
1826-1830	0.0	30260	29.9	1881-1885	0.0	24570	23.7
1831-1835	0.0	29491	28.1	1886-1890	0.0	24365	23.5
1836-1840	0.0	29340	27.2	1891-1895	0.0	24722	23.7
1841-1845	4.7	29030	26.4	1896-1900	0.0	26159	24.8
1846-1850	11.4	27575	24.9	1901-1905	0.0	25776	24.1
1851-1855	6.4	26045	24.0				

TABLE 3 FEMALE POPULATION ESTIMATES,
DISTRIBUTION BY AGE: 1801 TO 1906

AGE	1801	1806	1811	1816	1821	1826	1831	1836	1841	1846	1851
0- 4	22915	22277	22144	22661	20239	23217	24166	23186	23405	23307	21804
5- 9	19432	20518	19803	19730	20612	18657	21368	22048	21192	21372	21035
10-14	17732	18688	19504	18802	19045	20089	18225	20768	21322	20397	20384
15-19	16166	17045	17756	18510	18141	18552	19614	17704	20073	20512	19379
20-24	14598	15387	16043	16699	17704	17526	17957	18882	16970	19158	19224
25-29	13077	13780	14368	14973	15857	16987	16841	17156	17974	16089	17921
30-34	11631	12260	12785	13327	14135	15129	16227	15991	16238	16949	15019
35-39	10283	10827	11298	11781	12502	13406	14362	15308	15044	15225	15743
40-44	9021	9511	9916	10348	10987	11790	12652	13467	14319	14027	14072
45-49	7874	8286	8650	9020	9586	10292	11051	11782	12513	13262	12883
50-54	6747	7112	7413	7744	8226	8844	9498	10129	10781	11418	12003
55-59	5618	5916	6183	6454	6874	7393	7943	8466	9027	9589	10068
60-64	4454	4685	4900	5134	5473	5910	6344	6754	7216	7690	8084
65-69	3259	3444	3606	3787	4062	4398	4730	5022	5378	5754	6060
70-74	2146	2257	2379	2507	2701	2948	3173	3369	3611	3880	4097
75-79	1183	1249	1315	1399	1517	1669	1805	1912	2061	2223	2353
80+	618	638	670	711	779	866	946	1010	1090	1185	1261

AGE	1856	1861	1866	1871	1876	1881	1886	1891	1896	1901	1906
0- 4	20116	21680	22772	21419	20545	21114	20256	20070	19999	21712	21920
5- 9	19166	18404	19736	19675	19874	18707	19518	18672	18684	18486	20430
10-14	19580	18588	17665	18069	19355	19082	18140	18894	18341	18098	18090
15-19	18678	18957	17638	15098	18035	18186	18295	17241	18895	17411	17639
20-24	17130	17893	17535	13293	15421	16153	16967	16775	17710	17268	16758
25-29	17314	16323	16715	14704	13169	14156	15226	15868	16598	16561	16625
30-34	16317	16425	15345	14933	14170	12344	13452	14438	15277	15773	15935
35-39	13630	15389	15392	13795	14248	13296	11697	12733	13763	14499	15116
40-44	14260	12784	14374	13948	13041	13368	12573	11061	12012	13050	13836
45-49	12685	13286	11377	13025	13074	12187	12575	11837	10336	11344	12378
50-54	11460	11639	12175	10683	12001	12066	11317	11692	10872	9652	10622
55-59	10399	10237	10398	10654	9577	10799	10932	10269	10466	9906	8836
60-64	8312	8876	8736	8587	9159	8217	9366	9481	8837	9114	8722
65-69	6234	6622	7087	6732	6888	7356	6686	7618	7631	7225	7560
70-74	4219	4480	4783	4926	4870	5007	5430	4932	5544	5664	5463
75-79	2426	2576	2760	2824	3026	3022	3166	3430	3060	3529	3693
80+	1305	1389	1492	1530	1631	1765	1853	1941	2034	1988	2217

TABLE 4 MARRIED WOMEN ESTIMATES,
DISTRIBUTICN BY AGE: 1831 TO 1901

AGE	1831	1836	1841	1846	1851	1856	1861	1866
15-19	354	331	390	415	411	416	343	348
20-24	4136	4487	4174	4881	5080	4696	5108	4295
25-29	8713	9077	9743	8928	10175	10039	9689	10144
30-34	10769	10772	11127	11795	10604	11650	11900	11258
35-39	10243	11031	10993	11254	11753	10227	11671	11766
40-44	9370	10007	10738	10581	10661	10776	9724	10967
45-49	7746	8285	8907	9509	9282	9090	9600	8607

AGE	1871	1876	1881	1886	1891	1896	1901
15-19	383	561	564	485	405	418	652
20-24	3698	5014	5173	5266	5313	5565	5374
25-29	8233	7904	9197	9580	9797	10589	10683
30-34	11047	10087	9088	10290	10824	11337	11962
35-39	10561	10980	10063	9001	9968	10626	11127
40-44	10576	9909	10210	9454	8370	9138	9824
45-49	9335	9385	8803	9115	8568	7439	8128

TABLE 5 DEMOGRAPHIC INDICES AND FEMALE SINGULATE MEAN AGE
AT MARRIAGE: 1831 TC 1901

DATE	IF OVERALL FERTILITY	IG MARITAL FERTILITY	IH ILLEGITIMATE FERTILITY	IM PROPORTION MARRIED	SINGULATE MEAN AGE AT MARRIAGE
1831	0.300	0.635	0.028	0.448	26.3
1836	0.291	0.588	0.036	0.463	26.1
1841	0.287	0.563	0.041	0.472	26.0
1846	0.273	0.536	0.038	0.473	25.8
1851	0.259	0.493	0.041	0.483	25.6
1856	0.270	0.497	0.047	0.495	25.4
1861	0.278	0.501	0.053	C.502	25.5
1866	0.285	0.515	0.052	0.504	25.5
1871	0.301	0.532	0.050	0.521	25.1
1876	0.292	0.529	0.042	0.513	24.7
1881	0.288	0.516	0.045	0.515	24.8
1886	0.273	0.490	0.047	0.510	25.0
1891	0.271	0.478	0.048	0.517	25.0
1896	0.264	0.465	0.050	0.516	24.8
1901	0.269	0.459	0.053	0.532	

[464]

MORTALITY PATTERN: NORTH
MIGRATION: GRADUAL, WITH CHILD MIGRANTS SUBTRACTED AFTER 1866, AND OTHERWISE
UNCORRECTED POPULATION TOTALS

TABLE 1 FEMALE POPULATION ESTIMATES: 1801 TO 1906

DATE	R/CB RATIO	% COR-RECTION	FINAL POPULATION ESTIMATE	DATE	R/CB RATIO	% COR-RECTION	FINAL POPULATION ESTIMATE
1801	1.005	0.0	162621	1856	0.969	0.0	184633
1806	1.029	0.0	164686	1861	0.967	0.0	184768
1811*	1.027	0.0	166786	1866	0.967	0.0	185442
1816*	1.011	0.0	168887	1871	0.952	-0.3	181638
1821	0.988	0.0	170987	1876	0.948	-0.7	178171
1826*	0.994	0.0	174942	1881	0.937	-1.0	175436
1831	1.004	0.0	178897	1886	0.932	-1.4	173378
1836	0.997	0.0	179988	1891	0.912	-1.7	168510
1841	0.993	0.0	182977	1896	0.902	-2.0	163006
1846	1.000	0.0	187725	1901	0.886	-2.2	156954
1851	1.000	0.0	190180	1906	0.882	-2.7	152630

NOTE: R/CB RATIO REFERS TO THE POPULATION COMPUTED BY THE BALANCE OF BIRTHS
AND DEATHS OVER THE REPORTED POPULATION
* INTERPOLATED VALUES

TABLE 2 FEMALE BIRTH ESTIMATES: 1801-1805 TO 1901-1905

DATE	% COR-RECTION	FINAL BIRTH ESTIMATE	CRUDE BIRTH RATE	DATE	% COR-RECTION	FINAL BIRTH ESTIMATE	CRUDE BIRTH RATE
1801-1805	0.0	23974	29.3	1856-1860	0.0	20879	22.6
1806-1810	6.6	24967	30.1	1861-1865	0.0	20041	21.7
1811-1815	5.7	26499	31.6	1866-1870	0.0	18774	20.5
1816-1820	0.0	24246	28.5	1871-1875	0.0	17660	19.6
1821-1825	-10.7	22304	25.8	1876-1880	0.0	16982	19.2
1826-1830	0.0	23262	26.3	1881-1885	0.0	16086	18.4
1831-1835	0.0	23162	25.8	1886-1890	0.0	15041	17.6
1836-1840	0.0	22282	24.6	1891-1895	0.0	13649	16.5
1841-1845	0.0	22702	24.5	1896-1900	0.0	12688	15.9
1846-1850	0.0	23385	24.8	1901-1905	0.0	12060	15.6
1851-1855	0.0	21702	23.2				

TABLE 3 FEMALE POPULATION ESTIMATES,
DISTRIBUTION BY AGE: 1801 TO 1906

AGE	1801	1806	1811	1816	1821	1826	1831	1836	1841	1846	1851
0- 4	22309	17018	18349	19642	18971	17894	18542	18422	18508	19134	19425
5- 9	18115	18612	14351	15492	17065	16877	15874	16314	16631	16917	17283
10-14	16388	17378	17548	13438	14540	16377	16210	15032	15590	16060	16192
15-19	15120	16131	16726	16750	12793	14150	15962	15559	14513	15204	15513
20-24	13896	14818	15465	15905	15891	12407	13744	15269	14975	14110	14608
25-29	12686	13499	14100	14601	15002	15323	11980	13073	14627	14492	13518
30-34	11481	12181	12721	13191	13675	14365	14689	11318	12455	14080	13828
35-39	10273	10883	11357	11783	12259	12994	13660	13774	10719	11920	13357
40-44	9127	9642	10060	10433	10875	11569	12270	12724	12968	10200	11245
45-49	8051	8506	8855	9184	9574	10205	10862	11365	11915	12276	9572
50-54	7014	7397	7711	7983	8334	8885	9473	9950	10537	11169	11407
55-59	5941	6222	6505	6753	7070	7551	8047	8477	9040	9681	10167
60-64	4759	4942	5179	5407	5728	6138	6544	6904	7428	8016	8494
65-69	3508	3569	3761	3952	4267	4630	4944	5234	5690	6201	6612
70-74	2246	2230	2355	2505	2780	3078	3318	3535	3908	4310	4630
75-79	1170	1120	1194	1285	1487	1695	1857	2011	2275	2558	2772
80+	561	539	547	584	677	805	920	1027	1198	1395	1557

AGE	1856	1861	1866	1871	1876	1881	1886	1891	1896	1901	1906
0- 4	17610	17660	17346	16132	15158	14815	14196	13371	11781	11109	10587
5- 9	17033	16008	16289	15771	14716	13967	13781	13117	12275	10843	10359
10-14	16046	16272	15380	15438	15052	14105	13461	13168	12614	11781	10512
15-19	14974	15343	15590	14278	14532	14184	13367	12315	12500	11803	11372
20-24	13952	14074	14401	13810	12864	13091	12915	11210	11205	11030	11156
25-29	13368	13216	13356	13229	12850	11959	12284	11688	10501	10339	10559
30-34	12500	12718	12634	12585	12562	12252	11460	11671	11192	10021	9977
35-39	12754	11849	12129	11918	11948	11988	11755	10949	11172	10720	9651
40-44	12286	12046	11267	11451	11309	11403	11500	11293	10471	10718	10296
45-49	10306	11554	11408	10616	10838	10767	10908	11043	10767	10027	10252
50-54	8703	9609	10852	10678	9978	10248	10228	10426	10449	10243	9512
55-59	10154	7963	8869	9979	9853	9273	9572	9617	9687	9766	9548
60-64	8706	8968	7109	7864	8880	8838	8373	8672	8620	8732	8814
65-69	6840	7257	7581	5968	6618	7549	7573	7207	7348	7362	7469
70-74	4822	5193	5614	5823	4588	5154	5938	5994	5574	5746	5769
75-79	2911	3180	3509	3766	3901	3125	3555	4130	4037	3811	3939
80+	1668	1858	2110	2335	2524	2718	2512	2637	2813	2905	2859

[466]

TABLE 4 MARRIED WOMEN ESTIMATES,
DISTRIBUTION BY AGE: 1831 TO 1901

AGE	1831	1836	1841	1846	1851	1856	1861	1866
15-19	590	597	582	640	696	714	996	989
20-24	5110	5857	5947	5811	6247	6203	6527	7338
25-29	8097	9006	10294	10408	9891	9960	10026	10298
30-34	11601	9027	10066	11509	11402	10387	10655	10646
35-39	11202	11342	8914	9985	11229	10754	10039	10295
40-44	10221	10563	10832	8547	9408	10259	10074	9401
45-49	8644	9003	9532	9872	7683	8253	9279	9134

AGE	1871	1876	1881	1886	1891	1896	1901
15-19	779	751	747	630	502	552	701
20-24	6848	6399	6640	6146	5030	5406	5344
25-29	10446	10029	9437	9821	9045	8006	8266
30-34	10637	10688	10381	9748	9986	9467	8462
35-39	10098	10120	10189	9960	9275	9471	9059
40-44	9487	9331	9406	9458	9258	8537	8720
45-49	8415	8544	8489	8569	8637	8354	7716

TABLE 5 DEMOGRAPHIC INDICES AND FEMALE SINGULATE MEAN AGE
AT MARRIAGE: 1831 TO 1901

DATE	IF OVERALL FERTILITY	IG MARITAL FERTILITY	IH ILLEGITIMATE FERTILITY	IM PROPORTION MARRIED	SINGULATE MEAN AGE AT MARRIAGE
1831	0.281	0.467	0.026	0.578	24.8
1836	0.276	0.457	0.030	0.576	24.4
1841	0.276	0.444	0.034	0.589	24.1
1846	0.280	0.443	0.033	0.602	23.9
1851	0.271	0.424	0.031	0.610	23.7
1856	0.265	0.410	0.028	0.619	23.4
1861	0.255	0.390	0.030	0.626	23.0
1866	0.241	0.359	0.032	0.638	22.9
1871	0.232	0.342	0.033	0.644	22.9
1876	0.225	0.335	0.028	0.643	22.8
1881	0.219	0.322	0.031	0.645	22.8
1886	0.210	0.309	0.032	0.642	23.0
1891	0.206	0.305	0.030	0.639	23.0
1896	0.195	0.289	0.030	0.637	22.9
1901	0.191	0.277	0.033	0.645	

3. Présentation de l'Ouvrage au Lecteur Français

Le bref résumé qui va suivre vise à rendre l'ouvrage accessible au lecteur français. Nous indiquons ici dans quel chapitre il pourra trouver les développements méthodologiques qui expliquent et justifient les estimations présentées dans la seconde partie de l'ouvrage, et nous décrivons le contenu des tableaux qui la composent.

L'objet du présent volume est une reconstruction de la population féminine des départements français, à l'exception des suivants: Alpes-Maritimes, Bouches-du-Rhône, Belfort (Territoire de), Meurthe-et-Moselle, Rhône, Savoie, Savoie (Haute-), Seine, et Seine-et-Oise. L'exclusion de certains départements a été imposée par les problèmes techniques soulevés soit par l'immigration massive vers des zones urbaines, soit par des changements de frontière. La reconstruction couvre l'ensemble du siècle, de 1801 à 1901. Elle vise à donner des résultats valables à l'échelon départemental là où les données officielles (recensements ou état civil) sont incomplètes ou inexactes. En particulier, elle propose des répartitions par âge et état matrimonial avant 1851, là où elles n'étaient pas disponibles auparavant, et elle suggère les corrections à appliquer aux séries postérieures. De plus, une méthode d'évaluation et de correction des résultats de l'état civil (naissances) est appliquée systématiquement aux données des départements.

Les commentaires et l'exposé des méthodes sont divisés en huit chapitres, dont nous présentons brièvement le contenu ci-après.

Chapitre 1: Le cadre de l'étude.

Sont traitées successivement: la théorie de la transition démographique appliquée à la France, et les recherches sur l'histoire démographique française.

Chapitre 2: Les données.

Ce chapitre passe en revue l'histoire des recensements et de l'état civil en France, examine l'opinion des contemporains et les résultats des chercheurs concernant leur qualité, et soumet les résultats publiés à quelques tests élémentaires concernant leur cohérence.

Chapitre 3: Reconstruction de la population féminine par âge.

A partir du nombre de décès et de naissances de chaque période de cinq ans, du chiffre de la population d'après les recensements, et de tables types de mortalité, il est possible de projeter à travers le siècle une population stable qui aurait la natalité et la mortalité de 1801. Les différences entre l'accroissement naturel et l'augmentation du chiffre recensé de la population peuvent servir d'estimation du nombre total de migrants (moyennant des corrections pour la qualité des recensements); ces migrants sont répartis par âge selon une pondération standard. Jusqu'à ce point, la reconstruction dépend de la validité d'hypothèses que nous discutons en détail. Mais les chiffres ainsi obtenus sont confrontés systématiquement avec les répartitions par âge des recensements détaillés existant depuis 1851. Il devient ainsi possible d'attribuer les divergences entre le modèle et les résultats des énumérations soit aux hypothèses initiales, soit à la qualité des données d'état civil, soit aux biais du recensement. La matrice totale de la reconstruction offre de nombreuses possibilités de comparaison avec les données officielles. En gros, après vérification des hypothèses de départ (par exemple le rôle des migrations et leur effet par âge), les biais se partagent entre ceux qui sont systématiques par âge et doivent être attribués aux erreurs des recensements, et ceux qui caractérisent les générations et sont dûs aux déficiences de l'état civil.

Chapitre 4: Reconstruction de la population féminine par état matrimonial.

Les résultats de l'état civil rapportés au nombre de femmes par âge dans la reconstruction permettent de calculer les fréquences des premiers mariages à partir de 1861. Ces fréquences sont utilisées pour reconstruire par cohorte les proportions des femmes qui ont été mariées et, en soustrayant une estimation du nombre des veuves et divorcées, les proportions mariées tous les cinq ans. La méthode

[469]

utilisée, celle de Coale, modifie une courbe modèle de nuptialité en fonction de trois paramètres: a_0, l'âge auquel les femmes commencent à se marier; k, marquant le rapport entre l'échelle verticale de la courbe envisagée et celle de la courbe modèle; et C, la proportion qui se mariera dans la cohorte. C s'obtient à partir des recensements, a_0 et k à partir de l'état civil.—Pour les mariages d'avant 1861, il faut recourir à des approximations d'a_0 et de k.

Chapitre 5: La population totale de la France.

Nous illustrons par le cas de la France le format des tableaux présentés plus tard pour chaque département, décrivons les indices de fécondité et de nuptialité utilisés, et discutons les résultats obtenus, notamment en les comparant à la reconstruction faite par Bourgeois-Pichat.

Chapitre 6: Types d'erreurs dans les départements.

Les erreurs décrites comportent en ordre principal la sous-estimation des naissances au début du siècle et les inconsistences des répartitions par âge de la population totale et mariée. Le chapitre examine aussi l'influence globale des erreurs sur les indices de fécondité et de nuptialité calculés pour chaque département.

Chapitre 7: Evolution générale de la fécondité et de la nuptialité par département.

Nous présentons ici un résumé graphique des principales tendances, tant des taux de natalité entre 1801 et 1901, que de la fécondité matrimoniale, illégitime et totale, et de la proportion mariée, entre 1831 et 1901.

Chapitre 8: Résultats supplémentaires concernant la mortalité et les migrations.

Des tables présentent l'espérance de vie à la naissance et un indice de migration nette pour l'ensemble du siècle dans chaque département.

La seconde partie de l'ouvrage se compose de cinq tables uniformes présentées pour chaque département. Voici une description sommaire du contenu de ces tables:

Table 1: Population féminine totale. Trois colonnes à chaque date quinquennale entre 1801 et 1906:

Colonne 1: R/CB RATIO. Donne le rapport entre la population énumérée au recensement et celle qui aurait résulté de l'accroissement naturel (naissances moins décès) par rapport à 1846.

Colonne 2: % CORRECTION. Donne la différence entre le chiffre énuméré et celui utilisé dans l'étude.

Colonne 3: FINAL POPULATION ESTIMATE. Donne la population féminine totale acceptée dans l'étude.

Table 2: Naissances féminines. Trois colonnes pour chaque période quinquennale entre 1801-1805 et 1901-1905:

Colonne 1: % CORRECTION. Donne la correction appliquée au chiffre des naissances d'après l'état civil.

Colonne 2: FINAL BIRTH ESTIMATE. Donne le nombre corrigé des naissances.

Colonne 3: CRUDE BIRTH RATE. Donne le taux brut de natalité féminin (naissances corrigées pour mille personnes dans la population moyenne aux dates entourant la période quinquennale).

Table 3: Répartition par âge, 1801 à 1901. Donne le résultat détaillé de la reconstruction de la population féminine.

Table 4: Femmes mariées par âge, 1831 à 1901. Donne les nombres par âge entre 15 et 49 ans.

Table 5: Indices de fécondité et de nuptialité, 1831 à 1901. Cinq colonnes à chaque date quinquennale entre 1831 et 1901.

Colonne 1: *IF*, fécondité totale $= B \Sigma F_i w_i$

Colonne 2: *IG*, fécondité légitime $= BL \Sigma F_i m_i$

Colonne 3: *IH*, fécondité illégitime $= BI \Sigma F_i u_i$

Colonne 4: *IM*, proportion mariée $= \Sigma F_i m_i \Sigma F_i w_i$

Dans les formules ci-dessus, *B*, *BL* et *BI* représentent les naissances totales, légitimes et illégitimes; F_i est la fécondité

[471]

des femmes mariées huttérites, et w_i, m_i et u_i sont respective-
ment le nombre de femmes totales, mariées et non mariées à
l'âge i.

Colonne 5: SINGULATE MEAN AGE AT MARRIAGE.
Donne l'âge au premier mariage calculé d'après la proportion
des célibataires.

Les indices I_f, I_g, I_h et I_m sont utilisés systématiquement dans
l'étude du déclin de la fécondité en Europe entreprise à l'Université
de Princeton, et ils expriment la fécondité comme une fraction de
celle qu'auraient eu les femmes considérées avec la fécondité la plus
haute connue, celle des Huttérites. Empiriquement, des I_g (fécondité
légitime) inférieurs à 0.6 indiquent avec quasi-certitude l'usage de
la contraception dans le mariage.

References, including Official Statistical Sources

Andorka, Rudolf, 1971. "La prévention des naissances en Hongrie dans la région 'Ormansag' depuis la fin du xviiie siècle," *Population 26*: 63-78.

Angeville, Adolphe d', 1969. *Essai sur la statistique de la population française*, reedition, with an introduction by Emmanuel Le Roy Ladurie, Paris, The Hague: Mouton.

Ariès, Philippe, 1948. *Histoire des populations françaises*, Paris.

Armengaud, André, 1961. *Les populations de l'Est-Aquitain au début de l'époque contemporaine*, Paris, The Hague: Mouton.

————, 1964. "Les nourrices du Morvan au xixe siècle," *Etudes et chronique de démographie historique 1964*, pp. 131-139.

————, 1971a. *La population française au xixe siècle*, Paris: Que Sais-je? P.U.F.

————, 1971b. "Un siècle délaissé: le xixe (1815-1914)," *Annales de démographie historique 1971*, pp. 299-309.

Belgium, 1885. *Exposé de la situation du Royaume de 1861 à 1875*, Statistique générale de la Belgique, Brussels.

————, 1870 to 1900. Annuaire Statistique de la Belgique, Brussels.

Bergues, Hélène, et al, 1960. *La prévention des naissances dans la famille. Ses origines dans les temps modernes.* I.N.E.D., Travaux et Documents, Cahier n° 35, Paris: P.U.F.

Bertillon, Adolphe, 1880. "France," in *Dictionnaire encyclopédique des sciences médicales*, ed. A. Dechambre, Paris.

Biraben, Jean Noël, 1962. "Etude de la population pendant la Révolution et l'Empire (M. Reinhard, Gap 1961)," *Population 17*: 329-333.

————, 1963. "Inventaire des listes nominatives de recensement en France," *Population 18*: 305-328.

————, 1966. La fécondité dans l'Europe occidentale prémalthusienne. In *Official Documents of the European Population Conference*. Vol. 1. Council of Europe. Strasbourg, pp. 1-29.

————, 1970. "La France à l'époque napoléonienne." *Revue d'histoire moderne et contemporaine 17*: 359-372.

REFERENCES

Biraben, Jean Noël, Fleury, Marcel, and Henry, Louis, 1960. "Inventaire par sondage des registres paroissiaux en France," *Population 15*: 25-50.

Blayo, Yves, 1970. "La mobilité dans un village de la Brie vers le milieu du xix⁰ siècle," *Population 25*: 573-605.

Blayo, Yves, and Henry, Louis, 1967. "Données démographiques sur la Bretagne et l'Anjou de 1740 à 1829," *Annales de démographie historique 1967*, pp. 91-171.

Bougard, P., and Reinhard, Marcel, 1964. *Les sources de l'histoire démographique du département du Pas-de-Calais (1789-1815)*. Ministère de l'éducation nationale, Commission d'histoire économique et sociale de la Révolution française, Paris.

Bourgeois-Pichat, Jean, 1951. "Evolution générale de la population française depuis le xviiiᵉ siècle," *Population 6*: 635-662.

———, 1952. "Note sur l'évolution générale de la population française depuis le xviiiᵉ siècle," *Population 7*: 319-329.

———, 1965. "The General Development of the Population of France since the Eighteenth Century," in *Population in History*, eds. D. V. Glass and D.E.C. Eversley. Chicago: Aldine, pp. 474-506. (Translation of Bourgeois-Pichat, 1951 and 1952.)

Camp, Wesley D., 1961. *Marriage and the Family in France since the Revolution*, New York: Bookman Associates.

Chasteland, Jean-Claude, and Henry, Louis, 1956. "Disparités régionales de la fécondité des mariages," *Population 11*: 653-672.

Chasteland, Jean-Claude, and Pressat, Roland, 1962. "La nuptialité des générations françaises depuis un siècle," *Population 17*: 215-240.

Chevalier, Louis, ed., 1958. *Le choléra—la première épidémie du xixᵉ siècle*. Bibliothèque de la Revolution de 1848, Vol. xx, La Roche-Sur-Yon.

———, 1950. *La formation de la population parisienne au xixᵉ siècle*. I.N.E.D., Travaux et Documents, Cahier n° 10, Paris: P.U.F.

Coale, Ansley J., 1969. "The Decline of Fertility in Europe from the French Revolution to World War II," in *Fertility and Family*

Planning: A World View, ed. Samuel J. Behrman, Leslie Corsa and Ronald Freedman. Ann Arbor: The University of Michigan Press, pp. 3-24.

———, 1971. "Age Patterns of Marriage," *Population Studies 25*: 193-214.

Coale, Ansley J., and Demeny, Paul, 1966. *Regional Model Life Tables and Stable Populations*, Princeton: Princeton University Press.

Coppolani, Jean, 1953. *Toulouse, étude de géographie urbaine*, Toulouse.

Courgeau, Daniel, 1970. *Les champs migratoires en France*, I.N.E.D., Travaux et documents, Cahier n° 58, Paris: P.U.F.

Davis, Kingsley, 1963. "The Theory of Change and Response in Modern Demographic History," *Population Index 29*: 345-366.

Delaporte, P., 1941. *Evolution de la mortalité en Europe depuis les origines des statistiques de l'état civil*, Statistique générale de la France, Etudes démographiques, n° 2, Paris.

Delore, 1879. "Nourrices," "Nourissons," in *Dictionnaire encyclopédique des sciences médicales*, ed. A. Dechambre. Paris.

Deniel, Raymond, and Henry, Louis, 1965. "La population d'un village du nord de la France, Sainghin-en-Mélantois, de 1665 à 1851," *Population 28*: 563-602.

Depoid, Pierre, 1941. *Reproduction nette en Europe depuis l'origine de l'état civil*, Statistique générale de la France, Etudes démographiques, n° 1, Paris.

Dumont, Arsène, 1890. *Dépopulation et civilisation*, Paris.

Dupâquier, Jacques, 1965. *Département de Seine-et-Oise. Archives départementales. Répertoire numérique de la Série M*, Fac. 3. Sous-série 9M (Dénombrements de la Population), Versailles.

Dupâquier, Jacques, and Lachiver, Marcel, 1969. "Sur les débuts de la contraception en France, ou les deux malthusianismes," *Annales E.S.C. 24*: 1391-1406.

Duplessis-Le Guelinel, G., 1954. *Les mariages en France*, Paris.

Esmonin, E., 1964. "Statistiques du mouvement de la population en France de 1770 à 1789," *Etudes et chronique de démographie historique 1964*, pp. 27-130.

REFERENCES

Flaubert, Gustave, 1856. *Madame Bovary*, Paris.

Fleury, Marcel, and Henry, Louis, 1958. "Pour connaître la population de la France depuis Louis XIV. Plan de travaux par sondage," *Population 13*: 663-686.

France, Bureau de la Statistique générale, 1837. *Statistique de la France*, Paris: Imprimerie Royale.

————, 1855. *Statistique de la France. Territoire et Population*, Deuxième Série, Vol. 2, Paris: Imprimerie Impériale.

————, 1856. *Statistique de la France. Mouvement de la population en 1851, 1852 et 1853*, Deuxième Série, Vol. 3, Strasbourg: Vve Berger-Levrault.

————, 1857. *Statistique de la France. Mouvement de la population pendant l'année 1854*, Deuxième Série, Vol. 4, Strasbourg: Vve Berger-Levrault.

————, 1859. *Statistique de la France. Résultats du dénombrement de la population en 1856*, Deuxième Série, Vol. 9, Strasbourg: Vve Berger-Levrault.

————, 1861. *Statistique de la France. Mouvement de la population pendant les années 1855, 1856 et 1857*, Deuxième Série, Vol. 10, Strasbourg: Vve Berger-Levrault.

————, 1863. *Statistique de la France. Mouvement de la population pendant les années 1858, 1859 et 1860*, Deuxième Série, Vol. 11, Strasbourg: Vve Berger-Levrault.

————, 1864. *Statistique de la France. Résultats généraux du dénombrement de 1861 . . . ,* Deuxième Série, Vol. 13, Strasbourg: Vve Berger-Levrault.

————, 1869. *Statistique de la France. Résultats généraux du dénombrement de 1866*, Deuxième Série, Vol. 17, Strasbourg: Vve Berger-Levrault.

————, 1870. *Statistique de la France. Mouvement de la population pendant les années 1861, 1862, 1863, 1864 et 1865*, Deuxième Série, Vol. 18, Strasbourg: Berger-Levrault.

————, 1872. *Statistique de la France. Mouvement de la population pendant les années 1866, 1867 et 1868*, Deuxième Série, Vol. 20, Paris: Imprimerie nationale.

————, 1873. *Statistique de la France. Résultats généraux du dénombrement de 1872*, Deuxième Série, Vol. 21, Paris: Imprimerie nationale.

————, 1874 to 1907. *Statistique de la France. Statistique annuelle*, Nouvelle Série, Vol. 1 to 36, Paris: Imprimerie nationale. (Yearly volumes containing the vital statistical data.)

————, 1878. *Statistique générale de la France. Résultats généraux du dénombrement de 1876*, Paris: Imprimerie nationale.

————, 1883. *Résultats statistiques du dénombrement de 1881*, Paris: Imprimerie nationale.

————, 1888. *Résultats statistiques du dénombrement de 1886*, Paris: Imprimerie nationale.

————, 1894. *Résultats statistiques du dénombrement de 1891*, Paris: Imprimerie nationale.

————, 1899. *Résultats statistiques du dénombrement de 1896*, Paris: Imprimerie nationale.

————, 1906. *Résultats statisiques du recensement général de la population, 1901*, 5 Volumes, Paris: Imprimerie nationale.

————, 1910. *Résultats statistiques du recensement général de la population, 1906*, 3 Volumes, Paris: Imprimerie nationale.

————, 1915. *Résultats statistiques du recensement général de la population, 1911*, 2 Volumes, Paris: Imprimerie nationale.

————, 1923. *Résultats statistiques du recensement général de la population, 1921*, 3 Volumes, Paris: Imprimerie nationale.

Freedman, Ronald, 1961-1962. "The Sociology of Human Fertility," *Current Sociology 10-11*: 35-121.

Frost, W. H., 1940. "The age selection of mortality from tuberculosis in successive decades," *Milbank Memorial Fund Quarterly 18*: 61-66.

Galliano, Paul, 1966. "La mortalité infantile (indigènes et nourrissons) dans la banlieue sud de Paris à la fin du xviiie siècle (1774-1794)," *Annales de démographie historique 1966*, pp. 139-177.

Ganiage, Jean, 1963. *Trois villages de l'Ile de France*, I.N.E.D., Travaux et Documents, Cahier n° 40, Paris: P.U.F.

Gautier, Etienne, and Henry, Louis, 1958. *La population de Crulai, paroisse normande. Etude historique*, I.N.E.D., Travaux et documents, Cahier n° 33, Paris: P.U.F.

REFERENCES

Guillard, Achille, 1855. *Eléments de statistique humaine ou démographie comparée*, Paris.

Henry, Louis, 1967. *Manuel de démographie historique*, Centre de recherches d'histoire et de philologie, V, Hautes études médiévales et modernes, 3, Geneva-Paris: Droz.

Hollingsworth, T. H., 1964. *The Demography of the British Peerage*. Supplement to *Population Studies 18*.

Houdaille, Jacques, 1967. "La population de Boulay (Moselle) avant 1850," *Population 22*: 1055-1084.

―――, 1971. "La population de sept villages des environs de Boulay (Moselle) au xviiiᵉ et xixᵉ siècles," *Population 26*: 1061-1072.

Huber, Michel, 1938. *Cours de démographie et de statistique sanitaire*, 6 Volumes, Paris: Hermann et Cie.

Lallemand, Léon, 1885. *La question des enfants abandonnés et délaissés au xixᵉ siècle*, Paris.

Landry, Adolphe, 1934. *La révolution démographique*, Paris: Sirey.

―――, 1945. *Traité de démographie*, Paris: Payot.

Legoyt, Alfred, 1843. *La France statistique*, Paris.

―――, 1862. "Le dénombrement de 1861," *Journal des économistes 2, 23*: 261-279.

Le Play, Frederic, 1866. *La réforme sociale en France*, Paris.

Leroy-Beaulieu, Paul, 1913. *La question de la population*, Paris.

Le Roy Ladurie, Emmanuel, 1965. "Démographie et 'funestes secrets': Le Languedoc (fin xviiᵉ-début xixᵉ siècle)," *Annales historiques de la Révolution Française 37*: 385-400.

Levasseur, Emile, 1889-1892. *La population française*, 3 Volumes, Paris.

Lévy, Claude, and Henry, Louis, 1960. "Ducs et Pairs sous l'Ancien Régime. Caractéristiques démographiques d'une caste," *Population 15*: 807-830.

Marion, Marcel, 1928. *Histoire financière de la France depuis 1715*, 7 Volumes, Paris.

Moheau, 1912. *Recherches et considérations sur la population de la France–1778*. Reedited by René Gonnard, Paris.

Moreau de Jonnès, A., 1856. *Eléments de statistique*, second edition. Paris.

Pinchemel, Philippe, 1957. *Structures sociales et dépopulation rurale dans les campagnes picardes de 1836 à 1936*, Centre d'études économiques, Etudes et Mémoires, Paris: Armand Colin.

Pouthas, Charles, 1956. *La population française pendant la première moitié du xixe siècle*, I.N.E.D., Travaux et Documents, Cahier n°. 25, Paris: P.U.F.

Reinhard, Marcel, 1950. "La statistique de la population sous le consulat et l'Empire–Le Bureau de statistique," *Population 5*: 103-120.

————, 1959-1960. "Etude de la population pendant la Révolution et l'Empire," *Bulletin d'histoire économique et sociale de la Révolution Française, 1*: 21-88.

Reinhard, Marcel, Armengaud, André, and Dupâquier, Jacques, 1968. *Histoire générale de la population mondiale*, Paris: Montchrestien.

Seine, Préfecture de la, 1882-1924. *Annuaire statistique de la ville de Paris*. (One volume each year.) Paris: Imprimerie nationale.

Spagnoli, Paul, 1971. "The Demographic Work of Charles Pouthas," *Historical Methods Newsletter 4*: 126-140.

Spengler, Joseph J., 1938. *France Faces Depopulation*, Durham: Duke University Press.

Tabah, Léon, 1947. "La répartition par âge de la population française en 1851," *Population 2*: 349-354.

Toutain, Jean-Claude, 1963. "La population de la France de 1700 à 1959," *Cahiers de l'institut de science économique appliquée*. Suppl, n°. 133.

Tugault, Yves, 1970. "La mobilité géographique en France depuis un siècle: une étude par générations," *Population 25*: 1020-1036.

Vidalenc, Jean, 1956. "Observations sur la population du département de l'Eure au XIXe siècle," *Annales de Normandie 6*: 159-173.

Visaria, Pravin M., 1963. "The Sex Ratio of the Population of India," unpublished Ph.D. dissertation, Princeton University.

REFERENCES

van de Walle, Etienne, 1972. "De l'usage des modèles en démographie historique," *Annales de démographie Historique 1972*, pp. 153-177.

van de Walle, Etienne, and Knodel, John, 1967. "Demographic Transition and Fertility Decline: The European Case." In I.U.S.S.P. *Contributed Papers, Sydney Conference*, Sydney, pp. 47-55.

Geographical Index